The Branch

The Branch

A Plausible Case for the Substructure of the Four Gospels

PRESTON T. MASSEY

WIPF & STOCK · Eugene, Oregon

THE BRANCH
A Plausible Case for the Substructure of the Four Gospels

Copyright © 2018 Preston T. Massey. All rights reserved. Except for brief quotations in critical publications or reviews, no part of this book may be reproduced in any manner without prior written permission from the publisher. Write: Permissions, Wipf and Stock Publishers, 199 W. 8th Ave., Suite 3, Eugene, OR 97401.

Wipf & Stock
An Imprint of Wipf and Stock Publishers
199 W. 8th Ave., Suite 3
Eugene, OR 97401

www.wipfandstock.com

PAPERBACK ISBN: 978-1-5326-4277-7
HARDCOVER ISBN: 978-1-5326-4278-4
EBOOK ISBN: 978-1-5326-4279-1

Manufactured in the U.S.A.

I dedicate this book to the loving and grateful memory of my parents: John L. Massey (1915—2004) and Mildred Lorraine Massey (1918—2011).

Although neither lived to see the publication of this book, they both gave me great encouragement to write.

Contents

Acknowledgments | ix
Abbreviations | x
Introduction | xvii

Chapter 1: A Plausible Case for Divine Revelation | 1
Chapter 2: Disagreement in the Greco-Roman Literary Tradition and the Implications for Gospel Research | 31
Chapter 3: Minor Matters: Redaction, Allusions, Grids, and Silence | 58
Chapter 4: The Gospel of Matthew: The King Branch | 88
Chapter 5: The Genealogy of Jesus in Matthew | 120
Chapter 6: The Gospel of Mark: The Servant Branch | 127
Chapter 7: The Absence of a Genealogy in Mark | 155
Chapter 8: The Gospel of Luke: The Man/Priest Branch | 159
Chapter 9: The Genealogy of Jesus in the Gospel of Luke | 187
Chapter 10: The Gospel of John: The LORD God Branch | 205
Chapter 11: Rev 4:6–7 and the Four Living Beings around the Throne | 229
Chapter 12: Conclusion | 255

Bibliography | 277
Author Index | 319
Scripture Index | 325
Ancient Document Index | 329

Acknowledgments

I BEGIN MY INDEBTEDNESS TO others by recalling my PhD days at Indiana University in Bloomington, IN. Although my degree comes from the Department of Classical Studies and not New Testament, my dissertation director, my *Doktor Faktor*, Prof. Timothy Long (now emeritus) was an invaluable help in my growth as a scholar. Prof. Long was willing to meet with me on a regular basis for two whole years while we read and translated some difficult German. His time and mentoring was a key help in building my confidence that I could actually read German. He also pushed me to develop a more scholarly prose style. I also feel indebted to Dr. Judith M. Lieu who, as editor of the Cambridge journal *New Testament Studies* in 2007, escorted me through the process of getting my first article published.

Gratitude is hereby expressed to Dr. Everett Ferguson (also emeritus), from Abilene Christian University, who read chapter 2 and encouraged me to submit it for publication. On that note, I hereby also acknowledge appreciation to Dr. Craig S. Keener, professor at Asbury Theological Seminary, who read chapter 2 as published in *BBR* and actually wrote me a nice letter of encouragement (not an email!).

For the kind and generous comments which appear on the back cover of this book, I wish to express deep appreciation to Dr. Craig A. Evans, professor at Houston Baptist University, and to Dr. David E. Garland, professor at Baylor University.

To the staff at Wipf & Stock, I desire to express great gratitude to the following: to Jim Tedrick, managing editor, for his wanting to publish this book; to Matt Wymer, assistant managing editor, for his answering my questions and giving me direction; to Shannon Carter, graphic designer, for her work in creating a fine front cover; and to Calvin Jaffarian, typesetter, for his patience and expertise in working with a rather challenging manuscript. Working with this staff exceeded all my expectations.

I would like to express heartfelt gratitude to my wife, Laura, for her many hours of reading through the entire manuscript and for giving me helpful feedback. I also want to thank my daughter, Melinda, a PhD student in English at Claremont Graduate University. Her suggestions regarding style improved the quality of several chapters. A friend, Nancy Shewmaker, deserves mention for reading the first three chapters and making helpful comments.

ACKNOWLEDGMENTS

Finally, for their help in obtaining needed books, I would like to express gratitude to the library staff at Indiana Wesleyan University, in particular: Lynn Crawford, Mary Beth Dolmanet, Jessica O'Neal, and Jule Kind for carrier assistance.

Preston T. Massey

Bloomington, Indiana
12 December 2018

Abbreviations

AB	The Aramaic Bible
ABD	Anchor Bible Dictionary
ABRL	Anchor Bible Reference Library
AC	*Acta Classica*
AGAJU	*Arbeiten zur Geschichte des antiken Judentums und des Urchristentums*
AnB	*Analecta Biblica*
ANCTTBS	Ashgate New Critical Thinking in Theology & Biblical Studies
ANRW	Aufstieg und Niedergang der römischen Welt
ASBT	Acadia Studies in Bible and Theology
ASOR	American Schools of Oriental Research
ATR	*Anglican Theological Review*
BAGD	Bauer, Arndt, Gingrich, and Danker, *A Greek-English Lexicon of the New Testament and Other Christian Literature*
BAR	*Biblical Archaeological Review*
BAT	Die Botschaft des Alten Testaments
BBC	Broadman Bible Commentary
BBR	*Bulletin of Biblical Research*
BECNT	Baker Exegetical Commentary on the New Testament
BETL	Bibliotheca Ephemeridum Theologicarum Loveniensium
Bib	*Biblica*
BIS	Biblical Interpretation Series
BJ	*Bellum judaicum*
BJRL	*Bulletin of the John Rylands Library*
BLS	Bible and Literature Series

ABBREVIATIONS

BNTC	Black's New Testament Commentaries
BRBS	Brill's Readers in Biblical Studies
BRS	Biblical Resource Series
BS	Biblical Series
BSRLL	*Bulletin de la Société Royale des Lettres de Lund*
BTB	*Biblical Theology Bulletin*
BWANT	Beiträge zur Wissenschaft Neutestament
BZNW	Beihefte zur Zeitschrift für die neutestamentliche Wissenschaft
CAT	Commentaire de L'Ancien Testament
CBQ	*Catholic Biblical Quarterly*
CBTSSup	Classics in Biblical and Theological Studies Supplement Series
CEP	Contemporary Evangelical Perspectives
CJAS	Christianity and Judaism in Antiquity Series
CNT	Companions to the New Testament
CO	Christian Origins
COQG	Christian Origins and the Question of God
CSHJ	Chicago Studies in the History of Judaism
CW	*Classical World*
DSBS	Daily Study Bible Series
DSD	*Dead Sea Discoveries*
DSS	Dead Sea Scrolls
DSSCOL	Dead Sea Scrolls & Christian Origins Library
ECC	Eerdmans Critical Commentary
EGT	Expositor's Greek Testament
ET	English translation
EUS	European University Studies
FOTL	Forms of Old Testament Literature
FPSJCO	The First Princeton Symposium on Judaism and Christian Origins
FRLANT	Forschungen zur Religion und Literatur des Alten und Neuen Testaments
FSCS	Faith and Scholarship Colloquies Series
GBS	Guides to Biblical Scholarship
GNS	Good News Studies

HAT	Handkommentar Alten Testament
HeyJ	*Heythrop Journal*
HTS	Harvard Theological Studies
HTS/TS	Hervormde Teologiese Studies/Theological Studies
HNTC	Harper's New Testament Commentaries
ICC	International Critical Commentary
IDB	Interpreter's Dictionary of the Bible
Int	*Interpretation: A Journal of Bible and Theology*
IRT	Issues in Religion and Theology
ISBL	Indiana Studies in Biblical Literature
JBL	*Journal of Biblical Literature*
JETS	*Journal of Evangelical Theological Society*
JJS	*Journal of Jewish Studies*
JQ	*The Jewish Quarterly*
JR	*Journal of Religion*
JSHJ	*Journal for the Study of the Historical Jesus*
JSJSup	Journal for the Study of Judaism Supplements
JSNT	*Journal for the Study of the New Testament*
JSNTSup	Journal for the Study of the New Testament Supplement Series
JSPSup	Journal for the Study of the Pseudepigrapha Supplement Series
JTS	*Journal of Theological Studies*
KAT	Kommentar zum Alten Testament
LCL	Loeb Classical Library
LEC	Library of Early Christianity
LHG&L	*Lexicon Historio-graphicum Graecum et Latinum*
LNTS	Library of New Testament Studies (formerly JSNTSup)
LSJ	Liddell, Scott, and Jones, *A Greek-English Lexicon with a Supplement*
LXX	Septuagint
MB	Le Monde de la Bible
MHUC	Monographs of the Hebrew Union College
MNTS	McMaster New Testament Studies
MT	Masoretic Text
NCBC	New Cambridge Bible Commentary

NeoT	*Neotestamentica*
NCBC	The New Cambridge Bible Commentary
NGS	New Gospel Studies
NICNT	New International Commentary on the New Testament
NIB	New Interpreter's Bible
NIBC	New International Biblical Commentary
NICOT	New International Commentary on the Old Testament
NIV	New International Version
NIB	New Interpreter's Bible
NKS	Neukirchener Studienbücher
NovT	*Novum Testamentum*
NSBT	New Studies in Biblical Theology
NTL	New Testament Library
NTS	New Testament Series
NTS	*New Testament Studies*
NTT	New Testament Theology
OBS	Oxford Bible Series
OLD	Oxford Latin Dictionary
OTG	Old Testament Guides
PBM	Paternoster Biblical Monographs
PC	Proclamation Commentaries
PG	*Patrologicia graeca*
PGL	Patristic Greek Lexicon
PRR	Princeton Readings in Religions
PRS:SSS	Perspectives in Religious Studies: Special Studies Series
PTMS	Pittsburgh Theological Monograph Series
PTS	*Perspectives in Religious Studies*
PVTG	Pseudepigrapha Veteris Testamenti Graece
RHPR	*Revue d'Histoire et de Philosophie Religieuses*
RILP	Roehampton Institute London Papers
RLS	Rockwell Lecture Series
RevQum	*Revue Qumran*
SNGN	Studies in Ancient Greek Narrative

SBLEJL	Society of Biblical Literature Early Judaism and its Literature
SBLDS	Society of Biblical Literature Dissertation Series
SBLMS	Society of Biblical Literature Monograph Series
SBLSCSS	Society of Biblical Literature Septuagint and Cognate Studies Series
SBLSBS	Society of Biblical Literature Sources for Biblical Study
SBLSP	Society of Biblical Literature Seminar Papers
SBLSS	Society of Biblical Literature Symposium Series
SBTh	*Studia Biblica et Theologica*
SCB	Septuagint and Cognate Studies
SCK	Studies in Classical Kinds
SJC	Studies in Judaism and Christianity
SJT	*Scottish Journal of Theology*
SLI	*Studies in the Literary Imagination*
SNTS	Studiorum Novi Testamenti Societas
SNYW	Studies of the New Testament and Its World
SP	*Studia Patristica*
SR/SR	*Studies in Religion/Sciences Religieuses*
SSEJC	Studies in Scripture in Early Judaism and Christianity
SSJHC	Stanford Studies in Jewish History and Culture
SSN	Studia Semitica Neerlandica
STDJ	Studies on the Texts of the Desert of Judah
TAPA	*Transactions of the American Philological Association*
TB	*Theologische Beiträge*
TC	Tyndale Commentaries
TCB	A Theological Commentary on the Bible
TDNT	Theological Dictionary of the New Testament
TEG	Traditio Exegetica Graeca
Tg	Targum
TLJS	The Taubman Lectures in Jewish Studies
TP	Testament of the Twelve Patriarchs
TPIC	Trinity Press International Commentaries
TQ	*Theologische Quartalschrift*
TRINJ	*Trinity Journal*

ABBREVIATIONS

TSAJ	Texte und Studien zum Antiken Judentum
TST	Toronto Studies in Theology
TynB	*Tyndale Bulletin*
VC	*Vigiliae christianae*
VD	*Verbum domini*
VE	*Vox evangelica*
VT	*Vetus Testamentum*
WBC	Westminster Bible Companion
WBC	Word Bible Commentary
WTJ	Westminster Theological Journal
WUNT	Wissenschaftliche Untersuchungen zum Neuen Testament
ZECNT	Zondervan Exegetical Commentary on the New Testament
ZNW	*Zeitschrift für die Neutestamentliche Wissenshaft*
ZST	*Zeitschrift für systematische Theologie*
ZTK	*Zeitschrift für Theologie und Kirche*

Introduction

THIS BOOK ATTEMPTS TO answer the following questions:

Regarding the Four Gospels:

- Why do we have *four* canonical Gospels—not three, not five?
- Why do we have these four *particular* Gospels?
- Why do we have this particular *order* of the Gospels (Matthew, Mark, Luke, John)?
- Why do Matthew and Luke have a genealogy?
- Why do Mark and John omit a genealogy?

Regarding the Four Branches

- Why do we have *four* Branches—not three, not five?
- Why do we have these four *particular* Branches (King Branch, Servant Branch, Man Branch, LORD God Branch)?
- Why does no Old Testament text ever speak of any of them as fulfilled?
- What connection, if any, do these Branches have in relationship with the Gospels?

Regarding the Four Living Beings around the Throne in Revelation 4.6–7:

- Why do we have *four* living Beings around the throne in Rev 4.6–7—not three, not five?
- Why is their *order* given specifically as first, second, third, and fourth?
- What relationship, if any, exists between the present order of the four Gospels and the order of the four living Beings?

- What is the total relationship, if any, between the four Gospels, the four Branches, and the four living Beings?

- Finally, what is the implication, if any, from the total constellation of four prophetic texts, four Gospels, and four living Beings?

The aim of this book is to provide a plausible explanation for the additional following question: upon what basis can we formulate the four images of Jesus in the Gospels as complementary and supplementary, rather than competitive or contradictory? International academic scholarship currently and typically dismisses revelation and inspiration as a possible causation behind biblical texts. One of the approaches taken up by such scholarship for dismissing Scripture as the Word of God is a strategy known as *vaticinium ex eventu* ("prophecy after the fact"). Simply stated, this approach argues that anything in the Gospels with a tint or tone suggesting the fulfillment of prophecy is merely a retrojected polemical statement placed in the mouth of a given speaker or writer after the fact. As the argument goes, even though a prophetic text forecasts and predicts an alleged future event, this text is disqualified as legitimate if cited by any of the four gospel writers. This attempt to project backward into the past statements of prophetic content thus enables scholars to disable and dispose of prophetic pronouncements as fictitious efforts to authenticate the gospel record.

Furthermore, this skeptical argument maintains that these texts are only later insertions read back into the record in order to justify a community presentation of Jesus.[1] In other words, this questionable claim bases its logic on a belief that the four evangelists simply created their Gospels by reading back into them OT prophecies "after the fact." Thus current scholarly tendencies lean toward reading messianic statements as retrojected views of the early church placed in the mouth of Jesus or as statements alleging the fulfillment of events about Jesus.

These scholarly claims raise a question: how does one respond to the above objections? Given the current academic climate's coolness toward the subject of revelation, I come at the topic indirectly. The thesis I am proposing bases the argument upon an underlying thematic unity of the fourfold Gospels. This unity-argument is grounded upon a coherent substructure tying together four prophetic texts from the Old Testament. The preliminary aim of this book is to provide a plausible explanation for the following questions: 1) why do the Gospels of Matthew and Luke have a genealogy but Mark and John do not; 2) why do the genealogies of Matthew and Luke diverge; 3) why do we have four Gospels—not three or five; 4) why is the order of the current canon Matthew, Mark, Luke, and John; and 5) upon what basis can we formulate the four images of Jesus in the Gospels as complementary and supplementary, rather than competitive or contradictory? Ultimately and most importantly, this book is a defense

---

1. See, for example, J. H. Charlesworth, *Jesus within Judaism: New Light from Exciting Archaeological Discoveries* (1988) 153: "Can one be relatively certain that the passages brought forward from the New Testament are not the creations of the disciples' proclamations after Easter?"

of the divine inspiration of Scripture. In particular, it is a focused argument for the inspiration of the four Gospels.

Many individual studies of the four Gospels develop themes based upon the representation of Jesus in each respective Gospel as Matthew's royal king, Mark's servant, Luke's human portrait, and the Johannine view of Jesus as God. To my knowledge, no one has presented a scholarly and critical argument showing the unified and coherent relationship between these disparate views. A canvass of scholarly literature turns up zero references.

The thesis of the book may be stated simply: it is an argument based upon the four prophetic texts of Jer 23:5; Zech 3:8; 6:12; and Isa 4:2 as a foundational pattern for the four Gospels. This study seeks to show how, respectively, Matthew presents Jesus as the King Branch, Mark depicts Jesus as the Servant Branch, Luke portrays Jesus as the Man/Priest Branch, and John reveals Jesus as the LORD God Branch. Given this sequence of literary facts, the conclusion of this book proposes that the gospel writers could not have written *vaticinium ex eventu*.[2] Rather, these four gospel writers wrote under the influence of the Holy Spirit so that the above four prophetic texts from the Old Testament, like the keel of a ship, provide supporting structure to the fourfold Gospel.

The self-imposed binding logic and the obligatory nature of Scripture require that these four Branches find fulfillment in Jesus in some way. Consequently, they must be fulfilled in either the first coming of Jesus or the second. If the first coming, there should be some definable way for discerning this compliance. From a canonical point of view, the integrity of Scripture is at stake; there is no other option available. This is the consistent position maintained by Jesus himself: Scripture "cannot be broken" (John 10:35), *everything* must be fulfilled or accomplished (Matt 5:18), and the Greek text of Luke 24:25–28 with its triple emphasis: *everything* (ἐπὶ πᾶσιν) that *all* the prophets spoke (ἀπὸ πάντων τῶν προφητῶν) in *all* the Scriptures (ἐν πάσαις ταῖς γραφαῖς) regarding himself (τὰ περὶ ἑαυτοῦ) must be fulfilled. Thus there are implications to the four prophetic texts of this investigation: were they ever fulfilled; is it important that they were fulfilled; what plausible reasons can we offer that they were fulfilled?

The specific proposal here is a hypothesis based upon the number four. The number four will be examined in its linkage to four prophetic statements containing the metaphor of Branch in biblical texts and the four canonical Gospels. Consideration will also be given to the four heavenly Images as found in Revelation 4:7. The argument thus sets out to demonstrate that this numerical phenomenon is too unusual to be brushed aside as mere human coincidence—or "a fortuitous series of episodes."[3]

---

2. For a defense of this "after-the-fact" proposition, see John Reumann in his Introduction to Hans Conzelmann's *Jesus* (1973) x. For a rebuttal to such claims, see George Eldon Ladd, *A Theology of the New Testament* (1974) 141 and 177.

3. Albert Schweitzer, *The Quest of the Historical Jesus: A Critical Study of Its Progress from Reimarus*

The thesis not only involves the number four but, concurrently, it explores a significant theological symmetry employed within this number. The analysis, therefore, will be based upon both a quantitative and qualitative evaluation of the sources.

In order to validate this unified substructure, the investigation will utilize two principal criteria for advancing the plausibility case of the foregoing unity argument. First, the criterion of a fourfold attestation: do all four prophetic texts serve in the proposed substructure? This principle will be adopted in the following manner: all four prophetic texts must serve as a substructure, but each in a different way. If it can be established that one or more of the texts does not suitably fit as a background piece, the thesis will lose credibility. If it can be shown that one of the subtexts is clearly and substantially used for more than one Gospel, the thesis will be placed in doubt. This criterion requires that each prophetic subtext function in a singular and unrepeated manner. Two Gospels using the same subtext or two prophetic texts applying equally well to a single Gospel will break down the claim for uniqueness. A cognate objective will also focus upon answering the following subordinate questions: 1) does the proposed unity-substructure account for the various emphases in each of the four Gospels; 2) does this substructure explain omissions in a particular Gospel which is recorded in the others, and 3) does the proposed substructure help to resolve divergent accounts in the four Gospels?

Second, do the individual elements of each prophetic text find correspondence in a respective Gospel? This is an extension of the first criterion but with a narrower focus. If a substantial number of details of a prophetic subtext do not provide matching characteristics for the appropriate Gospel, the thesis will be weakened. Conversely is the opposite: if it can be shown that the individual details of each prophetic subtext do find a reasonable match in a respective Gospel, this should constitute probative evidence of a weighty nature. As an extension of the first criterion, its goal is to establish emphasis or singularity by means of detailed analysis. Overlapping is expected from one Gospel to another (especially in the synoptic tradition). But evidence of overlapping does not equal emphasis or cancel out its uniqueness. It is hoped that this second criterion will provide a check on the dangers of simplification.

Tangentially to the aforementioned is the intent to explain the unprecedented nature of a fourfold Gospel. These arguments will also be based upon the concept of plausibility rather than "proof texting."[4] Since there is no specific claim in any of the four Gospels making use of any of the proposed subtexts, "proof" is automatically eliminated; plausibility thus becomes the goal of this study. If the plausibility case as

---

to Wrede (1968) 7. I borrow Schweitzer's wording but intend a different application. Schweitzer must be credited, however, with recognizing a valuable truth: if the Gospels are products of random and happy chance, then it is hopeless to understand the principles behind their composition.

4. John S. Kloppenborg Verbin, "The Theological Stakes in the Synoptic Problem," in *The Four Gospels 1992* (1992) 93: "Since purely logical considerations do not resolve the Synoptic problem, the second issue—that of the plausibility of the editorial scenarios implied by each solution—becomes important. Here, clearly, we are dealing only in the realm of probability rather than 'proofs.'"

presented in this investigation can be established, then the subsequent challenge will be directed toward accounting for the *cause* that has generated the singular phenomenon of a fourfold Gospel. In other words, if a case for a unified substructure for the four Gospels can be established, what then is the *implication* of such a unity? This final stage of the investigation, deferred until the end, will be to explore the potential implications of a unified substructure as it relates to the issue of divine revelation.

1

A Plausible Case for Divine Revelation

AMONG ACADEMICS, THE CONCEPT of divine revelation has fallen upon hard times. The past century was not kind to this viewpoint as an ever escalating number of scholars concluded that supernatural inspiration was indefensible. As a consequence, this increasingly larger coterie of academics has turned to issues of historicity, literary relationships both inside and outside the sacred text(s), and social backgrounds.[1] Paul Tillich may serve as an entry point for the prevailing pessimism: "The idea of revelation is a creation of Hellenistic philosophy."[2] H. Richard Niebuhr, a Yale professor of theology and a representative voice from the 1940's intellectual climate, weighed in from the American side with an even more dismal appraisal. After dubbing belief in revelation as "fanciful," Niebuhr expanded his criticism into the following judgment: "It seems to be a part of the general flight of a troubled generation to fairy-tales and historical romances."[3] Two representative quotations from the 1960s underscore a similar point. F. Gerald Downing claimed, "The word 'revelation' is a source of great confusion. A theology

---

1. See Ronald F. Thiemann, *Revelation and Theology* (1985) 1, though defending the proposition of revelation, Thiemann acknowledges: "A sense of revelation-weariness has settled over the discipline and most theologians have happily moved to other topics of inquiry." See also Werner E. Lemke, "Revelation through History in Recent Biblical Theology," *Int* 36.1 (1982) 35: "It may be said, therefore, that the concept of revelation through history, which once enjoyed great popularity among theologians, has become problematic for many in recent years. Some have stopped talking about it altogether."

2. P. Tillich,"Die Idee der Offenbarung," *ZThK* 8 (1927, reprinted in *Offenbarung und Glaube* [1970] 8.31–39) 403: "Der Offenbarungsbegriff ist eine Schöpfung der hellenistischen Philosophie." For the view that Christians and pagans shared similar views of inspiration, see Robert J. Hauck, *The More Divine Proof: Prophecy and Inspiration in Celsus and Origin* (1989).

3. R. Niebuhr, *The Meaning of Revelation* (1941) 4. In 1944, Ned B. Stonehouse published his *The Witness of Matthew and Mark to Christ* in which he optimistically expressed the following view (vii): "Although many efforts have been put forth to discover a Jesus other than the divine Christ of the gospels to whom men might pledge fealty, the history of that search appears more and more clearly to have demonstrated its futility." Little did Stonehouse foresee what was coming around the corner: a reenergized "search," an ever expanding membership in the Society of Biblical Literature, and a proliferation of international journals in biblical research containing studies of the widest diversity on the subject of Jesus. However, Ronald S. Hendel, "Farewell to SBL: Faith and Reason in Biblical Studies," *BAR* 36.4 (July/August 2010) 28, acknowledges his personal disenchantment with recent SBL policy decisions to admit "fundamentalist groups" into annual meetings. For the brouhaha that this has created, see the follow-up issue in *BAR* 36.6 (November/December 2010) 12.

based on it is inadequate for the exposition of the traditional faith of Christians."[4] In a similar vein, Emil Bruner referred to revelation as a "scandal" to the modern mind.[5] Moving into more recent times, J. J. M. Roberts pronounced a funeral oration over the subject of revelation suggesting not just a decline but a "demise" in biblical theology.[6] As if rendering a coroner's verdict, his judgment placed the subject of revelation in the coffin of academic dead bones. More recently, William J. Abraham writes: "If truth be told, the contemporary academy does not find the appeal to divine revelation at all attractive. Outside theology, and often within theology itself, the appeal to revelation is simply not permissible."[7] Most recently, Bart D. Ehrman has registered his own personal disillusionment with inspiration by advocating that Scripture is simply and purely a "very human book."[8] Whether labeled as confusing, outdated, offensive, impossible, or impermissible, the concept of revelation is no longer considered relevant in theological discourse.[9] Thus, judging from the above selected examples, the academic study of Scripture for the past seventy-five years has been marinating in a sauce of humanistic ingredients. Although

---

4. F. Downing, *Has Christianity a Revelation?* (1964) 274.

5. E. Brunner, *The Scandal of Christianity: The Gospel as a Stumbling Block to Modern Man* (1965) 28. John L. McKenzie, *The Old Testament without Illusion* (1979) 8, upon raising the issue of inspiration, admits that there is "no solution to the problem, and therefore it is not worth pursuing."

6. J. Roberts, "Myth Versus History," *CBQ* 38.1 (1976) 1. For the effects of biblical/historical criticism upon theology during the 1970s, see also R. S. Barbour, "The Bible—Word of God?" in *Biblical Studies* (1976) 29. See also James Barr, "The Theological Case against Biblical Theology," in *Canon, Theology, and Old Testament Interpretation* (1988) 4, where Barr argues that biblical theology has lost its "power to persuade." For an interesting study comparing Catholic with Protestant theology on the subject of inspiration, see Thomas A. Hoffman, "Inspiration, Normativeness, Canonicity, and the Unique Sacred Character of the Bible," *CBQ* 44.3 (1982) 459: "Protestants have talked for years about degrees of inspiration as a way of handling the perceived differences in religious value between, say, Romans 8 and the Epistle of Jude, or between Ps 23 and Ps 109."

7. W. Abraham, "The Offense of Divine Revelation," *HTR* 95.3 (2002) 254. See also his *Divine Revelation and the Limits of Historical Criticism* (1982). For a confirmation of Abraham's view, see James Barr, *The Concept of Biblical Theology* (1999) 605: "the concept of biblical theology is a *contested* concept." For an analysis of Barr's position, see Robert W. Yarbrough, "James Barr and the Future of Revelation in History in New Testament Theology," *BBR* 14.1 (2004) 105–26.

8. B. Ehrman, *Misquoting Jesus* (2005) 11: "This became a problem for my view of inspiration . . . Now I no longer saw the Bible that way. The Bible began to appear to me as a very human book . . . . This was a human book from beginning to end."

9. For a rare scholarly dialogue on the subject of inspiration, see Wolfgang Speyer, "Falschung, Pseudepigraphische freie Erfindung und 'echte religiöse Pseudepigrahphe,'" in *Pseudepigrapha I: Entretiens sur l'antiquité classique*, 18 (1972) 333–66, followed by the response from M. von Fritz, 367–72. For views on inspiration in the early church, see the two essays in *Studies in Early Christianity* (1993) 2–46, "On The Primitive Doctrine of Inspiration," by Brooke Foss Westcott, and 47–62, and "Theology of Scripture in St. Irenaeus," by Dennis Farkasfalvy.

precise data may not be possible to determine,[10] there are exceptions to this consensus at the academic level.[11]

Probing into the Present State of Affairs: Dogmas and Dogmatics

For the benefit of some readers, it may be worthwhile to inquire into this state of affairs. Why has contemporary theology abandoned the discussion of divine inspiration? In short, the answer is that the claims of Scripture are no longer viewed as authoritative and, as a result, they cannot be used as decisive evidence in the forum of international scholarship. This objection may be summed up accordingly: the idea that Scripture makes a valid claim on its own behalf for its unique divine origin is no longer tenable; Scripture as a self-authenticating text is thus dismissed. Or, to state this otherwise: just because Scripture says something does not automatically make it true.[12] Furthermore, the self-witness of Scripture does not exempt such auto-proclamations from being studied critically as any other book. It is difficult, therefore, in today's academic climate to argue that Scripture is divinely inspired—regardless of the Bible's own particular claims.[13] This means that no given biblical text can be accepted at face

---

10. It appears that conservative scholars see an abundance of liberals, while liberals are surprised at the number of conservatives. I note the observation by P. J. Du Plessis, "Fundamentalism as Methodological Principle," in *Text and Interpretation* (1991) 201: "Despite the academic attitude towards the matter, it is remarkable to note that fundamentalism is either totally or partially practised, surprisingly, by more scholars then one would imagine, all over the world." Du Plessis defines fundamentalism as an attitude that takes Scripture as the inspired Word of God.

11. See C. P. Price, "Revelation as Our Knowledge of God: An Essay in Biblical Theology," in *Faith and History* (1990) 333: "A Christian theologian is obliged to do justice to the new element in the New Testament. Revelation is recognized as revelation because it is a disclosure of God's power over human limits. New revelation discloses God's power in a new dimension. Otherwise, it does not break the categories found adequate for the former revelation." F. F. Bruce, *The Canon of Scripture* (1988) 281, was simply unapologetic: "The work of the Holy Spirit is not discerned by means of the common tools of the historian's trade." See also Leon Morris, *I Believe in Revelation* (1976), for similar confessional statements. Such confessions are atypical at the academic level. Morris, however, acknowledges (4): "We can no longer take revelation for granted." Most recently, I note the confessional position by Mark L. Strauss, *Four Portraits, One Jesus* (2007) esp. 84, 228, 253. See the earlier article by Brevard S. Childs, "The *Sensus Literalis* of Scripture: An Ancient and Modern Problem," in *Beiträge zur Alttestamentlichen Theologie* (1977) 80–93. See the collection of essays edited by Jack Rogers in *Biblical Authority* (1977). Finally, see John W. Wenham, *Christ and the Bible* (1972), and D. A. Carson, *The Gagging of God* (1996) 141–91.

12. In a sense, this is true. We do not accept something as true because "something" says so. Other considerations must come into play. For example, non-Mormons do not accept the book of Mormon as true simply because that book makes a claim for revelation. Similarly, non-Muslims do not accept the Qu'ran/Koran as true just because that book claims to be a revelation.

13. See John H. Leith, "The Bible and Theology," *Int* 30 (1976) 228: "The situation has now changed. The Bible can be and is regarded by many as just another book. In a highly pluralistic, secular society, and after the last century of critical-historical study of the Scripture, the role of the Bible can no longer be taken for granted in theology." A similar view is expressed by A. O. Dyson, *Who Is Jesus Christ?* (1969) 21: "I take the view that we cannot in fact begin our enquiry about Jesus Christ from a supposed revelation." See also Robert M. Price, *The Incredible Shrinking Son of Man* (2003) 13, who refers

value; all must be interpreted in light of various scholarly disciplines. In fact, some would even argue that unless Scripture is corroborated elsewhere outside the sacred text, it is probably not true.[14]

In scholarly literature the theological concept of dogmatics is often introduced and set at odds with history.[15] While "dogmatics" can be a sobriquet for a branch or discipline of study,[16] it can also convey a sense of naïveté. In this sense, a dogma may represent something personally and subjectively believed in contrast to something objective or reasonable. Furthermore, dogmatic labels often end up being used like stickers to attach to a gullible person. For example, in the Hellenistic Greek tradition Polybius coined the term λαοδογματικός to describe "people's opinions" or "popular notions."[17] The geographer Strabo made use of similar language to describe similar postures.[18] The idea that inheres within the word is that of a simpleton who clings to strong opinions supported by little or no evidence. There is yet another use, not often mentioned in biblical studies, but apparent. A dogmatic attitude can describe a stubborn and unbudging position.[19] Quite often, though, scholars using the term "dogma" may consciously present themselves as objectively innocent and bipartisanly neutral, when, in fact, such neutrality is impossible. Dogmatic agendas exist on both sides of the aisle. As Eric Lane Titus once said, "It has always been one of the pitfalls of historico-critical research that there are hidden dogmatic interests."[20]

---

to the dogmatic application of Scripture as an attempt to "bully the skeptic." Finally, there is the recent assumption by George Aichele, "Jesus's Two Fathers: An Afterlife of the Gospel of Luke," in *Those Outside: Non-canonical Readings of the Canonical Gospels* (2005) 23: "The Bible no longer controls the meanings of its constituent texts." This present study, by contrast, is an attempt to interpret the Bible on its own terms.

14. For this point of view, see Philip R. Davies, "'House of David' Built on Sand: The Sins of the Biblical Maximizers," *BAR* 20.4 (1994) 54–55.

15. In an unusual exception, the late Carl F. H. Henry in his *Frontiers in Modern Theology* (1965) 41, in referring to Continental dogmatics as those who formed an exclusive private club, stated: "Membership was restricted mainly to scholars who shared the speculative dogma that spiritual truth cannot be unified with historical and scientific truth." See also Neil J. McEleney, "Authenticating Criteria and Mark 7.1–23," *CBQ* 34 (1972) 431, in which he refers to "eminent authorities" who "exercise a lord-like arbitrariness" in dismissing as authentic given statements in the Gospels.

16. F. H. Klooster, "Dogmatics," *Evangelical Dictionary of Theology* (2001) 350–51: "Dogmatics. That branch of theology which attempts to express the beliefs and doctrines of the Christian faith . . . in an organized and systematic way . . . this discipline is now more commonly called 'systematic theology' or simply 'theology.'"

17. Polybius, *Histories* 35.14.

18. Strabo, *Geography* 2.4.2.

19. A witness to this particular usage is the opening sentence by M.-E. Boismard, "The Two-Source Theory at an Impasse," *NTS* 26.1 (1979–80) 1, in which the author refers to the "unassailable dogma in Germany" that the Two-Source theory had finally and decisively won the day.

20. E. L. Titus, "The Fourth Gospel and the Historical Jesus," in *Jesus and the Historian* (1968) 115. See also Stanley E. Porter, *John, His Gospel, and Jesus* (2015) 35, who refers to "a subtle, hidden agenda" by some scholars to relocate the Gospel of John into the second century.

From my own viewpoint, I consider the notion that Mary remained a virgin for all of her life an idea (or "dogma") that is foreign to the biblical text and, therefore, an unreasonable claim. Yet, I consider the idea that Jesus was not born of a virgin also an unreasonable dogma, since that, too, is foreign to the biblical text. A case in point is Amand Puig i Tàrrech's treatment of Mary in his recent *Jesus: A Biography*.[21] While discussing the reference to the brothers and sisters of Jesus as recorded in Mark 6:3, Tàrrech finds it difficult to believe that Mary had biological sons and daughters after the birth of Jesus. In other words, he believes that Mary remained a virgin for all of her married life. I would add only that a dogma such as the *perpetual* virginity of Mary is foreign to the biblical text while her virginity is not an alien and extraneous element. Admittedly, then, this delineation serves to highlight that the word "dogma" can be a handy tag to describe others. As already stated, a dogma can be used to describe an unreasonable or stubborn attitude that resists fresh information.[22] Moreover, the pejorative use of the word usually results in the words "dogma" or "dogmatic" being employed to describe the unacceptable premise that reason must give way to the authority of Scripture.[23] As the skeptical argument goes, the theological cost of believing in divine revelation is purchased at the high price of forfeiting one's personal autonomy.[24]

The Influence of the Enlightenment

The erosion of confidence can be attributed to further antecedent causes. The impetus for this clashing view is generally traced back to the intellectual goal of the Enlightenment in which the scholar's conscience is liberated and protected against

---

21. A. Puig i Tàrrech, *Jesus: A Biography* (2011) 167–75.

22. See, for example, Bo Reicke, "Die Enstehungsverhältnisse der synoptischen Evangelien," *ANRW* 25.2 (1984) 1760: "später jedoch als seine Entdeckung des Markus bei Matthäus und Lukas von zahlreichen Forschern übernommen und hat sich wie ein Dogma über alle Länder verbreitet."

23. James H. Charlesworth, *Jesus within Judaism* (1988) 24: "Historical perception and methodology are the only means for separating dogma from superstition." Depending on your point of view, this statement can be slightly misleading. Some would actually equate dogma with superstition or even with the specious claims of historical Jesus research. For example, Heinz Zahrnt, *The Historical Jesus* (1963) 13, uses dogma in a reversal of its current application by affirming: "The attempt to use dogma as it were to overrun history has proved a failure." This statement sounds very much like a comment from Geza Vermes or Burton Mack; in reality, Zahrnt has turned the concept of dogma against historical Jesus scholarship.

24. See the comment by Edgar Krentz, *The Historical-Critical Method* (1975) 12: "Orthodoxy demanded instead a *sacrificium intellectus* in the face of the Bible's statements." See also Rudolf Bultmann's sustained and lengthy argument, "New Testament and Mythology," in *Kerygma and Myth* (1953) 3–4, in which Bultmann hammers away at his theme by postulating the view that NT cosmology is the language of mythology and, therefore, "A blind acceptance of the New Testament mythology would be irrational, and to press for its acceptance as an article of faith would be to reduce Christian faith to the level of a human achievement." Karl Jaspers, *Philosophical Faith and Revelation* (1967) 10, believed that belief in revelation was a detriment to human freedom.

the constraints of extraneous religious authority. Although his life has been variously assessed, the usual scapegoat for the avant-garde view of throwing off biblical authority and replacing it with faith in reason is David Hume. Hume essentially constructed the argument from Analogy by proposing that "firm and unalterable experience" is an established law and is, consequently, a proof against miracles.[25] The key concern that comes into view from an Enlightenment perspective is to allow the conscience the freedom to follow the evidence wherever it leads.[26] Writing in 1784, eight years after the death of David Hume and definitely living in his shadow, Immanuel Kant defined what that age understood by enlightenment:

> Enlightenment is man's emergence from his self-imposed immaturity. Immaturity is the inability to use one's understanding without guidance from another. This immaturity is *self-imposed* when its cause lies not in lack of understanding, but lack of resolve and courage to use it without guidance from another. *Sapere Aude!* "Have courage to use your own understanding!"—that is the motto of enlightenment.[27]

---

25. See *Enquiries Concerning Human Understanding and Concerning the Principles of Morals: Reprinted from the 1777 Edition with Introduction and Analytical Index* by L. A. Selby-Bigge (1902)114. For a review and discussion of Hume's rejection of the supernatural, see Ernst and Marie-Luise Keller, *Miracles in Dispute* (1969) 48–66. For a critique of some of David Hume's ideas, see Antony Flew, "Neo-Humean Arguments about the Miraculous," in *In Defense of Miracles* (1997) 45–58. Flew identified Hume as the first of two great philosophers of the Enlightenment. Flew, until recently, was an acknowledged atheist. For a recent response to Hume, see John C. Collins, *The God of Miracles* (2000) 147–51. For a positive application of the principle of freedom, see Brevard S. Childs, *Biblical Theology of the Old and New Testaments* (1993) 11, in which the author rightly mentions the dissatisfaction resulting from the imposition of dogmatic rubrics which are "foreign" to the biblical text. For a discussion of the relationship between dogma and historical criticism, see Robert Morgan, "The Hermeneutical Significance of Four Gospels," *Int* 33.4 (1979) 376–88.

26. The domino effect of the Enlightenment has been very energetic and enduring. In fact, the word "Enlightenment" is a commonplace in scholarly studies. For a discussion of how the Enlightenment affected the particular scholarly work of Ernst Troeltsch (1865–1923) who served as a philosophical bridge between David Strauss and Rudolph Bultmann, see Van Austin Harvey, *The Historian and the Believer* (1966) 3–5. For further influence of the Enlightenment on the Bible, see especially the two essays in *The Bible and the Enlightenment: A Case Study—Dr. Alexander Geddes (1737–1802)* [2004]: "Introduction: The Bible and the Enlightenment" by William Johnstone (1–34); and "What Do We Mean When We Talk about '(Late) Enlightenment Biblical Criticism'?" by Christopher Bultmann (119–34).

27. Immanuel Kant, "An Answer to the Question: What Is Enlightenment?" in *Perpetual Peace and Other Essays on Politics, History, and Morals* (1983) 41. The motto s*apere aude* comes from Horace (*Epistles* I.2.1.56: *dimidium facti qui coepit habet; sapere aude; incipe!* ["He who begins is half done. Dare to get started. Begin!"]). Although *sapio* can mean "be wise" or "be discerning," it appears that this mantra of the Enlightenment may have been misunderstood as the Latin line more accurately means "do not procrastinate" (as the verb preceding [*differs*] and the verb following [*prorogate*] suggest). For further discussions on the influence of the Enlightenment on biblical studies, see Henning Graf Reventlow, *The Authority of the Bible and the Rise of the Modern World* (1985); James E. Bradley and Dale K. Van Kley (eds.), *Religion and Politics in Enlightenment Europe* (2001); Luke Timothy Johnson, "The Humanity of Jesus," in *The Jesus Controversy* (1999) 48–74; in the same volume, see also Werner H. Kelber, "The Quest for the Historical Jesus," 75–115. See also N. T. Wright, *The Last Word: Scripture and the Authority of God* (2006) 82–105.

A fair and more up to date description of this enlightened autonomy is provided by Jack Dean Kingsbury as he assesses how contemporary scholarship interprets Matthew 1.18–25:

> Prior to the Enlightenment and rise of historical consciousness, the principal way in which commentators outlined the text was dogmatic in nature.... The focal theme of the text, therefore, is that of God's fulfillment of ancient prophecy, and all parts of the text undergird this theme. With the coming of the Enlightenment and the rise of rationalism and then liberalism in the 18th, 19th, and 20th centuries, commentators in droves forsook the dogmatic approach to 1:18–25 and replaced it with a radically historical approach.[28]

The influence of the Enlightenment further develops into the discipline of historical criticism and this, in turn, results in the abandonment of divine inspiration as a valid subject for serious inquiry.[29] Bart Ehrman articulates the modern position of the critical historian:

> Historians try to reconstruct what probably happened in the past on the basis of data that can be examined and evaluated by every interested observer of every persuasion. Access to these data does not depend on presuppositions or beliefs about God. This means that historians, as historians, have no privileged access to what happens in the supernatural realm; they have access only to what happens in this, our natural world. The historian's conclusions should, in theory, be accessible and acceptable to everyone, whether the person is a Hindu, a Buddhist, a Muslim, a Jew, a Christian, an atheist, a pagan, or anything else.[30]

---

28. J. D. Kingsbury, "The Birth Narrative of Matthew," in *The Gospel of Matthew in Current Study* (2001) 157–58. Kingsbury clearly does not adopt the dogmatic view but proceeds to show how literary and narrative analysis can circumvent the "dogmatic" label (as well as the historical one), and arrive at a proper understanding of the text.

29. For a nineteenth-century reaction to historical criticism, see William Sanday, "Methods of Theology: The Historical Method," in *Essays in Biblical Criticism and Exegesis* (2001, reprint from 1894) 22: "The historical method must not be employed as a covert means of getting rid of the supernatural. Wherever it has been so used, the use is wrong. It is no longer really the historical method. In itself that method is just as applicable to supernatural facts as to facts which are not supernatural. It is concerned with them only as facts. On the question of the cause of the facts it does not enter. To reject that for which the evidence is otherwise good, merely because it is supernatural, is a breach of the historical method; and where this is done the cause is sure to be ultimately traceable to that which is the direct opposite of this method, viz., philosophical presupposition." See also N.T. Wright, "The Surprise of the Resurrection," in *Jesus, the Final Days: What Really Happened* (2009) 105–6. More recently, see the monograph by Craig S. Keener, *The Historical Jesus of the Gospels* (2010) who examines the issue of whether the information in the Gospels is invented. For a sympathetic view of the ancient world, see John Killinger, *Hidden Mark: Exploring Christianity's Heretical Gospel* (2010) 13: "Miracles, strange occurrences, did not strain credulity then as they do now."

30. B. Ehrman, *The New Testament* (1997) 14. See also Dale C. Allison, "Explaining the Resurrection: Conflicting Convictions," *JSHJ* 3.2 (2005) 117.

From these self-imposed limitations of the discipline, historians decline to investigate the supernatural as a possibility.[31] This restricted view of history, however, is in many cases a post-Enlightenment development owing to the pressures of modern philosophical attitudes.[32] In this viewpoint an impossible dichotomy exists between revelation and the discipline of historical inquiry. A parallel may be found in the 1990 movie *Ghost*, starring Patrick Swayze who plays Sam Wheat, and Demi Moore who plays Molly Jensen. In the movie, Sam is fatally shot on the streets of New York and then as a departed spirit he spends the rest of the story trying to make physical contact with his surviving lover. These two souls, however, exist in separate worlds and thus can never touch the world of the other. This analog illustrates the construct as built up by the principles of historical criticism; for some scholars, perhaps many, the topic of divine revelation is seemingly like the movie *Ghost*: one dimension is off-limits to the other. It is not clear to me how or why inspiration should be placed off limits for investigation when it is an essential element contained in the biblical record. Yet, such is the state of academic affairs on the subject.

Consequently, the purpose of this study is to reverse the implication of the movie metaphor. Since the NT does not categorize Jesus on the level of a ghost, this study will advocate that the discipline of history should be a search for understanding not only what happened but also the cause or causes behind particular events—regardless of causation.[33] The position adopted in this present study is actually an application

---

31. For the rationale behind anti-supernaturalism as applied to NT research, see Rudolf Bultmann, "Is Exegesis without Presuppositions Possible?" in *Existence and Faith* (1966) 289–96. Not all historians disclaim the supernatural, but certainly an overwhelming majority. A small minority are willing to write as historians and, at the same time, defend the proposition of an inspired sacred text. Generally, though, this conservative defense of Scripture takes the form of defending the historical data of the biblical text as opposed to an outright defense of inspiration. See, for example, the survey article by Alanna Nobbs, "What Do Ancient Historians Make of the New Testament?" *TynBul* 57.2 (2006) 285–90. For a very recent survey of the problem and the trend away from the defense of revelation to an argument based upon historical reliability, see Paul Rhodes Eddy and Gregory A. Boyd, *The Jesus Legend: A Case for the Historical Reliability of the Synoptic Jesus Tradition* (2007). See also Craig L. Blomberg, *The Historical Reliability of the Gospels* (1987). From a slightly different perspective, see Birger Gerhardsson, *The Reliability of the Gospel Tradition* (2001) and H. E. W. Turner, *Historicity and the Gospels* (1963).

32. See, for example, James H. Charlesworth, "What has the Old Testament to Do with the New?" in *The Old and New Testaments: Their Relationship and the "Intertestamental" Literature* (1993) 62: "Living in a pluralistic society demands developing a position that can be defended academically." For a response to these modern philosophic and academic pressures, see E. Earle Ellis, "The Synoptic Gospels and History," in *Authenticating the Activities of Jesus* (1999) 49–57. See also James D. G. Dunn, *Jesus Remembered* (2003) 28: "But the increasing secularism of modernity more and more reflected the triumph of autonomous human reason as axiomatic." Finally, I note John P. Meier, "The Present State of the 'Third Quest' for the Historical Jesus: Loss and Gain," *Bib* 80.4 (1999) 463: "All too often, the first and second quests were theological projects masquerading as historical projects."

33. See Ernst Troeltsch, "Historiography," *Encyclopaedia of Religion and Ethics* (1961) 6.718: "What is it, then, that constitutes the essential element of pure historical knowledge? . . . .The sole task of history in its specifically theoretical aspect is to explain every movement, process, state, and nexus of things by reference to the web of its causal relations. That is, in a word, the whole function of purely

of the Enlightenment principle of freedom but one which follows the evidence to an opposite conclusion. Hence, an attempt will be made to reseat the issue of revelation at the table of theological discussion.[34]

The Analogy Argument

Another major reason for the modern rejection of the concept of biblical inspiration may be summed up and expressed by the word *hostile*. I use the word "hostile" here in the sense of something alien, foreign, and suspicious to normal human experience.[35] Philosophically, this hostility is expressed by the anti-term *Analogy*. Historical criticism defends this analogy-argument upon the basis that in order for a modern interpreter to accept anything as true from the ancient past, such an event must possess a corresponding analogy to present human experience.[36] If there is no analogy or correspondence, this event must be consigned to the status of a myth.[37] In such a model,

---

scientific investigation." For the view that an "explanation" behind a particular historical event is impossible to safely arrive at, see Charles E. Carlston, "Prologue," in *Studying the Historical Jesus* (1994) 7: "Whatever the description of Jesus is supposed to yield, we must be very cautious about imagining that description is equivalent to explanation."

34. As in other aspects of life, scholarly debates often occur in cycles. Leander E. Keck, "Toward the Renewal of New Testament Christology," *NTS* 32.2 (1979–80) 362, relies upon the appeal of such cycles and the need to reopen old issues by affirming that "the time is at hand to take up again what was set aside—an explicitly theological approach to NT Christology."

35. See Albert Wifstrand, "Die wahre Lehre des Kelsos," *BSRLL* (1941–42) 398: "Der Fehler der Christen besteht darin, dass sie sich absondern und sich gegen die von alters her üblichen Vorstellungen empören" (quotation cited by Robert J. Hauck, *The More Divine Proof* [1989] 10). For a negative visceral reaction to a recent sermon in which "God sent His only-begotten Son to be the unique God-man," see Wesley J. Wildman, *Fidelity with Plausibility* (1998) xvii. See also his reason (80): "supernaturalism itself cannot compete as an account of the world."

36. For an aggressive defense of the Analogy argument, see Robert M. Price, *The Incredible Shrinking Son of Man* (2003) 19–20. After stating that "All historical and scientific judgments are *probabilistic* in nature, provisional and tentative, because they are inevitably based on analogy (19)," Price then asks how the historian can deal with the "wildcard" of an act of God. He answers his own question by responding (20): "Merely because some ancient text says so? If we do not use the criterion of analogy with contemporary experience as our shibboleth for what *probably* did and did not happen in the past, we will be at the mercy of every medieval tale, every report that a statue wept, or that someone changed lead into gold or turned into a werewolf." For an updated version of the above, see Robert M. Price, "Jesus at the Vanishing Point," in *The Historical Jesus: Five Views* (2009) 56. For a more moderate view of Analogy, see Paul N. Anderson, *The Fourth Gospel and the Quest for Jesus* (2006) 178, where the author suggests a mediating approach between strident interpretations which "fail to correspond to general human experience" and recent cosmological views (those involving quarks, chaos theory and quantum mechanics) "that have caused the best of scientists to challenge mechanistic cosmologies and entirely predictable understandings of nature." For a rigorous examination and rebuttal to the argument of Analogy, see Charles Stephen Evans, *The Historical Christ and the Jesus of Faith* (1996) 197–200.

37. For the philosophical underpinnings of the Analogy argument, see Ernst Troeltsch, "Über historische und dogmatische Methode in der Theologie," in *Gesammelte Schriften zur religiosen Lage, Religionsphilosophie und Ethik* (922) 2.732: "Die Übereinstimmung mit normalen, gewöhnlichen oder doch mehrfach bezeugten Vorgangsweisen unter Zuständen, wie wir sie kennen, ist das Kennzeichen der Wahrscheinlichkeit für die Vorgänge, die die Kritik als wirklich geschehen anerkennen oder übrig

scriptural expressions such as revelation come under immediate suspicion of being a vehicle or instrument for deceiving others, to exaggerate one's own sense of importance, or to avoid responsibility for actions committed illegally.[38] In the third-century theological debate between Celsus and Origen, this is the salvo fired at Christians by Celsus who charges that Christians were deceiving the people by relying upon the argument that the OT is divinely inspired.[39] Present attitudes, therefore, are not restricted to our age; modern views have precedents in antiquity and they are connected to what can be known and experienced solely by means of what is characteristic of all humans. Thus, many of these modern attitudes are simply an old mannequin dressed up in a new skirt.

The Analogy-argument presumes that the supernatural must be rejected in light of a scientific attitude and in view of normal human experience.[40] This presupposition by Analogy,[41] however, contains two major weaknesses. First of all, it makes it difficult,

---

lassen kann. Die Beobachtung von Analogien zwischen gleichartigen Vorgängen der Vergangenheit gibt die Möglichkeit, ihnen Wahrscheinlichkeit zuzuschreiben unter das Unbekannte des einen aus dem Bekannten des anderen zu deuten." See Van E. Harvey's comments in his *The Historian and the Believer* (1966) 10, on David Strauss's *Life of Jesus Critically Examined* (1906): "Strauss undermined all of these alternatives by arguing that the writers of the New Testament—in fact, the people of the entire age—were naïve and mythologically-minded folk without any conception of natural law or order. They lived in a mythological time in which unusual events of nature and history were attributed to supernatural being of all kinds. The standard of reality was different than ours; their writings expressed a picture of the world which, though natural to them, is entirely alien to our own. Strauss, in short, began to think historically . . . . It is clear, for example, that Strauss' concept of myth is predicated on the view that 'all things are linked together by a chain of causes and effects, which suffers no interruption.'" Another example, perhaps milder by comparison, is Oscar Cullmann, *Christ and Time* (1965) 94.

38. Josephus in his *Jewish War* (2.13.45/258–63) and *Jewish Antiquities* (20.8.6/167–72) indicates that the guise of "divine inspiration" can be used to seduce people into insurrection. This is also often the case involving modern cults. An example of this aberration of biblical revelation may be found in the recent cult situation in Eldorado, Texas involving the sect of the Fundamentalist Church of Jesus Christ of Latter Day Saints (FLDS) and the alleged abuse of children. For a popular yet helpful essay dissecting these issues, see "How Polygamy Cleaved the Mormon Church," by Kimberly Winston, *USA Today* (April 21, 2008) 7D.

39. For a discussion of the issues dividing Celsus and Origen, see Robert J. Hauck (1989) 26, in which he cites an old work by Louis Rougier, *Celse contre les Chrétiens: la réaction païenne sous l'empire Romain* (1926): "Le *Discours vrai* inaugure le conflit séculaire de la science et de la religion."

40. What Paul Veyne, in *Did the Greeks Believe in Their Myths?* (1988) 14, calls the doctrine of present things: "The past resembles the present, or, in other words, the marvelous does not exist." The task, as he sees it, involves eliminating everything that has "no proven equivalent in our historical era" (71). See also Rudolph Bultmann, "New Testament and Mythology," in *Kerygma and Myth* (1953) 7, in which Bultmann, on the basis of Analogy, raises his own objections to accepting the NT view of reality and contends that modern science has rendered our world as a "self-subsistent unity immune from the interference of supernatural powers."

41. I do not mean to imply that *all* applications of the argument by Analogy are flawed. Austin Farrer, "Inspiration: Poetical and Divine," in *Promise and Fulfillment* (1963) 97, provides the following balanced view: "We look about for analogies, with which to support our belief: for though religious faith deals with mysteries which are *sui generis*, because God himself is absolutely unique; at the same time we expect religious mysteries to bear some analogy with natural realities, because they are revealed in the stuff of our human experience." Farrer, as I understand him, is using the concept of

if not impossible, for those who hold to this view to examine all the evidence. John Dominic Crossan's assessment may illustrate the point:

> First, it is important to emphasize clearly what my argument does not propose. It does not propose that history equals faith. It does not propose that history replaces faith. It does not propose that history creates faith. If two individuals saw and heard everything that the historical Jesus said and did in the first century, they could still respond like this. The one: he is a subversion of the Roman gods of law and order, he is dangerous and criminal; he should be executed. The other: he is an incarnation of the Jewish God of justice and righteousness, he is Messiah and Lord; he should be worshipped. The same applies to us today if we had a complete video tape of all that data. It would not be faith. It would not force faith. It would not guarantee faith. In other words, there can be history without faith. But, and this is the question, *can* there be *faith without history*?[42]

Is Crossan saying that even if someone were to see a video tape of the resurrection of Jesus, this person would not believe? If such is the case, this is the dilemma of those who hold to the Analogy argument—whether living in the ancient world or the modern. Not even a video tape would persuade them. However, Crossan is correct on one point: it is true that there can be no faith without history.

Given the state of contemporary affairs on the subject of inspiration, discussion is difficult—perhaps for some impossible.[43] As acknowledged above, there is a certain polarizing power to the subject of divine inspiration. Nevertheless, this difficulty should not be construed as sufficient justification for the abdication of either belief in divine revelation or the discussion of its merits. Regrettably, however, under the self-imposed limitations of the Analogy argument, an unfortunate upshot is unavoidable: if the claim for the resurrection of Jesus is valid, there is no way to verify it when clinging to the Analogy presupposition. Hence, the supernatural remains a major flashpoint in biblical studies.

Secondly, this Analogy perspective assumes that everyone in the ancient world was of the same mythological mindset, with no powers of critical judgment, with no exceptions. This is most unfortunate as there are exceptions. A notable exception is

---

Analogy to undergird biblical truth, not to undermine it. A positive application of Analogy in this sense would be that Jesus experienced both birth and death. How he experienced these two realities would fall into the category of *sui generis*.

42. J. D. Crossan, "Historical Jesus as Risen Lord," in *The Jesus Controversy* (1999) 1. I do agree with Crossan on one other point: the Gospels indeed show opposite responses of faith to Jesus.

43. See Van Austin Harvey, *The Historian and the Believer* (1966), who examines the work of Ernst Troeltsch (1865–1923) 5: "If the theologian believes that the events of the Bible are the results of the supernatural intervention of God, the historian regards such an explanation as a hindrance to true historical understanding." Troeltsch serves as a philosophical bridge between David Strauss and Rudolf Bultmann. A further result from the Enlightenment can be seen in such studies as the argument that Scripture is a book of fantasy tales; see, for example, George Aichele, "Literary Fantasy and the Composition of the Gospels," *Forum* 5 (1989) 42–60.

the case of Hippocrates in his *Airs, Waters, Places* (22.5–13). In this text it is possible to observe an ancient author penetrating through the then prevailing superstitious belief that God was the cause of male impotency. Empirically, he draws the following logical conclusion:

> Now the natives put the blame on God, and they reverence and worship its victims, fearful of being stricken by it themselves. I, too, think that these diseases are divine in nature as are all others and that no single phenomenon is more divine or more human than the others; but all are alike and all are divine. Each has its own nature, and none arises without its natural cause.

Hippocrates says that there is uniformity in nature and that this general uniformity permits no exceptions. In turn, this consistent method gives him a reliable tool for understanding the cause of disease. At 22.53, after concluding he has diagnosed the real cause of male impotency among the Scythians (horseback riding), Hippocrates says: "But the truth is, as I said above, these affections are neither more nor less divine than any others, all and each are natural." This is an early scientific method at work. It contains observation and examination of the data at hand, followed by repetition, comparison, and confirmation. By adopting a scientific method, Hippocrates concludes that the affliction of male impotency arises from natural causes.

A further case in point is the moralist Plutarch. Although he is generally sympathetic to reports involving unusual phenomena, Plutarch does have limits. In his *Numa* (4.3), he expresses doubt that an immortal god can have intercourse with a human. Even more to the point, Plutarch actually states the view that virgins do not give birth to babies.[44] Furthermore, Plutarch affirms as "very childish" (παιδικὸν κομιδῇ) the belief that a god can inspire prophetic utterances.[45] Hippocrates and Plutarch are not alone; others possessed similar critical powers of judgment.[46]

I cite three others who illustrate that the ancients were capable of a "scientific" point of view. Dionysius of Halicarnassus may be consulted as evidence that ancients could penetrate through myth to truth. In his *Critical Essays: Thucydides* (7), Dionysius is aware that an uncritical view of history can lead to deceiving the people. Among his examples of incredible and ignorant tales is the idea of the sexual union between mortals and gods.[47] Hence, the claim that naïve ancients could be duped by

---

44. Plutarch, *Advice to the Bride and Groom* 145D.

45. *Obsolescence of Oracles* 414E.

46. Pausanias may also serve as an example of such critical thinking. In his *Description of Greece: Attica* (1.30.4) Pausanias says that he is prepared to believe that a musician can become a king, but it is impossible to believe that a bird grows out of a man.

47. Dionysius does, however, show some ambivalence on this subject. In his *Roman Antiquities* (4.2.2) he relays the account of one Acrisia who allegedly has sex with a phantom (φάσμα). After narrating the strange tale, he writes: τοῦτο τὸ μύθευμα οὐ πάνυ τι πιστόν εἶναι ("This myth is not very [somewhat] believable"). He then proceeds to recount a fabulous version of fire shooting out of Tullius's head. Although it does not appear as though his intention was to make a comparison between the two incidents, he makes it clear that the case of fire shooting out of man's head is more credible

the story of a virgin birth because of their mythological view of reality does not stand up to the testimony of those ancients. Also among them is Justin Martyr who was of the understanding that a virgin birth falls clearly in the category of things considered "impossible" (ἀδύνατα).[48]

Yet, the ancients did, in fact, report very unusual miracles or prodigies. This can be seen from both Greek and Roman historians. Appian in his *Roman History: The Civil Wars* (1. 83) describes mysterious terrors falling upon the people because of the chaos of war. Among these terrors was the report of a woman giving birth to a snake instead of a child. Appian does not question the report. He says simply that this was but one of many such prodigies occurring at that time (τέρατά τε πολλὰ ἐγίνοντο). Dionysius of Halicarnassus in his *Roman Antiquities* (1.67.1–2) reports that a marvelous sign (θαῦμα) is said to have occurred when the statues within a temple dedicated to Aeneas miraculously changed positions during the night. He apparently takes the report at face value. Even Plutarch in his *Alexander* (14.5) reports that a wooden image of Orpheus at Leibethra broke out in a profuse sweat when Alexander set out on one of his expeditions. Plutarch does not question the credibility of the account. Of course, Polybius (10.5.8; 9.2) categorically rejects any explanation of historical events due to supernatural causation. On the NT side, there are reports that the early disciples witnessed Jesus alive and resurrected after his death. The rationalist rejects both the secular and sacred accounts as fabulous fictions. Supernaturalists, however, reject the former secular accounts but accept the latter sacred accounts. What is the difference? It has to do with one's view of Scripture, and one's view of Scripture ultimately traces back to cause and result.

The text of Matt 1:18–24 presents the reader with a test case. This biblical event capsizes normal analogical experience and illustrates the above point.[49] Within the account itself, the description shows Mary either blinded by this mythological mist or, conversely, she is conniving to take advantage of it in order to cover up her sin. Joseph, however, is neither persuaded nor pigeonholed into the same box. He questions her version of events because he does not see an analogy. There is nothing in his experience that corresponds to her account of what allegedly has happened. In short, he does not believe in virgin births,[50] sees no analogy and, therefore, considers her

---

than a woman having sex with a phantom.

48. Justin Martyr, *Apologiae pro Christianis* 33.2: ἃ γὰρ ἦν ἄπιστα καὶ ἀδύνατα νομιζόμενα παρὰ τοῖς ἀνθρώποις. See also Origen's *Contra Celsum* 2.20 for his statement that it is impossible for conception to occur without intercourse.

49. For other exceptions, see Alexander Globe, "Some Doctrinal Variants in Matthew 1 and Luke 2, and the Authority of the Neutral Text," *CBQ* 42 (1980) 57: "From the first, Jewish and pagan disbelief posed problems." For his references, see fn. 19 on the same page.

50. For the view that Joseph lacked the critical acumen to really understand what happened, see W. D. Davies and Dale Allison, *A Critical and Exegetical Commentary on the Gospel According to Saint Matthew* (1988) 221: "Matthew's thoughts are not our thoughts: he could hardly have operated with modern ideas of history and fiction." I believe to the contrary: Joseph's thoughts (and Matthew's thoughts) are our thoughts. Because of Joseph's world view, he originally rejected Mary's explanation;

unfaithful to him. According to Matthew, it takes an intervention from God to help Joseph overcome his worldview of natural law. Outside the account itself but within the mental world of Matthew, it may be questioned why he begins his Gospel with this inclusion of a doubting Joseph. If everyone in the ancient world was disposed to a mythological view of reality, why introduce a skeptical Joseph? Of course, it may be countered that this biblical narrative is simply a fictional disguise to mask the unpleasant truth of a promiscuous pregnancy.[51] This criticism, however, does not stand up to scrutiny since Joseph is clearly described as rejecting Mary's explanation for her conception. Initially, he thinks that he sees through the fabrication and concludes there is a legitimate basis for divorce. If this was meant to be taken as a genuine myth because people could extract some meaning from it, why involve Joseph as a foil in the narrative? If the account is a fiction, his presence does not simplify it with a plausible explanation but actually complicates the narrative.[52] Why not simply allow Mary's account to stand alone or, at least, present Joseph as naïvely accepting her story? The answer must be that Matthew's Joseph is allowed to have a voice because he speaks for all who understand that virgins do not conceive without a male partner. In other words, Joseph does not operate in a symbolic world of ancient myth but, rather, thinks in accordance with a real world view identical to our own.[53] Joseph's initial resistance is based upon his belief in the Analogy argument; his eventual acceptance of the pregnancy is based upon divine intervention—the only means available to him which would allow him to set aside his analogy preconceptions. The modern scholarly view that ancients, such as Joseph, could offer only a palliative diagnosis of the real situation does not accord with the facts.

The Questionable Case for Science

One of the more salient aspects of contemporary biblical scholarship and academic publishing is the claim to be scientific. It is very common to read the word "scientific"

---

only divine intervention allowed him to see things otherwise.

51. Livy in his *Ab urbe condita* (1.4.1) mentions the Vestal who, upon being raped and giving birth to twin boys, credited Mars as the father of the boys. Livy is not sure why she claimed Mars as the father; perhaps she really believed this or maybe it was simply less troublesome to deal with the unfortunate truth. Livy makes it plain in his Prologue (9) that he will attach no significance to such tales.

52. Marcus Borg, *Jesus: Uncovering the Life, Teachings, and Relevance of a Religious Revolution* (2006) 57, proposes that the gospel records narrating the miraculous, such as the virgin birth of Jesus, are "purely metaphorical narratives." That is, the Gospels were not meant to be taken seriously as real and literal events but only as fictions expressing symbolic truth. For an examination of this possibility, see Dale C. Allison, *Constructing Jesus: Memory, Imagination, and History* (2010) 435–62. Allison, at times, places himself in the same skeptical camp as Borg (456–58); at other times, he questions his own skepticism, but seems to have no secure place to go.

53. Paul Veyne, *Did the Greeks Believe in Their Myths* (1988) 28, claims that ancients were "not shaken by fictions that contradicted no known science." This is a confusing statement, actually attesting to the contrary. In Matthew's account, Joseph appears "shaken."

as applied to NT studies.⁵⁴ The word "scientific" presumes a claim to a certain objectivity which precludes the supernatural.⁵⁵ The assumption is that something "scientific" protects objective study from exaggerated one-sided theological enthusiasm. Consequently, the word *scientific* may serve as a catchword for dismissing the idea of the supernatural.⁵⁶ It is clearly not "scientific" for a substantial number of scholars to view Jesus in any transcendent manner.⁵⁷ To be sure, Jesus is placed on a human pedestal as an individual of remarkable influence, but he is not viewed in categories that

---

54. For a validation and celebration of the scientific method in biblical research, see James W. Robinson, "Introduction: The Dismantling and Reassembling of the Categories of New Testament Scholarship," in *Trajectories through Early Christianity* (1971) 2, where Robinson uses the words "science," "scientific," and "scientifically," four times in a single page to describe NT methodology. For the identification of scientific with historical and objective scholarship, see also James W. Robinson's verdict, "The Impossibility and Illegitimacy of the Original Quest," in *A New Quest of the Historical Jesus and other Essays* (1983) 26. For recent attempts to validate scientific research as applied to NT studies, see Philip F. Esler, "Models in New Testament Interpretation: A Reply to David Horrell," *JSNT* 78 (2000) 107–13; and David G. Horrell, "Models and Methods in Social-Scientific Interpretation: A Response to Philip Esler," *JSNT* 78 (2000) 83–105. Both Esler and Horrell make use of modern anthropological models to obtain insight into NT texts. There is nothing wrong with such an approach, but it is not to be identified with pure scientific research. See also John H. Elliot, "Social-Scientific Criticism of the New Testament: More on Methods and Models," *Semeia* 35.1 (1986) 1–34. For a critique of some of the issues involved in the "socio-scientific" attempt to span two thousand years, see Zeba A. Crook, "Reflections on Culture and Social-Scientific Models," *JBL* 124.3 (2005) 515–20. See also Bruce J. Malina, "Social-Scientific Methods in Historical Jesus Research," in *The Social Setting of Jesus and the Gospels* (2002) 3–26.

55. George E. Ladd, "The Search for Perspective," *Int* 25 (1971) 43, says: "Many American scholars vigorously rejected the new biblical theology in the name of scientific objectivity. A 'scientific' methodology means that we must study the Bible as a purely human document."

56. See especially Rudolf Bultmann's defense of the scientific approach in his "Is Exegesis without Presuppositions Possible?" (1966) 289–96. See also the observation of how a modern Jew looks at current NT scholarship in Matthew Hoffman's *From Rebel to Rabbi* (2007) 14. Hoffman's assessment is correct, although he falls prey to the same device by trying to make a non-supernatural Jesus palatable to Jewish culture. See also C. C. McCown, "The Current Plight of Biblical Scholarship," *JBL* 75 (1956) 12–18, for the argument that modern science and philosophy have no place for miracles and special providences. In other words, there are neither demons nor angels. *Par contre*, see Robert A. Gundry's brief assessment in *Matthew: A Commentary on His Literary and Theological Art* (1982) 622: "Apart from entering a philosophical discussion inappropriate to a commentary, there remains only the observation that refusal to accept the possibility of miracles may force a cavalier treatment of historical and literary data. Treated more naturally, these data may favor the miraculous in Jesus' life and therefore call in question a rigidly anti-supernaturalistic presupposition."

57. A survey of international publications reveals widespread doubt regarding the transcendent qualities of Jesus. For example, see E. P. Sanders, *Jesus and Judaism* (1985) 10–11, who lists eight "indisputable" facts about Jesus. Notably absent from his list is any reference to his transcendent qualities. Sanders acknowledges that he is not a theologian and prefers not to make a judgment on the issue of Christology. To his credit, however, Sanders endeavors to anchor these eight to actual historical events. For discussion and evaluation of these eight points plus two additional ones, see Craig A. Evans, "Authenticating the Activities of Jesus," in *Authenticating the Activities of Jesus* (1999) 3–29. For a recent argument questioning the actual existence of Jesus, see Richard Carrier, *On the Historicity of Jesus* (2014). For a response to such arguments, see Bart Ehrman's *Did Jesus Exist? The Historical Argument for Jesus of Nazareth* (2012). To his credit, Ehrman defends the historical existence of Jesus.

defy human understanding.[58] Additionally, the word can leave the impression that historical research is conducted in the same manner as a genuine scientific methodology with similar precisely measured results.[59] This is most unfortunate.[60] In its purest form, scientific investigation implies research under carefully controlled conditions that can be subjected to repeated testing, rigorous scrutiny, and independent corroboration.[61] Investigation into the past cannot measure up to such demanding standards.[62] When applied to biblical research and writing, the word "scientific" is thus a misnomer.[63] To state this in stronger language: the word "scientific" has actually been hijacked from the laboratory of hard science and misapplied to literary studies in which the principal workplace is the library.[64] Alex Berezow, holder of a PhD in microbiology and editor of the journal *Real Clear Science*, states this well: "Dressing up one's personal ideology in the language of science is an affront to the scientific method."[65]

58. Geza Vermes in his *The Religion of Jesus the Jew* (1993) 210, speaks of "The disappearance of the Master," and then places the resurrection in dubious quotation marks ("resurrection"). Yet he capitalizes the word "Master," indicating a tone of respect for Jesus. But the resurrection of Jesus is clearly off limits for him. A notable exception is C. H. Dodd's appraisal in his *About the Gospels* (1958) 7–8, who suggests that a proper understanding of Jesus "cannot be defined in plain words, but must be hinted at in the exalted language of the imagination . . . with the opening up of God's presence, and with the ultimate victory of the Spirit." Although Dodd uses the word "imagination," I focus upon his conclusion, "the ultimate victory of the Spirit."

59. An example of hidden dogmatic interests under the cover or guise of alleged objective historical research is that of James D. Tabor's recent *Jesus and Paul* (2012) 237, in which he refers to "our tools of critical historical research," as if such tools were a microscope and a petri dish, yielding scientifically verifiable results. This is clearly not the case.

60. I note John H. Leith's comment in "The Bible and Theology," *Int* 30 (1976) 233: "Theology is wisdom, not precisely defined scientific knowledge."

61. Rosalind Picard, "Living Machines: Can Robots Become Human?" in *A Place for Truth* (2010) 205, says: "In science we only consider those things that are measurable, repeatable and clearly specifiable in some way that others can identify." Picard, who has written numerous peer-reviewed scientific articles, is founder and director of Affective Computing Research at MIT.

62. See James H. Charlesworth, *Jesus within Judaism* (1988) 27, who says: "Historical research is scientific by a critical method but not necessarily by conclusion. The historian at best can provide us not with certainty, but with relative probability." I have no difficulty with this statement from Charlesworth. The premise of this book, therefore, is not one of certainty but of probability. However, the four gospel writers were not working with these limitations.

63. Loveday Alexander, *The Preface to Luke's Gospel* (1993) 21, although adopting the word "scientific," Alexander disclaims that she is doing research from a purely scientific stance; rather, she is making use of the term via the German *wissenschaftlich* or *Fachprosa*, suggesting a genre of technical or specialist prose. Hence, Alexander later on (104) actually contrasts scientific with historical modes of writing. See also her earlier article, "Luke's Preface in the Context of Greek Preface-Writing," *NovT* 28.1 (1986) 57, fn. 31: "The term 'scientific' is not ideal." See also Eve Paquette, "Religion as the Academic's Enemy: A Case Study of an Ineffective Discursive Strategy," SR/SR 35.3 (2006) 442, especially for her conclusion: "Am I suggesting that we simply drop the question of the 'scientific' quality of our academic undertaking, along with the question of the religious or theological underpinnings of our work? Yes . . ." See also John C. Meagher, *Clumsy Construction in Mark's Gospel* (1979) vii–ix.

64. See Robert F. Shedinger, "Kuhnian Paradigms and Biblical Scholarship: Is Biblical Studies a Science?" *JBL* 119.3 (2000) 466–69, for the distinction between biblical studies and the natural sciences.

65. A. Berezow, "When 'Science' Looks for Sexism, Guess What? It Finds it," *USA Today*, 11A, July

A better case can be made for encapsulating the practice of NT research by means of the word "objective,"[66] although this term, too, has been questioned as unrealistic and inappropriate.[67] In fact, at the 1984 SBL Seminar, Irvin W. Batdorf called for dispensing with the term altogether because objectivity is unattainable in biblical studies.[68] To be sure, William R. Farmer has labeled the results of so-called scientific research as "unintelligible."[69] A much more suitable word, and perhaps less pretentious, to capture the essence of NT scholarship is either the word "specialist" or the term "technical." These two words do not require that the bar of truth be set at either the scientific or objective level; they also allow the fact that scholarship is often personal, subjective, and far from truth—yet technical and complex. A simple return to the word "critical" as adopted by the ICC would also be suitable.[70]

The one supporting prop that a pseudo-scientific perspective leans upon is the conception that since we do not witness, for example, either a virgin birth or a resurrection from the dead taking place right now, this leads to the conclusion that such events have never taken place in history. History is thus considered to be a closed and sealed system, not permitting an exception to its physical laws, and not admitting the possibility that God has acted supernaturally in history.[71] This is an extension of

---

27, 2011.

66. For an optimistic assessment of the scientific view as being objectively neutral, see Werner Kahl, *New Testament Miracle Stories in their Religious-Historical Setting* (1994) 12. The question, of course, occurs: how "neutral" and how guaranteed are the investigative procedures? For a distinction between objectivity and neutrality, see Paul Helm, "Understanding Scholarly Presuppositions: A Crucial Tool for Research," *TynBul* 44.1 (1993) 153. See also John Barton, *The Nature of Biblical Criticism* (2007) 6: "Biblical Criticism strives to be 'objective in the sense that it tries to attend to what the text actually says and not read alien meanings into it." I have no quarrel with Barton's definition.

67. For the view that biblical exegesis demands objectivity, see Rudolf Bultmann, "Is Exegesis without Presuppositions Possible?" (1966) 296, in which Bultmann makes the argument, consistent with the scientific approach, that objectivity does not demand definitive results. For a more modest view of objectivity, see Samuel Sandmel, "Parallelomania," *JBL* 81.1 (1962) 4: "Furthermore, each of us operates within certain biases, and since I have one about Christianity, I must expose it here." See also John Dominic Crossan, *The Birth of Christianity* (1998) 96, who is willing to acknowledge that all have presuppositions when it comes to the subject of Jesus. The issue is not whether one has presuppositions; rather, the issue turns on what kinds. I have already stated mine: I believe that the ultimate source behind the Gospels is an inspired revelation. It should also be admitted that objectivity is not devoid of the subjective. Ideally, subjectivity must come under the discipline of an objective analysis.

68. I. W. Batdorf, "Interpreting Jesus since Bultmann: Selected Paradigms and Their Hermeneutic Matrix," *SBLSP* 23 (1984) 212, for his conclusion: "We ought to acknowledge that none of us can be scientifically objective." A follow-up to this admonition is the strong likelihood that anyone who comes to the study of either the resurrection or divine inspiration will not arrive with a blank mind on the subject. For a critique and summary of current scholarly presuppositions on the subject of the historical Jesus, see Joel Willitts, "Presuppositions and Procedures in the Study of the 'Historical Jesus': Or, Why I Decided Not to Be a 'Historical Jesus' Scholar," *JSHJ* 3 (2005) 61–108.

69. W. R. Farmer, "State *Interesse* and Marcan Primacy," in *The Four Gospels 1992* (1992) 2484.

70. Raymond E. Brown, *The Birth of the Messiah* (1977), in his Foreword mentions the "relentless advance of the scientific (critical) approach to the Gospels."

71. Floyd F. Filson, *The Gospel according to Matthew* (1971) 303: "What kind of world is this? If it

the argument by Analogy and is also an old view, having roots in the ancient past. A contemporary case in point is the recent book by James D. Tabor in which he argues the following *a priori* view:

> Historians are bound by their discipline to work within the parameters of a scientific view of reality. Women do not get pregnant without a male—ever. So Jesus had a human father, whether we can identify him or not. Dead bodies don't rise—not if one is clinically dead—as Jesus surely was after Roman crucifixion and three days in a tomb. So if the tomb was empty the historical conclusion is simple—Jesus' body was moved by someone and likely reburied in another location.[72]

The claim for a bodily resurrection is absolutely unique and unequivocally defies all the known laws of nature. If we could see bodily resurrections taking place all the time (and thereby conform to natural law and satisfy the demands of Analogy), the commonality of such occurrences would render the uniqueness of the NT claim frivolous and inconsequential. Efforts to reduce Jesus to the status of a non-unique character and fully compatible with natural law are not convincing.[73] It is the singularity of the Jesus-event that gives the resurrection its unique quality, its troublesome and stunning significance, and its enduring transforming power. The response, as recorded in the book of Acts, reveals first-century attitudes toward the claim for a resurrection as on the same emotional and philosophical footing as today's unbelief. That is, the narrative of Acts chronicles the reaction of first-century unbelief based upon much the

---

is an impersonal machine, if reality is limited to what man can grasp and state, then the resurrection makes no sense." It is the contention of this book, however, that God has interrupted the natural law of death and decay through the resurrection of Jesus and then revealed the meaning of resurrection through divine inspiration.

72. J. D. Tabor, *The Jesus Dynasty* (2006) 233–34. I note also his views on page 59: "But history, by its very nature, is an open process of inquiry that cannot be bound by the dogmas of faith. Historians are obligated to examine whatever evidence we have, even, if such discoveries might be considered shocking or sacrilegious to some. The assumption of the historian is that all human beings have both a biological mother and a father, and that Jesus is no exception." Tabor has taken seriously his own conclusion on this matter, and it has propelled him on the rather exotic quest to locate the actual bones of Jesus. I pause only to make one comment at this point: Joseph held the same view—women do not get pregnant without a human father. According to the record in the Gospel of Matthew, something changed his mind. Of course, the historian's major task is to examine causes. One approach is to dismiss evidence on the basis that a particular event could not happen—ever. This line of reasoning is one form of the improbability argument. The argument is not so much that the event in question could not have happened but, rather, it is impossible for it to happen at all—ever. Tabor argues that Jesus had a human father—the likely candidate being Panthera. Panthera, of course, was identified by Morton Smith in his famous/infamous book *Jesus the Magician* (1978) 67. Going back further, Ethelbert Stauffer, *Jesus and his Story* (1960) 17, refers to the "gossipy anecdotes about Mary and the legionary Panthera." For an even earlier work, one may consult Origen's *Contra Celsum* (1.32).

73. A. N. Wilson, *Jesus, A Life* (1992) 66–69, while totally dismissing the resurrection accounts as historically true, nevertheless, is still mystified by the person of Jesus and can even affirm: "I am speaking of those moments when imagination and instinct are shocked into recognition, and he stands before us."

same principles as modern unbelief, indicating a similar if not identical world view. Claiming that the discipline of historical investigation cannot consider the evidence for resurrection is an arbitrary decision. The resurrection of Jesus can be investigated just like any other historic event in the past.[74] Although there is no eye-witness testimony in the NT claiming to have seen the resurrection at the moment of its actual occurrence, this does not mean that the NT is speaking of something invisible, wholly based upon imagination, and, therefore, incapable of investigation. Similarly, it is granted that divine revelation is humanly impossible and cannot be demonstrated in a laboratory experiment under controlled conditions. This is not to claim, however, that something supernaturally revealed is not open to critical investigation and rational analysis or that it cannot be supported by rational analysis.[75] Reason may be elevated above revelation or subjected to it, but there is no inherent contradiction between reason and revelation. Reason and revelation are not necessarily arch rivals. Belief in revelation, therefore, is not irrational. Admittedly, an objection to the subject of divine revelation is that it inserts into the Analogy argument a polarizing influence.[76] As is peculiar to the nature of legitimate debate, there are two sides; resistance should be expected.[77] In tug-of-war fashion, scholars on both sides of the question strain to

---

74. For the argument that the resurrection of Jesus can be investigated as any other historical event, see Francis J. Beckwith, "History and Miracles," in *In Defense of Miracles* (1997) 86–98. See also N. T. Wright, *The Resurrection of the Son of God* (2003) 21: "There is no reason, no principle why the question, what precisely happened at Easter, cannot be raised by any historian of any persuasion." See as well Richard B. Hays, *The Moral Vision of the New Testament* (1996) 165: "I part company with many New Testament scholars and theologians who think it inappropriate to describe the resurrection as a historical event."

75. Hans Conzelmann, *Jesus* (1973) 5: "The historical and substantive presupposition for modern research into the life of Jesus is emancipation from traditional Christological dogma on the basis of the principle of reason." The same principle of reason can be applied to work in the opposite direction—not necessarily to recover "dogma," but to restore confidence that the NT documents transcend the human elements of research, compiling, editing, imagination, memory, and reflection. See also Matthew Day, "Let's Be Realistic: Epistemic Probabilism, and the Cognitive Science of Religion," *HTR* 100:1 (2007) 54, for the argument, from a so-called realist point of view, that "the best science reveals the world as it really is." I am adapting Day's language and formatting it to fit the purpose of this book in order to discover and develop an explanatory theory that accounts for the gospel texts as they *really* are.

76. For an interesting admission by James Charlesworth, see his personal statement and its context, "Hillel and Jesus: Why Comparisons Are Important," in *Hillel and Jesus* (1997) 5: "Frankly, I am willing to admit that in some ways the historical Hillel is more appealing than the historical Jesus." Since Charlesworth uses the word "historical" to apply to both Hillel and Jesus, we must assume that he is employing the term in its technical sense of a modern academic construct. Perhaps this is an oblique confession that modern so-called scientific views of Jesus are really boring. See also his personal exegetical goal as stated in "What Has the Old Testament to Do with the New?" in *The Old and New Testaments* (1993) 47. See also Jeremy Begbie, "Who Is This God?—Biblical Inspiration Revisited," *TynB* 43.2 (1992) 259: "So well-worn is the topic, and so sensitive the associated ideas, one's natural inclination is to give the topic a very wide berth."

77. I note Samuel Sandmel's defense of sincere debate, "Parallelomania" (1962) 13: "We do not want to arrive at some pallid unanimity, but rather to be the market place in which vigorously held viewpoints, freely expressed, vie with each other for acceptance."

pull back the other side. For example, years ago Wilhelm Pauck claimed: "It is a fact that the supernatural authority of old theology is dead. The miracles of God's personal appearance in Jesus Christ and of the divine inspiration of the Bible are dead."[78] Yet E. Earle Ellis has claimed with equal conviction that historical criticism of the Bible is "a failure and bankrupt."[79]

The skeptical side in the debate does not hesitate to make known its views. It is appropriate and natural that the believing side should do no less. Accordingly, although liberal scholarship has consigned the subject of divine revelation to the status of being on life support or in preparation for burial, perhaps the time has come for rehabilitating an old subject by proposing a new approach.

In an attempt to not only revive interest in a moribund subject but also to present a counter argument to current academic constructs,[80] my intention is to present an approach which shows the plausible reasons that the four Gospels are on a unique and supernatural level. This book takes its place among other current scholarly monographs which argue for transcendence in the person of Jesus.[81] Thus, this study ultimately will attempt to understand the canonical Scriptures on their own terms.

The Argument for a Plausible Case

In order to take into consideration skeptical views, both ancient and modern, and to address some issues that have been neglected, unexplored, or unsuspected, I will develop a case for inspiration based upon the concept of plausibility. The word "plausibility," first of all, has its roots and origin among ancient historians such as Herodotus, Thucydides, and their successors. An example of the principle of plausibility at work

---

78. W. Pauck, *Karl Barth: Prophet of a New Christianity* (1931) 212.

79. E. E. Ellis, *History & Interpretation in New Testament Perspective* (2001) 2–3. From a publishing point of view, such a judgment appears to be rather premature. I see no signs of the methodology dying out.

80. For a completely different analysis of the evidence issue from a physical scientist's point of view which challenges current philosophical consensus, see Michael G. Harvey, "Science, Rationality, and Theology," *JR* 87.1 (2007) 225–47. Harvey offers a counter view on the basis that empirical evidence does not justify a scientific triumph over theology.

81. One such monograph is the recent work by Simon J. Gathercole, *The Preexistent Son* (2006). Gathercole is clear about his thesis (17): "This should, however, be tempered by two considerations. First, there are still a minority who are much less skeptical. Second, there is also a growing school of thought which acknowledges that the portrayal of Christ in the Gospels in fact shows strong signs of including heavenly and divine contours to identity. This tendency in current scholarship may indicate—despite the majority report—that the time is ripe for a reconsideration of preexistence in Matthew, Mark, and Luke." I note also the comment by Charles Talbert in the Preface to *The Many Faces of the Christ* by Ben Witherington (1998) vii: "This means that the New Testament is studied in terms of its own time and place. It is allowed to speak in its own terms, out of its own assumptions, espousing its own values . . ." One of the assumptions or "values" of the New Testament is that it is a divine revelation. See also Craig S. Keener, *Miracles: The Credibility of the New Testament Accounts* (2011). I do agree with Craig Keener when he states in his monograph *The Gospel of John* (2003) 1.115: "A claim to divine authorship is not, strictly speaking, empirically verifiable."

among in an ancient writer is that of Strabo in his *Geography* in which he uses two of his favorite words for plausibility (πιθανότης and εἰκός) and then follows this up with a series of eight investigative questions, all with the word "how" (πῶς or τίς).[82] The search for what is plausible is a quest for the probable cause of *how* something has happened. The concept of plausibility is intrinsically linked to reasonable explanations. However, I do not equate "reasonable" solely with what is natural. A further ancient model is that of Aristotle in his *Poetics*. At 1451a/12.1, he twice uses the expression κατὰ τὸ εἰκὸς ἢ τὸ ἀναγκαῖον ("according to probability or necessity") in order to describe a proper sequence of events that likely could have happened. This is the probable part. The element of necessity or inevitability is the second part, and requires a proper explanation for this sequence. My intention is to adapt Aristotle's model but with a reverse twist in order to demonstrate the *im*plausibility of the four Gospels as having their origin in a purely human causation.

This term, along with its companion term *hypothesis*, provides scholars the acceptable language for doing research and sharing their results with others.[83] These two terms convey the temporary nature of academic consensus as well as a measured modesty in not claiming to know all truth. This approach eliminates any claim for failsafe or foolproof results.[84] Thomas Korteweg adds to this: "the only way for a hypothesis to prove its value is by explaining in the most convincing manner the facts that present themselves, without at the same time being seriously contradicted by those that it fails to account for."[85] Therefore, I follow current NT scholarly conventions by pursuing the goal of what is plausible. I adopt and make use of the same understanding of plausible as do Theissen and Winter: "*Plausible*, from the Latin *plausibilis* (also related to the English word 'applause') means 'deserving applause,' and may be defined or paraphrased by the English words 'illuminating, understandable, credible, sound, well-founded, convincing.'"[86]

---

82. 2.3.5: πῶς . . . τίς . . . τίς . . . πῶς . . . πῶς . . . πῶς . . . πῶς . . . πῶς ("how? . . . how? . . . how? . . . how? . . . how? . . . how? . . . how? . . . how?").

83. For example, see Géza Xeravits, "Précisions sur le texte original et le concept messianique de CD 7:13–8.1 et 19:5–14," *RevQum* 19 (1999) 52: "Je pense que S.A. White a décrit le plus plausiblement la formation des variants textuelles de CD . . . . Cependent cette hypothèse . . ." See also Jens Schröter, "Die Frage nach dem historischen Jesus und der Charakter historischer Erkenntnis," in *The Sayings Source Q and the Historical Jesus* (2001) 208: "Die Jesusfrage ist somit innerhalb der Theologie al seine *historische* Frage aus *theologischer* Perspective zu betrachten. Beide Aspekte der Frage müssen deshalb in ein plausibles Verhältnis zu einander gesetzt werden." What is deemed "plausible" is tied to the language of historical discourse.

84. As H. E. W. Turner, *Historicity and the Gospels* (1963) 72, states appropriately, the results of historical investigation cannot produce results which are capable of "slide-rule" precision.

85. Thomas Korteweg, "Further Observations on the Transmission of the Text," in *Studies on the Testaments of the Twelve Patriarchs* (1975) 161.

86. Gerd Theissen and Dagmar Winter, *The Quest for the Plausible Jesus: The Question of Criteria* (2002) 202. The OLD defines *plausibilis* as "likely or able to win applause." Applause is commendable when given sincerely and accepted graciously. No one writes in order to be ignored.

At no point along the way in this study will the concept of inspiration be granted as a fact;[87] the idea of inspiration will be presented as a thesis whose verisimilitude must be established. The burden of proof will rest upon establishing the concept of inspiration as the probable cause behind the four Gospels. A concomitant objective of not denying or explaining away evidence that appears contrary to the thesis of this study will trailer the primary pursuit for plausible evidence. Possible alternative rivals to the thesis of this study will be mentioned but kept to a minimum. The focus will be upon laying down the lines of evidence for divine inspiration rather than exploring every competing idea.

Those who are comfortable with the idea of some form of divine inspiration and desire to communicate with those outside this circle are forced to find footing that relies upon supports that do not build upon the premise that something is true simply because the authors of Scripture make a claim for it. For example, a frequent complaint lodged against the four evangelists is that they simply tailored their Gospels to fill out the "categories." In a recent *BAR* article this is the conclusion reached by Sean Freyne.[88] A. N. Wilson makes a similar claim when he states that Matthew "has been through the Scriptures cheerfully lifting details, and then inventing the 'facts' to fit the 'prophecies.'"[89] In other words, the skeptical claim bases its logic on a belief that the four evangelists simply created their Gospels by reading back into them OT prophecies "after the fact."[90] Craig A. Evans voices a similar view: "I believe that the passion predictions were not made prior to entry into Jerusalem. The Markan evangelist has retrojected them into Jesus' Galilean ministry (Mark 8.31; 9.12) and journey south for literary and theological reasons."[91] Alan F. Segal operates on a similar parallel principle: "For a fact about Jesus to be accepted as unassailable, it must *not* be in the interest of the church to tell us."[92] Since the "church" cannot be trusted, according to the prevailing academic view, it remains for critical scholarship to discover what can be trusted through the principles of historical criticism. Because of the current

87. I note Richard J. Erickson, "Joseph and the Birth of Isaac in Matthew 1," *BBR* 10.1 (2000) 35, in his very first sentence says: "That the NT portrays Jesus both as the Son of God and as the Son of David, designations carrying heavy Christological freight for first-century readers, is clear to anyone who reads it." The approach taken in this study is to assume the opposite—nothing is clear to the reader, nothing is taken for granted, and everything must be established by evidence.

88. S. Freyne, "Jesus of History Vs. Jesus of Tradition," *BAR* 36. 6 (2010) 45: "Jesus is made to fill all the categories."

89. A. N. Wilson, *Jesus, A Life* (1992) 62. A similar view is espoused by Walther Zimmerli and Joachim Jeremias, *The Servant of God* (1965) 99, who, under the rubric, "Can Jesus Have Referred The Servant Passages Of Deutero-Isaiah to Himself?" maintain: "Many of these passages are wholly or in part the work of the church." They do, however, acknowledge that some passages exhibit the strongest historical probability behind them.

90. I note that Origen in his *Contra Celsum* (2.13) includes the objection raised by Celsus that prophecies are simply words projected back into the mouth of Jesus and the prophets after the fact.

91. Craig A. Evans, "Diarchic Messianism in the Dead Sea Scrolls and the Messianism of Jesus of Nazareth," in *The Dead Sea Scrolls: Fifty Years after Their Discovery* (2000) 565–66, fn. 25.

92. Alan F. Segal, *Life after Death* (2004) 388.

academic climate, I must take into account the lingering suspicion that the evangelists may have retrospectively tailored their accounts to conform to OT predictive statements. This skepticism has forced me to approach the subject from a different point of view. Essentially, the task will be to demonstrate that the four evangelists do not consciously and deliberately compose their respective accounts in order to match the fourfold view as presented here. A quick acknowledgment is in order: it is no stunning proposal to argue that some predictive statements found in the Gospels were made after the fact. However, the suggestion that Jesus never predicted his own death seems more fictional than factual. Yet, the always present question is: are these predictive/fulfillment statements wild fabrications and gross misrepresentations of both the OT and the life of Jesus; or, conversely, are these statements legitimate, truthful, and accurate accounts? For those statements that reasonably appear to be later post event observations by the evangelists, one still has to arrive at some personal conclusion as to *how* they made those observations.[93] My own view is that these understandings go back to Jesus or the Holy Spirit as the original source.[94]

A disclaimer is appropriate. This investigation will not explore the following three current scholarly issues. First, the need to inquire into a speculative source such as Q (from the German word *Quelle*, "source") will not be entertained.[95] Inasmuch as no Q document has ever been discovered and consequently suffers in that it is heavily

---

93. For example, John 12:41 appears to be a case in point. John did not arrive at this conclusion during the actual earthly ministry of Jesus. This is likely a post-resurrection observation. I agree with Richard B. Hays in his well-written monograph, *Echoes of Scripture in the Gospels* (2016) 354, who says: "Strikingly, John tells his readers explicitly that Scripture can be understood only retrospectively after the resurrection; readers are instructed to 'read backwards' in light of the illumination provided by the Spirit who will come after Jesus' departure. And that retrospective reading will be explicitly *figural* in character." Oddly, though (p. 348), Hays includes a disclaimer that a "figural interpretation" does not allow for reading OT texts as actually and deliberately "*predicting* events in the life of Jesus." On this point I would have to disagree.

94. Another case is Matt 1:21–23. At v. 21 an angel of the LORD appears to Joseph and informs him that Jesus "will save his people from their sins." At vs. 22–23 the angel is no longer speaking; as it were, the voice of Matthew takes over and completes the narrative by informing the reader that this is the fulfillment of prophecy (Isa 7:14). How does the evangelist Matthew know this? Skepticism says that these are mere human fabrications. This book is a response to such skepticism.

95. The research on Q is mountainous. All the way from the confident assertion that Q is indispensable to the equally strong contention that Q is a pure fiction, the issue is debated on both sides. Darrell L. Bock, "Questions about Q," in *Rethinking the Synoptic Problem* (2001) 41: "To be assigned an essay about a document we do not have is a daunting task." The linchpin of optimistic Q research is summed up by the often repeated statement of G. Theissen and A. Merz, *Der historische Jesus: Ein Lehrbuch* (1996) 45: "Q ist zweifellos die wichtigste Quelle zur Rekonstruktion der Lehre Jesu." The list of those endorsing Q is endless. Gerhard Krodel, editor of the popular Proclamation Commentaries (*Luke*, 1976, vi) believes that Luke "certainly" used Mark and Q in his sources. Frederick W. Danker, the author of the aforementioned *Luke* (19) is equally clear in his conviction about Q: "Apart from Luke's own tipping of his editorial hand, we are able to use Luke's modifications of his sources, Mark and Q, as controls for our study." For a conservative evangelical assessment of the Q issue, see Kenneth Schenck, *Jesus Is Lord* (2003) 209–22; and David Alan Black and David R. Beck (eds.), *Rethinking the Synoptic Problem* (2001). For a clear and concise one-page summary of the arguments for Q, see Jack Dean Kingsbury, *Jesus Christ in Matthew, Mark, and Luke* (1981) 3.

weighted with speculation, its current role in modern research will be left out of this study.[96] Indeed, Robert Kysar now claims that Q "is a skyscraper built upon the end of a toothpick."[97] Regarding Q, therefore, this investigation will not pursue the fictional notion of Q.

Second, the human experience of reflection and imagination is also omitted from this study. This is not to suggest, though, that the evangelists lacked such capacity or that they did not make use of it. It is only to propose that reflection does not provide a fully sufficient explanation for the origin of the four Gospels.[98] Consequently, I do not see the four Gospels as a development due to reflection as if each Gospel represented a different stage along the way to a step-by-step sequence of R1, R2, R3, finally culminating in R4.[99]

Third, the human explanation of memory will not be explored.[100] James D.G. Dunn, a strong advocate of the role of memory in oral tradition, says:

---

96. A. Lindemann is objective enough to admit in his "Die Logienquell Q Fragen an eine gut Begründete Hypothese," in *The Sayings Source Q and the Historical Jesus* (2001) 3: "Die Annahme, daB es die Logienquelle als einen von Lukas und von Matthäus verwendeten schriftlichen Text gegeben hat, ist eine *Hypothese*" (italics his). Robert Grant in his *A Historical Introduction to the New Testament* (1963) 113–14, recommends: "On the other hand, the notion that there was a single written source to be designated as Q is also untenable . . . Perhaps the letter Q should be dropped." For the recent recommendation that Q be discarded, see Mark Goodacre, *The Case Against Q* (2002). The essential argument of Goodacre's book is the contention that the hypothetical document Q never existed and that, instead, Luke relied upon Matthew and Mark. For an insightful and undogmatic rebuttal to the Goodacre thesis, see Paul Foster, "Is it Possible to Dispense with Q?" *NovT* 45.4 (2003) 313–37. Foster ultimately charges as "unfair" the claim that requires the discovery of an extant manuscript identifiable as Q (337). For a slightly different approach to Goodacre, see John S. Kloppenborg, "On Dispensing with Q?: Goodacre on the Relation of Luke to Matthew," *NTS* 49 (2003) 210–36. See also Beverly Roberts Gaventa and Richard B. Hays, "Seeking the Identity of Jesus," in *Seeking the Identity of Jesus* (2008) 10: "It is important to emphasize that there is no extant manuscript of Q and there are no references in any ancient texts to such a document." Eight years later, Hays still stands by this judgment in his *Echoes of Scripture in the Gospels* (2016) 13. The entire search for Q may eventually turn out to be a wearisome academic wasteland. For an optimistic assessment of Q, see Edwin K. Broadhead, "The Extent of the Sayings Tradition (Q)," in *The Sayings Source Q* (2001) 719–28. For the faulty assumption that Q implies Markan priority, see John C. Poirier, "The Synoptic Problem and the Field of New Testament Introduction," *JSNT* 32.2 (2009) 179–90.

97. Robert Kysar, "What's the Meaning of This? Reflections upon a Life and Career," in *What We Have Heard from the Beginning* (2007) 173.

98. For the argument that imagination and aesthetic creativity must be allowed a place in an adequate theology, see William A. Beardslee, *Literary Criticism of the New Testament* (1970) 75–76.

99. C. F. D. Moule, *The Origin of Christology* (1977) 3, used the word "perception" to describe the process of "drawing out" something that was already there in the person of Jesus. Whether perception or reflection, I do not believe such a human enterprise can fully explain the fourfold nature of the Gospels.

100. For recent work on the role of memory, see James D. G. Dunn, *Jesus Remembered* (2003), and the subsequent debate sparked by Dunn's book: Bengt Holmberg, "Questions of Method in James Dunn's *Jesus* Remembered," *JSNT* 26.4 (2004) 445–57; Samuel Byrskog, "A New Perspective on the Jesus Tradition: Reflections on James D. G. Dunn's *Jesus Remembered*," *JSNT* 26.4 (2004) 459–71; Birger Gerhardsson, "The Secret of the Transmission of the Unwritten Jesus Tradition," *NTS* 51.1 (2005) 1–18, and his earlier seminal work, *Memory and Manuscript* (1998). See also the recent monograph

> For the prevailing characteristic of oral tradition is its flexibility. The same stories are retold with seemingly endless variation; the substance or core of the story is stable, but the detail can vary with each telling. The same teaching is repeated in seemingly endless permutations and combinations, with varying emphases presumably deemed appropriate to the differing circumstances in which performance of the tradition takes place.[101]

I have no objections to Dunn's understanding of memory and oral tradition. Obviously, Jesus was remembered in various ways during the first twenty or thirty years. However, I do not believe that oral tradition preserved by memory is an adequate accounting for the fourfold portrait of Jesus. People can remember certain events of the vividly or intensely experienced past. For example, those who lived through the bombing of England during WWII, the attack on Pearl Harbor in December of 1941, the assassination of JFK in November of 1963, and most recently the terrorist attack of the Twin Towers on 9/11/2001, can recall hearing the news, what they were doing at the time, and some details. This is not to argue that they can retain a full account of the details of these events in their memory; the passage of time often leads to fading memories and sketchy details. Although how a person *felt* at that time may continue, time takes its toll. Stated differently, I do not believe that the four Gospels are to be understood as M1, M2, M3, and M4, as if each Gospel represented a different stage in the human memory process. Although the association of the Holy Spirit with memory can be found in the Jesus tradition and is integral to the importance of eye-witness testimony,[102] nonetheless, memory does not figure as a primary source in this study for

---

by Richard A. Horsley, *Jesus in Context* (2008). Part of the Jesus tradition, however, does include both memory and creativity (the Spirit will bring to remembrance and will take the words of Jesus and make them known to the disciples, and will assist them when speaking before magistrates: Matt 10:19–20; John 16:13). For a continuation of the memory debate, see Michael F. Bird, "The Formation of the Gospels in the Setting of Early Christianity: The Jesus Tradition as Corporate Memory," *WTJ* 67 (2005) 113–34; Samuel Byrskog, "A New Quest for the *Sitz im Leben*: Social Memory, the Jesus Tradition and the Gospel of Matthew," *NTS* 52 (2006) 319–36; and Dennis Ingolfsland, "Jesus Remembered: James Dunn and the Synoptic Problem," *TrinJ* 27.2 (2006) 187–97. For the view that faith "overpowered" memory (thus creating a distortion), see Robert W. Funk and Roy W. Hoover, *The Five Gospels* (1993) 21–25. For the weakness and unreliability of memory, see John Dominic Crossan, *The Birth of Christianity* (1998) 59–84. And most recently, see the collection of essays in tribute to the pioneering work of Birger Gerhardsson: Werner Kelber and Samuel Byrskog (eds.), *Jesus in Memory* (2009). For a new approach to memory, see Anthony Le Donne, *The Historiographical Jesus* (2009); and Chris Keith, "The Claim of John 7.15 and the Memory of Jesus' Literacy," *NTS* 56.1 (2010) 44–63.

101. J. D. G. Dunn, "Living Traditions," in *What Is It That the Scripture Says?* (2006) 280.

102. For the new debate sparked by Richard Bauckham's recent book *Jesus and the Eyewitnesses* (2006), see Jens Schröter, "The Gospels as Eyewitness Testimony: A Critical Examination of Richard Bauckham's *Jesus and the Eyewitnesses*, *JSNT* 31.2 (2008) 195–209; Craig A. Evans, "The Implications of Eyewitness Tradition," *JSNT* 31.2 (2008) 211–19; and the reply by Richard Bauckham, "Eyewitnesses and Critical History: A Response to Jens Schröter and Craig Evans," *JSNT* 3.2 (2008) 221–35. See also Michael F. Bird, "The Purpose and Preservation of the Jesus Tradition: Moderate Evidence for a Conserving Force in Its Transmission," *BBR* 15.2 (2005) 161–85.

explaining the unique nature of the four Gospels.[103] Although the role of memory has been a trendy topic in recent scholarly research,[104] I see no possible way that memory could account for the fourfold portrait of Jesus as presented in the Gospels. Terrence W. Tilley has written of Jesus: "Whatever he may have been, he is far more as a human being than the impact he had on his followers. Even I am far more as a human being than the impact I have on my students that they might record."[105] I agree with Tilley's observations that the role of memory does not account for the full presentation of any person—let alone Jesus as we have in the Gospels. Therefore, the argument of this book goes beyond memory.

A candid admission is now acknowledged. The standard for determining inspiration is more difficult than the standard for establishing historical fact. The bar of truth is set higher, the stakes are greater, and the burden of proof is heavier for the one who champions the claim for the divine inspiration of Scripture. This is true also, for example, in forensic science as applied to solving a crime. Criminal investigators called to the scene of a homicide can immediately observe a historical fact—a crime has been committed. There may be traces of blood, signs of a struggle, and the obvious—a dead body. However, the crime is far from being solved. Besides a prime suspect, what is missing at the moment is a motive. Finding and establishing a motive will be paramount in locating and successfully prosecuting a suspect. In fact, the greater the success in establishing a motive, the higher will be the percentage for catching the culprit. Additionally, the veridical determination of motive will be critical in assessing severity of guilt. That is not all. Establishing a motive determines the gravity of the offense and directs the task force assigned to solve the crime. Unquestionably, a

---

103. The value of eyewitness testimony is currently under intense evaluation in the American judicial system. Because of the power of DNA to trump personal testimony, some 230 falsely accused prisoners, convicted principally on the strength of eyewitness testimonies, have been set free in the USA alone. For a review of the weakness of eyewitness testimony in a court of law, see Gary L. Wells, Amina Memon, and Steven D. Penrod, "Eyewitness Evidence: Improving Its Probative Value," *Psychological Science in the Public Interest* 7.2 (2006) 45–75. The claim of evangelists, especially John, is not that they have perfectly reliable memories. Rather, their testimony is that of memory aided by inspiration. See also Richard Bauckham's new book *Jesus and the Eyewitnesses* (2006) which has three noteworthy pages (355–57) bearing on the topic of eyewitness testimony and the courts.

104. See, for example, the following: Dale C. Allison, *Constructing Jesus: Memory, Imagination, and History* (2010) 2–8, who lists nine reasons for his own disillusionment with the role of memory in reconstructing the historical Jesus. For a continuation of the memory debate from the vantage point of psychological research with regard to the Gospels, two articles have recently appeared: Judith Redman, "How Accurate Are Eyewitnesses? Bauckham and the Eyewitnesses in the Light of Psychological Research," *JBL* 129 (2010) 177–97, who takes a more dissenting view. The second one: Robert K. McIver, "Eyewitnesses Guarantors of the Accuracy of the Gospel Traditions in the Light of Psychological Research," *JBL* 131.3 (2012) 529–46, takes a more positive view as McIver responds to Redman's earlier article.

105. Terrence W. Tilley, "Remembering the Historic Jesus—A New Research Program?" *JTS* 68.1 (2007) 17. For an "evangelical view" of memory, see Darrell L. Bock, "The Historical Jesus: An Evangelical View," in *The Historical Jesus* (2009) 252, in which he offers a slightly different assessment of memory than that of Tilley.

homicide receives greater attention than a suicide. If a homicide, the offender needs to be apprehended. Likewise, as applied to biblical studies, the claim for inspiration takes us into the heart of motive or cause. Discovering the deepest level of cause facilitates the assigning of value and worth.[106] With regard to Scripture, the reader has three clear-cut choices: 1) purely a human causation, 2) purely divine or supernatural causation, or 3) a mixture of both.[107] While most current studies focus solely upon human explanatory factors to account for the four Gospels, this study will attempt to provide reasons for a divine factor. This study assumes some human elements, eliminates others, and allows for divine influence.[108] Although this present study does not tackle the issue of the historical reliability of the Gospels, the issues of historicity and revelation are like the opposite sides of the same coin. Suffice it to say, historical veracity is of critical importance. If a particular biblical event did not in fact happen, divine revelation does not make it true. The flip side is equally true: just because an historical event is true and accurately reported does not make that report divinely inspired. Furthermore, if a particular event—like the resurrection—did occur in the past, we should be able to investigate its evidence.

This book proposes that the guiding force behind the composition of the four evangelists was the singular and primary influence of the Spirit of God revealing the meaning of Jesus, rather than four individuals reacting to what one, two, or three of

---

106. For an opposite view on value, see James H. Charlesworth, "A Prolegomenon to a New Study of the Jewish Background of the Hymns and Prayers in the New Testament," *JJS* 33.1–2 (1982) 267: "An historian of earliest Christianity must not approach 'non-canonical' texts with a theological bias or with methods different from those employed in the study of 'canonical' writings." In support of his view, Charlesworth cites a line from S. Holm-Nielsen, "The Importance of Late Jewish Psalmody for the Understanding of Old Testament Psalmodic Tradition," *ST* 14 (1960) 2: "This implies an unspoken value judgment which—perhaps under the influence of the old dogma of inspiration, of which research has hardly ever been able to rid itself completely—regards the canonical books as 'sacred,' while everything else is of secondary importance." The view presented in this book, however, does seek to establish a value. Reading Charlesworth can be like riding a roller coaster: occasional breathtaking highs followed by periodic plunges into nothing. See, for example, his "Jesus Research Expands with Chaotic Creativity," in *Images of Jesus Today* (1994) 10, for his assessment that Jesus' prediction about the time of God's rule was not fulfilled.

107. Without arguing the case for the human element, the premise in this investigation is that there are both human and divine factors at work in any given author of Scripture. Biblical writers compose in Hebrew, Aramaic, or Greek—not German, French, or English. Even within the Greek texts of the Gospels there are variations which must be attributed to human factors. Furthermore, biblical texts contain references to dress, manners, and attitudes of their times and places. In my judgment, biblical texts thus contain timeless truth expressed in time bound forms. For a brief treatment justifying the case that divine inspiration does not ignore the responsibility to interpret Scripture in its historical context, see Walter Kirchschläger, "Scripture and Inspiration," in *Understanding Scripture* (1987) 36–46; and George Eldon Ladd, *The New Testament and Criticism* (1967). For the view that purely human concerns must not be allowed to swallow up the authority of Scripture, see Robert H. Gundry, *Matthew* (1982) 623. See also David A. deSilva, *An Introduction to the New Testament* (2004) 174–77, who also allows for the Holy Spirit as a factor in composition.

108. See David E. Aune, "Charismatic Exegesis in Early Judaism and Early Christianity," in *The Pseudepigrapha and Early Biblical Interpretation* (1993) 126–50, for cautions that we must not try to prescribe the mechanics of divine revelation.

the others had already written.[109] This means that I am not trying to get back to the historical Jesus as reconstructed by current NT scholarship. Hence, this study may not support some current academic constructs for interpreting the Gospels. Consequently, the human elements of written records (Q), research, memory (oral tradition), and reflection will not be utilized as primary and determinative for causing the Gospels but only as secondary and subordinate to the deeper influence and revelation of the Spirit.[110] With "B" representing the four prophetic Branches, the formula of B1, B2, B3, and B4 better conveys the thesis of this book. James H. Charlesworth frames a question that is very applicable to this investigation:

> We must not inadvertently overlook the simplest of questions: How can we explain the appearance of a gospel? What preceded it? How was it possible for Mark to do what in fact he did, if all that preceded him were proclamations (kerygmata) *devoid* of any historical interest and content?[111]

Charlesworth, who is eminently qualified to speak on the subject of the DSS, raises an important question: why a Gospel? He finds the appropriate answers to his own questions in Qumran backgrounds. This investigation travels a different road. Ronald A. Piper asks a question parallel in importance: "Why precisely *these four* gospels, though? This is a difficult question to answer convincingly."[112] The two questions: why a Gospel and why four Gospels are interlocked. Part of the purpose of this study is to seek an answer to the above two questions. In actuality, we have a matrix of four

---

109. Robert M. Grant, *The Earliest Lives of Jesus* (1961) 7–8: "How do the evangelists actually know the words and deeds they report? . . . . It would be natural to assume that he knew the true teaching because of the resurrection and the gift of the Spirit." I take Grant's comment to indicate that this is how Mark would explain his Gospel. Given the context of Grant's entire book, this cannot reflect his own personal view.

110. Frederick C. Grant, *The Earliest Gospel* (1943) 23, admits to what he calls a "major control set up by the fact of the Resurrection" in Gospel composition, but he does not develop this idea. I follow F. F. Bruce, *Tradition: Old and New* (1970), who contends that even an unfailingly accurate memory cannot fully account for the presentation of Jesus in the Gospels. His main contention argues the following (71): "That this freedom should not clash with the spirit of His own teaching was safeguarded not so much by painstaking memorizing (although this played its part in the handing down of the gospel tradition) as by the gift of the Spirit. No account of the transmission of His message is adequate if it fails to reckon with the role of the Spirit to which the hearers of this tradition themselves bear witness."

111. J. H. Charlesworth, *Jesus within Judaism* (1988) 13. Charlesworth, however, makes it clear that divine revelation is very low on his list of concerns (23): "Devout Christians who claim to take the New Testament literally and uncritically are blind to three necessary insights: They fail to perceive that God's revelation is always directed toward imperfect humanity and that revelation can never be more than imperfectly perceived and even more imperfectly recorded." It is true that we should not allow confessional bias or agendas to befog our historical lenses.

112. R. A. Piper, "The One, the Four and the Many," in *The Written Gospel* (2005) 272. See also Piper's comment (at p. 268) regarding an implication from the views of Irenaeus: "The appeal to 'the Gospel in four forms but united with one spirit' implies a significant claim. It is not just an indication that the tensions or discrepancies in the case of these four works can be accommodated. It is also a positive insistence upon theological unity."

important questions: 1) why a *Gospel*, 2) why *four* Gospels, 3) why these four *particular* Gospels, and 4) why in this particular *order*?

The specific proposal here is a hypothesis based upon the number four. The word "hypothesis" is appropriate because nowhere does the NT present in actual statements an alignment of texts documenting the interconnectedness of the number four as developed in this study.[113] The goal, however, is to allow the theory to reflect reliable data rather than allowing theoretical ideas to trump the data. The number four will be examined in its linkage to four prophetic statements containing the metaphor of Branch and the four canonical Gospels.[114] Cognate to the Branch metaphor will be consideration of the four heavenly images as found in the book of Revelation. Since the OT mentions four prophetic Branches, since there are four canonical Gospels, and inasmuch as Rev 4:7 mentions four heavenly images, this study seeks to explain the significance of these relationships. The argument suggests that this numerical phenomenon is too unusual to be brushed aside as a mere human or pedestrian coincidence—or "a fortuitous series of episodes."[115] This proposal not only involves the number four but, concurrently, it explores a significant theological symmetry employed within this number. The analysis, therefore, will be based upon both a quantitative and qualitative evaluation of the sources. The final conclusion will claim that the *only* adequate and satisfactory explanation for the existence of the four Gospels is to be found within the biblical canon which reveals four prophetic Branches, four Gospels, and four living Beings around the throne. No other explanation will suffice.[116]

---

113. I note the relevant comment by Al Wolters, "The Messiah in the Qumran Documents," in *The Messiah in the Old and New Testaments* (2007) 89: "it is undeniably true that speculative hypotheses are the lifeblood of creative scholarship and are indispensable for suggesting new lines of investigation."

114. A suitable working definition of canon (from the Greek κανών, meaning "rule") as applied to the Gospels may be found in Joseph A. Fitzmeyer, "Judaic Studies and the Gospels: the Seminar," in *The Relationships Among the Gospels: An Interdisciplinary Approach* (1978) 245: "'Canonization' of the Torah means nothing more than 'authorized to be read in the synagogues' (to paraphrase the title page of the King Kames Version of the Bible). Hence 'canon' became something about which the community could rally, the centerpiece of its teaching. The same would have been true of the gospels. Out of a variety of gospels, four came to be regarded as authorized to be read publicly." See also Albert C. Sundberg, "The Bible Canon and the Christian Doctrine of Inspiration," *Int* 29 (1975) 356: "My proposal is that the term 'scripture' should be used to designate writings that are regarded as in some sense authoritative, and the term 'canon' used to designate a closed collection of scripture to which nothing can be added, nothing subtracted." For Augustine's view that only the canon of Scripture should be read in church, see Anne-Marie La Bonnardière, "The Canon of Scripture," in *Augustine and the Bible* (1997) 35.

115. Albert Schweitzer, *The Quest of the Historical Jesus* (1968) 7. I borrow Schweitzer's wording but intend a different application. Schweitzer must be credited, however, with recognizing a valuable truth: if the Gospels are products of random and happy chance, then it is hopeless to understand the principles behind their composition.

116. For the view that critical scholarship should be open-minded, see Paul N. Anderson, *The Fourth Gospel and the Quest for Jesus* (2006) 176: "If critical scholars are scandalized by the assessment of critical views critically, one questions the degree to which they are indeed 'critical' scholars, for the trademark of critical scholarship is to welcome all good questions, assessing claims on the basis of their merits rather than their implications."

In other words, the argument of this book raises the relevance of the number four to a level indicative of divine revelation and invites the reader to respect the significance of this number as an adequate explanation for the fourfold Gospel. Since it is a commonplace among the guild of NT scholars to claim that one evangelist contradicts another (and thus undermines any rightful claim to inspiration),[117] this investigation now turns to the issue of contradiction in ancient literature.

---

117. Over a hundred years ago, Paul Wendland in his *Die hellenistisch-römische Kultur in ihren Beziehungen zu Judentum und Christientum: Die urchristlichen Literaturform* (1912) 222, staked out his own personal view that the genealogy of Jesus was characterized by contradictions, legends, and interpolations.

2

Disagreement in the Greco-Roman Literary Tradition and the Implications for Gospel Research[1]

ALTHOUGH THE SPECIFIC SUBJECT of contradictions is rarely undertaken,[2] a frequent claim among NT scholars is that the Gospels are tainted with contradictions and discrepancies.[3] Current criticism generally stereotypes and stigmatizes the evangelists for outright disagreement with the intent to replace or displace a prior Gospel. This modern scholarly construct usually proceeds along the following lines: Matthew writes to correct Mark; Luke then edits Matthew and Mark; finally, John revises them all. It is a commonplace in NT scholarship to read that one or two of the four evangelists were motivated by the desire to replace Mark. John B. Gabel and Charles B. Wheeler represent well this position by offering this reading of the synoptics: "As in the case of Luke, we must assume that Matthew found Mark's gospel inadequate and intended to replace it with his own, not merely to supplement it."[4] John Barton, likewise, echoes the prevailing view: "It is hard to imagine that any of the redactors of the gospels wrote with the intention that his version should stand alongside others in a multi-gospel canon. Rather, each

---

1. For permission to include this chapter, I wish to thank Richard Hess and Craig S. Keener, past and present editors of *The Bulletin of Biblical Research*, for granting permission to publish this material which appeared originally in volume 22.1 (2012) 51–80. Since Penn State University now owns the rights to *BBR*, I wish to thank Sheila Sager Reyes, rights manager of Penn State University Press, for granting permission to reprint this article.

2. Nils Alstrup Dahl, "Contradictions in Scripture," in *Studies in Paul* (1977) 159–77. Dahl took a positive position on contradictions alleging that they serve a useful purpose. See also Martin Hengel's *The Four Gospels and the One Gospel of Jesus Christ* (2000) 167. For a conservative attempt to resolve apparent contradictions from a plausible point of view, see Craig L. Blomberg, *The Historical Reliability of the Gospels* (1987) chapter 4, "Contradictions among the Synoptics?" For a substantive discussion of contradictions, see Helmut Merkel, *Die Widersprüche zwischen den Evangelien: Ihre polemische und apologetisch Behandlung in der Alten Kirche bis zu Augustin* (1971).

3. For the frequent charge that the Gospels are tainted with contradictions and discrepancies which cannot be accounted for, see Robert Morgan, "The New Testament Canon of Scripture and Christianity Identity," in *The Unity of Scripture and the Diversity of the Canon* (2003) 152, in which Morgan includes a concise one-page summary of David Strauss's influential work *Life of Jesus* and then concludes with its impact: "Far from a harmonious symphony we find conflict and disagreement in the first as in every generation of Christianity." See also James E. Brenneman, *Canons in Conflict: Negotiating Texts in True and False Prophecy* (1997) 13–27.

4. J. B. Gabel and C. B. Wheeler, *The Bible As Literature* (1990) 196.

is an attempt to supersede its predecessors."[5] Regarding the viewpoint of the evangelist Luke, D. Moody Smith writes regarding the third Gospel: "Apparently, Luke wrote his Gospel to supplant earlier and less adequate accounts, which in all probability included Mark."[6] Mark Goodacre parallels a similar view: "Luke is making clear that he is critical of his predecessor's work and that his radical reordering of Matthew is in Theophilus's best interest."[7] Regarding the Gospel of John, Harold W. Attridge offers a further exemplar view that John "is not simply an extension of other narratives. This Gospel offers a judgment on whatever predecessors there may have been, be they a Signs Source or a Synoptic Gospel. They were not to be supplemented, but displaced."[8] An even stronger view is that of Mary Ann Tolbert who suggests that "the later writers had more malign than benign intentions in relationship to Mark and actually wished to supplant Mark's interpretation of Jesus with their own."[9]

Current criticism also comes packaged with the charge that the Gospels engage in the actual concealment of damaging evidence.[10] These claims allege that critical scholarship has irreparably damaged the idea of their canonical unity and any attempt to repair such damage is tantamount to patching holes on a sinking ship.[11] In comparison to previous assessments, recent NT scholarship has raised the issue of contradiction to a more aggressive level, escalating the intensity within the fourfold Gospel to a deliberate and intentional motive to disagree. The present trend has characteristics of a borderline official academic protocol: in the literary relationship between the Gospels contradictions are assumed; such assumptions witness to a speculative agenda to displace a prior Gospel; such displacements are evidence of a hypothetical antagonism among the four evangelists.

To simplify the above sequence, present scholarly trends may be reduced to a refined twofold premise: 1) a literary relationship between the Gospels, and 2)

---

5. John Barton, "Marcion Revisited," in *The Canon Debate* (2002) 348. See also Stefan Alkier, "From Text to Intertext: Intertexuality as a Paradigm for Reading Matthew," *HTS/TS* 61.1 (2005) 6, fn.5: "As a reader of Mark, Matthew thus implies that his (Mark's version) of the story of Jesus Christ is incomplete."

6. D. Moody Smith, *John* (1976) 8. See also his "When Did the Gospels Become Scripture?" *JBL* 119.1 (2000) 10, in which he states: "Obviously he intended to supersede Mark, as well as whatever other Gospels or Gospel-like writings he knew. Matthew's appropriation of 90 percent of Mark indicates that he had the same intention—to displace Mark. (Evidently, Matthew, as well as Luke, did not regard Mark as scripture.)."

7. M. Goodacre, *The Synoptic Problem* (2001) 27.

8. Harold W. Attridge, "Genre Bending in the Fourth Gospel," *JBL* 121.1 (2002) 18–19. See also Antonio Piñero, "Interaction of Judaism and Hellenism in the Gospel of John: Elucidating the Ideological Frame of the Fourth Gospel," in *Hellenic and Jewish Arts* (1998) 98.

9. M. A. Tolbert, *Sowing the Gospel* (1989) 81.

10. For the case of distortion or concealment of evidence (cover up), see Byron R. McCane, *Roll Back the Stone: Death and Burial in the World of Jesus* (2003) 101, where McCane then cites John Dominic Crossan (*The Historical Jesus* [1991] 394) that these efforts for the sake of improvement are all part of "damage control."

11. Thomas A. Hoffman, "Inspiration, Normativeness, Canonicity, and the Unique Sacred Character of the Bible," *CBQ* 44.3 (1982) 452.

consequent *intentional* disagreement. This interconnection creates a conditional link or dependence between these two premises: the first is able to exist and survive without the second; the second, however, cannot survive or succeed unless the first is granted. In this investigation it will be argued that the first does not assume the second. The thesis of this chapter assumes *a priori* the first premise, but challenges the second. A disclaimer is appropriate here. I do not want to distort the current state of affairs; there are scholars who defend in print the premise of supplementation. But the particular focus of this investigation takes a slightly different approach to supplementation. My purpose will argue that, when measured against the motif of disagreement in Greco-Roman authors, deliberate contradictions and intentional disagreements are not to be found in the canonical Gospels.

Inasmuch as presupposition should not eclipse objectivity, the optimism of this study's premise requires a realistic question, followed by rigorous testing. In respective order, we start first with an appropriate query: what do we mean by contradiction? Admittedly, one person's contradiction may be another person's variation; one scholar's suspicion may be another's conviction.[12] By what objective criteria can a consensus be established on what is an incontestable contradiction? Using the ancient model of Greco-Roman conventions, a contradiction in this study will be considered legitimate which is stated in clear and point-blank language. This investigation is thus a specific and narrow focus upon *intentional* contradictions which evidence deliberate and, in some cases, even adversarial intent to disagree and displace a peer.

Correlatively, this study does not seek to resolve from the Gospels alleged, falsely contrived, or imaginary contradictions. It is not my purpose to debate oblique subtleties and mundane minutiae.[13] For example, this study does not seek to resolve such cases as when the sun was setting (Mark 1:32 or Luke 4:40), or how many sandals the disciples were to wear (Mark 6:9 or Matt 10:10). Although these are often cited texts for those who favor a skeptical position, I leave the resolution of such questions to the

---

12. Or, as Amy-Jill Levine in her Introduction to *The Historical Jesus in Context* (2006) 1, states: "Comparison is often an extremely subjective judgment: where one scholar finds a connection, another finds disjunction." See also John Barton, "Unity and Diversity in the Biblical Canon," in *The Unity of Scripture and the Diversity of the Canon* (2003) 11–26. Barton alternates back and forth from a cluster of words trying to maintain his position that there are contradictions, inconsistencies, tensions, and variety, yet all within a framework of unity: "In so far as it (Scripture) is read as *Scripture*, however, this variety is to be subsumed in a higher unity."

13. Joseph A. Fitzmyer, "Judaic Studies and the Gospels: The Seminar," in *The Relationships among the Gospels* (1978) 252, refers to "the nonconformity in a large number of sayings, such as Mark 6:9 and Matt 10:10 with their conflicting statements about whether Christian disciples on their evangelical missions were to wear sandals." I refer the reader to William L. Lane, *Commentary on the Gospel of Mark* (1974) 207–8. See also Craig L. Blomberg, "The Parables of Jesus: Current Trends and Needs in Research," in *Studying the Historical Jesus* (1994) 254, who says: "In an age of increasing specialization, scholars need to be able to step back from the investigation of minutiae to grapple with the larger foundational questions about presuppositions and methodology." For a recent example of minutiae exploration, see J. Lionel North, "Reactions in Early Christianity to Some References to the Hebrew Prophets in Matthew's Gospel," *NTS* 54.2 (2008) 254–74.

individual exegetical commentaries,[14] or to specialized studies for such issues.[15] My focus will concentrate on the specific task of identifying the literary conventions of contradiction. Once identified, the next task will be to consider the implications for such conventions in gospel research.

The overall argument of this study contends that in comparison with the language of disagreement as conventionally used in the Greco-Roman literary tradition, Luke, for example, does not contradict either Matthew or Mark. From the perspective of the Greco-Roman literary tradition, a case in point is the death of Pompey's child. Both Velleius Paterculus and Suetonius record that the child was a son. Dio Cassius, however, records that it was a daughter. How could there be a disagreement on such a basic issue? Obviously, this is not a detail that really concerned any of these three Roman historians. In other words, these three Roman historians do not stop to consider the evidence; they are not interested in reconciling any divergency; they make no comment upon another possibility. Clearly, though, the sources for the life of Pompey indicate that a child suffered a premature death. The variation in the tradition obviously still needs clarification. By extension, how can this information apply to the Gospels? A similar case in point may be the actual time the sun is setting when Jesus enters Jericho. Although the timing of Jesus' entrance is a valid question for study and does need explanation, its value for this present investigation is not of material importance because, like the issue of Pompey's child, there is an absence of literary convention signaling an intention to disagree.

We arrive now at the proposed testing. It will be salutary to analyze how ancient critics express dissent and how they clearly and unequivocally contradict their literary predecessors. Within the parameters or conventions of contradiction, how do critics in antiquity present their opposing points of view? To answer this question, the four evangelists will be placed within the larger context of Greco-Roman authors in order to compare how disagreement with a predecessor or a peer is conventionally expressed. Although the relationship of the four Gospels and modern literary criticism is not a new subject,[16] I would like to approach the topic from an unexplored vantage

---

14. See, for example, Richard T. France, *The Gospel of Mark* (2002) 249; Adela Yarbro Collins, *Mark: A Commentary* (2007) 299; Robert H. Stein, *Mark* (2008) 291–93; and William L. Lane, *Commentary on the Gospel of Mark* (1974) 207. Lane refers the reader to E. Powell, "The Staff of the Apostles: A Problem in Gospel Harmony," *Bib* 4 (1923) 241–66. For an equally optimistic approach for understanding variations in the gospel record, see Robert Stein, *Difficult Passages in the New Testament* (1990) 131.

15. See, for example, Tjitze Baarda, "'A Staff Only, Not a Stick': Disharmony of the Gospels and the Harmony of Tatian," in *The New Testament in Early Christianity* (1989) 312: ". . . there is at least one discrepancy that cannot be explained so easily: Mt and Lk forbid the ῥάβδος; Mk allows it: εἰ μὴ ῥάβδος μόνον."

16. See Christopher D. Stanley, "The Social Environment of 'Free' Biblical Quotations in the New Testament," in *Early Christian Interpretation of the Scriptures of Israel* (1997) 18–27. Also by the author in the same volume is his "The Rhetoric of Quotations: An Essay on Method" (44–58). See also the volume of essays edited by William O. Walker, *The Relationships among the Gospels* (1978).

point. For the most part, the efforts of literary critics have been directed toward locating the Gospels within the genres of history, biography, encomium, or science.[17] The approach taken here is a more limited and telescoped view: to ascertain the essential characteristics of pinpoint disagreement, whether by historian, biographer, scientist, encomiast, philosopher, or even poet.[18] In biography, for example, it is true that the conventions of this genre do not call for disagreement to the degree that the genre of history does. However, whenever disagreement surfaces in biography, it follows along the lines developed in this present study.

Since disagreement is not a respecter of genre,[19] this investigation will consider how disagreement and contradiction function over several genres. Examination will be made of sixteen different Greco-Roman authors utilizing over forty texts.[20] In order to provide a workable model, albeit modern, Morton S. Enslin may be helpful as he records his own personal objection against divine revelation in the following statement:

> But there are equally clear variations and flat contradictions, known to every student of the gospels and evident to every reader who will take the trouble to read the accounts in a modern Harmony of the Gospels. Thus the convenient explanation that the gospels are unique writings, a part of Holy Scripture, and not to be judged by usual literary standards, but that, like the Old Testament, they were divinely inspired, and thus the authors were supernaturally guided and controlled . . . shivers on the rock of contradiction.[21]

---

17. For a still useful study locating the Gospels within the genre of biography, see David E. Aune, *The New Testament and Its Literary Environment* (1987) 1–70, and his "Greco-Roman Biography," in *Greco-Roman Literature and the New Testament* (1988) 107–26. For a more recent work, see Richard A. Burridge, *What Are the Gospels? A Comparison with Graeco-Roman Biography* (2004). Burridge builds upon the earlier work of Clyde Weber Votaw, *The Gospels and Contemporary Biographies in the Graeco-Roman World* (1970; reprint from *AJTh* 19 [1915] 45–73). See also the collection of essays edited by David P. Moessner, *Jesus and the Heritage of Israel* (1999) 9–143. For an informative summary of the issues, see Adela Yarbro Collins, *Mark* (2007) 15–43.

18. I include poetry even though the objective of a poet is not to present particular historical truth (Aristotle, *Ars poetica* 1451a/9.1–3). Nevertheless, poets do criticize one another as, for example, Horace does in *Satirae* 1.10.51–52, when he even asks: "Come now, I ask, do you a scholar find nothing to fault in the great Homer?" (*age, quaeso, tu nihil in magno doctus reprehendis Homero?*). Horace indicates that not even Homer is exempt from criticism, implying that if the great Homer is not safe then no one can escape from the barbs of critics. Of course, it should not be left unsaid that Horace found great pleasure in reading Homer. See also W. D. Davies, "Canon and Christology," in *The Glory of Christ in the New Testament* (1987) 28: "A sophist could even call Homer a liar and hold him up to ridicule: so Dio of Prusa, *Discourse* 11."

19. R. Burridge, *What Are the Gospels?* (2004) 53, states: "Genre is a crucial tool for the study and interpretation of a text in that it provides a form of contract between author and reader, giving a set of expectations for both composition and interpretation." This certainly applies to genre, but crossing genres does not require additional refinement of how contradiction is expressed.

20. The following authors are included: Appian, Arrian, Cicero, Dio Cassius, Diodorus Siculus, Dionysius of Halicarnassus, Herodotus, Horace, Josephus, Livy, Pausanias, Plutarch, Polybius, Strabo, Thucydides, and Velleius Paterculus.

21. M. Enslin, "Luke and Matthew: Compilers or Authors?" *ANRW* 25.3 (1984) 2359.

Enslin, in a most engaging and energetic manner, raises the issue of literary standards. As a result of his views, I would like to appeal to Enslin's own colorful expressions. Three pivotal elements in his protest stand out: 1) he clearly and pointedly makes known his disagreement with those who champion divine revelation; 2) he explains his own reasoning: anyone who will take the time to read a Harmony of the Gospels will reach the same conclusion; and 3) he even provides a metaphor—a view such as supernatural revelation will "shiver on the rock of contradiction." Enslin's objection to divine revelation suggests three useful criteria for determining a contradiction: 1) language characterized by plain statement and direct disagreement [a "flat contradiction"],[22] 2) reasons given, and 3) obvious displeasure—even colorfully and metaphorically expressed. The only omission in this threefold classification is the specific mention of whom he is refuting. Enslin simply uses the umbrella expression "the convenient explanation that" which he may have used obliquely in order to avoid giving offense. However, he has attached his own name to the document thus providing another marker in the language of disagreement.

I submit Enslin's manner of writing in order to investigate the language of disagreement and the rhetoric of correction. The above example will be adopted as an amiable model in order to compare it with the language of contradiction as found in ancient Greek and Roman authors. The reason for setting the investigation up in this fashion is to compare ancient expressions with modern in order to set the results alongside the four Gospels.

Plain Statement and Direct Disagreement

An informative starting point is Diodorus Siculus, a compiler of Greek history, lore, mythology, and topography who lived approximately 80–20 BC. In his *Bibliotheca historiae* (4.2.1), he describes the difficulties involved in compiling accurate information about Greek mythology: the sheer antiquity of these myths complicates the task of discovering the real truth; the variety of the different kinds of heroes and multitude of demi-gods tempts readers to treat these stories with contempt; but "the greatest obstacle of all" (τὸ δὲ μέγιστον καὶ πάντων ἀτοπώτατον) is the number of disagreements

---

22. An equally passionate view of the Gospels as full of "flat contradictions" is that of Geza Vermes, *The Authentic Gospel of Jesus* (2004) 370, who says: "They patently represent irreconcilable variations; indeed again and again they display flat contradictions." Vermes and Enslin use very similar language and thought; they are both equally convinced that the Gospels contain *flat contradictions* and anyone with a measure of intelligence should be able to recognize such conflicts. Furthermore, their expressions also support my thesis that serious contradictions, whether modern or ancient, contain the overlapping characteristics of clear disagreement, reasons given, and emotion expressed. Thus, their very own conventions are a suitable exhibit of how disagreement actually functions. Although Vermes and Enslin provide ample evidence from their own objections that genuine disagreement is voiced in the definite language of clear statement, reasons given, and displeasure visibly expressed, such concrete and unambiguous expressions are not to be found in the four Gospels.

among the mythmakers.[23] Diodorus then proceeds to his first myth, that of the god Dionysus (4.3.4–5.6). In this account, he mentions unknown sources of the myth by using the verb "they say" (φάσι) eight times,[24] and by using the alternate verb "they say" (λέγουσιν) five times.[25]

It is conventional to mention alternate versions without in any way minimizing the value of one's own work. All historians and biographers do this; whether one considers the Gospels as bio or history is immaterial. The point is that none of the four evangelists ever use the conventional expression "some say . . . others say." Luke 1:1–3 cannot be used to imply this. There are other ways of interpreting Luke at this point. Generally, the inclusion of statements such as "some say . . . others say" is used to acknowledge either diversity in the tradition or it is a subtle way of admitting that the writer himself does not know and neither do others. Therefore, the absence of such conventional expressions may suggest that the four evangelists are not writing under the handicap of ignorance. Four people standing on the four corners of an intersection who witness an accident in the center will offer four different versions of the same wreck. This does not imply contradiction or disagreement. It is a matter of perspective. Other than direct disagreement, variations in the four witness accounts are to be expected. Although there seems to be no significance to the change of verbs other than variety, the more salient point is that informational dissonance in a narrative can be characterized by the presence of confusing sources in which one source claims one thing and a second source claims another.

Returning now to Diodorus, toward the end of this narrative account of the exploits and achievements of Dionysus, he stops to assist the reader with an explanation for how there could exist two separate versions of this god. Here is his understanding: "and so the men of later times, being unawares of the truth and being deceived because of the identity of their names, thought there had been but one Dionysus."[26] Diodorus in direct and point-blank language states his view: "the men of later times, being ignorant or unawares of the truth, were deceived" (ἀγνοοῦντας μὲν τἀληθές, πλανηθέντας).[27] In other words, dissonance in the tradition is due to ignorance. This ignorance, then, is spelled out for the reader. This kind of language or reader assistance is not found in Matthew to describe Mark, nor in Luke to describe Matthew or Mark,[28]

---

23. The word Diodorus uses for "disagreements" is ἀσύμφωνος, suggesting that a disagreement is an unharmonious and dissonant clash. See also 5.6.1 where he uses the verb διαφωνεῖν to describe disagreements among historians. LSJ list the following definitions for this word as: musical "dissonance," architectural "displeasure to the eye," and literary "contradiction" or "disagreement."

24. 4.2.1, 5; 4.3.4; 4.4.2, 3, 4; 4.5.3–4.

25. 4.1.7; 4.4.2, 4, 5; 4.5.3.

26. Translation by C. H. Oldfather in the LCL.

27. 4.4.5. A similar complaint can be found in Polybius (12.4d.1): "Timaeus, while making a great parade of accuracy, in my opinion, falls very far from the truth."

28. See Eric Franklin, *Luke: Interpreter of Paul, Critic of Matthew* (1994) 370: "Luke's handling of Matthew is seen to be one controlled by caution: it amounts to no more than a guarded use of the first

nor in John to describe the other three.[29] Especially is this language absent from Luke's genealogy to describe that of Matthew's.[30] Inasmuch as ignorance of the real facts has been lodged against the evangelists,[31] this omission of assistance to the reader explaining disagreement in a tradition may be raised as a red flag against current and repetendous scholarly contentions lodged against the Gospels.

Livy's *Ab urbe condita* (1.24) may serve as another notable contrast to the Gospels. Livy, as it were, allows us to look over his shoulder and view him working on a problem as he endeavors to decide to which people (the Curiatii or the Horatii) a set of triplet brothers belonged:

> *Horatios Curiatiosque fuisse satis constat, nec ferme res antique alia est nobilior; tamen in re tam clara nominum error manet; utrius populi Horatii, utrius Curiatii fuerint. Autores utroque trahunt.*

> That they were Horatii and Curatii is clear enough, and hardly any other ancient tradition is more notorious; nevertheless, in spite of the celebrity of the affair, an uncertainty remains in regard to the names—to which people, that is, the Horatii belonged, and to which the Curiatii. Historians are drawn to both sides.

Livy, we are informed, is trying to sort out a discrepancy in his sources. What complicates his choice is the combination of the number of variations and the fame of the affair: "there is nearly none more notable" (*nec ferme res antique alia est nobilior*). Nevertheless, there still remains in the tradition an error or uncertainty regarding these names (*tamen in re tam clara nominum error manet*).[32] The presence of *tamen* ("nevertheless") suggests that the historical value of the affair should have created

---

Gospel's perspective and exhibits a critical attitude to much that it contains. Luke is in fact a critic of Matthew."

29. Indeed, language of this kind can be found within the NT but only to describe either those outside the community of faith, or to describe the past behavior of those now inside the family of faith. The language of clear disagreement, however, is not in any of the four evangelists to register objections against the others.

30. For one possible way to interpret the texts, see F. Gerald Downing, "A Paradigm Perplex: Luke, Matthew and Mark," *NTS* 38.1 (1992) 22, where Downing reviews M. D. Goulder's monograph *Luke— A New Paradigm* (1989). Downing alleges that Goulder sees Luke as a harmonizer between Matthew and Mark; Downing sees quite the opposite.

31. See W. D. Davies and E. P. Sanders, "Jesus: From the Jewish Point of View," in *The Cambridge History of Judaism* (1984) 3.622, who argue that the evangelists are "ignorant" about the birth of Jesus and that Luke "differs substantially" from Matthew and Mark regarding the death of Jesus. See also Dennis E. Smith, "Jesus and the Gospels" in *Chalice Introduction to the New Testament* (2004) 124: "Certainly 'what really happened' is part of what they are after, but they may not know the facts for certain."

32. Livy uses *error* in both senses: either "error" (27.16.6) or "uncertainty" or "perplexity" (9.45.16). Although the Latin *error* tempts one to jump to the conclusion that Livy has in mind the idea of "error," the context argues more for "uncertainty." However, I have left the word "error" in the text as a possibility. It is true that Luke wants Theophilus to know the "certainty" of things he has learned (Luke 1:4); this, however, does not insinuate that Theophilus is uncertain about anything he believes because of something he may have read or heard from another Gospel.

a more unified tradition, but this is not the case; an error or uncertainty prevents agreement. This unsettled issue causes a split decision among the historians (*auctores utroque trahunt*). As we place these Livian admissions alongside the fourfold Gospel, the following cardinal contrasts emerge: no evangelist confesses to a similar dilemma of having to decide between two compelling options; no evangelist acknowledges confusion in the tradition, either in a previous Gospel or the hypothetical document Q;[33] no evangelist admits to division among his peers. Likewise, there are no nebulous point-blank assertions (such as "they err") in the Gospels of an accusing nature directed toward an unnamed evangelist.

There is one further example demonstrating the rubric of disagreement. The Roman historian Velleius Paterculus in his *Historia Romana* (1.7.2–4), writing during the age of Augustus Caesar, reports that there are "many errors and discrepancies among the authorities" (*maximique erroris et multum discrepantem auctorum opinionibus*) regarding the distant past of Rome. With some of these authorities Paterculus is in agreement (*quibus equidem adsenserim*). But there is one in particular that is in grave error and must be singled out for correction. This is the mistaken view of Marcus Cato (*sed M. Cato quantum differt!*) regarding the issue of a date. Although Paterculus concedes that Cato is known for his conscientiousness, nevertheless, he cannot side with him on the dating of Capua. Judgments such as this from Paterculus cannot be found in the four Gospels. Although there have been claims of "sharp" disagreements alleged against the evangelists,[34] these claims, so far in this investigation, do not measure up to the standards of Greco-Roman convention.

What, therefore, do these contrasts suggest? One possible answer is that the Gospels occupy unique genre ground which exempts them from having to resolve such issues as variations. That is, the gospel writers give no evidence of being under obligation to tackle variations in the tradition. A second option is the one raised recently by Michael R. Licona who suggests that the conventions of ancient biographical writing do not require technical precision.[35] Another possible solution is that the four writers were completely unaware of fellow evangelists and their respective Gospels.[36] This present investigation, however, assumes the contrary; there is a literary relationship. Yet another possible explanation is that the four evangelists have utterly failed in their

---

33. Going all the way back to Herodotus (1.95.1), it was customary to admit different versions or "paths" (ἄλλας λόγων ὁδούς) regarding the subjects an author was treating. For a discussion of how Herodotus sorts out the truth, see David Branscome, "Herodotus and the Map of Aristagoras," *CA* 29.1 (2010) 34.

34. See James D. Tabor and Michael O. Wise, "4Q521 'On Resurrection' and the Synoptic Gospel Tradition," *JSP* 10 (1992) 161, for their example of a sharp disagreement between the texts of Luke 4:16–30 and Mark 6:1–6.

35. M. R. Licona, *Why Are There Differences in the Gospels?* (2017) 197–202.

36. For an exception, see, for example, Ulrich Luz, *Matthew 1–7* (2007) 75: "That neither of the evangelists tries to reconcile the differences must be seen as an indication that the classical assumption of the literary independence of Matthew and Luke is correct."

responsibility to confront alleged contradictions in the gospel tradition. What, therefore, some modern scholars see as flagrant violations, the four gospel writers have blindly missed owing to their weaknesses in critical judgment. There is yet one other option still on the table: the apparent face value of the data in light of Greco-Roman conventions. That is, absence of direct disagreement in the gospel tradition indicates no legitimate reason to disagree or even intent to do so. Stated otherwise, there is not one single statement in the fourfold Gospel of an evangelist saying, "I disagree with . . ." Nor is there a single statement in which an evangelist says of another, "He contradicts himself." This absence of point-blank criticism discredits the suspicion of an intention to disagree and places in doubt the judgment of historical criticism on this particular matter.

Reasons Given

When Greco-Roman writers openly disagree with a peer or a predecessor, they usually explain the reason for this disagreement. Strabo is a suitable example for this rubric. Strabo, born 64/63 BC, and living to about 21 AD, writes in book 1.2 of his *Geography* that he feels it necessary to correct the errors of Eratosthenes so that his readers will know what teachers they should follow. Strabo at 1.2.2 faults Eratosthenes for a "serious weakness of judgment" (ἱκανὴν ἀσθένειαν . . . γνώμης); at 1.2.3 Strabo claims that Eratosthenes "contradicts himself" (ἑαυτῷ μάχεται); at 1.2.7 he instructs the reader that his predecessor "makes many mistakes" (πολλὰ διαμαρτάνει); and at the end of 1.2.7, Strabo feels that the mistakes of Eratosthenes now require a more detailed exposure. Thus at 1.2.8 there begins a series of treatments prefaced with the word "first of all" (καὶ πρῶτον). This method of itemizing is characteristic of Strabo as he tends to order his objections in a sequential manner. He has a critical mind; it is orderly, analytical, and systematic in judgment. At 1.3.22 he begins a series of objections with an orderly structure: ἐπὶ τὰ ἑξῆς . . . ἑξῆς δέ . . . ἑξῆς δέ . . . ἑξῆς δέ ("next in order . . . next").[37] In between, he hammers and chips away at the mistakes of his predecessor. In book 2 he varies his sequences with a literary change of pace: "first of all . . . again" (πρῶτον μέν . . . πάλιν); or "neither . . . nor" (οὔτε . . . οὔτε).[38] This internal variation is bracketed by the outer and more familiar ἐν τοῖς ἑξῆς . . . ἑξῆς δέ ("in what follows . . . next").[39] In all these systematic and specific objections, Strabo constantly registers his disapproval of Eratosthenes by enumerating reasons.

Toward the end of his first book (1.2.35), Strabo mentions a plurality of writers who create their compositions with a tendency to confuse myth with history. This is his initial objection: they fashion free creations (οἱ δὲ πλάττοντες). He then passes quickly to mention an even greater reason for dismissing these writers: they

---

37. 1.3.21, 22, 23; 1.4.2, 7.
38. 2.1.12–13; 2.2.21.
39. 2.1.22–23.

"contradict one another" (τὸ ἐναντιοῦσθαι ἀλλήλοις). Strabo does not stop there but proceeds to offer additional insight into how these writers demonstrate their opposition to one another: they add their *reasons why* for disagreement (προστιθέντας καὶ διὰ τί). It should be noted, however, that Strabo is not claiming that the insertion of "reasons why" proves contradiction; rather, he suggests that by indicating such reasons this further compounds the case for disagreement and makes it easier to fault errors. His statement clearly suggests that, when one writer wants to contradict another, providing "reasons why" is part of the convention of disagreement.

There is more. In book 2 Strabo expresses his personal displeasure with a writer named Hipparchus: sometimes Hipparchus makes false assumptions about Eratosthenes; at other times he is correct in his censure. Strabo, however, faults Hipparchus for not correcting Eratosthenes! In other words, Strabo may be the only reliable source for faulting critics. Clearly, Strabo is out to protect his readers from an anaclitic trust in unreliable writers. By linking together the two geographers (Eratosthenes and Hipparchus), Strabo is taking on two leading authorities who are best viewed as competitors. This follows his programme as stated in the prologue (1.2); he desires to instruct his readers in who to follow. By naming names, Strabo can undermine his predecessors while at the same time elevate his own stature. From Stabo's point of view, credibility is damaged, opportunity is missed, and authority weakened when rival names are left out of the record. In his judgment, it is inappropriate to leave out the opposition. Nothing can be gained by such a tactic; it is, therefore, advantageous to include names and identify competitors. Furthermore, reasons supplied bolster his case and commend him to his reading public. From this Strabean data, I see no parallel evidence supporting the view that Luke wrote to supplant Mark, or that any of the four wrote to replace any of the others. Given the conventions of bio, geography or history, authors make known their intentions when they are supplanting, correcting, or finding fault.

The above viewpoints fail to answer a needed question: if Matthew and Luke absorbed ninety percent of Mark in order to displace him, why do *both* evangelists engage in the task of allegedly replacing an inferior Mark? Was Luke dissatisfied with both Mark and Matthew? Does Luke think that Matthew's effort to undermine Mark was a failure and now he must correct the corrector? The direction of this study pursues a different route by counter-proposing that Luke does not acknowledge disappointment with either Mark or Matthew because he experienced none.

Polybius may also serve as an adequate guide for understanding the convention of disagreement from the perspective of reasons given. In book 2.56.1 of his *Histories*, Polybius introduces Phylarchus into his narrative because he is a rival at variance with the more reliable historian, Aratus. Since Aratus is the preferred source, Polybius finds it necessary (ἀναγκαῖον ἡμῖν) to "minutely examine" (διευκρινεῖν) the failings of Phylarchus as they are measured against the more dependable Aratus. First of all, Phylarchus continually brings before his readers unnecessary horrors in order to sensationalize (2.56.2–16). Phylarchus not only sensationalizes his narratives but he includes falsehoods out of ignorance (2.58.12–13). There is then a short break in the narrative. This break is subsequently followed at 2.59.1 in which Polybius resumes his resumé of Phylarchian errors by the word πάλιν ("again" or "furthermore"). He thus indicates that he is not yet finished with Phylarchus. At 2.59.3 there is a passing note that what has been shown about the weaknesses of Phylarchus is now sufficient; yet at 2.59.7 Polybius must include more corrections. This list of shortcomings, however, is not complete; at 2.61.1 the account continues with χωρίς τε τούτων ("apart from these things"), hinting that there are still more failings to report: exaggeration and elaboration. At 2.62.1 the list of complaints continues to roll on: "further" (οὐ μὴν ἀλλὰ τούτοις ἑξῆς). When he arrives at 2.63.1, a final conclusion appears imminent. He guides the reader with a τούτῳ ("to this"); then, he takes off again, finally laying to rest the subject at 2.63.6. Polybius also reveals his motives for this visceral dissecting of Phylarchus. It is twofold: 1) he desires to explain why he prefers the tradition as passed down from Aratus, and 2) he desires to demonstrate the faulty historical principles of Phylarchus. In order to do this he must itemize and defend his reasons. In all of this, Polybius presents himself as one who feels the weight of responsibility pressing upon him to protect his reading public.

Velleius Paterculus in his *History of Rome* provides another motive for supplying reasons. After listing the age of Pompey at his death as fifty-eight years, Paterculus refers to writers who, owing to "excessive preoccupation" (*nimium occupatos*), have failed to give the correct age of the great man. Paterculus cannot allow this error to go uncorrected and unmentioned. He feels slightly apologetic, though, for bringing up the failures of others and adds: "I have added this remark not for the sake of criticizing others, but to avoid criticisms of myself."[40] As a writer who has uneasy qualms about criticizing fellow authors, Paterculus feels justified in protecting himself by setting the record straight.

When we compare a convention such as this with gospel narratives, what are we to conclude? As compared to the Hellenistic practice of stating reasons, there is no evidence that any of the four evangelists openly disagrees with another evangelist by validating such a disagreement with an explanation as to why. Yet, criticism accompanied by reasons given often characterizes ancient historical writing of almost any kind. Praise and criticism of the tradition inheres as part of the individual historian's craft—almost as if a default position.[41] Indeed, it is often expressed as a moral obligation to readers. For example, Strabo, addressing Polybius as if that man were still alive, informs him that correcting errors in the historical tradition is obligatory for

---

40. Velleius Paterculus, *History of Rome* 2.53.4: *Quod adieci, non ut arguerem, sed ne argerer.*

41. For references to the historian's duty, see John Marincola, "ἀλήθεια," *LHG&L* (2007) 2.28: "He is expected to have a certain completeness in his account, and, in those places where there is controversy, to lay out for his audience conflicting accounts so that they may be decided." An appropriate example of this fairness to readers may be found in the prologue to Arrian's *History of Alexander* (1.1–2). Arrian explains who the two most reliable sources are and what he will do if they disagree.

the historian.[42] But the comparative data under the present rubric suggests that no evangelist directly disagrees with another (especially in an orderly sequence). Furthermore, there is no apology for such a censure because it seemed necessary to do so in order to protect his credibility or his audience.

Up to this point, the data suggest provisionally that the Gospels contain no evidence of direct disagreements openly stated; and, tangentially, there are no reasons given. Yet, the four evangelists are not without a model for doing so. In Mark 12:18–27 the text records the conflict between the Sadducees and Jesus over the subject of resurrection. The text includes these words (24): "Are you not in error because you do not know the Scriptures or the power of God?" And (27): "You are badly mistaken!" Here we find in the narrative direct disagreement and reasons given. Although this blunt dialogue is credited to the Markan Jesus,[43] this kind of point-blank statement cannot be found in one gospel writer directed against another.[44] So, according to the Markan text, although the disciples could find precedent in Jesus' manner of criticizing the Sadducees for their lack of correct biblical knowledge, we find no such criticism as directed toward a fellow evangelist. As a negative example, it will be instructive to introduce a finding from the Jesus Seminar regarding the above text (Mark 12:18–27). The Seminar claims: "For these reasons, many Fellows concluded that the words could not have originated with Jesus." This judgment by the Jesus Seminar team turns the evangelist Matthew into the originator of a tactic that he does not even use against Mark (assuming the priority of Mark). My argument, to the contrary, is that Jesus is the true source of the statement and thus he provides a potential model and precedent for criticism. But the fact is that no evangelist found it necessary to follow this model in order to fault another evangelist.

What is the implication of such literary silence? One possible answer is that no evangelist was actually aware of another Gospel in circulation. Given the general consensus on literary dependence in the Gospels, this would be a hard sell in today's academic climate. This, of course, is not an argument that consensus equals truth. Consensus, however, cannot be ignored. In fact, this investigation is a response to consensus. An acknowledgement is accordingly repeated here: this investigation is based upon the premise that there is, indeed, a literary relationship between the Gospels. The prologue to Luke's Gospel leads in the direction of such awareness. A more likely solution, therefore, is the proposal advocated here: the absence of reasons given is a tacit argument that the evangelists were not actively engaged in correcting a peer.

42. *Geography* 10.3.5.

43. Robert W. Funk, Roy W. Hoover, and, The Jesus Seminar, *The Five Gospels* (1993) 237.

44. Another example may be Matthew's account of Jesus responding to ancient views with the correction, "You have heard that it was said to the people long ago" (5:21, 27, and 33). This series of counter-statements has Jesus looking back upon a remote past and offering corrections to mistaken views. Nowhere does the author of Matthew, as it were, adopt this pedagogic model and then, facing his readership, pen the words, "You have heard it said (or read in the Gospel of Mark) that an evangelist said."

Obvious Displeasure

Emotion negatively expressed is often present in ancient texts when one author contradicts or corrects another. Positive pleasure would be the opposite—an emotion that some contemporary scholars eschew in their own work.[45] Some academics, however, do not disdain a scholarly scoff.[46] In order to illustrate this category, Polybius and his assessment of Timaeus may serve as a strong didactic indicator. This evaluation is found in book 4.12.1–16.14 of his *Histories* and is one of the more caustic criticisms from antiquity in faulting the failings of a fellow historian. Not only does Polybius acknowledge his own motives for writing, but he feels capable of evaluating the motives of others. This is especially the case regarding Timaeus. The *OCD* (1995) lists the dates for Polybius at 200–118 BC., and the dates for Timaeus at 350–260 BC. At the minimum, Polybius is writing eighty years after the death of Timaeus; yet he faults Timaeus for a number of reasons—often questioning the very motives of his predecessor. Although Timaeus is not a contemporary, his reputation, like a ghost, may have haunted Polybius. Polybius, it appears, feels some sort of inner compulsion to judge Timaeus for his carelessness with facts—for what he calls "random" or "scattered" (ἀπεσχέδιακεν) comments on Africa. Polybius is unsparing in censure and relentless in criticism as he lodges numerous pungent complaints. His most telling comments about this rival occur when he delves into motives. Polybius believes that Timaeus's judgments are colored or darkened by prejudice.[47] Even worse, Timaeus deliberately lies.[48] The strongest metaphor of obvious displeasure comes into play when Polybius accuses Timaeus of using language and descriptions that are not even to be found in a house of prostitution.[49] Polybius clearly has a taste for expressing strong and biting language toward a rival. What should not remain unsaid is Polybius' own expression

---

45. For such expressions, see Larry W. Hurtado, "Devotion of Jesus and Historical Investigation: A Grateful, Clarifying and Critical Response to Professor Casey," *JSNT* 27.1 (2004) 99; Maurice Casey's review, "Lord Jesus Christ: A Response to Professor Hurtado," *JSNT* 27 (2004) 83–96. For yet another contemporary example of clear disagreement and emotion expressed, see Bruce Chilton and Craig A. Evans, "Jesus and Israel's Scriptures," in *Studying the Historical Jesus: Evaluations of the State of Current Research* (1994) 302–3, and their critique of Michael Goulder's treatment of Mark 4:12.

46. For a classical scholar's reaction to a fellow classicist, see J. P. Gould, "Law, Custom and Myth: Aspects of the Social Position of Women in Classical Athens," *JHS* 100 (1980) 42: "When Gomme sums up his position by saying, 'there is nothing remarkable about the position of women in Athens, except perhaps the special honor paid to them,' I can only gasp!" For NT scholars, see the review by L. De Blois and E. A. Hemelrijk in *Mnemosyne* 45 (1992) 279, of Ben Witherington's book *Women in the Earliest Churches*. See also N. T. Wright, *Jesus and the Victory of God* (1996) 464, in which he says Schweitzer was "disastrously wrong" and Bultmann "utterly mistaken." See also John P. Meier, "The Present State of the 'Third Quest' for the Historical Jesus: Loss and Gain," *Bib* 80.4 (1999) 473, also on Bultmann: "The master skeptic of form criticism can be oddly subjective, not to say romantic, when evaluating the historicity of individual sayings."

47. Polybius, 12.7.1.

48. For some of the more trenchant statements accusing Timaeus of deliberate lying, see 12.7.6; 9.1; 10.6.

49. 12.13.2. Literally: "neither (would) anyone among those who under the roof employ the body."

of actual bitterness toward Timaeus (12.15.12). Although he tempers his displeasure with a claim that he is refraining from giving full vent to his hostility (ἀπεχθεία), nonetheless, he is quite open and transparent about his feelings.

A further example may reinforce the point. Dionysius of Halicarnassus composed his *Roman Antiquities* during the reign of Augustus Caesar, writing perhaps up to the year 7 BC.[50] At 2.58.1 Dionysius raises the issue of contradictions and disagreements in regard to his predecessor's treatment of Numa. Dionysius alerts the reader that he is now going to engage in the task of contradicting (ἀντειπεῖν) previous historians. He even expresses his displeasure and dismay at these former treatments.[51] He then mentions how many earlier historians have written incorrectly about the date in which Numa lived, thereby erroneously placing him in the lifetime of Pythagoras and consequently contradicting the known facts of universal history.[52] Dionysius next proceeds to provide yet stronger evidence making it impossible that Numa and Pythagoras could have been contemporaries. This he does by showing that the city of Croton did not exist during the time of Numa. Dionysius does stop to consider the possibility that another wise man by the name of Pythagoras could have been the center of the controversy. This he dismisses since the sources do not allow such a conclusion. Dionysius offers his own view of the confusion: it is the result of erroneously combining two traditions into one. The historical method of Dionysius reveals definite conventions when faced with conflicting information in the tradition. There is often an expression of displeasure, either preceded or followed by reasons given. Other examples could be supplied.[53] As applied to the four gospel accounts, this Greco-Roman literary principle of stating reasons why with expressions of displeasure when demurring with a peer or predecessor is revealing.

A brief mention of another case may be helpful. J. Enoch Powell, staking out a claim that Matthew was the first Gospel, offers the view that Mark was "flummoxed" over what he read in Matthew.[54] The word "flummoxed" suggests strong bewilderment. Unless direct statement is present in a text, emotion of this sort cannot be as-

---

50. On the dates for Dionysius, see Earnest Cary in the Loeb edition, vol.1, xi.

51. ("In what follows next I am somewhat at a loss of what to say").

52. μάχεται πρὸς τὸν λόγον ("[the date of Pythagoras] contradicts this account").

53. See Dionysius of Halicarnassus, *Roman Antiquities* 4.6.1, in which he indicates the need to explain his reasons (αἰτίας) for disagreeing with Fabius and other historians. I note also the essay by Plutarch in his *On the Malice of Herodotus*. Plutarch makes it plain from the outset his purpose: he intends to expose Herodotus as a clever and charming distorter of facts—even an outright liar. Plutarch views his effort in this regard as a pursuit in the cause of truth (854F/1). What is worse (καὶ οὐ τοῦτο δεινόν [857E/14]), Herodotus combines blasphemy with malice. Plutarch, relentless in building his case, provides example after another, piles up metaphor upon metaphor, and at the very end (874B/43) acknowledges the literary gifts of Herodotus only to illustrate his point: these artistic gifts are like the rose-beetle; they may have an external charming quality but in the end they are harmful.

54. J. Enoch Powell, *The Evolution of the Gospel* (1994) xiii, in which Powell says: "In addition to passages where Matthew presents difficulties due to corruption or error, proof of Mark's resort to Luke when flummoxed by Matthew is provided where Matthew's narrative is deliberately symbolical."

sumed. Since we are not in a position to read Mark's body language (such as facial expressions), the plain meaning of words must be our guide in understanding his state of mind. Intentionality that is unexpressed is normally considered to be an ulterior motive. Without clearer evidence, Mark should not be faulted as possessing such ulterior motives. In my judgment, a fair and amenable analysis of Powell's assertion of Markan bewilderment at Matthew deserves dismissal as misguided and unfortunate.

I affirm, therefore, that hostility or even a lesser displeasure expressed from one evangelist against another is notably and ostensibly missing in gospel texts. This absence of acerbic attacks, bitter rebukes, and chilling challenges adds further weight to the thesis of this study that there are no deliberate disagreements in the fourfold gospel tradition. Indeed, not even gentle corrections, mildly expressed, may be found. Furthermore, this omission of such criticisms may suggest an unusual unity.

As I close this section, it may be helpful to bring in one of the main criteria for establishing authenticity in Jesus research; this is the criterion of embarrassment. We begin with Anthony Le Donne's recent description:

> The supposition that the Gospels contain invented material is predicated upon the notion that early Christianity had motive to invent material as they commemorated Jesus' post-Easter significance. This commemoration tended to exalt Jesus in several ways and decrease or eliminate details that cast him in an embarrassing light. Because of this, episodes that do indeed contain such details are not easily explained as Christian invention.[55]

Further in his book, Le Donne then illustrates how his understanding of the criterion of embarrassment functions. He compares the details of Mark 8:22–26 with Matt 9:27–31 and says: "As briefly discussed, Mark 8:22–26 seems to have embarrassed Matthew. Luke has likely omitted this story altogether for similar reasons."[56] Since the Markan text reveals a case of progressive rather than instantaneous healing, and Matthew never records a case of progressive healing, this supposedly indicates redactional invention on Matthew's part (due to feelings of embarrassment) and memory on Mark's part. In other words, Matthew, due to his own offended sensitivities, actually sanitizes the episode by omitting Markan material from the tradition; whereas Mark, for his part, is relying upon the tradition as he has received it. I will confine my comments here only to the notion of embarrassment. If this is a literary situation of genuine embarrassment on the part of Matthew for the alleged awkward details in Mark, this is an unusual way of recording such embarrassment. Feelings of embarrassment are evidence of displeasure. Writers truly experiencing embarrassment over details or defects found in a peer normally register such reactions. In such cases,

---

55. Anthony Le Donne, *The Historiographical Jesus* (2009) 89. Le Donne lists six criteria. In his judgment, the criterion of embarrassment is especially important for establishing historical reality in Jesus research. See also Darrell L. Bock, "The Historical Jesus: An Evangelical View," in *The Historical Jesus* (2009) 249–81, for his use of the embarrassment criterion.

56. Bock (2009) 176.

expressions of displeasure are the norm. This holds true for both ancient and modern writers. For example, I note James D. G. Dunn's reaction to Robert M. Price's view that Jesus is a myth: "Gosh! So there are still serious scholars who put forward the view that the whole account of Jesus' doings and teachings are a later myth foisted on an unknown, obscure historical figure."[57] I take Dunn's "Gosh" as a mild and subtle tongue-in-cheek emotional expression of ironic amazement originating in embarrassing feelings of surprise. Such expressions are absent in the four evangelists' literary relationships with one another.

The Name of Addresser and Addressee(s)

There is one last category to discuss: the issue of identity. Not all Greek historians identify themselves.[58] The tendency, however, is to acknowledge one's personal name. an example of this tendency is Cicero's *Pro Archia* (26) which mentions how philosophers will heap scorn upon the pursuit of seeking glory and fame, yet they will still attach their name to their own essays: *Ipsi illi philosophi etiam in eis libellis quos de contemnenda gloria scribunt nomen suum inscribunt; in eo ipso in quo praedicationem nobilitatemque despiciunt praedicari de se ac se nominari volunt* ("Even philosophers themselves in the very books in which they censure [the pursuit of] glory, include their own names. By the very thing in which they deem as worthless—fame and notability—they wish to have their names attached").[59] That is to say, a chief means for building up one's reputation in order to acquire fame was to attach one's name.

The power of literature to confer "immortality" can be traced back to Homer in poetry,[60] and in prose to both Herodotus (1.1) and Thucydides (1.22.4; 2.43.3, 64.5). Herodotus states in the prologue that he does not want the great deeds of men to fall into oblivion. Thucydides is clearly aware of the enduring power of literature to confer fame as well as simultaneously to establish an author in the national consciousness by writing of the greatest war ever fought (1.4); he envisions his work as being a "possession forever" (κτῆμά τε ἐς αἰεί, 1.22). Hence, both historians hang onto the coattails of great deeds. The Hellenistic poet Callimachus is also aware of the power of poetry to confer immortality when he referred to his deceased friend Heracleitus' verses as not

---

57. J. D. G. Dunn, "Response to Robert M. Price," in *The Historical Jesus: Five Views* (2009) 94.

58. See T. Hidber's comparison "Arrian," and "Appian," in *Narrators, Narratees, and Narratives in Ancient Greek Literature* (2004) 1.165–74, 175–85. As Hidber shows, Arrian clearly identifies himself in the first person; Appian, as if in direct contrast to the former, leaves unsaid his identity but assumes everyone knows who he is.

59. See also Velleius Paterculus (2.16.2) where he will not allow a false sense of modesty to deprive his kin of "glory" (*gloria*) by not acknowledging the loyalty of his great-grandfather toward Rome. See also Mary Jaeger, "Cicero and Archimedes' Tomb," *JRS* 92 (2002) 49: "A great mound bears witness to Achilles' death at Troy, but the outburst of the competitive Alexander testifies that a poem is a better memorial than a tomb."

60. *Iliad* 9.525.

being subject to death.⁶¹ Diodorus Siculus at 1.1.5 records the ability of history to confer "the glory of immortality" (τῷ διὰ τῆς δόξης ἀθανατισμῷ); at 1.2.3 he mentions the voice of history as able to keep alive the deeds of men "for evermore" (ἅπαντα τὸν αἰῶνα); at 4.1.4 he refers to the power of history to sing appropriate praises "for all time" (εἰς τὸν αἰῶνα). I note Cicero's letter addressed to Lucceius in which he is searching for a qualified author to write his biography.⁶² Cicero presents this historian with the proposal to write an embellished account of the famous orator's life. Cicero's ultimate quest is for literary immortality. A further extravagant tribute to the power of prose to confer immortality is to be found in Velleius Paterculus, 2.66.3–5. Paterculus reveals, like a two-edged sword, how literature glorifies Cicero and vilifies Marc Antony. Clearly, poets of Latin verse and writers of Latin prose were cognizant, like the Greeks, of the power of literature to confer a kind of immortality.

Regarding poetry, Horace, in *Epodi* 3.30, after the opening two lines in which he refers to his poetry as a "monument more lasting than bronze and more impressive than a pyramid" (*monumentum aere perennius regaliqu siu pyramidum altius*), goes on to say: "I will not completely die, for many parts of me will escape the death-goddess. On and on shall I grow, ever fresh with the glory" (*non omnis moriar multaque pars mei vitabit Libitinam; usque eos postera rescam laude recens*); at 4.8 he further praises poetry: "Nor has time destroyed what Anacreon once celebrated" (*Nec siquid olim lusit Anacreon delevit aetas*); and at 4.9 he continues: "Many heroes lived before Agamemnon, but all were unmourned for and unknown, overwhelmed by a long night because they lacked a sacred poet" (*vixere fortes ante Agamemnona multi; sed omnes inlacrimabiles urgentur ignotique longa nocte, carent quia vate sacro*).

Given the fact that Greco-Roman authors seek glory, fame, and literary immortality through the written and published word, it is a striking and stunning anomaly that none of the four evangelists attach their names to their respective Gospels. Authors and literary critics who want to be taken seriously and who are writing to offset, correct, or overthrow something previously written in a similar genre include their name. The significance of this omission is that it tells against any intentional contradiction, especially one aimed at correcting an alleged error in the tradition. Previous publications about a notable person provide subsequent authors the opportunity to enrich their own portfolio by disparaging their antecedents. The converse is also true: an author's self-definition can be enhanced by attaching his name to the well-established reputation of a predecessor, as long as the predecessor's fame does not undermine the successor.⁶³ The extraordinary person of Jesus offers the evangelists the occasion to elevate their prestige by pointing out the shortcomings of rival writers. This attempt to denigrate is noticeably absent from gospel texts. Furthermore,

---

61. *Epigram* 2.

62. *Ad familiares* 5.12/15. See also Cicero's *Pro Archia*, passim.

63. For criteria in establishing an author's self-definition, see John Marincola, *Authority and Tradition in Ancient Historiography* (1997) 217–57.

each evangelist was aware that he was writing about a truly transformational figure. With so much at stake in terms of potential personal prestige, are we to believe that in the guise of subtleties they would camouflage their true intention to contradict one another? Are we to believe that overt objection has been concealed beneath the sheath of covert criticism? The literary conventions of Greco-Roman writers and, indeed, the proclivities of human nature do not suggest such a conclusion.[64]

If their motive was to correct or replace a current alternate version, is it possible that four authors could write four independent accounts of the same impacting person (Jesus) without attaching their name to their respective documents? Although this is theoretically possible, it does not strike me as plausible. Yet, if part of their purpose was to counter a Gospel already in circulation, is it realistic to believe that four independent writers could write of the same influential person without acknowledging one of these gospel writers?[65] Is it possible to contemplate that they would contradict the others without a specific reference to a name? Considering the contemporary belief among many scholars that the evangelists contradict one another, one needs to ask: if this is true, why the omission of names? Concealment of identity for the sake of personal protection does come to mind. This motive, however, would only account for the writer, not for the absence of an alleged evangelist in error.

We must consider further how this rubric of naming names actually works by means of example. Appian in his *Roman History* mentions his name in the Preface (15) and indicates some of his qualifications to write on the chosen subject: he has reached the "highest places" (πρῶτα ἥκων) in his native country, as an orator has pled cases before emperors (βασιλέων), and has served as a procurator by the will of emperors. Undoubtedly, this accolade of achievements serves the intended purpose of establishing authorial credibility. The example of Polybius may further reinforce the point. He indicates that he has selected as his theme the great document (the Roman Constitution), the greatest achievement (the Roman Republic), and some of the greatest men (among them, Scipio). By hitching his wagon to the star of such outstanding luminaries he has thereby increased the potential for his own distinction and celebrity. He accomplishes this literary achievement by attaching his name.[66] Furthermore,

---

64. A possible exception may be noted. Catullus 49 is perhaps an example of stinging criticism couched in ironic flattery. If taken as a piece of irony, it is clearly aimed at Cicero as his name is included in the poem. Catullus identifies himself as the author. For a discussion of this poem, see W. Jeffrey Tatum, "Catullus' Criticism of Cicero in Poem 49," *TAPA* 118 (1988) 179–84.

65. Thucydides in his prologue (1.2, 22) to the Peloponnesian War most likely makes an oblique reference to Herodotus. The two historians are not covering the same subject, but Thucydides makes it clear that he is not writing a book that will bring pleasure to the ear. If he has Herodotus in mind, his quarrel is with style, content, and perhaps even purpose. It is to be noted that Thucydides prefers to write a more austere work than a work with the capacity to entertain. He is surely contrasting styles and purposes with the expression μᾶλλον ἤ ("rather than"). Such a contrasting insinuation is not expressed in the four Gospels.

66. Although Polybius prefers the use of the plural "we," he does not avoid using his own name (12.2.1).

Polybius clearly sets out to establish his own credentials for writing a new history of Rome by distancing himself from the two most notable predecessors: Philinus and Fabius. He singles out Philinus four times, with other references implied.[67]

As Polybius views it (ὡς ἐμοὶ δοκεῖ), the account of Philinus is "full of inconsistencies" (τῆς πάσης ἐστὶν ἀλογίας πλήρης). Polybius then tops off his introduction or "digression"[68] by asserting that he will always follow "the order of events" (τὸν ἑξῆς λόγον) and so guide his readers into a true understanding of the war. A comparison between Polybius and Luke in their respective programmatic statements yields both contrast and likeness. Regarding the likeness, both claim to give an orderly account and both use the expression ἐμοὶ δοκεῖ ("it seems to me"). Luke, however, directs these impressions toward himself, while Polybius directs these impressions toward the failings of his predecessors. Regarding the contrasts, Polybius names his competitors, mentions their faults, and seeks to justify why his readers should prefer his version of events to all others. Luke does none of this.

The absence of any attempt to promote one's name and to advance one's literary reputation in the four Gospels is a strange silence. Of course, Luke comes quickly to mind, especially since he refers to Theophilus as "most excellent." Although Luke records (1.1-3) "it seemed good to me *also* to write up an account" (ἔδοξε κἀμοὶ παρηκολουθηκότι), this statement reveals only Luke's personal response to the gospel tradition. There are no pejorative tones or insinuations of displeasure. Rather, the opposite is really the case; whatever qualities the gospel forerunners possessed, Luke attributes the same to his own work.[69] Clearly, the presence of καθώς indicates correlation rather than correction. He concedes, though, that "many others" (πολλοί ... οἱ ἀπ' ἀρχῆς αὐτόπται) have written respective accounts concerning Jesus.[70] Luke,

---

67. 1.14.1, 3; 15.1, 1, 12.

68. What he calls a παρέκβασις (1.15.13).

69. I. I. Du Plessis, "Once More: The Purpose of Luke's prologue (Lk I 1–4)," *NovT* 16.4 (1974) 266: "The κἀμοί puts Luke into the same category as his predecessors and thus his own effort can hardly imply open criticism on the πολλοί." See also Richard J. Dillion, "Previewing Luke's Project from His Prologue (Luke 1:1–4)," *CBQ* 43 (1981) 208: "The κἀμοί of v. 3 will suggest solidarity with previous efforts, not odious comparison with them."

70. It is not clear how we are to take the πολλοὶ ἐπιχείρησαν of the opening verse. For a pejorative take on the "many," see Ambrose, *Expositio Evangelii secundum Lucam* 1.1: *sic et nunc in novo testamento multi evangelia scribere conati sunt, quae boni nummularii non probarunt, unum autem tantummodo in quattuor libros digestum ex omnibus arbitrati sunt eligendum.... Non conatus est Matthaeus, non conatus est Marcus, non conatus est Iohannes, non conatus est Lucas.* Dom Gabriel Tissot, in his *Traité sur l'évangile de S. Luc* (1956) 44, n.1, says: "Comme son guide, Ambroise distingue les évangiles canoniques de leurs contrefaçons apocryphes." This explanation by Ambrose is not impossible. Tissot has rightly interpreted Ambrose's words. But the question arises: is Ambrose correct? Against his reading is the pronoun κἀμοί. Whatever his predecessors have undertaken, Luke claims the same for himself—no less, no more. Luke admits that he is further down the literary line but not that he is any better. The verb ἐπιχείρησαν, however, requires comment. Does it imply that the "many" attempted to write a narrative but failed? The references listed by BADG lead in that direction. If this is the case, the κἀμοί makes it difficult to avoid the conclusion that any alleged shortcomings would also apply to Luke and make him vulnerable to the same attributed failings. Or, does the verb suggest that the

therefore, places himself later in the sequence but other than his admitted distance from the original eyewitness source(s), he does not explain how his link in the series varies from the others.[71] He especially does not acknowledge that he is correcting anything already circulating in a text format.[72] Neither does Luke suggest that his account is necessarily more reliable. François Bovon, however, views the situation differently: "Luke begins with a reference to his predecessors (v. 1), but the manner in which he mentions them shows that he is, at the same time, more or less refuting them."[73] This is a strange argument by Bovon inasmuch as he acknowledges: "All exegetes agree that the author is making use of the literary forms of the time."[74] Bovon's claim does not square with the facts of literary convention. Indeed, with the single exception of Luke's superlative description of Theophilus as κράτιστε ("most excellent"), there are no other comparatives or superlatives in the prologue, especially none situating Luke in a superior position. If Luke felt that his account was more accurate and more dependable, he certainly did not make use of the right vocabulary to express such a contrast.[75] This implies that the third Gospel makes no claim to be either more accurate or the most accurate. Nor does the prologue hint that any rivalry exists between these writers.

It appears that Luke's intention is to focus uniquely on the person of Jesus without minimizing the value of the other accounts. To be more precise, Luke does not even return later to the vague reference in his prologue to specify any author or oral witness as a possible problem. He acknowledges only that it seemed *good* to him also to write an orderly account, thus attributing to himself and to his predecessors the positive motive of "good."[76] Taken at face value, his prologue does not reveal the presence of

---

"many" simply took in hand the task of composing a narrative with no implications of an unsuccessful attempt? Luke's language does not imply that others have tried and failed but now he will succeed. It is my judgment that the verb ἐπιχείρησαν simply suggests the idea of "to put pen to pad" and lacks any hint of a failed undertaking. The verb need not be problematic; the positive power of κἀμοί neutralizes and offsets the negative potential of ἐπιχείρησαν. Unless, of course, one wants to argue that none, including Luke, has succeeded. Alternately, another option is simply to acknowledge that Luke is not referring to either Matthew or Mark; rather, he is simply referring to non-canonical writers.

71. I understand the prologue to chronicle three separate phases: eye-witnesses, the many, and Luke.

72. For an opposite conclusion, see David Laird Dungan, *A History of the Synoptic Problem* (1999) 16, where Dungan argues that Luke set out to write an account that would be "more orderly, accurate, and true." Dungan is convinced that the prologue to Luke implies a criticism of rival narratives. As stated above, however, Luke's language does not reveal an implied criticism. There is no adverb or adjective of comparison in the prologue.

73. François Bovon, *A Commentary on the Gospel of Luke 1.1–9.50* (2002) 19.

74. Ibid., 17.

75. Luke could have easily, if he had intended so, engaged in combative comparisons such as "more accurately," "more orderly," and "more securely." I note that Polybius in his *Histories* (12.4.4) does not hesitate to fault Timaeus for his lack of careful inquiry.

76. Whether the verb δοκέω should be translated as "it seems good to" or simply "it occurs to" is not relevant. Whatever motive the third evangelist ascribes to his predecessors, he attributes the same motive to himself. Relative to motive, he does not distinguish himself from the others. For a

any negative motives in the third Gospel.[77] Consequently, rivalry and competition should not be introduced as a plausible explanation for why Luke is writing.

Authors engaged in the enterprise of writing of an illustrious and world-impacting personality or events do not normally conceal their own personal identity.[78] Although his name ("Luke") may have been attached externally in some way to the third Gospel, for example, a cover letter,[79] the more salient fact is that his name is not included anywhere in the text. The argument presented here is that such absence is significant. This absence suggests two possible factors: 1) the desire to subordinate one's personal identity in order to keep the focus on the person of Jesus, and 2) the secondary factor indicating that there was no motive to undermine a previous Gospel. Regarding the first reason, an author's own self-definition is thus submerged into the greater purpose of highlighting the importance of Jesus. Regarding the second reason, the evangelist does not engage in polemic in order to accent the virtue of his own work over that of others. This would suggest that, although Luke sees himself as continuing or complementing the tradition, he does not see himself as culminating the tradition with the final or most authoritative account. Once again, a disclaimer is appropriate: the argument that the Gospels themselves do not identify actual authors is not intended to serve the form-critical view that the Gospels were produced by communities rather than individuals.

As a concluding contrast, I mention two writers who offer alternate prologues on the use of names. Arrian in his *Anabasis Alexandri* (1.1–3) explains to his readers the merits of two predecessors: Ptolemy and Aristobulus; their accounts have surpassed all others in the field. Whenever possible, Arrian will follow their narratives; when they differ (ὅσα δὲ οὐ ταὐτά), Arrian will select the more trustworthy account of the

---

convincing argument that ἔδοξε κἀμοί should be understood as "it seemed good to me" (or, "I decided"), see Loveday Alexander, *The Preface to Luke's Gospel* (1993) 127.

77. For establishing Luke within a scientific or *Fachprosa* literary tradition, see Loveday Alexander's, "Luke's Preface in the Context of Greek Preface-Writing," *NovT* 28 (1986) 48–74.

78. See Theo K. Heckel, *Vom Evangelium des Markus zum viergestaltigen Evangelium* (1999) 81–90.

79. For the reasonable view that, at the least, a personal cover sheet of some kind would have accompanied a Gospel, see Hans Freiherr von Campenhausen, *The Formation of the Christian Bible* (1972) 126, for his observation, following Dibelius, that it would indeed be an extraordinary omission for Luke not to include his name in a work dedicated to Theophilus. Campenhausen (282) further observes how Tertullian rejected Marcion's gospel because it was nameless. Working backward from Tertullian's judgment against Marcion, we would have to conclude that his basic premise for genuine gospel inclusion was that of antiquity. Therefore, he must have felt confident that he had sufficient evidence to trace the authorship of the fourfold Gospel back to the traditional names of Matthew, Mark, Luke, and John. See also Martin Hengel's *The Four Gospels and the One Gospel of Jesus Christ* (2000) 48–56, for his convincing arguments that the names of gospel authors are not later additions but accompanied the Gospels from the very beginning. See also Richard Bauckham, *Jesus and the Eyewitnesses* (2006) 300–305; esp. 415, for his argument that the name "John" indeed accompanied the fourth Gospel, but this does not necessarily prove or imply John, the son of Zebedee. For the contrary view that the Gospels were completely anonymous from the very beginning, see K. Aland, "The Problem of Anonymity and Pseudonymity in Christian Literature of the First Two Centuries," *JTS* 12 (1961) 42.

two. However, Arrian makes it transparently clear to his readers that his history will surpass theirs. Since he is writing about the deeds of the greatest Greek who ever lived, his narrative will match the extraordinary deeds of Alexander (1.12.5). Thus, Arrian claims for himself the ability to outshine his rivals and the capacity to do justice to the accomplishments of the greatest Greek, perhaps even implying that no other authority will ever exceed his. When compared to Luke, several dissimilarities stand out: Luke lays no claim to superiority in the tradition, feels no need to mention names, and does not hint of weaknesses in the tradition that are in need of correction.

Josephus's prologue to the *Bellum judaicum* also contrasts sharply with Luke's prologue. Josephus openly identifies himself as the author and mentions several groups of writers worthy of criticism: some were witnesses to actual events, while others were not; whether absent or present, none of them have reported accurately the events they describe; they have even recorded contradictory accounts of the same events in a rhetorical style (ἀσύμφωνα διηγήματα σοφιστικῶς ἀναγράφουσιν). Not only that, Josephus judges that their motives are impure for they composed out of flattery for the Romans or hatred for the Jews. We thus notice three characteristics of Josephus in this prologue that find no correspondence with Luke: the mention of his name, faulting the failures of predecessors for lack of accuracy in presentation, and the impurity of their motives. On the literary ledger sheet, Luke is clearly on one side and Josephus on the other. Other examples could be provided.[80] Consequently, we have an unusual set of facts: no evangelist mentions himself and no evangelist mentions the name of another gospel writer.[81]

Tracking the data on the personalities of the four evangelists, the following dots can be connected: In Matt 20:20, the mother of the sons of Zebedee comes to Jesus with a request for a privileged position at his throne. When the ten learn of this request, they are indignant. They do not blame this impertinent request on a doting mother but, rather, zero in on the two sons (James and John) and their desire for preeminence. The implication, as perceived by the other disciples, is that the two brothers have used their mother as an advantageous lever to gain a higher position and to out-maneuver the other disciples. Dionysius of Halicarnassus reports an analogous incident in his *Roman Antiquities* (2.61.1). Right after the death of Romulus, Dionysius reports that the Roman senate lapsed into quarreling among themselves as to who would have greater authority. It is interesting that the four evangelists do not fall victim to seeking a prominent place for themselves in their respective Gospels. Once again, we are brought face to face with another crossroads decision: since the disciples are pictured as vying for prestige and prominence, and since the four evangelists do not identify themselves, does this not create a wall of separation between disciples and evangelists?

---

80. For example, see Plutarch's *Solon* 27.1.

81. Inasmuch as the Gospels have been compared to OT historical books, this is unusual even in the comparison against 1 and 2 Kings. The two books of Kings make use of at least eight different sources.

How can we remove the disparity between the profile of the disciples seeking honor for themselves and anonymity of the Gospels?

Inasmuch as men of letters define themselves in contrast to or in relationship to others, what does one do with such omissions? Several possibilities emerge: rivals are not mentioned because to do so would possibly endanger or diminish the credibility of the author as captious and caviling; rivals are omitted because it would draw unwelcomed attention to them; rivals are omitted because there are, in fact, none to be included.

Conclusion

At this juncture of the investigation, necessity dictates a critical query: is it possible to nail down any valid observations for gospel research? Does a substantive implication present itself? Throughout this chapter constant reference has been made to the contrasts between the four Gospels and disagreement within the Greco-Roman literary conventions. Given the nature of ancient literary dissent, I propose four additional implications.

THE LIMITS OF THIS INVESTIGATION. The inquiry of this chapter has at least three preliminary limitations. First, what is the possible implication(s) of the unusual omission of names in the fourfold Gospel? The limits of this investigation—at this point—do not permit a positive answer to that question. Other than the elimination of dissent, data from this chapter do not explain the absence of names in the Gospels.[82] I will revisit this question in the concluding chapter. Second, the absence of an adversarial spirit in the four Gospels cannot adequately explain variation in the fourfold Gospel. This chapter principally establishes what the Gospels are not; however, these findings open the door to consider what the fourfold Gospel is. The information extracted can, therefore, provide a spur to further engage the gospel texts for understanding the value of variations. Third, a question is left begging: do the above data completely eliminate the possibility of minor, oblique, or subtle contradiction? No, not completely.[83] This admission, however, should not detract from the major premise of the study in that the rhetoric of dissent is by nature openly candid, often bluntly direct, and clearly

---

82. The likelihood that the omission of authorial names is simply a characteristic of the tradition does not satisfy. In order to put this claim for the tradition-argument on solid footing it would have to be established that such a tradition existed prior to the first Gospel. In other words, I would not argue the case that Mark (for example) is the original model and the other three, out of a blind conformity, fell in line lock-step. To me, a more satisfying explanation is to be found in what D. Moody Smith refers to as "the protective aura of canonicity." For an opposite conclusion, see John Barton, "Two Types of Harmonization," in *What Is it that the Scripture Says?* (2006) 266–74.

83. If the supposition is that the author of the Gospel of John was not aware of the synoptics, it cannot be established, therefore, that deliberate disagreement is in mind.

straightforward. In this case, the artifice of subtle sleight of hand disagreement does not offer great promise for deciphering the significance of variations in the tradition.

THE DATA GIVE A BASIS FOR QUESTIONING CURRENT SCHOLARLY TRENDS. Viewed strictly from the specific vantage point of direct disagreement from the Greco-Roman literary tradition, the assertion that the evangelists contradict one another must be considered suspect. Such a claim for gospel dissension is a worthy candidate for doubt and a cause for complaint against such claims. The premise that no gospel writer, in clear and direct language, quarrels with any other evangelist does not appear as an arbitrarily forced conclusion. Neither does this conclusion qualify as simplistic. Rather, the premise has emerged naturally from the comparative study of the texts themselves. Specifically, when placed alongside the measuring stick of Greco-Roman literary models, it cannot be established, for example, that Matthew was out to replace Mark—a common contention in NT scholarship.[84] Neither has John purposed to replace the synoptics—another common assertion among NT scholars.[85] It is an axiom of current New Testament scholarship that specialists operate on the premise that there is a literary connection in the synoptics from one Gospel to another.[86] Without staking out a position—at this point—on the issue of literary relationship but simply

---

84. Donald Senior, "Directions in Matthean Studies," in *The Gospel of Matthew in Current Study* (2001) 13. See also Graham N. Stanton, "The Fourfold Gospel," *NTS* 43 (1997) 317–46.

85. See D. Moody Smith, "John and the Synoptics in Light of the Question of Faith and History," in *Faith and History* (1990) 74–89. Moody begins with reflections on Hans Windisch's *Johannes und die Synoptiker: Wollte der vierte Evangelist die älteren Evangelien ergänen oder ersetzen?* (1926) 76: "Windisch proceeded on the traditional view that John knew and was familiar with all the synoptic gospels, but because they were inadequate representations of the gospel as John understood it, he wrote a gospel to supersede them and in doing so found most of their content useless." After surveying the literature and the problem of the differences between John and the synoptics, Moody returns to the challenge raised by Windisch (83): "As we earlier observed, the major differences between John and the other gospels have traditionally been understood in terms of supplementation. Either John was to supplement the other gospels, or vice versa, or both. Windisch has shown the difficulties of that perspective once the protective aura of canonicity is allowed to fall away. (By 'aura of canonicity' I mean the implication, tacitly drawn from the canonical status of the other Gospels, that John would have accepted their adequacy and authority.)." Moody goes on to argue that the term "supplementation" is too weak and "displacement" may be too strong; he observes (87) that "with the rise of higher criticism and the questioning of the tradition of apostolic authorship, John's differences from the synoptics began to count against its historical reliability." See also D. Moody Smith's, "John and the Synoptics," *NTS* 26.4 (1980) 429: "So it comes about that the only satisfactory resolution of the conundrum posed by John's wide divergence from the synoptics is the one Windisch adopts, namely, that John wrote to *displace* the other gospels, because he found them inadequate vehicles for the Christian proclamation as he understood it." Smith acknowledges the difficulty of this position (John never recognizes the existence of the synoptics, let alone "polemizes" against them) but in the end finds it less troublesome.

86. E. P. Sanders and Margaret Davies represent well the consensus in their *Studying the Synoptic Gospels* (1989) 51: "Whatever the reasons, the synoptics are so close to one another that virtually all students of them have concluded that the relationship depends on direct literary copying from one gospel to another, or from common sources. It is especially to be noted that there is extensive verbatim (word-for-word) agreement in Greek, which can hardly be explained by independent knowledge of the saying of Jesus in Aramaic."

making use of it, the conclusion seems unavoidable that the omission of direct disagreement is a striking anomaly.

GRECO-ROMAN CONVENTIONS ALLOW US TO DEFEND CANONICAL UNITY. Another contrast to the absence of point-blank disagreement in the fourfold Gospels may be found in the style of the *Gospel of Philip* (17): "Some say Mary was impregnated by the Holy Spirit. They err. They do not know what they say."[87] Two characteristics of this post-fourfold Gospel document stand out: 1) the reference of an unidentified "some," and 2) the accusation that they are in error. Noticeable in the four Gospels is the absence of any reference to a nebulous "some say."[88] Such an oblique referent would leave the reader wondering who these "some" could be. Equally significant is the absence of criticism ("they err"). This twin set of indicators helps to mark a distinct boundary line which facilitates the distancing of the Gospel of Philip from the canonical unity of the fourfold Gospel. Likewise, the more popular Gospel of Thomas may be introduced, not for the presence of direct disagreements, but for the attribution of a personal name.[89] If it is conventional for a particular genre (as, for example, the Gospels) to dispense with the name of the writer, then the subsequent presence of a name such as Philip or Thomas creates a wall of separation from the original pattern.

Unless further research in the area of the Greco-Roman literary traditions can clearly overthrow the major findings of this study, the canonical unity of the four Gospels is worthy of confidence.[90] This would suggest that, instead of contradictions in the gospel record, canonical unity leads more in the direction of complementation.[91]

---

87. *The Gospel of Philip: Jesus, Mary Magdalene, and the Gnosis of Sacred Union, Translation from the Coptic and Commentary by Jean-Yves Leloup* (2004) 51. See also 21: "Those who say that the Lord first died, and then was resurrected, are wrong," as well as 69: "Those who say that there is someone in the sky are mistaken."

88. The closest we come to a "some" is the vague reference in Luke 1:1 to the "many" (πολλοί).

89. For a discussion of this attribution, see April D. Deconick, *The Original Gospel of Thomas in Translation* (2006) 44–46. See also Stephen J. Patterson, *The Gospel of Thomas and Jesus* (1993) 9–16, where the author disclaims literary dependence of Thomas from the synoptic tradition in order to demonstrate that this gospel represents a completely different stream of Christianity.

90. The early church was aware of variations within the gospel tradition. These variations, though troublesome, did not overthrow their confidence in the Gospels as unified products of divine inspiration. For associations with the concept of canonical unity, see James C. Vanderkam, "Questions of Canon Viewed through the Dead Sea Scrolls," *BBR* 11.2 (2001) 269–92. Parallel associations usually admit such theological concepts as inspiration, revelation, and authoritative Scripture.

91. For a moderate or intermediate view, see Christopher W. Tuckett, "Jesus and the Gospels," in *The New Interpreter's Bible* (1995) 74: "Are we to believe that Jesus entered Jerusalem on a donkey three or four times in almost (but not quite) identical circumstances and each evangelist recorded a different occasion accurately? And such an idea becomes even more ludicrous with other events.... Much more plausible, then, is the view that these different accounts in our Gospels represent different reports of the *same* incident, and the differences may reveal something more about the way in which a tradition was told and used later." Tuckett is using variations in the tradition to trace development within the tradition. However, there is another way to cut the cake. Variations may not necessarily connect to development in the tradition but to purpose, perspective, and selectivity. Variations, also,

The most identifiable finding of this study is that, in comparison to Greco-Roman conventions, point-blank disagreement does not characterize the fourfold Gospel. Or, we may state this conclusion in a softer tone: given the nature of these conventions, it is most likely the case that when two biblical texts (such as the genealogies in Matthew and Luke) *appear* to contradict, this must not be viewed as a case of outright contradiction but, rather, may suggest a relationship of complementation.[92]

SCHOLARLY WORK ALLEGING CONTRADICTIONS IN THE GOSPELS IS EXCESSIVE. The results of this investigation recommend restraint. Recognition of Greco-Roman literary practice would caution us to tone down the language of contradiction, especially the use of such abrasive adjectives as "sharp" and "blatant." If the results of this study stand up to the scrutiny of cross-examination, it would indicate the further necessity to refine the language of scholarly discourse and return to such terms as variation and complementation. Modern scholarly language to describe gospel variations as "blatant disagreements," "flat contradictions," and "sharp contrasts" is unsatisfying, unnecessary, and unsubstantiated when compared to the practice and profile of the Greco-Roman literary tradition of dissent. Inasmuch as current New Testament scholarship continues to assume contradiction, those who see the issue otherwise may find some comfort that the matter is not so cut and dried. For those who are hesitant to jump on the scholarly band wagon that claims contradictions in the Gospels, perhaps the above investigation will offer an alternative explanation worth considering. We now turn to examine an alternative explanation for variation within the fourfold Gospel.

---

need not point to contradictions or disagreements. See also C. H. Dodd, *The Interpretation of the Fourth Gospel* (1953) 446, who, in evaluating the issue of whether the fourth Gospel is complementary to the synoptics, says: "I believe that the course which was taken by *Leben-Jesu-Forschung* ('The Quest of the Historical Jesus') during the nineteenth century proves that a severe concentration on the Synoptic record, to the exclusion of the Johannine contribution, leads to an impoverished, a one-sided, and finally an incredible view of the facts—I mean, of the *facts*, as part of history." See also Beverly Roberts Gaventa and Richard B. Hays, "Seeking the Identity of Jesus," in *Seeking the Identity of Jesus* (2008) 8: "we should receive all four together as complementary testimonies, about the complex figure of Jesus the Christ. If this is so, it follows that no single historical reconstruction of Jesus of Nazareth can supplant the fourfold testimony of the Gospels as a more adequate account of his identity." A similar conviction may be found on p. 19.

92. In this light, a more plausible explanation may be that four Gospels mirror the narrative sections of the Old Testament. See, for example, Edwin A. Abbott's *The Fourfold Gospel: Introduction* (1913) 15, who noted a hundred years ago: "It comes nearly to this, that the Fourth Gospel was, in one respect, related to the Three as the Book of Chronicles was related to the Books of Samuel and Kings. In the LXX, the Book of Chronicles is entitled *Paraleipomena*, 'Things Passed Over', or 'Things Omitted', that is to say, things omitted in Kings and added (as a supplement to Kings) in Chronicles. Somewhat similarly it was supposed by 'the ancients' that John supplemented the Synoptists. 'The ancients' did not indeed mention Kings and Chronicles. Had they done so, they would doubtless have recognised that the tone and the spirit of the Evangelist were very different from the tone and the spirit of the Chronicler. But they said that the Evangelist supplemented the earlier gospels. And the title of Chronicles in the LXX implies that the Chronicler supplemented Kings."

3

Minor Matters: Redaction, Allusions, Grids, and Silence

THIS CHAPTER INTRODUCES SOME minor matters relevant to the study of the first Gospel. These issues have overlapping applications to the other three Gospels. My initial concern is with Matthew. Current scholarly work on the Gospel of Matthew shows great diversity, little agreement. The points of perhaps greatest agreement are that Matthew is the most Jewish of the Gospels and it was likely written in Galilee or Syria.¹ To a lesser degree, current scholarly interests find the Matthean presentation of Jesus centered in royal kingship.² Outside of these points of contact, there is great diversity of interpretation. Aside from attention given to individual chapters or selected pericopes, I note the following eight topics characteristic of modern research on Matthew that potentially impinge upon the subject of this study, with their respective efforts: 1) to explain Matthew in terms of his community;³ 2) to connect Matthew to the larger environment of a

---

1. See W. D. Davies and Dale Allison, *A Critical and Exegetical Commentary on the Gospel According to Saint Matthew I–VII* (1988) 10–11, for their chart showing how Matthean scholars from 1886 to 1985 (Holtzmann to Luz) line up regarding Matthew's identity. The majority view clearly falls on the side of "Matthew" as not the apostle but, rather, someone who is at least Jewish. See also Richard C. Beaton, "Isaiah in Matthew's Gospel," in *Isaiah in the New Testament* (2005) 63: "Matthew's gospel is the most Jewish of the gospels and, not surprisingly, one of the most referential texts in the NT, in that it is replete with references to the Jewish Scriptures." See also Donald Hagner, "Matthew: Christian Judaism or Jewish Christianity," in *The Face of New Testament Studies* (2004) 263: "One of the virtually firm conclusions in Matthean studies is that the Gospel was written to Jews who had come to faith in Jesus as the Messiah." For a similar recent view, see Anders Runesson, "Rethinking Early Jewish-Christian Relations: Matthean Community History as Pharisaic Intragroup Conflict," *JBL* 127.1 (2008) 95–132. For a discussion on the Syrian-hypothesis, see Bas ter Haar Romeny, "Hypothesis on the Development of Judaism and Christianity in Syria in the Period after 70 C.E.," in *Matthew and the Didache* (2005) 13–33. For a modern Jewish point of view assessing the value of Matthew for things Jewish, see Alan F. Segal, "Matthew's Jewish Voice," in *Social History of the Matthean Community* (1991) 3–37. Finally, for Qumran and Matthew, see John Kampen, "The Significance of the Scrolls for the Study of the Book of Matthew," in *The Dead Sea Scrolls* (2000) 157–69.

2. Notables examples are: Donald Verseput, *The Rejection of the Humble Messianic King* (1986) 304; Alan Hugh M'Neile, *The Gospel According to St Matthew* (1961) xvii; and William Barclay, *Introduction to the First Three Gospels* (1975) 171.

3. David L. Turner, *Matthew* (2008) 5, mentions four times in a single page the importance of seeing the Gospels as calculated to meet the needs of its respective audience. That there is a "need" is a

Roman background;[4] 3) to utilize Matthew and history in the "quest" for the historical Jesus;[5] 4) to understand the particular genre for this Gospel; 5) to identify Matthew's Christology;[6] 6) to comprehend Matthew's use of the OT;[7] 7) to establish to what degree Matthew is an editor/redactor, composer, or narrator in his own right.[8] Most of these subjects also serve as a template for the other three evangelists. Of these seven current

---

safe assumption; that this need explains the origin of a particular Gospel may be questioned. Because of the thesis of this book, I am not advocating that Matthew's audience needed to know particularly about a King Jesus, or Mark's audience about a particular Servant Jesus.

4. See Warren Carter's *Matthew and Empire* (2001) 1, in which he sets out to challenge the dominant paradigm for understanding the first evangelist: "Overlooked in this discussion, and almost completely absent from it, is the simple observation that the Gospel comes from and addresses a world dominated by the Roman Empire." See also Joe E. Barnhart and Linda A. Kraeger, *In Search of First-Century Christianity* (2000) 108: "the emergence of first-century Christianity cannot be profoundly comprehended unless the Jesus figure and Christology are viewed against the background of Caesar worship." See also the series of essays in *The Gospel of Matthew in its Roman Imperial Context*, John Riches and David C. Sim, eds. (2005) 107–27, 143–65.

5. See Leander E. Keck, "Toward the Renewal of New Testament Christology," *NTS* 32 (1986) 362–77, and also his *Who Is Jesus?* (2000) 11. See also Robert Morgan, "The Historical Jesus and the Theology of the New Testament," in *The Glory of Christ in the New Testament* (1987) 190: "The saying that the Son of man *must* suffer was probably an early Christian inference from what *had* happened." For the view that places Jesus within an accurate historical environment, see Craig A. Evans, *Jesus and His Contemporaries* (1995).

6. See Jack Dean Kingsbury's sustained interest in identifying the significance of Jesus as the Son of God: "The Title 'Kyrios' in Matthew's Gospel," *JBL* 94 (1975) 246–55; "The Title 'Son of Man' in Matthew's Gospel," *CBQ* 37 (1975) 193–202; *Matthew* (1977); *Matthew: Structure, Christology, Kingdom* (1975), and also the volume edited by him, *Gospel Interpretation: Narrative-Critical & Social-Scientific Approaches* (1997).

7. See Steve Moyise, *The Old Testament in the New* (2001) 34–44; and John M. Court, "The Birth of Jesus Christ According to Matthew and Luke," in *New Testament Writers and the Old Testament* (2002) 13–25. Court seeks to show that Matthew and Luke diverge at the point of the genealogies because of cultural issues owing to provenance. See also D. Moody Smith, "The Use of the Old Testament in the New," in *The Use of the Old Testament in the New and Other Essays* (1972) 45, where Smith remark: "In view of the unsettled state of research, is it possible to characterize Matthew's use of the Old Testament with any felicity?"

8. J. Barnhart and L. Kraeger, *In Search of First-Century Christianity* (2000) 84: "The issue among contemporary biblical scholars, therefore, is not whether the biblical writers practice redaction and editing, but whether all the redactors possessed the same image of Jesus and used the same theological premises in composing their narratives. The working hypothesis of redaction criticism is that most of the biblical writers were either weaving a narrative with a plot or saw themselves as operating within a theological narrative. Redaction critics mine the texts in the hope of discovering themes and plots that helped give the biblical authors focus in sifting, selecting, and arranging their material." In principle, I agree with this definition. The ultimate question is to what degree the evangelists were actually aware of composing a particular "plot" or "saw themselves as operating within a theological narrative." I note David Barrett Peabody's comment in his book *Mark as Composer* (1987) 22: "However, some caution must be maintained in attributing all apparently compositional features of the text of Mark to the author of the gospel, since the exact nature of all of the source material utilized by the author of Mark remains unknown." For an excellent example of narrative analysis, see the narrative-critical analysis by David R. Bauer, "The Kingship of Jesus in the Matthean Infancy Narrative: A Literary Analysis," *CBQ* 57.2 (1995) 306–23.

subjects for research, three are of particular interest: Matthew's use of the OT, his Christology, and to what degree he is a redactor.

Matthew as a Redactor

I begin with Matthew as a redactor. In this view, we allegedly learn more about Matthew and his community than we do about Jesus. This is actually a two-part interpretive approach: one part stressing Matthew as redactor and the other part stressing the community that Matthew represents.[9] Geza Vermes suggests that some "Son of Man" sayings in Matthew (as well as Mark and Luke) "are unlikely to be traceable to Jesus" and other statements indicate "editorial interference on the part of the early church."[10] This "editorial interference" as alleged by Vermes implies the need to bypass Jesus as a source and attach certain sayings to the creativity or selectivity of a redactor. This redactor, in turn, represents the concerns of his community at that time.[11] Redaction critics also focus upon separating tradition from redaction.[12] Leander Keck in a study focusing on Matthew's own community and the role of the Holy Spirit writes:

> Nor will it do to attribute the silence to the fact that this evangelist, not knowing Luke and John but using Mark, which had no appearance story, simply had no precedent to guide him. True as this may be, that did not inhibit him from replacing Mark 16:1–8 altogether in order to end the Jesus story the way he thought it ought to end.[13]

---

9. See Norman Perrin, *What Is Redaction Criticism?* (1976) 56, where Perrin emphasizes how redaction criticism seeks to correct false views in the community. For the similar view that Matthew is a "window through which the critic might catch glimpses of the society, culture, and history of the Matthean community," see Huub van de Sandt, "Introduction," in *Matthew and the Didache* (2005) 2. See also Richard A. Burridge, "Who Writes, Why, and for Whom?" in *The Written Gospel* (2005) 99–115, who sums up this view (102): "The crucial implication for our study here is that the stress on the oral tradition meant that there was no author to speak of, no individual mind behind the text. The evangelists were seen as merely stenographers at the end of the oral tunnel, stringing together the pearls of wisdom composed by various early preachers. This is authorship by committee, with notes from a secretary."

10. G. Vermes, *The Religion of Jesus the Jew* (1993) 159.

11. See Robert H. Stein, "What Is Redaktionsgeschichte?" *JBL* 88.1 (1969) 49, for a variation of this view. Stein holds that Mark portrays the views of the evangelist himself, while Matthew may represent a school. For the view that *redaktionsgeschichte* is no more than a modern scholarly construct, see Judith M. Lieu, *Christian Identity in the Jewish and Graeco-Roman World* (2004) 87. See also Craig A. Evans, "Images of Christ in the Canonical and Apocryphal Gospels," in *Images of Christ* (1997) 37: "Redaction critics hope to infer from this editorial activity information about the circumstances of the evangelists and their communities." It is perhaps more accurate to view the situation as G. D. Kilpatrick stated long ago in his *The Origins of the Gospel according to St. Matthew* (1946) 2: "While we may not say that the Gospel was created by community, yet it was created in a community and called forth to meet the needs of a community."

12. For a criticism of this application as being both misleading and unrealistic, see Donald H. Juel, *A Master of Surprise* (1994) 92.

13. L. E. Keck, "Matthew and the Spirit," in *The Social World of the First Christians* (1995) 148.

Keck thus sees Matthew as having no inhibition in correcting Mark and no hesitation in rewriting Jesus the way that seemed right to him. This approach, common in New Testament studies,[14] focuses upon the human elements of dissatisfaction and authorial rewriting to suit one's own viewpoint.[15] Or, as Bruce Metzger suggests: the existence of or need for four Gospels "is as good as admitting that none of them is perfect."[16] Graham N. Stanton, who represents well this position, writes: "When Matthew wrote his Gospel, he did not intend to supplement Mark: his incorporation of most of Mark's Gospel is surely an indication that he intended that his Gospel should replace Mark's, and that it should become *the* Gospel for Christians of his day."[17] Francis Watson inclines to the same view, using similar language but with italics: "More likely he expects to *replace* Mark."[18] A rather acerbic view of this position is that of Mary Ann Tolbert who suggests that "the later writers had more malign than benign intentions in relationship to Mark and actually wished to supplant Mark's interpretation of Jesus with their own."[19] Anthony J. Saldarini who writes of Matthew's connection with Judaism, offers this additional corresponding view:

> This study of the Gospel of Matthew presupposes the widely held position that the final author exercised strong compositional and creative control over the documents and traditions at his disposal. He ordered and edited them to fit the needs of his group, to convey his understanding of the Jesus movement,

---

14. See, for example, the very recent work of Anthony Le Donne, *The Historiographical Jesus* (2009) 182–83: "I am convinced that Matthew did not see his alterations of Mark and Q in terms of 'distortion' or 'refraction;' his story was to him simply a better interpretation of the events and their significance . . . but he does refract the Jesus tradition in a way that makes it 'more authentic.'" Richard C. Beaton, "How Matthew Writes," in *The Written Gospel* (2005) 120; and W. R. Telford, *The Theology of the Gospel of Mark* (1999) 46. For an earlier effort to explain differences in Matthew and Mark as due to the fact that Mark was unacceptable, see William G. Thompson, "An Historical Perspective in the Gospel of Matthew," *JBL* 93.2 (1974) 254. See also James H. Charlesworth, "Jesus Research Expands with Chaotic Creativity," in *Images of Jesus Today* (1994) 10, where he concludes that Matthew and Luke "edit" Mark 9:1, presumably out of embarrassment.

15. See John Barton, "Two Types of Harmonization," in *What Is it that the Scripture Says?* (2006) 269, for his assessment of how Matthew, allegedly dissatisfied with Mark and desiring to compose a superior Gospel, was able to write his improved Gospel based upon the premise that Mark had not yet attained canonical status.

16. Bruce M. Metzger, *The Canon of the New Testament* (1987) 262.

17. G. Stanton, "The Fourfold Gospel," *NTS* 43 (1997) 341. See also David C. Sim, "Matthew's Use of Mark: Did Matthew Intend to Supplement or to Replace His Primary Source?," *NTS* 57 (2011) 192, for his conclusion: "Matthew's redaction and expansion of Mark reveal his deep dissatisfaction with that text."

18. F. Watson, *The Fourfold Gospel* (2016) 6. On the same page, Watson continues: ". . . he is also an editor who takes upon himself the task of preparing an enlarged and improved second edition of the earlier gospel text." See also Larry W. Hurtado, *How on Earth Did Jesus Become a God? Historical Questions about Earliest Devotion to Jesus* (2005) 147, where he seems to indict either Matthew or Mark for unhistorical editorializing.

19. M. A. Tolbert, *Sowing the Gospel* (1989) 81.

and to promote his solutions to group problems. Thus the story of Jesus in Matthew reflects the experience of Matthew's group and its social situation.[20]

What Saldarini does is root Matthew's presentation of the Messiah to "strong compositional and creative control over the documents." This frame of reference presupposes that Matthew himself is the principal influence in the work.[21] Saldarini's thesis is a frequent contention in Matthew/Gospel criticism which emphasizes how each evangelist has total redactive control over their material.[22] Tangential to the notion of total control over the material is the view that each subsequent evangelist was out to supplant and supersede a previous Gospel.

Part of the purpose of this investigation is to raise the following question: is it possible that the premise of "total" control is flawed? Or, stated less obtrusively: is it possible that this premise is simply inadequate? Although my aim is not to discount the full value of redaction criticism,[23] my purpose is to question whether redaction criticism as exemplified in the above examples is methodologically sufficient to account for the distinctiveness of each Gospel. In my judgment, there is a more attractive alternative than the argument that Matthew is a remedial correction for the alleged shortcomings of Mark. The thesis presented here is that the decisive influence in this

---

20. A. Saldarini, *Matthew's Christian-Jewish Community* (1994) 5. Generally speaking, arguments of this kind are rooted in the premise that the Gospels tell us more about the community of believers than about Jesus. For such an argument, see Yigal Levin, "Jesus, 'Son of God' and 'Son of David': The 'Adoption' of Jesus into the Davidic Line," *JSNT* 28.4 (2006) 415–42, who believes that Jesus is a Gentile construct. For the counter argument that it is fallacious to read back into the Gospels the issue of community concerns, see N. T. Wright, *The New Testament and the People of God* (1992); Michael F. Bird, "The Formation of the Gospels in the Setting of Early Christianity: The Jesus Tradition as Corporate Memory," *WTJ* 67 (2005) 113–34; M. Eugene Boring, "The Convergence of Source Analysis, Social History, and Literary Structure in the Gospel of Matthew," *SBLSP* 33 (1994) 587–611; Donald Senior, "Between Two Worlds: Gentiles and Jewish Christians in Matthew's Gospel," *CBQ* 61 (1999) 1–23; and Douglas R. A. Hare, "How Jewish Is the Gospel of Matthew?" *CBQ* 62 (2000) 264–77.

21. An example of this is Hans Conzelmann, "Jesus Christus," in *Jesus* (1973) 26–27, who argues that the first two chapters of Matthew are strictly non-historical of an "*ad hoc*, artistic construction." In Conzelmann's view, Matthew is charged with participating in the first of a series or "cycles of legends," and even adds his own "artistic construction" to the picture of Jesus. None of this, according to Conzelmann, is to be equated with historical truth. Similarly, see also Ulrich Luz, "Fiktivität und Traditionstreue im Matthäusevangelium im Lichte griechischer Literatur, *ZNW* 84 (1993) 153–77, for his argument that Matthew's narrative art is based upon weaving fictional legends into the text.

22. See also Wolfgang Roth, "To Invert or Not to Invert: The Pharisaic Canon of the Gospels," in *Early Christian Interpretation of the Scriptures of Israel* (1997) 70: "What distinguishes Matthew's from Mark's Gospel are thorough-going compositional differences . . . . Closer study shows that the first evangelist is a freely working composer indeed."

23. A moderate view may be found in R. H. Stein, "What Is Redaktionsgeschichte?" (1969) 52–53: "Redaktionsgeschichte is concerned with the theological conception of each gospel as an individual entity . . . it is the attempt to ascertain the unique theological purpose of purposes, views, and emphases which the evangelists have imposed upon the materials available to them." I would question, however, to what extent the evangelists "have imposed" their views on the material. This question relates only to the degree, not whether their own personal views may also be found. For Stein's own method of combining redaction criticism with divine revelation, see his article "Luke 1.1–4 and Traditionsgeschichte," *JETS* 26.4 (1983) 429.

Gospel is not the total human control of Matthew but the same Spirit that enabled Peter to confess Jesus to be the Messiah (the Christ).[24] Indeed, the concept of a similar dynamic of revelation was current within the early Jesus movement to describe the process of how Jesus was to be understood.[25] As already stated, however, it is not my intention to argue from the assumed premise of revelation but to present a case for the plausibility of revelation based upon other factors than an *a priori* starting point of citing proof texts.

Allusions

We glance now at the literary concept of intertextuality with its subordinate ally of allusion. The last forty years have seen a vigorous interest in how NT authors make use of the OT. Steve Moyise observes that scholars working in the area of OT quotations in the NT find it helpful to classify these references into three categories: quotations, allusions, and echoes.[26] Quotations, as Moyise defines them, are generally indicated by the formula "it is written." An author's use of an echo, by contrast, is when "the allusion is so slight that conscious intention is unlikely."[27] Max Wilcox views an allusion or a quotation without an introductory formula as tending "to assume that the readers or hearers have a certain familiarity with the wider context and probably with current exegetical interpretations(s) also."[28] Some scholars, such as Joel Marcus, use allusion and echo interchangeably; or, without explanation, they simply assume the reader knows the difference.[29] Allusions for their part may perhaps make use of only one word.[30] Most allusions, however, contain more than a single word. This study will

---

24. Some scholars consider Peter's confession a later creation of the church inserted back into the Jesus tradition. Rudolf Bultmann believed Peter's confession to be attributed to a "legend of faith" (*History of the Synoptic Tradition*, 258). The position advanced here is that the same principle of revelation accredited to Peter is no less effectual and no less prominent in the authorship of Matthew.

25. This is the implication of such texts as 1 Pet 1:10–12; 2 Pet 1:20–21; Matt 13:17; 16:17; John 11:51; 14:26, and 16:13. My intention, however, is not to base the investigation upon these texts.

26. See Steve Moyise, *The Old Testament in the New* (2001) 5; Joseph A. Fitzmyer, "The Use of Explicit Old Testament Quotations in Qumran Literature and in the New Testament," *NTS* 7 (1960-61) 297–333; reprinted in *Essays on the Semitic Background of the New Testament* (1971) 5. Richard Bauckham, *The Theology of the Book of Revelation* (1993) 4, commenting on the book of Revelation, simply notes: "The whole book is saturated with allusions to Old Testament prophecy, though there are no formal quotations."

27. Moyise, *The Old Testament in the New* (2001) 6. Moyise admits that some scholars regard echoes as being too tenuous.

28. Max Wilcox, "On Investigating the Use of the Old Testament in the New Testament," in *Text and Interpretation* (1979) 237.

29. As for example, Anthony Le Donne, *The Historiographical Jesus* (2009), who without defining either term, says (120): "There are multiple echoes (and at least one allusion) of Psalm 72 in *Psalm of Solomon* 17."

30. Craig A. Evans, "The Old Testament in the New," in *The Face of New Testament Studies* (2004) 130: "The OT is quoted or alluded to in every NT writing except Philemon and 2 and 3 John . . . .

keep essentially to one or two words. On the task of precisely defining an allusion, Morna D. Hooker acknowledges: "It is notoriously difficult to decide what is and what is not an allusion to another text."[31] Klyne Snodgrass asks, "What constitutes an allusion? Is one word in common between NT and OT texts sufficient? Not unless there is something in the NT context that suggests dependence on the OT text."[32]

While limiting his comments to allusions in Mark from the OT, Willem S. Vorster observes that there are so many that "it can be said that the passion narrative, for example, is told in the language of the Old Testament."[33] Vorster does not define an allusion but simply uses the synonym "language." Richard B. Hays uses the term "symbolic field" to describe how the OT becomes the great precursor for the NT.[34] Nathan Lane, building somewhat upon Hays, sees an author's use of echo as an effort "to capture the theological ideas imagined in the original text."[35] Roger Nicole, treating the whole of the NT, provides the following suggestive list for appreciating the role of allusions: "If clear allusions are taken into consideration, the figures are much higher: C. H. Toy lists 613 such instances, Wilhelm Dittmar goes as high as 1640, while Eugene Huehn indicates 4105 passages reminiscent of Old Testament Scripture."[36]

Joel Marcus uses the term allusion generously in his monograph, *The Way of the Lord*. (I personally counted 135 uses of the word by Marcus.) Although Marcus never defines the concept, he freely substitutes for it with synonymic expressions such as "overlaps in vocabulary,"[37] "close linguistic relationship,"[38] "common features,"[39] and

---

Sometimes the allusions comprise no more than a word or two."

31. M. D. Hooker, "Mark," in *It is Written: Scripture Citing Scripture* (1988) 224.

32. K. Snodgrass, "The Use of the Old Testament in the New," in *The Right Doctrine from the Wrong Texts?* (1994) 46, fn. 54.

33. Willem S. Vorster, "The function of the Use of the Old Testament in Mark," *NeoT* 14 (1981) 62–72, reprinted in *Speaking of Jesus* (1999) 150. See also Howard Clark Kee, "The Function of Scriptural Quotations and Allusions in Mark 11–16," in *Jesus und Paulus* (1975) 165–88.

34. Richard B. Hays, *Echoes of Scripture in the Letters of Paul* (1989) 15. See also pp. 29–33 where Hays argues (29) that some echoes "will be so loud that only the dullest or most ignorant reader could miss it; other times there will be room for serious differences of opinion . . ." Hays offers seven tests for detecting an echo: availability, volume, recurrence, thematic coherence, historical plausibility, history of interpretation, and satisfaction. See also the more recent works by Hays, *Echoes of Scripture in the Gospels* (2016) 1–14, as well as his *Reading Backwards* (2014).

35. Nathan Lane, "An Echo of Mercy: A Rereading of the Parable of the Good Samaritan," in *Early Christian Literature and Intertextuality* (2009) 75. See also Sanghee M. Ahn, *The Christological Witness Function of the Old Testament Characters in the Gospel of John* (2014) 48–51, who surveys various authors in their use of allusion and echo. See as well Stanley E. Porter, "The Use of the Old Testament in the New Testament," (1997) 79-96, who recommends that scholars use more precise language when using terms such as "echo" and "allusion."

36. Roger Nicole, "The New Testament use of the Old Testament," in *The Right Doctrine from the Wrong Texts?* (1994) 14. Nicole does not cite references to Toy, Dittmar, or Huehn.

37. J. Marcus, *The Way of the Lord* (1992) 8.

38. Ibid., 52.

39. Ibid., 57.

"language strikingly familiar."[40] As Robert Horton Gundry shows, Matthew's use of allusion or "striking verbal resemblances" usually involves more than one word.[41] Howard Clark Kee, using substitute language for the idea of allusion, adopts terminology such as "influence," "clear verbal agreement," and "oblique reference" as co-equal replacements for allusion.[42] Richard B. Hays also offers a very useful expression for allusions by defining them as "embedded fragments."[43] Bruce Chilton and Craig Evans argue that beneath gospel strata lie what they call "underpinnings,"[44] and that these underpinnings are not always self-evident. Whether using the analogy of embedded fragments, voices, frequencies, or underpinnings, one thing is clear: scholars operate on the premise that below the surface of a gospel text there is an underlying influence of some kind. David M. Hay suggests that some allusions, "if they exist at all, lie so far below the surface of our documents that they cannot be recognized with any confidence."[45] David Hay's contention represents a challenge to this study that cannot be bypassed: can the proposed four prophetic texts be recognized as subtexts for the four Gospels? Also, can they be recognized with any confidence?

On a more optimistic note, Dale C. Allison has shown by his examination of Martin Luther King's speech ("I Have a Dream") that an allusion may be a deliberate attempt by means of a rhetorical maneuver on the part of a writer/speaker to evoke or trigger a mental association with some significant event in the past. Among his examples: he cites King's opening words "Five score years ago" from Abraham Lincoln's memorable *Gettysburg Address* ("Four score and seven years ago").[46] The use of the single word "score" combined with a mere mention of "years" is a significant trigger to enable the memory to make the desired association. Allison then applies the use of allusions to the biblical text. I cite just one: Mark's description in 6:30–44 of Jesus' feeding of the five thousand. This text from Mark mentions the grass at that time as "green." Allison argues that this is a subtle allusion to the "*green* pastures" of Psa 23.[47]

Allison's observation merits further comment. He observes that a conscious attempt was made by Martin Luther King to connect to the earlier statement by President Lincoln. We might ask: what associations are possibly evoked by such an allusion? I assume that King did not randomly select the words "score" and "years" as an act of pure happenstance. There had to be a recognizable and substantial purpose in his choice

---

40. Ibid., 65.

41. Robert H. Gundry, *The Use of the Old Testament in St. Matthew's Gospel* (1967) 127–50.

42. Howard Clark Kee, "The Function of Scriptural Quotations and Allusions in Mark 11–16," in *Jesus und Paulus* (1975) 166, 171, 175.

43. R. B. Hays, *Echoes of Scripture in the Letters of Paul* (1989) 14–16.

44. Bruce Chilton and Craig A. Evans, "Jesus and Israel's Scriptures," in *Studying the Historical Jesus* (Brill, 1994) 281–82: "the sense of his (Jesus) teaching is often inaccessible unless its scriptural underpinnings are appreciated. Those underpinnings are not always evident, for several reasons."

45. David M. Hay, *Glory at the Right Hand: Psalm 110 in Early Christianity* (1973) 17.

46. Dale C. Allison, *Scriptural Allusions in the New Testament* (2000) 1.

47. Ibid., 4.

of words. A likely guess is the following: King's own intuition that his speech would have an impact of similar historic significance. The association would likely evoke a corresponding sense of impending dramatic importance for the African-American community. Hence, the simple use of the word "score" is striking. It is also notable that King did not refer to either Lincoln or the *Address*. The allusion without citation of reference was mnemonically sufficient. Richard B. Hays in his recent monograph (2016) does a similar thing by comparing a statement from then President Barack Obama echoing Martin Luther King Jr:

> This is not some arcane theory-driven methodology. It is a matter of simple attention to the way that human language and storytelling ordinarily work. I offer by way of illustration a single elegant contemporary example. In his eloquent victory speech on the night of his initial election to the presidency of the United States in 2008, Barack Obama declared that his hearers could put their hands "on the arc of history and bend it once more toward the hope of a better day." The phrase echoes a maxim from the speeches of Martin Luther King Jr: "The arc of the moral universe is long, but it bends toward justice." Obama's declaration was not a direct quotation of King; the verbal link between the two utterances depends on just two words, *arc* and *bend*.[48]

The power of single-word allusions is used by authors for effect. The crucial issue in this investigation, however, will not necessarily be the search and discovery for an isolated allusion but, rather, will there be a substantial number of relevant and necessary allusions that fit into a coherent whole or a reasonable picture portraying the antecedent text in question? Davies and Allison make a helpful observation which can be extended to the entire Gospel: "Nothing could make plainer the folly of interpreting the individual pericopae of the gospel in isolation from each other. The many pieces of Matthew hang together and were intended to shed light upon one another. Meaning resides not just in the parts but in the whole."[49] L. Hartman suggests that in order for a given allusion to communicate there must be a "set of associations."[50] In this present investigation, it is this framework of sets that is of special interest. One of the benefits of such associative sets is that it has the potential to reduce or eliminate the possibility of literary coincidence as an explanation for the fourfold Gospel.[51]

---

48. R. B. Hays, *Echoes of Scripture in the Gospels* (2016) 11.

49. W. D. Davies and Dale Allison, *A Critical and Exegetical Commentary on the Gospel According to Saint Matthew* (1988) 2.141.

50. L. Hartman, "Scriptural Exegesis in the Gospel of St. Matthew and the Problem of Communication," in *L'Évangile selon Matthieu: Rédaction et théologie* (1971) 146.

51. Martin Pickup, "New Testament Interpretation of the Old Testament: The Theological Rationale of Midrashic Exegesis," *JETS* 51.2 (2008) 359: "Similarities of wording or subject matter between passages in different OT books could be treated as mere happenstance, or as the result of a later writer borrowing material, perhaps even unconsciously, from an earlier writer. In any case, such interconnections between biblical passages might easily be viewed as carrying little or no exegetical weight."

This survey of scholarly usage reveals that the literary concept of allusion has certain parameters that require caution and respect. Yet, some flexibility is in order;[52] allusions are not absolutes, conforming to a rigid mold or standard. What is indisputable about allusion is that there must be an original precursor and a follow-up successor text.[53] This goes without saying: a later text containing references signals a compatible link to an earlier text. This linkage could then serve to enliven the narrative and to ground the later text with a scriptural underpinning that would resonate with the reader. This present study will endeavor to establish such verbal similarities, whether single or multiple, subtle or striking, that are reasonable in their resonance and do not take unfair or inadmissible liberties with the allusion concept. In order to advance the thesis of this book, it is incumbent to inquire if there is evident use of allusions from the text of Jer 23:5 in Matthew, and if established, what does this evidence imply?[54]

In working through Matthew's use of allusions, one of the goals will be to ascertain to what degree the first Gospel engages in subtly implicit or clearly explicit allusions. Although a mere single-word allusion may be considered as suspect for a true allusion, the compilation of several single-word allusions cannot be ignored. I will present evidence that the Gospel of Matthew offers ten such single-word associations imaging the text of Jer 23:5–6.[55] These allusions do not develop sequentially but

---

52. For yet another perspective on allusions, see Michael A. Lyons, "Marking Innerbiblical Allusion in the Book of Ezekiel," *Bib* 88.2 (2007) 245, in which Lyons asks an appropriate question: "How did ancient Israelite authors make it clear that they were purposefully alluding to other texts?" Lyons suggests that such allusions could be attributed to coincidence or to unconscious dependence; these employments, however, would not fall under the category of deliberate or purposeful. Lyons, therefore, commends two techniques for identifying deliberate allusion: 1) "inversion of elements," and 2) the splitting and redistribution of such elements. Lyons provides the following example for cataloging inverted elements: Lev 26:4 says, "And the land will give its produce, and the trees of the field will give their fruit;" and Ezek 34:27, "And the trees of the field will give their fruit, and the land will give its produce."

53. See David C. Sim, "Matthew and the Pauline Corpus: A Preliminary Intertextual Study," *JSNT* 31.4 (2009) 402: "At a basic level it is concerned with the relations between precursor and successor texts, especially when later documents make use of embedded elements from earlier, and how these relationships serve to generate meanings from each of these texts." Sim acknowledges indebtedness to S. Alkier, "From Text to Intertext: Intertextuality as a Paradigm for Reading Matthew," *HvTSt* 61 (2005) 1–18. We shall return later to both Sim and Alkier and their model for understanding Matthew.

54. An ancient model to be adapted in this study is that of Aristotle's *Poetics*. At 1451a/12.1 of his *Poetics*, Aristotle twice uses the expression κατὰ τὸ εἰκὸς ἢ τὸ ἀνακαῖον ("according to probability or necessity") in order to describe a proper sequence of events that likely could have happened. This is the probable part. The element of necessity or inevitability is the second part and requires a proper explanation or pre-condition for this sequence. My intention is to adapt Aristotle's model but with a reverse twist in order to demonstrate the *im*plausibility of the four Gospels as having their origin in a purely human causation. On the explanation and importance of a necessary condition, see R. Latourelle, "Critères d'authenticité historique des Evangiles," *Greg* 55.4 (1974) 628: "Bien qu'ignoré de la plupart des auteurs qui s'intéressent au problème de la critériologie évangélique, ce critère nous paraît capital. Nous le considérons même comme le plus important des critères fondamentaux."

55. The verb πληρόω is used twenty-seven times in the NT. Of this number sixteen are found in

thematically. Taking into consideration all four Gospels, a total of twenty-eight such references will be studied throughout this investigation. Also, the mere mention of particular and isolated words by themselves does not in and by itself establish an allusion.[56] What I will be searching for is a meaningful and associative correspondence of identical ideas and matching motifs.[57]

In the next chapter I will attempt to anchor the text of Jer 23:5–6 to verbal similarities in Matthew by taking up three key elements in Matthew's presentation of Jesus: 1) the specific vocabulary of Matthew as it relates to Jer 23:5–6, 2) the genealogy with its all-important references to David, 3) and the response of people to Jesus. A final section will engage the question of whether the King Branch provides a plausible explanation for variations within the first Gospel as compared to Mark and Luke.

Grids

Another preliminary issue is that of a so-called "grid." Various attempts have been made to find a grid or background template for each of the Gospels.[58] Although James

---

Matthew as he is clearly interested in showing promise and fulfillment. The Index to Nestle's *Novum Testamentum Graece* lists eight references to Jeremiah in Matthew. However, the number of possible allusions in the margin of Nestle's text yields a count of twenty. Additionally, Matthew is the only Gospel to actually cite Jeremiah by name (vv. 2:17 and 27:9). Craig A. Evans, *Jesus and His Contemporaries: Comparative Studies* (1995), commenting specifically upon Jer 23:5–6, bypasses Matthew completely, for he says (169–70): "There may be allusions to the passage in the New Testament. Paul's description of Christ Jesus as the believer's 'wisdom' and 'righteousness' may echo the prophetic text (1 Cor 1.30)." I am puzzled by Evans's passing over Matthew. It is not clear to me how 1 Cor 1:30 can contain evidence of allusion to Jer 23:5–6, while he implies that the Gospel of Matthew does not.

56. For example, David C. Sim, "Matthew and the Pauline Corpus," (2009) 412, uses the expression σάρξ καὶ αἷμα in Matt 16:17, as compared to Paul's similar statement in Gal 1:16–17, to demonstrate that Matthew is reacting to Paul's more liberal theology of grace and freedom. In this model as advocated by Sim, Matthew is thus pitted against Paul; in the present investigation the search is not for conflicting ideas but to identify correspondence of ideas.

57. Gian Biago Conte, *Genres and Readers* (1994) 108, accents the importance of not isolating words (or "facts") in order to make them fit into an unnatural mold: "Facts acquire meaning only in connection with each other . . . as a totality of reciprocal structured relations. The single element must enter into constellation with others if it is to be transvalued."

58. For the argument that it is the prophet Isaiah who determines the proper interpretation of Matthew, see Warren Carter, "Evoking Isaiah: Matthean Soteriology and an Intertextual Reading of Isaiah 7–9 and Matthew 1.23 and 4.15–16," *JBL* 119.3 (2000) 503–20; and Richard Beaton, "Isaiah in Matthew's Gospel," in *Isaiah in the New Testament* (2005) 63–78. For the view that the grid for Matthew is to be found in the Pentateuch, see B. W. Bacon, *Studies in Matthew* (1930). For the specific view that it is Deuteronomy, see Helen Milton, "The Structure of the Prologue to St. Matthew's Gospel," *JBL* 81.2 (1962) 175–81. For the recent view that Matthew is refuting the Pauline theology of grace and freedom from the Law, see David C. Sim, "Matthew and the Pauline Corpus," (2009) 401–22. For the view that it is a great mistake to imagine that a particular Gospel exhibits a singular Christology, see Birger Gerhardsson, "The Christology of Matthew," in *Who Do You Say That I Am?* (1999) 17–18. For the view, now discounted, that Gnosticism forms the background, see Rudolph Bultmann, *The Gospel of John* (1971) 7–9.

H. Charlesworth does not cite specific examples, he mentions a number of critical principles that should be observed when treating a particular text:

> We must avoid myopic focus on methodology in the concerted effort "to place textual and intertextual concerns within a comprehensive theoretical framework."[59] We must also see what is before us, a particular text, and not simply understand it as a mirror image of another text or family of texts. Its own unique voice must be heard, even if intertextuality helps us hear it within a chorus of supporting voices.[60]

Charlesworth refers to the "myopic focus" of imposing a "comprehensive theoretical framework" upon a specific text. In essence, this warning is directed against the arbitrary imposition of a grid system.[61] Since this present inquiry is predicated upon an attempt to gain a comprehensive understanding of not just four particular texts but four complete Gospels,[62] the question, then, becomes: is this investigation "myopic" and, consequently, (changing the metaphor) does it leap to false inferences because of a theoretical framework? Or, on the contrary, will the data uncovered admit safe conclusions about the fourfold nature of the Gospels? That, in part, is the central challenge of this study. I freely acknowledge the hazard of trying to understand the four Gospels on the basis of the four proposed prophetic OT texts.[63] Thus the challenge will be to deal with counter claims that the thesis of this book is an illusory correlation which falsely perceives a relationship between texts when no such relationship exists.

Charlesworth warns of the inherent danger in treating a particular text as a "mirror image" of another text. Inasmuch as the task of demonstrating that the four Gospels mirror four prophetic texts, it is absolutely essential to the success of this study to

---

59. This quotation, as Charlesworth acknowledges, is from G. A. Phillips, "Sign/Text/Différence. The Contribution of Intertextual Theory to Biblical Criticism," in *Intertextuality* (1991) 79.

60. J. H. Charlesworth, "Intertextuality: Isaiah 40.3 and the Serek ha-Yahad," in *The Quest for Context and Meaning* (1997) 200–201.

61. See Robert P. Carroll, "Intertextuality and the Book of Jeremiah: Animadversions on Text and Theory," in *The New Literary Criticism and the Hebrew Bible* (1993) 56, where he expresses his own apprehensions at other scholar's reading of Jeremiah when these interpretative strategies are the "underwriting of their own programmes." For the view that biblical texts do not stand alone all by themselves but form part of an ongoing discourse, see William M. Schniedewind, "The Davidic Dynasty and Biblical Interpretation in Qumran Literature," in *The Dead Sea Scrolls* (2000) 83.

62. For the contrary argument that a comprehensive understanding of the four Gospels is required in order to understand their nature, see Richard A. Burridge, "Who Writes, Why, and for Whom?" in *The Written Gospel* (2005) 113: "Therefore we need a Christological hermeneutic where every passage and verse is interpreted in the light of that gospel's presentation of Jesus' teaching, life, death and resurrection." Burridge goes on to claim that the current redaction-critical approach with its emphasis upon "certain problems for specific communities" does not do justice to the subject of the Gospels—namely Jesus of Nazareth. On this score, I concur.

63. Leon Morris, *I Believe in Revelation* (1976) 30, summarizes the challenge: "Let the Bible speak for itself without our man-made unities. But that carries with it the additional consequence that where the Bible has its own unity the exegete is not at liberty to deny it on the grounds that he perceives some diversity."

question the validity of Charlesworth's assertion. It is my contention that the aspect of a "mirror image" quality cannot be dismissed out of hand simply on the basis of one literary critic's assessment. Texts often appear in relation to other texts; rarely do they stand entirely alone. Therefore, the crucial issue at stake is whether there is genuine evidence of a coherent picture of four Gospels actually reflecting four prophetic texts and, if so, what does this imply? In essence, establishing a réseau approach to the Gospels will serve as a litmus test for this investigation. Joel Marcus also fires a warning shot against imposing a particular grid of OT texts upon the Gospel of Mark. He makes an observation (from two 1980 scholarly works) that applies equally well to any of the four Gospels:

> J. D. M. Derrett, came out with a two-volume commentary on Mark that attempted to show that the entire Gospel was based on an Old Testament "grid" provided in the main by Exodus, Numbers, and Joshua. Near the end of the decade, similarly, W. Roth claimed to have "cracked the code of Mark" and to have discovered that it was based on the paradigm of the Elijah/Elisha narratives of 1 Kings 17 to 2 Kings 13 . . . both tend to force the Markan evidence arbitrarily into the grid provided by the particular Old Testament passages that each author considers important. It must be questioned, moreover, why Derrett and Roth come up with such different grids and why neither grid corresponds to sections of the Old Testament that are extensively utilized in Mark's overt Old Testament citations.[64]

Inasmuch as the approach of this investigation makes use of a grid paradigm, it will be necessary to succeed where Derrett, Roth, and others have failed.[65] If this investigation is to succeed in provoking new thought, it will have to justify a grid approach. Marcus raises valid objections against a grid system that does not coincide with clear citations in a Gospel. Derrett and Roth seek to provide a substructure only to a single Gospel (Mark). This investigation makes a claim for a grid or template system that justifies a substructure for all four Gospels. Therefore, the degree of difficulty increases considerably; the climb becomes steeper accordingly; the stakes rise higher substantially. If successful, however, the benefit of such an approach becomes apparent. In a recent monograph (2006), Paul N. Anderson notes the following diversity in the four Gospels (the italics are mine):

> Despite having a common subject—Jesus, the four canonical gospel tradition all have distinctive sets of perspectives to contribute. Mark shows him as a Jewish Rabbi, taking his band of followers on itinerant tours of ministry and

---

64. Joel Marcus, *The Way of the Lord* (1992) 4. The reference to J. Derrett is *The Making of Mark* (1985), and W. Roth, *Cracking the Code of Mark* (1988).

65. See Morna D. Hooker, "Mark," in *It is Written: Scripture Citing Scripture* (1988) 220. See also David P. Moessner, *Lord of the Banquet: The Literary and Theological Significance of the Lukan Travel Narrative* (1989). Moessner attempts to develop a type of grid structure between Luke's travel narrative and Deuteronomy.

calling them to count *the cost of discipleship* while at the same time calling them to follow him . . . Luke presents Jesus as a just *man*—one caring for the needs of the poor, women and Samaritans . . . Matthew shows Jesus as the ultimate teacher of *righteousness*. . . John presents Jesus as the revelatory agent from heaven . . . . Despite a common subject, these perspectives are impressively diverse.[66]

Anderson's substantive observation, composite in scope and panoramic in view, is of considerable interest. In a single compressed paragraph, he isolates four subordinate elements that meld themselves into the design of my theoretical grid: righteousness in Matthew, the cost of discipleship in Mark, man in Luke, and Jesus as the revelatory agent from heaven in John. Anderson portrays the four Gospels as diverse, with distinctive sets of perspective. What he implies as evidencing diversity, I will develop as a unity for unlocking the unified substructure of the four Gospels. In a nearly identical manner, another recent publication is the monograph by Mark L. Strauss who outlines a similar portrait of Jesus in the following schematic:[67] Matthew presents Jesus as a royal Davidic Messiah;[68] Mark reveals Jesus as the suffering Servant;[69] Luke writes of a Savior for all mankind;[70] John pictures Jesus as the divine Son of God who reveals the Father.[71] These profiles, from only a slightly different angle, cohere well into the unified substructure as presented here. The principal difference is that this present study endeavors to show that a fourfold prophetic background is the template

---

66. Paul N. Anderson, *The Fourth Gospel and the Quest for Jesus* (2006) 182. For another recent scholarly approach, see Dennis E. Smith, "Jesus and the Gospels," in *Chalice Introduction to the New Testament* (2004) 133, where Smith interprets the death of Jesus from Mark as suffering, from Luke as modeling forgiveness, and from John as emphasizing divinity. Since Smith is not seeking a coherent grid understanding of the Gospels, his incidental portrayal cannot be faulted as forced. Yet, at the same time, it connects easily to the thesis of a fourfold grid as proposed here.

67. Mark L. Strauss, *Four Portraits, One Jesus* (2007) 24. See also Darrell L. Bock, *Jesus according to Scripture: Restoring the Portrait from the Gospels* (2002) 27–28, 32, 36–37, and 41; and also Kenneth Schenck, *Jesus Is Lord!* (2003) 144, who both develop similar approaches to the four Gospels.

68. Strauss (2007) 239: "Jesus is the promised king from David's line who will bring salvation to his people. This identification of Jesus as the royal or Davidic Messiah takes center stage throughout the birth narrative, functioning as Matthew's foundational category for Jesus." See also 240: "the Davidic Messiah serves as Matthew's foundational category."

69. Ibid., 177, 183, 185, 193, and 200. Strauss continues from beginning to end of his chapter on Mark to focus on the suffering servanthood of Jesus. Strauss categorizes Mark's narrative of servanthood into three major themes [199–200]: 1) the kingdom of God, 2) Jesus as the Servant-Messiah, and 3) Discipleship: Following the Servant's Suffering Path.

70. Ibid., 260, 268, and 281. Strauss acknowledges that Luke presents varied pictures of Jesus, but focuses principally upon Jesus as the Savior for all people. Inasmuch as this connection between priesthood and salvation is developed in Hebrews (5:9–10; 7:24–25; 9:24–26; 10:10), the possibility presents itself that the author of Luke also wrote Hebrews, but this is by no means certain.

71. Ibid., 328: "While the Gospel speaks of Jesus as equal with God (5.18; sometimes called ontological equality), there is also a strong functional subordination . . . . The role of the Son is to reveal the Father and bring others into a relationship with him."

for this fourfold view of Jesus. Thus, this investigation sets out to demonstrate *why* we have these four particular Gospels.

Moving from monograph to a recent multi-authored collection of essays, we can see similar identifying characteristics as the Anderson and Strauss citations above. In the Cambridge publication *The Written Gospel* (2005), four separate scholars tackle issues of Christology in the four respective Gospels. Each scholar finds significant and corresponding emphatic traits of Jesus that illuminate the primary claim of this present chapter. Richard Beaton finds in Matthew "a more sustained explication of Jesus as the ideal Davidic messiah . . . the author seeks to demonstrate that, above all, this one is the Davidic messianic king."[72] Although Craig Evans's major focus in this volume concentrates on Markan style, he does find in Mark an emphasis upon discipleship.[73] David P. Moessner begins his discussion of Luke with a stunning opening quotation from Ambrose: "'This Gospel is represented fittingly by the calf, because it begins with priests and ends with the Calf who, having taken upon himself the sins of all, was sacrificed for the life of the whole world.'"[74] Although Ambrose, I believe, has misidentified the calf with the role of priest, the more important fact is that Moessner identifies Jesus with a high priestly role.[75] Only Judith Lieu, in her treatment of John, prefers to conceal her own personal view of Jesus as recorded in the fourth Gospel.[76] Three of the four writers provide views of Jesus that fit into the grid approach as developed here. A similar approach may be found in the recent collaborative monograph *Seeking the Identity of Jesus* (2008).[77] Other notable authors may be enlisted: Dale C. Allison in his contribution on the Gospel of Matthew focuses primarily upon Jesus as King;[78] Joel Marcus isolates Markan information as it relates to a suffering Servant;[79]

---

72. Richard Beaton, "How Matthew Writes," in *The Written Gospel* (2005) 123.

73. C. Evans, "How Mark Writes," in *The Written Gospel* (2005) 148.

74. David P. Moessner, "How Luke Writes," in *The Written Gospel* (2005) 149. The citation from Ambrose comes from *Exposition from the Gospel of Luke* 1.4.7.

75. Moessner continues (157): "Now resounding the resolve of Ezekiel—priest, 'son of man'—to declare God's judgment against an idol-sated Jerusalem."

76. Judith Lieu, "How John Writes," in *The Written Gospel* (2005) 171–83. Instead, she reels off a litany of scholarly views, often presenting only contrasting points without making any firm statement about how Jesus is presented in John. Lieu, it may be said, does not really describe "How John Writes," but how others write about John.

77. Beverly Roberts Gaventa and Richard B. Hays, eds., *Seeking the Identity of Jesus* (2008).

78. D. C. Allison, "The Embodiment of God's Will: Jesus in Matthew," (2008) 117–32. Although Allison disclaims that a single title can adequately define Jesus (118), he does affirm (122): "Jesus' status as king is prominent in Matthew, and it unites much of Matthean theology."

79. J. Marcus, "Identity and Ambiguity in Markan Christology," (2008) 133–47. Marcus focuses primarily upon Jesus as a Suffering Servant throughout his contribution. Interesting enough, Marcus does reference Zech 3:8 in a parenthetical format. He does not, however, make a direct connection for Zech 3:8 serving as a possible substructure for the Gospel of Mark.

Beverly Roberts Gaventa zeroes in on the "departed" aspects of Jesus;[80] and Marianne Meye Thompson narrows John's Gospel down to Jesus as God.[81]

There is one more grid approach worth bringing into the discussion. Richard A. Burridge, in his study championing narrative biography with its stress upon the individual author's point of view rather than representing community concerns, distills the individual characteristics of each Gospel to the following portraits: Mark shows Jesus as the Messiah who will suffer;[82] Matthew shows Jesus as a king and teacher; Luke shows Jesus as "the man of prayer;"[83] and John shows Jesus as one who was with God in the beginning. I agree with each individual assessment that Burridge has isolated. What Burridge does not do, however, is to explore why the four Gospels focus upon these particular characteristics.

In summary, combining the conclusions from the above eleven scholars into a composite, it is possible to see that they have independently arrived at the following significant parallel results: they single out for emphasis such characteristics of Jesus as a king, Jesus as a servant model for discipleship, Jesus as possessing priestly qualities, and Jesus as identified with God. Hence, a number of individual studies of the four Gospels develop themes based upon the representation of Jesus in each respective Gospel as Matthew's royal king, Mark's servant, Luke's human portrait as a priest, and the Johannine view of Jesus as God. To my knowledge, however, no one has presented a scholarly and critical argument showing the unified and coherent relationship between these disparate views.[84] A canvass of scholarly literature turns up zero references. The purpose of this present study is to demonstrate how these independent accounts can justifiably cohere into a plausible unity by appealing to the proposed substructures of Jer 23:5–6, Zach 3:6 and 6:12–13, and Isa 4:2. Conversely, while modern scholarship does not recognize these four prophetic texts as decisive for

---

80. B. R. Gaventa, "Learning and Relearning the Identity of Jesus from Luke–Acts," (2008) 161–63, where Gaventa pays special attention to the activity of Jesus in heaven. Although Gaventa avoids such terms as temple and high priest, she ends up describing Jesus in ways that are consistent with a heavenly high priestly role.

81. M. M. Thompson, "Word of God, Messiah of Israel, Savior of the World: Learning the Identity of Jesus from the Gospel of John," (2008) 166–79. Thompson never loses sight of the fourth Gospel's presentation of Jesus as LORD God.

82. Richard A. Burridge, "About People, by People, for People: Gospel Genre and Audiences," in *The Gospels for All Christians: Rethinking the Gospel Audiences* (1998) 128

83. Ibid., 129.

84. See Craig L. Blomberg, *Jesus and the Gospels* (1997) 119 for Mark: "For Mark, however, 10.45 may be the most important verse in the Gospel in summarizing his emphasis on Jesus' road to the cross;" see esp. 129 for Matthew: "*Son of David, King, and Royal Messiah*. One of the most distinctive titles for Jesus in Matthew is 'Son of David';" see esp. 145 for Luke: "None of the titles such as 'Christ', 'Son of God', or 'Lord' is nearly as prominent. Rather, what strikes most readers of Luke's Gospel is how Jesus' humanity shines through;" and see esp. 163 for the Gospel of John where Jesus is identified as God. Likewise, Blomberg makes no attempt at a connection with the four prophetic texts of this investigation.

understanding the four Gospels, these texts are often found as references in a documented form as footnote or a parenthesis.[85]

Given the above modern scholarly overlappings, it is the argument of this chapter that such synchronicity cannot be construed as an attempt to force an arbitrary and artificial grid upon the four Gospels. Rather, these mirror images in the Gospels may give evidence of a true reflection originating from the proposed four prophetic texts. The contribution, therefore, of this study will not be so much the individual assessment of each Gospel but, rather, the collective patching together of the four evangelistic pieces into a whole cloth.[86]

This investigation utilizes two principal criteria in order to advance the plausibility case for the proposed substructure.[87] These criteria, if established, lend support to the case for plausibility. First, do all four prophetic texts serve in the proposed substructure? All four subtexts must be present in the substructures, yet in a diversified manner. If it can be shown that one of the subtexts is used for more than one Gospel, the thesis will suffer a loss of credibility. If it can be established that one or more of the selected prophetic texts does not suitably fit as a background piece, the thesis will also weaken. This criterion requires that each prophetic subtext function in a singular and unrepeated manner. Two Gospels using the same subtext or two prophetic subtexts applying equally well to a single Gospel will break down the claim for uniqueness.

The second criterion is that of particularity or specificity. That is, do the individual elements of each prophetic text find correspondence in a respective Gospel? This criterion differs slightly from the first in that the focus is upon specific details. This criterion is based upon a mutual reciprocity of mirror and reflection. If it can be

---

85. Michael Knowles in his book *Jeremiah in Matthew's Gospel* (1999) does not explore this metaphor at all except for one small reference to Jer 23:6 in a footnote (233, fn. 3). See also Nicole Chibici-Revneanu, *Die Herrlichkeit des Verherrlichten: Das Verständnis der δόξα im Johnnesevangelium* (2007) 443–46.

86. See H. E. W. Turner, *Historicity and the Gospels* (1963) 17: "Different aspects of the same fact will acquire a special significance according to the context in which it is placed. Thus the coronation of a king may be viewed from the political, social, economic or ecclesiastical angle, and in each case the use made of the available material will be different."

87. For a clarification and discussion of literary criteria as applied to studies of the Gospels, see Morna D. Hooker, "Christology and Methodology," *NTS* 17 (1970–71) 480-87; Neil J. McEleney, "Authenticating Criteria and Mark 7.1–23," *CBQ* 34 (1972) 431–60; D. G. A. Calvert, "An Examination of the Criteria for Distinguishing the Authentic Words of Jesus," *NTS* 18 (1971–72) 210; Richard Longenecker, "Literary Criteria in Life of Jesus Research: An Evaluation and Proposal," in *Current Issues in Biblical and Patristic Interpretation* (1975) 217–29; R. Latourelle, "Critères d'authenticité historique des Evangiles," *Greg* 55.4 (1974) 609–38; Craig A. Evans, *Jesus and His Contemporaries: Comparative Studies* (1995) 213–26; Craig A. Evans, "Authenticating the Activities of Jesus," in *Authenticating the Activities of Jesus* (1999) 3–29; Gerd Theissen and Dagmar Winter, *The Quest for the Plausible Jesus: The Question of Criteria* (2002); and most recently, Anthony Le Donne, *The Historiographical Jesus* (2009) 88–91. For the double criteria of compositional function and distribution in the Gospel of Mark, see David Barrett Peabody, *Mark as Composer* (1987) 22–24. For an example of how to create criteria in handling texts from the Pseudepigrapha, see James H. Charlesworth, "Biblical Interpretation: The Crucible of the Pseudepigrapha," in *Text and Testimony* (1988) 66–78.

shown that the individual details of each prophetic subtext find a reasonable correlate in a respective Gospel, this, I believe, will constitute evidence of a weighty nature.[88] Conversely, however, is the opposite: if it can be demonstrated that a substantial number of details from a prophetic subtext do not provide meaningful and matching characteristics for the appropriate Gospel, the thesis will wane in its vitality to convince and will be vulnerable to a quick dismissal. Hence, the aspect of resemblance functions somewhat like the manner of a mirror: the prophetic image and prefiguration reflected in the mirror of the Gospel should reveal a close likeness, not a distortion. Such an analogy does not imply an exact photocopy, only a resemblance. These cameo-like characteristics, however, need to show reasonable correspondence. The goal of this criterion is to establish emphasis or singularity by means of detailed analysis. My intention is not to atomize or to exploit by means of isolating smaller parts to the exclusion of the whole but to respect all the words and lines of each prophetic text. In the four prophetic texts under consideration there are a total of eleven lines of Hebrew script comprising nearly one hundred words. The task is not to pursue a pick-and-choose methodology by discarding what may appear as either unexplainable or non-supportive. It is hoped that this criterion will provide a further check on the dangers of abuse or oversimplification, thus preventing theology from leaping over exegetical barriers.[89] Overlapping from one Gospel to another is expected; indeed, it cannot be avoided.[90] Overlapping, however, does not negate a particular emphasis. Although there is obvious overlapping, the thesis of this study is that there is clearly a distinctive emphasis within each of the four Gospels.

Silence

A final concern in this chapter is the objection that the present argument contains too much silence and not enough hard evidence. Silence is often an obstacle that scholars must overcome.[91] Some attempts are very bold as, for example, the ambitious

---

88. I am making use of some encouragement by Samuel Sandmel, "Parallelomania," *JBL* 81.1 (1962) 2: "The issue for the student is not the abstraction but the specific. Detailed study is to be the criterion, and the detailed study ought to respect the context and not be limited to juxtaposing mere excerpts."

89. Rudolf Bultmann, "Prophecy and Fulfillment," in *Essays on Old Testament Interpretation* (1960) 55: "Furthermore, what then is the criterion by means of which it becomes possible to find prophecies in the Old Testament? What safeguard is there that the sense one wishes to find is not being arbitrarily imported?" Although Bultmann rails against what he considers the abuse of OT texts, the merit of his complaint cannot be denied.

90. The claim of this study is not an argument for exclusivity but, rather, emphasis. Of course, some texts are exclusive to a particular Gospel. The exclusive appearance of a particular passage as, for example Matt 11:28–30, is not essential to my argument. However, exclusivity, when apparent, can contribute to the overall case for emphasis.

91. For a systematic fourfold procedure to cope with silence or omissions (when one evangelist omits material as found in the synoptic tradition) in redaction criticism, see the scheme proposed by Frank Connolly-Weinert, "Assessing Omissions as Redaction: Luke's Handling of the Charge against

enterprise of trying to determine various stages of composition in the alleged Q document,[92] (once again, Robert Kysar's statement is appropriate here: Q is a "skyscraper built upon the end of a toothpick"[93]), or the attempt to reconstruct gospel narratives with extraneous details that are completely foreign to the biblical record.[94] The word "silence," though frequently used to describe a paucity of evidence, may not be an appropriate metaphor to describe the methodology as applied in this study. This investigation makes use of the term "substructure" to explain the foundational nature of the fourfold Gospels. A substructure more accurately portrays something out of sight, rather than something silent. However, just because something is out of sight does not indicate that it is not there. If it is there, then there should be some evidence of the fact. The challenge is to discover what is there, not to assume it must be there because of a superimposed theory. This study will fail in the end if it appears that there has been a concerted effort, as it were, to force ideas through cracks in the main flooring.[95] Hugh Anderson refers to what he calls "imaginative typologists" who see, for example, that "the stone rolled back" of Mark 16:5 is a symbol of the removal

---

Jesus as Detractor of the Temple," in *To Touch the Text* (1989) 359: "omission usually forces interpreters to argue from silence. From a redaction-critical standpoint, then, evaluating omissions demands special care."

92. See, for example, Norman Perrin, "The Christology of Mark: A Study in Methodology," in *The Interpretation of Mark* (1985) 104, where Perrin argues from a redactional standpoint that Luke 22:24–27 had its origin in a Hellenistic milieu, while Luke 19:10 originated perhaps "in a moment of solemn reflection at a very early Christian Eucharist." In other words, neither passage can be traced back to Jesus; they are both products of early church creativity. Yet, both conclusions seem to me to be based upon pure speculation. The same weakness may be faulted for much research on Q. See also Arland D. Jacobson, "The Literary Unity of Q," *JBL* 101.3 (1982) 374: "Again, redactional activity is observable in Q, namely at the end of the collection of woes. The older woes accuse Jewish leaders of hypocrisy; those woes reflect inner-Jewish debate. To those woes have been added an expanded woe." Then (at 382) we have a similar statement: "In Q, the saying has undergone at least two stages of expansion." See also Burton Mack, *The Lost Gospel: The Book of Q and Christian Origins* (1993), who postulates a similar two-stage development in the Q material. These overt speculations, lacking textual evidence, leave such theoretical interpretations vulnerable to severe and justifiable criticism. An example of such criticism is that of Michael Bird's recent review of Helmut Koester's book *From Jesus to the Gospels* (2007). Bird, in *JSNT* 31.5 (2009) 43–44, expresses his dismay: "I remain confused, however, as to how Koester can advocate the impossibility of uncovering a 'historical Jesus' and yet he barely bats an eyelid in consenting to literary approaches that divide Q into various layers and accretions and attempts to map the contours of a 'Q community.'"

93. Robert Kysar, "What's the Meaning of This? Reflections upon a Life and Career," in *What We Have Heard from the Beginning* (2007) 173.

94. James D. Tabor's recent book, *The Jesus Dynasty* (2006) 71–72, may serve as an example. Tabor offers up the historical reconstruction that Panthera, a Roman soldier, got Mary pregnant.

95. The hypothesis of this present study must survive fair and legitimate testing. I have no quarrel with a particular judgment by John Dominic Crossan, *The Birth of Christianity* (1998) 96: "Superstructures are built on top of foundations. Conclusions and decisions about the historical Jesus are built, by *everyone*, atop their presuppositions about the gospels. Mistakes about foundations can bring superstructures tumbling down either partially or totally." The converse, I may add, is also true: adequate and justifiable foundations can support superstructures.

of Pharisaic legal righteousness.[96] His point is well taken. Excessive typology (or allegory) leads to the misinterpretation of Scripture. Allegorical interpretation opens the door for an anything-goes subjective analysis. A more controlled approach is in order. I note the comment by the late C. F. D. Moule: "Their understanding of the person of Jesus, indicated by the titles they attach to him and the role he plays, is far deeper than is suggested by most of their express citations of scripture."[97] Moule's use of the word "deeper" points us in a more fruitful direction.

There are two critical questions facing the issue of silence: 1) is the interpreter trying to make something out of nothing, and 2) has the interpreter ignored evidence that would contravene his or her proposed thesis? In the case of this present investigation, I acknowledge that not one of the four evangelists mentions *in extenso* any of the four prophetic texts in this study. The objection, therefore, may be raised that this militates against the premise of this book in that without specific and full textual confirmation through explicit citation it is impossible to build a credible case. For example, Peter's interpretation of Joel 2 on the day of Pentecost provides us with an interpretive key for how the early church understood the text of Joel 2. Peter even says, "This is that which was spoken by the prophet" indicating that such a scriptural explanation enables the reader to understand how an OT text has been understood by the early Christian movement.[98] This interpretative key, known in Qumran circles as *pesher*,[99] is expounded by Richard Longenecker as beyond human ability; only

---

96. H. Anderson, "The Old Testament in Mark's Gospel," in *The Use of the Old Testament in the New and other Essays* (1972) 281. See also James H. Charlesworth, "What has the Old Testament to Do with the New?" in *The Old and New Testaments* (1993) 47, where the author, warning of pressing typology too far, asks: "Are we dangerously close to creating texts?" Charlesworth, although admitting that typology is valid in principle, swings the pendulum to the opposite extreme by objecting to such applications as seeing the Passover lamb as a type of Christ.

97. C. F. D. Moule, "Fulfillment-Words in the New Testament: Use and Abuse," *NTS* 14 (1967–68) 301.

98. In essence, this is the objection raised by Robert H. Gundry, *Matthew: A Commentary on His Literary and Theological Art* (1982) 629: "Did Matthew have more than one intent in writing a passage? What are the boundaries of the passage characterized by his intent? How high a level of consciousness is required for authorial intent? Answers do not always come easily. But they do come, and the difficulty of these and similar questions pose far less a hermeneutical problem than the difficulty of discovering meanings unintended by an author and therefore wholly unfalsifiable. Though God intended more than the authors of the OT had in their minds, apart from the NT we would not have known that he did so. To find additional meanings in either the OT or the NT would require us to have the kind of inspiration the NT authors had in interpreting the OT. But the closing of the canon implies that we have only illumination for interpreting scriptural truth, no inspiration for adding to it, much less changing it."

99. For specialized studies on Pesher or Peshat, see David Instone Brewer, *Techniques and Assumptions in Jewish Exegesis before 70 CE* (1992) 14: "Peshat is a term indicating the 'plain' meaning of a text, in contrast to the 'Derash' or 'hidden meaning.'" It may also be seen as the distinction between the primary meaning and any secondary or allegorical meaning which may be found in the text. For a challenge to such distinctions, see James H. Charlesworth, *The Pesharim and Qumran History: Chaos or Consensus?* (2002) 68. I note as well the observation by Donald Juel, *Messianic Exegesis* (1988) 51: "It is possible to overstate the differences between pesherim and midrashim, however, or at least

revelation from God can vouchsafe such a claim.[100] To a certain extent, this is true. But a counter-argument may be justifiably presented in the defense of silence (or more accurately hiddenness). From the point of view of current NT scholarship, this objection collapses when one considers the amount of research that is devoted to proving theories based upon Q. Although the scholarly assumption continues in the belief that a Q document existed, no material document has ever been discovered. Darrell L. Bock soberly acknowledges the following challenge when dealing with Q: "To be assigned an essay about a document we do not have is a daunting task."[101] The linchpin of optimistic Q research is summed up by the often repeated statement of Gerd Theissen and Anne Merz that the most important source for Jesus research is Q.[102] That document, however, is materially non-existent, being only a hypothetical construction.[103]

The substructure, however, of this present investigation is undergirded by documents we do have: Jer 23:5–6, Isa 4:2, Zech 3:8 and 6:12–13.[104] Therefore, in my judg-

---

to misunderstand the differences." See also (55): "The differences between midrashim and pesherim should be understood properly . . . but they cannot be pressed." Juel also states (51): "what is unique at Qumran is the consistency of the interpretive program aimed at uncovering secrets in the text." This definition or description is often attributed to midrash as well. However, as Juel points out (52), at Qumran interpretations of the text were based upon revelation not reason. For further distinctions, see also F. F. Bruce, *Biblical Exegesis in the Qumran Texts* (1959). For very recent work highlighting some of the differences between pesher and midrash, see George J. Brooke, "Pesher and Midrash in Qumran Literature: Issues for Lexicography," *RevQ* 93.1 (2009) 79–95. For a possible application of the pesher method to the first Gospel, see James E. Patrick, "Matthew's *Pesher* Gospel Structured around Ten Messianic Citations of Isaiah," *JTS* 61.1 (2010) 43–81.

100. R. N. Longenecker, "Can We Reproduce the Exegesis of the New Testament?" *TynBul* 21 (1970) 36: "But apart from a revelatory stance on our part, I suggest that we cannot reproduce their pesher exegesis." See also Longenecker's *Biblical Exegesis in the Apostolic Period* (1975) 43–44.

101. D. L. Bock, "Questions about Q," in *Rethinking the Synoptic Problem* (2001) 41. For one of the most severe criticisms of Q, see Stewart Petrie, "'Q' Is Only What You Make It," *NovT* 3.1 (1959) 28–33. For a recent statement casting additional doubt upon the material document Q, see Stephen Hultgren, "The Apostolic Church's Influence on the Order of Sayings in the Double Tradition," *ZNW* 99.2 (2008) 185–212. See also M. Enslin, "Luke and Matthew: Compilers or Authors?" *ANRW* 25.3 (1984) 2361: "Q we do not have, nor do we have the slightest evidence that it ever existed."

102. G. Theissen and A. Merz, *Der historische Jesus: Ein Lehrbuch* (1996) 45: "Q ist zweifellos die wichtigste Quelle zur Rekonstruktion der Lehre Jesu."

103. Editors James M. Robinson, Paul Hoffmann, and John S. Kloppenborg of *The Critical Edition of Q* (2000) claim on page xv: "The text of Q need no longer be just an imaginary black box lurking somewhere behind certain Matthean and Lukan verses as their source, but can emerge as a text in its own right." Their claim, however, must be considered speculative as it lacks material evidence. This is tantamount to claiming there has been a murder when no physical body has yet been found. See also Robinson's earlier claim, "The Sayings Gospel Q," in *The Four Gospels* (1992) 361: "It is in fact possible, in the analysis of Q, to move beyond individual sayings and discourses, and to discern the compositional intentionality of this part of Q with a clarity that is remarkable." That is clearly an amazing claim. For the earlier and pioneering work on the possibility of recovering the various layers of Q (Q1, Q2, and Q3), see John S. Kloppenborg, *The Formation of Q* (1987). For a more moderate claim for the possibilities of Q, see Craig A. Evans, "Images of Christ in the Canonical and Apocryphal Gospels," in *Images of Christ: Ancient and Modern* (1997) 38.

104. Numerous studies include these texts in footnotes as possible messianic references. In other words, many interpreters do not find a hopeful solution to this fourfold Branch identity in the

ment, I am not advocating a thesis from a speculative case fraught with no evidence. Kenneth Kitchen aptly states a helpful principle: "Absence of evidence is *not* evidence of absence."[105] As an archaeological principle, absence of evidence above the ground does not necessarily equate to absence of evidence below the ground. As a biblical principle, absence of direct citation in a gospel text does not necessarily equate to evidence of absence behind the text. An ultimate question in this investigation is the following: does the fourfold Gospel require the four prophetic prefigurations as an adequate explanation for their existence or simply permit this interpretation? A modern analogy may be helpful at this point: because an accused murderer does not confess to the alleged crime does not end the matter. Honest investigation is still under obligation to satisfy justice. Law enforcement must follow the clues without rushing to judgment. By collecting and interpreting all relevant circumstantial evidence as best it can and by finally presenting a justifiably plausible case, officers of the law are carrying out the intent of the law. The position taken up in this study is that, taking into consideration the entirety of the biblical canon, the evidence not only allows but even requires an interconnectedness between prophetic and gospel texts.

I must return for a moment to the implications of research into the alleged document Q. I do not want to use the difficulties involved for establishing the case for Q as a red herring. As a defensive strategy, deflection works in sport but not in scholarship. Casting doubt on Q does not safeguard the thesis of this book. In chapter 2, I argue that we cannot impute, for example, alleged feelings of embarrassment onto the evangelists without expressed statements from the evangelists. In other words, if Matthew does not expressly acknowledge embarrassment over a statement in Mark, it is unfair, unwise, and inaccurate for us to do so. Consequently, can the principle of silence be turned against this study? The ultimate answer to this question is the relevance of allusions. Allusions, as utilized in this present study, serve as indicators pointing to substructures. Matthew, I would argue, does not allude to imagined embarrassments over statements in Mark. Conversely, Matthew, sharing in a symbolic field of conceptual Branch categories, does allude to ideas and motifs as found in Jer 23:5–6. Another analogy may be enlisted at this point. William Sanford LaSor offers the following word picture to illustrate the concept of *senus plenior*:

> An ordinary seed contains in itself everything that will develop in the plant or tree to which it is organically related: every branch, every leaf, every flower.

---

immediate historical situation of the respective prophet but, rather, in a future person designated as "messianic." Therefore, the propositional claim that Jesus fulfills the role of an expectant Messiah is no surprise. What is novel about the present investigation is the claim that the Gospel of Matthew uniquely develops this claim. The debate on whether these four prophetic texts contain a hidden meaning does not apply to this study.

105. K. Kitchen, "The Patriarchal Age: Myth of History?" *BAR* (March/April 1995) 50. Leander E. Keck, "On the Ethos of Early Christians," *JAAR* 42 (1974) 448, says: "Two issues emerge: (1) Given the occasional character of the NT literature, can we convert silence into absence?" Keck suggests, for example, that "silence" in a text cannot infer absence in the community from which the text came.

> Yet no examination by available scientific methods will disclose to us what is in the seed. However, once the seed has developed to its fullness, we can see how the seed has been fulfilled.[106]

In light of the full and complete development of the fourfold Gospel, it is my conviction that the original four prophetic "seeds" revealing the metaphor of a future fourfold Branch find their fulfillment in Christ who is subsequently presented in the fourfold Gospel. This, I contend, is not an arbitrary forcing of extraneous ideas upon Scripture but, rather, a simple act of overlaying one set of congruent biblical data upon another. In my judgment, it is unreasonable to argue that the NT must specifically claim that an OT prophecy has been fulfilled in Christ in order to establish fulfillment. Such passages as Isa 9:6 would then remain unfulfilled. If we follow the suggestion as given by LaSor above that "once the seed has developed to its fullness, we can see how the seed has been fulfilled," we should be able to look back and see that Christ is the fulfillment, not our own personal ideas.

To pursue the metaphor of substructure one step further, the assumption is that if there is a visible floor, there must be a supporting substructure underneath. But the question then becomes: what kind of substructure? By extension, the metaphor of a floor does not necessarily prove that there is a unified interlocking fourfold substructure beneath the four Gospels. That is yet to be demonstrated. Whether the metaphor is substructure or silence, the issue of caution must be applied.[107] A premature verdict must not precede the trial; analysis must go before conclusion.[108]

A disclaimer is appropriate here. Academic studies on the Gospels assume some precursorial substructure, whether oral tradition, a written tradition such as Q, or testimonia. Such studies do not imply secret or occult meanings. Likewise, this study does not make a claim for occult meanings in a text.[109] Rather, reliance will be upon the plain sense of Scripture. Consequently, the critical issue is not just meanings but also sources. The meanings should be plain, but the sources may remain uncited, be-

---

106. W. S. LaSor, "Prophecy, Inspiration, and *Sensus Plenior*," *TynB* 29.1 (1978) 56. LaSor does admit to the possibility that not everything was understood by the original human author.

107. George J. Brooke, "Shared Intertextual Interpretations in the Dead Sea Scrolls and the New Testament," in *Biblical Perspectives* (1998) 35: "There is indeed a certain danger inherent in this task. It is often difficult to be certain that particular scriptural passages lie behind certain Qumran or New Testament phrases." Although Brooke tries to mine the Dead Sea Scrolls for possible connections with New Testament texts, what he applies to Qumran must also apply to the Gospels and the prophetic texts in this present study. See also C. H. Dodd, *According to the Scriptures: The Sub-Structure of New Testament Theology* (1953) 28, who offered the following challenge: ". . . we have had many learned essays upon the old theme, 'Novum testamentum in vetere latet, vetus in novo patet,' but some of them, I think have not altogether avoided the dangerous ground of speculation and fancy, where associations of ideas arising in the critic's own mind have been treated as evidence for original connections."

108. This is not to claim that our mind is a *tabla rasa*. Exegesis is impossible without some presupposition. Presupposition, however, should proceed by objective analysis.

109. An example of such occult readings is the recent article by Jonathan Cahn, "The Paradigm," *Charisma* (September 2017) 26, in which he claims that OT prophecies predicted the years of Barack Obama and Hillary Clinton.

low the surface, and out of sight. In my view, I am not claiming that there is a secondary meaning in the four prophetic texts which was unknown to the original human author.¹¹⁰ The early Christian movement understood that the OT prophets could see foreshadowed a figure with messianic characteristics. According to NT texts, what puzzled the OT prophetic luminaries was the time of fulfillment.

There are two implications to this NT observation: the first is that OT prophets were not looking for a fulfillment in the immediate future of their own times; the second is that they could see a messianic figure foreshadowed beyond their own times. In other words, the specific metaphor of a Branch must have been known to the prophets as the Messiah.¹¹¹ The metaphor of a Branch as applied to Jesus was certainly known to the early church and to the Qumran Covenanters.¹¹² To claim that a future figure (the Messiah) would fulfill the original intention of the prophets as the proper fulfillment of the Branch does not go beyond the single intention of the human authors.¹¹³

It will be argued in this investigation that Zech 6:12–13, for example, does not have in mind the contemporary Zerubbabel as the historical fulfillment. Rather, the person envisioned is the Messiah. This, it will be argued, is the plain meaning of the text, not an arbitrarily enforced meaning. What is new in this investigation is the claim that Matthew, Mark, Luke, and John write uniquely about this fourfold view of Christ as King, Servant, Priest, and LORD God as a reflection of these four prophetic texts. Obviously, we cannot defend the notion that Jeremiah was told of Matthew, Zechariah of Mark and Luke, and Isaiah of John. That fact, however, does not negate the premise of this study.¹¹⁴ Even a liberal scholar such as John M. Allegro acknowledges the com-

---

110. I am not claiming that such secondary meanings or levels are illegitimate. For a defense of midrash hermeneutics as applied to the NT, see Martin Pickup, "New Testament Interpretation of the Old Testament: The Theological Rationale of Midrashic Exegesis," (2008) 353–81. In a similar vein, W. S. LaSor, "Prophecy, Inspiration, and *Sensus Plenior*," (1978) 57, argues that Hosea could not have understood the line (11:1) "out of Egypt, I have called my son" in the same sense as Matthew. LaSor refers to the Matthean messianic interpretation as a deeper meaning or the *sensus plenior*. In the case of the four prophetic texts under consideration in this study, it is likely that the human authors were puzzled by the vagueness of the language. However, my argument is that they did not have in mind any historical fulfillment from their own times.

111. It would seem a strange and unusual phenomenon if the Qumran Covenanters could identify the Branch with a messianic interpretation but the OT prophets could not. From 1 Pet 1:10–11 it is obvious that the early church understood that some OT prophecies regarding the Messiah had no immediate historical fulfillment.

112. As Luke 1:78; Rom 15:12; and Rev 5:5 indicate. Although the word ἀνατολή in Luke 1:78 is justifiably translated as "rising sun," depending upon context, this metaphor may also be translated as "branch."

113. Although this book is not a fully focused engagement with the inspiration-inerrancy-hermeneutical debate, certain points of contact are unavoidable. See Walter A. Kaiser, "The Single Intent of Scripture," in *The Right Doctrine from the Wrong Texts?* (1994) 55, where Kaiser takes exception to the issue that Scripture contains two authors: God and the human author, and prophecy has at least two meanings: the prophet's understanding and God's surprise meaning in the distant future.

114. Given the conclusions of this study, a purely midrashic approach could find in Zech 6:12–13 an application to Luke.

plexity of the Gospels: "In the Gospels we are dealing with highly complex creations, offering several levels of interpretation."[115] Allegro's observation, if pursued, alerts us to another way of possibly understanding the thesis of this book: one of these "levels," I would argue, is the undergirding of the four prophetic texts advocated in this study."[116] It is not uncommon for scholars to refer to "levels" in sacred texts.[117] Craig Keener has acknowledged the reality that scholars have to work with layers: "Most scholars agree that the Gospel depends on several layers of tradition and reworking of sources or earlier drafts."[118] The notion of substructure implies a layer of some sort, not necessarily an editorial reworking of a previous gospel writer's autographs. A layer may indicate either a source or a redaction. My claim applies only to the source.

A follow-up question is left begging: does the claim for the first Gospel, for example, as a narrative about Jesus fulfilling the King Branch prophecy go beyond the knowledge of Matthew? Although Matthew does not specifically cite the full text of Jer 23:5–6, this study advances the case that the Gospel of Matthew does indeed fulfill the King Branch prophecy by means of a substantial number of allusions.[119] It is my

---

115. J. Allegro, *The Dead Sea Scrolls and the Christian Myth* (1984) 193. Allegro brackets this positive recognition of complexity with a long series of negative statements: "however lacking they may be in chronological consistency or unsupportable in matters of fact, historical, geographical, topographical, sociological, political, philological, or religious . . . and they often involve the kinds of unrestrained exegesis of biblical texts evidenced in the Essene scrolls. Embedded in these narratives are scraps of real history, fleeting glimpses of actual persons and events. Proper names may be reckoned the least authentic elements."

116. Origen even suggests such a possibility (*Contra Celsum* 2.6): "The prophets also do not limit the meaning of their sayings to the obvious history and to the text and letter of the law. For in one place, when about to recount supposed history, they say: ἀνοίξω ἐν παραβολαῖς τὸ στόμα μου, φθέγξομαι προβλήματα ἀπ' ἀρχῆς. While I would not espouse Origen's allegorical method of interpreting Scripture, the above statement is not off target.

117. Brevard Childs in his commentary on Isaiah (2001), for example, makes an interesting personal observation on the nature of Scripture in his comment on Isa 4:2–6 (p. 36): "Indeed, the very expansive, overlaid style of the unit is a further sign that this passage has acquired multilayered connotations when construed in the light of the larger corpus of scripture." Most recently, Urban C. von Wahlde, in *The Gospels and Letters of John* (2011), has written a prodigious 609 page introductory commentary on John, setting out to prove that there are three layers behind the fourth Gospel (1): "The Gospel in its present form is not the work of a single individual but has gone through a series of three editions at the hands of three different individuals." Without endorsing this three-edition theory, this citation does point out the probability of layers. My own investigation, however, focuses upon only one single human hand, yet guided by the divine Spirit.

118. Craig S. Keener, *The Gospel of John* (2003) 1.112. An example of a scholarly work dependent also upon layers is that of J. Louis Martyn, *History and Theology in the Fourth Gospel* (2003) 40 and 46. An exception to the premise of layers is that of literary criticism. Literary criticism rejects the notion of layers, eschews the idea of sources, and works only with the text as we have it. See R. Alan Culpepper, *Anatomy of the Fourth Gospel: A Study in Literary Design* (1983) 3: "Relying on the standard critical methods, Johannine scholars have generally approached the text looking for tensions, inconsistencies, or 'aporias' which suggest that separate strains or layers of material are present in the text." Culpepper, however, does not subscribe to this layered view of Scripture; rather, he adopts the methods of literary criticism which leave no place for what he calls "stratification" (5).

119. I note that Steve Moyise, *The Old Testament in the Book of Revelation* (1995) 20, fn. 30,

contention that when the sum total of all allusions is calculated, these tabulations will add up to a substructure of Jer 23:5–6 as a legitimate and plausible way of understanding the first Gospel. However, I have not answered the question: does the King Branch prophecy go beyond the knowledge of Matthew.

A comment upon authorial intention deserves some attention. John 11:49–51 may illuminate the point. John records in this text that Caiaphas prophesied that one man would die for the nation. John then adds: "He [Caiaphas] did not say this on his own." Without defending the historical factualness of this statement but assuming it, John's own understanding presumes that Caiaphas was not able to come up with this statement on his own. In other words, knowing an author's intention does not necessarily plumb the depths to the point of a given statement's origin. John attributes this statement to either a non-human source or a source outside of the high priest. According to John, Caiaphas did not *intend* to attribute to Jesus the notion of a sacrificial savior. Yet, John takes that statement as conveying precisely that content. As C. K. Barrett once wrote, "Caiaphas was made an unconscious vehicle of truth."[120] Therefore, prophecy cannot be tied to an author's conscious intention. The upshot of this leads me to believe that efforts to sound out the depths of a given author's intention may not be possible. Accordingly, Donald Juel raises the following objection to arguments based upon a lack of citations and allusions:

> The weakness of such arguments is that they build on silence; there is little to exercise constraints on the imagination of the interpreter. . . .Beginning with explicit citations at least provides some control over imagination. Yet such risks notwithstanding, reconstruction of christological exegesis in its earliest stages cannot rely solely on such criteria as frequency of citation. The choice of a point of departure must arise from an imaginative proposal that seeks to comprehend the tradition as a whole.[121]

Juel does not eliminate imagination; in fact, at the end he endorses the concept of an "imaginative proposal" that thinks holistically. His holistic approach expands enough to make room for the reasonable use of imagination in order to "comprehend the tradition as a whole." Thus, the mere counting up of the number of citations is not determinative for understanding the Christology of a Gospel. Yet these references may serve as a starting-point. The purpose of these starting-points is to provide a reasonable and imaginative basis "that seeks to comprehend the tradition as a whole."

Admittedly, this investigation relies upon actual citations only in subtexts. The interpretation of allusions to these prophetic subtexts as found (or not found) in the Gospels will be crucial to surmounting difficulties and establishing a convincing case for the thesis of this book. Because of the primary place of allusions, this has the

---

suggests that it is better not to try to restrict the use of the word "allusion" to conscious choice.

120. C. K. Barrett, *The Gospel According to St. John* (1965) 339.

121. D. Juel, *Messianic Exegesis* (1988) 60.

advantage of circumventing the complex manner of how later rabbinic Judaism could accept their own view of biblical contradictions while at the same time holding to a belief in divine inspiration.[122]

Another appropriate question surfaces: if these four prophetic texts had actually been written in citation form and in a promise-fulfillment/pesher format, would the presence of such texts in the four Gospels prove the thesis of this book? For some, the argument would remain that these texts were only later insertions read back into the record in order to justify a community presentation of Jesus.[123] John Meier has noted that for some scholars the presence of OT Scripture as cited in the Gospels is "a clear sign that it is a creation of the early church."[124] This was the argument, articulated for the first time by Celsus in the second century, that statements about Jesus were later fictions fabricated by the disciples and read back into the Gospels.[125] Rudolf Bultmann in modern times resurrected the Celsus claim that gospel material was only "prophecies after the fact" (*vaticinium ex eventu*).[126] More recently, A. N. Wilson has made a similar claim: Matthew "has been through the Scriptures cheerfully lifting details, and then inventing the 'facts' to fit the 'prophecies.'"[127] In other words, this skeptical claim bases its logic on a belief that the four evangelists simply created their Gospels by reading back into them OT prophecies "after the fact."[128]

This "after-the-fact" approach for assessing contents of the fourfold gospel record can take a variety of forms. For example, Bultmann assigns Peter's confession of Jesus as the Christ to a creation of the evangelist Matthew. In other words, this confession never happened on the coasts of Caesarea Philippi. It is only a fictitious projection back into the past to enliven the narrative. Craig Evans does a similar thing by rewriting

---

122. On the issue of the Jewish interpretation of Scripture, see Fredrick C. Holmgren, *The Old Testament and the Significance of Jesus* (1999) 27: "The New Testament understanding of the Old Testament is similar to that of the rabbis in that both present a non-literal, 'creative' interpretation of scripture." See also Klyne Snodgrass, "The Use of the Old Testament in the New," in *The Right Doctrine from the Wrong Texts?* (1994) 43.

123. See, for example, J. H. Charlesworth, *Jesus within Judaism* (1988) 153: "Can one be relatively certain that the passages brought forward from the New Testament are not the creations of the disciples' proclamations after Easter?" A rather noteworthy and legitimate attempt to understand how to correctly read "backwards" is that of Richard B. Hays, *Reading Backwards: Figural Christology and the Fourfold Gospel Witness* (2014), and his more recent, *Echoes of Scripture in the Gospels* (2016). In neither case, however, does Hays pursue the interpretative approach as laid out in this present investigation.

124. John Meier, "The Debate on the Resurrection of the Dead: An Incident from the Ministry of the Historical Jesus?" *JSNT* 77.1 (2000) 3.

125. Origen, *Contra Celsum* 2.13, 26.

126. R. Bultmann, *The History of the Synoptic Tradition* (1963) 24.

127. A. N. Wilson, *Jesus, A Life* (1992) 62.

128. See also Richard A. Burridge and Graham Gould, *Jesus Now and Then* (2004) 196: "For example, we know that some of the Gospel statements that Jesus fulfilled prophecy—and the events in his life that are alleged to have done so—were probably created in the light of the belief that he was the Messiah, and cannot be used as evidence to support the belief."

the narrative of Mark. Evans sees Jesus actually being blindsided by the rejection of the High Priest. Most recently, I cite another author articulating a similar claim. James D. Tabor writes: "I know of no responsible scholar who denies the historicity of the Roman crucifixion of Jesus, even though one might conceivably argue that it arose as a post-mortem creation of loyal followers based on their reading backwards from Zech. 12.10."[129] Finally, Matthew Neujahr has assembled a number of ancient Mediterranean texts with the goal of demonstrating an entire genre of using *vaticinium ex eventu* as a literary technique for taking past historical phenomena and creating an alleged prediction of future events.[130]

In keeping with current scholarly tendencies to read messianic statements as retrojected views of the church placed in the mouth of Jesus or as statements alleging the fulfillment of events about Jesus, Geza Vermes, an apt representative of such perspectives (while commenting upon the question of whose Son is the Christ, Matt 22:44), says:

> We are faced here with a kind of quibbling biblical exegesis. If Jesus actually indulged in this sort of hair-splitting, its only possible aim would have been to embarrass the other party. It is more likely, however, that such an exegetical argument did not originate with him, but is evidence of subsequent Judaeo-Christian polemic.[131]

In order to make Jesus' reply a *later* creation of the church ("subsequent Judaeo-Christian polemic"), Vermes must label it "quibbling biblical exegesis" (if actually said by Jesus). But Vermes's suggestion makes the church more creative than its Founder, misses the import of the argument, and dilutes the significance of the actual statement. As Amy-Jill Levine rightfully maintains, it is exceedingly difficult to establish that Jesus did *not*, in fact, say certain things.[132]

In order to respond to this "after-the-fact" claim, I rest my case upon the contention that some degree of silence actually facilitates this investigation. By this logic, the

---

129. James D. Tabor, "Are You the One? The Textual Dynamics of Messianic Self-Identity," in *Knowing the End from the Beginning: The Prophetic, the Apocalyptic and their Relationships* (2003) 188.

130. Matthew Neujahr, *Predicting the Past in the Ancient Near East: Mantic Historiography in Ancient Mesopotamia, Judah, and the Mediterranean World* (2012).

131. G. Vermes, *The Authentic Gospel of Jesus* (2004) 62–63. Later in his book (189), Vermes returns to the same point, with slightly different language: "It goes without saying that the evangelist (impersonating Jesus) takes it for granted that David was a prophet, the ancestor of the Messiah and the author of the Psalm. The final question—how can someone called by David his Lord be his son?—is rhetorical. It is not intended to produce an answer but rather to confuse the Pharisees. Biblical exegesis and anti-Pharisee argument of this kind are more likely to express the mentality of a Christian 'scribe' of the Palestinian church than the thinking of Jesus."

132. A. Levine, "Introduction," in *The Historical Jesus in Context* (2006) 3: "The positivistic side regards the Gospel accounts as accurate or at least relatively accurate reports, and the burden of proof is placed on those who would claim something attributed to Jesus was not historical (although the demand to 'prove a negative' creates a logical fallacy: it is impossible, in most cases, to prove that Jesus did *not* say or do something the Gospels attribute to him)."

gospel writers cannot be accused of taking the four prophetic texts and explaining them after the fact. It is clear that they do not consciously and overtly undertake to capitalize on this fourfold prophetic identification. Furthermore, it is the thesis of this book that the ultimate source of the four Gospels is not the individual minds of Matthew, Mark, Luke, and John. The narrative art of Matthew or the literary skills of John will not be decisive in understanding the fourfold Gospel. The ultimate source, I will argue, belongs to the Spirit of God, not to the artistic achievement of human authors.

I want to pursue the Celsus objection one step further. Celsus claims that authors were simply projecting back into the NT the fulfillment of OT prophecies after the fact. In other words, NT authors were reading back into OT texts simply what they wanted to interpret. To this I offer the following counterproposal: the internal logic of the biblical canon (and Jesus himself) is that *everything* in the prophets concerning Jesus had to be fulfilled. The following line of evidence is hereby submitted. The NT interpretive key for understanding OT texts can be summarized and paraphrased from 2 Cor 1:22: *all* the promises of God find their fulfillment in Christ.[133] Pursuing this claim for completeness further, the Greek text of Luke 24:25–28 has a triple emphasis: *everything* (ἐπὶ πᾶσιν) that *all* the prophets spoke (ἀπὸ πάντων τῶν προφητῶν) in *all* the Scriptures (ἐν πάσαις ταῖς γραφαῖς) regarding himself (τὰ περὶ ἑαυτοῦ) must be fulfilled. What are some possible conclusions from this Lukan text? I mention six: 1) these four Branches are part of the overall claim of Scripture that everything about Jesus must be fulfilled; therefore, it is incumbent upon Scripture to show this fulfillment in some way. 2) Jesus taught his disciples about the four Branches as applying to him, but they did not record this just as they did not record the fulfillment of other prophecies. 3) These four Branches do apply to Jesus; but Jesus did not mention this to his disciples because these Branches had no real relevance in explaining his mission to them. 4) Jesus did not mention the four Branches because they did not apply to him. 5) Jesus was not aware of the four Branches as applying to him and, consequently, he remained silent regarding their value. 6) The text of Luke 24:25–28 was never spoken by Jesus at all; it is a fictitious saying falsely attributed to Jesus. Of these six options, the first and second leave open the possibility that the four prophecies are not only fulfilled in the person of Jesus Christ but these also undergird the four Gospels. I

---

133. For the argument that the NT cannot be used to properly interpret the OT, see Rolf Rendtorff, "A Christian Approach to the Theology of Hebrew Scriptures," in *Jews, Christians, and the Theology of the Hebrew Scriptures* (2000) 149: "Here things must be clearly separated. The pattern of promise and fulfillment in this field can only be a Christian one, which goes beyond the exegesis of the Hebrew Scriptures." Rendtorff does not acknowledge the exegetical role of the targums or the Dead Sea Scrolls as evidence of Jewish exegesis of an expected Messiah. See also Bultmann's, "Prophecy and Fulfillment," (1960) 52–53, who, likewise, denies that the NT can be used to interpret the OT. For the opposite case, see Walter Brueggemann, *Theology of the Old Testament* (1997) 620: "It is Christian interpretive work to claim the promise for Jesus. It is, moreover, Christian work to claim the promise exclusively—to eliminate all other claimants to this role, which may have many occupants, and to attach it singularly and exclusively to Jesus . . . . But then, that is the nature of this material from the Old Testament: It invites such daring reuse."

would now like to take this one step further: I am going to adopt the *first* option as the most viable and most preferred. The self-imposed unbreakable logic and the obligatory nature of Scripture require that these four Branches find fulfillment in Jesus in some way. Consequently, they must be fulfilled in either the first coming of Jesus or the second. If the first coming, there should be some definable way for discerning this compliance. The integrity of Scripture is at stake; there is no other option available from a canonical point of view. This is the consistent position maintained by Jesus himself: Scripture "cannot be broken" (John 10:35) and *everything* must be fulfilled or accomplished (Matt 5:18).[134]

There are significant implications to the four prophetic texts of this investigation. Questions remain: were they ever fulfilled; is it important that they are or were fulfilled; what plausible reasons can we offer that they were fulfilled? I will now argue, Gospel by Gospel, that these four Branches are best fulfilled in Matthew, Mark, Luke, and John and that the best explanation as to why we have these four Gospels is to be found in the four prophetic texts of Jer 23:5–6; Zech 3:6, 6:12–13;[135] and Isa 4:2.

---

134. David E. Garland, *Luke* (2011) 974, charts a number of events in the life of Jesus pointing to a divine "must" or a "divine necessity" by which these events call for fulfillment. While Garland focuses upon the necessity of such fulfillment, I focus upon the all-encompassing nature of Scripture with its emphasis upon "all" or "everything" (πάντα) as needing fulfillment. Walter Kasier, "The Single Intent of Scripture," in *The Right Doctrine from the Wrong Texts? Essays on the Use of the Old Testament in the New* (1994) 55–69, makes the case that Scripture has only one meaning. Assuming that is indeed the case, could not, for example, the Gospel of Luke be the "single" meaning of fulfillment for understanding Luke's narrative of Jesus?

135. An enticing question arises: would the prophet Zechariah, upon reading the third Gospel, find a resonating fulfillment of 6:12–13 in Luke's account? I see no compelling reason why not.

4

The Gospel of Matthew: The King Branch

THE SINGULAR PICTURE OF the King Branch as a possible background for the Gospel of Matthew has not been raised.¹ Although the study of the Branch in both the OT and the DSS has acquired the attention of scholars in the last few years, no work has been done tying together Old Testament Branch passages and the Gospels. Such a connection is still lacking. In particular, a specific association is lacking between the King Branch and the Gospel of Matthew. It is the purpose of this chapter to offer a plausible case for making such a linkage. Also, it is the burden of this chapter to produce evidence that the details of Jer 23:5–6 serve as the substructure to Matthew by adequately supporting the weight of the first Gospel's superstructure in a distinctive way. Tangentially, this chapter will attempt to demonstrate that the text of Jer 23:5–6 not only undergirds the foundation of the Gospel of Matthew but that it, consequently, does not serve as a substructure for any of the other three Gospels. We turn now to explore the plausibility of such a unique substructure and the specific OT prophetic metaphor of a King Branch and its relationship to the Gospel of Matthew. I begin with an English and Greek (LXX) translation of Jer 23:5–6.

> MT: הנה ימים באים נאם־יהוה והקמתי לדוד צמח צדיק ומלך מלך והשכיל ועשׂה משפט וצדקה בארץ: בימיו תושׁע יהודה וישׂראל ישׁכן לבטח וזה־שׁמו אשר־יקראו יהוה צדקנו:

> LXX: Ἰδοὺ ἡμέραι ἔρχονται, λέγει κύριος, καὶ ἀναστήσω τῷ Δαυιδ ἀνατολὴν δικαίαν, καὶ βασιλεύσει βασιλεὺς καὶ συνήσει καὶ ποιήσει κρίμα καὶ δικαιοσύνην ἐπὶ τῆς γῆς. ἐν ταῖς ἡμέραις αὐτοῦ σωθήσεται Ιουδας, καὶ Ισαηλ κατασκηνώσει πεποιθώς, καὶ τοῦτο τὸ ὄνομα αὐτοῦ, ὃ καλέσει αὐτοῦ κύριος Ιωσεδεκ.

---

1. Jack Dean Kingsbury's collection of essays in *Gospel Interpretation: Narrative-Critical & Social-Scientific Approaches* (1997) bases this work on the fourfold canon but the index omits any reference to the King Branch. I note Craig A. Evan's passing comment from his chapter, "The Recently Published Dead Sea Scrolls and the Historical Jesus," in *Studying the Historical Jesus* (1994) 549, where he identifies the "branch of David" with Jer 23:5. However, no commentary is given and no connection is made with Matthew's presentation of Jesus. See also Frederick W. Danker, "Matthew: A Patriot's Gospel," in *The Gospels and the Scriptures of Israel* (1994) 98: "It is quite probable that a passage such as Jer 23.1–6 specifically inspired some of Matthew's interest in critique of Israel's spiritual leadership." Danker pursues this suggestion no further than to say simply, "It is quite probable that . . ."

NIV: "The days are coming," declares the LORD, "when I will raise up to David a righteous Branch, a King who will reign wisely and do what is just and right in the land. In his days Judah will be saved and Israel will live in safety. This is the name by which he will be called: the LORD our Righteousness."

Elements of vital interest from the text of Jer 23:5–6 may be briefly noted; there are ten rubrics in all: 1) a formulaic exclamatory opening ["Behold," הנה, or Ἰδού]; 2) YHWH is speaking ["declares the LORD": יהוה, or κύριος]; 3) a reference to an indefinite future ["the days are coming," LXX: ἡμέραι ἔρχονται]; 4) a specific reference to the time when [LXX: ἐν ταῖς ἡμέραις αὐτοῦ]; 5) a reference to the plant metaphor "Branch" [צמח/*Zemah*, LXX: ἀνατολή/*anatolē*]; 6) the mention of King David; 7) the Branch as righteous [δικαίαν], lawful, or perhaps legitimate to rule, which will include the very puzzling and obscure reference to a cryptic Ιωσεδεκ; 8) a king who will reign wisely [βασιλεύσει βασιλεὺς καὶ συνήσει καὶ ποιήσει κρίμα καὶ δικαιοσύνην ἐπὶ τῆς γῆς]; 9) a reference to salvation, "Judah will be saved" [σωθήσεται Ιουδας]; 10) finally, a reference to the role or impact on the land [ἐπὶ τῆς γῆς . . . καὶ Ισαηλ]. Of significance to this investigation is the fact that all ten of these prophetic rubrics are found in the Gospel of Matthew in either clear statements or shadow-like allusional references. We examine now the particulars of Jer 23:5–6.

The Formulaic Exclamation: "Behold"

MT: הנה, LXX: ἰδού, ESV: "Behold!"

At this point, I will break down the opening line into smaller units in order to focus on the single word "Behold" (הנה/*hinneh*). While the ESV includes the exclamation, the NIV omits this attention-getting particle of exclamatory interjection. A check with three different NIV editions (1988, 2005, and 2011) reveals a consistent omission in both Jeremiah and Matthew. Regarding the Greek text of Matthew, the NIV leaves untranslated all sixty-one references to ἰδού. This is a rather glaring deletion, considering such passages as Matt 2:13 ("Behold, an angel of the LORD appeared to Joseph") which omit this exclamation. John Nolland in his commentary on Matthew likewise declines to translate this Greek particle.[2] The LXX, however, preserves ἰδού in Jeremiah. Is it worth the effort to defend its preservation in a modern translation? Or, is this a case of literary hardscrabble—much ado about nothing? In my judgment, it is a mistake not to insist upon its value to the reader; the reasons for maintaining it in translation outweigh the aesthetic logic of dropping it. הנה/*hinneh* ("Behold!") by itself is used some forty-five times in Jeremiah in a variety of ways, the principal usage being directed to a listener to pay careful attention. The particle הנה/*hinneh* in the OT

---

2. J. Nolland, *The Gospel of Matthew: A Commentary on the Greek Text* (2005) xx: "An example of the impact of this policy on the translation is my decision to leave untranslated most of Matthew's uses of ἰδού."

can also point to a truth, either "newly asserted or newly recognized."[3] Additionally, this interjection can allow or invite the reader "to enter into the surprise or satisfaction of the speaker or actor concerned."[4]

What is the significance of this exclamatory term and what is the value of preserving it in translation? Of the four key prophetic texts involved in this investigation three of them employ such an interjection: the texts of Jer 23:5–6, Zech 3:8, and Zech 6:12.[5] When we turn to the Gospels, the influential presence of ἰδού (or the alternate ἴδε) in all four Gospels is striking.[6] This is especially the case with the first Gospel. Of the sixty-one references in Matthew, approximately thirty-one of these may be construed as Matthean points of emphasis. The numerical merit of this mention is that it may, if only in a minor introductory way, facilitate situating Jer 23:5–6 into the substructure of Matthew. Likewise, if only by means of anticipation at this point, this exclamation in both Zech 3:8 and 6:12 may also serve as subtexts for Mark and Luke. These emphases function in order to call attention to either a result owing to a supernatural cause or something of a surprising or extraordinary nature.[7] The translation of "Behold!" is somewhat archaic, although I have retained it in translation. A more dynamic and contemporary equivalent would be: "Wow!" "Look!" or "See!" Of the relevant thirty-one references in Matthew (out of sixty-one), a further point of emphasis may be noted in that they all contain ideas or suggestions that Jesus is a king.[8] The best example is found at 21:5 where Matthew says: "Behold, your king is coming" (ἰδοὺ ὁ βασιλεύς σου ἔρχεται).[9]

3. William Gesenius, "הנה," *A Hebrew and English Lexicon of the Old Testament* (1975) 244.

4. Ibid., 244.

5. Jeremiah uses הנה apart from the entire formulaic expression a total of forty-five times by itself.

6. Matt (61), Luke (55).

7. I assign the following texts to either a supernatural cause or an extraordinary result: 1:20, 23; 2:9, 13,19; 3:16,17; 4:11; 8:2, 24, 32, 34; 9:18; 12:41, 42; 15:22; 17:3, 5; 21:5; 27:51; 28:2, 9, 20.

8. Six references occur in Matt 1–2: an angel of the LORD appearing to Joseph (1:20), the announcement of Mary's virgin birth (1:23), the arrival in Jerusalem of magi from the East to worship the newborn king (2:12), the description of the star (2:9), a second appearance of an angel to Joseph (2:13), and another appearance of an angel to Joseph (2:23). All references point to either supernatural or extraordinary events. All references call special attention to the identity of Jesus as an eventual king. Benedict T. Viviano, "The Genres of Matthew 1–2: Light from 1 Timothy 1.4," *RB* 97.1 (1990) 32, notes these six references in Matt 1–2, but then proceeds to a modern scholarly conclusion: "It is rather disconcerting to the historically-minded reader that an evangelist who otherwise shows a sober historical interest ... should here seem to deviate so markedly from historical plausibility." Viviano concludes that Matt 1–2 falls into the category of myth and that the text of 1 Tim 1:4 labels the Matthean genealogy as "mythopoetic" (52).

9. MT of Zech 9:9: הנה מלכך יבוא לך צדיק ונושע; LXX: ἰδοὺ ὁ βασιλεύς σου ἔρχεταί σοι, δίκαιος καὶ σῴζων αὐτός. Matthew has clearly omitted "righteous and saving/victorious." In view of Matthean emphasis upon the qualities of a king who is both righteous and victorious, what can account for this obvious omission? For possible solutions, see Robert A. Gundry, *Matthew: A Commentary on His Literary and Theological Art* (1982) 408, who simply says that Matthew's omission of these two words is "surprising in view of his fondness for δίκαιος and σῴζω." Since he emphasizes these characteristics elsewhere, how do we account for this omission? Several options present themselves: First, Matthew

Statistics may be suggestive. A comparison with the Gospel of Mark hints at possibilities. Although the second Gospel uses ἰδού (or its alternate, such as ἴδε) a total of sixteen times, it never does so in a manner recognizing Jesus as a king. Matthew offers a distinct contrast to Mark. The majority of uses of the particle ἰδού in Matthew serve to call attention to Jesus as a king. One other observation may be made: in the first two chapters of Matthew, the interjection ἰδού is mentioned six times.[10] All six references point to an event of unusual circumstances and all six connect in some way in order to identify Jesus as a coming king.

The remaining references in Matthew contain phrases of an imperatival nature directed toward someone in the text itself. For example, at 10:16 Jesus tells his disciples: "Behold, I am sending you out as sheep" (ἰδοὺ ἐγὼ ἀποστέλλω ὑμᾶς ὡς πρόβατα), or 7:4 where Jesus tells the crowd to "behold"/"look at" the beam that is in their own eye. The meaning of these imperatival texts is a translation expressing the idea of "Look!" or "Consider!" or "See!" The critical point to be made is that Matthew dominates in references to Jesus as King.

The Speaker: The LORD

MT: נְאֻם־יְהוָה; LXX: λέγει κύριος; NIV: "declares the LORD"

Matthew pays the highest respect to Old Testament Scripture by honoring it as the Word of the LORD. In the first two chapters there are five OT prophetic references. In two of these (1:22 and 2:15) Matthew adds specifically that these citations were spoken by the LORD (ἵνα πληρωθῇ τὸ ῥηθὲν ὑπὸ κυρίου διὰ τοῦ προφήτου λέγοντος).[11] Of course, there is no specific citation in Matthew from Jer 23:5–6. However, there is the recognition and acknowledgment by Matthew of how he understands the nature of Scripture. He clearly understands the OT texts to be fulfilled in the person of Jesus. Yet, at this point, there is no way of knowing if these two passages would actually

---

has used a different *Vorlage* (or text form) than either the MT or the LXX. Second, Matthew deliberately omits these two identification markers as if not to call attention to these two elements of the king. The motive in this case would be to call attention to the meekness of Jesus. Third, Matthew has accidentally left out these words due to a "lapse in memory" (suggested as a possibility by W. D. Davies and Dale C. Allison, *Matthew: A Shorter Commentary*, [2004] 345). Fourth, Matthew, in the final analysis, has no real interest in presenting Jesus as a righteous and saving king; thus, this omission tells against the particular argument of this chapter and the overall thesis of this investigation. Fifth, by means of omission, this figure of speech actually ends up calling greater attention to δίκαιος and σῴζω as properties integral to a divine king.

10. Matt 1:20, 23; 2:1, 9, 13, 19.

11. τὸ ῥηθὲν ὑπὸ κυρίου διὰ τοῦ προφήτου λέγοντος may be translated in one of two ways: "the word spoken by the LORD who said through the prophet," or "the word of the LORD which was spoken through the prophet who said." The potential confusion is caused by both nouns being a genitive linked to λέγοντος, also a genitive. It is best, however, to allow λέγοντος to attract to the nearest noun, in this case τοῦ προφήτου. Either way, though, the origin of the word is attributed to the LORD; the prophet is not the origin but the instrument.

evoke a mental association with the Branch. A further note may be mentioned with profit. These two statements mark a distinction between Matthew's use of the OT as contrasted with Qumran. The Qumran interpreters never use fulfillment formulae.[12] Furthermore, the prophetic statement contains the affirmation that it is YHWH who is speaking and it is YHWH who will initiate the action that will bring forth the Branch.

The Vision of an Indefinite Future

> MT: הנה ימים באים; LXX: ἰδοὺ ἡμέραι ἔρχονται; NIV: "Behold! Days are coming," ESV: "Behold, the days are coming."

This formulaic expression is used a total of fourteen times in Jeremiah.[13] Of these fourteen, only two may arguably qualify as belonging to an indefinite future: 23:5 and 31:31–34 (the promise of a new covenant). The language of this opening formulaic expression is vague, suggesting an undefined period of time. Its very opaqueness has prevented scholars from reaching agreement whether Jeremiah has a contemporary historical person in mind or a mysterious future figure. However, arguments for the fulfillment of this promise as coming true in a historical figure belonging to Jeremiah's time have not fared well.[14] The interpretative path I will follow leads to a period yet-to-come as there are seven verbs stated in the future. The seven are: "and I will set up" (והקמתי), "and will reign" (ומלך), "and act wisely" (והשכיל), "and will do" (ועשה), "will be saved" (תושע), "will dwell" (ישכן), and "will be called" (קראו). These verbs bolster the case that this prophetic text is not declaring an immediate fulfillment in the days simultaneous to those of Jeremiah.[15]

A Specific Reference to His Days

> MT: בימיו; LXX: ἐν ταῖς ἡμέραις αὐτοῦ; NIV: "in his days," ESV: "in his days."

---

12. C. M. Tuckett, "Micah 5.13 in Qumran and in the New Testament and Messianism in the Septuagint," in *Messianism and the Septuagint* (2004) 89.

13. Jer 7:32; 9:15, 25; 16:14; 17:6; 23:5; 31:27, 31, 38; 33:14; 48:12; 49:2; 51:47; 51:52.

14. For a discussion of this issue, see William McKane, *A Critical and Exegetical Commentary on Jeremiah* (1986) 559–65. McKane argues that the current Davidic monarchy was in danger of imminent historical collapse. For the view that an OT prophet must have some historical fulfillment in the prophet's own times as well as an extended application ("historical antecedents as well as the realities yet to come"), see Walter C. Kaiser, "The Promise to David in Psalm 16 and its Application in Acts 2.25–33 and 13.32–37," *JETS* 23.3 (1980) 222.

15. J. A. Thompson, *The Book of Jeremiah* (1980) 489, observes: "The expression *days are coming* is very general and has no particular time reference." John L. McKenzie, "Royal Messianism," *CBQ* 19.1 (1957) 25–52, states (44): "The passage in Jer 23 is more probably eschatological than any passage we have hitherto considered; the introductory formula, 'Behold, the days are coming,' suggests the eschatological future." For an opposite view that the language implies the future but not necessarily an eschatological end, see Werner Dommershausen, "Der 'Spross' als Messias-Vorstellung bei Jeremia und Sacharja," *TQ* 148 (1968) 321–41.

The Synoptics present a different situation. All three provide striking language making use of some form of expression containing a reference to "days." The Gospel of John is an exception which will be treated later. Matthew 3:1, a text which occupies a pivotal position, is indicative of such an allusion: "*in those days* John the Baptist came preaching in the desert of Judea" (ἐν δὲ ταῖς ἡμέραις ἐκείναις παραγίνεται Ἰωάννης ὁ βαπτιστὴς ἐν τῇ ἐρήμῳ τῆς Ἰουδαίας). But to what period of time do the three words ταῖς ἡμέραις ἐκείναις ("in those days") in Matt 3:1 refer? First of all, these words serve as a contrast to the earlier statement at 2:1: "in the days of King Herod" (ἐν ἡμέραις Ἡρῴδου τοῦ βασιλέως). Matthew has now moved temporally away from Herod to a focused attention upon Christ. Herod has passed away; Jesus is about to begin his public ministry. Of greater importance, however, is the opening statement at 3:1: "in those days" (ἐν δὲ ταῖς ἡμέραις ἐκείναις) which is very close to the wording in the LXX of Jer 23:5–6: ἐν ταῖς ἡμέραις αὐτοῦ ("in the days of him").[16] This is not to suggest that Matthew is copying directly from the LXX; my observation is intended to point only in the direction that similar language is indicative of corresponding ideas. The demonstrative pronoun "those" (ἐκείναις) points not to the days of Herod but to those of Jesus. Matthew states that John the Baptist appeared in "those" days.

John Nolland acknowledges that this shadowy reference could point "to the times in which the revelation of the kingdom of God takes place."[17] Indeed, the texts of the MT, the LXX, the Tanakh,[18] and the Targum,[19] all agree that it is not just "in those days," but the time is further defined and circumscribed as belonging to "in *his* days"—the days of the Branch, thus imposing upon the prophecy a limitation which confines the very time to the days of the Branch and none other. The Hebrew text is emphatic: "the days are coming . . . in *his* days" (ימים באים . . . בימיו).[20] Judging from

---

16. Although this study is most certainly not a defense of the LXX, the LXX does offer some helpful guidelines for the interpreter. I suggest three: 1) the LXX offers insight into translating Hebrew into Greek; 2) the LXX provides evidence of a kind showing the development or non-development of messianic thought from pre/post-Exilic Judaism down to the time of translation; 3) the LXX reveals how its text has potentially influenced the NT.

17. J. Nolland, *The Gospel of Matthew* (2005) 135.

18. The Tanakh: "See, a time is coming"—declares the LORD—"when I will raise up a true branch of David's line. He shall reign as king and shall prosper, and he shall do what is just and right in the land. In *his* days Judah shall be delivered and Israel shall dwell secure. And this is the name by which he shall be called: 'The LORD is our Vindicator.'"

19. *The Targum of Jeremiah: Translated, with a Critical Introduction, Apparatus, and Notes* (1987) 111, translated by Michael Maher, who translates Jer 23:5–6: "Behold the days are coming, says the Lord, when I shall raise up for David an Anointed One of righteousness, and he shall reign as king and prosper, and he shall perform true justice and righteousness in the land. In *his* days those of the house of Judah shall be redeemed, and Israel shall dwell safely, and this is his name which they shall call him: Righteous deeds shall be done for us before the Lord in his days." See also Merrill P. Miller, "Targum, Midrash and the Use of the Old Testament in the New Testament," *JSJ* 2 (1971) 31–36. See also Craig A. Evans, *Word and Glory: On the Exegetical and Theological Background of John's Prologue* (1993) 31, where he acknowledges that the Targum on Jer 23:5 interprets the passage in a messianic sense.

20. For a most intriguing observation, see Gerhard von Rad, "βασιλεύς," *TDNT* (1964) 1.566–67: "A sharp distinction is to be made between even the most extravagant of the courtly language of

the Psalm of Solomon, a document likely composed for the most part in the period prior to the NT,[21] the expression "in his days" was a watchword for the coming Messiah.[22] Furthermore, in Matt 2:6 there is a double reference to Judah; this, in turn, is reinforced by the LXX of Jer 23:5 and its mention of Judah who will be saved "in the days of *him*" (ἐν ταῖς ἡμέραις αὐτοῦ σωθήσεται Ἰουδας). It may not be an unreasonable contention that Matthew's reference to "in those days" would be a sufficient mnemonic phrase to evoke valid associations with the "in his days" of Jer 23:6.[23]

Notable also is the following comment by Shemaryahu Talmon; he observes the failed and unfulfilled expectations at Qumran: "The Teacher was born out of intense emotional stress, triggered by the profound disappointment that the unrealized hope for an imminent onset of the millennium had evoked in the initial nucleus of Covenanters when the pre-calculated date passed uneventfully."[24] In other words, what the record at Qumran shows as a failed disappointment within that community, the NT reveals as a fulfilled expectation. A justifiable conclusion may be in order at this point: from the perspective of the OT prophet, the expression "in his days" points to a future date; from the perspective of the Qumran community, this intriguing reference indicates that the time had not yet come; from the perspective of Matthew and the NT, the time has now been fulfilled and it has been fulfilled in the person of Jesus.

Israel and faith in the Messiah . . . . The whole complex of religious and political ideas linked with the empirical king; what was expected of him; how he was addressed; what wonderful deeds were ascribed to him—all these form the soil for Messianic belief. The connection is natural, for the expected king was of the house of David. Yet it is still a question how the eschatological element came into the simple language of court. Thus far there has been no satisfactory explanation for the rise in Israel of this mysterious eschatology, no comparable expectation of a Deliverer King at the end of the age, in Babylon or Egypt, the classical lands of courtly address."

21. See *The Old Testament Pseudepigrapha* (1985) 2.641.

22. Psalm of Solomon 17:32: καὶ αὐτὸς βασιλεὺς δίκαιος διδακτὸς ὑπὸ θεοῦ ἐπ' αὐτούς, καὶ οὐκ ἔστιν ἀδικία ἐν ταῖς ἡμέραις αὐτοῦ ἐν μέσω αὐτῶν, ὅτι πάντες ἅγιοι, καὶ βασιλεὺς αὐτῶν χριστὸς κυρίου. See also 18:1-7 which is perhaps more emphatic about a future Messiah called the "LORD's Christ/Messiah" (τοῦ χριστοῦ κυρίου), who is further designated as "the one and only firstborn son" (υἱὸν πρωτότοκον μονογενῆ) and "God will raise up this Christ, and all who live 'in those days' (ἐν ταῖς ἡμέραις ἐκείναις) will be blessed." The significance of this text is that it shows at least some in pre-first century Judaism expected a messiah to come at a time specifically designated by the expression "in his days." It is clear, however, that from the perspective of the writer that "those days" had not yet arrived. See also Walter Brueggemann, *Theology of the Old Testament* (1997) 616-17: "Interpreters are at a loss to know why this promise, now removed from political reality and carried only in Israel's liturgical, visionary, ideological hopes, continued to have shaping power for the life and imagination of Israel; but unarguably it did."

23. Gerard Mussies, "'In Those Days': Some Remarks on the use of 'Days' in Matthew 2:1; 3:1, and Luke 2:1," in *Early Christianity and Classical Culture* (2003) 89-101, is silent regarding a possible connection with the prophetic text of Jer 23:5.

24. Shemaryahu Talmon, *The World of Qumran from Within* (1989) 284.

The LORD Will Set Up a Davidic King Branch

MT: והקמתי לדוד צמח צדיק ומלך מלך; LXX: καὶ ἀναστήσω τῷ Δαυιδ ἀνατολὴν δικαίαν . . . βασιλεύς; "NIV: "when I will raise up to David a righteous Branch, a King."

The promise in Jer 23:5–6 is that YHWH himself will establish a king for David, a righteous Branch. I am calling this metaphor the *King Branch*. The Hebrew word מלך (*melek*) leaves no doubt that the text describes a king.[25] The Matthean presentation of Jesus as a king has been long recognized in scholarly studies on this Gospel.[26] Of course, this scholarly observation does not establish a clear cut connection between Jeremiah and Matthew, but it does add some momentum to the cause of making such an association.

To substantiate and solidify the concept of a kingship link between Jer 23:5–6 and Matthew's account of Jesus, I now investigate the following key words that describe this role: "Son of David,"[27] "king" (βασιλεύς),[28] "kingdom" (βασιλεία),[29] "to rule" or

---

25. As 1 Sam 8:5 shows.

26. For an overall view of Jesus as king, see Alan Hugh M'Neile, *The Gospel According to St Matthew* (1961) xvii: "The four portraits are those of the same Person, but in each is seen a dominant aspect . . . . But the special impression which S. Matthew embodies is that of royalty: Jesus is the Messiah." Unfortunately, M'Neile did not comment upon what he thought the other three portraits embody. See also William Barclay, *Introduction to the First Three Gospels* (1975) 171: "When we are looking for one final characteristic of Matthew's gospel, a characteristic which will in some sense contain and sum up all the others, it may well be that we will find Tasker right when he claims that Matthew is supremely *the royal gospel* . . . . Even in the closing scenes, rather, especially in the closing scenes, Jesus moves through his trial, his humiliation, his crucifixion like a king." The reference to Tasker is R. V. G. Tasker, *Matthew* (1961) 19. More recently, see the discussion in Justin J. Meggitt, "The Madness of King Jesus: Why was Jesus Put to Death, but his Followers were not?" *JSNT* 29.4 (2007) 379–413; and Joel Marcus, "Meggitt on the Madness and Kingship of Jesus," *JSNT* 29.4 (2007) 421–24. See also Donald Verseput, *The Rejection of the Humble Messianic King: A Study of the Composition of Matthew 11–12* (1986) 304: "It is immediately clear upon reading the First Gospel that the kingly theme is important to the Matthean christology. From the very beginning, the representation of Jesus is peculiarly marked by a royal element."

27. The number of references to Son of David in the Gospels is: Matt (9); Mark (3); Luke (3); John (0).

28. βασιλεύς: Matt (22); Mark (12); Luke (10); John (15). Matthew dominates any of the other three Gospels by a wide margin.

29. βασιλεία: Matt (56); Mark (18); Luke (45); John (4). Matthew nearly equals the sum total of the combined other three Gospels (56/67); yet the total from Luke is also significant. Robert H. Stein, "The Matthew-Luke Agreements Against Mark: Insight from John," *CBQ* 54 (1992) 490–91, calls attention to the fact that in Mark 11:9, Luke 19:38, and John 12:13 in the so-called triumphal entry, "Jesus is referred as 'King' in Luke and John and, in Mark, there is a reference to the coming of the '*King*dom of our Father David.' There is no mention of 'King' or 'Kingdom,' however, in Matthew." Stein may be overstating his case. As noted above, at 21:5 Matthew says: ἰδοὺ ὁ βασιλεύς σου ἔρχεται ("Behold, your king is coming to you").

"to reign" (βασιλεύω),³⁰ "authority" (ἐξουσία),³¹ "it is permitted" (ἔξεστιν),³² "throne" (θρόνος),³³ "judgment" (κρίσις),³⁴ "recompense" (μισθός),³⁵ "law" (νόμος),³⁶ "Christ/Messiah" or "Anointed" (Χριστός),³⁷ and "LORD" (κύριος).³⁸ This unique cluster of terms is of cardinal importance. What, then, is the numerical significance of these tabulations and how does it influence this study? All of these terms, like smaller tribu-

30. βασιλεύω: this verb is not used in Matthew. Luke, however, uses it twice. This is an isolated verbal instance which demonstrates overlapping from one Gospel to another.

31. ἐξουσία: Matt (9); Mark (9); Luke (15); John (6). Luke outnumbers any of the other three. Matthew and Mark tie for second. For a different approach detailing the supremacy in Matthew to the issue of "authority," see Simon Gathercole, *The Pre-existent Son* (2006) 245: "Immediately striking is the sheer extent of Jesus' authority in Matthew's Gospel. This is no surprise, as Matthew has thematized the fact that the Father has handed over *all* things to the Son (Matt. 11.27). At various points it is said that Jesus heals *all* the ailments of *all* who came to him (4.23-24; 9.35); he even raises a girl from the dead (9.18-26)." Gathercole's intention (p. 17) is to examine the Synoptic Gospels "in the sense that it is an analysis of the Gospels as they stand."

32. ἔξεστιν: Matt (10); Mark (6); Luke (5); John (2). Matthew nearly equals the sum total of the other three.

33. θρόνος: Matt (4); Mark (0); Luke (3); John (0). Matthew exceeds the sum total of the other three.

34. κρίσις: Matt (12); Mark (0); Luke (4); John (11). Matthew exceeds each of the other three and comes close to equaling their total count. For a contrast between what is innocent or lawful/unlawful as pitted against understanding the real function of mercy and what is truly righteous, see Matt 12:18-42. Notice the word "righteous" and "justice" (κρίσις). Gerhard Barth, "Matthew's Understanding of the Law," in *Tradition and Interpretation in Matthew* (1963) 58-59: "In none of the other Gospels is the expectation of judgment and the exhortation to the doing of God's will so prominent as in Matthew . . . . Among the Gospels only Matthew contains detailed descriptions of the final judgment."

35. μισθός: Matt (9); Mark (1); Luke (3); John (1).Thus Matthew exceeds the sum total of the other three. Daniel Marguerat, *Le jugement dans l'évangile de Matthieu* (1981) 25, observes: "La comparaison synoptique révèle que le thème du salaire (μισθός) promis à l'obéissance émerge, ici, avec une fréquence inhabituelle: 10 emplois de μισθός, contre 1 seul chez Mc et 3 chez Lc; son corollaire verbal, μισθοῦσθαι, est singulier (seulement Mt 20.1, 7)." See also Marguerat's conclusion (563): "sur les 148 péricopes que l'on dénombre dans l'évangile, pas moins de 60 traitent du jugement eschatologique ou s'y réfèrent." See also Blaine Charette, *The Theme of Recompense in Matthew's Gospel* (1992).

36. νόμος: Matt (9); Mark (0); Luke(9); John (13). The Gospel of John turns out to be a surprise by leading the pack. Both Matthew and Luke tie for second. Also, once again, Mark tends to omit many of the significant terms which find paramount expression in the first Gospel. What is critical, though, is the interpretative value placed upon Matthew's use of the Law. It is in Matthew alone (5:17) that Jesus does not "come to destroy the Law but to fulfill it."

37. Χριστός: Matt (17); Mark (8); Luke (12); John (18). Obviously all four Gospels in some sense attribute to Jesus the characteristic of an anointed person. See Kim Paffenroth, "Jesus as Anointed and Healing Son of David in the Gospel of Matthew," *Bib* 80.4 (1999) 551: "There is one final, but all-important observation to be made about Jesus' healing in Matthew. As observed above, Matthew omits Mark 6.13, thereby making Jesus the only person anointed in Matthew's Gospel. Just as importantly, however, this omission removes any reference to anyone other than Jesus healing in Matthew's Gospel."

38. κύριος: I cite only the difference between Matthew (76) and Mark (17, counting the controversial ending). The role of κύριος in the Gospel of John will be critical. Donald Hagner, "Matthew: Christian Judaism or Jewish Christianity," in *The Face of New Testament Studies: A Survey of Recent Research* (2004) 263-82, observes (269): "Although in certain contexts the word can be merely a term of respect, like our word 'sir,' for Matthew and his community *kyrios* identifies Jesus as sovereign 'Lord,' or ruler, who functions as deity."

taries feeding into a larger stream, contribute to the overall concept of kingship. The references to "king" and "kingdom" carry significant weight as they describe both title and domain. Matthew is preeminently the Gospel that presents Jesus as a king reigning over a kingdom.[39] David as the greatest king in ancient Israel became the idealized figure who would foreshadow an even greater person. According to 2 Sam 7, God had promised to King David a throne which would last forever. Jesus is presented as the one who is to sit on this throne. And this is underscored by the fact that Jesus is specifically called a king.

Although the kingdom is mentioned in all four Gospels, its length, breadth, and depth are uniquely developed in Matthew. Matthew shows how the kingdom grows (13:1–9), overcomes such obstacles as "weeds" (13:24–30), and eventually triumphs over all opposition (7:21–23; 13:41–43; 19:28; 24:30–31; 25:34). The theme of a king sitting in judgment is of eye-catching interest in Matthew. The ultimate vindication of Jesus as a king is never in doubt. The above five parenthetical texts describing the final victory of the kingdom are distinctive to Matthew alone. Of the twenty-eight chapters in Matthew, only chapters 15, 17, and 28 omit either the word king or kingdom. This emphasis is so dominant in Matthew that the expression "kingdom of heaven" is found *only* in the first Gospel. Also, in comparison with the law, the temple, and the prophets, Jesus is presented in the first Gospel as having priority and sovereignty over all these iconic institutions, including symbols and human subjects of the OT (Moses, David, Solomon, and Jonah).[40] To this impressive list I would also include Matthew's claim that Jesus will deliver his people from sin (1:21).

This is an appropriate place to initiate the discussion on David. Of the four prophetic texts under discussion in this study, only Jer 23:5–6 contains a mention of David. The language of Jer 23:5–6 builds upon the earlier promise to David and his lineage of a perpetual representative upon the throne (as found in 2 Sam 7:8–11).[41] Both language and ideas also find support in the later Psalm of Solomon in which the expectation for a future Davidic king may be found.[42] Furthermore, of the four Gos-

39. I note the comment by Klyne Snodgrass, "The Gospel of Jesus," in *The Written Gospel* (2005) 40: "But Jesus' language was unique in at least two respects: no one prior to Jesus spoke of the kingdom as already here and no one spoke of the kingdom with expressions such as having drawn near, as coming, or as being sought, entered into, or seized." Without Jesus, there is no kingdom.

40. See Terence L. Donaldson, "The Vindicated Son: A Narrative Approach to Matthean Christology," in *Contours of Christology in the New Testament* (2005) 109, who isolates some relevant observations from Matthew that enable us to advance our argument: "Jesus also makes a number of statements in which he asserts his superiority over various Jewish institutions or Old Testament saints: the temple (12.6), the temple tax (17.24–26), the Sabbath (12.8), the law (5.21–48), David (22.41–43), Jonah (12.41), and Solomon (12.42)."

41. Dennis C. Duling (1973) 56–57, refers to what he calls a "prophetic perpetuation formula" going back to 2 Sam 7:5–16. Duling breaks down the oracle of Nathan to David into three key components: 1) descent of the king from the seed of David, 2) a father-son relationship between God and king, and 3) the promise of an eternal reign on the throne.

42. See Marinus De Jonge, "The Use of the Word 'Anointed' in the Time of Jesus," *NovT* 8.2 (1966) 134–35: "The last expression does not mean more than that the expected king will be a true son of

pels Matthew dominates the total number of references to the ancient Judean king. Of the total fourfold Gospel count of thirty-eight references to David, Matthew gets the lion's share—sixteen altogether. Six come in the first chapter alone (vv: 1, 6, 6, 17, 17, 20)—a chapter which pointedly directs the reader to King David. By contrast, Mark uses the title Son of David only three times (10:47, 48; 12:35); and Luke also has only three references (18:38, 39; 20:41). Once again, Matthew leads the count with a total of nine references alone to the Son of David.

Moreover, although Matthew mentions a total of fifteen kings in his genealogy,[43] only David is singled out as a king. As a contrast, Luke does not identify David specifically as a king in his genealogy; nor does Luke list any other king. He does not even follow David with a mention of Solomon. (I will explore the implications of Solomon's omission in chapter 8.) Building upon this initial introductory and programmatic connection with David, Matthew records seven specific addresses in which an individual calls upon Jesus as the "Son of David."[44] Jack Dean Kingsbury correctly assesses the implications of the tabulated data in the following conclusion: "Of all evangelists, none occupies himself more with the Davidic sonship of Jesus than does Matthew."[45] As a second contrast, Jesus is not called the Son of David one single instance in the Gospel of John. The upshot of this contrast is that in Matthew the reader is invited to see Jesus as King,[46] whereas in John, it will be argued, the reader is challenged to see Jesus as God. In the Gospel of John, because of the lofty Christology of Jesus as God, there is no need to demonstrate a link to King David. To further reinforce this interpretation is the illuminating fact that David was considered a type of messiah.[47]

In Matthew this associative link is critical to the development of the image of Christ as a king. Therefore, Matthew presents the kingship of Jesus from a number of telling angles. First, there is Matthew's own account of the genealogy (1:1–17). Second, the genealogy is then followed by the announcement from the angel of the LORD to Joseph, son of David (1:20). Finally, the magi inquire where is he who was born

David, another link in the long chain which began with David and had been interrupted in the days of the author of Psa 17 (see vv. 1–20, esp. vv. 4–8). Just because no son of David has been king over Israel for a long time, the return of the Davidic kingship is expected with so much fervour."

43. David, Solomon, Rehoboam, Abijah, Asa, Jehoshaphat, Jehoram, Uzziah, Jotham, Ahaz, Hezekiah, Manasseh, Amon, Josiah, and Jeconiah/Jehoiachin. According to 2 Chronicles, four are omitted: Ahaziah, Athaliah, Joash, and Amaziah.

44. 1:1; 9:27; 12:23; 15:22; 20:30, 31; 21:9, 15; 22:42. For the argument that the title "Son of David" cannot be a creation of the Hellenistic church but must go back to Palestine, see A. J. B. Higgins, "The Old Testament and Some Aspects of New Testament Christology," in *Promise and Fulfillment* (1963) 130.

45. J. D. Kingsbury, *Jesus Christ in Matthew, Mark, and Luke* (1981) 65.

46. See Graham Stanton, "The Origin and Purpose of Matthew's Gospel: Matthean Scholarship from 1945 to 1980," *ANRW* 25.3 (1985) 1923–24, where Stanton acknowledges confusion—perhaps by others—("Matthew's use of this title remains something of an enigma"), followed by confidence—perhaps his own—("The title is used positively to characterize Jesus as the royal Messiah from the house of David promised and specifically sent to Israel").

47. See Craig A. Evans, "The Old Testament in the New," in *The Face of New Testament Studies* (2004) 136.

"king of the Jews" (2:2). To further augment the weight of this triplet testimony is the added description of David himself as "*the* king."[48] These references do not die out or fade away. From chapters 9–22 there are eight additional occasions where the title reappears.[49] Rudolf Schnackenburg offers a strong justification for the thesis of this by providing support for one of the criterion adopted for this study (the criterion of unique emphasis): "Jesus, therefore, the shoot of David, is presented as Israel's promised 'king of salvation' in Matthew as nowhere else."[50]

To follow up on Schnackenburg's claim, I offer a further check on the thesis as proposed in this book. In between chapters 9–22 there falls the text of Matt 17:24–27, a text which contains a reference to the kings of the earth not collecting taxes from their own sons. First of all, this text is not found elsewhere in the Synoptics or in John. Donald Hagner says, "It is difficult to know why Matthew has inserted this pericope just at this point . . . . The pericope is unique to Matthew and was probably drawn from his special fund of oral tradition."[51] Although it may not be possible to know exactly why Matthew has placed this material at this point, I would like to offer a suggestion based upon the overall contents of this Gospel: this pericope illustrates, once again, the kingship of Jesus.[52] It does this in a subtle way by suggesting that Jesus is the King and the disciples are the sons of the King. Plus, the instructions in the pericope emphasize the wisdom of the King.

I pause here to examine a corollary consideration. Matthew notably presents people responding to Jesus with an attitude and posture of worship. Jack Dean Kingsbury, in comparing Matthew with Mark, states: ". . . when it comes to the matter of distinctiveness, it can hardly be stressed enough that Matthew possesses a character all its own."[53] Although Kingsbury isolates several unique elements distinct to Matthew, there is one in particular that applies to this investigation: the use of προσέρχομαι

---

48. The Greek is emphatic: τὸν Δαυὶδ τὸν βασιλέα ("David, *the* king"). Luke 3:31 omits the mention of David as a king, but Luke 1:32 does say that Jesus will inherit the "throne" of David. See also David R. Bauer, *The Structure of Matthew's Gospel: A Study in Literary Design* (1988) 76. For the view that David is a fairy tale, see Peter D. Miscall, "Moses and David: Myth and Monarchy," in *The New Literary Criticism and the Hebrew Bible* (1993) 184–200.

49. Matt 9:27; 12:23; 15:22; 20:30, 31; 21:9, 15; and 22:42.

50. R. Schnackenburg, *The Gospel of Matthew* (2002) 8.

51. D. Hagner, *Matthew 14–28* (1982) 510.

52. See Grant R. Osborne, *Matthew* (2010) 663, for his conclusion that the true King is God and the "sons" refers to Jesus and his followers. I would counter that Jesus is the "true King." Perhaps this is a minor distinction, but I feel it is worthwhile to state it. Ulrich Luz, *Matthew 8–20* (1989) 415, takes the entire pericope as a creation of the church.

53. J. D. Kingsbury, "The Gospel in Four Editions," *Int* 33.4 (1979) 367. See also Robert A. Gundry, *Matthew: A Commentary on His Literary and Theological Art* (1982) 8: "He constantly receives the designation 'Lord'. Repeatedly, people worship him. He has angels. Even kingdoms belong to him as the Son of Man. All these represent special and sometimes exclusive emphases of Matthew."

("to approach" or "to come to") when combined with προσκυνέω ("to worship"). As Kingsbury points out, both of these verbs indicate positions of respect due a king.[54]

The verb προσέρχομαι offers a useful starting point. Matthew uses the verb a total of fifty-three times. By contrast, Mark uses this verb only three times. However, the situation is not quite as skewered as Kingsbury depicts. Although Mark uses προσέρχομαι only three times, he does use ἔρχομαι πρός or an equivalent fifteen times. But this still leaves Matthew out in front by a wide margin. Of the Matthean number, forty-two refer to various people approaching Jesus; most of these references simply describe either the disciples or others approaching Jesus to ask a question or make a request. Jesus is shown only once approaching anyone: that occasion occurs in the garden of Gethsemane while praying to his Father (26:39). Proceeding further inside the relevant references, the verb προσέρχομαι is accompanied four times by the unusual verb προσκυνέω.[55] For its part, προσκυνέω occurs an additional seven times without προσέρχομαι for a total of eleven references. Of this number, the verb προσκυνέω is used a total of eight times with a specific reference to worship of Jesus:[56] once with a reference to YHWH or the LORD God (4:10), once with a reference to Satan who tempts Jesus to worship him (4:9), and once with a reference to a slave imploring his master for mercy in a parable (18:26). This composite number must be supplemented by five additional alternate expressions such as the desperate father, in a kneeling position before Jesus, interceding for his son (17:14),[57] or the disciples falling on their faces before Jesus in a posture of worship (17:6). This bumps up the total number of significant referents to around thirteen. Heinrich Greeven in the TDNT points out the verb προσκυνέω consistently describes the physical action of bowing in the LXX.[58] Matthew alone adds the verb πίπτω ("to fall") to supplement the posture

---

54. J. D. Kingsbury, "The Gospel in Four Editions," 368. See also Kingsbury's *Jesus Christ in Matthew, Mark, and Luke* (1981) 76: "Thus, in forty-nine instances Matthew utilizes the verb *proserchomai* ('to come to,' 'to approach'), which in the LXX is cultic in coloration and in Josephus is used of stepping before a king, in order to portray persons as approaching Jesus with the same reverence that would be due to a deity or king." See also John Nolland, "No Son-of-God Christology in Matthew 1.18–25," *JSNT* 62 (1996) 9, fn. 28: "In Mark προσκυνεῖν means only to show deferential respect to (5.6; 15.19); in Luke it denotes religious worship (4.7, 8) and is used with Jesus as object only after the resurrection (24.52); in Matthew it clearly can mean religious reverence (4.9, 10), at times seems clearly to involve worship directed towards Jesus (14.33; 28.9, 17) . . ." See Crispin H. T. Fletcher-Louis, "The Worship of Divine Humanity as God's Image and the Worship of Jesus," in *The Jewish Roots of Christological Monotheism* (1998) 113, where he has argued that historically within ancient Judaism there was a precedent for the worship of humans and, consequently, the worship of Jesus is not to be considered as unthinkable or insurmountable. This assumes that Matthew was perhaps influenced from the environment of a larger literary community in which such conceptions were current rather than reporting something that happened in the ministry of Jesus as a spontaneous reaction to Jesus.

55. Matt 8:2; 9:18; 20:20; 28:9.

56. Matt 2:2, 8, 11; 8:2; 9:18; 14:33; 15:25; 20:20; 28:9, 17.

57. See also Matt 27:29.

58. Heinrich Greeven, "προσκυνέω," *TDNT* (1968) 6.760. Greeven translates προσκυνέω as the consistent translation in the LXX for the Hebrew שחה (*shahghah*).

of worship (2:11; 18:26). It may be added that none of the above actions occurs in a formal ceremonial setting; there is no music, no commands, no stage directions or theatrical trappings, and no coaxing or coaching. These postures of worship are pictured as occurring voluntarily and spontaneously.

By tracking the verb προσέρχομαι ("to approach") and its companion προσκυνέω ("to worship") through all four Gospels, further distinct colorations emerge. Mark uses προσκυνέω only once (5:6);[59] Luke likewise has only a single reference (24:52) and that occurs after the resurrection. John, similarly, has only a single reference (9:38). Clearly, Matthews stands out among the four evangelists as describing various people in a singular posture of offering worship to Jesus. One reference in particular bears special mention: Matt 9:18: ἰδοὺ ἄρχων προσελθὼν προσεκύνει αὐτῷ λέγων ("Behold, a ruler, coming to him and worshiping him, said"). Matthew, it may be noted, is the only evangelist who reports a "ruler" bowing down to Jesus in a posture of worship. Secondly, the verb προσεκύνει is an imperfect, indicating some kind of repetitive or ongoing action. Matthew, therefore, is calling attention to an expression of devotion while it occurs, indicating a special point of emphasis. Since this was not a single one time act of worship but a sequence of such expressions, Jesus would have been in a position to stop such devotion if it was excessive or inappropriate. Third, as characteristic of Matthew, he introduces such striking statements conveying royal implications with the appropriate "Behold" (ἰδού). At the risk of wearying the reader, I repeat: this text is found only in Matthew.

A useful and more complete accounting for the unusual word προσκυνέω still needs some attention. The following data may fill out the profile. The verb προσκυνέω seems to imply the physical posture of bowing before someone with face to the ground.[60] Sometimes this act of bowing is a formal expression of etiquette, political correctness, or deference of one party to another.[61] It is not always easy, however, to discern whether the act of worship is implied or if it is simply honor and respect.[62] In the OT, Jews rarely fall down or bow down before men, but two occasions do stand out. The first reference

---

59. Mark does use the verb γονυπετέω twice: 1:40; 10:17. BADG translates this verb as "to fall on one's knees." See also Matt 17:14 and 27:29 for the only other usages. This behavior does not necessarily indicate worship; it is more a position of desperate pleading. BADG cites Tacitus' *Annals* 11.30: *genibus Caesaris* ("on her knees before Caesar") as a Roman parallel. This text is of similar tone; Messalina, in dire distress, is pleading for mercy.

60. If I have counted correctly, there are 168 references to שחה (*shahghah*) in the Hebrew Bible, of this total the LXX translates with προσκυνέω 149 times. Sometimes the meaning is clearly a demonstration of respect or perhaps only a polite and courteous greeting (Gen 23:7). At other times, however, these two verbs openly reveal an attitude of worship before deity (Gen 18:2; 2 Chr 33:3).

61. Gen 23:7 illustrates the point. Abraham bows down (προσκυνέω in the LXX) before the Hittites. The scene involves a business transaction to purchase the cave at Machpelah as a burial site for Sarah.

62. For example, the NIV is not always consistent with this verb. In Matt 2:2, 8, and 11, the NIV translates προσκυνέω with "worship," but at Matt 8:2; 9:18; 15:25; and 20:20, the translation is one of "kneeling."

is that of the brothers of Joseph bowing down before him with faces to the ground.[63] This act is not done as to a brother but as to a lord or high official. In the combined texts of 1 Sam 20:41 and 24:9, David bows before Jonathan and then Saul. These are acts of respect and honor, not worship. A very unusual case is reported in 2 Sam 18:26 in which Ahimaaz, coming from the battlefield with a report of victory, falls down before King David with his face to the ground and proclaims: "Praise be to the LORD your God!"[64] Clearly, even though on his face before the king, he is praising the LORD. A similar text is that of 1 Chr 29:23 in which the people bow down before the LORD and King Solomon. It appears that Solomon, newly crowned and now sitting upon the throne in regal ceremony, represents the presence of YHWH and, accordingly, the people pay their due respects. The people are also responding to directions from King David to worship the LORD. Therefore, the bowing down in this enthronement scene is not a spontaneous act. The reference in Matt 9:18 to an ἄρχων ("leader" or "ruler") probably describes a Jewish leader, perhaps a leader or ruler of a synagogue.[65] This behavior by a Jew would be highly unusual. A final reference may be noted; although last in sequence, it is not last in significance. In Genesis 24 the servant of Abraham falls down in worship before the LORD on three separate occasions (26, 48, 52).[66]

Turning now to information in the Greek historians, it is possible to see that Greeks do not fall down and worship other men.[67] One of the ways that Greeks distinguished themselves from barbarians (Persians) is by the way that they do not worship their leaders.[68] On the Roman side, neither the Roman Republican historian Livy nor the Imperial Tacitus use the verb *adorare* to describe Romans in the sincere worship of men.[69] Tacitus, however, does record one instance when Otho feigns obeisance to

---

63. LXX Gen 43:26: προσεκύνησαν αὐτῷ ἐπὶ πρόσωπον τὴν γῆν.

64. Josephus, *Jewish Antiquities* 7.250, uses the verb προσκυνέω to narrate the following scene which reads: καὶ προσεκύνησεν τῷ βασιλεῖ ἐπὶ πρόσωπον αὐτοῦ ἐπὶ τὴν γῆν.

65. This is the position taken by W. D. Davies and Dale C. Allison, *Matthew: A Shorter Commentary* (2004)139.

66. The LXX uses προσκυνέω for all three verses.

67. See, for example, Xenophon, *Anabasis* 3.2.9, where we find the expression "they worshiped god" (προσεκύνησαν τὸν θεόν), and especially 3.2.13: οὐδένα γὰρ ἄνθρωπον δεσπότην ἀλλὰ τοὺς προσκυνεῖτε ("You worship no human despot but the gods [only]"). However, Xenophon does claim that some men fell at his feet (προσπίπτω, *Anabasis* 7.21) beseeching him for leadership. Philostratus in his *Life of Apollonius* uses the word fifteen times, mostly in the sense of worship. Although Philostratus records claims or rumors of worship of Apollonius, Apollonius is never actually shown being worshiped. The text of 7.22.25 cannot be used to prove this. The principal idea for worship from Philostratus may be found at 7.14.4: τὰς τυραννίδας προσκύνουσιν ("they worship tyrants"). See also 1.27.2, 4; 1.31.6; 2.11.55; 2.21.24; 2.42.11; 7.11.38; 7.14.4; 7.21.20, 22, 25; 8.15.40.

68. See, for example, Arrian, *History of Alexander* 4.11.9: τοὺς Ἕλληνας τοὺς ἐλευθερωτάτους προσαναγκάσεις ἐς τὴν προσκύνησιν ("will you force the Greeks, the most free of men, to bow down to [you]?"). Greeks considered such bowing down to another person an act of humiliation.

69. Livy, *Ab urbe condita* 7.40.4; 6.12.7; 21.17.4; and 38.43.5, shows only the Roman gods being worshiped.

the common people.[70] A notable exception is reported by Polybius (30.18).[71] As he narrates the entrance of King Prusias into the Roman senate, Polybius records the offensive behavior of Prusias bowing down with face to the ground in a humiliating posture of worship (προσεκύνησε). Polybius describes this servile gesture as degrading to a man, characteristic of both "unmanliness" (ἀνανδρίας) and "womanish" (γυναικισμοῦ). It is clear from the account that this bowing down was construed as an attempt to manipulate.

Turning to Josephus, he uses this verb nearly one hundred times, with the basic meaning of "to worship" God, or "to reverence" the holy place (the temple in Jerusalem) as a sacred and legitimate place of worship.[72] Exceptionally, Josephus does use προσκυνέω to describe the submissive act of yielding to Roman sovereignty.[73] This, of course, would not be a voluntary act.

Finally, what is perhaps most significant about the worship of Jesus is that this posture is neither required nor sought. This action of worship is wholly spontaneous and unforced. It never occurs in a formal or scripted ceremony and, furthermore, it seems to leave the worshiper with a sense of awe (Matt 28:9), never demeaning the man or woman, or leaving that person with feelings of regret. In the case of the leper at Matt 8:2, there are further details that conform to the picture presented here. The narrative opens with the interjection "Behold" (ἰδού) followed by the leper approaching Jesus, then bowing down in an attitude of worship, and finally crying out, "LORD, if you will, you can cleanse me."[74] This is just one of the many images in Matthew that illustrates the motif of kingship, thus providing at a fundamental level a possible allusional link to the prophetic text of Jer 23:5–6. A final comment should not be superfluous: while the NT consistently shows both men and angels rejecting worship,[75] Jesus, however, never rejects worship, never rebukes or cautions the worshipper, and never expresses embarrassment or dismay over such overt acts of devotion."[76]

With the disparity between Matthew, Mark and Luke on the number of references to people in various positions of bowing down to Jesus, a question thus must be faced: upon what critical grounds can the preponderance of references in Matthew be assigned to the historical Jesus? Or, has Matthew touched up his narrative with fictional and imaginative strokes of the brush? In short, did these people really worship

---

70. Tacitus, *Histories* 1.36: *Nec deerat Otho protendens manus adorare vulgum, iacere oscula et omnia serviliter pro dominatione.*

71. Livy at 44.45.20 provides a similar account. Dio Cassius, *Roman History* 59.27.5, shows Vitellius bowing down to a jealous Gaius in an act of worship in order to save his life.

72. *Jewish War* 4.262, 324; 5.402; 6.123.

73. *Jewish War* 2.361. See also his *Jewish Antiquities* 11.333 in which Josephus records Alexander bowing down before God.

74. Although I have used the capitalized form of "LORD," it is possible that "Lord" is also admissible.

75. Acts 10:26; Rev 19:10; 22:9.

76. Richard Swinburne, *Was Jesus God?* (2008) 103: "Jesus, on the other hand, is never reported as rejecting worship."

Jesus? Dale C. Allison, noting the numerical differences between Matthew and Mark regarding this position of worship, clearly harbors misgivings about the historicity of Matthew's account.[77] He also believes that Matthew is correcting the record as found in Mark.[78] I grant that a theological tint is present in the texts. Does that necessarily discredit historical reality? A question is left begging: if Greek, Roman, and Jewish culture disdained such acts as unworthy of men for other men, why would Matthew create fictional accounts of men worshiping Jesus? In my judgment, fiction does not explain these exceptional actions of bowing down. If Matthew has recorded what actually happened, Mark, it may be argued, has simply omitted these references because of a different presentation of Jesus. Neither narrative may be faulted as literary fictions or untrue and untrustworthy historical accounts. Furthermore, I propose an alternative solution to the diversity: the diversity may be caused by the prophetic King Branch of Jer 23:5–6.

Although arguments continue to reach publication articulating the premise that the Gospels of Mark and Luke also present Jesus in the role of a king,[79] the distinctive kingship vocabulary in Matthew presents Jesus emphatically in this role. This study, therefore, is an attempt to place in doubt the current notion in NT scholarship that each subsequent Gospel is an effort to improve upon a prior Gospel by composing a better version of Jesus. The view, as developed here, aims at showing each Gospel representing Jesus from the distinctly unique perspective of King, Servant, High Priest, and LORD God.

A further demarcation may be observed, especially between Matthew and Luke. While Matthew presents Jesus from the dominant aspect of a King Branch, I will argue that Luke presents Jesus as a High Priest Branch. One of the ways in which this can be seen is the singular manner in which Jesus must confront the antagonist Satan. Mark Allan Powell argues that the main plot of Matthew is *God's Plan and Satan's Challenge*.[80] This plot, if accepted, partially coincides with the presentation of Jesus as a king. Kings by their very nature must subdue hostile threats, defeat attacking armies, and deal with the threat of menacing enemies. High priests for their part must intercede for people. Kings have to deal with aggression; high priests have to deal with

---

77. Dale C. Allison, *Constructing Jesus Memory, Imagination, and History* (2010) 225. Allison is clearly pessimistic about gauging the reliability of the sources for the life of Jesus. Yet, ironically, "despite our primary sources being consistently wrong, we can nonetheless get it right" (232).

78. Ibid., 454–55.

79. Among recent attempts, see Robert D. Rowe, *God's Kingdom and God's Son* (2002); Joel Marcus, *The Way of the Lord: Christological Exegesis of the Old Testament in the Gospel of Mark* (1992). This book by Marcus is well written, but in my judgment some of his explanations about Jesus and kingship are overstated (pp. 80–93). See also Mark L. Strauss, *The Davidic Messiah in Luke–Acts* (1995) 317: "The present section is limited to Luke's Christological presentation, and seeks to show that two themes are most prominent: *Jesus' kingship and his role as Isaianic servant*" (italics his). In chapter 6, I will present reasons why Mark does not reveal Jesus in the role of a king. On the contrary, evidence suggests that Mark narrates Jesus as the obedient Servant and Son of God.

80. M. A. Powell, "The Plot and Subplots of Matthew's Gospel," *NTS* 38.1 (1992) 199.

transgression. Simplistically stated, kings slay and priests pray.[81] Part of the Matthean presentation of Jesus involves the dominant role of dealing with enemies and their opposition to the kingdom of God. Matthew is different from the other three Gospels by virtue of victory over the forces of evil and the judgment of hostile intentions. A summary comment may be inserted here regarding the difference between Matthew and Mark: Matthew, it appears, does not emphasize the servanthood of Jesus, while Mark does.[82] Conversely, Mark does not emphasize the concept of Son of David, while Matthew does. It is a matter of emphasis. The final epithet bears closer scrutiny as the title "LORD" (κύριος) cannot be avoided.[83]

The Metaphor of a Branch

MT: צמח צדיק; LXX: ἀνατολὴν δικαίαν; NIV: "a righteous Branch."

The text of Jer 23:5 introduces us to a person called a *Branch*. Without a doubt, the single most indispensable concept to this study is the Hebrew word צמח (*Zemah, Tsemah,* or *Ṣemaḥ*), ἀνατολή or *anatolē* in the LXX, or "Branch" in English translations.[84] Qumran texts demonstrate unequivocally that this Branch was a metaphor with messianic connotations.[85] Although עמח (*Zemah*) is principally a figurative term

---

81. A Lukan exception may be noted. In Luke 19:27 Jesus is presented as giving the order to slay his enemies (κατασφάξατε αὐτοὺς ἔμπροσθέν μου). These words, actually more characteristic of Matthew but omitted by him, are not incongruent with the picture of the high priest in ancient Israel. Gen 49:5 indicates that one of the weapons of Levi is the sword. Deuteronomy 33:11 pictures God striking down those who oppose Levi. Nevertheless, the text of Luke 19:27 is an example of some overlapping within the Gospels. Matt 22:7 does, however, contain the words: "the *king* was angry, and sent his army and destroyed those murderers."

82. See Charles E. Carlston, "Christology and Church in Matthew," in *The Four Gospels* (1992) 2.1285, who suggests that the term "Servant" is probably not central to Matthew.

83. For a discussion of Matt 22:41–45 in which an interchange between "Son of David" and "LORD" occurs, see Georg Strecker, *Der Weg der Gerechtigkeit: Untersuchung zur Theologie des Matthäus* (1965) 118–19: "Da der Evangelist 'Davidsohn' durchaus als positive christologische Bezeichnung verwendet, ist von vornherein ausgeschlossen, daB er—wenn dies auch die ursprüngliche Aussage gewesen sein könnte—den Titel abgelehnt wissen wollte. Tatsächlich sagt der Wortlaut des Textes nichts von einer Alternative zwischen υἱὸς Δαυίδ und κύριος." See Günther Bornkamm, "The Stilling of the Storm in Matthew," in *Tradition and Interpretation in Matthew* (1963) 55, where he noted that κύριος is used in a distinctive way in Matthew. Whereas in Mark, Jesus is referred to by the disciples as διδάσκαλε and in Luke as ἐπιστάτα, both are human titles of respect. In Matthew κύριε is used. Other examples of Matthew's use of κύριος confirm that it is "a very divine predicate of majesty."

84. The King James (1608), the American Standard (1908), the Revised Standard (1952), and the recent NIV (2005) all have Branch.

85. See especially 4Q252 V.13: "The scepter shall [no]t depart from the tribe of Judah. While Israel has the dominion, 2) [will not] be cut off someone who sits on the throne of David. For 'the staff' is the covenant of royalty, 3 [and the thou]sands of Israel are 'the standards'. *Blank*. Until the messiah of righteousness comes, the branch of David" (משי הצדק צמח דויד), [eds. and trans. by Florentino García Martínez and Eibert J. C. Tigchelaar, *The Dead Sea Scrolls Study Edition*, QI–4Q273 (1997)].

illustrating a type of vegetative growth,[86] this word is also used to describe the kind of growth that produces a tree.[87] Alternately, the verb form (ἀνατέλλω) can describe the rising of the sun or the action of lighting.[88] More importantly is the fact that this metaphor describes a person. By what criteria can we look ahead and apply this to Jesus? In the sense of being a "branch," Jesus obviously qualifies as he came forth from the Jewish nation like a branch from a tree. As a Branch he has a family tree, a tribal tree, and a national tree.

The messianic concept of "Branch" as applied to Jesus is known to NT writers. Rom 15:12, referring to Isa 11:1, describes the "root of Jesse springing up" (ἡ ῥίζα τοῦ Ἰεσσαί... ἀνιστάμενος). Rev 5:5, also using the synonym "root" (ῥίζα), describes Jesus as "the Lion of the Tribe of Judah, the Root of David."[89] This text from Rev 5:5 provides a scriptural connection joining together three integral motifs: Lion, Judah, and Root (or Branch) of David. Of no less importance, though, is the currency of this word in first-century Judaism. Heinrich Schlier in the *TDNT* offers the view that on the basis of Jer 23:5, Zech 3:8, and 6:12, this word "became a name for the Messiah in the Synagogue."[90] It is the Gospel of Matthew, though, that is presently in view.

It must acknowledged that nowhere does Matthew consciously and overtly indicate that he has set out to demonstrate that the word "Branch" applies directly to Jesus. This, however, is not the end of the matter. At the same time it must be equally affirmed that there are allusions to the Branch in the first Gospel.[91] Rudolf Pesch,

---

86. For the argument that צמח/Zemah has been incorrectly translated as "Branch" and should be understood as referring only to "growth," see Wolter H. Rose, *Zemah and Zerubbabel* (2000) 107–20. I am not persuaded by the importance that Rose attaches to this hairsplitting.

87. For example, Eccl 2:6: יער צומח עצים ("the forest shooting forth/growing trees"); LXX: δρυμὸν βλαστεῶτα ξύλα.

88. Indeed, the verb ἀνατέλλω ("to arise") is used at Matt 4:16 to describe a great light breaking over people who are sitting in darkness and on those living in the land of the shadow of death a light has dawned.

89. The text of Rev 5:5 also introduces Jesus with the exclamatory ἰδού ("Behold!"). Rom 15:12 also employs the metaphor of "root" as springing up from Jesse.

90. H. Schlier, "ἀνατολή," *TDNT* (1974) 1.352–53. Schlier does not refer to documentation to support his point. Perhaps he was assuming that his point was common knowledge. The Eighteen Benedictions is likely the referent. On the role and function of the targums in the synagogue, see Bruce D. Chilton, *A Galilean Rabbi and His Bible* (1984) 39. Essentially, the meturgeman (or translator) would first read the text from the original Hebrew, close the scroll, and then give his paraphrased interpretative reading to the congregation. Chilton comments (39): "These interpretations were popular." See also Bruce Chilton and Craig A. Evans, "Jesus and Israel's Scriptures," in *Studying the Historical Jesus* (1994) 281–335.

91. Floyd V. Filson, *The Gospel according to St. Matthew* (1971) 25, suggests the possibility of linking the Hebrew *netzer* ("shoot") from Isa 11:1 with the "Nazorean." If so, this is a very remote allusion. Alan Hugh M'Neile, *The Gospel according to St. Matthew* (1961) 21, after considering this option, dismisses it as improbable: "Mt's reference to the OT is sometimes improbably explained as giving a play on *nēzer* 'a shoot' in Isa xi.1 (where the Targ. refers it to the Messiah)." See also John Nolland, *The Gospel of Matthew* (2005) 130, who, admitting that it may be possible to exploit more than one link to OT texts, suggests that *Nazarios* may connect to Isa 4:3 as well as Isa 11:1 via *nsr*. This concession, however, requires among the readers in the original community some who knew Hebrew. This, of

in a rather bold and daring exegetical leap, makes the intriguing connection from the Hebrew *neser* ("shoot") from Isa 11:1. Then, linking it to the *Zemah* (or *Sproß* in German) of Jer 23:5–6, he finally identifies it as equivalent to the word "Nazarene" in Matt 2:23.[92] E. Earle Ellis follows up this suggestion from Pesch by also identifying the reference to Jesus as a Nazarene in Matt 2:23 as a possible double-entendre for "branch."[93] Others have drawn similar conclusions.[94] No less tantalizing, yet possibly more viable and illuminating, is the reference in Matt 2:1–9 (vv. 1, 2, 9) where the OT word for Branch (ἀνατολή) is found twice in the singular, once in the plural, with all three describing the star. Such references to a star rising in the East (ἀνατολή) would clearly evoke images of the Branch.[95] To think of one would likely trigger mental images of the other. In fact, the text of Luke 1:78–79 ("the rising sun will come to us from heaven") uses the LXX word for "branch" (ἀνατολή), but with the alternate meaning of "sun" (or possibly "star"), thus evoking a possible messianic connection.[96] Similarly, Matt 4:16–17 uses the verb ἀνατέλλω ("to rise") to describe a bright light rising upon those who sit in darkness. Consequently, the noun ἀνατολή (anglicized to *anatolē*),

---

course, is not unlikely or impossible. See also W. D. Davies, "The Jewish Sources of Matthew's Messianism," in *The Messiah: Developments in Earliest Judaism and Christianity* (1987) 494–511.

92. R. Pesch, "'Er wird Nazoräer heissen': messianische Exegese in MT 1–2," in *The Four Gospels* (1992) 1392–93: "Auch wenn nur Jes 11.1 vom *neser*, so ist doch der Äquivalentbegriff *ṣemaḥ* (aus dem Parallelismus des Prophetenspruchs) in der Ankündigung weiterer Propheten zu finden: Jes 11.1 ... Jer 23.5 ... Jer 33.15 ... Sach 3.8 ... Sach 6.12! Auch die frühjüdische Überlieferung kennt diese Prophetie; vgl. TestJuda 14.5f ... Die Exegese des Matthäus setzt voraus, daß auch der Äquivalentbegriff *neser* die messianische Bedeutung des 'Namens' Sproß (*ṣemaḥ*) trägt. Deshalb darf der Evangelist von 'den Propheten' (im Plural) sprechen! Die Verwendung des Begriffs 'Sproß' setzt voraus, daß die Familie wie ein Baum vorgestellt wird, dessen Kraft in der Wurzel liegt." H. H. Schaeder, "Ναζαρηνός/Ναζωραῖος," *TDNT* (1965) 4.878, disputes the likelihood of any substantial connection. He discounts the linkage by saying: "But apart from the substitution this does not carry with it any connection of signification, but is a pun which only experts in Rabbinic interpretation can unravel. Mt., however, was trying to make himself understood by Gk. readers."

93. E. E. Ellis, *History & Interpretation in New Testament Perspective* (2001)104.

94. See, for example, Craig A. Evans, *Jesus and His Contemporaries* (1995) 164: "The Matthean fulfillment, 'He shall be called a Nazarene' (Matt 2.23), probably has something to do with the נצר of Isa 11:1. These are allusions at best; in Rom 15:12 Paul quotes LXX Isa 11:10 and explicitly applies the passage to Jesus. From this we may infer that the messianic interpretation of Isaiah 11 was known to Christians no later than the middle of the first century."

95. See Dennis C. Duling, "The Promises to David and Their Entrance into Christianity—Nailing Down a Likely Hypothesis," *NTS* 19 (1973) 61, in which Duling concludes: "Perhaps the best known example is the translation ἀνατέλλω and its noun form ἀνατολή. Thus, the 'shoot' of Isa 4.2, Jer 23.5, and Zech 3.8, 6.12 is consistently rendered by the unusual ἀνατολή, 'East,' apparently a reflection on the verb which translated 'shoots up' not only in Zech 6.12, but is found with the 'star' of Num 24.17, the 'horn' of Psa 132.17, and the 'Sun of Righteousness' in Mal 3.20."

96. For the argument that the noun ἀνατολή in Luke 1:79 insinuates notions of a heavenly messiah, see Simon J. Gathercole, "The Heavenly ἀνατολή (Luke 1:78–9)," *JST* 56.2 (2005) 471–88. For the view that Luke 1:78 speaks only of origin, see Gregory Lanier, "'From God' or 'from Heaven'? ἐξ ὕψους in Luke 1,78," *Bib* 97.1 (2016) 121–27. For a very intriguing but cautious insinuation that this ἀνατολή is messianically in the background to Matt 2:1, 2, 9, see W. D. Davies, "Appendix IV: Isaiah XLI.2 and the Pre-existent Messiah," in his *The Setting of the Sermon on the Mount* (1963) 445.

which comes from the verb ἀνατέλλω (*anatellō*), not only suggests growth springing up from the ground or a branch bursting forth from a tree, but the relationship between the verb and noun hint linguistically at a rising star or sun. Justin Martyr makes this very connection by using the metaphor of star and sprout interchangeably as he applies both of them to Christ.[97] Clearly, the word ἀνατολή has polysemic characteristics. At its intrinsic core it describes something that rises, whether sun, star, vegetative growth, or a branch from a tree.

The relationship between the words "east," "arising," and "branch" is strong enough that it could create confusion, if only by association. A testimony to the potential for confusing these terms can be found in Philo's appropriately named *The Confusion of Tongues*. At XIV–XV/60–64, Philo first uses ἀνατολή in the genitive plural to describe some men who moved from the east (or "rising") and settled in the plain of Shinar. Philo follows this first reference with an immediate mention of another ἀνατολή but suggests a figurative or allegorical meaning for the word, giving it the sense of "rising" as in the increase of evil in the soul. At the beginning of the next paragraph (XV/64), Philo uses ἀνατολή two more times. Sandwiched in between these four texts, Philo proceeds with this account:

> I have heard also an oracle from the lips of one of the disciples of Moses, which runs thus: "Behold, a man whose name is the rising," strangest of titles, surely, if you suppose that a being composed of soul and body is here described. But if you suppose that is that Incorporeal one (ἀσώματον), who differs not a whit from the divine image, you will agree that the name of "rising" assigned to him quite truly describes him.

The above translation by Colson and Whitaker in the LCC prefers "rising" over "Branch." But they acknowledge in a footnote that "Branch" is an alternative translation. This illustrates my point: the terms (branch, east, or rising) are close equivalents, nearly interchangeable, each pointing to the other. More significant, though, is Philo's identification of the ἀνατολή with what he calls the ἀσώματον ("Incorporeal One").

---

97. See Justin Martyr, *Apologia* 1.32.10, where he paraphrases the prophet Isaiah: ἀνατελεῖ ἄστρον ἐξ Ἰακώβ, καὶ ἄνθος ἀναβήσεται ἀπὸ τῆς ῥίζης Ἰεσσαί, καί . . . ἄστρον δὲ φωτεινὸν ἀνέτειλε, καὶ ἄνθος ἀνέβη ἀπὸ τῆς ῥίζης Ἰεσσαί, οὗτος ὁ Χριστός ("a star will arise from Jacob, and a flower [sprout] will come forth from the root of Jesse, and . . . a bright star arose and a flower [sprout] came forth from the root of Jesse; this is the Christ"). Justin clearly identifies the star with the branch and then connects both to Christ. See also *Dialogus cum Tryphone* 106.4: καὶ ἄλλη δὲ γραφή φησιν: "Ἰδοὺ ἀνήρ, ἀνατολὴ ὄνομα αὐτῷ." Justin equates two things as near equals: ἀνατελεῖ ἄστρον (a star with arise or shine) equals ἄνθος ἀναβήσεται (a sprout or flower will spring up). Obviously, Justin is aware of the Christian application of the Branch prophecy to Christ. What we do not know is how early this application can be dated. In this same text, however, Justin bases his identification of star and sprout to the person of Christ by appealing to the memoirs of the apostles, suggesting the Gospel of Matthew. See also Ambrose, *Expositio evangelii secundum Lucam* 3:22, where he shows himself aware of the prophecy of Zech 6:12 and applies this to Christ. He interprets the word *oriens* as applying more to light than to vegetative growth.

This is very likely a messianic association.[98] Thus a first-century Jew, reading from the Greek text of Matt 2:1–12, could connect the notions of east, rising, or branch.[99] To further underscore the point, *TLevi* 18.3 says: καὶ ἀνατελεῖ ἄστρον αὐτοῦ ἐν οὐρανῷ ὡς, φωτίζων φῶς γνώσεως ὡς ἐν ἡλίῳ ἡμέρας ("and his star will arise in heaven as enlightening the light of knowledge as [though] in daylight").

The LORD will set up for David a righteous Branch, a King who will reign

> MT: והקמתי לדוד צמח צדיק ומלך מלך; LXX: ἀναστήσω τῷ Δαυιδ ἀνατολὴν δικαίαν . . . καὶ βασιλεύσει βασιλεύς, NIV: "I will raise up to David a righteous Branch, even a king [who] will reign".

The promise in Jer 23:5–6 is that the LORD will establish a king for David, a righteous Branch who will do justice. His name is further elaborated in that he will be called "the LORD our righteousness." This cluster of words focuses upon the inner character qualities of doing right, being righteous, establishing righteousness, capped off with the epithet of righteousness. The words וצדקה (*tsedaqah*, LXX: δικαιοσύνη) and צדיק (*tsaddiq*, LXX: δίκαιος/"righteous") occur four times in Jer 23:5–6 and they are further defined by qualifying ideas that a righteous king will act wisely.[100] The LXX of Jer 23:5 can be read with profit both frontwards and backwards: the *Zemah* or ἀνατολή is "righteous," or the "righteous one" is an ἀνατολή or *Zemah*. Jer 23:5–6 is emphatic that the coming king will be defined by a distinctive righteousness. The Gospel of Matthew is equally emphatic that Jesus measures up to that standard. The word group of "right," "righteous," and "righteousness" (or "justice") in Matthew overshadows the other three Gospels.[101] In fact, Matthew exceeds the sum total of the other three.

The doublet "righteousness and justice" is a frequent pair in the OT.[102] Psalm 97:3 says that righteousness and justice are the foundation of God's throne. Isaiah 16:5

---

98. Although not mentioned in the Testament of the Twelve Patriarchs, the NT, or the Apostolic Fathers, Philo also uses ἀσώματος in *De specialibus legibus* (2.176) for the "incorporeal image of God."

99. To further add to this mysterious mix is the description in Num 2:3 of the camp arrangement of ancient Israel. Judah is mentioned *first* in the configuration. Upon breaking camp, Judah sets out *first*. Also, its position faces eastward. Furthermore, of the twelve tribes, only four carry a standard. It is tempting to think that Judah's standard is the image of a lion.

100. For the argument that the Hebrew *tsedaqah* and the LXX translation of δικαιοσύνη are essentially equivalents, see Benno Przybylski, *Righteousness in Matthew and his World of Thought* (1980) 77. Unfortunately, Przybylski does not discuss Jer 23:6. However, he does propose that righteousness in Matthew is used to stress righteous behavior, not righteousness as a gift (105).

101. δίκαιος: Matt (16); Mark (2); Luke (11); and John (3). Matthew equals the combined totals of the other three. δικαιοσύνη: Matt (7); Mark (0); Luke (1); John (2). Matthew exceeds the sum total of the other three.

102. For the view that this pair of terms does not have a juridical sense but should be understood as a manifestation of kindness, see Moshe Weinfeld, "'Justice and Righteousness'—וצקה משפט—The Expression and its Meaning," in *Justice and Righteousness: Biblical Themes and their Influence* (1992) 228–46.

states that the future house of David will have an occupant upon the throne who will seek justice and speed the cause of righteousness. Isaiah 32:1 indicates that an ideal king will reign and rule in both righteousness and justice. This word pair epitomizes the essence of divine kingship. This couplet is especially prominent in Jeremiah and equally paramount in Matthew. The language of Jer 23:5 portrays a king who is righteous to rule, suggesting that this king will be legitimate or qualified to rule based upon the quality of righteousness.[103] Although the suggestion has been questioned,[104] the larger context of the entire book of Jeremiah (especially 21:1–5 and 52:2) and the smaller context of Jer 23:1–6 may imply a contrast with the ancient Judean king Zedekiah.[105] Where Zedekiah was a failure in righteousness, the new king will succeed; where Zedekiah proved unfaithful and disqualified to reign, the new king will be legitimate to rule with justice. A further contrast may be observed from the aspect of time. There is no indication given of an immediate fulfillment to be sought in a historical figure contemporary with the time of Jeremiah.[106] As a very clear antithesis to Zedekiah, there is an ostensible stress on the quality of righteousness as characteristic

---

103. William L. Holladay, *Jeremiah 1: A Commentary on the Prophet Jeremiah Chapters 1–25* (1986) 618, advances evidence that although the expression צמח צדיק is a technical term for a future Davidic king who would restore the monarchy, the term should be more broadly interpreted in the wider context of Northwest Semitic languages since it appears in a Phoenician inscription of the third century B.C. In this inscription the phrase conveys the idea of "legitimate scion." Holladay concludes (618): "This is not to say that the meaning 'righteous' is absent from the present passage, but that the nuance of 'rightful' is central." See also J. A. Thompson, *The Book of Jeremiah* (1980) 489: "The metaphor is of a shoot (Ṣemaḥ) bursting forth from the Davidic tree which, though cut off, is not dead. English versions have generally translated the word as *Branch*. In postexilic times the term became the classic technical one for the expected ideal king (Zech 3.8; 6.12) . . . .The precise description in Hebrew is a ṣemaḥ ṣaddiq, which could mean a 'righteous shoot,' or 'a true shoot' of David's line as distinct from one who pretended to be such." See Wolter H. Rose, *Zemah and Zerubbabel* (2000) 110–14, for arguments that צדיק is best understood as "righteous" rather than "legitimate." For additional arguments, see also Werner Dommershausen, "Der 'Spross' als Messias," (1968) 323.

104. For the view that no contrast with Zedekiah is required, see Ernest W. Nicholson, *The Book of the Prophet Jeremiah, Chapters 1–25* (1973) 192; William McKane, *A Critical and Exegetical Commentary on Jeremiah* (1986) 564.

105. David R. Bauer, *The Structure of Matthew's Gospel* (1988) 67: "Jesus is throughout Matthew the model of the obedient Son. In contrast to this portrait of Jesus, Matthew presents the opponents of Jesus as those who disobey the will of God." Bauer also says (69): "in all the Gospels, and especially Matthew, there are only two positions: the right, which is the way of God; and the wrong, which is the way of the devil." See also W. Dommershausen (1968) 324: "Zedekia war unselbständig und ängstlich und geriet ganz in die Abhängigkeit von seinen Hofbeamten, die hohe dynastische Hoffnungen auf ihn setzten und ihn schließlich sogar zum Treubruch gegenüber Nebukadnezar veranlaßten. Der Chronist tadelt Zedekia, weil er 'sich nicht unter Jeremia demütigte' und hartnäckig sich nicht bekehrte zum Gotte Israels. Diesem illegitimen, rechsbrüchigen und Unheil bringenden Schwächling stellt Jeremia im Konstrast den Ideal-könig der Zukunft gegenüber. Dieser ist nänlich der 'gerechte' SproB aus dem Hause Davids."

106. For arguments that early Christians did not feel a loyal obligation to find only one meaning in OT Scripture, see also Fredrick C. Holgren, *The Old Testament and the Significance of Jesus* (1999) chapter 2, "Finding Jesus in the Depth of the Old Testament." For similar views, see also Richard B. Hays, *Echoes of Scripture in the Letters of Paul* (1989) 133.

of this unidentified figure and a prediction of his success based upon that righteousness.[107] Joel F. Drinkard comments:

> The clear interest in צדק, "righteous(ness)," and the word play in naming the king both point to a comparison with Zedekiah. This pericope apparently is intended to give a reversal of Zedekiah's reign and fate. Whereas Zedekiah had sought some miraculous intervention from Yahweh but was told only defeat and death would follow (21.1–10), this new king will have success and will see the deliverance of the people from their captivity. The name of this new king reverses the elements of Zedekiah's name (צדקיהו, "Zedekiah," יהוה צדקנו, "Yahweh is our righteousness"), indicative perhaps that all the aspects of Zedekiah are here reversed. The implication is that even the righteousness of this new king contrasts with Zedekiah; his name said "Yahweh is righteousness/ my righteousness," but the king himself was anything but righteous.[108]

Drinkard suggests that the mention of Zedekiah is an intended contrast to the Branch: where one fails, the other succeeds. The LXX offers tantalizing support for this contrast. The Hebrew text of Jer 23:6 ends with the line: "and this is the name by which he will be called: *the LORD our Righteousness*" (יהוה צדקנו).[109] The word צדקנו (*tzahdaknu*) unquestionably means "our righteousness."[110]

The LXX, however, offers the reader an unexpected twist with a bizarre translation of Ιωσεδεκ (*Iosedek*). Upon reading this for the first time in Greek, I was completely caught off guard. How could the LXX translators mistake the well-known noun

---

107. James Leo Green, *Jeremiah* (1971) 121: "*The Lord is our righteousness* . . . a deft play on 'Zedekiah'. In short, the righteous ruler of the future will succeed in his service to God and men, will make possible salvation and security, and will completely carry out all covenantal stipulations in his relationship with God's people as king."

108. J. Drinkard, *Jeremiah* (1991) 329. This is a composite work by three separate authors; I have listed only Drinkard as he was responsible for writing chapters 17 through 25. See also Norman C. Habel, *The Land Is Mine: Six Biblical Land Ideologies* (1995) 94. For the view that only God could legislate law in the OT and not kings (with exceptions noted), see Hans Jochen Boecker, *Law and the Administration of Justice in the Old Testament and Ancient East* (1980) 41–49. The implication for this study suggests that for God's people "law" originates in divine initiative and that Jesus is a righteous and wise legislator.

109. The LXX: καὶ τοῦτο τὸ ὄνομα αὐτοῦ, ὃ καλέσει αὐτοῦ κύριος Ιωσεδεκ ("and this [is] his name by which the LORD will call him, 'Iosedek'"). The Vulgate of Jer 23:6 reads: *et hoc est nomen quod vocabunt eum Dominus iustus noster*. The Vulgate translation steers clear of the LXX. On the problem of what precisely is the Septuagint, see J. Ross Wagner, "The Septuagint and the 'Search for the Christian Bible,'" in *Scripture's Doctrine and Theology' Bible* (2007) 17–28. For a reverse argument detailing reasons why messianism declined in Egypt during the Second Temple period, see J. Lust, "Messianism and the Greek Version of Jeremiah," in *VII Congress of the International Organization for Septuagint and Cognate Studies: Leuven 1989* (1989) 87–122; a slightly revised edition of this study appeared in "Messianism and the Greek Version of Jeremiah: Jer 23.5–6 and 33.14–26," in *Messianism and the Septuagint* (2004) 41–68.

110. The MT of Jer 51:10 reads: את־צדקתינו ("the LORD our righteousness"). This text has been omitted in the LXX. The Vulgate of Jer 51:10 reads: *Dominus iustitias nostras* ("the LORD our righteousness").

"righteousness" (צדק/*tzahdak*) with such a name as Ιωσεδεκ (Iosedek)? Clearly, this is not a mistake; rather, it is a deliberate mistranslation. It is my view that the name Iosedek, which is a personal name, appears to be coded language cryptically coined in reverse. A hint of this creative reversal is found in the LXX of Jer 1:3 as it reads: Σεδεκια υἱοῦ Ιωσια (*Sedekia son of Iosia*). In other words, the name at Jer 23:6 reverses a part of the father's name (*Io*) with a part of the son's name (*sedek*), giving us, in opposite order, Ιωσεδεκ or *Iosedek*. From the viewpoint of the LXX translation, the intentional reversal seems to be that the envisioned Branch will be a moral opposite and a definite contrast to Zedekiah. Instead of duplicating Zedekiah's character flaws (as subsequent kings often did by following in the unfaithful footsteps of their predecessors), the coming Branch will succeed by virtue of his righteousness.[111] Although Matthew does not make use of the name Ιωσεδεκ, he does do something that mirrors the moral failures of this ancient Judean king: he mentions the name of the infamous King Herod nine times in chapter 2, with three of these references specifying that Herod is indeed a king (2:1, 3, 8). Herod is an antithesis of a righteous king, a mirror image of the failings and flaws of King Zedekiah. The juxtaposition of Jesus and Herod side by side thus serves as an apt contrast between righteousness and its opposite of unrighteous or unjust.[112] Matthew is the only evangelist to include this information.

The verbal association (allusion) of righteousness forms yet another visible connection between Jer 23:5–6 and the first Gospel. Matthew presents us with a very striking case where righteousness characterizes Jesus. This occurs at his baptism when Jesus responds to the reticence of John the Baptist to immerse him. Jesus alleviates John's anxiety and hesitation by saying that it is "necessary to fulfill all *righteousness*" (3:15). The baptism of Jesus is a major moment in his life; all four Gospels report Jesus being baptized. However, only Matthew records that Jesus must be baptized in order to fulfill all righteousness. Although it has been typical of NT scholarship to interpret such a statement as originating in Matthew's mind as a response to his community's concerns over the abuse of grace, another way of understanding this text is to allow it not only to stand as a true statement coming directly from Jesus himself but also as connecting tightly to the motif of the King Branch. The word in translation "the LORD our righteousness" is not found in this exact form in the first Gospel; however,

---

111. For a full discussion of Near East announcement oracles and whether the LXX or the MT regarding this line is preferable, see John M. Wiebe, "The Form of the 'Announcement of a Royal Savior' and the Interpretation of Jeremiah 23.5–6," *SBTh* 15 (1987) 16, for his conclusion: "While Zedekiah did not rule effectively and brought on the exile, *Yōṣedeq* would do just the *opposite*. In his days Judah would be saved and Israel would dwell securely. So in order to convey this, the author repeated what looked to be the genuine Judean coronation oracle of Zedekiah. He proclaimed the new age the king would usher in but he altered the name in such a way that its similarities with Zedekiah would still be noticed. The way he changed the name was also significant. Holladay's suggestion is convincing that by reversing the divine element in the name from the back to the front of the root the author was saying the savior king would be just the *reverse* of Zedekiah."

112. For recent efforts to rehabilitate the character of Herod, see Byron R. McCane, "Simply Irresistible: Augustus, Herod, and the Empire," *JBL* 127.4 (2008) 725–35.

Matt 6:33 does come close with "seek first the kingdom of God and *his righteousness.*" These words are found only in Matthew. Since Matt 7:24 equates the words of Jesus with wisdom and righteousness, an implicit notion might lead to the conclusion that Jesus thus becomes the personal righteousness for the disciples. An additional Matthean reference to righteousness or righteous may be found at Matt 27:19;[113] only Matthew contains the information that Pilate's wife warned her husband not to have anything to do with that "righteous man" (δίκαιος).

Although Matthew does not make use of the verb βασιλεύω ("to reign"), he does provide a synonym with the verbs ἡγούμενος ("to lead") and ποιμάνω ("to shepherd") as found in 2:6: "And you, Bethlehem of the land of Judah, in no way are you the least in the clans/tribes of Judah, for out of you will come a ruler (ἡγούμενος), who will shepherd (ποιμάνω) Israel my people." This text contains several key concepts which further buttress the argument of this chapter. There are several references to the land, particularly the land of Judah, a critical reference to a "ruler" (one who leads) who will *shepherd* his people,[114] and the town of Bethlehem which has important associations with David. This citation does not conform to either the MT or the LXX,[115] and naturally forms a fertile field for exegetical plowing.[116] Especially notable is the sub-

---

113. A textual variant at v.24 also mentions that Jesus is δίκαιος.

114. See also Ezek 34:23–24: "And I will raise up over them one shepherd. And he shall feed them; my servant David, he shall feed them; and he shall be to them for a shepherd. And I, Yahweh, will be their God; and my servant David a ruler among them." The motifs of ruler, shepherd, and David as a servant are all linked together in a promised future idyllic figure.

115. A glance at the Greek text of the United Bible Society quickly reveals several significant details; the LXX/MT quotation is printed in bold letters, while the Matthean additions are in italics, of which there are two: Matthew transforms Ephratha into γῇ Ἰούδα ("land of Judah") and then adds the adverb οὐδαμῶς ("in no way"), thereby elevating the status of Bethlehem from "least" among the clans (Mic 5:2) to a position of being not least at all. How can we justify or even understand such a transformation? Davies and Allison (*Matthew: A Shorter Commentary*, [2004] 227) say: "No persuasive explanation seems forthcoming." For cautionary warnings not to jump to hasty conclusions, see John A. Emerton, "Messianism and Septuagint," in *Messianism and the Septuagint* (2004) 13: "The messianic interpretation in the LXX is not necessarily due to the Greek translator. It may have been a characteristic of his Hebrew *Vorlage*." Emerton's caution is due to his thesis that the LXX does not show development toward messianism. If his thesis is correct, then statements regarding the Branch must be considered extraordinary. For a balanced judgment on the issue of messianism in the Septuagint, see L. Desrousseaux, "David dans La Septante: Remarques préliminaires sur la Septante" in *Messianism and the Septuagint* (2004, reprint from *Lectio divina* 177 [1999] 243–63) 171: "La Septante n'est le travail ni d'une seule personne, ni d'une école. Plusieurs traducteurs et réviseurs ont participé à cette enterprise de longue haleine, et cettte pluralité se vérifie même pour tel ou tel livre biblique pris isolément. Il est donc hasardeux de parler de 'tendances théologiques de la Septante,' comme si cette traduction formait un bloc homogène." One possible way of answering part of the question is to follow the trail back to the text of Jer 23:6.

116. For a likely background to this text, see H. Heater, "Matthew 2.6 and Its OT Sources," *JETS* 26 (1983) 395–97;" and A. J. Petrotta, "A Closer Look at Matthew 2.6 and OT Sources," *JETS* 28 (1985) 47–52. For the origin of this citation and the argument for a diminishing role of the LXX on NT messianism, see Christopher W. Tuckett, "Micah 5.13 in Qumran and in the New Testament and Messianism in the Septuagint," in *Messianism and the Septuagint* (2004) 100: "Here it may suffice to say that the author of the gospel most likely did not use the LXX since he chose צעיר as a translation

stitution of Ephratha in the MT with "Judah" by Matthew. John Nolland is probably correct in assigning this alteration as due to Matthew's interest in Judah as the tribe from which the royal line came.[117]

A subsidiary question presents itself: why would Matthew substitute the verb βασιλεύω with the less attractive verbs ἡγούμενος and ποιμάνω? Of course, it is possible that he found one of these verbs in the text he was using.[118] There are other possibilities. First, there is the likely association with King David; David was not just a king but also a shepherd.[119] Jesus thus would fulfill the idealized role of a king who will shepherd his people with wisdom and justice. Second, the text of Jer 23:1–4 describes false shepherds who are abusing the people. In order to reverse the curse of poor shepherding, the LORD makes a promise to raise up faithful shepherds who will care for the flock.[120] Jesus would then fulfill the requirement of a very wise and just shepherd. Third, there is further reinforcement by the words of Zech 13:7 in which the LORD says, "I will strike the *shepherd* and the sheep will scatter." Notable is the fact that this text is omitted in Luke but contained in Matthew (26:31). To further underscore the nexus of connections between Jesus, kingship, and King David, there is the Matthean identification of Jesus as a shepherd (9:36). In this scene, while Jesus is preaching the "gospel of the kingdom," he has compassion upon the multitude because they are ὡσεὶ πρόβατα μὴ ἔχοντα ποιμένα ("like sheep without a shepherd").[121]

---

of ἐλαχίστη and not LXX's ὀλιγοστός, which is an unusual equivalent of the Hebrew term in question. Matthew's emphatic negative οὐδαμῶς ἐλαχίστη εἶ may be due to a free interpretation, or to the reading of הצעיר as a rhetorical question, or to a different *Vorlage*." For some unknown reason, Timothy R. McLay, *The Use of the Septuagint in New Testament Research* (2003), does not list Matt 2:6 in his Index.

117. J. Nolland, *The Gospel of Matthew* (2005) 114.

118. For the use of the LXX in Matthew, see Maarten J. J. Menken, *Matthew's Bible* (2004) 35, where Menken outlines some of the difficulties: it's not always easy to establish what text Matthew is using or if he is translating freely from the MT.

119. For further connections with David, kingship and riding a donkey, see James E. Patrick, "Matthew's *Pesher* Gospel Structured around Ten Messianic Citations of Isaiah," *JTS* 61.1 (2010) 73.

120. F. F. Bruce, in *This Is That: The New Testament Development of Some Old Testament Themes* (1968) 100, offered the following connection: "In the Old Testament not only is the relation between a ruler and his subjects repeatedly expressed in terms of a shepherd and his sheep, two of the greatest leaders of Israel in Old Testament history, Moses and David, served their apprenticeship by keeping sheep—a fact which might prompt a course of meditation on the characteristics shared in common by sheep and human beings, which call for similar qualities of leadership."

121. L. Hartman, "Scriptural Exegesis in the Gospel of St. Matthew and the Problem of Communication," in *L'Évangile selon Matthieu: Rédaction et théologie* (1971) 147, while discussing allusions in Matthew, acknowledges that the word "shepherd" is an allusion to the OT. Since Hartman operates on the principle of "a set of associations" that identify a given text as an allusion, strangely he does not mention Psa 23:1 or Jer 23:1–6. His omission of these two striking texts is puzzling.

A Wise King

MT: וּמָלַךְ מֶלֶךְ וְהִשְׂכִּיל; LXX: βασιλεύσει βασιλεὺς καὶ συνήσει καὶ ποιήσει κρίμα καὶ δικαιοσύνην ἐπὶ τῆς γῆς; NIV: "a king who will rule wisely and do judgment and righteousness."

Matthew presents Jesus uniquely as both righteous and wise.[122] In the four Gospels there are a total of five different words expressing various shades of meaning for the virtue of wisdom. These five are: συνίημι ("to understand"),[123] νοέω ("to understand," or "to comprehend"),[124] σοφία ("wisdom"),[125] σοφός ("wise"),[126] and φρόνιμος ("wise").[127] Matthew leads the way in the sum total of all five words.[128] The idyllic king in the OT embodies a spirit of wisdom and sound counsel.[129] Proverbs 8:14–15 is a proclamation by Wisdom (σοφία) who says: "Counsel and sound judgment are mine; I have understanding and power. By me kings reign and rulers make laws that are just".[130] In Matt 12:39–42, I find perhaps the climactic statement regarding the wisdom of Jesus. Verse 39 indicates that this is a statement directly from Jesus, although the Jesus Seminar assigns the saying to the Matthean community.[131] Without contesting the Seminar claim, I note that a contrast is made between Jesus and King Solomon on the score of wisdom: the Queen of the South came to hear of Solomon's wisdom, but one greater than Solomon is here. By comparison, this places Jesus above Solomon in respect to wisdom. As Kenneth Schenck says, "But Jesus was not just an ordinary king to Matthew. Like King David's son, Solomon, who was known for his wisdom, Jesus the 'Son of David,' was as the supreme teacher of God's wisdom."[132] Significant also is the emphatic ἰδού ("behold")—a term of exclamation found in the LXX of

---

122. On the role of wisdom in Matthew, see Celia Deutsch, "Wisdom in Matthew: Transformation of a Symbol," *NovT* 32 (1990) 36–39.

123. συνίημι: Matt (9): 13:13, 14,15,19, 23, 51; 15:10; 16:12; 17:13; Mark (4): 4:12; 7:14; 8:17, 21; Luke (4): 2:50; 8:10; 18:34; 24:45; John: (0). The noun σύνεσις is not significant, with only two total references: Mark 12:33 and Luke 2:47.

124. νοέω: Matt (4): 15:17; 16:9, 11; 24:15; Mark (1): 13:14; Luke (0); John (1): 12:40.

125. σοφία: Matt (3): 11:19; 12:42; 13:54; Mark (1): 6:2; Luke (6): 2:40, 52; 7:35; 11:31, 49; 21:15; John (0).

126. σοφός: Matt (2): 11:25; 23:34; Mark (0); Luke (1): 10:21; John (0).

127. φρόνιμος: Matt (7): 7:24; 10:16; 24:45; 25:2, 4, 8, 9; Mark (0); Luke (1): 12:42; John (0).

128. Matt (25); Mark (10); Luke (13); John (1). Matthew thus exceeds the sum total of the other three evangelists.

129. For a discussion of wisdom and righteousness as key components of Son of David and Solomon typology, see Anthony Le Donne, *The Historiographical Jesus* (2009) 93–127. Le Donne's focus is upon Solomon more than David.

130. LXX: δι' ἐμοῦ βασιλεῖς βασιλεύουσιν.

131. Robert W. Funk, Roy W. Hoover, and The Jesus Seminar, *The Five Gospels: The Search for the Authentic Words of Jesus* (1993) 189: "Since Luke does not seem to know this interpretation, we must assume it did not appear in Q, but is a Christian reinterpretation provided by Matthew. It certainly did not originate with Jesus."

132. Kenneth Schenck, *Jesus is Lord!* (2003) 160.

Jer 23:5–6. Most likely the wisdom of Jesus in this context applies to the power to vanquish evil spirits.[133] M.J. Suggs suggested "it would not greatly overstate the case to say that *for Matthew* Wisdom has 'become flesh and dwelled among us' (John 1.14)."[134] On this note, I cite an extended observation by Anthony Le Donne who, after stating that Psalm of Solomon 17 has made explicit what was implicit in Isaiah 11 (Solomon typology), then concludes: "It is specifically typological because the psalmist hopes for a Davidic figure that embodies both the characteristics and legacy of Solomon.... In other words, this Solomonic figure will possess all of Solomon's admirable qualities and none of his faults."[135]

Salvation

MT בימיו תושע יהודה; LXX: ἐν ταῖς ἡμέραις αὐτοῦ σωθήσεται Ιουδας; NIV: "In his days Judah will be saved."

This salvation will include both Judah and Israel and it will occur "in *his* days."[136] Matthew 1:21 portrays an angel of the LORD speaking to Joseph to the effect that Mary will give birth to a son and Joseph is to call this son Jesus "for he will save his people" (σώσει τὸν λαὸν αὐτοῦ). This is another striking allusion to the text of Jer 23:5–6 and it involves the promise of salvation. Accordingly, Ulrich Luz does not hesitate to propose that the demographic term "the people" (τὸν λαόν) refers to Israel, the OT people of God.[137] The concept of a Davidic king bringing salvation to Israel was not unknown or unexpected at Qumran;[138] historically, however, it did not materialize in that community. Proceeding on this assumption, the value of identifying "the people" (τὸν λαὸν) with Israel is that both are mentioned in Hebrew parallelism of Jer 23:6.

Rudolf Schnackenburg takes the Matthean concept of salvation a step further: "Jesus, therefore, the shoot of David, is presented as Israel's promised 'king of salvation' in Matthew as nowhere else."[139] Schnackenburg's concluding words bear isolating for special repetition in italics: "*as nowhere else.*" This claim for exclusivity, if accepted, can strengthen the thematic case for seeing a plausible substructure in Matthew. It is necessary now to inquire if this contrast "as nowhere else" can stand up to scrutiny. To begin with, the trio of words σωτήρ ("Savior"), σωτηρία ("salvation"), and

---

133. For the argument linking the wisdom of Jesus with power over the demonic forces of evil, see Larry Perkins, "'Greater than Solomon,'" *TRINJ* 19 (1998) 207–17.

134. M. J. Suggs, *Wisdom, Christology and Law in Matthew's Gospel* (1970) 57.

135. A. Le Donne, *The Historiographical Jesus* (2009) 121. See also P. A. Torijano, *Solomon the Esoteric King: From King to Magus, Developments of a Tradition* (2002) 106–8.

136. For the use of "his," see Isa 65:20: אתימיו ("his years/days").

137. U. Luz, *Matthew 1–7: A Commentary* (2007) 95.

138. For a discussion of this expectation at Qumran, see George J. Brooke, *Exegesis at Qumran: 4QFlorilegium in its Jewish Context* (1985) 197–205.

139. R. Schnackenburg, *The Gospel of Matthew* (2002) 9.

σώζω ("to save") are not exclusive to Matthew. In fact, Luke actually has a higher word-count.[140] Schnackenburg, however, has qualified his observation by referring to Jesus as "king of salvation." This is helpful but not quite accurate enough. In Matthew, Jesus is presented uniquely as the King who brings salvation to his people; in Luke (it will be argued), Jesus is presented as the High Priest who ministers salvation. Salvation characterizes both roles, not one. Thus, as though through a single prism, they are refracted into two separate rays.

The Land

MT: בָּאָרֶץ, LXX: ἐπὶ τῆς γῆς, NIV: "in the land."

There remains a final category not covered in this category of rubrics. That rubric is the land. Jeremiah 23:6 says that this Branch will do what is right *in the land*. Matthew is dominated by geographical names and places; this is especially evident in chapters 2 and 4.[141] To be more precise, in chapter 2 alone, the word "the land" (ἐπὶ τῆς γῆς) is mentioned three times (2:6, 20, 22). Moving from the general to the particular, there are twenty additional references to places in Palestine: Bethlehem of Judea is mentioned six times (2:1, 5, 6, 8, 10, 16); Judea three times (2:3; 3:1, 5); Jerusalem three times (2:1, 3; 3:5); the Jordan River or its region three times (3:5, 6, 13); the land of Israel twice (2:20, 22); the region of Galilee twice (2:23; 3:13) and Nazareth once (2:23). Expanding upon these locations, the following serried references occur in Matthew: Capernaum (4x), Galilee (17x), Jerusalem (12x), and Nazareth (4x). Of special interest is a text already mentioned, Matt 2:6: "And you, Bethlehem of the land of Judah, in no way are you the least in the clans/tribes of Judah, for out of you will come a ruler. Jer 23:6 specifically mentions that a king would come out of Judah. The name "Judah" is polysemic. It can refer to the individual Judah, one of the sons of Jacob; it can refer to the tribe of Judah; it can also refer to the land of Judah. Judah can clearly represent either the people proper or it can be a synonym for the land. In all fairness, I do not see a way to separate the two. Matthew 1:2–3 mentions the individual Judah twice, while the reference in Matt 2:6 links Judah to Bethlehem, thereby connecting Judah to the land. I have applied the reference to the land, but this by no means excludes the people. The salient point is that Jesus is thereby firmly anchored to the land of Israel.

On a wider front, in comparison with the other Gospels, Matthew's greater numerical count of references includes those of Bethlehem, Galilee, Judah, Judea,

---

140. σωτήρ: Matt (0); Mark (0); Luke (2); John (1). σωτηρία: Matt (0); Mark (0); Luke (3); John (1). σώζω: Matt (4); Mark (4); Luke (3); John (3). Combining all three words, we have Matt (4); Mark (4); Luke (8); John (5). The Gospel of Luke doubles Matthew. There seems to be a reticence among all four Gospels to use the word σωτήρ.

141. Krister Stendahl, "*Quis et Unde?*: An Analysis of Matthew 1–2," in *The Interpretation of Matthew* (1983) 57.

Nazareth, and the River Jordan.[142] At the very least, Matthew seems intent on identifying Jesus with the land of Israel. The land itself was an integral ingredient to the traditional faith of Israel. Moshe Weinfeld observes: "No other people in the history of mankind was as preoccupied as the people of Israel with the land in which they lived. The whole biblical historiography revolves around the Land."[143] The promise of land goes all the way back to Abraham, continues through the Prophets, and influences Matthew's narrative. This I state in spite of the fact that at the end Matthew includes the commission to disciple all the nations.[144] Luz suggests: "Much of the evidence suggests that the Matthean community comes from a Judaism that belonged to the 'people of the land' . . ."[145] Hans Conzelmann writes, "Matthew takes up Mark's idea of Galilee as the chosen district and emphasizes it further by introducing a scriptural proof showing Galilee as the promised land of fulfillment."[146]

The word γῆ ("land") stands out in Matthew when compared to the other three Gospels. The word γῆ (ge, the basis of geography or "land writing") is mentioned only eleven times in John but forty-two in Matthew. Mark (19) and Luke (26) fall in between. The first four references in Matthew are instructive: at 2:6 Bethlehem is described as being in "the *land* of Judah;" in 2:20–21 an angel of the LORD tells the family to leave Egypt and return to "the *land* of Israel." At 4:15 Jesus begins his ministry preaching to the people in the *land* of Zebulun. At this point, though, Matthew cites from Isaiah not Jeremiah: "to fulfill what was said through the prophet Isaiah: 'Land of Zebulun and land of Naphtali . . .'" It is clear that Matthew intentionally ties his gospel narrative to the land of Israel.[147] Jesus was born in the land, ministered in the land, and was put to death in the land of Judah. J. R. C. Cousland makes a compelling case that the data in Matthew regarding the land does not require a date post-70 but, rather, conforms to conditions more indicative of the period A.D. 44–66.[148] He does not stop

---

142. References to the land of Judah are the following: Matthew (4); Mark (0); Luke (2); John (0). References to Judea are: Matt (8); Mark (4); Luke (10); John (6). References to Galilee are: Matt (16); Mark (12); Luke (14); John (17). References to the Jordan River are: Matt (6); Mark (4); Luke (2); John (3). The totals equate to: Matt (34); Mark (20); Luke (28); John (26).

143. M. Weinfeld, *The Promise of the Land* (1993) 183.

144. Judith M. Lieu, *Christian Identity in the Jewish and Graeco-Roman World* (2004) 229, says: "as the closing verses of the Gospel make clear, this gives the land no privilege for the future." See also W. D. Davies, *The Gospel and the Land* (1974).

145. U. Luz, *Matthew 17: A Commentary* (2007) 48. See also James H. Charlesworth, "What has the Old Testament to Do with the New?" in *The Old and New Testaments* (1993) 52.

146. H. Conzelmann, *An Outline of the Theology of the New Testament* (1969) 144.

147. Of course, the above profile does not do full justice to geographical issues in the Gospels. Seán Freyne, "The Geography, Politics, and Economics of Galilee and the Quest for the Historical Jesus," in *Studying the Historical Jesus: Evaluations of the State of Current Research* (1994) 80, has shown that with non-Jewish writers there is a "strange detachment from the geography of Palestine. We never get any authorial interjection to explain details." Freyne also includes the observation that Josephus possessed a sharp awareness of such details.

148. J. R. C. Cousland, *The Crowds in the Gospel of Matthew* (2002) 65: "Taken as a whole then, the geographical features of Matthew's gospel can hardly be said to conform to the period after the

with first century observations only but proceeds to develop the additional proposal that land descriptions in the period of A.D. 44–66 also reflect geographical conditions current during the time of David. This is a claim of potential interest; if true, it would lend credibility to the claim of this book. If untrue, it would imply that artistic license has taken priority over geographical fact. Michael E. Fuller in a succinct statement aptly says, "geography matters, for it is profoundly theological."[149] It needs to be stated, however, that the focus of the Jer. 23:6 prophecy is not about the Jews returning from exile or the Diaspora to the land of Israel. Rather, the salient point is that the Davidic messiah is to arise, sprout, or come from that land.

Conclusion

Even though the Gospel of Matthew does not contain a full citation of Jer 23:5–6, this does not close the door to possible options. Other factors invite consideration. The ironical fact is that of the total number of twenty-eight individual Hebrew words in this prophetic text, twenty-seven of them conceivably find an equivalent place in the Greek text of Matthew. A visual indicator of this correspondence can be observed by opening a Greek text to the first three chapters of Matthew. As one reads the Greek text from Matt 1:1 to 3:17, highlighting with color coding the key words as found in the Greek text of Jer 23:5–6 in the LXX version, a verbal and visual scene opens up before the eyes. There are a total of thirty-two color-coded words from Jer 23:5–6 in these three chapters alone. This number bumps up to forty-one by counting the nine references to King Herod as a substitute for Zedekiah (both a moral opposite of righteousness). The number further increases to sixty-one, if the twenty specific references to places in chapters 2 and 3 are included. This number of sixty-one relevant words occurs in a space of just sixty-five total verses in the first three chapters of Matthew alone. The imprint of Jer 23:5–6 is everywhere in the first three chapters of Matthew and, consequently, may serve as a thematic template for the entire Gospel.[150] By further expansion, I count some twenty-four prophetic passages that Matthew cites from the OT. Of these twenty-four texts, I do not believe that there is a single one that surpasses the explanatory power of Jer 23:5–6 for understanding the structure of the first Gospel. Taking into consideration the entire contents of Matthew, no other prophetic text in the Old Testament contains so many matching motifs, accounts for so many thematic issues, and encompasses so many foundational elements as does the text of Jer 23:5–6.

Jewish revolt."

149. Michael E. Fuller, *The Restoration of Israel: Israel's Re-Gathering and the Fate of the Nations in Early Jewish Literature and Luke–Acts* (2006) 26. I note also his intriguing comment (209): "That is, the author of Luke–Acts claims Israel's reconstitution in a time *when the Land lies in ruins*" (italics his).

150. Benedict T. Viviano, "The Genres of Matthew 1–2" (1990) 32, suggests that the first two chapters of Matthew "constitute an overture to the rest of the gospel."

5

The Genealogy of Jesus in Matthew

MATTHEW BEGINS HIS GOSPEL with what could be perceived as a rather blasé opening. This has tempted some to consider this genealogy of little interest.[1] Before considering the purpose of the genealogy, a relevant question intervenes: why even begin the Gospel in this supposedly mundane manner? Matthew could have easily left out these first seventeen verses and begun his Gospel at v.18. A typical response to the above question is to say merely that this information must have been important to the original readers. But does this fully answer the question? Commentators, both ancient and modern, have struggled with its historicity, with attacks in modern times being relentless.[2] There is evidence, though, that Jewish family histories were kept intact up to the first century.[3] One biblical example is that of Paul himself who claims lineage through the tribe of Benjamin.[4] On a scale of Jewish values, however, the tribe of Benjamin would not carry the same weight as the tribe of Judah.

Although there has been no lack of research on the purpose, function, and design of Matthew's account of the birth of Jesus,[5] one question is always missing: why do Matthew and Luke contain a genealogy, while Mark and John omit one? Craig L. Blomberg, under the rubric of *Variations in Names and Numbers*, observes, "By far the most complicated divergence under this heading is the seemingly hopelessly muddled

---

1. On a popular level, see the advertisement in *Christianity Today*, 52.7 (July 2008) which promotes the book *Four Gospels, One Story: Savior*, by enticing the buyer with this line: "No long genealogical lists."

2. Representative of this view is Ulrich Luz, *Matthew 1–7: A Commentary* (2007) 82: "However, too much speaks against the historicity of this genealogy for us to take it seriously." Also (93): ". . . it is hopeless to ask about the historicity . . . we do not need to assume that it contains information from the circle of Jesus' family."

3. Josephus, *Against Apion* 1.36, makes this claim for the lineage of the high priests.

4. For this observation, see Herman C. Waetjen, "The Genealogy as the Key to the Gospel According to Matthew," *JBL* 95.2 (1976) 207. He also mentions Josephus' own table of ancestry (*Life* 1.1.6).

5. For example, John Mark Jones, "Subverting the Textuality of Davidic Messianism: Matthew's Presentation of the Genealogy and the Davidic Title," *CBQ* 56 (1994) 256–72. For a more objective view, see John Nolland, "Genealogical Annotation in Genesis as Background for the Matthean Genealogy of Jesus," *TynBul* 47.1 (1996) 115–22.

genealogies of Jesus as record by Matthew and Luke."[6] By the expression "seemingly hopelessly muddled," Blomberg suggests that the lack of congruence between Matthew and Luke seems to be a hopeless mess, perhaps beyond hope of reconciliation. He does not explore the issue which I am raising here. Bo Reicke suggests that Matthew and Luke diverge from one another in their respective birth narratives because Matthew wanted to stress instruction to men, while Luke wanted to emphasize the emotion of joy from the women.[7] A rather novel and idiosyncratic view of Matthew's account is that of J. A. (Bobby) Loubser who argues that ultimately the Matthean genealogy is so constructed as to produce an "altered mind state" and in this altered state of mind the participating audience could, in solidarity with their host of ancestors, become immediate participators in the life of the Messiah.[8] Although Loubser does make some valuable observations on the general nature of biblical genealogies, he does not confront the issue of why Matthew and Luke are the only two evangelists with such texts.

Matthew's Genealogy Points in the Direction of Kingship

The proposal offered here is predicated upon the idea of kingship. Although it is conventional to mention that Mark omits a genealogy while Matthew contains one, the significance of the presence in one and absence in the other is often ignored. Raymond E. Brown, in his monumental study of the birth narratives, is one of the few to consider a solution to this difference between Matthew and Mark. He proposes an answer based upon a combination of process and time: Mark does not require a genealogy because at that time it was not necessary to meet the needs of the church, but as time passed and the early church engaged in further reflection upon the mystery of Jesus' identity, a more developed view became both necessary and dominant.[9] The advantage of such a position, admittedly, is that it seeks an explanation grounded in the historical conditions of the developing church.[10] One of the disadvantages of such a view, however, would be the necessity to distance the composition of Matthew sufficiently later in time. It is doubtful that such a short gap in time would account for this alleged need. Another explanation is the view that the genealogy fits better or is "more at home in Greco-Roman culture than it was in Jewish culture."[11]

---

6. C. L. Blomberg, *The Historical Reliability of the Gospels* (1987) 150.

7. B. Reicke, "Christ's Birth and Childhood," in *From Faith to Faith* (1979) 151–65.

8. J. A. Loubser, "Invoking Ancestors: Some Socio-Rhetorical Aspects of the Genealogies in the Gospels of Matthew and Luke," *NeoT* 39.1 (2005) 137.

9. R. E. Brown, *The Birth of the Messiah* (1977) 27–32. He thus concluded (29): "This addition to the Gospel is best explained in the light of the development of Christology."

10. This view, of course, presumes the priority of Mark.

11. Anthony Le Donne, *The Historiographical Jesus* (2009) 187. Le Donne follows the lead marked out by Y. Levin, "Jesus, 'Son of God' and 'Son of David'," *JSNT* 28.4 (2006) 424–42.

I would like to propose an alternative solution. Another way of answering the above question (why Matthew has a genealogy and Mark does not) is to suggest a solution based upon OT precedence: for the most part, kings in the OT have a genealogy. To be more specific, the OT kings of Judea *always* have a genealogy, even though in most cases it is only a single reference to the king's father. The OT historical books contain the accounts of forty-two kings, three while Israel was united in monarchy (during the reigns of Saul, David, and Solomon) and after the division: twenty-one for Judea in the south and eighteen for the kings in the north. These accounts are similar in many ways: one of the most striking characteristics is the consistent pattern of always listing the father. In some cases, the name of the mother is even included. I could find only two exceptions.

In order not to be faulted for dodging a potentially uncomfortable fact, it will be necessary to examine the two cases involving an exception. In the entire registry of OT kings, only two men surface as fatherless; the first is Zimri. Recognizing this anomalous omission, H. B. MacLean comments, "No mention is made of his father."[12] James A. Montgomery in the ICC describes Zimri as "a nobody, as his father is not named."[13] In similar language, Charles G. Martin describes Zimri as an "upstart, taking advantage of a drunken stupor to succeed his master."[14] The absence of patronym becomes significant in light of the fact that this is a clear departure from the normal pattern. Why the omission and what, if any, is the relevance to this study? Zimri first appears in 1 Kgs 16:9. Salient facts of his very short reign are the following: he came to power through treachery and murder; he was never anointed or recognized by any official body politic or any ceremonial anointing; he lasted only seven days before he ended his life by shameful suicide. In short, he is an ignominious figure. So low and ignoble is his name that in 2 Kgs 9:31 the name of Zimri becomes a byword for an assassin.

Zimri is followed by Omri, who also is apatronymic. Simon J. DeVries notes: "It is important to note that Omri was made king and that he did not simply seize power in a conspiracy."[15] Given this additional information, what can possibly tip the balance? H. B. MacLean offers a reason for the absence of patronym for Omri: "The probable explanation is that Omri, like Zimri, was a foreigner, a non-Israelite, who had achieved his position through his own efforts and abilities."[16] If this is the case,

---

12. H. B. MacLean, "Zimri," IDB (1962) 4.958.

13. J. Montgomery, *A Critical and Exegetical Commentary on the Books of Kings* (1951) 282.

14. C. Martin, *1 and 2 Kings* (1979) 444.

15. Simon J. DeVries, *1 Kings* (1985) 200.

16. H. B. MacLean, "Omri," IDB (1962) 3.601. For Omri's place of origin, see B. D. Napier, "The Omrides of Jezreel," *VT* 9.4 (1959) 366–78. For Omri's posterity, see Julian Morgenstern, "Chronological Data of the Dynasty of Omri," *JBL* 59.3 (1940) 385–96. For the significance of Omri's reign, see C. F. Whitley, "The Deuteronomic Presentation of the House of Omri," *VT* 2.2 (1952) 137–52. For the description of Omri as a "hapless rebel," see Francisco O. Garcia-Treto, "The Fall of the House: A Carnivalesque Reading of 2 Kings 9 and 10," *JSOT* 46 (1990) 48.

then Zimri and Omri suffer a similar biblical fate. They are both foreigners and, therefore, as foreigners they are treated with a less than normal respect. More relevant to this study, however, is the particular fact that neither one is from the tribe of Judah. The kings from Judah occupy a unique and exceptional status in that they are *always* recognized with the appropriate patronym.

The two chapters of 1 Kings 14–15 may serve as an example. At 14:1, Abijah is listed as the son of Jeroboam and he becomes king at 15:1; Jeroboam himself is the son of Nebat (15:1); Rehoboam, king over Judah, is the son of Solomon (14:21). The significance of this unvarying formula is that it paves the way for a better understanding of Matthew 1:1–25. The relationship between the OT catalog of kings and the genealogy of Matthew provides potential illumination into the prophecy of Jer 23:5. The genealogy of Matthew suggests that in order for Jesus to be considered the rightful or legitimate king who sits on David's throne, he must establish this claim, at the minimum, upon the basis of his human ancestry. Yet, as Francis Watson points out,[17] this registry is not the biological ancestry of Jesus. Matthew's record shows that it is Joseph's family tree, but Joseph is not the real father of Jesus. How then does the alleged genealogy of Jesus legitimize the claim to be the Son of David?

Beyond the issue of human ancestry, the fact that Matthew includes a genealogy at all deserves a deeper probe. More specifically, why does Matthew include the family tree of Jesus while the Gospel of Mark omits such information? Is Matthew dealing with rumors that Jesus was illegitimate? Is he dispelling doubts about the paternity of Jesus? Are there perhaps even questions whether Jesus was a real person?[18] Matthew takes the reader back through David, through Judah, all the way back to Abraham. Although the presence of the four ladies in Matthew's account has attracted considerable scholarly attention, we should not lose sight of the fact that the very first verse begins: "the origin/genealogy of Jesus Christ, son of *David*, son of *Abraham*." Therefore, going beyond the simple to the more complex, the purpose of the genealogy also serves to identify Jesus as a descendant of both King David and the patriarch Abraham. More particular, however, is the number of references to David in Matthew's first chapter. There are six in all: 1:1, 6, 6, 17, 17, and 20. Of King David, Jack Dean Kingsbury notes: "in Jewish circles it was the acknowledgment of the male child by a man that made that child his son, and not the physical act of procreation as such, the fact Matthew depicts Jesus as being adopted into the line of David does not mean that his Davidic lineage is therefore in any sense questionable."[19]

H. C. Waetjen suggests that David is mentioned because he (along with Jeconiah) is a transitional figure who both terminates and inaugurates historical periods

---

17. F. Watson, *The Fourfold Gospel* (2016) 31

18. This is the assessment of Ulrich Luz, *Matthew 1–7* (2007) 87: "A basic affirmation of Christian faith is contained here—the knowledge that Jesus is a human, historical figure." Luz is unable to go much further than to affirm that Jesus is a real human being.

19. J. D. Kingsbury, "The Title 'Son of David' in Matthew's Gospel," *JBL* 95 (1976) 597–98.

of time.[20] Although demarcation in the timeline by the use of the number fourteen is part of Matthew's overall scheme, the fact that David is mentioned twice in name and specifically singled out once as a king indicates something more substantive than mere transition. David is a key marker indicating a possible allusion or echo behind the promise and fulfillment of the Branch prophecy.

Even though there are fourteen kings mentioned in Matt 1:6–12,[21] all of them coming through the seed of David, only one is actually mentioned as a king—King David. Matthew thus begins his Gospel by subtly hinting at a kingship link with King David; in fact, the genealogy of Christ in Matthew comes strategically through the lineage of King David. Jesus, as a king, is proleptically positioned as the anticipated Son of David. Ulrich Luz writes:

> There is little to be gained from inquiring into the roots of the "Son of David" title in religious history . . . . In the Prologue the title quite clearly had a "genealogical" significance: Jesus, through his adoption by Joseph, truly is the Son of David and for this very reason a claimant for the title of Israel's King-Messiah (1.18–2.12). Matthew therefore engages his Jewish-Christian readers at the level of their own expectations of the Messiah.[22]

Kingsbury and Luz offer a way for understanding Matthew's frame of reference. They both suggest that legal adoption qualifies Jesus to take on Joseph's family linage as his own. Is this interpretation correct? If the answer is yes, this affirmation must be qualified. It can only be true legally; it is not true biologically. Since it is not true in a biological sense, the upside means that Jesus does not inherit Joseph's genetic weaknesses; the downside is that Jesus cannot be a son of David by virtue of Joseph's seed. Matthew's account, however, shows no concern that Jesus is not the Son of David by virtue of Joseph's blood. There is no anxiety on Matthew's part that this linage is a non sequitur. How could this be accepted as true? To borrow a modern analogy, when a child is adopted into another family, that child does not possess the DNA of the new parents. Yet, the child does inherit the last name of the adopting parents. If Joseph is a son of David, the title transfers to Jesus as well.

Advancing on, Matthew does want to connect his narrative as a bridge back to the OT in order to show that Jesus is the Messiah who was promised to sit on the throne of David. This is the language of promise and fulfillment, even of king and kingdom. In fact, Matthew 2:1–2 says, "Magi from the east came to Jerusalem and asked, 'Where

---

20. H. C. Waetjen, "Genealogy as the Key" (1976) 212–3. See also Christof Landmesser, "Interpretative Unity of the New Testament," in *One Scripture or Many? Canon from Biblical, Theological, and Philosophical Perspectives* (2004) 171, who says: "These three sections span the entire history of Israel from Abraham to Jesus. Each of the three parts concludes with an extraordinary event in the history of Israel."

21. Grant R. Osborne, *Zondervan Exegetical Commentary on Matthew* (2010) 67, suggests that the nine names from Abiud down to Jacob, covering a period of 500 years, contains gaps.

22. U. Luz, *The Theology of the Gospel of Matthew* (1995) 71.

is the one who has been born king of the Jews? We have seen his star in the east and have come to worship him.'" Matthew is the only Gospel that contains this information of the Magi coming to worship a king. This information, unique to Matthew, helps to buttress the premise of this chapter in that the first Gospel gives evidence suggesting a link to Jesus as the fulfillment of the Branch prophecy as the King of kings.

To this writer, the issue of priority does not resolve the absence of a genealogy in Mark and the presence of a different genealogy in Luke. If Mark is first in order and Matthew has followed him, this would account for Mark not containing one, but it would not explain a different one in Luke. If, however, Matthew is first in priority, this would lead to confusion as to why Mark did not follow him and why Luke adopts a different one. In other words, the question of literary priority does not provide a sufficient explanation behind three separate approaches to the family line of Jesus. The explanation as presented in these pages gives a more accurate account of the variations.

Conclusion to Chapters 4 and 5

I acknowledge that nowhere does Matthew cite the full text of Jer 23:5–6. Although Jeremiah is frequently alluded to by Matthew, the fact is that the text of Jer 23:5–6 is never cited *in extenso*. In view of the thesis as developed in this book, what, if anything, can be made of this minimal use? Does the fact of minimal use undermine or vitiate the thesis? Or, conversely, can this relative silence actually underscore the thesis? The point of view adopted here is that this omission does not create a disabling handicap and, therefore, does not hamstring the investigation. On the contrary, this silence can potentially work in favor of discovering the substructure and, consequently, even the ultimate source of inspiration. In this sense I am using silence as an ally. To state this in stronger language, this silence is actually necessary to the thesis as presented here. Inasmuch as proof-texting by means of direct quotations from the OT is often faulted as being an "after-the-fact" addition, silence actually serves a positive and constructive role. Because of this silence, Matthew cannot be accused of inventing the fulfillment of OT prophecies after-the-fact regarding Jer 23:5–6, of participating in a duplicitous conspiracy, or employing Jewish haggadic imagination.[23] Nor can Matthew be faulted for twisting Scripture by misunderstanding OT texts.[24] In other words, it would not

23. W. D. Davies and Dale Allison, *A Critical and Exegetical Commentary on the Gospel According to Saint Matthew* (1988) 221 and 252, are rather restrained in a subtle promotion of the notion of haggadic exegesis rather than historical fact regarding the details of the birth of Jesus. They are held in check by the counsel of their editor, C. E. B. Cranfield. See also Robert H. Gundry's apologetic and Herculean effort to establish Matthew's artistic methods as "haggadic and midrashic techniques" in his monograph *Matthew: A Commentary on His Literary and Theological Art* (1982) xi.

24. For an example of such accusations, see S. Vernon McCasland, "Matthew Twists the Scriptures," *JBL* 80.2 (1961) 143–48, in which the author faults Matthew for a number of alleged mistakes. Among them is Matthew's treatment of Zech 9:9; he does not understand the nature of Hebrew poetry which shows "Matthew's lack of literary appreciation" (145). For a specific response to McCasland's study, see Norman Walker, "The Alleged Matthean *Errata*," *NTS* 9 (1962) 391–94.

necessarily advance the case if a full citation of Jer 23:5–6 were quoted along with fulfillment formulae. The more significant fact is that, once the relevant data is brought forward, the text of Jer 23:5–6 and the overall contents of Matthew invite the interpreter to visualize plausible connections. Once these connections are recognized, the interpreter must come to terms with his or her own understanding of their relevance.

Although other OT models have been advocated as a possible background to Matthew, the combination of details from Jer 23:5–6 along with the ensemble of the three other prophetic OT texts (Zech 3:8; 6:12–13; Isa 4:2) is eligible for consideration as a striking singularity. Above and beyond this fourfold constellation of prophetic texts there is the more isolated phenomenon of the various details of Jer 23:5–6 serving as an adequate substructure for the entire Gospel of Matthew. This inner consistency shows a remarkable whole cloth texture admitting few exceptions. There are more than twenty quotations from the OT in Matthew. Yet, none of them explains the contents of Matthew more accurately than Jer 23:5–6. This is not to argue that Matthew has the very schemata of Jer 23:5–6 before his eyes and is using them as a guide. Rather, the salient point is that the Jeremiah schemata do explain the major emphases of the first Gospel. C. K. Barrett once made use of the English proverb "two swallows do not a summer make" as a reminder that a mere two words cannot establish a case for the background of a biblical text.[25] Chapters 4 and 5 examine ten separate rubrics containing a total of fourteen individual key words or phrases indicative of allusions to Jer 23:5–6. The sum of the data, I suggest, indicates it is plausible that the text of Jer 23:5–6 dictates the structure of the first Gospel. This proposal recommends that the concept of the Branch must be assigned pride of place as the single most important idea undergirding and providing a literary substructure for the Gospel of Matthew.[26] These separate and individual allusional pieces, when assembled together into this theological latticework, do not create a misleading mirage but coalesce into a homogeneous mirror image of Jer 23:5–6. To further augment the contention of this study, there is nothing in Matthew's presentation that contradicts Jer 23:5–6. Neither is there anything in Jer 23:5–6 that runs counter to the Gospel of Matthew. Furthermore, when all the allusions from Jer 23:5–6 in Matthew (especially the first three chapters) are pieced together, there is integration and harmony, not disarray, confusion, or needless fripperies. Additionally, no integral piece from Jer 23:5–6 is missing from the Matthean picture of Jesus. This substructure comes to the surface particularly in the first three chapters of Matthew where all ten rubrics inform the narrative. If this organizational pattern is correct, it suggests the notion of a literary foundation or substructure.

25. C. K. Barrett, "The Background of Mark 10.45," in *New Testament Essays* (1959) 2.

26. David R. Bauer, *The Structure of Matthew's Gospel: A Study in Literary Design* (1988), mentions in three separate references (7, 54, 135) that there is no consensus among scholars on the structure of Matthew's Gospel. This would suggest that such a structure is beyond recovery. Or, conversely, this could possibly suggest that the thesis presented in this investigation merits consideration on the basis that Jer 23.5–6 provides sufficient structural details for understanding Matthew's main ideas.

6

The Gospel of Mark: The Servant Branch

INTEREST IN THE GOSPEL of Mark continues to attract an astounding number of scholars.[1] Perhaps because of its assumed priority as the first written Gospel, Mark offers scholars an opportunity to explore issues of tradition, sources, genre, redaction, and purpose. Markan research since the publication of the special *ANRW* edition in 1985 has continued to focus upon these major issues: 1) the priority of Mark,[2] 2) Mark's literary style,[3] 3) the Christology of Mark,[4] 4) the purpose and origin of Mark,[5] 5) Mark and the OT, 6) Mark as a compiler, redactor or an interpreter,[6] 7) Mark as history,[7] 8) the

---

1. See Wilford Telford, "Introduction," in *The Interpretation of Mark* (1985) 1, where he mentions his editorial task of having to review over 250 books, articles, and essays most of which were written between 1960 and 1985. Morna D. Hooker, *The Gospel According to St Mark* (1991) 398, relays the information from H. M. Humphrey's *A Bibliography for the Gospel of Mark 1954–1980* (1980) in which he lists 1,599 items for this period of time alone. Ben Witherington, *The Gospel of Mark* (2001) 1: "The study of Mark today is an ever expanding growth industry."

2. Gottfried Rau, "Das Markusevangelium: Komposition und Intention der ersten Darstellung christlicher Mission," *ANRW* 25.3 (1985) 2039.

3. See Dean B. Deppe, *The Theological Intentions of Mark's literary Devices* (2015) who takes a twofold approach to Mark: the first is an on-the-surface plain meaning of the text; the second is a more subtle one going below the surface to discover how Mark tries to answer the needs of the early church. I note his comment (475): "One needs bifocals to appropriately read the Gospel of Mark." Also, I note (477): "Through literary devices Mark speaks at two levels."

4. For the view that a Hellenistic background is behind Mark 10:41–45, see David Seeley, "Rulership and Service in Mark 10.41–45," *NovT* 35.3 (1993) 234–50.

5. H. N. Roskam, *The Purpose of the Gospel of Mark in its Historical and Social Context* (2004) 209–11. See also his statement (220): "Mark's Gospel is not just a random selection of traditional stories, but has a clear message and purpose."

6. See Robert H. Stein, "The Proper Methodology for Ascertaining a Markan Redaction History," *NovT* 13.3 (1971) 181–99.

7. For a defense of Mark as historically reliable, see P. M. Casey, "Culture and Historicity: The Cleansing of the Temple," *CBQ* 59 (1997) 306–32. For a dismissive treatment of Mark as being historically unreliable, see Herbert N. Schneidau, "Literary Relations among the Gospels: Harmony or Conflict?" in *SLI* 18 (1985) 17–32. See also the collection of essays in *Redescribing the Gospel of Mark*, edited by Barry S. Crawford and Merrill P. Miller (2017) which proposes a speculative model for understanding Christian origins by claiming it is a fantasy, not history, to trace early Christian beginnings back to Jesus.

background to Mark,[8] 9) the community behind Mark,[9] and 10) the genre of Mark.[10] Many of the specialist concerns regarding Matthew find similar points of contact in Mark. Items of important interest for this present study are Mark as a redactor, his purpose in writing, his use of the OT, his relation to the other synoptic Gospels, and his Christology.[11] Regarding purpose, Paul Achtemeier has written: "The need to understand Mark's structure as a way of finding his theological intention is more acute in the case of Mark than it is in the case of Matthew and Luke."[12] I see no reason to disagree with Achtemeier's contention. When we come to Mark, the task of discerning his purpose is more difficult than that of locating the center of interest for Matthew or Luke. Almost a century ago, Paul Wendland took this view to an extreme position arguing that Mark had no theological point of view at all.[13] Since then, research into this Gospel has continued to produce mixed results. Some would add that these disparate results are "confusing."[14]

---

8. See Joel Marcus, *The Way of the Lord: Christological Exegesis of the Old Testament in the Gospel of Mark* (1992) for his presentation of the wilderness theme for the key to unlocking the message of Mark. For a defense of Mark's provenance as Rome and the exegetical importance implied in this place of origin, see Brian J. Incigneri, *The Gospel to the Romans: The Setting and Rhetoric of Mark's Gospel* (2003) 59–115.

9. Dwight N. Peterson, *The Origins of Mark* (2000) 3, asks: "Scholars have produced a bewildering variety of Matthean, Markan, Lukan and Johannine communities from which to choose. How are we to know which is the correct one?" For a completely different and clearly dissenting view, see Richard Bauckham, *Jesus and the Eyewitnesses* (2006). Bauckham's overall argument is to establish that the Gospels are based upon eyewitness information, not community theological interests.

10. For a helpful summary on the genre issue involving the second Gospel, see Adela Yarbro Collins, *Mark: A Commentary* (2007) 15–44. I note the concise comment by Hans Conzelmann, *An Outline of the Theology of the New Testament* (1969) 98: "The gospel as a literary form was created by Mark." See also Eduard Schweizer, "Mark's Contribution to the Quest of the Historical Jesus," *NTS* 10 (1964) 421–32, here 421: "In this situation, Mark wrote his gospel. The most astonishing fact is this decision in and of itself. For there are almost no prototypes."

11. For example, Gunther Bornkamm, *Jesus of Nazareth* (1960) 227, regards the statement in Mark 10:45 ("For the Son of Man also came not to be served, but to serve, and to give his life as a ransom for many") as a "homiletical saying of the primitive Church in Palestine." For an opposite view, see T. W. Manson, *The Servant-Messiah: A Study of the Public Ministry of Jesus* (1961) 61–62. See also P. J. Achtemeier, *Mark* (1975) 41: "It would be quite accurate to say that to solve the problem of Jesus would be to solve the problem of the Gospel of Mark. Scholars have as yet reached no agreement that the problem of Mark has been solved, but a good deal of recent research approaching Mark from a wide variety of perspectives has pointed unmistakably to the fact that a major reason—if not *the* major reason—for the writing of Mark centers around this christological problem."

12. P. J. Achtemeier, *Mark* (1975) 31.

13. P. Wendland, *Die hellenistisch-römische Kultur in ihren Beziehungen zu Judentum und Christentum* (1912) 267: "Eine schriftstellerische Individualität ist er nicht . . . . Er hat keinen ausgeprägten theologischen Standpunkt." See also Morna Hooker, *The Gospel According to Mark* (1991) 19, who echoes a similar but more personal thought: "we cannot claim to be able to present Mark's theological position with any certainty."

14. As does Wilford Telford, "Introduction," in *The Interpretation of Mark* (1985) 8. See also Petri Merenlahti, *Poetics for the Gospels? Rethinking Narrative Criticism* (2002) 21, where he refers to the "split within Markan studies" over the issue of whether Mark is a clumsy editor or a genuine artist.

Compounding the picture of confusion is the view that Mark is frequently faulted as a defective Gospel, in need of correcting, upgrading and refining.[15] This line of logic, of course, presumes the priority of Mark as a major source for both Matthew and Luke.[16] According to this argument, Mark suffers for its lack of finesse and literary sophistication and, consequently, Matthew and Luke become remedial responses to the deficiencies of Mark. John B. Gabel and Charles B. Wheeler represent well this position by offering this reading of the Synoptics: "As in the case of Luke, we must assume that Matthew found Mark's gospel inadequate and intended to replace it with his own, not merely to supplement it."[17] It will be argued here that the above pessimistic view is not the case. In between one may find mediating positions.[18] This investigation pursues a new and different path.

The proposal that the text of Zech 3:8 informs the substructure of Mark has not been raised.[19] D. Moody Smith has even remarked, "Mark's use of the Old Testament is hard to isolate and characterize."[20] Willem S. Vorster remarked that the relationship between the Old and New Testaments (and the eventual connection with Mark)

---

15. See, for example, the article by Stefan Alkier, "From Text to Intertext: Intertexuality as a Paradigm for Reading Matthew," *HTS/TS* 61.1 (2005) 6, fn.5, who suggests that Mark is incomplete. See also Paul J. Achtemeier, *Mark* (1975) 13: "Thus, the clear historical impression given by the Lukan narrative is due, not to better historical information Luke had, but to his desire to eliminate some ambiguity in Mark's narrative. The resulting account in Luke is thus due to literary polishing, not historical accuracy." This line of logic, of course, assumes that Luke had Mark before him as a source and that Luke feels a need to correct its alleged deficiencies. See also Craig A. Evans, "Jesus and Zechariah's Messianic Hope," in *Authenticating the Activities of Jesus* (1999) 382: "Mark's failure to exploit an important proof text argues both for his Gospel's priority and for the essential historicity of the account." Evans, it must be stated, is making an argument for historicity. The argument of this present investigation, however, is not just for historicity but also for divine revelation. Is it possible that Mark omits something for other reasons than a "failure to exploit" a given text? Furthermore, why does Mark include information that others omit?

16. For an opposite reading of Mark in which Matthew is the precursor, see J. Enoch Powell, *The Evolution of the Gospel* (1994) xiii, where Powell says: "In addition to passages where Matthew presents difficulties due to corruption or error, proof of Mark's resort to Luke when flummoxed by Matthew is provided where Matthew's narrative is deliberately symbolical."

17. J. B. Gabel and C. B. Wheeler, *The Bible As Literature* (1990) 196.

18. Rudolf Bultmann, *The History of the Synoptic Tradition* (1963) 349, was almost as pessimistic, contending that a search for any leading ideas in Mark was a misguided use of energy. For a more optimistic appraisal, see Petri Merenlahti, *Poetics for the Gospels? Rethinking Narrative Criticism* (2002) chapter 2, "Why Do Modern Readers Value Mark?" Merenlahti argues, from a narrative-critical point of view, that Mark possesses a literary unity. Most recently, however, is the excellent work of Richard B. Hays, *Echoes of Scripture in the Gospels* (2016) 15–103, who finds Mark's presentation of Jesus anchored to "echoes" as revealed in the Old Testament. Although citing a number of texts from the prophet Zechariah, Hays does not mention 3:8.

19. For the suggestion that Zechariah may have contributed to Jesus' messianic understanding, see C. A. Evans, "'The Two Sons of Oil': Early Evidence of Messianic Interpretation of Zechariah 4.14 in 4Q254 4 2," in *The Provo International Conference on the Dead Sea Scrolls* (1999) 575. Evans does not focus upon Zech 3:8 but Zech 4:14.

20. D. M. Smith, "The Use of the Old Testament in the New," in *The Use of the Old Testament in the New and Other Essays* (1972) 40.

"remains an unsolved riddle."[21] Craig Evans also notes, "The scholarly literature that has investigated the extent, if any, of Zechariah's influence on Jesus is modest."[22] Evans, in another monograph, actually claims that there are no allusions at all to Zech 3:8 in the NT.[23] Rather than jumping *media res* into the subject, a fairer approach is to begin with Rex Mason's ominous caution that may serve as an entry point: speaking of Zech 3:8, he issues a cautionary warning suggesting that "it would be a rash commentator who claimed to be able to explain satisfactorily the varying signals of 'messianic hope' that confront us here."[24] He then follows up with this additional personal sentiment: "We must each make what we can of this. It would be a brave exegete who would claim to know the one, true meaning of it."[25] Mason, however, does venture far enough away from safe waters to say, "Twice in these chapters, someone called 'Branch' is mentioned (3.8; 6.12). In each case he is unnamed and his coming seems to be envisaged as an event some distance in the future."[26] David L. Petersen says, "Zechariah's visions remain some of the most enigmatic literature in the Hebrew Bible."[27] On the opposite extreme is the position that the text is a gloss.[28]

OT scholars working in the area of prophetic texts may be faulted for their reluctance to look ahead for possible fulfillment in the individual Gospels.[29] NT scholars, for their part, do not look back at how the NT might make use of the Branch

---

21. W. S. Vorster, "The Function of the Use of the Old Testament in Mark," *NeoT* 14 (1981) 62–72.

22. C. A. Evans, "Jesus and Zechariah's Messianic Hope," in *Authenticating the Activities of Jesus* (1999) 380.

23. C. A. Evans, *Jesus and His Contemporaries* (1995) 175. Dean B. Deppe, *Theological Intentions of Mark's Literary Devices* (2017) 24, fn. 95, although mentioning such allusions as the Spirit descending like a dove (1:10) as a reference to Noah after the Flood experiencing a new world, Deppe does not mention the Branch from Zech 3:8.

24. R. Mason, "The Messiah in the Postexilic Old Testament Literature," in *King and Messiah in Israel and the Ancient Near East* (1998) 343. For a similar view, see Mark Cameron Love, *The Evasive Text: Zechariah 1–8 and the Frustrated Reader* (1999) 14: "I begin with a confession. I do not understand Zechariah 1–8." Later we find this admission (105): "The symbols weave the narrative together in a blatant abuse of artistic license while pulling the narrative apart by refusing to declare their significance." See as well Michael H. Floyd, *Minor Prophets: Part 2* (2000) 305: "Zechariah does more than most texts to foster humility in its interpreters."

25. R. Mason, *The Messiah* (1998) 346.

26. Ibid., 345. Mason does suggest that Joshua and his men are not the fulfillment of the promise but "guarantors" that eventually the Branch will come. For an opposite view implying a more immediate historical fulfillment, see Michael H. Floyd, *Minor Prophet* (2000) 375.

27. D. Petersen, "Zechariah's Vision: A Theological Perspective," in *Prophecy in the Hebrew Bible: Selected Studies from* Vetus Testamentum (2000) 188.

28. For the view that the Branch is a later gloss, see H. G. Mitchell, *Zechariah* (1912) 156, who argued that this insertion was added "by a reader of a later time, feeling that it was incomplete, and not taking pains to examine the context, to see if he understood the drift of the passage, added as a gloss, *for I will bring my servant Shoot*."

29. Von Rad, in his classic introduction to OT theology, includes three indices at the end of his book: one for Scripture passages, one for Hebrew words, and one for names and special subjects. None of these three sources list the Branch as a topic of interest for discussion (G. von Rad, *The Message of the Prophets*, 1967).

metaphor. Have these scholars missed something? Of course, it can be countered that the reason for this absence of NT scholarly commentary on the Branch is the simple fact that no Branch text is explicitly cited by any NT writer. A partial purpose of this chapter is to provide evidence that a connection between the Branch of Zech 3:8 and the Gospel of Mark is more substantial than mere speculation, more organically based than mere imagination. I offer this reading as a plausible paradigm for understanding the Gospel of Mark. The continuing investigation will comprise a total of four major rubrics, all anchored to the prophetic text of Zech 3:8. The following information offers a plausible proposal for understanding the substructure of the Gospel of Mark in light of the Servant Branch as found Zech 3:8. We turn now to that prophetic text.

Joshua and the Associates Who Are Sitting before him

MT: שמע־נא יהושע הכהן הגדול אתה ורעיך הישבים לפניך; LXX: ἄκουε δή, Ἰησοῦ ὁ ἱερεὺς ὁ μέγας, σὺ καὶ οἱ καθήμενοι πρὸ προσώπου σου; NIV: "Listen, O high priest Joshua and your associates seated before you."

Of the four prophetic texts under investigation, Zech 3:8 is unique in that it has a double focus: first, men who are a sign or portent and who are associated with this Branch come into view; secondly, the Servant Branch is then mentioned. I begin with these associates or colleagues who are sitting before Joshua.

THE SIGNIFICANCE OF THE ASSOCIATES SEATED BEFORE JOSHUA. In the text of Zech 3:8, Joshua the high priest is mentioned along with some of his "associates" (רעיך, *rea*).[30] The Hebrew ו (*waw*) "and" should not be ignored. The address is directed to both Joshua *and* his colleagues as both parties are to listen to the forthcoming proclamation. Yet, at this juncture, there is a separation. Even though both parties are admonished to listen to the address, it appears that only the associates are a sign. The text says: "your associates who are sitting before you, *they* (המה מופת) are a sign." The LXX correctly translates the Hebrew: διότι ἄνδρες . . . εἰσί ("for *they* . . . are"). A separation thus occurs between Joshua and his associates. The singular reference to Joshua is followed by a plural to the associates, thus excluding Joshua as a sign. However, he is clearly responsible for paying attention to the address. The word "associates" רעיך (*rea*), also translated as "fellows," "friends," "companions," or simply as "men" is found ten times in the OT with no special attachment to an elevated office or duty.[31]

THE SIGNIFICANCE OF SITTING. These men are further qualified as associates or companions *sitting* before Joshua. As a contrast, the overall context of Zech 3:1–8 contains a

---

30. The LXX simply says that they are "men" (ἄνδρες).
31. Exod 2:13; 7:13, 14, 22; 1 Sam 14:20; 2 Sam 2:16, 16; Isa 34:14; Jonah 1:7; Zech 3:8.

verb depicting the posture of *standing* six times.³² Obviously, the contrasting positions of sitting and standing are intentionally juxtaposed in this vision. The associates sit; everyone else is standing. Added to this descriptive mix is the specific reference to Joshua as a "high" (הגדול) priest. This could possibly suggest that these men are simply priests, but that is by no means certain. What is more notable is that Joshua as the *high* priest is standing and that these men before him are sitting. David L. Peterson says: "Despite this focus on Joshua, one does wonder about the identity of those sitting before Joshua . . . . Nor does the syntax of the clause itself require a formal deliberative setting, though it does suggest that the high priest has a higher status."³³ Also, the physical posture of *all* other individuals seems to be a point of emphasis. After the six references to the standing personages of Joshua, the angel of the LORD, and a person identified as Satan (all in a position of standing), the single reference to these associates as sitting comes unexpectedly into view. The unexpectedness of their sudden appearance in a sitting posture probably indicates an even more pronounced point of emphasis, or better yet—a point of contrast. This numerical ratio of six to one is striking. What, if anything, is the significance? I suggest that the vision of these men as occupying a sitting position implies subordination or servanthood.

THE POSTURE OF SITTING IN THE GOSPEL OF MARK. Proceeding farther, does the posture of *sitting* offer any interpretative links to the Gospel of Mark? The second Gospel narrates a series of scenes containing references or suggestions about various people in sitting positions.³⁴ A critical question thus surfaces: is there theological intention behind Mark's mention of people in a sitting position? First of all, a comparison between Mark and the Synoptics is in order at this point. Since the LXX uses the expression οἱ καθήμενοι ("those sitting"), I begin with the verb κάθημαι ("to sit"). Matthew employs this verb eighteen times,³⁵ Luke thirteen,³⁶ but Mark only twelve.³⁷ One point of similarity is that all the Synoptics show Peter sitting among attendants and guards

---

32. At v.1 Joshua the high priest is standing before the angel of the LORD, and Satan is also standing there to accuse him (Joshua). At v.3 Joshua is described a second time as standing before the angel. At v.5, the angel of the LORD is also portrayed as standing. At v.7 there is a promise that Joshua, if faithful to the LORD, will be given a place among those standing there.

33. D. L. Petersen, *Haggai and Zechariah 1–8* (1984) 208–9. Petersen discounts these men as part of a formal priestly assembly: "Many commentators suggest that they comprise a group of priests. Unfortunately, there is little warrant for this assertion. The texts proffered in its defense, 2 Kings 4.38 and 6.1, do not yield evidence of a priestly assembly with a high priest at its head."

34. Mark 6:39–40; 8:6; 9:35; 10:38, 40, 48; 12:41; 13:3 (Matt 24:3 says that Jesus was sitting; Luke 21:6 mentions only that Jesus looked up); 14:3, 18, 32 (Jesus does not say, "wait here" but "sit here") 54, 62; and 16:5, 19. Standing is mentioned at: 11:25; 14:47, 57, 60. The position of *sitting* can indicate that one is in league with those sitting nearby.

35. Matt 4:16; 9:9; 11:10; 13:1, 2; 15:9; 19:28; 20:30; 22:44; 23:22; 24:3; 26:58, 64, 69; 27:19, 36, 61; 28:2.

36. Luke 1:79; 5:17, 27; 7:32; 8:35; 10:13; 18:35; 20:42; 21:35; 22:30, 55, 56, 69.

37. Mark 2:6, 14; 3:32–34; 4:1; 5:15; 10:46; 12:36; 13:3; 14:54, 62; 16:5.

as he warms himself by the fire while Jesus is interrogated by Caiaphas. Points of dissimilarity reveal Matthew alone showing the following: Pilate sitting in judgment of Jesus (27:19), the soldiers sitting before the cross (27:36), the women sitting before the tomb (27:61), the children sitting in the market place (11:10), and the people sitting in darkness (4:16). The composite of these sitting positions does not yield a consistent picture. A conclusion from the data at this point suggests caution. Further points of dissimilarity may be noticed. Two stand out. First, Mark never depicts Jesus in a standing position.[38] Matthew, Luke, and John all offer a contrast showing Jesus in standing positions.[39] Secondly, Mark alone pays distinctive attention to the disciples as sitting before Jesus.[40] I repeat: it is only Mark who pays distinctive attention to the disciples in a sitting position before Jesus. Two texts in a touchstone manner may advance this observation. I begin with a vignette from Mark 3:31–32. The scene is the familiar event of Jesus' mother and brothers standing outside a house and calling for him. Matthew, Mark, and Luke all include information that these family members are standing outside as they call for Jesus. The Markan text, however, does not stop there as it provides the unique detail that indoors there is a crowd *sitting* (ἐκάθητο) around Jesus. Thus the crowd indoors occupying a sitting position is contrasted to those standing outside. That is not all. Verses 34–35 bring the pericope to a conclusion with yet more exclusive Markan touches: "Then he looked at those *seated in a circle around him* and said, 'Behold (ἴδε), my mother and my brothers. Whoever does God's will is my brother and sister and mother.'" Mark is the only Gospel that records a crowd sitting in a circle around Jesus. This sitting position is accordingly pictured as a model of discipleship. A safe assumption is that the disciples are included in this group. Thus a threefold contrast emerges: one group is outside the house, the other inside. The outside group is standing while the inside group is sitting. The outside standing group is further away from Jesus while the inside sitting group is closer—a possible suggestion of greater devotion.

It is generally assumed that ninety percent of Mark is contained in Matthew and Luke;[41] but since the above pericope is contained only in Mark, a series of questions would now be appropriate: if Mark is first in order of composition and there is a literary relationship between the three Gospels, why have the latter two in their redacted

---

38. Mark 1:35 and 7:24 both contain the verb ἀνίστημι ("to get up"). In neither case is Jesus portrayed as standing. In both cases he got up and went somewhere. Mark 10:49 comes close; Jesus simply stops (ἵστημι) and addresses blind Bartimaeus. R. T. France, *The Gospel of Mark* (2002) 424, comments: "Given Jesus' urgency in 10:32, his stopping (and presumably bringing the whole crowd to a halt) for a beggar is remarkable."

39. Matt 27:11 shows Jesus standing before Pilate. Luke 4:16 depicts Jesus standing up to read in the synagogue; 5:1 shows him standing by the lake; 6:17 shows him standing on a level place; and 24:36 shows Jesus standing among the disciples. John 7:37 shows Jesus standing in the Temple area.

40. An exception may be noted: Luke 10:39 describes Mary sitting (παρακαθεῖσα) at the feet of Jesus. This is an isolated incident in the third Gospel.

41. Some assume a count as low as fifty percent; others go as high as ninety-five.

version omitted the specific details? Or, if Mark is placed in a different order, why has he included these details? Is it possible that the Markan passages referencing people in a sitting position are unique to this ten percent for a specific reason?

There is clearly a disparity between Matthew and Mark regarding references to people in various positions of either bowing down to Jesus (Matthew) or people in a sitting position around Jesus (Mark). In view of this, another series of questions is in order: upon what critical grounds can the preponderance of references in a bowing position (Matthew) and the references to sitting positions (Mark) be assigned to the historical Jesus? The never ending question will not go away: what, if any, do these references have to do with the actual facts? Did some of these people actually worship Jesus? Did others simply sit down around him? I grant that a theological tint is present in the texts. Does that obligate us to discredit historical reality? Would that not place Mark in the risky and dubious position of altering facts? If Matthew has recorded what actually happened, it may be argued, that Mark has simply omitted these references because of a different presentation of Jesus. If this is the case, why would Mark be motivated to drop references to Jesus being worshiped? The proposal offered here is that, by such omissions, Mark's characterization of Jesus conforms to the prophetic profile of Jesus as a Servant Branch who is defined by servanthood. I propose therefore that neither narrative may be faulted out of hand as untrue. Alternately, the picture of those in a bowing position may describe an initial response; those in sitting positions may describe the continuing attitude of discipleship. Once again, neither narrative need cancel out the other as a fiction.

Depending upon the context, the posture of "sitting before" or "seated around" suggests an attitude of learning or a subordinate position, perhaps a formal position of being a disciple.[42] One of the Greek words used frequently to describe the disciples in the Gospels is the number δώδεκα ("twelve"). Although containing the least amount of pages, the Gospel of Mark contains the greatest number of references to the disciples as the Twelve.[43] Notable is the fact that Mark has almost three times the references as does the Gospel of John. Of particular interest is Mark 9:35. This text describes Jesus, in a sitting position himself, addressing the Twelve. This is similar to Matt 5:1, except that Mark confines his narrative to disciples only. The situation is also not a hillside but a house (a more intimate setting). It is perhaps implied that if Jesus sat down, so did the disciples.[44] The text also suggests a learning environment. In this classroom atmosphere, Jesus desires to teach them about servanthood. In order to do

---

42. Carl Schneider, "κάθημαι," *TDNT* (1976) 3.440–44, delineates several motifs for the sitting position: 1) sitting as a mark of particular distinction [gods, rulers, and judges]; 2) teachers; 3) sitting as a psychological attitude (grief, begging, sitting for practical reasons: some people have to sit because of their occupation, for example, a tax collector). Schneider (443) then says: "We are to regard it as purely practical that scholars usually sit (Mk 3.32)."

43. Matt (9); Mark (11); Luke (6); John (4).

44. At Mark 4:1, Jesus gets into a boat and sits down in order to teach. It is difficult to visualize the audience in a sitting position at water's edge.

so, Jesus both sits down and then places a child in their midst. This is a likely invitation for the disciples to sit down as well and assume a servant position. Richard T. France calls attention to another aspect of this scene: "The contrast between insiders and outsiders is vividly depicted by the spatial imagery."[45] However true this may be, I would suggest that the body-position imagery is a feature highlighting servanthood more than the spatial distinctions.

There is one remaining issue that must be addressed. Heinrich Greeven in the *TDNT* calls attention to a difference between Matthew and Mark on the subject of *proskynesis* (the act of worship in a bowing position). He argues that Matthew has "altered or expanded his Marcan original in no less than five passages in order to describe the gesture of those who approach Jesus explicitly as proskynesis."[46] He cites five examples: the leper (Matt 8:2/Mark 1:40); Jairus (Matt 9:18/Mark 5:22); the disciples in the boat (Matt 14:33/Mark 6:45); the woman of Canaan (Matt 15:25/Mark 7:25); and the mother of James and John (Matt 20:20/Mark 10:35). One possible way to analyze the data is to conclude, as does Greeven, that the two evangelists have either made an alteration by addition (Matthew) or made a subtraction (Mark). Furthermore, while Mark 15:18 shows the soldiers in a mocking posture of feigning worship of Jesus, Matthew omits this description. Supposedly then, in Matthew there are five cases of addition and one case of subtraction; in Mark there is just the opposite: five cases of subtraction and one instance of addition. Regarding the particular case of Matthew's omission of the soldiers feigning worship, it can be explained on the grounds that Matthew does not include this incident of insincerity because it is not befitting of Jesus as a legitimate king. By contrast, Mark's inclusion of these soldiers engaging in feigning and sarcastic worship can be explained on the basis that he does not portray Jesus in the role of a genuine king but rather a humble servant who suffers such mocking mimicry.

What more can we make of the data? Greeven does not attempt an explanation for the variation. Two factors strike me as highly unusual. First, if Matthew's presentation is historically accurate in that people did actually fall down and worship Jesus, then it becomes most significant that Mark would not mention such behavior. In other words, he would have needed a compelling reason for omitting these actions. Secondly, it is not characteristic for humans to worship another human unless under the compulsion of a forced obligation. Therefore, I do not see Matthew inventing a literary fiction in order to embellish his account of Jesus. Consequently, the following issue comes to the front: why the Matthean inclusions and the Markan exclusions of such striking responses to Jesus? It is clear that theological intention must be at work. However, I would insist that neither clear disagreement nor historical fabrication is at play. This, therefore, presents an opportunity to analyze a noted and significant difference between two Gospels by appealing to the thesis as developed in this book.

---

45. R. T. France, *The Gospel of Mark* (2002) 179.
46. H. Greeven, "προσκυνέω," *TDNT* (1968) 6.763.

I propose that the explanation may be found in the fact that Matthew rightfully presents Jesus in the role of a king; Mark, on the other hand, by presenting Jesus as a servant rightfully omits references to worship. In this light, it is inappropriate to show a servant being worshiped. Hence, Mark simply drops these descriptions. Matthew, for his part, has not altered the facts.

In a similar way, Craig Keener observes that Mark does not mention Jesus riding into Jerusalem on a donkey during the triumphal entry narrative (Mark 11:1–11). Keener first says, "Mark seems not to have exploited and perhaps not to have noticed."[47] One page later, Keener further comments on the absence of reference to Jesus riding on the colt in Mark by suggesting, "That knowledge of the Zechariah allusion seems lost on Mark." I would ask: is there some other possible explanation for this Markan omission? What other plausible reason could there be for Mark omitting information that Jesus entered Jerusalem riding on this colt? The intended symbolism as reflected from the Zech 9:9 image is that of a *king* riding into the city. It may be that Mark does not want to portray Jesus in the image of a king; his interests lie elsewhere.

Men Who Are a Sign or Symbol

> MT: כִּי־אַנְשֵׁי מוֹפֵת הֵמָּה, LXX: διότι ἄνδρες τερατοσκόποι εἰσί, NIV: "who are men symbolic of things to come."

These associates are further described as "men of a *sign*." The NIV translation of "symbolic of things to come" is really an interpretation, not a true translation. The Hebrew word translated as "sign," "symbol," or "portent" is מוֹפֵת (*mopet*). John D.W. Watts notes that the English translation of "symbol" (NIV) is less desirable than the word "wonder."[48] He cites as apt examples the following texts: various passages in Exodus, texts in Isa 8:18; 20:3; and Ezek 12:6. Isaiah 8:18 is significant as Watts observes that those who bore symbolic names were as "signs and wonders in Israel."[49] Peterson further elaborates the identity of these men:

> Whoever these individuals are, they are called, in this emphatic parenthesis, men of portent. This is an odd phrase. What sort of sign or portent they are, or are to be, is not indicated. However, on the basis of the way in which this phrase is used elsewhere (Isa 8.18; Ezek 12.6; 24.24, 27), for Yahweh to declare that they are a sign means we must conclude that Yahweh himself has designated them as a sign.[50]

---

47. C. S. Keener, *The Historical Jesus of the Gospels* (2009) 258.
48. J. D. W. Watts, *Zechariah* (1972) 322.
49. Ibid., 322.
50. Peterson, *Haggai and Zechariah 1–8* (1984) 209.

Pursuing this further, Carol and Eric Meyers, upon translating *mopet* as "portent," view this word as a difficult challenge for the translator.[51] They offer three primary angles from which to view this noun: 1) when used with *otot* ("sign"), the word refers to God's miraculous intervention in delivering Israel from Egyptian captivity;[52] 2) the word is also used to describe God's "intended actions which will be carried out in the future;" 3) the proposal adopted by both Meyers is that *mopet* does not denote a predictive element, but only a role in communicating the divine will. I would add a fourth to this list: when מופת (*mopet* or *mohphehth*) is used by itself apart from *otot* ("sign"), it tends to drop the sense of "wonder" and take on more the sense of "sign."[53] However, it must be emphasized that these two words share a common semantic field. They are like the opposite sides of the same coin. Since the text before us omits *otot* ("sign") but retains the partner term מופת (*mopet/mohphehth*), the significance of this singularity should not be lost.

These men are only a sign. But what are they a sign of? Two possibilities present themselves: 1) either they are a sign or witness of some coming event or person—the Branch—or, 2) they are a sign based upon their sitting relationship to Joshua and the others standing in the court. Watts, mentioned above, concludes: "These men are witnesses to the saving work of God,"[54] and that this saving work of God is that of bringing "his servant called Branch, undoubtedly a messianic name."[55] Is this observation by Watts correct? In the interest of objectivity, the text does not spell out precisely what they are a sign of. However, the central idea of a portent is the expectation that something momentous is going to take place.

The LXX translation of τερατοσκόποι suggests that they are observers of signs.[56] The Latin Vulgate is closer, suggesting that these men are "portents" (*viri portendentes sunt*). The Hebrew text indicates only that these men are a sign. In other words, they do not observe signs; rather, they are to be observed as a sign. Also, the word "sign" is singular, not plural. A similar passage is that of Isa 20:3: "Then the LORD said, 'Just as my servant Isaiah has gone stripped and barefoot for three years as a sign and

---

51. C. L. Meyers and E. M. Meyers, *Haggai, Zechariah 1–8* (1987) 199.

52. Ibid., 199.

53. For example: 1 Kgs 13:3; 2 Kgs 19:29; Isa 7:11.

54. Watts, *Zechariah* (1972) 322. See also Ben C. Ollenburger, *The Book of Zechariah* (1994) 766: "Joshua and his colleagues are signs or omens that God is bringing an unnamed scion of David's house: a king." Ollenburger is only partially correct. The person that God is bringing is specifically identified as a servant.

55. Watts (1972) 322.

56. In the LXX these men (ἄνδρες) are identified as τερατοσκόποι. This unusual word is used only in one other place in the LXX and that is Deut 18:11, in which the word is best understood as one who practices divination, a "diviner." It may be contrasted with "prophet," used at v.15. Thus τερατοσκόποι in the LXX is translated from two different Hebrew words, the first from קסמים ("diviners"), the second from מופת ("portent"). Literally, τερατοσκόποι describes one who observes signs. Thus, it appears that the LXX translators took the Hebrew word as having an active meaning of one who is observing something.

portent against Egypt and Cush." By virtue of being "stripped and barefoot," Isaiah was a "sign," a "wonder," or a "portent" (מוֹפֵת/*mohphehth*). His physical condition pointed to something spiritual. In a sense, therefore, he was a symbol.

A sign points to something. As a sign, what could these associates possibly indicate? It appears that two viable explanations present themselves: 1) either their position of sitting reflects subordination, or 2) they in some sense point beyond themselves to the Branch. That is, either these men point to something or someone in the future (the Branch), or they themselves are a sign of something. In view of the total number of references to the physical postures of standing, plus the contrasting description of these men as sitting, the interpretation which best suits the context is, indeed, that of subordination.

By extension, one additional angle must be pursued. As a sign, do these sitting men portend that the Branch will also sit in subordination? The Hebrew עַבְדִּי ("*my servant*") may indicate yet another comparison. As the men sitting before Joshua are a sign of subordination or servanthood, so YHWH's Branch will likewise be a servant. If this is a valid connection, the description of the Branch as a servant coheres well with the picture of the associates before Joshua. As the associates occupy a sitting servant position before Joshua, so the Branch will occupy a servant (and perhaps sitting position) before YHWH.

Another relevant question arises: in what sense can data be extracted from Mark giving corresponding evidence linking to these men as a sign? In the interest of fairness, it will not be advantageous to press the point. The more promising course of interpretation is not to force the issue. However, a few things may suggest plausibility. On this score, what relationship if any, does this Zechariah scene have to do with Mark? The Gospels contain a variety of words describing companions, followers, and disciples. Mark 1:36 describes Peter following Jesus along with those "with him" (καὶ μετ' αὐτοῦ). Mark 2:25 is a similar text, describing those with Jesus (καὶ οἱ μετ' αὐτοῦ), but it contains an interesting side note: Jesus adds that David, "during the days of Abiathar the high priest, also gave food to those with him" (τοῖς σὺν αὐτῷ).

This Zechariah prophecy points to a time in the future. It not only involves the Branch, but also these men who are a sign or symbol. The Gospel of Mark not only has an emphasis upon Jesus as a servant, but also there is an emphasis upon the disciples and discipleship. Adding to this profile is this observation by Jane Schaberg: "In Mark, for example, all three passion-resurrection predictions are followed by teaching on the subject of discipleship, as though the term Son of Man has been associated with the disciples ... as model."[57] Mark is continually pointing out the failings and successes, the ups and the downs, the doubts and understanding of the disciples. These disciples uniquely associate with Jesus, sit at his feet, and learn from him. They also follow him.[58]

---

57. J. Schaberg, "Daniel 7.12 and the New Testament Passion-Resurrection Predictions," *NTS* 31 (1985) 217.

58. Donald J. Verseput, "Jesus' Pilgrimage to Jerusalem and Encounter in the Temple: A

Closely linked to the mission and purpose of Jesus in Mark is the tangential idea of how this messianic mission is to effect the disciples. In Mark, the themes of messiahship and discipleship are linked.[59]

The Exclamation: Behold!

> MT: כִּי־הִנְנִי מֵבִיא אֶת־עַבְדִּי צֶמַח; LXX: διότι ἰδοὺ ἐγὼ ἄγω τὸν δοῦλον μου Ἀνατολήν; ESV: "Behold, I will bring my Servant, the Branch."

They are told to "Behold" (הִנְנִי/hgg, an alternate form of הִנֵּה/hinneh, which occurs at v.9). The LXX renders the Hebrew as ἰδού ("Behold"). Since the NIV omits this particle, just as it did in its translation of the Gospel of Matthew, I have used the translation from the English Standard Version (2011). Is it worth the effort to defend its preservation? Once again, just as claimed in chapter 4 dealing with Matthew, it is my judgment that it is a mistake not to insist upon its value to the reader. YHWH is speaking (Zech 3:7, 9), and the text indicates that he wants Joshua and his men to pay attention to something that he is going to do. This divine activity will involve the bringing forward of an anonymous person identified only as the Branch.

Mark uses this very word and he also makes use of a variation of this interjection. First of all, he uses ἰδού a total of eight times (six spoken by Jesus).[60] Twice this word is used to describe the imminent event of betrayal and death (Mark 14:41, 42). Secondly, the alternate form of ἴδε ("Behold") is also found eight times in Mark.[61] The first of these references is found at 3:34, which was discussed above. The word ἰδού is a very unusual word to be found in narrative texts. Josephus never uses it. It is found only rarely among Greek historians.[62] In other words, the preponderance of references is confined to the Old Testament, Philo, the Testament of the Twelve Patriarchs, and the Gospels. The word ἰδού thus occurs in texts in which authors exhibit a consciousness of the extraordinary work of God.

Geographical Motif in Matthew's Gospel," *NovT* 36.2 (1994) 106, in making a contrasting comment upon the travel motif in Mark, says: "Securely joined to this travel motif is the exacting lesson of discipleship under the looming shadow of the cross, for those who accompany Jesus 'on the way' are those who follow him to his rejection and death (8.27, 34; 10.17, 21)."

59. See also Suzanne Watts Henderson, *Christology and Discipleship in the Gospel of Mark* (2006) 241–61, for her conclusions which balance together the motifs of Christology and discipleship. Although not a book dealing with the various aspects of the identity of Jesus (but, rather, eyewitness testimony), Richard Bauckham, *Jesus and the Eyewitnesses* (2006) 171, pauses to consider the "focused purpose" of Mark: true messianic identity and discipleship, the messianic exemplification of service and suffering.

60. The six occasions are: 1:2 (God); 4:3; 10:33; 13:23; 14:41, 42.

61. 2.24; 3:34; 11:21; 13:1, 21; 15:4, 35.

62. The interjection ἰδού is not found in Diodorus Siculus, Herodotus, Josephus, Pausanias, Polybius, Strabo, and Thucydides; neither does Plutarch make use of it in the Lives.

Another relevant detail requires attention. The NIV, omitting the word "Behold" as it does also in Zech 3:8, translates ἴδε at Mark 3:34 as, "Here are..." I have, however, retained the sense of "Behold," suggesting a tone of amazement. It is worth mentioning also that an alternate form of ἴδε is ἰδού, which is the Greek equivalent of *hinneh* as found in Zech 3:8. Thus, three corresponding connections emerge between Zech 3:8 and Mark 3:31–34. These are: 1) as men sit before Joshua, so men are sitting around or before Jesus; 2) as both groups occupy a position indicative of a listening and subordinate attitude, so they may characterize servanthood or discipleship; and 3) as there is the presence of the interjection "Behold" in both texts, special attention is given to each group, possibly indicative of amazement.

The Servant Branch

> MT: כי־הנני מביא את־עבדי צמח; LXX: διότι ἰδοὺ ἐγὼ ἄγω τὸν δοῦλόν μου Ἀνατολήν; ESV: "Behold, I will bring my Servant, the Branch."

YHWH is speaking and he announces something that he is going to do. Although a future perspective is most likely intended, the inevitable result is so real that it is expressed in present tense language as if occurring at that moment. As suggested above, this servant is the servant of YHWH himself. This is perhaps a contrast to the servants of Joshua. This Branch is also singular in form. The key phrase is את־עבדי צמח/*ebed yod Zemah* ("My Servant the Branch"). The expression "my servant" (עבדי/*ebed yod*) is used some forty times in the Hebrew Bible in the singular person to identify a lone individual. These references usually describe an outstanding OT personage such as Abraham (Gen 26:24), Caleb (Num 14:24), David (1 Kgs 11:38), Isaiah (Isa 20:3), and Job (Job 1:8). Jacob as a simile for the nation may also be found (Jer 30:10; Isa 41:9). By far, David has the greatest references (sixteen).[63] In all these references, it is YHWH who is speaking. The personal pronoun "my" identifies the servant as belonging to YHWH. Of particular interest is the single reference to Zerubbabel (Hag 2:23).

The language points to an undefined future. Wolter H. Rose comments: "Only an identification of Zemah with an unidentified future figure has the explanatory power to deal satisfactory with all the features of the double portrait of Zemah in Zechariah 3 and 6."[64]

---

63. 1 Kgs 11:32, 34, 36; 14:8; 2 Kgs 20:6; 21:8; 1 Chr 17:4, 7; Psa 89:3, 20; Jer 33:21, 22, 26; Ezek 34:23, 24; 37:24.

64. Wolter H. Rose, "Messianic Expectations in the Early Post-Exilic Period," *TynB* 49.2 (1998) 374.

The Servant Motif in Mark.

I begin with a critical observation: the description of the Branch as a Servant was not unknown in Second Temple Judaism.[65] The argument of this chapter contends that Mark presents Jesus as an ideal Servant. This premise contrasts sharply but does not disagree with Matthew's presentation of Jesus as an ideal King. This is not to say that there is a clash of presentations, as if one was contradicting the other. Matthew adopts the language of authority, power, kingship, and majesty; Mark makes use of a contrasting list of terms focusing upon servanthood, such as: rejection (ἐξουδενθῇ, "be rejected," Mark 9:12, 31; 10:33; 14:21), the experience of betrayal (παραδοθῆναι, "be betrayed," Mark 10:45), serving (διακονῆσαι, "to serve," Mark 10:45), ransom: δοῦναι τὴν ψυχὴν αὐτοῦ λύτρον ἀντὶ πολλῶν, "to give himself as a ransom for many," and ἐκχυννόμενον ὑπὲρ πολλῶν, "poured out for many" (Mark 14:24), as well as the "crucified one" (τὸν ἐσταυρωμένον in Mark 16:6). All of these words point toward eventual death. In fact, from Mark 8:31 onward death is in the air.[66] Yet this death is never constructed as symptomatic of severe depression, misguided calculations, or mental illness; rather, it is presented as a voluntary and sacrificial act of servanthood on behalf of others.[67]

Crispin H. T. Fletcher-Louis has offered a formidable thesis advocating the view of Jesus as the High Priestly Messiah as an aspect of Jesus distinctively presented in the Gospel of Mark.[68] Of relevant interest is his explanation of Mark 1:24 in which the man who is suffering from an unclean spirit cries out, "I know who you are Jesus . . . *the holy one of God* (ὁ ἅγιος τοῦ θεοῦ)." Fletcher-Louis subsequently argues from Psa

---

65. See Eduard Löhse, "Der König aus Davids Geschlecht: Bemerkungen zur messianischen Erwartung der Synagoge," in *Abraham unser Vater* (1963) 342: "Auch im Habinenugebet, das in knapper Form die wichtigsten Gebetsanliegen zusammenfaBt, wird für den SproB Davids bzw. das Aufsprossen eines Horns 'für David, deinen Knecht' gebeten." For a counter view, see John J. Collins, "Teacher and Servant," *RHPR* 80.1 (2000) 37–50. Collins devotes himself to a single issue: did the Teacher of Righteousness conceive of himself as a messianic figure in fulfillment of Isaiah 53? He states his thesis (38): "We should be wary, then, of assuming that the modern construct of the Servant was also recognized in antiquity. . ." Collins further refines his view (48) that the role of vicarious suffering "is never clearly attested in pre-Christian Jewish texts."

66. John F. O'Grady, *The Four Gospels and the Jesus Tradition* (1989) 205: "Mark seems to always have the pall of the cross hanging over the ministry of Jesus."

67. Geert Van Oyen, "The Vulnerable Authority of the Author of the Gospel of Mark: Re-Reading the Paradoxes," *Bib* 91.2 (2010) 183, emphasizing the main theme of Mark, says: "In a unique way he has shown what it means to serve. Serving and being the slave of all can imply the gift of one's life for others."

68. C. H. T. Fletcher-Louis, "Jesus as the High Priestly Messiah: Part 1," *JSHJ* 4.2 (2006) 155–75; and his second installment, "Jesus as the High Priestly Messiah: Part 2," *JSHJ* 5.1 (2007) 62 in which he says: "Mark has *carefully* chosen material in the opening chapters of his life of Jesus so as to encapsulate themes that *dominate* the Jesus tradition and that he regards as *definitive* of his historical life" (italics mine). For the issue of whether this expression is messianic, see Max Botner, "The Messiah Is 'The Holy One': ὁ ἅγιος τοῦ θεοῦ as a Messianic Title in Mark 1:24," *JBL* 136.2 (2017) 417–33.

106:16 that the only precedent for a singular "*the* Holy One of God" is Aaron.[69] This pedimentary piece forms the basic structure for the rest of his study as the author presents compelling additional support that Mark reveals Jesus as the Messiah High Priest (especially from texts involving the healing of the unclean and contagiously sick).[70] His two-part study is judicious, insightful, and arresting.

How is it possible to respond to the exegetical difficulties that Fletcher-Louis has developed? One of the several criteria adopted for this study is that a prophetic text cannot serve as a substructure for more than one Gospel. Does this study by Fletcher-Louis have an Achilles heel? In both of his studies he acknowledges a weakness: although Jesus thought of himself as the nation's king and priest, he was not of priestly lineage. Fletcher-Louis has made a telling admission. This admission creates an opening for possible passage through an impasse. I will take up his claim (that Jesus has no priestly lineage) in chapter 8 which deals with the Gospel of Luke. For now, though, what else can be said in direct response to the Fletcher-Louis study? I would raise two objections. First, he leaves the impression that the text of Mark 1:24 is unique to Mark. This is not true—Luke 4:24 contains the identical words (as does John 6:69). This is significant because it places Luke in the position to potentially develop the motif of the Priest Branch. Secondly, Fletcher-Louis does not deal with the absence of a genealogy in Mark.

Although scholars continue to argue that Mark presents Jesus in the role of a king,[71] the unique emphasis in Mark does not support a kingship presentation. William R. Telford, endeavoring to reconcile divergent descriptions of Jesus in Mark, says: "He speaks of himself, however, as the 'Son of Man' and defines his role as that of a servant (10:45). Given this multi-faceted representation, how then do we determine Mark's Christology, his understanding of the person of Jesus?"[72] Telford further elaborates his understanding of the Markan Jesus by proposing that Mark tilts away from a Messianic "Son of David" Christology while at the same time promoting a "Son of God" Christology.[73] Ralph Martin outlines chapter 8 of his book on Mark

---

69. This was previously noticed by Morna Hooker, *The Gospel According to Mark* (1991) 64.

70. Fletcher-Louis (2007) 64–71.

71. For example, Robert D. Rowe, *God's Kingdom and God's Son: The Background to Mark's Christology from Concepts of Kingship in the Psalms* (2002). However, in spite of Rowe's book title, he admits (230): "Thus Mark wishes to show that following Jesus, in a life of faith and commitment (involving service and suffering), is the way to realizing who he is." See also Gottfried Rau (1985) 2157: "Als weiteres christologisches Leitmotiv steht am Anfang des Abschnittes—vor den Toren Jerusalem und außerhalb des Tempels—die Huldigung der Begleiter Jesus für ihn als den einziehenden König."

72. W. R. Telford, *The Theology of the Gospel of Mark* (1999) 30. See F. F. Bruce, *This Is That: The New Testament Development of Some Old Testament Themes* (1968) 97, where Bruce identifies the Servant in four profiles: a) "Son of Man," b) "suffering Son of Man," c) the suffering of the Son of Man was "something which was 'written,'" and d) the Son of Man's suffering was "a ransom for many."

73. Telford, *The Theology of the Gospel of Mark* (1999) 52. He further elaborates (52): "'Son of God' is not therefore a synonym for 'Messiah' in Mark, and hence there is in Mark strictly speaking not a 'Messianic' secret but a 'Son of God' secret, and when this is acknowledged, many of the conflicting

with five italicized topical headings at the head of the first paragraph; the third topic significantly called, "*The form of a servant as a paradigm for the persecuted church.*"[74] Martin, however, does not highlight this topic in his treatment and does little more than mention "Jesus as a Servant of God."[75]

The First Chapter of Mark. The beginning of the second Gospel is unusual in comparison with the other Gospels. One of the more striking features is the abundant use of the conjunctive expression καὶ εὐθύς ("and immediately"). This expression is used thirty-three times in the NT; strikingly, twenty-seven are found in Mark. Furthermore, nine are found in the first chapter alone, with two additional references to the single word εὐθύς (1:28, 43). Is there any special significance to this unusual count? More specifically, is Mark actually typecasting Jesus as routinely in a hurry? Robert Stein advises: "the expression is little more than a mild conjunctive, meaning 'and then'. In such instances it is unwise to associate a strong temporal meaning with the expression."[76] R. T. France further elaborates how the adverb (εὐθύς) is used: "It adds to the graphic force of the narrative, and serves to keep the reader/hearer alert and aware of the dramatic development of the story."[77] Later on, France tacks on this supplementary observation: "Its role is more to keep the story going with vigour than to comment on the specific nature of their response."[78] This is entirely possible. Others have often noted the rhetorical use of "immediately" to grab the attention of the reader/listener. If this is the case, no historical implications may be implied. That is, we are not to suppose, historically speaking, that Jesus was always in a hurry. Both Matthew and Mark record that Jesus came forth from his baptism immediately. This is entirely normal for anyone undergoing baptism by immersion. Mark is clearly not contrasting Jesus' baptism with those who remained under water for longer periods of time. The fact that Luke uses this adverbial expression only once (Luke 6:49) perhaps strengthens this conclusion. If this is a rhetorical plot device, engaging the narrative in a lively manner, then I conclude that the Markan Jesus is not at odds with Jesus as presented in the Gospel of John. That is, John is not trying to correct Mark. In the fourth Gospel, Jesus resists external human circumstances which impinge upon him to act; in the second Gospel, Jesus responds more to internal promptings, perhaps indicative of his obedience to the Father.

That being said, a possible implication is hereby proposed. Of these nine first-chapter references to εὐθύς in Mark, six of them suggest possible connections to the

---

elements in the Markan presentation begin to come together."

74. R. P. Martin, *Mark: Evangelist and Theologian* (1973) 206.
75. Ibid., 208.
76. Robert H. Stein, *Mark* (2008) 56.
77. R. T. France, *The Gospel of Mark* (2002) 76.
78. Ibid., 97.

notion of servanthood.⁷⁹ A characteristic of a faithful servant is the attitude of prompt obedience. Although the Greek adverb εὐθύς is not used in the LXX, there is a helpful text in Gen 18:1–7 which illuminates ideal servant-like behavior. In this text the LORD appears to Abraham while he was *sitting* in his tent in the heat of the day. Suddenly, he sees three men standing before him. Verse 2 says, "When he saw them, he *hurried* from the entrance." At v. 5 Abraham describes himself as a *servant* ("you have come to your servant"). Verse 6 continues the narrative: "So Abraham *hurried* into the tent to Sarah." Then he says to her, "*Quick*, get three seahs of fine flour." It could be that Mark, consciously or not, is portraying the qualities of a Son who is the model for ideal servanthood by virtue of his single-minded obedience.

THE BAPTISM OF JESUS IN MARK. The baptism of Jesus is recorded in all four Gospels, and in all four Gospels John the Baptist is the administrator of this baptism. Here the similarities end and the differences begin. In Matthew (3:13–17) the emphasis is upon Jesus fulfilling all righteousness. This fulfillment of righteousness upon submission to baptism is unique to Matthew. This obedience to baptism in order to fulfill such righteousness thus coheres well with the Matthean characterization of Jesus as a just and righteous king. Luke provides an additional piece of information. Luke alone adds that while being baptized, Jesus was praying (3:21). The picture of Jesus praying at his baptism conforms to the image of a priest. Mark, however, simplifies the entire event by stressing only the voice from heaven: "You are my Son, whom I love, with you I am well pleased." Morna D. Hooker makes the following observation about Jesus' baptism as presented in Mark:

> What we do find in Mark's prologue is the reason that Jesus, *as* "the Son of Man," can claim authority—namely, because he is also "the Son of God," who is pleasing to God because he is obedient to God's will and so fulfills Israel's vocation. That very obedience, however, may lead to suffering. There is, perhaps, also a hint of this coming suffering in Jesus' baptism, a hint that is made plain when we come to 10.38–39.⁸⁰

Robert Guelich comments that the "coming of the Spirit and the voice from heaven identify Jesus as the Spirit-equipped servant of Isa 42.1 . . . . By explicitly identifying the 'beginning of the gospel' with Isaiah, Mark connects the gospel to its Old Testament Jewish roots."⁸¹ William L. Lane further adds to this profile:

> The declaration provides a unique appraisal of Jesus. The designation 'Son' is enriched by the concept of the Servant of the Lord of Isa. 42:1, but the primary emphasis is upon sonship. In this context 'Son' is not a messianic title, but is to

---

79. Mark 1:10, 12, 18, 20, 21, 29.

80. Morna D. Hooker, "'Who Can This Be?' The Christology of Mark's Gospel," in *Contours of Christology in the New Testament* (2005) 83.

81. R. Guelich, "The Gospel Genre," in *The Gospel and the Gospels* (1991) 196.

be understood in the highest sense, transcending messiahship. It signifies the unique relationship which Jesus sustains to the Father, which exists apart from any thought of official function in history.[82]

Lane's description of Jesus is valuable as it focuses upon relationship rather than function. Yet, it must also be noted that this relationship includes obedience as a son willing to the do will of the Father (Mark 14:36).

THE WORD "KING" IN CHAPTER 15:2–32. Before examining the role of Jesus' eventual suffering on the cross, I pause to consider an unusual characteristic of Mark. This characteristic has led some to draw misleading conclusions. I speak of the six references in chapter 15 to Jesus as a king (15:2, 9, 12, 19, 26, and 32).[83] Ben Witherington observes the following: "It should not be seen as puzzling that the title King does not appear in Mark until chapter 15."[84] I would caution that it depends upon how one uses the word "puzzling." If the conclusion is that this fourteen-chapter delay should not detour us from seeing Jesus portrayed as a king, I disagree. If, however, this delay until chapter 15 correctly points us in the direction that Jesus is not to be viewed as a king in the Gospel of Mark, then I do agree. In other words, this fourteen-chapter silence is important because it enables us to follow the narrative through a different lens. This view (or silence), I believe, points out a difference between Matthew and Mark as it de-emphasizes kingship. This means, then, that Mark has not been stringing us along only to jolt us at the end with a surprise twist.

Additionally, there is the more salient issue of how the word "king" is used in chapter 15. There is clear and pellucid consistency in the ironic manner in which all six references to a king are used in 15:2–32. None of them are positive in tone; none are confessional; all exhibit tongue-in-cheek sarcasm. Furthermore, all of them come together in a single chapter. Edwin K. Broadhead captures the emotional import of these uses:

> The images associated with the King title are wholly negative. The title is first assigned by a Roman magistrate and is employed by him to bait the religious authorities (15.2, 9, 12). This taunting accusation is taken up and amplified by

---

82. William L. Lane, *Commentary on the Gospel of Mark* (1974) 57.

83. Among recent attempts, see Robert D. Rowe, *God's Kingdom and God's Son* (2002); Joel Marcus, *The Way of the Lord: Christological Exegesis of the Old Testament in the Gospel of Mark* (1992). This book by Marcus is well written, but in my judgment some of his explanations about Jesus and kingship are overstated (see pp. 80–93). See also Mark L. Strauss, *The Davidic Messiah in Luke–Acts* (1995) 317: "The present section is limited to Luke's Christological presentation, and seeks to show that two themes are most prominent: *Jesus' kingship and his role as Isaianic servant*" (italics his). More particularly, for the view that Mark presents Jesus as a king based upon the six-fold use of βασιλεύς in chapter 15, see Frank J. Matera, *The Kingship of Jesus: Composition and Theology in Mark 15* (1982) 61. I am relying not only on statistical or quantitative analysis but also qualitative. On both of these counts, therefore, I do not assign the theology of Mark to a kingship motif.

84. B. Witherington, *The Many Faces of the Christ* (1998) 137.

the violent mockery of the soldiers (15.18) and the sarcasm of the religious leaders (15.32). The leaders connect the term to the Christ title and seem to understand both in political terms (15.32). This image of the failed pretender to the throne of Israel is made public by the inscription (15.26). These associations produce a wholly negative aura around the title of King.[85]

The upshot of Broadhead's analysis of chapter 15 is that this chapter in Mark cannot be used to defend kingship in the second Gospel. I rest my case with a further comment from Broadhead : "No disciple or defender employs the title, and the narrator does nothing to salvage the term."[86]

THE LAST WEEK AND THE LAST TWO CHAPTERS: SUBMISSION TO THE CROSS. Ben Witherington aptly comments: "Mark devotes some 19 percent of his narrative to the passion narrative, compared to 15 percent by Matthew or Luke. There is, in short, proportionally more emphasis in Mark on the last week of Jesus' life than in the other Synoptics."[87] What one evangelist omits, another may include; what one evangelist merely mentions, another may emphasize. This contrast in omission and its counterpart of inclusion provides additional clues for understanding Jesus in the Gospel of Mark. Darrell L. Bock, I believe, isolates well the difference between Matthew and Mark: "However, Jesus' authority is not one of raw power. In terms of proportion, Mark highlights Jesus as *the suffering Son of Man and Servant* more than the other Gospels. In fact, nine of thirteen uses of this language look to Jesus' suffering."[88] Jack Dean Kingsbury points out that Matthew drops Markan references to "feelings" such as anger (Mark 3:5), pity (Mark 1:41), wonder (Mark 6:6), indignation (Mark 10:14), and love (Mark 10:21).[89] The literary effect of these omissions in Matthew is to make Jesus more remote, perhaps more regal, while in Mark they make Jesus more human. Kingsbury also offers two further points of contrast: Mark's Gospel, on the surface, seems "to intimate a lack of knowledge or perception on Jesus' part," and Markan expressions appear "to circumscribe his authority or allude to the fact that some desire of his went unfulfilled."[90] These observations on the qualities of Jesus as presented in Mark not only accentuate human characteristics but also indicate a profile befitting a servant.

Wayne Rollins simply says, "The suffering and death of Jesus lay hold of Mark's mind."[91] Or, to state this in different terms: for Mark, the suffering of Jesus on behalf of others is an inescapable necessity that continually drives the narrative towards its

---

85. Edwin K. Broadhead, *Naming Jesus: Titular Christology in the Gospel of Mark* (1999) 78.
86. Ibid., 78.
87. Ben Witherington, *The Gospel of Mark: A Socio-Rhetorical Commentary* (2001) 5.
88. D. L. Bock, *Jesus According to Scripture: Restoring the Portrait from the Gospels* (2002) 32.
89. J. D. Kingsbury, *Jesus Christ in Matthew, Mark, and Luke* (1981) 76.
90. Ibid., 76.
91. W. G. Rollins, *The Gospels: Portraits of Christ* (1963) 34.

painful climax.⁹² Indeed, the Markan narrative tenaciously holds to this theme of sacrificial suffering; it is a suffering or service "on behalf of many" (10:45). Everything in Mark's Gospel leads to this inexorable journey to the cross. To compose a narrative which would conclude with such a shameful and horrifying conclusion is an anomaly. This means that death is not just the end but also the narrative goal. To illustrate the uniqueness and singularity of Mark's Gospel, Plutarch may serve as a contrast. To be sure, Plutarchean biographies end with a final note on how a subject faces death or how he comes to the end of his life. But these narratives are not driven by frequent forecasts of impending death. Christopher Pelling remarks: "Is death the end? Often it is; but it is striking how often a Life ends with someone else's death, not the principal's. Thus *Caesar* ends with the death of Brutus, and *Crassus* with that of King Orodes. More than a quarter of Plutarch's forty-six Parallel Lives fit this pattern."⁹³ Pelling then goes on to observe: "The Parallel Lives average forty-five Teubner lines devoted to posthumous material, between one-and-a-half and two pages. That is something like 4% of the Lives' total bulk. And that is quite a lot."⁹⁴ The Gospel of Mark shows a noticeable difference. If we begin the count at 14:32 when Jesus enters Gethsemane and terminate the count at 15:47 when Jesus is buried, the number of verses from this arbitrary selection is eighty-eight. The percentage of material focusing on his death comes to around 13% of the total 661 verses in Mark. If 4% is "quite a lot" in Plutarch, 13% must be a staggering sum.

W. R. Telford, after assembling a number of descriptions of Jesus that are made by others, singles out the Markan description by Jesus himself: "He speaks of himself, however, as the 'Son of Man,' and defines his role as that of a servant (10.45)."⁹⁵ Telford in an earlier essay acknowledged that "there is nowadays a gathering consensus among Marcan scholars that the emphasis by the evangelist on the divine necessity of Jesus' suffering and death ('the way of the cross') represents a major thrust of his Christological presentation."⁹⁶ Edwin Broadhead, connecting together several key texts, provides a comprehensive description of Jesus from the Gospel of Mark:

---

92. P. Achtemeier, *Mark* (1975) 47: "If there is, for example, a characteristic difference between the first and second halves of the Gospel, it lies precisely in the fact that once Jesus' suffering is announced (8:31), it dominates the narrative from that point on." See also H. J. Bernard Combrink,, "Salvation in Mark," in *Salvation in the New Testament: Perspectives on Soteriology* (2005) 50. See also D. W. Geyer, *Fear, Anomaly, and Uncertainty in the Gospel of Mark* (2002) 1, who says: "Yet here it is in Mark, precisely the main event, to which every other detail in Mark is directed and around which the whole story is composed." However, it must be acknowledged that Geyer's thesis is to demonstrate that Mark's Gospel is, among other things (76), the result of "mistakes made by an excited, if not somewhat befuddled, storyteller." These mistakes, supposedly, lead to a clumsy narrative, bewilderment, uncertainty, and massive misunderstanding for the reader.

93. Christopher Pelling, "Is Death the End? Closure in Plutarch's Lives," in *Plutarch and History: Eighteen Studies* (2002) 365.

94. Ibid., 366.

95. W. R. Telford, *The Theology of the Gospel of Mark* (1999) 30.

96. W. R. Telford, "Introduction," in *The Interpretation of Mark* (1985) 18. Telford (15) also isolates

This link between service and suffering is not incidental. Jesus speaks of his own service on one occasion (Mk 10.45). The service of Jesus is given precise definition: he has come to give his life on behalf of the people . . . . Seen in this light, Mk 10.45 becomes a verbal hinge which takes up the initial characterization of Jesus as an obedient servant and connects it to the death of Jesus: he has come to serve, to give his life as a ransom on behalf of the many. . . .Only in the closing verses of this Gospel is the suffering of Jesus given titular expression. Mark 16.6 refers to Jesus as τὸν ἐσταυρωμένον, the Crucified One, and confirms the fulfillment of the service proposed in Mk 10.45.[97]

If the evidence leads to the conclusion that Mark presents a particular view of Jesus congruent with the Suffering Servant, the question must be asked if this is a unique emphasis characteristic only of Mark? This present chapter champions the view, indeed, that Mark is distinct in his manner of presenting Jesus as a Suffering Servant.[98] Proceeding further, what justification is there for linking the text of Zech 3:8 to the Gospel of Mark? After all, it must be admitted that nowhere does Mark specifically make such a clear identification. Additionally, it could be argued that the foundation for the Servant motif in Mark is not Zech 3:8 but Isaiah 52–53.[99]

---

eight significant interests in Mark that dominate scholarship. Of these eight, two are connected with suffering and servanthood. In the same collection of essays, see the following contributions (each offering a slightly different perspective, yet all calling attention to the motif of Jesus as a suffering Servant): Eduard Schweizer, "Mark's Theological Achievement" 42–63, esp. his conclusion at 57: "So Mark is the Gospel of the amazing, incomprehensible condesension and love of God which in Jesus seeks the world;" Theodore J. Weeden, "The Heresy that Necessitated Mark's Gospel," (1985) 68, where Weeden develops his thesis of a Markan suffering messiah pitted against a false *theios aner* Christology; Norman Perrin, "The Christology of Mark: A Study in Methodology," (1985) 99, where Perrin redactionally follows the lead of Weeden, reinforcing the view that Jesus is a suffering Servant set off as a corrective to a false *theios aner* Christology; Robert C. Tannehill, "The Disciples in Mark: The Function of a Narrative Role," (1985) 140, where Tannehill uses narrative criticism to take issue with redaction criticism but still places in the forefront the same focus upon servanthood. See also M. Eugene Boring, "The Birth of Narrative Theology," in *Chalice Introduction to the New Testament* (2004) 145: "In both his christology and his picture of the discipleship, Mark's emphasis falls on the cross."

97. E. K. Broadhead, *Naming Jesus* (1999) 106.

98. Two scholars, although from completely different points of view, advocating Mark's presentation of Jesus as a Servant are Luke Timothy Johnson, *The Real Jesus: The Misguided Quest for the Historical Jesus and the Truth of the Traditional Gospels* (1996); and Robert J. Miller, "The Jesus of Orthodoxy and the Jesuses of the Gospels: A Critique of Luke Timothy Johnson's *The Real Jesus*," *JSNT* 68 (1997) 101–20. Johnson sees the suffering Son of Man as *the* single pattern from which all four Gospels are cut. Miller confines this pattern only to Mark and finds fault with Johnson for imposing this view on the others. As the title implies, Miller is out to challenge Johnson's book. In the process, he advances his own understanding of Luke (esp. 113) as a presentation of Jesus as a prophet-martyr. For the view of a suffering messiah in the DSS, see John J. Collins, "A Messiah before Jesus?" in *Christian Beginnings and the Dead Sea Scrolls* (2006) 21–31. Although not suggesting a background to the Gospel of Mark, Collins does argue for a messianic view that eliminates the so-called Teacher of Righteousness of Qumran (*contra* Michael Wise).

99. See R. Frank Johnson, "Christ the Servant of the Lord," in *The Old and New Testaments: Their Relationship and the "Intertestamental" Literature* (1993) 107: "The fourth Servant Song in Isaiah 52.13ff. may well have served as a prototype for interpreting (and perhaps reconstructing) Jesus' life

David Rhoads offers a more pointed analysis of Mark's purpose, "A study of standards of judgment shows that the Gospel of Mark is a tightly woven narrative reflecting two contrasting ways of life."[100] These two contrasting ways of living are respectively: "saving one's life out of fear" or "losing one's life for others out of faith."[101] Paul Achtemeier points to a trail of evidence that would be a mistake not to follow. He assembles a number of interpretive clues that point in the direction of servanthood as the controlling Christological viewpoint of the Second Gospel:

> There is one title, however, that Mark found eminently suited to his purposes. That title is "Son of Man"....The title can also be used to refer to Jesus as the one who was betrayed (14:21), arrested (14:41), who suffered (9:12), and who died (10:45) . . . Mark presents this one christological designation as the favorite title of Jesus for himself....It is in fact this understanding of Jesus as one who must suffer, die, and who will rise, that represents the controlling christological emphasis in Mark's Gospel.[102]

Robert Stein has argued that one of the major seams in Mark is the "unique Galilean emphasis."[103] Elizabeth Malbon, building upon the Galilean motif, offers yet another instructive way of understanding how to read Mark. She isolates all the passages connected with the Sea of Galilee and then extracts the significance as pointing directly to lessons on servanthood for the disciples, as well as the suffering of Jesus.[104] In this construct, the Sea of Galilee becomes, as it were, the training ground for developing a servant-spirit in the disciples. Jesus is the model for such obedience, and the sea is the boot camp for such training. Etienne Trocmé has observed, "in Mark, more than any of the other gospels, Jesus is everywhere in the company of his disciples."[105]

---

in the Gospel narratives." Johnson does add (108): "Isaiah 53 is not the only Old Testament text that could have served as a 'proof' for a suffering messiah." Finally, Johnson (129) affirms: "In Mark 9.12, Jesus predicts that he is to suffer many things and be treated with contempt (Isa 53.3, *nibzeh*)." He also cites Mark 9:13; 10:33; and 14:21.

100. D. Rhoads, "Losing Life for Others in the Face of Death: Mark's Standards of Judgment," in *Gospel Interpretation: Narrative-Critical & Social-Scientific Approaches* (1997) 83. See also Francis D. Weinert, "Luke, the Temple and Jesus' Saying about Jerusalem's Abandoned House," *CBQ* 44.1 (1982) 68–76.

101. D. Rhoads, "Losing Life," (1997) 84.

102. P. Achtemeier, *Mark* (1975) 45–47.

103. R. H. Stein, "The Proper Methodology for Ascertaining a Markan Redaction History," (1971) 183: "In order to join these pericopes together Mark had either to create the seams we find in his gospel or rework the original introductions which introduced the isolated pericopes." Although Steins's article is highly speculative in its attempt to reconstruct the various stages of Markan composition history, his observation on Galilee is valuable.

104. E. S. Malbon, "The Jesus of Mark and the Sea of Galilee," *JBL* 103.3 (1984) 363–77. Here she enters into debate with W. H. Kelber, *The Kingdom in Mark: A New Place and a New Time* (1974) over the purpose of the sea-narratives. Kelber finds the sea as a place for failure among the disciples until after the resurrection. Malbon does not so understand the incidents involving the sea—they are, rather, places of success.

105. Etienne Trocmé, *The Formation of the Gospel According to Mark* (1975) 142, cited by Suzanne

These emphases do not imply contradictions, only variations in selectivity.[106] I must now state a theme running through Mark: the second Gospel shows a strong emphasis, first, upon Jesus as a suffering Servant; secondly, this Gospel shows almost an equal emphasis upon discipleship and serving.

It is often noticed that Mark emphasizes Jesus as a teacher. Is there any special significance to this distinction? One possibility is that Jesus assumes the role of a teacher in order to instruct his disciples on the issues involved in serving.[107] Adela Yarbro Collins, noting that in Mark Jesus is addressed ten times as a teacher, adds, "This activity or social role seems at first glance to be incompatible with the office of royal messiah."[108] She then attempts a reconciliation between the two roles. It is not necessary, however, to resolve this apparent incompatibility. Jack Dean Kingsbury, noting a difference between Matthew and Mark, observes:

> Again, the disciples and those who come to Jesus in the attitude of faith do not simply address him as teacher, as in Mark's Gospel, but Lord (*kyrie*), which is a title that characterizes him as one of exalted station and divine authority (8.2, 6, 8, 21, 25; 14.28, 30).[109]

Watts Henderson, *Christology and Discipleship in the Gospel of Mark* (2006) 3.

106. W. D. Davies, *The Gospel and the Land* (1974) 221, where Davies is of a slightly different persuasion arguing that "in the ancient Jewish sources" there is no connection between the Messiah and Galilee.

107. For example, John Killinger, *Hidden Mark: Exploring Christianity's Heretical Gospel* (2010) 72–73, sketches out "twelve warnings for twelve disciples," indicating challenges the disciples would face if they would follow him. See also Charles A. Bobertz, *The Gospel of Mark: A Liturgical Reading* (2016) 186, who connects Simon of Cyrene's taking up the cross at 15:21 with the "narrative fulfillment" of 8:34, thus personalizing the disciple's call to carry his or her own cross.

108. A. Collins, *Mark: A Commentary* (2007) 66.

109. J. D. Kingsbury, "The Gospel in Four Editions," 368. See also Kingsbury's *Jesus Christ in Matthew, Mark, and Luke* (1981) 76: "Thus, in forty-nine instances Matthew utilizes the verb *proserchomai* ('to come to,' 'to approach'), which in the LXX is cultic in coloration and in Josephus is used of stepping before a king, in order to portray persons as approaching Jesus with the same reverence that would be due to a deity or king." See also John Nolland, "No Son-of-God Christology in Matthew 1.18–25," *JSNT* 62 (1996) 9, fn. 28: "In Mark προσκυνεῖν means only to show deferential respect to (5.6; 15.19); in Luke it denotes religious worship (4.7, 8) and is used with Jesus as object only after the resurrection (24.52); in Matthew it clearly can mean religious reverence (4.9, 10), at times seems clearly to involve worship directed towards Jesus (14.33; 28.9, 17)." See Crispin H. T. Fletcher-Louis, "The Worship of Divine Humanity as God's Image and the Worship of Jesus," in *The Jewish Roots of Christological Monotheism*: (1998) 113, where he has argued that historically within ancient Judaism there was a precedent for the worship of humans and, consequently, the worship of Jesus is not to be considered as unthinkable or insurmountable. Since some pious Jews were comfortable worshiping "a particular righteous humanity" this, supposedly, provides the rationale for understanding the worship of Jesus. Note also his conclusion (128): "Yet, that *certain righteous individuals were deemed worthy of worship because they were God's Image, his living idols*, is, I submit a key to the history-of-religions (and theological) context for the worship of Jesus" (italics his). This is perhaps making a mountain out of a mole hill. This kind of exaggeration also assumes that Matthew was influenced from the environment of a larger literary community in which such conceptions were current rather than reporting something that happened in the ministry of Jesus as a spontaneous reaction to Jesus.

Kingsbury, I believe, offers a way out, a path to reconciliation. The Gospel of Matthew emphasizes kingship; the Gospel of Mark highlights the servant attitude of the king. Neither needs to cancel out the other.

In the Gospel of Mark, Jesus tells us that he did not come to be served, but to serve and to give his life as a ransom for many (10:45). This places Jesus in the potentially relevant position of being the fulfillment of the Servant Branch. As C. H. Dodd says: "As Servant, he deliberately associates himself with sinful humanity and offers his life as λύτρον ἀντὶ πολλῶν (Mk 10.45)."[110] R. T. France adds: "The term διακονέω is not used with Jesus as subject elsewhere in the gospel tradition."[111] Jesus, who should have enjoyed the service of others, is the servant of all. Further adding to this configuration of Jesus as presented in Mark is the contrast between Matthew and Luke in terms of worship. It is rare to find Jesus worshiped in Mark; he uses προσκυνέω only once (5:6),[112] while this extravagant devotion is abundantly evident in Matthew.[113] This is not to argue that Jesus is not worshiped at all in Mark but, rather, the emphasis upon the worship of Jesus is diminished. What could account for this disparity of references? One possibility is the view that in Mark Jesus is presented as a servant.[114] Servants characteristically offer worship rather than receive worship. Yet, it must be asserted, the term servant carries significance as a messianic concept.[115]

---

110. C. H. Dodd, *According to the Scriptures: The Sub-Structure of New Testament Theology* (1953) 118.

111. R. T. France, *The Gospel of Mark* (2002) 419.

112. Mark does use the verb γονυπετέω twice: 1:40; 10:17. BADG translates this verb as "to fall on one's knees." See also Matt 17:14 and 27:29 for the only other usages. This behavior does not necessarily indicate worship; it is more a position of desperate pleading. BADG cites Tacitus' *Annals* 11.30: *genibus Caesaris* ("on her knees before Caesar") as a Roman parallel. This text is of similar tone; Messalina, in dire distress, is pleading for mercy.

113. Simon Gathercole, *The Pre-existent Son* (2006) 69: "The question, however, is not particularly which term is used, but whether one is to understand the obeisance/devotion/worship offered to Jesus *as that which is specifically due, and also offered to the one God*. There is little evidence of this in Mark's Gospel, where the language of προσκυνεῖν is not present, although we do see the leper (Mark 1.40) and the rich man (10.17) falling on their knees before Jesus, and Jairus similarly falls at Jesus' feet (5.22). Matthew and Luke, however, offer a somewhat clearer picture. Matthew uses προσκυνεῖν repeatedly."

114. For arguments that Mark focuses upon servanthood both in Jesus and the disciples, see E. Schweizer, "The Portrayal of the Life of Faith in the Gospel of Mark," *Int* 32 (1978) 387–99; and P. J. Achtemeier, "Mark as Interpreter of the Jesus Traditions," *Int* 32 (1978) 339–52.

115. For the view that the concept of "Servant" is a messianic term, see J. Jeremias, "παῖς θεοῦ," *TDNT* (1967) 5.681–86; Walther Zimmerli, "παῖς θεοῦ," *TDNT* (1967) 5.666–73. See also Theodore J. Weeden, "The Heresy that Necessitated Mark's Gospel," in *The Interpretation of Mark* (1985) 68, where Weeden develops his thesis of the suffering messiahship of Jesus as a contrast to the disciples' mistaken notion of a *theios aner* Christology. He then proceeds to tie this "heresy" to Mark's community of believers. In other words, the *theios aner* controversy has no historical basis in the lives of the actual twelve disciples; therefore, the controversy must be situated in the turmoil of Mark's community. See also H. H. Rowley, *The Servant of the Lord and other Essays on the Old Testament* (1965) 63–93, for his chapter, "The Suffering Servant and the Davidic Messiah."

The Branch

MT: צמח (*Zemah*), LXX: Ἀνατολή (*Anatolē*), NIV: Branch

A critical question cannot be avoided: who is this Branch? The NIV capitalizes the word suggesting a messianic reference. This interpretation, however, has been challenged. A likely candidate who has often been proposed is the person of Zerubbabel.[116] Since he is specifically identified by the prophet Haggai as a servant of YHWH (2:23), this possibility must be considered. The proposal, however, that this mysterious figure is Zerubbabel has met stiff resistance. There are four objections. First, James C. VanderKam expresses a measure of confidence by affirming: "The following clause in Zech 3:8 contains Zechariah's first reference to someone called 'my servant the Branch'. Clearly, he belongs to the future of which the priests sitting before Joshua (and perhaps Joshua himself) are portents. Jeremiah employed the same word Branch (צמח) for a Davidic ruler of the future."[117] Second, VanderKam offers the following correction:

> Yet, if Branch in 3.8 is an epithet for Zerubbabel, the text contains a puzzling feature: the LORD says that he is bringing or will bring a Branch. Zerubbabel, however, had been in Jerusalem for years, according to Ezra 2–5. It does seem peculiar that in the prophet's first reference to Zerubbabel, where he fails to name him, he predicts that he will be brought to a place where he has been for eighteen or nineteen years. In light of these unsettling facts, it is

---

116. For this argument, see Paul L. Redditt, "Zerubbabel, Joshua, and the Night Visions of Zechariah," *CBQ* 54.2 (1992) 249–60. For the argument that Zech 3:8 does not have indications of Davidic royal status, see Kenneth E. Pomykala, *The Davidic Dynasty* (1995) 53, where the author disclaims Davidic messianic associations on the basis of the expression "my servant" (עבדי). See also D. Winton Thomas, *The Book of Zechariah: Chapters 1–8* (IB, 1956) 6.1054: "The high hopes which Haggai had reposed in Zerubbabel as the long-awaited king-messiah find expression again in Zechariah."

117. J. C. VanderKam, *From Joshua to Caiaphas: High Priests after the Exile* (2004) 30. For a similar conclusion, see W. Rudolph, *Haggai-Sacharja 1–8* (1976) 99: "Da der zunächst so seltsame anmutende Name nicht weiter erläutert wird, muß er den Hörern vertraut gewesen sein, und es ist nicht zweifelhaft, daß damit auf die messianishc verstandene Weissagung Jeremias (Jer 23.5) angespielt ist, nach der Jahwe dem David eine echten (oder: gerechten) Sproß erwechen wird. Wir haben also eine traditionell gewordene Bezeichnung des Messias aus dem Hause Davids vor uns . . ." W. A. M. Beuken, *Haggai-Sacharja 1–8: Studien zur Überlieferungsgeschichte der frühnachexilischen Prophetie* (1967) 284, although acknowledging that v.9 contains a messianic reference, questions the unity of this prophecy. See also Benjamin Uffenheimer, *The Visions of Zechariah: From Prophecy to Apocalyptic* (1961), although the main text of the study is written in Hebrew, the Introduction contains a summary in English with the following capsulation (v): "The main conclusions of this first section are briefly as follows: Zechariah's visions (I–VIII) do not reflect a single but rather a series of experiences over a considerable period of time. As may be gathered from the passage where the so-called Branch (*Zemah David*) is mentioned (a term, incidentally which, does not relate to Zerubbabel but to the ideal king who is to come)." See also Gerard Van Groningen, *Messianic Revelation in the Old Testament* (1990) 880: "To state it pointedly: these are key messianic terms; they refer ultimately to the royal, divine Person, the Messiah." Finally, for additional arguments that the promotion of Zerubbabel is not in view, see Greg Goswell, "The Fate and Future of Zerubbabel in the Prophecy of Haggai," *Bib* 91 (2010) 77–90.

understandable that some have opted to say no more than that Zechariah, in his use of the title Branch, has in mind some future ruler from David's line.[118]

Indeed, the metaphor of branch suggests something that grows out of something or suddenly sprouts from a pre-existing condition, such as a branch from a tree or a blossom from a plant. Third, a further objection may be made with profit. The interjection "Behold" (הנה, or a variation[119]) is used a total of seventeen times in the first six chapters of Zechariah. The majority of these references point to a vision or an event of a surprising nature; in some cases they describe phenomenon such as a "flying scroll" (5:2). These texts have descriptions of a supernatural import. They do not describe pedestrian events or ordinary people. Joshua is mentioned specifically six times in Zechariah (3:1, 3, 6, 8, 9; 6:11); yet, nowhere does Zechariah ever write "Behold" when bringing forward the person of Joshua. In other words, the person of Joshua does not cause surprise to Zechariah. However, the mysterious figure of the Branch does cause wonder and amazement. Inasmuch as the argument has been made that the Branch is either Joshua or Zerubbabel,[120] I introduce this information as a possible benchmark creating a further wall of separation between the Branch and Joshua or Zerubbabel. The Branch causes wonder; neither Joshua nor Zerubbabel evoke surprise. Fourth, one additional observation may be made; Joyce Baldwin, calling attention to the absence of an article with the Hebrew word *Zemah*, observes:

> The absence of the article is important because attention is thereby drawn to the fact that someone other than either Joshua or Zerubbabel is meant. Emphasis is on the pronouns in the clauses that follow, again drawing a contrast between the present leaders and the future one."[121]

Although Zerubbabel is mentioned as a servant of YHWH as well as being a "signet ring" (Hag 2:23), he is never identified with the word *Zemah*.

Two complex issues must now be singled out for a response. The first is whether the text of Zech 3:8 speaks of the same identical role as envisioned in Zech 6:12. Or, do these two texts tell of a single individual fulfilling multiple roles? Of further particular interest to this study is the critical question of whether Zech 3:8, in an isolated manner, is speaking of an individual whose principal identity is that of a servant, rather than a priest in the manner of Zech 6:12. Both texts use the word צמח (*Zemah*) to describe a "branch," "shoot," or "sprout." The translations cited above capitalize the word

---

118. J. C. VanderKam, "Joshua the High Priest and the Interpretation of Zechariah 3," *CBQ* 53.4 (1991) 561. VanderKam, however, goes on to say: "It must be admitted, nevertheless, that Zerubbabel is probably intended, although the vagueness surrounding 'my servant Branch' hints that the emphasis here does not lie on Zerubbabel." This is hardly a resounding vote of confidence for Zerubbabel. See also R. J. Coggins, *Haggai, Zechariah, Malachi* (1984) 36.

119. For example, הנני at 3:8–9, and ראה at 6:8.

120. See, for example, Margaret Barker, "The Two Figures in Zechariah," *HeyJ* 18 (1977) 38–46, who argues that Joshua is the Branch.

121. J. G. Baldwin, "ṢEMAḤ as a Technical Term in the Prophets," *VT* 14.1 (1964) 95.

in their versions with "Branch." Thus, in the view of translators, these two Zecharian texts clearly have in common the same metaphor.

The Hebrew word צמח (*Zemah*) or "Branch" ends the sentence in Zech 3:8. Words that come at the very end often carry a note of emphasis. Such is likely the case here. At the very end, like a caboose on a train, the Branch appears. This Branch is a distinctive Servant Branch, unlike the other three Branches. Since my case rests upon the plausibility that the Gospel of Mark is a fulfillment of this branch prophecy, it is necessary to ask: is this word found in the second Gospel? The answer is a quick "no." That, however, does not conclude the matter. It is not my contention that the four evangelists have consciously set out to prove that their respective Gospels are a fulfillment of the four prophecies under investigation. My contention is only that these four prophetic texts provide an adequate explanation for the unique characteristics of each individual Gospel. Furthermore, these four prophetic texts undergird the four Gospels just as a substructure supports the weight of a framework—whether material or literary.

Conclusion

The Gospel of Mark offers a number of telling clues suggesting that this Gospel uniquely presents Jesus as the prophesied Servant of God.[122] The first chapter initiates this identity with programmatic details that separate Mark from the other three Gospels. As an emphasis, Mark distinctly portrays Jesus with the credentials of the Son of God Servant. Comparing the first chapters of Matthew, Mark, and Luke is an exercise in contrasts. Although they clearly describe a single person (Jesus), their portraits are vastly different. In the first forty-eight verses of Matthew (the first two chapters) Jesus does nothing. In the eighty verses of Luke's first chapter Jesus is not shown doing anything. In between these two Gospels is placed Mark, showing yet another contrast. In the first forty-five verses of Mark there are over forty verbs depicting Jesus in the act of ministry. What is startling is that Jesus is never depicted as doing anything for himself. Other than being baptized, every one of Jesus' actions is directed toward helping someone else or doing something to spread the Kingdom of God. Mark's portrait of Jesus is clearly one of very intense and immediate action. This portrait conforms to the obedient Servant Son of God. The premise that Matthew and Mark describe the same person may seem at first glance to be self-contradictory, paradoxical profiles. That may be the case on the surface, yet, as I propose, they are prophetically explainable.

---

122. A. B. Caneday, "Mark's Provocative Use of Scripture in Narration," *BBR* 9 (1999) 3: "The style of Mark's Gospel is to use the Hebrew Bible in a cryptic, enigmatic, and allusive manner that provokes the reader's imagination to uncover intertextual connections with those scriptures. It is a style that effectively draws the reader into Mark's narrative, but it also brings one to recognize that Mark has skillfully woven into his narrative many allusive words and phrases that subtly link the Jesus of his story with the Coming One of the Hebrew Bible."

7

The Absence of a Genealogy in Mark

ONE OF THE OBVIOUS characteristics of Mark is the starting point of his Gospel. Contrary to Matthew, he omits any formal reference listing the family history of Jesus. This omission has given rise to noticeable scholarly attention. Marcus Borg suggests: "At the very least, this indicates that it was possible to write a gospel without mentioning the birth of Jesus. There are two possible explanations. The tradition of a special birth was old, but these authors either didn't know about it or didn't consider it important enough to include."[1] Paul J. Achtemeier notes that Matthew and Luke include information that Jesus is from the Davidic line, while Mark is silent; Achtemeier, however, does not pursue the significance of this silence.[2] George Aichele notes simply that an absence of a genealogy in Mark is "problematic."[3] Charles H. Talbert, after studying the subject of the birth of important people in the ancient world, concludes that the Gospel of Mark without a birth narrative was subject to "an interpretation of a meritorious Jesus who is rewarded by God."[4] Given the entire context of this claim, Talbert alleges then that Matthew and Luke "added birth narratives with a miraculous conception as part of rewriting Mark."[5] Craig Evans, explaining his reason for accepting the priority of Mark, offers the view that the absence of the nativity is an indication that Mark was written first. His logic is based upon the premise that if Matthew had preceded Mark, Mark would have included the family record of Jesus.[6] John S. Kloppenborg Verbin has explored similar issues, suggesting that the adoption of a particular source theory/hypothesis has consequences for understanding each Gospel.[7] This presumption, however, overlooks the value of *not* including a genealogy. John B. Gabel and Charles B. Wheeler offer a

1. Marcus Borg and N. T. Wright, *The Meaning of Jesus: Two Visions* (1999) 180.

2. P. J. Achtemeier, *Mark* (1975) 43.

3. G. Aichele, "Jesus's Two Fathers: An Afterlife of the Gospel of Luke," in *Those Outside: Non-canonical Readings of the Canonical Gospels* (2005) 34: "For the Gospel of Mark, there is no Joseph and there is no Christmas story. Jesus' father is problematic throughout Mark."

4. C. H. Talbert, "Miraculous Conceptions and Births in Mediterranean Antiquity," in *The Historical Jesus in Context* (2006) 86.

5. Ibid., 86.

6. C. A. Evans, *Luke* (1990) 4.

7. J. S. Kloppenborg Verbin, "The Theological Stakes in the Synoptic Problem," in *The Four Gospels* (1992) 93–120.

reading of Mark which suggests that the omission of the birth material has the advantage of downplaying the human side of Jesus, "which Mark wished to deemphasize."[8] Leslie Houlden, endeavoring to account for the absence of a birth record of Jesus in Mark, offers an explanation hinting at what he calls "Mark's almost gratuitous hostility" to Jesus' family.[9] James D. Tabor, taking the argument even further, says: "Mark never refers to Joseph at all, by name or otherwise. He avoids the paternity issue altogether."[10] The context in which Tabor's observation occurs suggests that Mark omits the birth record of Jesus because of embarrassment that Jesus is illegitimate. Indeed, this is Tabor's view: Jesus was conceived by a human father before marriage. Laying aside Tabor's contention for the moment, is there any viable reason why Mark would omit the genealogy of Jesus?

Given the wide diversity of explanations for the absence of a Markan genealogy, can a new vista be opened on this intriguing absence? Darrell D. Hannah has observed that some "silences speak louder than others; in fact, some can be deafening."[11] The silence or omission of a genealogy in Mark must be considered quite loud, quite noticeable. If the Gospel of Matthew has a genealogy because kings in the OT have a genealogy, in light of the present investigation one strong possibility presents itself: in the OT, servants do not have a genealogy. Of course, suggestions do not prove possibility, and possibilities do not demonstrate actuality. Therefore, we must pursue this perspective further.

In the OT, there are over seven hundred references to servants. There are two principal words in the OT describing either a domestic or court servant. The first is נער (naar) and it is used fifty-two times. Of these fifty-two references, only four servants are given a name.[12] In these four particular cases, none of the four are given the name of their father. They are clearly referenced without benefit of a patronym. Their identity is not linked to the name of their father but to the one they now serve. For example, a man may be simply "the servant of Saul." The second word is the more familiar עבד (ebed) used over 700 times. In Gen 15:2 we are introduced to Eliezer, a servant of Abraham. His only identity is that he is from Damascus, and Abraham indicates that Eliezer could possibly be an heir to his estate. In Gen 24:2, Abraham is now advanced in years and requests that his "chief servant" go on a mission to find a wife for Isaac. Eliezer is never mentioned by name in this chapter. I can only surmise that it is Eliezer. His only identity is that he is a servant (an *ebed*) of Abraham. Five times he is referred to as "*the* servant" (העבד/*the ebed*), with the definite article perhaps describing his position as the chief servant. The most significant fact, though, is that his parents are never named. His identity is tied solely to the one he serves, in this case Abraham. Another notable case is Doeg the Edomite, Saul's head shepherd (1 Sam 21:7). His name comes belatedly after a hiatus of 190 references to prior nameless

---

8. J. B. Gabel and C. B. Wheeler, *The Bible as Literature: An Introduction* (1990) 192.

9. L. Houlden, "Jesus, Origins of," in *Jesus in History* (2003) 1.439.

10. J. D. Tabor, *The Jesus Dynasty* (2006) 61.

11. D. D. Hannah, "The Four-Gospel 'Canon' in the *Epistula Apostolorum*," *JTS* 59 (2008) 632.

12. Phurah (Judg 7:10); Ziba (2 Sam 9:9); Gahazi (2 Kgs 4:12); and Sanballat (Neh 6:5).

servants. The name of his father is not given, and his identity is linked to the master whom he serves. Another striking example is the Egyptian servant discovered out in a field, perhaps looking for food (1 Sam 30:13). Upon being brought to David, the king then asks, "To whom do you belong?" The man mentions only that he is the servant of an Amalekite. He has no anamnestic family history. In 2 Sam 9:2, David inquires into the identity of a servant named Ziba by simply asking, "Are you Ziba?" Ziba's connection to the narrative is that he served in the house of Saul. Outside of a first name, he actually has no other personal identification. His status, therefore, is that of a slave, although he himself has twenty servants (2 Sam 9:10). There are five additional servants listed with names; none are identified by their relationship to a father.[13] Only one exception to this list is found. This is Jeroboam, the son of Nebat (1 Kgs 11:26), who served for a time in the service of Solomon, later rebelled against the king, and eventually became king himself over the ten tribes. It is possible that the reason Jeroboam contains the name of his father is because he did serve as a king. The NIV describes Jeroboam as a "man of standing" and translates *ebed* with the word "official" rather than "servant."

A further detail merits mention. Notable personalities such as Abraham, Moses, David, and Elijah are often described as servants of YHWH. However, they are not to be classified as either domestic slaves or indentured servants to a man of higher rank. Additionally, their fathers are also included. For example, Abraham is the son of Terah (Gen 11:27) and also the servant of YHWH (Gen 26:24). Moses is the son of Amram (Exod 6:20) and also the servant of YHWH. David is the son of Jesse (1 Sam 16:1). Aside from the sole person of Moses, no servant in the OT has a record of an actual birth. The question then surfaces: if Mark begins without a genealogy because court and domestic servants in the OT do not have genealogies, but outstanding individuals such as Moses, David, and Elijah are portrayed as servants of YHWH, then why—according to the argument of this chapter—is Jesus not given similar genealogical consideration? A possible answer to this rightful question is indebted to the fact that Jesus does not have a genuine biological father. He is a servant of YHWH only. Hence, the genealogy is omitted because the logic of OT Scripture does not require servants to produce evidence of their human ancestry. In fact, the registry of their past is actually dispensed with as they transfer their identity to the one they now serve.

Conclusion to Chapters 6 and 7

It is obvious that the text of Zech 3:8 does not offer as many details as does Jer 23:5–6 or Zech 6:12. But the text of Zech 3:8 does introduce us to a metaphor identified as a Branch. This Branch is not a king but, rather, a servant. It has been the particular challenge of these two chapters to offer evidence that the Gospel of Mark portrays Jesus as

---

13. Abijah (1 Kgs 15:29); Zimri (1 Kgs 16:9); Ben-hadad (1 Kgs 20:32); Asaiah (2 Kgs 22:12); and Tobiah (Neh 2:10).

the fulfillment of the Servant Branch prophecy.[14] In my judgment, this prophecy is the most difficult one to unlock and the most difficult one to apply. This difficulty is not due to an abundance of cryptic terms but, rather, to the paucity of language.[15] A comparison between specific key words as employed by Matthew and Mark can be instructive for determining their unique presentation of Jesus. Words such as "throne," "law," and "judgment" dominate Matthew; they are not found in Mark. These Matthean words, characteristic and stereotypical descriptions of ancient kingship, are noticeably absent from Mark. The thesis as presented here is that this conception of Jesus in Mark is based upon the modest and simple role of the servant as described in the OT text of Zech 3:8. For example, servants in the OT are portrayed in language bare of ornamentation.

I acknowledge that nowhere does Mark cite the full text of Zech 3:8. Therefore, it would be unfair to advocate that Mark is consciously in dialogue with this text from Zechariah. Thus, it is not possible to maintain that the Gospel of Mark *requires* that we locate the prophetic text of Zech 3:8 as its substructure. That does not end the matter. A crucial question still remains: if we tone down the rhetoric to a more moderate word such as "allow," is it possible that the second Gospel *allows* us to see Zech 3:8 as the underpinning of this Gospel? The investigation leads in this direction based upon the premise of congruent allusions that suitably provide a corresponding match of converging ideas between the prophetic text of Zech 3:8 and the second Gospel. Furthermore, the central ideas of Zech 3:8 and the Gospel of Mark are not at loggerheads with each other. In fact, the opposite is the case. The former anticipates the latter; the latter mirrors the former.

My argument is not that Mark is consciously inviting the reader to understand that, for example, Mark 9:35 is a direct fulfillment of Zech 3:8. It is more reasonable to suggest that these cameo descriptions are simply compatible with the picture as presented in Zech 3:8. Although this fragmentary image is not a perfect one, neither is it pixilated. It is simply a reasonable correspondence. Stated differently and less aggressively, the Gospel of Mark does not *require* the above analysis but it does *allow* us to see a possible consonant relationship between the two texts.

---

14. For the argument that Jesus is the suffering Servant of Isaiah, see Ivan Engnell, "The 'Ebed Yahweh Songs and the Suffering Messiah in Deutero-Isaiah," *BJRL* 31 (1948) 58: "We need not speak of 'Ebed Yahweh as a 'parallel figure' of Messiah. 'Ebed Yahweh is the Messiah himself, the Saviour king of the dynasty of David waited for." For the view that ancient Israel could conceive of a servant king, see Moshe Weinfeld, "The King as the Servant of the People: The Source of the Idea," *JJS* 33 (1982) 189–94, and his discussion of 1 Kgs 12:7 ("If today you will be a servant to these people and serve them and give them a favorable answer, they will always be your servants") on the occasion when the people approached Rehoboam for a relaxation of taxes. As well as refuting the idea that a servant king owes its ideology to Hellenistic philosophy, Weinfeld demonstrates that the idea can be traced back to Israel in the OT.

15. Hans Conzelmann, *An Outline of the Theology of the New Testament* (1969) 141, offers the view that "Mark's understanding of revelation is clear from the structure of his book. In literary terms, its shaping is primitive. But from a theological point of view it proves to be astonishingly well thought out."

8

The Gospel of Luke: The Man/Priest Branch

GREG STERLING HAS ARTICULATED a view that purports to highlight Luke's own personal perspective: "the third evangelist reshaped the traditions that he inherited by self-consciously situating them in the context of the larger Greco-Roman world."[1] The specific form of this reshaping, as Sterling understands it, is to present Jesus in the role of a Socrates. But Sterling does not stop there; he also sees Luke completely in control of his material, reshaping it, and even reacting to another evangelist because "he was not satisfied with what he read in Mark."[2] Sterling thus imputes to Luke motives of dissatisfaction, an agenda to make Jesus into a second Socrates, and an author thoroughly in control of his own material. It is typical in Lukan research to present this evangelist in the role of a redactor, editor, and interpreter, sifting and selecting what was of interest to him.[3] As the argument develops, this places Luke in the elevated position of upgrading a supposed inferior Mark.[4] A secondary feature of this approach is to view Luke as also

---

1. G. Sterling, "*Mors philosophi*: The Death of Jesus in Luke," *HTR* 94.2 (2001) 394.

2. Ibid., 394. See also his conclusion (401): "That is, the evangelist carefully reworked the death of Jesus at critical points to remind the hearer/reader of Socrates, the paradigmatic martyr of his society."

3. François Bovon, *A Commentary on the Gospel of Luke 1.1–9.50* (2002) 19, states: "Luke begins with a reference to his predecessors (v. 1), but the manner in which he mentions them shows that he is, at the same time, more or less refuting them." See also I. Howard Marshall, *Luke: Historian and Theologian* (1971) 217.

4. See James D. Tabor and Michael O. Wise, "4Q521 'On Resurrection' and the Synoptic Gospel Tradition: A Preliminary Study," *JSP* 10 (1992) 161, for their example of a sharp disagreement between the two evangelists: "For example, his crucial and dramatic scene of the inauguration of the ministry of Jesus is set in the synagogue at Jesus' hometown Nazareth (Lk 4.16–30; in sharp contrast to Mk 6.1–6)." Although the word "contrast" in this quotation can be misleading, implying only emphasis rather than disagreement, the sense argues for disagreement between Mark and Luke on the point as to when Jesus began his ministry. A closer look at the two texts, however, may reveal congruence. In Luke, Jesus reads from the scroll at the synagogue in Nazareth (4:17), then he goes to Capernaum (4:31), and finally on to the home of Simon (4:38). It is not until 9:1 in Luke that the disciples are sent out. At this point, John the Baptist has already been beheaded (9:7–9). In Mark, Jesus goes to his hometown of Nazareth, "accompanied by his disciples" (6:1). There, presumably at Nazareth, Jesus teaches in the synagogue (6:2). Moving on from Nazareth, he travels about teaching from village to village (6:6). At 6:7, Jesus commissions the disciples to go out ministering in teams of two. As a direct result of their healing ministry, Herod hears reports of these miraculous powers at work and wonders if John the Baptist has been raised from the dead (6:13–14). Where, then, is the "sharp" contrast as alleged by Tabor and Wise? It centers upon the word "accompanied" (Mark 6:1). Mark may be thus

faulting the alleged failings of Matthew.[5] In a similar vein, Bradly Billings situates Luke in the social milieu of the Greco-Roman world, artfully shaping his narrative so as to parallel events linked to Caesar Augustus.[6] He concludes: "a Jewish Messiah foretold and longed for by the Old Testament Prophets is not enough."[7]

The argument of this study champions an alternate view that Luke is part of a series of four coherent pictures about Jesus that originate with the prophets in the distinctive metaphor of a Branch and continue in the other three evangelists so that there is a unified fourfold presentation of a single Messiah.[8] Luke is unique among the canonical Gospels in several respects. In order to anticipate the complete discussion, I offer the following preliminary outline for viewing Luke as the third fulfilling installment of four prophetic pictures of a future Messiah. First, the principal line of evidence is centered in the prophecy of Zechariah 6:12–13 which presents the Branch as a royal Davidic king combined with the archetype of a future high priest. Second, the investigation pursues the relevance of the genealogy of Jesus as found in Luke 3. Third, the investigation concludes in the next chapter by examining the relationship between the Gospel of Luke and Acts. We examine now the prophecy as found in Zech 6:12–13 which presents the following prophetic picture of a metaphorically distinct Branch.[9] The following nine major rubrics and five minor or secondary ones present evidence that the Gospel of Luke is unique among the Gospels in profiling Jesus as a Priest/Man Branch.

MT: ואמרת אליו לאמר כה אמר יהוה צבאות לאמר הנה־איש צמח שמו ומתחתיו יצמח ובנה את־היכל יהוה:
והוא יבנה את־היכל יהוה והוא־ישא הוד וישב ומשל על־כסאו והיה כהן על־כסאו ועצת שלום תהיה בין שניהם:

LXX: καὶ ἐρεῖς πρὸς αὐτόν Τάδε λέγει κύριος παντοκράτωρ Ἰδοὺ ἀνήρ, Ἀνατολὴ ὄνομα αὐτῷ, καὶ ὑποκάτωθεν αὐτοῦ ἀνατελεῖ, καὶ οἰκοδομήσει τὸν οἶκον κυρίου. καὶ αὐτὸς

---

implying that the disciples were already following Jesus in some informal way. Luke, however, may be viewing the calling from a more formal, official, or public manner. Or, is it possible that the two evangelists are not describing the same event? It would be a mistake to conclude that there is a sharp dissent between Mark and Luke on this point. More critical, though, is the absence of specific language detailing a point-blank disagreement.

5. See Eric Franklin, *Luke: Interpreter of Paul, Critic of Matthew* (1994) 370, who states: "Luke's handling of Matthew is seen to be one controlled by caution: it amounts to no more than a guarded use of the first Gospel's perspective and exhibits a critical attitude to much that it contains. Luke is in fact a critic of Matthew."

6. Bradly S. Billings, "'At the Age of 12': The Boy Jesus in the Temple (Luke 2:41–52), the Emperor Augustus, and the Social Setting of the Third Gospel," *JTS* 60.1 (2009) 88.

7. Ibid., 89.

8. Stated otherwise: my argument in this study is that there was another source available to him: divine revelation and that this source is the only way to fully and correctly understand the Gospel of Luke.

9. G. K. Beale, *The Temple and the Church's Mission* (2004) 194, mentions that this passage is "not expressly cited" anywhere in the NT; yet Beale does acknowledge that "broadly speaking" the text of Zech 6.12–13 is a fulfillment of Jesus building a new temple through his resurrection.

λήμψεται ἀρετὴν καὶ καθίεται καὶ κατάρξει ἐπὶ τοῦ θρόνου αὐτοῦ, καὶ ἔσται ὁ ἱερεὺς ἐκ δεξιῶν αὐτοῦ, καὶ βουλὴ εἰρηνικὴ ἔσται ἀνὰ μέσον ἀμφοτέρων.

NIV: "Tell him this is what the LORD Almighty says: 'Here is the man whose name is the Branch, and he will branch out from his place and build the temple of the LORD. It is he who will build the temple of the LORD, and he will be clothed with majesty and will sit and rule on his throne. And he will be a priest on his throne. And there will be harmony between the two.'"

Elements of special interest are: a third reference to a Branch, his identification as a "Man," his double role of holding a priestly ministry in order to build the temple of the LORD while sitting upon a throne, and the fact that there will be harmony between these two roles. Added to this prophetic profile is the Word of the LORD.

The LORD Is Speaking

MT: כה אמר יהוה צבאות; LXX: Καὶ ἐρεῖς πρὸς αὐτόν τάδε λέγει κύριος παντοκράτωρ; NIV: "this is what the LORD Almighty says;" ESV: "Thus says the LORD of hosts."

This oracle is very similar to those in Jer 23:5–6 and Zech 3:8 in that the prophet claims a direct word from the LORD. Zechariah is not speaking on his own authority but, rather, consciously expressing the will of YHWH. If we place the text of Zech 6:12 alongside the first chapter of Luke, similarities emerge from the point of view of who is directing the action. At Luke 1:11 an angel of the LORD (κυρίου) comes to Zachariah, the husband of Elisabeth, indicating some kind of divine intervention. At Luke 1:17 he clarifies his mission: he was sent by God to bring good news to this family—they will have a son who will prepare the way of or "for" the LORD (κυρίῳ). At Luke 1:19 the angel identifies himself as Gabriel who stands in the presence of God (θεοῦ). At 1:25 Elisabeth acknowledges that her conception is from the LORD (κύριος). At 1:26 Gabriel is sent by God (θεοῦ) to a virgin named Mary with news that she, too, will conceive and bear a son. At 1:32 the promise is made that the LORD God (κύριος ὁ θεός) will give to this son the throne of David. This litany of references continues to the end of the chapter, narrating the activity of God in bringing to fruition his plans and promises. In other words, divine intervention is not a thin patina of superficial coating but it is actually the principle dynamic which undergirds the narrative of Luke's Gospel, beginning with the first chapter.

The Exhortation to Behold a Man Branch

MT: הנה־איש צמח שמו; LXX: Ἰδοὺ ἀνήρ, Ἀνατολὴ ὄνομα αὐτῷ; NIV: "Here is the man whose name is the Branch;" ESV: "Behold, here is the man whose name is the Branch."

We begin with the first word in the address ("Behold") an expression of exclamation or interjection—הִנֵּה (*hinneh*) in the Hebrew or Ἰδού in Greek. Once again, as mentioned in chapters 4 and 6, the NIV leaves out this word in their translation, while the ESV includes it. Commentaries also consistently make little mention of this word.[10] I see the value of retaining ἰδού ("Behold") in translation because of its potential bonding power with Zech 6:12. The first chapter of Luke alone uses the word six times (1:20, 31, 36, 38, 44, 48). Five of these references point to something that the LORD is going to do or has done (1:20, 31, 36, 38, 48). Grounds for including ἰδού in translation outweigh reasons for excluding it; the presence of "Behold" in translation inclines more to the side of useful than to the side of needlessly pedantic.

Although this interjection can point to something already accomplished in the past,[11] it is also employed in order to evoke a focused attention on something forthcoming in the future. Verbs in the future tense in this context argue for the latter. In either case, attention is directed to the statement immediately following. Of the four key prophetic texts involved in this investigation three of them employ such an interjection: the texts of Jer 23:5, Zech 3:8, and Zech 6:12.[12] The numerical merit of this mention is that it may, if only in an introductory way, facilitate situating Zech 6:12 into the substructure of Luke. The influential presence of ἰδού in both Matthew and Luke is significant. Matthew has sixty-one references; Luke has fifty-five, many of them calling attention to a similar supernatural effect. These emphases, for their part, function in order to call attention to either a result owing to a supernatural cause or something of a surprising or extraordinary nature.[13] Of greater significance, however, is the aspect of time. The usage of ἰδού in Luke does not refer to a fulfillment in a way-off future, but to an event presented as fulfilled or in the act of being fulfilled.

Another observation regarding this word may be made with profit. The interjection "Behold" (הִנֵּה, or a variant[14]) is used a total of seventeen times in the first six chapters of Zechariah. The majority of these references point to a vision or an event of a surprising nature. In some cases, such as the mention of a "flying scroll" at 5:2, these texts have descriptions of a supernatural import. Furthermore, even though Joshua is mentioned specifically six times in Zechariah (3:1, 3, 6, 8, 9; 6:11); yet, nowhere does Zechariah ever write "Behold" when bringing forward the person of Joshua. Simply stated: the person of Joshua does not arouse surprise or cause excitement to Zechariah. However, the mysterious figure of the Branch does cause amazement. Inasmuch

---

10. I. Howard Marshall, *Luke* (1978) makes little comment upon the word other than it is septuagintal. Darrell Bock, *Luke* (1994) omits any reference, as does François Bovon, *Luke* (2002).

11. As in Gen 1:29.

12. Jeremiah uses הִנֵּה apart from the entire formulaic expression a total of forty-five times by itself.

13. I assign the following texts to either a supernatural cause or an extraordinary result: 1:20, 23; 2:9, 13,19; 3:16,17; 4:11; 8:2, 24, 32, 34; 9:18; 12:41, 42; 15:22; 17:3, 5; 21:5; 27:51; 28:2, 9, 20.

14. For example, הִנְנִי at 3:8–9, and רָאֹה at 6:8.

as others have made the argument that the Branch is either Joshua or Zerubbabel,[15] I introduce this information as a possible boundary line marking off a further wall of separation, distancing the Branch from either Joshua or Zerubbabel. The Branch causes wonder; Joshua and Zerubbabel do not evoke surprise. Yet another observation may be made: Joyce Baldwin, calling attention to the absence of an article with the Hebrew word *Zemah*, concludes: "The absence of the article is important because attention is thereby drawn to the fact that someone other than either Joshua or Zerubbabel is meant. Emphasis is on the pronouns in the clauses that follow, again drawing a contrast between the present leaders and the future one."[16]

The Man Branch

MT: איש צמח, LXX: ἀνήρ, Ἀνατολή, NIV: "the man whose name is the Branch."

The LORD orders Zechariah (6:9) to go to the house of Josiah and there Zechariah is to place a golden crown upon the head of the high priest, Joshua, the son of Jehozadak. The critical issue at stake in these words is whether Joshua is *the* person spoken of in the prophecy or is he simply a symbolic representation of a future figure. If the prophecy applies directly to him, how does he fulfill it? If he represents by virtue of his high priestly position an idealic future high priest, this symbolism moves the fulfillment into the future. On behalf of the latter interpretation is the address. Zechariah does not say to Joshua, "*You* are the man." Rather, the prophetic vision is "Behold, the Man!" However, it is very significant that Joshua, being of high priesthood lineage, does not descend from the tribe of Judah and the seed of David. On the contrary, he would have to come out of the tribe of Levi. The significance of this fact will be developed later. As in the previous two prophetic texts, it is the same LORD who speaks. Secondly, throughout the text the subject never varies. I cite the text from the NIV (italics mine): "Here is the man whose name is the Branch, and *he* will branch out from *his* place and *he* build the temple of the LORD. It is *he* who will build the temple of the LORD, and *he* will be clothed with majesty and will sit and rule on *his* throne. And *he* will be a priest on *his* throne." The subject remains the same throughout. The following will stake out a claim that a single individual fulfills a double role.

The description in Zech 6:12 is striking: he is a "Man Branch" (צמח איש/ ἀνήρ, Ἀνατολή), not just a Branch but a *Man* Branch. The text clearly identifies the human quality of the person envisioned; he is a man. In the second part of a towering tandem of two prophetic texts in Zechariah, we single out the third encounter with a figure described metaphorically as a Branch. He is further described as also a *Man*.[17]

---

15. See, for example, Margaret Barker, "The Two Figures in Zechariah," *HeyJ* 18 (1977) 38–46, who argues that Joshua is the Branch.

16. Joyce G. Baldwin, "ṢEMAḤ as a Technical Term in the Prophets," *VT* 14.1 (1964) 95.

17. J. Balwin (1964) 97: "Joshua knows that he cannot be the Shoot because he is not of the house of David, and Zerubbabel is not present."

Throughout the book of Zechariah the reader is frequently introduced to a mysterious figure who suddenly comes out of nowhere and is often identified as a "Man" (איש). At 1:8, Zechariah cries out "Behold," upon seeing a Man riding a red horse.[18] At 2:1, he looks again and says, "Behold, a Man;" this man has a measuring line in his hand to measure off Jerusalem. At the key text of 6:12, this Man is identified as a Branch; he will occupy a throne and build a temple. Finally, at 13:7, we read: "Awake, O sword, against my Shepherd, and against the Man (who is) my companion,[19] says YHWH of hosts; strike the Shepherd and the sheep will be scattered." In all four texts there are hints of a person with unusual qualities—even superhuman qualities.

Upon what critical grounds, then, can we assign this Man Branch to Jesus? Zech 6:12 follows 3:8 and also Jer 23:5 in calling this future figure a Branch. The LXX follows suit in the parallel texts of Zech 3:8 and Jer 23:5 in ascribing the Hebrew *Zemah* with the translation of Ἀνατολή. Among the Synoptics, Luke is the only Gospel that uses the term ἀνήρ ("man") to describe Jesus.[20] Furthermore, Luke specifically calls Jesus an ἀνατολή at 1:78. The argument of this chapter thus follows the format developed in the previous chapters (regarding Matthew and Mark) by understanding the third prophetic text (Zech 6:12–13) as a substructure for the third Gospel.[21] This, of course, states the thesis of the book. Statements alone do not establish proof; assumption does not guarantee a successful outcome. What is the evidence for such a claim? That is yet to be established.

Continuing the focus on Luke, Jack Dean Kingsbury has pointed out that Jesus is never addressed in Luke as the "Son of Man"—either by humans or by divine beings (including God).[22] Only Jesus refers to himself as Son of Man. Kingsbury then raises the question: what does "Son of Man" mean in Luke? The answer, he suggests, is that this is a technical term meaning "human being," or simply "man."[23] Craig A. Evans calls attention to a double aspect of Jesus as presented in Luke: Jesus identifies with man and he also has an interest in the synagogue.[24] Evans observes:

> Why does Luke provide us with a genealogy, and why does he locate it at this point in his Gospel? The answer to both parts of this question appears in the last (human) name on his list: *Adam* (v.38) . . . . By going back to Adam, Luke

---

18. He is also identified as an "angel" or "messenger" of the LORD. He clearly stands between Zechariah and YHWH.

19. The Hebrew word עמיתי is rendered variously as "companion," "someone close," a "neighbor," or "intimate." Keil Delitzsch, *Commentary on the Old Testament: Zechariah* (2006) 615, translated this as "the man who is my nearest one;" he is "essentially divine," the Messiah.

20. Luke 24:19.

21. For the contrary view that Zech 6:12–13 has no allusions in the NT, see Craig A. Evans, *Jesus and His Contemporaries: Comparative Studies* (1995) 125 and 175.

22. D. Kingsbury, *Conflict in Luke: Jesus, Authorities, Disciples* (1991) 74.

23. Ibid., 76.

24. Craig A. Evans, "Luke and the Rewritten Bible: Aspects of Lukan Hagiography," in *The Pseudepigrapha and Early Biblical Interpretation* (1993) 175, 190.

finds biblical support for his presentation of Jesus as Savior of all humankind. Moreover, the title "son of man," so popular in Luke's Gospel (Jesus is called "son of man" in Luke twice as often as in the other synoptic Gospels), may have suggested the propriety of including Adam's name in the first place, since *ādām* in Hebrew literally means "man." Therefore, Luke's genealogy concludes appropriately, the son of Adam (or "man").[25]

Evans has alerted us to one very important element: Jesus' association with mankind. Although Luke does, in fact, describe Jesus with the noun ἀνατολή in 1:78, his use of the word at this point indicates that he does not have before him the prophetic text of Zech 6:12. Thus, Luke's comment is not an exegetical explanation of Zech 6:12.

The MT suggests that this Branch will sprout or arise "from under himself" or "from his place"—a possible reference to his native soil.[26] The Lukan text of 1.78, however, says that the ἀνατολή or *anatolē* will arise from "on high" (ἐξ ὕψους) and visit his people, perhaps suggesting that the ultimate origin of the Messiah is divine and heavenly. As François Bovon says: "For Luke this tension is pregnant with content: Jesus will arise in the midst of humanity, within his people. Yet, it will happen 'from heaven' (cf. 1.35)."[27]

This verbal reference to a Branch in Zechariah that "will arise" (or "sprout") is the first in a series of seven future tense verbs, adding further support to the interpretation that Joshua the high priest is not in view. Although Hinckley G. Mitchell in the ICC acknowledges that the Branch/Shoot has connections with the Messiah, he takes the reference here to apply to Zerubbabel, but with some hesitation.[28] However, as Ben C. Ollenburger points out, Zerubbabel has been left out of the account: "His omission here is striking."[29] James VanderKam calls attention to further arresting details:

> It does seem peculiar that in the prophet's first reference to Zerubbabel, where he fails to name him, he predicts that he will be brought to a place where he

---

25. C. A. Evans, *New International Biblical Commentary: Luke* (1995) 58. For a similar conclusion, see Richard J. Erickson, "Joseph and the Birth of Isaac in Matthew 1," *BBR* 10.1 (2000) 35–51, who observes (40): "the genealogy is thus inserted between the baptism and the wilderness temptation. Taken together with the way the list ends with Adam and God, this gives the impression that Jesus is to be understood as the New Adam, who—the second time around—does not succumb to temptation. In this again, he represents all humanity."

26. C. F. Keil and F. Delitzsch, *Commentary on the Old Testament: The Minor Prophets: Zechariah* (2006, reprinted from 1866–1891) 554. They further elaborate: "He will grow from below upwards, from lowliness to eminence." The LXX pinpoints the location as "from under" his place. From where the Messiah was to arise was an important discussion question in first century Judaism. At the least, the Messiah was to come out of the land of Israel.

27. F. Bovon, *A Commentary on the Gospel of Luke 1.1–9.50* (2002) 76.

28. H. G. Mitchell, *Zechariah* (1912) 187. He acknowledges that the Shoot will build the temple of YHWH, but limits the application to a contemporary of the prophet—Zerubbabel being the likely choice. For similar thoughts, see Michael H. Floyd, *Minor Prophets* (2000) 406–7.

29. B. C. Ollenburger, *The Book of Zechariah: Introduction, Commentary, and Reflections* (1994) 787.

has been for eighteen or nineteen years. In light of these unsettling facts, it is understandable that some have opted to say no more than that Zechariah, in his use of the title Branch, has in mind some future ruler from David's line. It must be admitted, nevertheless, that Zerubbabel is probably intended, although the vagueness surrounding "my servant Branch" hints that the emphasis here does not lie on Zerubbabel.[30]

VanderKam is willing to admit that certain details create a rather "unsettling" set of facts and that the "vagueness" of the *Zemah* term is arresting to the point that the emphasis is not upon the human figure of Zerubbabel. VanderKam is even gracious in his footnote at the bottom of this cited page to acknowledge B. Uffenheimer's view that the prophets always have a future figure in mind when mentioning the Branch.[31]

Who then is this prophetic vision speaking of? While the text speaks primarily of a royal person, it also contains an oxymoron—a priest who will sit on a throne as a king. Although it has been argued that the text is not speaking of a king,[32] the language of royalty and the subsequent argument from the expected objection suggest otherwise. In fact, Luke 1:32 specifically says that Jesus will receive the "throne of his father David." Luke is the only evangelist to mention Jesus inheriting the throne of David.

"And He Will Sprout (or Branch) from His Place"

> MT: ומתחתיו יצמח; LXX: καὶ ὑποκάτωθεν αὐτοῦ ἀνατελεῖ; NIV: "and he will sprout from his place;" ESV: "For he shall branch out from his place."

This individual is further described as a Man Branch who will "branch out from under his place," indicating that this Branch will sprout, spring up, or arise from a place

---

30. James C. VanderKam, "Joshua the High Priest and the Interpretation of Zecharia 3," *CBQ* 53 (1991) 553–70; reprinted in *From Revelation to Canon: Studies in the Hebrew Bible and Second Temple Literature* (2000) 166.

31. VanderKam's footnote (n. 29) at the bottom of page 166 is instructive. He cites B. Uffenheimer (*The Vision of Zechariah, 1–7*, 1961, available in Hebrew) who argues from the biblical usage of *Zemah* that this word "never refers to an individual existing at the author's time; he is always a figure of the future."

32. Janet E. Tollington, *Tradition and Innovation in Haggai and Zechariah 1–8* (1993) 173–4: "Similarly, while משל (rule) occurs occasionally in regard to kingly rule (2 Sam 23.3) and to Yahweh's sovereignty (Psa 22.29; Isa 40.10) there are many more instances where it implies the power or authority exercised by ordinary humans over individuals, groups, or abstract forces (Gen 3.16), which suggest that it should not be understood as synonymous with מלך (reign, be king) but in a broader sense of having authority. The noun בסא (throne) is undeniably used for the seat of kings, the throne as a symbol of their rule (2 Sam 7.16), but it can also refer to the seat of a priest (1 Sam 1.9; 4.13, 16) . . ." Note: I have supplied some of the biblical references which are located, in full, in her footnotes. Yet, Tollington finally concludes on a surprising note (175): "The final clause of Zech 6.13 comments on the harmonious relationship which the two rulers will enjoy when this arrangement is constituted. The concept of diarchic rule is unknown in the classical prophetic literature and it had not been exercised throughout Israel's history, nor was it a system which pertained among its neighbours. Thus, if my interpretation of Zech 6:13 is correct, the prophet was proclaiming a totally new constitution."

below or underneath. Indeed, the root word תחת (*tahghath*) suggests a place "under." The Hebrew text does not indicate how we are to take the metaphor. The MT suggests only that this Branch will sprout or arise "from under himself" or "from under his place"—a possible reference to his native soil.[33] The old work of Keil and Delitzsch may be consulted here with some benefit:

> These words must not be taken impersonally, in the sense of "under him will it sprout," for this thought cannot be justified from the usage of the language, to say nothing of its being quite remote from the context, since we have ומתחיו, and not תחתיו ("under him") .... ומתחתו, "from under himself," is equivalent to "from his place" (Ex 10.23) i.e., from his soil.[34]

If the notion of native soil is the natural inference, the first chapter of Luke contains numerous references to places of origin. Luke mentions that Mary lives in Nazareth of Galilee (1:26) and that Elisabeth lives in the city of Judah (1:39). Subsequently, he mentions that Jesus is born in Bethlehem (2:4), then taken to Jerusalem to be dedicated to the LORD (2:22), is baptized in the River Jordan by John the Baptist (3:21), and then returns to Nazareth where he begins his ministry at around the age of thirty (3:23). All of these references, suggesting places indigenous in nature, anchor Jesus to the soil of Israel. Even though the Zechariah text does not specify the actual place, it does limit the fulfillment of the place to "his" place, perhaps indicating the notion of a native place. Indeed, Luke mentions Capernaum (4x), Galilee (15x), Jerusalem (32x), and Nazareth (8x) as places frequented by Jesus. Keil and Delitzsch further suggest a spiritual implication: "He will grow from below upwards, from lowliness to eminence." This, indeed, may be implied as the metaphor of sprouting not only points to something taking root from a place but also growing from that place. If this is the case, the Gospel of Luke is the only Gospel that records Jesus actually growing "in wisdom and stature" (2:52).

"And He Will Build the Temple of the LORD"

> MT: וּבָנָה אֶת־הֵיכַל יְהוָה: וְהוּא יִבְנֶה אֶת־הֵיכַל יְהוָה; LXX: καὶ οἰκοδομήσει τὸν οἶκον κυρίου; NIV: "and he will build the temple of the LORD; even he will build the temple of the LORD;" ESV: "and he shall build the temple of the LORD. It is he who shall build the temple of the LORD."

As the following phrase will indicate, the figure envisioned is first described in terms of a king but he is a king who will engage in building a temple. As a man, one of his

---

33. From where the Messiah was to arise was an important discussion question in first century Judaism. At the least, the Messiah was to come out of the land of Israel.

34. Keil & Delitzsch, *Commentary on the Old Testament: The Minor Prophets* (2006) 554. See also John D. W. Watts, *Zechariah* (1972) 330: "*He shall grow up* uses the same verb-root as *Branch*, thus making a word-play on the name. *His place* refers to his heritage as the Davidic heir to the throne."

functions is to perform the duties of a priest; he will build the temple of the LORD and will appropriately fulfill those priestly responsibilities in the temple. Donna Runnalls observes: "one of the signs of the authenticity of the chosen messiah would be his role in temple building or temple restoring."[35] Indeed, in the OT it is not the priests or even the high priest who build the temple but a king. David desires to build a sanctuary for YHWH but was prevented from doing so. It falls to his son, Solomon, to undertake and complete the task and so receive the honor. David M. Hay, commenting upon Psa 110:4, says: "Psa 110.4 announces an irrevocable divine decree that someone, presumably the king addressed in vs. 1, is a priest 'after the order of Melchizedek.' Ancient kings, including those of Israel, sometimes performed priestly functions."[36]

At this point, we must consider the special and unique role that the temple plays in Luke's narrative. J. Bradley Chance calls attention to a special Lukan temple characteristic: "Omitting the prologue (1.1–4) from consideration, fifty-two of the 128 verses describe activity which is taking place in the temple (Luke 1:2–25; 2:22–38, 41–51). Thus almost forty percent of the first two chapters are devoted to the setting of the temple."[37] Ron C. Fay, pursuing further the importance of the temple in Luke, argues that the temple functions as the narrative center of both Luke and Acts. He then throws in the following tantalizing tidbit:

> While the temple serves as the hub of the cultus, the center point of God's presence on earth, Jerusalem, is the seat of the Davidic dynasty, the place where Jewish kings once ruled. Beale argues for a unity of thought here, noting that the function of ruler and of priest were often combined in ANE thought and therefore in ANE institutions."[38]

What Beale advocates and Fay mentions should not end on a quiet note. Lukan references to either the temple (ἱερόν) or to a priest (ἱερεύς) show by a striking margin that the third Gospel has the greater emphasis upon the temple than the other three Gospels.[39] The first chapter is exhibit A of this emphasis. The following words abound, indicating priestly connections: the temple (ναός); temple duties (ἱερατεύειν);

---

35. D. R. Runnalls, "The King as Temple Builder: A Messianic Typology," in *Spirit within Structure* (1983) 15.

36. D. M. Hay, *Glory at the Right Hand: Psalm 110 in Early Christianity* (1973) 20. Hay cites 1 Sam 13:9–10; 2 Sam 6:14, 18; 24:25; 1 Kgs 3:4,15; 8:14, 52–65; 9:25; and 2 Kgs 16:12–15. See also Werner Dommershausen, "Der 'Spross' als Messias-Vorstellung bei Jeremia und Sacharja," *TQ* 148 (1968) 334: "Es dürfte einsichtig sein, daß auch hier mit dem Sproß nicht Serubbabel gemeint ist, sondern ein König der zukunftigen Heilszeit;" then 336: "Denn dieser König ist nicht nur Kriegsheld und gerechter Herrscher, er baut auch den Tempel, vollzieht das Opfer und signet das Volk;" and finally 338: "Er wird den Tempel bauen."

37. J. B. Chance, *Jerusalem, the Temple, and the New Age in Luke-Acts* (1988) 48.

38. R. C. Fay, "The Narrative Function of the Temple in Luke-Acts," *TRINJ* 27.2 (2006) 267.

39. The data are as follows (ἱερόν): Matt (9); Mark (8); John (10); Luke (14), for (ἱερεύς): Matt (3); Mark (2); John (1); Luke (6). Total references for the three other Gospels: 33, but for Luke: 20.

requirements such as serving in his "division" (ἐν τῇ τάξει τῆς ἐφημερίας);[40] descending from the tribe of Levi and thus qualified to serve as a temple priest (ἱερεύς). I count a total of fifteen. This information may serve as possible additional linkage for establishing that the third Gospel has an undercurrent pulling in the direction of Jesus as a priest. However, a disclaimer is appropriate at this point. David Petersen notices an omission in the Zechariah vision: "No explicit mention of the Jerusalem temple is ever made in the vision reports."[41] I cite this not to make a disconnect between Zechariah and Luke, but to suggest that the temple vision in Zechariah, in mirror-like fashion, will play off the temple at Jerusalem, thus using it as an analog. Although the second echoes the first, the latter will be different in nature.

"And He Will Bear the Majesty and Sit upon His Throne and Rule"

MT: והוא־ישא הוד וישב ומשל על־כסאו והיה כהן על־כסאו; LXX: καὶ αὐτὸς λήμψεται ἀρετὴν καὶ καθίεται καὶ κατάρξει ἐπὶ τοῦ θρόνου αὐτοῦ; NIV: "and he will be clothed with majesty and will sit upon his throne and rule;" ESV: "and shall bear royal honor, and shall sit and rule on his throne."

The Branch will not only sit but rule. This pleonastic construction simply expands the idea of sitting to include the notion of ruling.[42] This redundancy is unnecessary as a sitting king is also a ruling one, just as a sitting president is an incumbent one. The Hebrew והוא ("even he") which is translated by the LXX as καὶ αὐτός may indeed indicate an emphasis—"*even* he." The notion is that there is no change in subject. The prescient text indicates that "he will bear the majesty." Oscar Cullmann, writing on the high priestly qualities of Jesus, comments: "It is the idea that in his very self-sacrifice Christ manifests his high priestly *majesty* (italics his)."[43]

Sarah Harris has recently identified the many parallels between The Magnificat in Luke 1:46–55 and Hannah's prayer at the birth of Samuel in 1 Sam 2:1–10 by labelling the first as the "predominate model" and the second as an "intertextual echo."[44] Indeed, there are clear similarities between the two texts: Hannah prays to the LORD, so Mary does the same; Hannah acknowledges that the LORD is holy, so does Mary; Hannah gives thanks to the LORD for blessing and lifting up the humble, so Mary does the same. However, one significant difference is worthy of comment: Hannah does not give birth to a king, but to a priest. Yet, her prayer ends on the prophetic note

---

40. These "divisions" are stipulated in 1 Chr 24.

41. David L. Petersen, "Zechariah's Vision: A Theological Perspective," in *Prophecy in the Hebrew Bible* (2000) 196.

42. H. C. Leupold, *Exposition of Zechariah* (1971) 124, says: "Since in the Jewish commonwealth there was a clearly marked distinction of offices: the royal, the priestly, the prophetic—it surely marked an unexpected departure to hear it said of the high priest: 'He shall bear the (royal) glory.'"

43. O. Cullmann, *The Christology of the New Testament* (1959) 91.

44. Sarah Harris, *The Davidic Shepherd King in the Lukan Narrative* (2016) 48, 50.

of a future king, thus hinting at a possible link between the two roles of priest and king. This leads to the next rubric.

"And He Shall Be a Priest on His Throne"

> MT: וְהָיָה כֹהֵן עַל־כִּסְאוֹ; LXX: καὶ ἔσται ὁ ἱερεὺς ἐκ δεξιῶν αὐτοῦ; NIV: "and he shall be a priest on his throne;" ESV: "And there shall be a priest on his throne."

The LXX alters the Hebrew somewhat by translating the Hebrew as: καὶ ἔσται ὁ ἱερεὺς ἐκ δεξιῶν αὐτοῦ ("and a priest shall be at his right hand"). A critical translation issue thus confronts the interpreter here: is the priest a predicate nominative or a separate subject?[45] Do we translate this as "and he shall be a priest on his throne"? Or does the text require a translation of "and a priest shall be beside his throne"? The LXX translation of καὶ ἔσται ὁ ἱερεὺς ἐκ δεξιῶν αὐτοῦ ("and the priest shall be at his right hand") throws the text into confusion by implying that another individual other than the aforementioned king is in view. The Jewish Bible Tanakh follows the lead of the LXX by also inserting a second person: "and there shall also be a priest seated on his throne."[46] The ESV follows the same lead by implying that there are two separate individuals. In order to support both the ESV and the Tanakh translation, two words alien to the text must be inserted: the word "there" and the word "also." The adverb "there," not present in the Hebrew text, suggests an interpretation, not a translation.[47] The additional word "also" serves to buttress and shore up the weakness of the adverb of place. The LXX indicates that this person will be a priest occupying a position beside the throne of the ruling king. We are confronted, therefore, with the issue of deciding whether the Branch serves the double role of both king and priest, or is the Branch accompanied by a subordinate associate serving a secondary role as a priest. This is a contested issue.[48] It is also a critical issue of no little importance. On what jus-

---

45. For the argument that two separate individuals are in view, see W. A. M. Beuken, *Haggai-Sacharja 1–8: Studien zur Überlieferungsgeschichte der frühnachexilischen Prophetie* (1967) 277: "Nimmt man V.13 als Ganzes, dann kann wohl von einer neuen Gegebenheit gesprochen werden, falls man כהן nicht als Prädikat liest, sondern als Subjekt, so daB die zweite Vershälfte eine neuen Person einführt."

46. The full text from the Tanakh (1985) reads: "Thus says Yahweh of hosts, saying: "Behold the Man whose name is the Branch! He shall grow up out of his place and he shall build the temple of Yahweh. Even he shall build the temple of Yahweh. And he shall bear the majesty and shall sit and rule on his throne; and there shall also be a priest seated on his throne, and harmonious understanding shall prevail between them." See also Kevin J. Cathcart and Robert P. Gordon, *The Targum of the Minor Prophets: Translated, with a Critical Introduction, Apparatus, and Notes* (1986) 198, who translate: "Behold, the man whose name is Anointed will be revealed, and he shall be raised up, and shall build the temple of the LORD. He shall build the temple of the LORD and he shall assume majesty and shall rule upon his throne; and there shall be a high priest beside his throne, and there shall be peaceful understanding between the two."

47. David L. Petersen, *Haggai and Zechariah 1–8* (1984) 277, also inserts the adverb "there" in order to justify a second person interpretation.

48. On the side of two separate individuals, see Lester L. Grabbe, *Priests, Prophets, Diviners, Sages: A Socio-Historical Study of Religious Specialists in Ancient Israel* (1995) 49: "One called the Branch

tifiable grounds does the LXX translate this phrase implying two individuals, rather than one? Three options present themselves: 1) the LXX is based upon a Hebrew text other than the MT; 2) the LXX has misunderstood the Hebrew; 3) the issue does not fall within the domain of how to translate the Hebrew; rather, the LXX reveals a theological bias of a diarchic messiah. If this third option is indeed the situation, then theology trumps the lexicon.

How do we resolve this matter? Three linguistic factors commend themselves. The first is the manner in which the prophet Zechariah formulates a series of actions with a single subject. As a starting point, an example taken from Zech 12:10 may illustrate the point. The prophet, describing those who will look upon One who is pierced, portrays these visual responses in a sequence of three verbs as: "and they shall look" (והביטו); "and they shall mourn" (וספדו); "and they will grieve" (והמר). There is no change in subject; all three actions describe the same group of onlookers. Each verb is also preceded by an inseparable prefix "and" (ו), otherwise known in Hebrew grammar as a *waw* conversive (or "consecutive").[49] The purpose of a *waw* conversive is to establish the repetition of the same identical subject in a sequence of narrative descriptions. Unless interrupted by an obvious new subject, a series of *waw* conversives in a given narrative text dictates that the same subject is still under consideration. This pattern conforms precisely to the sequence found in Zech 6:13: "and he will build" (ובנה), "even he will build" (והוא יבנה), "and he will bear the majesty" (והוא-ישא הוד), "and he shall sit and rule" (וישב ומשל), "and he shall be a priest" (והיה כהן). Throughout the sequence there is no change in subject;[50] all five actions describe the same individual.[51]

Secondly, there is no signal indicating a sudden intrusion into the text of an extraneous second party. A sudden intrusion would be an adverb such as "there" or a pronoun. In all five cases the *waw* conversive is attached to a verb, with no exceptions, further underscoring the idea that only one individual is in view. Had the *waw* been joined to the noun "priest" (כהן), this would have opened the door for the introduction of a possible second person. As the text stands there is mention of only one single individual: "and he . . . and he . . . and he . . . and he." Marvin A. Sweeney correctly notes the emphasis of this text: "Again, the emphatic third person form suggests that the verse

---

would rebuild the temple and sit on a throne to rule; alongside him would also sit a priest. Joshua is obviously intended to be the priestly leader of the community, though the identity of the Branch is left indeterminate."

49. For a discussion of the *waw*, see Frank R. Blake, "The Hebrew Waw Conversive," *JBL* 63 (1944) 271–95.

50. For a similar conclusion, see Marko Jauhiainen, "Turban and Crown Lost and Regained: Ezekiel 21:29–32 and Zechariah's Zemah," *JBL* 127.3 (2008) 509, who calls attention to five third masculine singular imperfect verbs whose subject is Zemah.

51. Petersen, *Haggai and Zechariah 1–8: A Commentary* (1984) 276, makes use of the *waw* conversive argument to establish that a single subject is in view at v.12, but he does not follow his own argument to a logical conclusion in v.13.

applies to someone other than Joshua ben Jehozadak. It repeats the role of the 'Branch' as Temple builder."[52] Two roles have coalesced into one in order to define a single person: king and priest. There is, however, the Hebrew והוא ("even he") which is translated by the LXX as καὶ αὐτός and may indicate an emphasis upon the single subject—"*even he.*" The implied notion is that there is no change in subject, but an emphasis upon the same subject, thereby excluding a second and extraneous subject.[53] The upshot of this emphasis is that the Branch would have both royal and priestly qualities.[54]

Third, there is an absence of a modifier alerting the reader to a contrast or distinction in terms of a spatial relationship. In each case this Branch will occupy a single throne. This throne in both cases is "his" throne. Furthermore, this priestly king or royal priest will sit "on" his throne. He will not preside beside it, as though assisting as an auxiliary but will sit upon it.[55]

The book of Zechariah abounds with prepositions of every sort. In the first six chapters there are at least eleven different prepositions describing almost every conceivable spatial relationship.[56] When the prophet describes the nuanced position of "beside" (עליה), he adds the qualifying words "on the right side" or "on the left side" (על־שמאלה), as he does at 4:3 and 4:11–12. This qualifier, providing clarity as to whether the location is on the left or right side, protects the text from confusion and defends the description that I offer here. Inasmuch as a throne has a left and right side, the absence of such a description emphasizes that "on" or "upon" is the preferred translation. Additionally, in every case where "on" is a reasonable or unforced transla-

---

52. Marvin A. Sweeney, ברית אולם (*Berit Olam*): *Studies in Hebrew Narrative & Poetry* (2000) 631.

53. Wilhelm Rudolph, *Haggai-Sacharja 1–8* (1976) 128, strongly objects to the above conclusion: "Man darf nicht übersetzen: 'Und er wird Priester sein auf seinem Throne' als ob der 'Sproß' Herrscher und Priester zugleich wäre, denn nach 13b handelt es sich um zwei verschiedene Personen." A reasonable response to Rudolph is to affirm that the text does not mention two different people but two different roles.

54. Stephen G. Gempster, *Dominion and Dynasty: A Biblical Theology of the Hebrew Bible* (2003) 167, says: "It is important also to note that not only the throne will be ensured but so also will the Levitical priesthood (33:17-18)." Gempster goes on by underscoring the point (p. 179): "And Jeremiah also predicted a righteous plant growth (ṣemaḥ ṣĕdāqā) that would bring about justice, ensuring a lasting throne and Levitical priesthood. It would seem that the servant has combined both regal and sacramental functions in his person." I am not sure that Jeremiah is including the Levitical priesthood in the person of the Branch. Gempster may be reading too much into that promise. What is most interesting, though, is that he does ask how this could be accomplished or how would the Messiah fulfill this/these promises!

55. The Hebrew text (על־כסאו) is sufficiently clear to establish the spatial relationship of "on" rather than "beside." Zech 4:3 contains the word עליה, meaning "beside." The prophet makes a distinction between prepositions describing an object spatially "on" or "upon" as opposed to one positioned "beside" something.

56. For example: "among" (בין: 1:8, 10, 11; 3:7); "around" (סביב: 2:9); "before/in front of" (לפני: 3:3, 8, 9; 4:7; 5:1, 9; 6:1); "behind" (אחריו: 1:8), "between" or "among" (בין: 1:8; 5:9); "by/beside" (עליה: 4:3, 11–12); "from" or "out of" (מא: 10:10); "in" or "in the midst of" (בתוך: 5:8); "on" (על: 3:9; 4:3, 11; 5:3; 6:11, 13); "under" (תחת: 3:10); and "within" (בתוך: 5:4). The preposition על ("on"), depending upon qualifiers, shows flexibility. Coupled with nouns, the word can suggest the idea of "at," "over," or even "against" (12:3–4).

tion of צל, it is clear that "beside" is not a natural or smooth translation. For example, at 3:9 the LORD is about to engrave a stone which has seven eyes "upon" it. A translation at 3:9 such as "beside" would cause confusion to the reader.

The result of this prepositional survey is that the prophesied figure of a Branch sitting upon his own throne in the dual capacity of both priest and king justifies a conclusion that this particular text has in view one single individual.[57] Moving from preposition to subject strengthens this case. An italicized English translation from the NIV, consistent from beginning to end, highlights the point: "and *he* will branch out from *his* place and build the temple of the LORD. It is *he* who will build the temple of the LORD, and *he* will be clothed with majesty and will sit and rule on *his* throne. And *he* will be a priest on his throne. And there will be harmony between the two." It is perhaps worth repeating that Luke 1:32 specifically says that Jesus will receive the "throne of his father David." Luke is the only evangelist to mention Jesus inheriting the throne of David. This pronouncement comes in the midst of fifteen references to temple or priestly descriptions.

We stop to consider an objection to the above. Craig A. Evans offers a very ingenious reading of Zechariah in combination with his interpretation of Mark 11:11, arguing for separate priestly and royal dynasties "confirmed by prophetic promise in the Hebrew Bible and variously embellished and qualified in the writings of the intertestamental period. This diarchism is also reflected in the Dead Sea Scrolls, which speak of two 'anointed' personages (or two 'messiahs')."[58] Evans postulates a series of miscalculations on the part of Jesus (allegedly extracted from Mark). I single out two of them for consideration; neither so simple that an easy solution is obvious.

The first reconstruction by Evans has Jesus being guided by Zechariah's vision of diarchic restoration (a faithful anointed high priest serving alongside an anointed royal figure), entering the temple in Mark 11:11 with the expectation of being received by the High Priest. Jesus receives no such greeting but, on the contrary, is ignored. Even worse, subsequent to this rebuff, Israel's anointed High Priest actually condemns the anointed king Jesus. The second reconstruction by Evans is that "the diarchic government Jesus hoped to establish, prophesied by Zechariah and confidently awaited at Qumran, did not materialize."[59] This novel line of interpretation by Evans involves a number of challenging issues.

We begin with the matter of Mark 11:11 as it presents the lesser difficulty. Evans suggests that the action of Jesus looking around in the temple indicates an expectation to find the High Priest there. This alleged expectation for a meeting was to lead to an anticipated coalition between the two. This interpretation is creative. If Evans's

---

57. For a contrary view, see Eduard Lohse, "Der König aus Davids Geschlecht: Bemerkungen zur messianischen Erwartung der Synagoge," in *Abraham unser Vater* (1963) 340.

58. C. A. Evans, "Diarchic Messianism in the Dead Sea Scrolls and the Messianism of Jesus of Nazareth," in *The Dead Sea Scrolls* (2000) 561.

59. Ibid., 565–66.

understanding of a diarchic messiah is correct, then this historical reconstruction may have some merit. Or working backwards, if this historical reconstruction alleged by Evans is correct, then Evans's interpretation of diarchism may be on solid footing. What can be said in response? First of all, does the evidence from Mark's presentation of Jesus leave room for miscalculations? Although Mark does show Jesus being amazed at unbelief, this does not necessarily prove miscalculation. In fact, Mark 11:2 indicates that Jesus knows the future as he can tell the disciples exactly where to find a colt.[60] Although, as Richard Bauckham points out,[61] it is possible that Jesus had already pre-arranged with the colt's owner this eventual loaning, the Markan narrative taken as a whole does not allow for wholesale pre-arrangements.[62] A conceivable way out of this dilemma would be to argue that Mark has falsely portrayed Jesus as having knowledge of future events but misunderstanding past prophetic statements. Evans actually does this when he says:

> I believe that the passion predictions were not made prior to entry into Jerusalem. The Markan evangelist has retrojected them into Jesus' Galilean ministry (Mark 8.31; 9.12) and journey south for literary and theological reasons. It is more probable that Jesus began to speak of his suffering and death at the hands of ruling priests after it became apparent that rapprochement was impossible.[63]

Evans thus tries to see a human causation at work. In essence, Jesus, having been jolted by the High Priest's lack of a positive response, then surmises his own death as inevitable. If human causation is responsible for Jesus' anticipation of his own imminent death, what human reason would then explain his proceeding forward to such an expected shameful death? Would not a more human explanation be for Jesus to withdraw immediately from this danger? I am thus perplexed over this reconstruction by Evans as it creates the additional dilemma of Jesus advancing onward to the inevitable fatal event from an attitude of mental illness. My view, to the contrary, is that Jesus enters Jerusalem as a redemptive event. Fully expecting rejection by the High Priest and, after carefully explaining to his disciples that he would die, Jesus offers himself to save mankind from its mental illness.

The most devastating strike against the Evans's proposal, though, is that Mark 10:33 shows Jesus predicting that he would be handed over to the high priests. In fact,

---

60. For a completely different view of temple activity, see Emilio Chávez, *The Theological Significance of Jesus' Temple Action in Mark's Gospel* (2002) 69, who asks: "What did Jesus see? He would have seen one of the great wonders of the ancient world." I am not sure that this is the intent behind Mark's comment. Mark's comment that Jesus was looking around at the temple as a majestic wonder of the ancient world strikes me as a superficial reaction. See also Craig A. Evans, "Jesus' Action in the Temple: Cleansing or Portent of Destruction?" *CBQ* 51 (1989) 237–70. A view closer to mine is that of William L. Lane, *Commentary on the Gospel of Mark* (1974) 398: "The point is rather that Jesus is the Lord of the Temple, who must inspect its premises to determine whether the purpose intended by God is being fulfilled."

61. R. Bauckham, *Jesus and the Eyewitnesses: The Gospels as Eyewitness Testimony* (2006) 187.

62. Ibid., 188. Bauckham does not eliminate what he calls "providential timing foreseen by Jesus."

63. C. A. Evans, "Diarchic Messianism," (2000) 565–66, fn. 25

Mark 10:32 specifically states: "Again he took the Twelve aside and told them what was going to happen to him ... and the Son of Man will be betrayed to the chief priests." The Markan data do not add up to miscalculations or failed expectations.

Other Markan texts which indicate that Jesus correctly anticipates the future are the following: at 2:20 Jesus anticipates that the "bridegroom will be taken;" at 7:29 Jesus knows that a child will be healed; at 9:1 Jesus anticipates a manifestation of kingdom power (this is fulfilled at 9:2); at 8:31–32 and 9:31 we have more expectations of his own death; at 12:25 Jesus knows the nature of the age to come; at 13:2 he predicts that no two stones will be left standing in the temple; this is capped off at 13:23 with the prescient warning: "I have told you everything ahead of time." Finally, chapter 14 narrates a series of events in which Jesus possesses foreknowledge of future events: 14:13–16 presents Jesus as saying that a man carrying a jar of water will meet his disciples; 14:18 states that Jesus knows someone will betray him; 14:30 contains Jesus' reference to Peter's denial. These texts fail to show that Jesus miscalculates. In fact, from Mark 13:2 to 14:31 there are thirty-four statements in which Jesus anticipates, predicts, or prophecies that something will happen. In terms of fulfillment, most come to pass quickly, some are fulfilled later; a few still remain open and unfulfilled. But Mark shows no doubt about their ultimate fulfillment. In my judgment, it is more plausible to argue that Jesus is not expecting an alliance with the High Priest, that Jesus is prescient about these eventual priestly failings, and that Mark has accurately portrayed Jesus as not blindsided by an unexpected turn of events. To understand the data otherwise is to totally reconstruct the narrative along the lines of an arbitrarily imposed presupposition that runs counter to the actual information as provided in the second Gospel.

To further reinforce the point, Mark uses the verb περιβλέπομαι ("to look around") a total of six times; only one other use is found in the NT. When Jesus enters the temple at Mark 11:11, he "looked around" (περιβλεψάμενος). Evans argues that Jesus is looking for the High Priest. I would suggest, however, that Jesus, knowing what was going to transpire in the following day (or days) with his anticipated action of clearing out the money-changers, is simply looking around to imagine the fated scene.[64] His visit to the temple is somewhat similar to a modern athlete walking through a stadium the day before the actual competition. To borrow another metaphor, it is a dress rehearsal.

There is still an unresolved issue. We must now back up to the second of Evans's original points: his proposal alleges that the text of 1 Sam 2:35 contains hints of the first prophetic glimpse of a diarchic messiah. The LORD God of Israel is the speaker (1 Sam 2:30), and he declares (1 Sam 2:35):"I will raise up for myself (והקימתי לי כהן נאמן) a faithful priest, who will do according to what is in my heart and mind. I will firmly establish his house, and he will minister before my anointed one always".[65] A key

---

64. William Hendrickson, *Exposition of the Gospel According to Mark* (1975) 440: "He made a quick, all-around, sweeping survey. Nothing escaped his purview. He gathered the impressions that would lead to actions on the following day."

65. The LXX: καὶ ἀναστήσω ἐμαυτῷ ἱερέα πιστόν, ὃς πάντα τὰ ἐν τῇ καρδίᾳ μου καὶ ἐν τῇ ψυχῇ

question is: who is this "faithful priest"? The following options present themselves. The first, stoutly defended by Martin Buber, is that the logical candidate is Samuel himself.[66] Indeed, evidence that the selection is Samuel is not lacking. There are three key promises made. The first is that the LORD will raise up a "faithful" priest. Samuel meets this criterion: 1 Sam 2:11, 18, 21, 26; and 12:1–5. Although not technically a priest, Samuel fulfills priestly functions by virtue of wearing an ephod (2:18), ministering and waiting in the presence of the LORD (2:11, 18, 21), anointing King Saul (10:1), and anointing even David as King (1 Sam 16:13). The second is that the LORD will "firmly" establish his house. Although Samuel's sons are described at 8:3–5 as turning away after dishonest gain, at 12:2 these sons are still with Samuel in ministry. The text of 1 Chr 6:28, it may be added, seems to treat the sons of Samuel as a "sure" house; it would be inaccurate, therefore, to conclude that Samuel's house was not a sure or stable house. The third is that he will minister before the LORD's "anointed." Samuel meets this criterion (1 Sam 10:1; 16:13.) Everyone left in the family of Eli will come and bow down before him for a piece of silver and a crust of bread. Although not specifically mentioned during the lifetime of Samuel, the reader is left to conclude that this is the inevitable outcome of the Elide posterity. Everything else in the narrative prepares the reader to assume this outcome. As Eugene H. Peterson describes it: "As the curve of Eli's priesthood declines, the curve of Samuel's ministry rises."[67]

A second candidate is the eventual priest Zadok. Henry P. Smith advocates this position in the ICC series,[68] and it has been followed by a host of others.[69] If the line

---

μου ποιήσει καὶ οἰκοδομήσω αὐτῷ οἶκον πιστόν, καὶ διελεύσεται ἐνώπιον χριστοῦ μου πάσας τὰς ἡμέρας.

66. M. Buber, "Der Gesalbte," in *Werke II: Schriften zur Bibel* (1964) 727–845. Buber argues that Samuel is not simply a cultic priest; his birth bears the mark of divine intervention, suggesting a divine purpose and calling: he belongs to the LORD all the days of his life; he apprentices under Eli; he wears priestly clothing (1 Sam 2:18). Peter D. Miscall, *1 Samuel: A Literary Reading* (1986) 20–23, presents a series of narrative truths in tension with the idea of a perpetual high priest going in and out before the LORD's anointed. The first is that the promise of perpetuity, "forever" (àd òlam; 1 Sam 1:11, 22) is to be taken back, denied, because of sin (1 Sam 2.30). Miscall then concludes (20): "Retributive justice takes priority and cancels a divine election and promise; justice prevails over grace." The second is that the twin texts of Samuel and Kings do not mention a faithful high priest who has a sure house forever. Lyle M. Eslinger, *Kingship of God in Crisis: A Close Reading of 1 Samuel 1–12* (1985) 137: "Finally, it should be noted that Samuel builds an altar to Yahweh in 7.17 and survives through the remainder of the narrative as the only active priest (7.9; 9.12–14; 10.8; 12.23). He does, in fact, replace Eli at Yahweh's altar."

67. E. H. Peterson, *First and Second Samuel* (1999) 36.

68. H. P. Smith, *A Critical and Exegetical Commentary on the Books of Samuel* (1929) 23, says: "There can be no doubt therefore that the *faithful* priest is Zadok, who was made priest by Solomon in place of Abiathar. This is expressly stated to be the fulfillment of the prophecy, 1 Ki. 2.27. The family of Zadok maintained themselves in the sanctuary of Jerusalem until the final destruction of the temple."

69. For the majority view that the envisioned priest is Zadok, see P. Kyle McCarter, *I Samuel: A New Translation with Notes & Commentary* (1980) 92–93: at first, McCarter states that "Samuel emerges incontestably as the successor." McCarter then reverses his course to claim: "So the 'faithful priest' of v 35 is not Samuel but Zadok, David's second high priest (II Sam 15.24–37), who supported Solomon's cause (I kings 1.22–39 *passim*) and became the unrivaled leader of the Jerusalem priesthood after the banishment of Abiathar (I Kings 2.35) . . . .The Books of Samuel and Kings display a relentless march

of Zadok properly fulfills the prophecy, does this imply that they were faithful, doing all of God's will? If so, is it possible to place Jesus in this lineage? Craig A. Evans asks, "Did Jesus, hailed by his followers with the language of Psalm 118.26, see himself as the anointed son of David (Mk 10.47–48), ready and willing to cooperate with the high priest and so form a diarchy?"[70] Evans then proceeds to further reinforce this tantalizing possibility with the following probing question:

> If this is true, a provocative inference immediately suggests itself. Could it be that Jesus anticipated a blessing from the High Priest, but when he did not receive it, being initially ignored (Mk 11.11) and then later rebuffed (Mk 11.27–33), he criticized the Temple establishment both in his actions (Mk 11.15–17) and in his teaching (Mk 12.1–12, 38–40, 41–44; 13.1–2)?[71]

On the positive side of the ledger, what Evans does is offer a teasing possibility for making a link between Jesus and the priesthood. Mary J. Evans, after presenting reasons for assigning the high priestly role to either Samuel or Zadok, adjudicates the issue by saying: "Similarly, it points to the Christian understanding that sees both the most 'faithful priest' and the true 'anointed one' as Jesus Christ."[72]

A summary of the various options may now be stated: the high priest is Samuel; the high priest is the line of Zadok; the faithful high priest is an unknown figure not capable of a secure identification;[73] the high priest is a messianic figure fulfilled in the person of Jesus; the high priest is a non-messianic individual or series of individuals such as the faithful believer in the church (the "sure house" that God will build); or, finally, the prediction regarding this particular individual is nullified because of disobedience.[74]

The interpretation that best fits the original historical context favors Samuel as the faithful high priest. Whether the faithful priest is indeed Samuel, or Zadok, or an

---

of history toward not only David, the chosen king, but also Jerusalem, the chosen city, and along with the latter, Zadok of Jerusalem, the chosen priest." André Caquot and Philippe de Robert, *Les Livres de Samuel* (1994) 55: "Seul élément positif dans cet oracle, le v. 35 announce l'établissement d'une nouvelle dynastie sacerdotale, associée au roi-messie, avec mêmes expressions que pour la dynastie royale davidique en 2 Sam 7.11–16 ou en 1 R 2.31. Malgré le contexte où se trouve cet oracle, il est bien difficile de penser à Samuel. Comme on l'a le plus souvent reconnu, c'est le prêtre Sadoq et ses descendants attachés a la dynastie davidique." See also Ralph W. Klein, *1 Samuel* (1982) 27: "V 35 announces the establishment of a faithful priest, who is not to be Samuel, as one might expect, but clearly Zadok, David's other priest, who came to preeminence under Solomon. The Zadokites or sons of Aaron are the sure house (dynasty) referred to in the text." See also Ben F. Philbeck, *1–2 Samuel* (1970) 19.

70. C. A. Evans, "'The Two Sons of Oil': Early Evidence of Messianic Interpretation of Zechariah 4.14 in 4Q254 4 2," in *The Provo International Conference on the Dead Sea Scrolls* (1999) 574.

71. Ibid., 575.

72. M. J. Evans, *1 and 2 Samuel* (2000) 25. Evans's conclusion is based upon the logic that when one chosen line fails in its moral obligation, another one is chosen as a replacement.

73. Stephen B. Chapman, *1 Samuel as Christian Scripture* (2016) 83.

74. David H. Jensen, *1 & 2 Samuel* (2015) 35. For a further review of some of the issues, see James S. McLaren, "Corruption among the High Priesthood: A Matter of Perspective," in *A Wandering Galilean: Essays in Honour of Seán Freyne* (2009) 141–57.

unnamed figure, or a prophecy that is left unfulfilled because of disobedience in the priestly line, the evidence does not support the proposal that Jesus is the fulfillment. Before moving on, I would mention two secondary issues. The first is that Jesus is not likely the candidate because of the description of this high priest serving God's anointed. That would place Jesus in the awkward position of then serving himself. The second concern is that it is more likely the case that Jesus, knowing that the High Priest could not be relied upon to do anything other than act out of unfaithfulness, does not put his trust in a relationship doomed to failure. In this sense, the high priest corresponds to the historical development of the fraudulent priesthood as projected in 1 Sam 2:35–36.[75] If that is the case, this could explain why the LXX and the Dead Sea Scrolls anticipate a high priest serving alongside a Davidic king—they did not factor in the cancellation of the promise due to corruption in the priesthood. However, Jesus is aware of this disqualifying factor and, therefore, he is not looking for cooperation from the High Priest. But, wary of protracted priestly disloyalty, Jesus warns his disciples not to expect support either. Indeed, at 8:31 and 10:33, Mark twice records that Jesus specifically forecasts that he would be handed over to the High Priest.[76] Suffering, then, at the hands of the High Priest was his actual expectation.

However, difficulties remain. Nowhere is Jesus specifically identified as a high priest in Luke.[77] Does the absence of a specific high priestly title in the third Gospel block the way for understanding Jesus in a high priestly role? On one front, the fact that Jesus is never specifically called a high priest or even a priest would suggest that this Gospel is not a redactional interpretation of community interests but a faithful account of the real historic person. On another front, however, it must be admitted that a titular reference to a priestly function is clearly absent. Such an absence is a barrier to be overcome, not

---

75. John Nolland, *Luke 1–9:20* (1989) 170, notes: "Already in Solomon's day the high priesthood had been transferred from one line of Aaron's descendants to another (1 Kgs 2:27). Where the potential for the fulfillment of the Davidic promise along the Solomonic line had petered out, God would be free to carry forward the Davidic promise through another of David's descendants. Scripture is aware already of some role for the house of Nathan (Zech 12.12). So, it is no surprise that the messiah's ancestry is now traced through David's son Nathan and completely bypasses the line of the kings of Judah." For a similar application, see E. Jenni, "Messiah, Jewish," IDB (1962) 3.363, where Jenni argues that, upon the failure of the prophecy to materialize, "the wording was changed secondarily so that the high priest Joshua was to receive the crown as a sign that the Messiah would come (in the future). The unfulfilled imminent expectation of the Messiah thus became here again the expectation of a future Messiah."

76. Of course, it may be countered that texts containing references to suffering at the hands of the priests are simply later statements inserted back into the record. The thesis of this book does not support that view.

77. Jack Dean Kingsbury, *Conflict in Luke: Jesus, Authorities, Disciples* (1991) 14–15, in which Kingsbury emphasizes the "vastly different ways" in which Jesus is understood in Luke: David's scion, Israel's king, and God's royal son (1.32–35); LORD, David's greater son (1.69), Savior, Messiah, and LORD (2:11); the mightier One (3:16), my Son, Son of God, a prophet, and King (19:38). For a similar breakdown of categories, see Stanley E. Porter, "Scripture Justifies Mission" in *Hearing the Old Testament in the New* (2006) 114. Although conceding that the Lukan Jesus is a complex figure, Porter does not include the role of a priest. Neither does Kingsbury. In my judgment, this is an unfortunate omission.

one to be avoided. The following is an attempt to document the priestly characteristics which are uniquely presented in the third Gospel. There are a number of scenes in Luke which distinctly show Jesus as possessing high priestly qualities.

A PRIESTLY TITLE. In Luke 4:34 we find a titular reference to Jesus as *the holy one of God* (ὁ ἅγιος τοῦ θεοῦ). In John 6:69, Peter confesses Jesus to be "the holy One of God (ὁ ἅγιος τοῦ θεοῦ). Peter's confession conveys notions of a messianic title. Of equal interest to this investigation is the fact that this title appears in connection with the high priest Aaron, since a similar title can be found in the LXX at Psa 105:16: "Aaron, the holy one of the LORD" (Ααρων τὸν ἅγιον κυρίου). This connection with Aaron, of course, establishes a clear association with priestly characteristics. This title also appears in two texts in Acts (3:14; 4:27).

REFERENCES TO PRAYER. Alfred Plummer provides a helpful introduction to this section with the following observation: "More than any of the other Evangelists S. Luke brings before his readers the subject of *Prayer* . . . on seven occasions Luke is alone in recording that Jesus prayed."[78] The seven occasions are: at his baptism (3:21, as Luke is the only evangelist to record this), before his first conflict with religious leaders (5:16), before choosing the Twelve (6:12), before his first prediction of his eventual death (9:18), at the Transfiguration (9:29), before teaching the LORD's Prayer (11:1), and while on the cross (23:46). Also, there are a number of times that people call upon the LORD for mercy. The thief on the cross is a notable one. This happens only in Luke. It is Luke alone who records Jesus saying that he would pray for Peter in an act of intercession on his behalf (22:32). Intercessory prayer is characteristic of faithful priestly duties. Kyu Sam Han states it simply but securely: "Prayer materials in Luke's Gospel are rich and unique."[79] The verb προσεύχομαι (meaning "to petition"), for example, is used nineteen times in the Gospel of Luke alone. In fact, thirty-five of the eighty-six NT occurrences of the term are in Luke-Acts, whereas only ten occurrences are in Mark and fifteen in Matthew. When the noun προσευχή is included in the count, the Lukan writings use the term forty-seven times, whereas Matthew employs it seventeen times, Mark twelve, and it is not found in John.

THE NUMBER OF REFERENCES TO COMPASSION AND MERCY. Luke looks at things and understands them through the eyes and heart of compassion. Compassion is a salient characteristic of this Gospel. In chapter 1, mercy (τὸ ἔλεος) is mentioned five times alone (1:50, 54, 58, 72, 78). Only Luke records the instance of the thief on the cross calling upon Jesus for mercy. This places Jesus in the active role of functioning as a mediating high priest.

---

78. A. Plummer, *Luke* (1896, reprinted in 1975) xlv.
79. K. S. Han, "Theology of Prayer in the Gospel of Luke," *JETS* 43.4 (2000) 675.

Compassion (σπλαγχνίζομαι) is mentioned four times in Luke (1:78; 7:13; 10:33; 15:20). There are three parables that clearly set out the character quality of compassion. These three are the Prodigal Son, the rich man and Lazarus, and the two men who go to the temple to pray. In each case we are dealing with an identical and alternate pair of two men who serve as opposites. The prodigal son humbles himself desiring only to eat the "pods" from the pig pen; the poor man Lazarus yearns only to eat "crumbs" that fell from a rich man's table; and the third man of the trio goes up to the temple to pray (asking for mercy) but will not even look up to heaven. These men illustrate humility before God. Their opposites serve to highlight a contrast: the resentful elder brother judges his sibling harshly and is left outside the celebration taking place within the house; the rich man does nothing to alleviate the suffering of Lazarus and ends up in torment; the prideful man at prayer looks down his nose at others and has only himself to thank. These three examples illustrate a lack of compassion for their fellow man. The third evangelist reveals an interest in showing, alternately, dramatic indications of the absence of mercy and open expressions of compassion as, for example, the "Good Samaritan" in Luke 10. These are characteristics of an ideal high priest. Although a king may grant clemency, offer pardons, and free prisoners, everyday people in the ancient world commonly turned to the local priest for issues concerning mercy and forgiveness. Luke is preeminently a Gospel of mercy and compassion.

REFERENCES TO SIN, GUILT, AND THE FORGIVENESS OF SIN. Joseph A. Fitzmeyer offers the suggestion that the correct interpretation of the statement in Luke 4:18–19 containing the words "release of the captives" may contain the idea of release from the debt of sin.[80] In Luke 23:34, a controversial text which Bruce M. Metzger assigns as of "dominical origin,"[81] the text as it stands in the NIV has Jesus praying, "Father, forgive them for they do not know what they are doing."

THE UNUSUAL NUMBER OF REFERENCES TO THE TEMPLE OR SYNAGOGUES. Since I have already mentioned the special emphasis in Luke regarding the temple, I will not labor the issue. George J. Brooke, however, does call attention to an unusual aspect of Luke: "In Luke, Jesus' ministry begins in the synagogue at Nazareth rather than with the call of the disciples as in the other synoptic gospels. Alfred Plummer makes a similar observation: "The Third Gospel is also remarkable for the prominence which it gives to *Praise and Thanksgiving*. It begins and ends with worship in the temple (1.9; 24.53)."[82] There is a deliberate reordering of tradition at this point."[83] What might account for

---

80. J. A. Fitzmeyer, *The Gospel According to Luke I–IX* (1983) 532.

81. B. M. Metzger, *A Textual Commentary on the Greek New Testament* (1971) 180.

82. A. Plummer, *The Gospel according to St. Luke* (1975) xlvi.

83. George J. Brooke, "Shared Intertextual Interpretations in the Dead Sea Scrolls and the New Testament," in *Biblical Perspectives: Early Use and Interpretation of the Bible in Light of the Dead Sea Scrolls* (1998) 48.

this different starting place? Is there any explanation other than a "reordering of tradition"? I submit that these six secondary evidentiary indicators outlined above suggest correspondence in Luke with a view of the Messiah that is anchored to the prophetic picture of the Man/Priest Branch as found in Zech 6:12.

"And there will be Peace between the Two"

> MT: ועצת שלום תהיה בין שניהם; LXX: καὶ βουλὴ εἰρηνικὴ ἔσται ἀνὰ μέσον ἀμφοτέρων, NIV: "and there will be peace between the two;" ESV: "and the counsel of peace shall be between them both."

These words anticipate a possible objection and they resolve an apparent contradiction. In this NIV translation, possible confusion arises only at the end when the plural noun "two of them" (שניהם) enters the picture. To what or whom does the pronoun "them" refer? Two possibilities present themselves: either this is a reference to two separate individuals or this is a single individual fulfilling two distinct and unique roles. How can we resolve this difficulty?

We begin with the noun שלום, generally translated as "peace" or Anglicized to the popular word *shalom*. Shemaryahut Talmon offers the following commentary upon this noun: "The denominative adjective שלם means 'complete, unharmed' et sim. In reference to the individual, 'wholeness' spells physical and spiritual wellbeing. On the collective level, it indicates harmonious interpersonal and inter-group relations."[84]

The LXX, as in the above line, continues the confusion by translating the Hebrew as καὶ βουλὴ εἰρηνικὴ ἔσται ἀνὰ μέσον ἀμφοτέρων ("and there will be a peaceful counsel between both of them"). The LXX version suggests two people in separate but harmonious roles. The Hebrew text, however, can bear the translation of a single individual in a double role, rather than a description of two separate people. Several English versions reflect the translation of one individual occupying two separate roles. The Hebrew text, as revealed in the English translation from the NIV, clearly anticipates the potential confusion that a single individual serving in a dual capacity would create a superficial conflict of interest. This text, similar to Psa 110,[85] envisions a double role for the singular

---

84. S. Talmon, "The Significance of שלום and its Semantic Field in the Hebrew Bible," in *The Quest for Context and Meaning* (1997) 81. Talmon investigates the use of שלום in over two hundred OT texts. However, his only mention of שלום in Zech 6.12–13 comes in footnotes 134 and 138, with little or no discussion. In his conclusion (115), one gets a sense of how he would interpret Zech 6:12–13: "In the last count, the restorative national ideal, the future reconstitution of an Israelite polity patterned after the united monarch and the *pax salomonica*, inspired also the biblical authors' utopian-mythic visions of an ideal future age."

85. See the comment by Deborah Rooke, "Kingship as Priesthood: The Relationship between the High Priesthood and the Monarchy," in *King and Messiah in Israel and the Ancient Near East: Proceedings of the Oxford Old Testament Seminar* (1998) 188: "In support of the royal interpretation, it may be noted that the psalm clearly addresses a royal figure to whom priestly prerogatives are subsequently granted by divine oath, and not a priestly figure who is being granted some kind of kingly rule." This does appear to be the case. There is only a single reference to a priest, but multiple references to

figure of a future ruler.[86] James C. VanderKam, commenting upon differences between Qumran and the NT, writes: "Although the two literatures differ regarding how many messiahs there would be and who the one from the line of David was, they agree in considering the messianic work to be twofold—kingly and priestly."[87]

David L. Petersen points to the theological message of the prophet: "What Zechariah reports in these visions is initial restoration within the cosmic order.... What we see in the visions is the beginning of restoration on a cosmic plane. Things are being carried out over 'all the earth', not just in Judah ... He is not, in these visions, directly proposing or engaging in the mundane work of restoration."[88] By the use of the term "mundane work of restoration" Petersen implies the mundane work of *earthly* restoration. Petersen, we must call attention to, views Zech 3:8 and 6:12 as representing a single image. The argument of this chapter, however, presents a slight variation to the Petersen thesis. The evidence, I believe, leads to the conclusion that the two passages in question from Zechariah do describe a single individual but with separate images reflecting different roles. Petersen, in one respect, has pointed us in the right direction; his suggestion speaks not to a temporal temple but a spiritual one with no definite geographical location, no national identity, and no specified time. The ultimate theological point that Petersen articulates is that a restoration or creation of a new temple is not accomplished through the agency of human hands. On this point I completely agree. This premise advances the argument of this chapter and facilitates the placing of Zech 6:12 as the substructure to the Gospel of Luke.

Elizabeth Achtemeier in a similar manner compresses the two images of Zech 3:8 and 6:12 into a single "mysterious figure of the future,"[89] and sees the fulfillment in Jesus as developed in the NT letter of Hebrews. Indeed, in my opinion, the author of the Gospel of Luke may also be the author of Hebrews.[90] That suggestion, however, is a distraction at this point. The purpose of this chapter is to provide associative linkage between the third Gospel and Zech 6:12. In a recent monograph G. K. Beale, commenting upon the text of Zech 6:12–13, mentions that this passage is "not expressly cited" anywhere in the NT; yet Beale acknowledges that "broadly speaking" this text

---

language befitting a king (v.1 "right hand," and "footstool," v.2 "mighty scepter" and "will rule," v.3 "your troops," v.5 "he will crush kings," and v.6 "crushing the rulers."

86. C. H. T. Fletcher-Louis, "Jesus as the High Priestly Messiah: Part 1," *JSHJ* 4.2 (2006) 173, claims: "Psalm 110 is the *only* biblical text that *explicitly* speaks of a king who is also a 'priest.'" Fletcher-Louis does not see the text of Zech 6:12 *explicitly* speaking of both king and priest or he has overlooked this text.

87. J. VanderKam, *The Dead Sea Scrolls Today* (1994) 177.

88. D. L. Petersen, "Zechariah's Vision: A Theological Perspective," in *Prophecy in the Hebrew Bible: Selected Studies from* Vetus Testamentum (2000, reprint from *VT* [1984]) 194.

89. E. Achtemeier, *Interpretation: Nahum—Malachi* (1986) 122.

90. See R. Steven Notley, "Jesus' Jewish Hermeneutical Method in the Nazareth Synagogue," in *Early Christian Literature and Intertextuality* (2009) 46–59.

is a fulfillment of Jesus building a new temple through his resurrection.[91] What Beale advocates as "broadly speaking" I am endorsing. Whatever "broadly speaking" implies, I have no hesitation in adopting this kind of limiting language to describe the present investigation.

It is incumbent upon this study to face an issue in regard to the Messiah: how is it possible to reconcile the function of priest with the role of a king? Historically, in ancient Israel the temple and the throne were kept separate—similar to the separation of powers in the USA constitution. In this sense, the duties and roles of king and high priest functioned as a check-and-balance in order to provide accountability and protection against the abuse of power. In the ancient world the emergence of king and high priest into a single person could be construed as an overture to dictatorship. The text from Zech 6:12, however, indicates that there would be "peace," "harmony," or *shalom* between the two figures. Although the respective roles of priest and king are never combined in an actual person in the OT, the role of priest and king find common ground in that both are spoken of as anointed.[92] Yet, in the text before us, the objection is anticipated that the two roles would merge, without contradiction, in a single person. In the Gospel of Luke, right after being anointed by the Holy Spirit in his baptism (3:22), Jesus enters the synagogue at Nazareth and announces, "The Spirit of the LORD is on me because he has anointed me to preach good news to the poor" (4:18). It is not a great mental leap to move from synagogue to temple.

The consolidation of these two roles also has an antecedent in the text of Psalm 110:1–4, in which YHWH speaking to Adonai ("The LORD speaks to my Lord"), says: "The LORD will extend your mighty *scepter* from Zion." The imagery pictured begins first with a reference to that of a king, envisioned in possession of a ruling scepter. But suddenly at v.4 the imagery switches as once again YHWH speaks ("The LORD has sworn"): "you are a *priest* forever . . ." Psalm 110, which Jesus himself cited in his controversy with the Pharisees as recorded in Matt 22:43, contains the additional reference that David spoke these words "by the Spirit." This psalm therefore must be submitted as additional evidence that the OT contains prophetic hints of a future individual who would function in the dual capacity of both priest and king.

We return to the image of David. Although institutionally and ceremonially, the roles of priest and king were not merged in the OT, there is precedent for their roles

---

91. G. K. Beale, *The Temple and the Church's Mission* (2004) 194. Beale further comments (194): "In the Zechariah text, the messianic 'Branch' is prophesied to 'build the temple' and rule in glory." Even further (374), he says: "To see Christ and the church as the true end-time temple is neither an allegorical spiritualization of the Old Testament temple nor of prophecies of an eschatological temple, but is an identification of the temple's real meaning."

92. For a defense of the dual role of priest and king submerged into a single person, see F. F. Bruce, *Second Thoughts on the Dead Sea Scrolls* (1975) 83. See also Richard S. Hess, "The Image of the Messiah in the Old Testament," in *Images of Christ: Ancient and Modern* (1997) 33 for his conclusion: "The occurrences of these referents in the extrabiblical texts and in the uses of the root, משה, and of the form, משיה, in the Hebrew Bible provide an image of 'Christ' for both modern and ancient readers which places an emphasis on priestly and royal elements."

overlapping in specific actions. This occurs significantly and coincidentally in the life of David. Hans-Joachim Kraus observes:

> Of the priestly activity of David and of his descendants we hear in 2 Sam.6:14, 8; 24:17; 1 Kings 8:14, 56. The king wears priestly vestments (2 Sam. 6.14), blesses the people, intercedes for the cultic assembly in prayer, and presides over the rites. Yes, he even presents the offering (1 Sam. 13:9: 2 Sam.6:13, 17), draws near to God like the high priest (Jer. 30:21), and also, in the conceptions of Ezekiel concerning the "prince," he stands in the midst of the worship (Ezek. 44:3; 14; 14:16ff; 46:2ff).[93]

The only thing that the OT does not report regarding David's priestly activities is his actual entering the Tabernacle of Moses (which, according to the biblical record, stood outside of Jerusalem and was neglected by the priests during the reign of King Saul). As Daniel J. Hays says: "Instead, it appears that David blurs the image of priest and king together, as did many kings in the region. Thus, when a Davidic messianic figure begins to emerge in Scripture, it is no surprise that he is pictured as both priest and king."[94]

Only an explanation at the end anticipates a potential objection—there will be harmony between the two. My conclusion is to take this oblique reference to "two" not as describing two individuals, but as qualifying one individual in the respective roles of king and priest. Although this relationship of priest and king is not held up as the OT model, there is precedent for the image. The actions of David certainly demonstrate a kind of precedential compatibility.

The Issue of Luke-Acts

The Gospel of Luke presents a particular difficulty different from those found in the other three Gospels. Luke has a sequel known as "Acts" and, therefore, we must consider whether the theology of Acts is consistent with the Gospel of Luke. Schuyler Brown argues that any scholar writing on Luke who wants to be taken seriously must examine the two works as a whole.[95] Bovon voices a similar view: "When we approach Christology, the distinction between the gospel and Acts is hardly justifiable."[96] In light of the argument of this chapter, we must face up to the appropriate question: does Acts give indication of presenting Jesus in the role of a high priest? At this point, we are not interested whether Acts places an emphasis upon Jesus as a high priest, only if Acts shows Jesus in this role.

93. H-J. Kraus, *Psalms 60–150* (1989) 351.

94. D. Hays, "If He Looks Like a Prophet and Talks Like a Prophet, Then He Must Be . . .," in *Israel's Messiah: In the Bible and the Dead Sea Scrolls* (2003) 67.

95. Schuyler Brown, "The Role of the Prologues in Determining the Purpose of Luke-Acts," in *Perspectives on Luke-Acts* (1978) 99–111. Brown presents both sides of the issue. While these two works go together, this does not necessarily follow that they have an identical Christology.

96. F. Bovon, *Luke the Theologian* (2006) 134.

There are three sets of texts which reveal Jesus in a high priestly role consistent with the view as developed in this chapter. The first set is the doublet of 2:33 and 7:56. In 2:33 Jesus is shown at the right hand of God, receiving from the Father—in an intercessory role—the Holy Spirit and pouring this out upon the disciples. At 5:31 Peter is reported as claiming that "God exalted him (Jesus) to his own *right* hand as Prince and Savior that he might give repentance and forgiveness of sins to Israel." Again, we have a reference to the "right hand" of God, followed by the giving or granting of forgiveness of sins. These are preeminently prerogatives of high priestly activities. These proclamation statements echo Psa 110:1–5 in which the Messiah sits at the right hand of God and serves as a "priest forever." In 7:56 Jesus is also shown at the right hand of God, as it were, in the intercessory role of a priest, listening to and responding to the prayer of Stephen as he is being stoned. In the second set we also find twin texts describing Jesus as a "man" (Acts 2:22 and 17:31). These are the only texts in which Jesus is expressly called a man. Although Luke is often seen as a Gentile, a case can be made that Luke is also Jewish with a sensitivity to scriptural concerns of a Jewish nature.[97] Danker, in his short exposition of the Gospel of Luke, actually develops the theme of Jesus as the great Servant of God as the unifying thread between Luke and Acts.[98]

A further question regarding Luke is appropriate here: why is Luke separated from its companion, the book of Acts? Since the two books give evidence of being written by a single author and were likely intended for the same individual (Theophilus), yet they are separated in manuscripts and in our present Bibles by the Gospel of John.[99] This mysterious separation stimulates an additional question: why isn't the order Mark, Matthew, John, and then Luke, followed by Acts attached to its original traveling destination? There appears to be no reasonable human cause for this disconnect. The argument could even be made that this separation is unfortunate and may lead to confusion.[100] Thus, we not only have a mysterious separation but a strange silence regarding the position of Luke. This disjunction lacks a logical human explanation. The argument presented here is that Luke belongs in the third position because it is the rightful and most meaningful explanation given the fact it exhibits the greatest amount of characteristics befitting the human and high priestly aspect of Jesus.

---

97. Bo Reicke, *The Gospel of Luke* (1964) 21–22, proposed a case for Luke being Jewish. This, however, may be questioned on basis of Acts 1:19, which suggests that Luke did not know Hebrew or Aramaic. Even if Luke was not Jewish, he seems to have been fully aware of Jewish sensitivities. For the argument that all the missionaries (including Luke himself) in Acts are Jews, see David E. Garland, *Luke* (2012) 23.

98. F. W. Danker, *Luke* (1976) 89.

99. Matthias Klinghardt, "The Marcionite Gospel and the Synoptic Problem: A New Suggestion," *NovT* 50 (2008) 9, notes that "all manuscripts" (ancient implied) contain Luke and Acts in different sections. There is no evidence that the early church was confused about authorship and, therefore, made a mistake by displacing Acts from Luke. Some other concern was at work in this dislocation.

100. Kenneth Schenck, *Jesus Is Lord!* (2003) 313.

Conclusion

I now summarize. The argument advanced here is that the above ten rubrics (including the supplemental section on Luke/Acts) find an unforced matching correspondence with the Gospel of Luke. This is not to say that Luke consciously follows a ten point rubric outline from the text of Zech 6:12–13. My contention is only that these ten markers give indication of finding fulfillment in the Gospel of Luke by virtue of corresponding parallel ideas. Furthermore, these ten rubrics suggest a Lukan uniqueness in the sense that the other three Gospels do not. Luke alone presents Jesus as distinctly possessing both kingly and priestly qualities. Matthew, of course, narrates the royal aspect of Jesus, but it is Luke alone who reveals Jesus as uniquely possessing both characteristics. This double quality conforms to the dual aspect of a Man Branch in Zech 6:12–13. If one highlights with color coding the number of words or ideas in Luke 1:1–80 that match up well with Zech 6:12–13, a striking visual scene opens up. I count some thirty-six to forty-five key words that indicate a thematic connection between the texts of Zechariah and Luke. This tabulation counts only one chapter from Luke. These thirty-six indicators do not suggest a full body photograph; they are more like telltale fingerprints. But these fingerprints point to a person with definite characteristics. I conclude this chapter by emphasizing an ongoing theme of this investigation: my thesis is not that Luke is engaging directly with the text of Zech 6:12. Rather, the purpose of this book is to demonstrate that the details of Zech 6:12–13 provide an explanation, an accounting, a substructure for understanding the theology of Luke that cannot be found elsewhere. The *Index locorum* of Nestle's Greek New Testament lists twenty-eight texts from Zechariah found in the NT. The text of Zech 6:12–13 is not listed among them, indicating in the judgment of those editors that no NT author makes use of it. Yet, the facts are these: the text of Zech 6:12–13 does more to explain major Lukan themes than any other prophetic OT text. Furthermore, though the Gospel of Luke may contain as many as thirty explicit OT prophetic texts, none of them reveals as much, explains as much, or accounts for as much as does Zech 6:12–13.

9

The Genealogy of Jesus in the Gospel of Luke

This chapter begins with a primary question: whose ancestry does the genealogy contain: Joseph or Mary? Since space does not permit a full treatment of all the names listed in both Matthew and Luke, one name has been selected for discussion. Because of its place, relevance, and ultimate bearing on the subject of inspiration, the father of Joseph will be given special consideration. Some of the strongest pessimism about the Gospels containing reliable historical information concerns the birth record of Jesus.[1] This is the question of Matt 1:16 and Luke 3:23 and the father of Joseph. Raymond E. Brown may serve as a starting point: "This question, which may seem naively curious, is raised by the blatant disagreement between Matt 1.16, which identifies Joseph's father as Jacob, and Luke 3.23, which identifies that gentleman as Eli."[2] Brown's contention of a "blatant disagreement" between Matthew and Luke is inappropriate and need not stand. There are other options. In the face of how Greco-Roman authors express disagreement, Brown's alleging of a serious contradiction cannot be sustained. One possible way of resolving the difficulties is to view the lineage of Jesus in Matthew as a "legal line of descent from David," whereas the line in Luke is the "actual descendants of David."[3] A bigger issue is Luke's alleged disagreement with Matthew by stating that Jesus is the son of "Joseph son of Heli" (Ἰωσήφ τοῦ Ἠλί). Alfred Plummer in the ICC argues strongly that Luke had Joseph in mind, even stating his conviction in italics. He bases his principal reason upon ancient practice: "It is evident from the *wording* that Lk is here giving *the genealogy of Joseph and not of Mary*. It would have been quite out of harmony with either

---

1. For example, Ulrich Luz, *Matthew 1–7: A Commentary* (2007) 87, says: "Today we will have to do without its linguistic expression—that is, the genealogy—because scholarship, probably in this case with finality, has recognized that it is a fiction." See also his judgment that ". . . we do not need to assume that it contains information from the circles of Jesus' family. Nor are the signs favorable for the historicity of the virgin birth" (93). Luz further comments that "the two traditions are not only different but irreconcilable" (75).

2. R. Brown, *The Birth of the Messiah: A Commentary on the Infancy Narratives in Matthew and Luke* (1977) 86. Brown does not attempt a reconciliation of these two accounts. Instead, he outlines three major explanations for how Matthew may have come upon his list of names: a) he invented them; b) he copied them from a list of post-exilic royal lineage names from the House of David; or c) he copied them from Joseph's own family records.

3. See Howard I. Marshall, *Commentary on Luke* (1978) 158.

Jewish or Gentile ideas to derive the birthright of Jesus from His mother."[4] More recently, François Bovon in the Hermeneia series, after arguing that Luke also runs the lineage of Jesus through Joseph, says: "Even Jesus' grandfather is called Heli by Luke, and Jacob by Matthew. The despair of the scribes and theologians of the ancient church is quite comprehensible; in the Scriptures which they held to be inerrant, they suddenly found contradictions."[5] Inasmuch as this present investigation relies upon genealogies in order to support the thesis of a unified substructure, several troublesome problems found in the genealogies themselves face the interpreter.

The Different Names between Matthew and Luke

When we compare genealogies between Matthew and Luke, numerical difficulties confront us. George Brooke suggests "something Enochic" lies behind the genealogy of Jesus in Luke because there are seventy-seven generations from Adam to Jesus. He then cites a comment by Richard J. Bauckham: "It cannot be accidental that in the Lukan genealogy the name Jesus occurs not only in the seventy-seventh place, but also in forty-ninth place—where the only namesake of Jesus among his ancestors appears (Luke 3.29)."[6] Craig A. Evans calls attention to the disparity of seventy-seven total names in Luke's account as compared with the forty-two in Matthew; of this number from Abraham down to Jesus, only about half of the names overlap.[7] Evans then suggests: "The proposal made some 500 years ago (Annius of Viterbo, ca. 1490) that Matthew has given us Joseph's genealogy, while Luke has given Mary's, provides no real solutions to the problems enumerated above but only creates new ones."[8] Although Evans concedes that both Matthew and Luke did make use of real records and registries, Evans has abandoned the most viable solution. Not only does the possibility of separate genealogies avoid the thorny issue of having to reconcile different variations

---

4. A. Plummer, *A Critical and Exegetical Commentary on the Gospel According to S. Luke* (1896, reprinted in 1975) 103. Norval Geldenhuys in his *Commentary on the Gospel of Luke* (1960) 151, however, countered this argument from custom by calling attention to the overall context of the first two chapters: "He was not afraid that his readers would get the impression that the genealogical tree was that of Joseph and not that of Mary, for in Luke i and ii he had pointed out expressly that Jesus was solely the son of Mary and not of Joseph and Mary." Geldenhuys continues (152): "For Matthew throughout gives the antecedents (announcement of the birth itself, the childhood years) as seen from the standpoint of Joseph, while in Luke we feel from beginning to end that we are concerned with the course of events from Mary's point of view."

5. F. Bovon, *A Commentary on the Gospel of Luke 1.1–9.50* (2002) 135. See also John Nolland, *Luke 1–9:20* (1989) 169: "Although ὡς ἐνομίζετο does raise problems, this solution must finally be judged to be an artificial harmonization."

6. George J. Brooke, "Shared Intertextual Interpretations in the Dead Sea Scrolls and the New Testament," in *Biblical Perspectives: Early Use and Interpretation of the Bible in Light of the Dead Sea Scrolls* (1998) 49. The citation from R. J. Bauckham is *Jude and the Relatives of Jesus in the Early Church* (1990) 319.

7. C. A. Evans, *Luke* (1990) 57.

8. Ibid., 57. On this point, Evans follows Joseph A. Fitzmyer, *The Gospel According to Luke I–IX* (1981) 497.

from the same tradition, but this option, allowing for two independent family histories (maternal and paternal) of the same person, would then account for the variety of names. This observation, if followed, then accrues to a further advantage—the names from Luke's account include families from the tribe of Levi (Luke 3:24 and 29). In view of this, Howard I. Marshall's comment is striking: "the number of priestly names in the genealogy may indicate a desire to show that Jesus was a priestly Messiah."[9] Yet, Marshall D. Johnson argues that the OT clearly indicates that the Messiah could only come from one tribe and from one house, the House of David.[10] Janet E. Tollington, after surveying the numerous scholarly options for interpreting this text, finally concludes:

> The Jeremianic concept of the motif צמח (Zemah) cannot apply to Joshua, the high priest, who was not of David's lineage, and the context of the motif's occurrence in Zech 3.8 indicates that the compilers understood it to refer to a figure other than Joshua. Therefore, I suggest that Zechariah adopts the motif צמח (Zemah) to point away from current historical figures towards a future leader for the community.[11]

Is it possible, therefore, that within the bloodlines of Jesus there flowed two tribal streams? And, if so, is it possible that Luke is unique among the Gospels in that he gives us a record of such bloodlines? G.R. Beasley-Murray asks:

> Is it conceivable that an individual writer should at the same time advocate the appearance of a Messiah from the tribe of Judah as well as one from Levi? There seems to be no other conclusion possible from the statements of the Testaments. A refrain running through the various parts of the book is that the salvation of the Lord will arise from Levi *and* Judah; not from one tribe to the exclusion of the other but from both."[12]

9. H. I. Marshall, *Commentary on Luke* (1978) 161.

10. M. D. Johnson, *The Purpose of the Biblical Genealogies* (1969) 116.

11. J. Tollington, *Tradition and Innovation in Haggai and Zechariah 1–8* (1993) 172. Tollington goes on to say (172): "He appears to have no specific individual in mind but uses the motif as a typological identification for the ruler in the new age that Yahweh will inaugurate. In Zech 3.8 the oracle of Yahweh refers to the Branch as עבדי (my servant) a term which has Davidic dynastic connotations but which also has wider eschatological implications . . . . Thus it seems that the motif צמח is used by Zechariah to indicate a future Davidic ruler who will be raised up by YHWH and on whom a new dynasty will be founded." For the view that the Branch is not confined to Zerubbabel, but to a future and prophetic figure, see Carol L. Meyers and Eric M. Meyers, *Haggai, Zechariah 1–8: A New Translation with Introduction and Commentary* (1987) 203: "Rather, the prophet is employing lively prophetic imagery to point to a future time when kingship might well be reestablished."

12. G. R. Beasley-Murray, "The Two Messiahs in the Testaments of the Twelve Patriarchs," *JTS* 48 (1947) 7. See also 8: "This last quotation seems to show without doubt that the salvation which God will introduce in the last days, presumably including both a redeeming act and the settled state of the Messianic kingdom, will be through the agency of two distinct persons, High Priest from Levi and a King from Judah. There is no question of interpolation here nor can one person alone be in mind; the two Deliverers come from two tribes and have distinct functions to perform." See also John Martin Creed, *The Gospel according to St. Luke:* (1960) 17, fn. 27.

This is a critical issue; its importance cannot be overstated. This quotation from Beasley-Murray, first cited in chapter 3, but deferred until now for a response, is a vital focus of this chapter.

The Meaning of ὡς ἐνομίζετο

Pursuing further this possibility, we now consider the implications of the expression ὡς ἐνομίζετο ("as was supposed") at Luke 3:23. Only two realistic interpretations present themselves: either Luke intends the words to be understood as a corrective to a misinformed public opinion,[13] or Luke offers these preliminary words as reinforcing public opinion because the public view is justified. First of all, Luke may be using this formulaic expression to convey a false presumption. Without a doubt, the expression ὡς ἐνομίζετο can mean something falsely presumed.[14] If that is the case here, what is the false presumption? Marshall D. Johnson proposes the suggestion that Luke is casting suspicion over the entire genealogical line.[15] Such an impeachment, then, would place in doubt the ultimate conclusion at the end which finishes with God as the originator of the entire line. I do not see Luke setting out to discredit the entire line. There is more, however, to the definition than a simple false presumption. A

---

13. For this view, see Paul Strack and Herman Billerbeck, *Das Evangelium nach Markus, Lukas und Johannes und die Apostelgeschichte* (1924) 155: "Das Substantivum חזקה bezeichnet eine Annahme (Präsumption), die sich auf Grund gegebener Verhältnisse allgemein wie von selbst herausbildet u. festsetzt." See also Alfred Loisy, *L' Évangile selon Luc* (1924) 144: "La formule: 'comme on croyait' n'est pas pour suggérer un doute, et moins encore pour signifier que Jésus était réellement ce que on le croyait être, mais c'est une restriction gauche pour faire droit à la conception virginale, tout en maintenant une généalogie que impliquait originairement, comme celle de Matthieu, la filiation naturelle. Car il est évident que la généalogie de Luc, aussi bien que celle de Matthieu, n'a pas été composée pour déclarer avec solennité que Jésus était seulement le fils putatif de Joseph, mais la place que lui est assignée dans Luc ferait supposer qu'elle n'a pas été trouvée dans la meme source que les récits de la naissance." Loisy continues (145): "Mais la contradiction principale et irréductible consiste en ce que les deux généalogistes, énumérant les ancêtres de Joseph, qui sont par la même censés les ancêtres de Jésus." Loisy then makes a disclaiming yet tantalizing statement regarding the age at which Jesus began his ministry (144): "On ne peut guère supposer que le rédacteur aurait en égard à l'âge fixé pour l'entrée en fonctions des lévites (NOMBR 4.3, 23)."

14. The linguistic evidence in Josephus supports the above conclusion. As a contrast, the exact sequential couplet under investigation (ὡς + νομίζω +) is used by Josephus at *Ant*.6.195: δοὺς αὐτῷ χώραν ἀμείνονα μὲν ἀσφαλεστέραν δὲ ὡς ἐνόμιζεν αὐτῷ (LCL: "thus giving him [David] a better post, but one, as he thought, safer for himself [Saul]"). Saul, in order to do away with David, assigns to him a post of duty that was calculated to lead to David's death in battle. This plan, however, failed as Saul's designs for David's demise proved futile. This usage of ὡς + νομίζω invalidates the supposition and shows an error in judgment on the part of the one doing the supposing. Saul wrongly supposed that assigning David a particular duty would cause his death. This usage conforms to that of Luke 3:23. Notable also in both cases (Luke and Josephus) is the imperfect tense. See also Josephus, *Ant*. 7.196 for the same usage. Hippocrates, *Regimen in Acute Diseases* (65.12) does present an exception in which the expression (ἢ ὡς + νομίζω) is best translated "than is usual." Could Luke be suggesting that the genealogy is as usual or customary from a Jewish or human point of view? This does not seem likely.

15. M. D. Johnson, *The Purpose of the Genealogies* (1969) 230: "Perhaps the ὡς ἐνομίζετο is best taken as an indication of Luke's uncertainty concerning the historical value of the list."

construction which sets up a completely false assumption would likely require the following sequence: ὡς + νομίζω + the thing falsely presumed + the addition of a follow-up statement explaining the reason for the misplaced assumption. In other words, although grammatically this combination can stand alone as ὡς + νομίζω + for the thing in doubt, this would not yield a complete thought. One piece would still be missing. That piece would be the subsequent information explaining the false supposition. This complementary information would not be false, but true within the writer's own mind, thus enabling the reader to understand the contrast. The reliable data would begin right after Joseph's name. If this argument is valid, it implies that Joseph was falsely assumed to be the father of Jesus and the remaining names in the genealogy would bear this out.[16] This would imply a disconnect between Joseph and the names that follow. The line from Heli to Adam was clearly of definite interest to Luke. I see no purpose in disavowing all seventy-seven names. In fact, it is best to view this data as intentionally informing part of the Gospel's theology.[17]

The alternate expression, reversing the verb and conjunction (νομίζω + ὡς), means the opposite; the assumption is valid and post developments bear this out.[18] The upshot of Luke's language would be to interpret the Greek as applying *only* to Joseph. I do not believe that Luke has set out to discredit the entire family line, only the first name—Joseph. The common perception is that Joseph was the father; hence, in the public mind Jesus would have been considered illegitimate. This may be the intention behind the question at 4:22: "Isn't this Joseph's son?" Or, Luke could possibly be suggesting that Joseph was considered the real father but, in fact, it was God (Luke 3:38). The comma placed after ἐνομίζετο should be moved one word over to embrace Joseph in the thought. It would be a *reductio ad absurdum* to argue that the popular perception ap-

---

16. Alexander Balmain Bruce, *The Synoptic Gospels* (1974) 485, contends that if Luke had intended this meaning, he would have inserted the words ὄντως δέ before τοῦ Ἡλί.

17. Alfred Plummer, *Luke* (1975) 103. Plummer, responding to the option that Jesus was supposed to be the son of Joseph but in reality was the grandson of Heli, stated a serious obstacle to that position: "It is not credible that υἱός ("son") can mean both son and grandson in the same sentence."

18. Josephus uses νομίζω + ὡς only twice. The first is *Antiquities* 4.53: (adapted from the LCL: "at the sight of what had happened, they confirmed [νομίζοντες ὡς] the sentence, and, judging that Dathan and his followers had perished as miscreants, they refrained even from grief"). As the narrative from 4.1–53 indicates, Dathan is an adversary of both YHWH and Moses. Moses prevails upon the LORD to judge him or Dathan and the conspirators. As Dathan and his contingent are swallowed up by the earth, Moses includes the postscript that the fatal sentence is judged as acceptable without criticism since there was no outpouring of grief. However, the combination here is not that of ὡς + νομίζω, but just the reverse: νομίζω + ὡς and it can have only one meaning—to confirm, validate, or draw the right conclusion following a prior event. Moses, therefore, is not questioning the outcome or raising any suspicion about it but offering an affirmation or justification for the end result. Consequently, since Luke does not use this expression but the opposite, he is not validating Joseph as the actual father of Jesus. This is the grammatical state of affairs, even though Mary refers to Joseph as the father (2:48). See also *Antiquities* 7.43 for similar usage. Thucydides (3.88.3) also may serve as a useful example: the people of Hiera believe (νομίζουσι) that (ὡς) Hephaestus forges brass in their region because (ὅτι) a great flame is seen shooting up at night. Thucydides does not question this view (a possible volcano) but simply cites the reason for the belief.

plied to the entire genealogical line. Furthermore, if Luke intended the entire line from Joseph to Adam to be the legitimate family history, then the expression ὡς ἐνομίζετο would be unnecessary; in fact, this superfluous phrase would only cause confusion. Its purpose, however, must be to suggest doubt somewhere. Although Mary acknowledges Joseph as assuming the role of father (Luke 2:48); yet, in fact, Mary knows that Joseph is not the biological father of Jesus. Furthermore, Mary is the one who assumes leadership throughout the narrative.[19] Joseph never has a voice, never says a word, and he is never shown acting alone. It is Mary who is the center of consistent and focused attention.[20] That being said, Luke is careful to include that Joseph is a descendant of David (1:27, 69; 2:4).[21] Tangentially, Mary is never described as a descendant of David. The question, therefore, arises: which lineage dominates, if any?

Possible Solutions

Ray Summers reduces the major alternatives down to three strong options: 1) Matthew gives Joseph's physical lineage and Luke gives his legal lineage;[22] 2) Matthew gives Joseph's legal lineage and Luke gives his physical lineage;[23] and 3) Matthew gives Joseph's physical line through his father, Jacob, and Luke gives Mary's physical line through her father (or grandfather), Heli.[24] In the end, Summers prefers the third option because, as he understands, it presents less difficulties. Reinforcing this last point, John Nolland tacks on the additional possibility that Mary may not have had any brothers and, therefore, by virtue of her marriage to Joseph, Joseph was then adopted by Mary's father, whose genealogy "is thus reflected in the Lukan text."[25] Similarly, a very early attempt to reconcile the two genealogies is recorded by Eusebius as he recounts the contents of a letter he received from Africanus.[26] Africanus suggests that the Levirate law of remarriage would explain the sudden change from David to Nathan,[27] thereby omitting Solomon.

19. At Luke 1:34 Mary asks the angel a question; at 1:38 Mary answers; at 1:40–41 she greets Elizabeth; at 1:46 Mary speaks; at 2:48 Mary speaks to Jesus.

20. This is particularly noticeable at 2:33 where the "child's father and mother" marvel at Simeon's prophetic word, but then Simeon directly addresses only Mary. At 2:48 Mary says to Jesus "Your father and I have been anxiously searching for you." Jesus, however, replies, "I had to be in my Father's house."

21. Harald Sahlin, *Der Messias und das Gottesvolk* (1945) 98, notes a careful distinction: "ἐξ οἴκου Δαυίδ gehört, wie es jedem unbegangenen Leser sofort einleuchtet, lediglich zu Joseph, nicht *auch* zu Maria, und noch weniger *einzig* zu Maria."

22. R. Summers, *Commentary on Luke* (1973) 50–51. As Summers explains, this view can be traced back to Julius Africanus (ca. 240) via Eusebius.

23. Ibid., 51.

24. Ibid., 51.

25. J. Nolland, *Luke* (1982) 174.

26. Eusebius, *Ecclesiastical History* 1.2.1–17.

27. The mention of Nathan is perplexing and, in my judgment, not easy to resolve. We know little about him, based mostly on 1 Kgs 4:5 ("Zabud, the son of Nathan, was a priest"). For the argument

Norval Geldenhuys, in a near identical manner as Summers, advocates a similar reconciliation between Matthew and Luke by proposing that Luke gives Mary's genealogy while Matthew provides Joseph's.[28] He provides four reasons to justify the claim that Luke is focusing upon Mary rather than Joseph. His four reasons merit consideration: 1) it is not unreasonable that Mary's family would have such private birth records; 2) the words "as was supposed" are an explanation by Luke to forestall confusion on the part of his readers because Mary's lineage is the one envisioned and not Joseph's;[29] 3) Luke 1 and 2 plainly show that Luke is centering on Mary, not Joseph; the overall contents of Luke's first two chapters show a definite focus upon Mary, not Joseph; and 4) the absence of the definite article τοῦ before the name of Joseph (when all other names contain the article) shows that Joseph is not intended to be a part of the real list, but in the minds of some was only "supposed" to be the father of Jesus.

A Provisional Summary

What is the strength of the above arguments? In my judgment, Geldenhuys's emphasis upon the role of Mary accords well with the first three chapters of Luke. Also, this evidence would show that Jesus has a family lineage that intertwines with the tribes of both Judah and Levi.[30] Although a consensus appears impossible on how to correctly understand Luke's language, what does seem incontrovertible is the fact that names from both the tribes of Judah and Levi merge in the genealogy. It is significant that the fourteen names in Matthew that follow right after David are all kings, or in the case of Zerubbabel a son of a king; of the thirty-nine names that follow David

---

that this text is a *Zusatz* or "addition," see Johannes Fichtner, *Das Erste Buch von den Königen* (1964) 81. For the argument, based upon 2 Sam 8:18, that David's son, serving as priests, were not actually serving in a sacerdotal capacity, see James A. Montgomery, *The Book of Kings* (1915) 115. John A. Davies, *1 Kings* (2012) 96, supports the view that these priests of David or *cohen* were, indeed, secular in nature. Simon J. DeVries, *1 Kings* (1982) 69, says: "The priest is the royal chaplain." I note also *The Works of Aurelius Augustine: The Harmony of the Evangelists* (trans. by William Findlay and S. D. F. Salmond, 1873) 1.3.5, where Augustine mentions his own belief that Nathan, although technically a king, did eat the shew-bread, thereby giving him, under the law, priestly status. These interpretations focus upon function rather than bloodline. I am left wondering, though, if more is involved than mere function or duty.

28. Norval Geldenhuys, *Luke* (1960) 151–55. See also A. T. Robertson, *Word Pictures in the New Testament: The Gospel according to Luke* (1930) 46: "If we understand Luke to be giving the real genealogy of Jesus through Mary, the matter is simple enough." See also Craig A. Evans, *Luke* (1990) 57. For an opposite view, see H. I. Marshall, *Commentary on Luke* (1978) 158. Marshall also adds (159): "It is only right, therefore, to admit that the problem caused by the existence of two genealogies is insoluble with the evidence presently at our disposal."

29. For evidence from Josephus that it was possible for those priests living in the time of Jesus to trace their descent back to Aaron, see Daniel R. Schwartz, "Priesthood and Priestly Descent: Josephus, *Antiquities* 10.80," *JTS* 32 (1981) 129–35.

30. Ethelbert Stauffer, *Jesus and his Story* (1960) 45, called attention to this possibility years ago: "As a Davidite, Joseph belonged to the tribe of Judah. Mary was in all probability a Levite of the tribe of Aaron."

in Luke's account, as many as twenty-one may be considered names of priests. One possible reason for this unusual merging is the thesis of this book: Jesus fulfills the qualifications of not only kingly requirements but also priestly.

Why Include a Genealogy?

We come next to another vital question: why does Luke even include a genealogy? Considering for a moment the possibility that Luke is aware of Matthew's genealogy, why include one of his own? Would not two genealogies cause confusion? At the risk of such possible confusion, Luke shows no hesitation by including his. But why take a risk if Matthew's account is already available and in circulation? Or, if not available, why include one at all? One possible answer is, of course, the familiar refrain that Luke is out to correct Matthew and also to supply what is lacking in Mark. A more fruitful question is offered by Craig Evans who asks, "Why does Luke provide us with a genealogy, and why does he locate it at this point in his Gospel?"[31] Evans has raised the question as to what is the purpose of Luke's genealogy. He has alerted us to one very important element: Jesus' association with mankind. A second solution, and perhaps a more important one, is that priests, especially high priests in the OT, have genealogies.[32] J. D. G. Dunn in a most emphatic tone promotes a common misconception: "We can dismiss at once the second of the two messiah figures described above: the *priest* messiah. There is no indication whatsoever that this was ever canvassed as a possibility or seen as an option in the case of Jesus. Presumably Jesus was known to lack the basic qualification of belonging to the tribe of Levi."[33] Dunn is not alone in dismissing Jesus as having any legitimate claim to being a priestly Messiah on the basis of no Levitical ancestry.[34] Dunn, however, is mistaken in his claim that Jesus was never

---

31. C. A. Evans, *Luke* (1995) 58. For a similar conclusion, see Richard J. Erickson, "Joseph and the Birth of Isaac in Matthew 1," *BBR* 10.1 (2000) 40, who observes: "The genealogy is thus inserted between the baptism and the wilderness temptation. Taken together with the way the list ends with Adam and God, this gives the impression that Jesus is to be understood as the New Adam, who—the second time around—does not succumb to temptation. In this again, he represents all humanity."

32. For a bittersweet treatment of OT genealogies, see Gary A. Rendsburg, "The Internal Consistency and Historical Reliability of the Biblical Genealogies," *VT* 40.2 (1990) 185–206.

33. J. D. G. Dunn, "Messianic Ideas and Their Influence on the Jesus of History," in *The Messiah* (1987b) 373. For a counter-view, see Anders Hultgård, "The Ideal 'Levite,' the Davidic Messiah, and the Saviour Priest in the Testaments of the Twelve Patriarchs," in *Ideal Figures in Ancient Judaism* (1980) 93–110. See also J. Gnilka, "Die Erwartung des messianischen Hohenpriesters in den Schriften von Qumran und im Neuen Testament," *RevQum* 7 (1960) 408: "Wir müssen daher annehmen, dass die Erwartung eines Priesters aus Levi und eines Königs aus Juda zum älterren, jüdischen Bestand der *Testamente* gehörte, und der Vorschlag . . . dass er Christus als Hohenpriester mit dem Stamm Levi und als König mit dem Stamm Juda verband." See also his argument (409) that the role of forgiving sin was considered a function of a high priest within Second Temple Judaism.

34. See also Crispin H. T. Fletcher-Louis, "Jesus as the High Priest Messiah: Part 1," *JSHJ* 4.2 (2006) 157: "On the face of it, of course, it would seem impossible for Jesus to think in these terms because he is not of priestly lineage."

"canvassed as a possibility" for occupying the double role of both king and priest.[35] An interesting text to the contrary is the promise of *TSimeon* 7.2: ἀναστήσει γὰρ κύριος ἐκ τοῦ Λευὶ ὡς ἀρχιερέα καὶ ἐκ τοῦ Ἰουδὰ ὡς βασιλέα, θεὸν καὶ ἄνθρωπον, οὗτος σώσει πάντα τὰ ἔθνη ("And the LORD will raise up from Levi as a high priest and from Judah as a king, God and man, this one will save all the nations").[36] Besides the double reference to a high priest and to a king, there is the notation that a single individual (οὗτος) will fulfill this twofold role. An equally arresting text is that of *TLevi* 18.1: Καὶ μετὰ τὸ γενέσθαι τὴν ἐκδίκησιν αὐτῶν παρὰ κυρίου, ἐκλείψει ἡ ἱερατεία. Τότε ἐγερεῖ κύριος ἱερέα κανόν ("And after their punishment from the LORD, the priesthood will fail. Then the LORD will raise up a new priest"). From *TJudah* 24.1 comes similar language: καὶ μετὰ ταῦτα ἀνατελεῖ ὑμῖν ἄστρον ἐξ Ἰακὼβ ἐν εἰρήνῃ, καὶ ἀναστήσεται ἄνθρωπος ἐκ τοῦ σπέρματός μου ὡς ὁ ἥλιος τῆς δικαιοσύνης ("After this, a Star will arise for you from Jacob in peace, and a Man will rise up from my seed, the Sun of righteousness"). Elements of interest are: the verb ἀνατελεῖ from which the noun ἀνατολή ("Branch") comes, a reference to Man (ἄνθρωπος), and most significantly is the expression "from *my seed*" (ἐκ τοῦ σπέρματός μου).

Eusebius claims that Mary had to be born of Judah due to the inheritance law of Moses. This law, stated in Num 36:6–8, forbids intermarriage outside of one's clan or tribe. But Eusebius did not think this through. The logic behind the Mosaic prohibition was to prevent one tribe from accumulating land through the means of marriage. The law does not really prevent intermarriage; it only prohibits the transfer of land. Even within the genealogy of Jesus there are intermarriages. For example, King David not only married Bathsheba, a Hittite woman, he also married Michael (daughter of

---

35. The idea that the lineage of Jesus possessed two tribal seeds was known to early Christians. Hippolytus in his commentary on Daniel (1.12.5) states: "Those who were of the priestly seed from the tribe of Levi mixed with the tribe of Judah so that the blending together of two seeds from rightful tribes might demonstrate that the rightful seed of Christ according to the flesh might be demonstrated as even a priest of God who was born in Bethlehem." The Greek text may be found in *Studien zu den Kommentaren Hippolytus zum Buche Daniel und Hohen Liede* (1897). See also Marinus De Jonge, "Two Messiahs in the Testaments of the Twelve Patriarchs?" in *Tradition and Re-Interpretation in Jewish and Early Christian Literature* (1986) 150–62. One part of De Jonge's twofold thesis is (151, 156) that "whenever a human agent of divine deliverance comes into the picture, there is only one: Jesus Christ." His conclusion is of value to this present study (161): "There are no clear traces of two agents of divine deliverance, one from Levi and one from Judah. Every time a messianic figure appears, there is one, clearly Jesus Christ, who is connected with Judah, or with Judah and Levi." See also J. Gnilka, "Die Erwartung," (1960) 407–8. Gnilka argued that a Christian redactor took over the Jewish material of the Twelve Patriarchs and reworked it into a Christian tract. He follows De Jonge in disclaiming the TP as a purely Jewish work. The text of *TRub* 6.8 clearly shows an expectation of a priestly Messiah (ἀρχιερέως χριστοῦ). Gnilka (405), however, does propose that the Qumran community definitely expected a priestly and royal Messiah but identified them as separate figures.

36. On the issue of whether the Testaments are Christian or Jewish, see M. De Jonge, "Christian Influence in the Testaments of the Twelve Patriarchs, in *Studies on the Testaments of the Twelve Patriarchs* (1975) 198: "In the interpretation of a writing with such a complicated history as the Testaments many conclusions will necessarily remain hypothetical, but it seems right to assume that a particular passage is Christian until clear evidence of the contrary is adduced."

King Saul, a woman from the tribe of Benjamin). David also married Maachah (most likely also for political reasons) who was not an Israelite at all. Furthermore, one of the sons of Naomi married Ruth, a Moabite woman. It would be no surprise, therefore, if somewhere down the line there was a marriage between a Levite man and a woman from Judah. One thing is abundantly clear: if one presses for a strictly literal translation of the Greek word σπέρμα ("seed," Rom 1:3) or the word καρπός ("fruit," Acts 2:30), there is no way for Jesus to be from the tribe of Judah based solely upon Joseph's biological line, for Jesus did not have within him the *seed* of David by virtue of Joseph's sperm. Such a birth connection could have happened only through Mary. R. P. Nettelhorst, who defends the premise that both Matthew and Luke contain the genealogies of Joseph, states: "A simple explanation is readily available, one that involves neither strange customs nor textual twists. Both genealogies are clearly through Joseph's father, and that the other traces back through Joseph's mother."[37] Based upon a strict and literal translation of both σπέρμα and καρπός, Nettelhorst's view is untenable, indefensible, and unnecessary. In order for Jesus to be truly descended from the tribe of Judah by virtue of a blood line, this descent would have to occur through the blood line of Mary.

A Missing Piece Supplied

We turn now to further question and challenge Dunn's assertion. I will advocate a case that Jesus did, in fact, possess the necessary bloodlines for the priesthood. James D. Tabor in his monograph *The Jesus Dynasty* raises an interesting point that merits careful consideration. Tabor says:

> Finally, the names in Luke that run from King David down to Heli, Mary's father, offer us some very interesting clues that further explain why this particular Davidic line was uniquely important. There are listed no fewer than six instances of the name we know as Matthew: Matthat (twice), Mattathias (twice), Maath, and Mattatha. What is striking is that the name Matthew was one invariably associated with a priestly, not a kingly or royal, lineage. One of Jesus' Twelve Apostles was named Matthew, but was also called Levi. Two of the six "Matthews" in Jesus' lineage were sons of fathers named "Levi." Josephus records that his own father, grandfather, great-grandfather, and brother were all named Matthias, and they were all priests of the tribe of Levi from the distinguished priestly family of the Hashmoneans or Maccabees. Ancient Israel was divided into twelve tribes, descendants of the twelve sons of Jacob, the grandson of Abraham. The priests of Israel had to be descendants of Aaron, brother of Moses, who was from the tribe of Levi.[38]

---

37. R. P. Nettelhorst, "The Genealogy of Jesus," *JETS* 31.2 (1988) 169–72.
38. J. D. Tabor, *The Jesus Dynasty* (2006) 55–56.

We must commend Tabor for teasing out some important truth and for his insightful assembling of relevant data. The names by themselves do not add up to very much, but Tabor has correctly connected the dots and the picture he paints is tantalizing. It is imperative, therefore, that we not lose sight of the importance of the collage. Tabor's penetrating analysis continues:

> Remember, when Mary became pregnant and left Nazareth to stay with Elizabeth, mother of John the Baptizer, Luke notes that they were *relatives*, though he does not say how (Luke 1:36). But he also records that Elizabeth and her husband Zechariah were of the priestly lineage (Luke 1:5). This is further confirmation of the link between Mary's Davidic family and the priestly tribe of Levi. It is inconceivable that such a heavy prevalence of Levite or priestly names would be part of Mary's genealogy unless there was a significant influence from the tribe of Levi merging into this particular royal line of the tribe of Judah.[39]

The data that Tabor has pieced together conforms exactly to the information recorded in the Gospel of Luke. It is vitally important to acknowledge that this information appears in Luke, not Matthew or Mark. Matthew records the royal Davidic line, and that royal bloodline coming through the tribe of Judah bears witness to Jesus' rightful claim to be the prophetic heir to the throne of David. Matthew, therefore, focuses on the pedigree of Jesus to be called a legitimate king. Georg Kuhn calls attention to another helpful piece of information: the lineage of David in Luke 3 veers off and resumes under Nathan.[40] It is generally conceded that families in the line of Judah and Levi were most likely to preserve reliable records.[41] Cognate to the Matthean genealogy is the recognition by Jack Dean Kingsbury that Mary does not stand in the line of David.[42] Luke, however, is different. Luke shows how Jesus, coming through Mary's Levite side of the family, can rightfully be identified as a priest.[43] Tangential to this observation is the equally important connection with the tribe of Judah and the lineage of David. Tabor, I believe, has correctly identified Luke's record as belonging to Mary's genealogy.

---

39. Ibid., 56.

40. Karl Georg Kuhn, "Die Geschlechtsregister Jesus bei Lukas und Matthäus, nach ihrer Herkunft untersucht," *ZNW* 22 (1923) 206: "Die zwei Geschlechtsregister Jeus bei Matthäus (1.1–17) und Lukas (3.23–38) unterscheiden sich schon auf den ersten Blick dadurch, daB bei Mt die Geschlechtsreihe durch alle davidischen Könige geführt wird, während der Reihe bei Lc dieser äuBere Glanz mangelt und schon durch Natthan von David abgezweight wird."

41. F. Bovon, *A Commentary on the Gospel of Luke 1.1–9.50* (2002) 134, acknowledges that "Purity of bloodlines was especially important for the priestly families, and so precise genealogies were maintained."

42. J. D. Kingsbury, *Jesus Christ in Matthew, Mark, and Luke* (1981) 66.

43. Raymond E. Brown, *The Birth of the Messiah* (1977) 60, says: "In both Matthew and Luke we shall find an interesting mixture of Judah and Levi in Jesus' putative ancestry."

It is here, however, that I must part company with Tabor. He does not pursue the trail of evidence demonstrating that Jesus rightfully and scripturally fulfills the genealogical requirements to serve in the double role of priest and king. In this disappointing crossroads decision, Tabor extracts the data from the genealogy according to Luke to then apply it to John the Baptist. On this basis, he proceeds to develop the thesis of two separate messiahs in first-century Judaism. This, of course, is not a new thesis.[44] Tabor, however, has popularized it with a novel twist, principally by applying the priestly messiah to the lineage of John the Baptist who, in Tabor's reconstruction, becomes a second messiah.[45] Unfortunately, his thesis does not square with NT information. Tabor has not followed the evidence where it leads. Where then does this leave the issue? J. L. Houlden observes:

> The birth stories provide the major evidence, supported by the genealogy, which, however, transcends mere Jewishness, in tracing Jesus' ancestry back to Adam and so to God himself, Adam's creator-father. According to Luke, Jesus springs from the most unimpeachable and devout Jewish setting. Of David's line, he is related to a working priest of the temple, and his birth in such a context is endorsed by angels from on high. The Temple continues to figure in his infancy and childhood, as the holy man Simeon and the prophetess Anna, stepping out of the past in order to illuminate the present, endorses his role.[46]

Houlden's interpretation of temple connections with Jesus opens up intriguing possibilities for understanding Lukan Christology. I believe that Houlden has correctly pointed out a valid link. Luke associates Jesus uniquely with the temple, subtly identifying him with priestly attributes.[47]

---

44. Reputable scholars who document evidence for two messiahs are: James H. Charlesworth, "From Messianology to Christology: Problems and Prospects," in *The Messiah: Developments in Earliest Judaism and Christianity* (1987b) 3–35, esp. 7; and Klaus Berger, *Jesus and the Dead Sea Scrolls: The Truth under Lock and Key?* (1995) 82, who suggests the possibility of linking John the Baptist with one of the two expected messiahs at Qumran. See also Morton Smith, "What Is Implied by the Variety of Messianic Figures?" *JBL* 78.1 (1959) 66–72.

45. See also Tabor's article, "Are You the One? The Textual Dynamics of Messianic Self-Identify," in *Knowing the End from the Beginning* (2003) 181, in which he identifies John the Baptist also as a Suffering Servant in fulfillment of Isa 53.

46. J. L. Houlden, "The Purpose of Luke," *JSNT* 21 (1984) 55.

47. For additional connections between Jesus and the temple, see K. Baltzer, "The Meaning of the Temple in the Lukan Writings," *HTR* 58 (1965) 263–77; Jack Dean Kingsbury, "The Plot of Luke's Story of Jesus," *Int* 48.4 (1994) 369–77, who isolates the issue of "conflict" as the plot of Luke, and the first encounter of this conflict occurs in the temple—the place of God's presence and also the seat of authorities' power. See also Willard M. Swartley, *Israel's Scripture Traditions and the Synoptic Gospels* (1994) 185: "Though scholarly interpretations have varied, consensus holds that Luke has a place for the temple in God's salvation purpose, unknown to Matthew and Mark." Although Swartley does make a number of interesting observations on Luke's understanding of the temple, he does not mention the role of Zech 3:8. See also Louis T. Brodie, "A New Temple and a New Law: The Unity and Chronicler-based Nature of Luke 1:1—4:22a," *JSNT* 5 (1979) 520–39; and Francis D. Weinert, "Luke, the Temple and the Jesus' Saying about Jerusalem's Abandoned House," *CBQ* 44.1 (1982) 68–78; and

These temple connections, however, are only one piece of the puzzle. R. Alan Culpepper provides another piece by stating some significant numerical data:

> In Luke, Jesus speaks of himself as 'the Son of Man' more frequently than with any other form of self-reference. The title 'Son of Man' occurs 25 times in Luke (not counting the variant in 9:56). Moreover, with the possible exception of Luke 5:24, which may be a comment by the narrator, the term occurs only on the lips of Jesus in Luke.... Moreover, Luke has added the title to sayings where it does not appear in Mark or Matthew (e.g., 6:22; 9:22; 12:8, 40; 19:10).[48]

Two pieces come easily together: references in Luke uniquely tie Jesus to the temple and the unusual high count of references to "Son of Man" emphasize the humanity of Jesus.

There is more. Robert M. Grant notices yet another key piece contained in Luke: "In the Bible the term 'power of the Most High' occurs only in Gabriel's address to Mary. The atmosphere resembles the old stories about the births of Samson and Samuel."[49] Robert Grant then catalogs a list of related connections between Jesus and Samuel as narrated by Luke: that the child Samuel grew in the presence of the LORD (1 Sam 2:21) is paralleled with Luke 2:40 ("the child [Jesus] grew, and waxed strong in spirit;"), and "the boy Samuel continued to grow both in stature and in favor with the LORD and with men" (1 Sam 2:26) is paralleled with Luke 2:52 ("and Jesus increased in wisdom and in stature, and in favor with God and man").[50] Grant, however, associates these parallels with Samuel the prophet. I would like to suggest a more likely relationship: high priest. Yes, it is true that Samuel did function in the role of a prophet, but his principal identity was his high priestly role. In fact, the texts of 1 Chr 6:19, 28 identify Samuel specifically as from the tribe of Levi. This ascription has been questioned because Samuel's father was an Ephraimite. Yet, just as in the case with Mary, it is possible that Samuel's link to Levi is historically due to his mother, Hannah. Indeed, it is Hannah—not Elkanah—that dominates the first chapter of Samuel as she is mentioned pointedly entering the temple or house of the LORD on three separate occasions (1:7, 9, 24). A subtle fourth reference may be the most significant: Samuel will live "there" always (1:22 [and 28]), meaning in the temple of the LORD. Finally, she turns the child Samuel over to Eli the priest. Therefore, we have three additional connections between Samuel the high priest and Jesus: 1) Just as Hannah dominates

---

David Seeley, "Jesus' Temple Act," *CBQ* 55.2 (1993) 263–83, and his "Temple Act Revisited," *CBQ* 62.1 (2000) 55–63.

48. R. Alan Culpepper, *The Gospel of Luke* (1995) 18.

49. R. Grant, *Jesus after the Gospels: The Christ of the Second Century* (1990) 19–20.

50. Craig A. Evans, *Jesus and His Contemporaries* (1995) 162, also makes this connection: "That Luke intended the infancies of Samuel and Jesus to parallel one another seems clear enough.... Samuel's summary likewise appears in the context of the boy growing up in the Temple." Other than to connect the two temple scenes with the Aramaic paraphrase of Hannah's song, Evans does not explore why Luke might possibly want to make this connection between Jesus and Samuel.

the first chapter of Samuel, so Mary dominates the first chapter of Luke; 2) just as Hannah is from the tribe of Levi, so Mary is from the tribe of Levi; 3) just as Samuel is found in the temple at an early age, so Jesus is found in the temple at an early age.

My argument for a priestly lineage of Jesus as recorded in Luke's genealogy is grounded in the fact that OT priests have a genealogy. In order to serve as a priest it was necessary to have a record of one's family tree. The genealogy of Jesus in the Gospel of Luke is different from that of Matthew. In Luke, the genealogy goes all the way back (back, back, back) to the very first man—to Adam himself. The genealogy in Luke reveals that Jesus is identified with mankind in general—not just the Jews in particular.

Houlden, Culpepper, and Grant make valuable piece-meal contributions for the understanding of Luke's presentation of Jesus. However, there is a possible omission by all three. What is missing is a reference to Zechariah's prophetic statement about the Branch. By saying this, I am not claiming that Luke specifically mentions this particular text. In fact, it is clear that Luke does not offer an exegetical exposition of Zech 6:12–13, nor has he self-consciously entered into the first century debate regarding a double Messiah. I suggest, though, that this text of Zech 6:12 is an important missing piece to the Lukan puzzle.[51] At this point, it would not be appropriate to advocate that the Gospel of Luke *requires* the location of Zech 6:12 as the substructure for the third Gospel. But a critical question remains: is it possible that the Gospel of Luke *allows* such a connection? A further question can provide a valuable key for unlocking this interpretative door: does placing Zech 6:12–13 into the background of Luke cloud or clarify our understanding? Does the placement of Zech 6:12–13 into the substructure of the third Gospel block or unlock possibilities for additional analysis? Evidence of my assertion is the uncanny manner in which the very insertion of the Zechariah text as the background for Luke enables us to explain the third Gospel in a way that is consistent with Luke's theology. Tangentially, the details of Zech 6:12–13 do not butt heads with basic information as contained in Luke. This premise, if accepted, would thus give us the freedom to situate Zech 6:12 as an embedded or encoded substructure to Luke.[52] Arland J. Hultgren observes another important characteristic about Luke

---

51. E. Käsemann, *Essays on New Testament Themes* (1971) 29, states: "The outline of a chronological and geographical sequence determines this whole and gives it clarity of arrangement. But, in this careful ordering of what is immediately visible, we come to see the inward order created by the divine plan of salvation."

52. For an incorrect and misleading judgment by a team of respected scholars, see Gerd Theissen and Anne Merz, *The Historical Jesus: A Comprehensive Guide* (1998) 532: "This concept of a priestly Messiah occurs only in late texts (I Chron. 29.22; Sir. 45.15; Dan. 9.25f.; II Macc. 1.10)." See also 534: "It is clear that outside Qumran the expectation is predominantly only of a royal Messiah. The messianic diarchy of a priestly and royal Messiah is in opposition to the Hasmonean rule which combined the two offices. Elsewhere we find a comparable juxtaposition of a priestly and a royal messianic figure only in the Testaments of the Twelve Patriarchs." They list *T.Levi* 18 and *T.Judah* 24. Unfortunately, they have omitted the most critical passage of all. From the Roman quarter, it may be argued that Augustus Caesar combined the two offices of king and high priest into one. See the *Res Gestae Divi*

that conforms to the picture as presented here: "Contrary to Mark, in which Jesus conducts part of his ministry outside the temple (11.11–14, 19–26; 13.1–37), Luke has the entire section of the Judean ministry after the triumphal entry (19.28–44) take place in the temple."[53] Hultgren insightfully and correctly spotlights a cardinal contrast: Mark emphasizes what happens outside the temple (as a servant,[54] I might add), while Luke focuses upon the inside (thus calling attention to high priestly characteristics). Also, as Jack Dean Kingsbury points out, Luke locates the appearances of Jesus after the resurrection, not in Galilee (as in Matthew and Mark) but in Jerusalem. Luke does this, according to Kingsbury, because Jerusalem is the place of the temple.[55]

The Text of Hebrews 7:14

There is yet one additional obstacle to hurdle: the text of Heb 7:14: "For it is clear that our LORD descended from Judah" (πρόδηλον γὰρ ὅτι ἐξ Ἰούδα ἀνατέταλκεν ὁ κύριος ἡμῶν). Hebrews 7:14, by assuming and protecting only the lineage of Jesus through Judah, seems to eschew and eliminate an attribution of Jesus to the priestly tribe of Levi. How, then, can the apparent conflict between Heb 7:14 and the thesis as developed in this study be resolved? I now consider the following possibilities. 1) The thesis as developed in this investigation is incorrect due to an arbitrary forcing of extraneous data on the third Gospel.[56] 2) The insistence of the author of Hebrews on the exclusive evidence for Judah is in error, incorrectly relying upon faulty data, thereby removing a significant attribute of Jesus' blood line. 3) Neither Heb 7:14 nor the thesis of this book is incorrect; both are correct from their respective points of view. I will argue that this third option is indeed the case. If indeed the case, it is imperative to find a way to reconcile the divergent views.

One possible explanation is to argue that Hebrews shows the lineage of Jesus through the male line. Hence, paternity is the prime goal for protection; a matrilineal defense is not in view. Can such a proposal survive criticism? If we compare Luke 1 with Hebrews 7, a possible connection emerges linking the tribe of Levi with the mother of Jesus: Elizabeth is clearly a descendant of Aaron (1:5) and also a relative of Mary. At 1:36 she is called a συγγενίς, "a kinswoman."[57] A cognate of συγγενίς is

---

Augusti: The Achievements of the Divine Augustus (1989) 7.

53. A. J. Hultgren, "Interpreting the Gospel of Luke," *Int* 30 (1976) 361.

54. For an alternate view that posits a strong servant motif for Luke rather than Mark, see R. F. O'Toole, "How Does Luke Portray Jesus as Servant of YHWH," *Bib* 81 (2000) 328–58, who presents a compelling case for Jesus as the Servant of YHWH.

55. J. D. Kingsbury, "The Gospel in Four Editions," *Int* 33.4 (1979) 371.

56. Paul Ellingworth, *The Epistle to the Hebrews* (1993) 376, takes the position that there is no historical basis for the view that the genealogy of Jesus contains a Levitical bloodline.

57. συγγενίς suggests the idea of "the same kind." See BDAG. For a contrary view, see Alfred Plummer, *The Gospel according to S. Luke* (1975 reprint) 25, who inclines to the idea that this text does not prove Mary is of the priestly line. For a confirmation of such lineage, see I. Howard Marshall

found at Luke 1:61 where the word συγγένεια is used to further describe the relatives of Elizabeth. These two terms suggest relationship by blood, not by marriage. The difference between συγγενίς (a late feminine form of συγγενής) and συγγένεια is that the former is a gender specific smaller part comprising the larger latter part. Thus, συγγενίς describes one woman out of the whole constellation of family relationships. The vitality of this relationship places Mary in the same position as Elizabeth. If Elizabeth is a συγγενίς of Mary, then Mary becomes potentially related to the whole συγγένεια, thereby situating her among the descendants of Levi. But we are not quite finished; three key facts remain.

THE NAME OF MARY. Few scholars have paid serious attention to the actual name of Mary.[58] Due to the familiar and popular name of "Mary," familiarity has perhaps bred neglect. As a result, the significance of the original spelling has not been pursued to any significant degree.[59] Furthermore, those who do not read Greek may not be aware that Luke actually uses two different names to distinguish her. English Bibles (such as the NIV) mention "Mary" eight times in chapter 1.[60] However, the first five references in Greek are Μαριάμ (anglicized to "Marian," "Mariam," or "Miriam"), followed by the single mention of "Maria" or "Mary" (Μαρία) at 1:41 for the sixth reference. Luke then caps off this list with two additional references to Mariam (1:46, 56). Not only is Luke's spelling of Mariam preferred, but this name dominates the first chapter. Mary is only mentioned once, while Mariam is mentioned seven times. Can more be said on this score?

EVIDENCE FROM JOSEPHUS. Josephus records a number of women bearing the name Μαριάμη, which is his alternate spelling for Mariam. Josephus mentions the name of Mariam a total of seventy-six times. Abraham Schalit narrowed down these seventy-six references as applying to seven individual women.[61] Notably among these women we may count the following: Mariamme (Josephus' spelling), a grand-daughter of Hyrcanus,[62] who himself was of priestly descent.[63] This Mariamme had a brother

---

(1978) 71: "Mary's relationship to Elizabeth suggests that she too may have been of priestly descent."

58. Darrell L. Bock, *Luke 1–9:50* (1994) 107, suggests: "many argue that she has Levitical roots.... It is hard, in light of the limited data, to make a choice, though her Levitical roots are clearer in Luke 1 than her Davidic roots are, because of her tie to Elizabeth." See also Bock's excursus (918–23) in which he focuses on the difficulties of reaching a definite conclusion. For a discussion of the meaning of her name, see E. Vogt, "De nominis Mariae etymologia," *VD* (1948) 163–68.

59. François Bovon, *A Commentary on the Gospel of Luke 1:1–9:50* (2002) 49, can only comment: "Of course, only the name of Jesus' mother and the family's residence in Nazareth are historical for certain."

60. Luke 1:27, 30, 34, 37, 39, 41, 46, 56.

61. Abraham Schalit, *Namenwörterbuch zu Flavius Josephus* (1968) 82.

62. *Jewish War* 1.241.

63. See Victor Tcherikover, *Hellenistic Civilization and the Jews* (1979) 126, for arguments that Hyrcanus belonged to the period of the priests.

named Jonathan whom Herod appointed to the office of high priest.[64] There is also Mariamme, the daughter of Simon the high priest.[65] Of further special note is the fact that Josephus spells Mariam from Exod 15:20 as ("Mariamme"). The significance of this variation is that it makes it possible to identify other references as alternates to Mary.

THE CUSTOM OF NAMING CHILDREN ACCORDING TO TRIBAL TRADITION. Luke 1:61 mentions that Mary's relatives react adversely to the idea of naming the Baptist "John." Their objection merits citation: "There is no one among your relatives who has that name." This is not strictly true. Nehemiah 12:13 is a case in point where "Johanan" (a variation of John) is mentioned. Indeed, the LXX translates this Hebrew name (יהוחנן) as Ιωαναν ("John"). There are other exceptions as well.[66] Since this objection must apply to the family line of Levi, the objection may only refer to names in their recent memory or their own circle of immediate family members. Obviously, though, according to this complaint, certain names tended to follow definite tribal identities. It is possible to see this elsewhere. When we meet the apostle Paul, he is Saul from the tribe of Benjamin who is named after the first king of Israel, also from the tribe of Benjamin. Zechariah himself is most likely named after many OT Levitical priests,[67] among whom the prophet Zechariah is a likely member. I presume, therefore, that this logic may have been influential in the naming of Mary/Mariam. That is, her name had a long history of prior Levitical namesakes. This identification suggests that Mary/Miriam may have been named after the sister of Moses. In Exod 15:20, the LXX spells her name as Μαριαμ and identifies her as the sister of Aaron. The Hebrew name of מרים (*Miryahm*) is used fourteen times in the OT.[68] In all cases the LXX translates the Hebrew with Μαριαμ ("Mariam"); in all cases she is the sister of Moses. This correlation adds another link to the NT Mariam with the tribe of Levi. Furthermore, Mary or Mariam is never identified with David or the tribe of Judah.

Conclusion

I conclude that Luke intends a Levitical link to Mary. If she was only from the line of Judah, it is likely that Luke would have mentioned this for it would have bolstered his logic of Jesus being of Davidic descent. Clearly, though, at the very minimum, the

---

64. *Jewish War* 1.437.

65. *Jewish War* 1.562, 573.

66. 1 Macc 2:1: ἐν ταῖς ἡμέραις ἐκείναις ἀνέστη Ματταθιας υἱὸς Ιωαννου τοῦ Συμεων ἱερεὺς τῶν υἱῶν Ιωαριβ ("in those days Mattathias, son of John, son of Simeon, appeared [being] a priest from the sons of Joarib"). For a parallel to this text, see Josephus, *Jewish Antiquities* 12.266, and Josephus, *Jewish War* 2.575, where he mentions John, a son of Levi.

67. T. M. Mauch, in the IDB (1962) 4.941–43, lists as many as thirty-three different men in the OT with the name of Zechariah. Of this number, Mauch identifies fifteen from the tribe of Levi.

68. Exod 15:20, 21; Num 12:1, 4, 5, 10, 10, 15, 15; 20:1; 26:59; Deut 24:9; 1 Chr 5:29; Mic 6:4.

number of telling references to the tribe of Levi in Luke 1 leaves open the suggestion that Mary was a Levite. This, of course, is not to argue that somewhere back down the line there could not have been an intermarriage between a Levite and someone from Judah, thus introducing Judah into the bloodline of Mary. This is not impossible, even likely, perhaps even inescapable. In that case, it would still leave Mary as a descendant of Levi. It is only Joseph who is identified with David and the tribe of Judah (Luke 1:27; 2:4). Hebrews 7 pursues a different course; that chapter singles out only males: Melchizedek, Abraham, Levi, and Judah. The writer of Hebrews does not show a concern for the issue of Mary's lineage.

Furthermore, the writer of Hebrews does not recognize the role and relevance of the Law at the birth of Jesus. Luke, however, pays special attention to everything being done "according to the Law of the LORD" (2:22, 23, 24, and 27). From the perspective of the writer of Hebrews, the Law is now abrogated; from the perspective of the Gospel of Luke, Jesus must fulfill that Law. Although the priesthood of Melchizedek is of a higher order, Jesus still must fulfill the requirements for priesthood according to the Levitical order. Thus, it is a matter of perspective.

10

The Gospel of John: The LORD God Branch

Current scholarly work on the fourth Gospel shows wide speculation, very divergent views, little agreement. There is absolutely no consensus on the author's identity.[1] Some prefer that the author is the "Beloved Disciple" who is not the apostle John, possibly either Thomas,[2] or John the Elder.[3] Lazarus as the author, however, has not gained support.[4] Some interpreters propose that the fourth Gospel is a composite resulting from at least three editorial hands.[5] Others go so far as to assign authorship to an unknown Gentile writing at the end of the first century or the beginning of the second.[6] Finally, a number of conservative scholars do defend the longstanding view that

---

1. Harold W. Attridge, "Genre Bending in the Fourth Gospel," *JBL* 121.1 (2002) 3–21, refers to the Beloved Disciple as a "mysterious figure" (19), who "remains resolutely anonymous" (19), as someone who "either wrote, or perhaps caused to write" the fourth Gospel (20), but his identity "remains cloaked in secrecy" (20).

2. For the view that Thomas must be considered as "the beloved disciple" (but not the author of the Gospel of John), see James H. Charlesworth, *The Beloved Disciple* (1995) 423.

3. For the view that the author of the fourth Gospel is John the Elder, see Richard Bauckham, "The Beloved Disciple as Ideal Author," *JSNT* 49 (1993) 21–44, and his monograph, *Jesus and the Eyewitnesses: The Gospels as Eyewitness Testimony* (2006). For the similar view that John the Elder was the composer but John the Apostle as the real source, see J. H. Bernard's commentary on John in the ICC series (1928) lxiv: "John the presbyter was the writer and editor of the Fourth Gospel, although he derived his narrative material from John the son of Zebedee." Bernard takes the references at 19:35 and 21:24 to indicate the composer or narrator as opposed to the original witness. For an opposite view, see Craig S. Keener, *The Gospel of John* (2003) 1154.

4. Although Lazarus is mentioned three times in John (11:3, 5, 36) as loved by Jesus, his name as a possible author has not gained traction.

5. For the argument that the "author" was a composite of at least three editorial hands, see most recently Urban C. von Wahlde, *The Gospels and Letters of John* (2011) 3: "As a composite document, the present Gospel lacks the unity, coherence, and emphasis characteristic of the work of a single author." For the view that the essence of the fourth Gospel did not come from a "single mind" but was most likely organized by such a mind, see John Ashton, *Understanding the Fourth Gospel* (1991) 98. More remotely, see the thirty-six page exploration on the subject by C. K. Barrett, *The Gospel According to John* (1965) 83–119, who divides the composition of the fourth Gospel into four separate and distinct stages.

6. For example, see P. Maurice Casey, "The Deification of Jesus," *SBLSP* 33 (1994) 708: "We can now see what is wrong with the classic arguments of Westcott and Morris, that the author of the Fourth Gospel was a Jew."

the author is, indeed, the apostle John.[7] I count myself among this number and, accordingly, proceed on the basis that there is not enough evidence to set aside the traditional view of the apostle John as the human instrument behind its composition.[8]

Aside from authorship, current areas of interest for NT scholars working in the fourth evangelist are the following: 1) John as history,[9] 2) John and Q, 3) John and Christology, 4) John as a redactor or compiler,[10] 5) the origin and provenance, 6) the Johannine community,[11] and 7) John's use of the OT.[12] As developed in the three other Gospels, I will focus primarily on the issue of John's use of the OT, and John's Christology.

The Prophecy of the LORD Branch in Isa 4:2.

MT: בַּיּוֹם הַהוּא יִהְיֶה צֶמַח יְהֹוָה לִצְבִי וּלְכָבוֹד וּפְרִי הָאָרֶץ לְגָאוֹן וּלְתִפְאֶרֶת לִפְלֵיטַת יִשְׂרָאֵל׃

LXX: Τῇ ἡμέρᾳ ἐκείνῃ ἐπιλάμψει ὁ θεὸς ἐν βουλῇ μετὰ δόξης ἐπὶ τῆς γῆς τοῦ ὑψῶσαι καὶ δοξάσαι τὸ καταλειφθὲν τοῦ Ισραηλ.

NIV: "In that day the Branch of the LORD will be beautiful and glorious, and the fruit of the land will be the pride and glory of the survivors in Israel."

---

7. For the view that the apostle John wrote the fourth Gospel, see Leon Morris, *The Gospel According to John* (1971) 9; F. F. Bruce, *The Gospel of John* (1983) 4–5; Craig S. Keener, *The Gospel of John* (2003) 1.114: "It is somewhat surprising, then, to discover the degree to which internal and external evidence appear to favor John son of Zebedee as the Fourth Gospel's author." See also Mark L. Strauss, *Four Portraits, One Jesus* (2007) 333: "The weight of evidence, however, favors the church's traditional identification with the apostle John, son of Zebedee and one of the Twelve." Most recently, see also C. Marvin Pate, *The Writings of John* (2011) 21.

8. Hence, I side with such scholars as Andreas J. Köstenberger, *John* (2004) 1, fn. 2: "In any case, the summary way in which Johannine authorship is regularly dismissed in contemporary scholarship is without justification, for this theory of authorship has never been definitely refuted."

9. For a recent study of historiography and John, see Richard Bauckam, "Historiographical Characteristics of the Gospel of John," *NTS* 53 (2007) 17–36. For the view that John's descriptions of Jesus cannot be based upon historical fact, see D. Moody Smith, "John and the Synoptics in Light of the Question of Faith and History," in *Faith and History* (1990) 88: "The most impressive and central divergence of John from the synoptics is its impressive, christologically elevated portrait of Jesus, which no critical scholar any longer takes to depict the way the historical Jesus presented himself. If those aspects of the narrative that are parallel to the synoptics are taken to be derivative from them, one will conclude that where John moves away from the synoptics, he departs from historical reality." See also his *The Fourth Gospel in Four Dimensions* (2008) 47–56. For a defense of the fourth Gospel's historicity, see Thomas D. Lea, "The Reliability of History in John's Gospel," *JETS* 38.3 (1995) 387–402.

10. For an overview of such issues, see John Ashton, "Second Thoughts on the Fourth Gospel," in *What We Have Heard from the Beginning: The Past, Present, and Future of Johannine Studies* (2007) 1–18.

11. See the groundbreaking work by J. Louis Martyn, *History and Theology in the Fourth Gospel* (2003) 40. See also Judith Lieu, "How John Writes," in *The Written Gospel* (2005) 171–83.

12. See Robert Kysar, *The Fourth Evangelist and his Gospel* (1975) 104–106.

There are five rubrics that we will now isolate and examine for possible connections for understanding the substructure of the Gospel of John: 1) a reference to a day, 2) a reference to a Branch, identified with YHWH, 3) the glory of this Branch, 4) the glory of the fruit of the land, and 5) the meaning of the survivors. It is my argument that these five rubrics, in some fragmentary form, are all found in John's Gospel. Furthermore, I will argue that four of the five are found specifically in the Prologue (1:1–18). We turn now to examine each one.

Reference to a Day

>MT: ביום ההוא, LXX: Τῇ ἡμέρᾳ ἐκείνῃ, NIV: "in that day."

The Branch will appear at an indefinite point in time, limited by the particular word *day*. This prophetic word, although similar to that as found in Jeremiah, speaks only of a "day," as if a single day. While Jeremiah puts this word in the plural, Isaiah reduces it to a singular day. As noted above, Joyce Baldwin defends the text as messianic; one of her reasons is anchored to the mention of a unique day: "The words 'in that day' indicate that some new thing was to happen, whereas luxuriant wild growth and a good harvest were hardly so remarkable, even in Palestine. No, in this messianic passage the phrase is beginning to be used in a messianic sense."[13] Walter Brueggemann aptly comments that this day indicates "an imaginative reach into the future, beyond all present circumstance."[14] The particular expression "in *that* day" is found in Isaiah some forty-four times. Of these forty-four, I count twenty-six viewed as most likely coming to pass in the historic time of Isaiah.[15] A case in point is the pericope of 7:17–23. That leaves a remainder of nineteen references which could possibly be placed into an undefined and indefinite future beyond the days of Isaiah.[16] Many of these references may be construed as possible messianic statements. If we consider the NT perspective of 1 Pet 1:10–12, OT prophets sensed something was going to happen, but not during their lifetime. Regarding Isaiah in particular and given the nature of the foreboding catastrophe, it is not likely that he could foresee a national survival in his own lifetime. Thus, he would have had no difficulty visualizing a fulfillment of some of these promises after his death. Regarding the coming disaster itself, he may have sensed the fulfillment of this as occurring before his death, especially is this likely from a text such as 7:18–23 with its mention of Egypt and Assyria. Of these nineteen other key texts, Brevard Childs comments: "Not just ordinary time is being extended,

---

13. Joyce Baldwin, "ṢEMAḤ as a Technical Term in the Prophets," *VT* 16 (1964) 94.

14. Walter Brueggemann, *Isaiah 1–39* (1998) 41.

15. The following appear capable of some sort of close-at-hand fulfillment: 3:7, 18; 4:1; 5:30; 7:17–23; 17:4, 7, 9; 19:16–24; 20:6; 22:8, 20, 25; 27:12–13; and 31:7.

16. I place the following texts in a distant future: 2:11, 17, 20; 4:2; 10:20–21; 11:10–11; 12:1, 4; 13:6–7; 24:21; 25:8–9; 26:1; 27:1–2, 6; 28:5; 29:18; and 52:6. For a slightly different view of this breakdown, see J. Barton, *Isaiah 1–39* (1996) 66.

but God's time of eschatological judgment and salvation, which comprises one single reality without a fixed temporal sequence."[17] As we go further into the significance of this momentous day, Isaiah provides details which suggest a constellation of ideas. The text of 4:2 and its overall context of vs. 3–6 delineate motifs that connect this day with the Branch (11:10), with the remnant of Israel (10:20–21), with the glory of the LORD (28:5), and with the blind seeing out of the darkness (29:18). In other words, the motifs contained in 4:2 find resonance throughout the first thirty chapters of Isaiah and they speak of something extraordinary, encompassing not just Israel but the entire world.[18]

The LXX translates the Hebrew ביום ההוא with Τῇ ἡμέρᾳ ἐκείνῃ ("in that day"). I argue in chapter 4 that Jer 23:5 serves as the background to the Gospel of Matthew which uses the plural in describing "days." Here, however, the Gospel of John does not even once contain the same plural usage. Rather, we find the fourth Gospel using the unique expression "in that day" (τῇ δὲ ἡμέρᾳ ἐκείνῃ or ἐν ἐκείνῃ τῇ ἡμέρᾳ).[19] Of particular interest is the usage in John 14:20, "in *that* day you will know that I am in my Father and you are in me and I am in you." Joyce Baldwin may be repeated here without taxing the reader's patience: "The words 'in that day' indicates that some new thing was to happen, whereas luxuriant wild growth and a good harvest were hardly so remarkable, even in Palestine. No, in this messianic passage the phrase is beginning to be used in a messianic sense."[20]

The Branch of the LORD

> MT: צמח יהוה, LXX: ἐπιλάμψει ὁ θεὸς, NIV: "the Branch of the LORD."

This is the fourth significant OT reference to the Branch.[21] For the sake of clarity and consistency, I will anglicize the Hebrew expression צמח יהוה to *Zemah* of YHWH. This concludes references to *Zemah* in the OT. As well as the messianic issue, the above passage has been placed under a cloud of suspicion as not coming originally from the prophet Isaiah. Otto Kaiser in the OTL assigns the passage to the status of a scribal addition, non-messianic in nature, whose composition may be dated possibly to as late as the second century before Christ.[22] Kirsten Nielsen follows Kaiser with an

---

17. Childs, *Isaiah* (2001) 35.

18. Nicole Chibici-Revneanu, *Die Herrlichkeit des Verherrlichten: Das Verständnis der δόξα im Johnnesevangelium* (2007) 376, calls attention to the worldwide implications of the glory of God and anchors her observations to Isa 4:2: " . . . und auch seine endzeitliche Offenbarung in Herrlichkeit wird als öffentliches Geschehen dargestellt vor dem Volk Israel oder der ganzen Welt."

19. John 5:9; 14:20; 16:23, 26; 20:19.

20. Joyce G. Baldwin (1964) 94.

21. *The Targum of Isaiah: Translated, with a Critical Introduction, Apparatus, and Notes* (trans. Bruce Chilton; 1986) 10. Chilton translates Isa 4:2: "In that time the Messiah of the Lord shall be for joy and for glory, and those who perform the law for pride and for praise to the survivors of Israel."

22. Otto Kaiser, *Isaiah 1–12* (1972) 53–55.

equally skeptical reading of Isa 4:2 by affirming: "This redactional work clearly took place during the Exile."[23] More recently Wonsuk Ma also views the text as post-exilic: "It can be easily assumed that the passage has been inserted by later hands, possibly in the postexilic period."[24] However, Brevard Childs defends the text as integral and original to the context: "The dominant eschatological emphasis of 2:1–4 and 2:6ff. reverberates strongly in 4:2."[25] It is obvious that some see evidence of later editorial handiwork. In defense of the authenticity of the Isaiah text, I would respond briefly by noting that the text of Isa 4:2 does not intrude, jar, or unsettle the train of thought in the immediate context. Secondly, the metaphor of branch, growth, and deliverance forms a part of Isaiah's sustained message from beginning to end. Therefore, I will proceed on the basis that the text, as handed down to us, is indeed part of the original autograph.

How one interprets the language of both prophetic texts and gospel references is a pivotal issue around which several key factors swing. Georges Barrois observes: "The dream of royal messianism in its temporal version remained in the consciousness of the people as an elusive mirage, a pretext for insurrection against foreign rulers, or the positive appeal of a higher and broader ideal."[26] I would like to isolate from this helpful observation by Barrois two important expressions: "temporal version" and "a pretext for insurrection against foreign rulers." The first leads to the second. In other words, a literal or *temporal* interpretation of messianism leads to open conflict with the oppressor. Such is the case with first-century Judaism; this literal interpretation of a messianic hope set Israel on a fatal course of open warfare with Rome. Instead of netting justice and peace, the end result was the disintegration of the state.

We must now turn to John's Prologue. A prologue is a programmatic statement indicating in advance where an author intends to take the narrative. Prologues generally contain ideas both new and old; they help to place the author in some kind of literary context; they also prepare the reader for the major themes to be covered. Alan Culpepper offers the following commentary on the Prologue:

> Having drawn readers to his side by means of the prologue, the evangelist trusts them to pick up the overtones of his language . . . . What seems clear and simple on the surface is never so simple for the perceptive reader because of the opacity and complexity of the gospel's sub-surface signals. Various textual features, principally the misunderstandings, irony, and symbolism constantly lead the reader to view the story from a high vantage point . . . . It is

---

23. Kirsten Nielsen, *There Is Hope for a Tree: The Tree as Metaphor in Isaiah* (1989) 183. See also Marvin A. Sweeney, *Isaiah 1–4 and the Post-Exilic Understanding of the Isaianic Tradition* (1988) 180.

24. Wonsuk Ma, *Until the Spirit Comes: The Spirit of God in the Book of Isaiah* (1999) 137.

25. B. C. Childs, *Isaiah* (2001) 35. Childs, however, does enumerate the objections: 1) allegations that the style is clumsy, indicative perhaps of a later prose style; 2) the ideology of the unit suggests themes of later priestly literature; 3) ritualistic and ethical concerns may reflect or resemble Ezekiel; and 4) the text shows that the threat to Jerusalem had already passed.

26. G. A. Barrois, *The Face of Christ in the Old Testament* (1974) 100.

the discovery of sub-surface signals which had previously escaped the reader's notice that allows the gospel to be read again and again with pleasure and profit. Traffic on the gospel's subterranean frequencies is so heavy that even the perceptive reader is never sure he or she has received all the signals the text is sending.[27]

Culpepper's use of language, especially his metaphors of "subterranean frequencies" and "sub-surface signals" illustrate the very point that this investigation is based upon: signals, sources, and motifs that are hidden beneath the surface. It is my contention that the subtext of Isa 4:2 is below or behind the Prologue.

Craig Evans, in examining the case for Bultmann's old claim that Gnosticism was behind the Prologue of the fourth Gospel, suggests four useful criteria for detecting a legitimate source:[28] 1) antecedent documentation,[29] 2) contamination,[30] 3) provenance,[31] and 4) degree of coherence, which he explains: "Finally, the degree of *coherence* between the New Testament passage and the proposed parallel must be considered. Is the parallel merely formal, perhaps even coincidental, or does it point to a genuine and meaningful relationship of language and conceptuality?"[32] Although Evans is looking for what he calls an "exegetical payoff" in post-New Testament sources, his criteria may be useful for this investigation. Three of the four are relevant and they do pass inspection. The text of Isa 4:2 is indeed antecedent to the NT; the charge of so-called contamination does not apply; the provenance is squarely within the milieu of the NT; the issue of coherence offers intriguing possibilities for connecting Isa 4:2 to the background of John's Prologue. The question is: do the language, the images, and the conceptual ideas contained in Isa 4:2 find resonance in the Prologue of John 1:1–18? Do they help to answer questions regarding sources? Do they fill in gaps and help to explain, clarify, or illuminate Johannine themes? While acknowledging that Genesis 1–2 and Exodus 34 assist us in providing the backdrop to John's Prologue, Evans then concludes: "Most interpreters have rightly recognized that the biblical parallels do not in themselves fully explain the ideas presupposed by the Johannine Prologue."[33] Evans makes no reference to the possible connection between Isa 4:2 and John 1:1–18. What he has left out, I propose to include. It is the claim of this chapter that the details of Isa 4:2 merit inclusion.

As noted above, *Zemah* as a messianic description in Isa 4:2 is disputed. Two questions have plagued this prophetic passage: 1) is the text indeed messianic, and 2)

---

27. R. Alan Culpepper, *Anatomy of the Fourth Gospel: A Study in Literary Design* (1983) 151.
28. Craig A. Evans, *Word and Glory* (1993) 19.
29. Ibid., 19: Does the later source reflect a tradition that probably existed earlier than the NT?
30. Ibid., 19: Are there indications that the later source has been influenced by the NT?
31. Ibid., 19: Do the respective documents contain traditions that were part of the milieu of the NT?
32. Ibid., 19.
33. Ibid., 100.

is the text part of the original autograph? Regarding the first objection, there are three principal arguments for dismissing *Zemah* as messianic. The first is that a non-messianic translation does not jar or disturb the flow of thought. A. S. Herbert translates the Hebrew as: "On that day the plant that the Lord has grown shall become glorious in its beauty."[34] On the surface, this translation is smooth and settles easily into the context without shocking the reader. The second argument is the evidence from the Targums and the Septuagint. Although the Targums give evidence of messianic understandings, some have contended that they do not support a messianic reading for Isa 4:2. However, this contention has been challenged.[35] The same can be said for the LXX. The LXX completely omits any reference to a branch. That being said, the LXX does not omit the text itself. Yet, the Vulgate does include it (*germen Domini*). What the LXX does is to translate the noun clause of the Hebrew into a verbal clause of "God will shine" (ἐπιλάμψει ὁ θεός). This translation is not necessarily untrue to the original; translators often transform noun clauses into verbs for the sake of variety. Yet, it must be said that the LXX unfortunately then diminishes the full impact of the noun *Zemah*. The third reason is the Church Fathers.[36] Robert O'Connell steers a middle course between simple vegetative growth and "messianic connotation" by suggesting that the "multivalence of prophetic language" can lead in both directions.[37] How does one resolve this issue? To begin with, it is not likely that a consensus will ever be achieved. All I can do is to offer my own view.

The book of Isaiah, much more so than either Jeremiah or Zechariah, contains an enormous amount of references to sapling-like growth, either springing forth from a tree, blossoming from a flower, or growing up from the ground like a bush. I count eight separate and distinct descriptions to this branch-like growth. For the sake of consistent clarity, I will use the NIV translation. These eight terms break down as

---

34. A. S. Herbert, *The Book of the Prophet: Isaiah 1–39* (1973) 45.

35. John D. W. Watts, *Isaiah 1–33* (1982) 49, says: "Tg translates משי חא דיהיה and understood it as a Messianic title." But then Watts adds that, arguments withstanding, there is no evidence that demonstrates a "fixed" messianic title. For a counter view, see E. W. Hengstenberg, *Christology of the Old Testament and a Commentary on the Messianic Predictions* (1861) 10–25. See also Samson H. Levey, *The Messiah: An Aramaic Interpretation. The Messianic Exegesis of the Targum* (1974) 43. See also Martin S. McNamara, *The New Testament and the Palestinian Targum to the Pentateuch* (1966) 253; for a defense of the Targums as having a weighty bearing upon NT interpretation, I note also that Bruce D. Chilton in his monograph *The Glory of Israel: The Theology and Provenience of the Isaiah Targum* (1983) 86–87, acknowledges that the Targum on Isa 4:2 is messianic, but because of the "bitter experience of the Bar Kokhba period" this messianic hope was more individualistic than national in application. The Tanakh reads: "In that day, the radiance of the LORD will lend beauty and glory, and the splendor of the land will give dignity and majesty to the survivors of Israel." Thus the Tanakh does not translate צמח as "Branch" but, instead, prefers "radiance." This follows closely the translation of the LXX: ἐπιλάμψει ὁ θεός.

36. See Théodoret de Cyr, *Commentaire sur Isaïe* (Sources Chrétiennes 276, 1980) 224; and Jean Chrysostome, *Commentaire sur Isaïe* (Sources Chrétiennes 304, 1983) 204.

37. Robert H. O'Connell, *Concentricity and Continuity: The Literary Structure of Isaiah* (1994) 90.

follows: "root" (שרשׁ/shoresh), used eight times;[38] "rod" or "shoot" (חטר/ghohter), used once;[39] "stump" (מצבת/matz-tzeveth), used twice;[40] "branch" (נצר/netzer), used five times;[41] "branch" (צמח/Zemah), used once;[42] the verb "to bud" or "to sprout" or noun (פרח/pahragh), used five times;[43] "blossom" (ציץ/tzeetz), used five times;[44] and "offshoot" or "root" (צפע/tzephag), used twice.[45] The total number of composite references comes to twenty-nine. What is most unusual about this count is that the key Hebrew word under investigation is found only once in the prophet Isaiah; Zemah is used only at 4:2. A further note may be included: many of these terms have messianic implications. In the book of Isaiah, the company of words that the Zemah keeps is messianic in nature.

A subsidiary point is whether the translation "Branch" is more accurate or should greater consideration be given to a word such as "Sprout."[46] Obviously, the idea of a branch suggests growth springing from a tree, while a sprout can come forth from the ground. Hugh Williamson in the updated ICC series argues that "the common translation 'branch' is certainly mistaken, as has been most recently demonstrated by the full and thorough analysis of Rose."[47] Williamson then translates Zemah with the word "vegetation." The translators of the LXX associate the word with light, suggesting perhaps a connection to the rising of the sun. I believe that Richard B. Hays is closer to the linguistic truth by calling attention to the double-edged nature of this word:

> The Greek word ἀνατολή, which literally means "rising" or "that which rises up," conveys a delicate ambiguity. It can refer to the rising of the sun . . . Yet, the same word can also have a botanical meaning, referring to the "branch" or shoot" arising from a plant.[48]

Whether a botanical or meteorological metaphor is intended, the precise translation of Zemah is really a secondary issue. More relevant is the question whether the term is messianic or simply a non-personal metaphor for what YHWH will cause to

---

38. Isa 5:24; 11:1, 10; 14:29, 30; 27:6; 37:31; 53:2. The verb is found at 27:6.
39. Isa 11:1, 10; 18:6; 18:5; 37:27.
40. Isa 6:13, 13.
41. Isa 11:1; 14:19; 17:6; 18:5; 60:21.
42. Isa 4:2.
43. Isa 17:11; 27:6; 35:2; 55:10. The noun is found at 5:24; 18:5.
44. Isa 27:6; 28:1; 40:6, 7, 8.
45. Isa 14:29; 22:24.
46. See George Buchanan Gray, *A Critical and Exegetical Commentary on the Book of Isaiah I–XXXIX* (1928) 78, who contends that צמח means not a branch, but whatever grows or shoots forth from the ground. Gray continues: "metaphorically it is used as a term for him who should re-establish the Davidic monarchy, and it has often been given a Messianic sense in this passage; but this is inconsistent with the parallel *the fruit of the ground* . . ." Gray thus argues that the word applies more to the "fruit of the land" as in Num 13:26.
47. H. G. M. Williamson, *A Critical and Exegetical Commentary on Isaiah 1–27* (2006) 301.
48. R. B. Hays, *Echoes of Scripture in the Gospels* (2016) 230.

rise up, spring up, or to grow.[49] English translations defend a messianic view from the King James, to the American Standard of 1901, to the Revised Standard of 1952, up to the recent NIV and ESV, preferring the word "Branch." It should be noted, however, that the American and Revised Standard versions do not capitalize the word at Isa 4:2. Clearly, though, the word "Branch" is entrenched in English Bibles. The anglicized and italicized *Zemah* avoids the difficulty by transforming a Hebrew word into flexible English. Joyce Baldwin defends the text as messianic for three reasons. First, 4:2–6 is not an abnormal intrusion into the context. Beginning back at 2:1, the pericope is a natural conclusion to the flow of thought.[50] Secondly, "the 'shoot of YHWH' is a man;"[51] the notion of vegetation does not do justice to the concept. Third, "The words 'in that day' indicate that some new thing was to happen, whereas luxuriant wild growth and a good harvest were hardly so remarkable, even in Palestine. No, in this messianic passage the phrase is beginning to be used in a messianic sense."[52]

In like manner with the three previous prophetic texts, the text of Isa 4:2 not only contains the term branch but also differs in description. One such difference is the inclusion of the personal name of YHWH. This Branch is a YHWH Branch, or using equivalent NT language a LORD God Branch.[53] This Branch will be clearly of the LORD or of YHWH. If of the LORD, this equates and identifies the Branch with God. Thus, the name of YHWH is not, as it were, dragged into the discussion by the scruff of the neck, but is brought easily into the text by Isaiah. This Branch can only be YHWH's Branch. As the Branch of YHWH, it complements the other three Branches of King, Servant, and Man/Priest. Each Branch has its own particular identity in the details; yet each Branch also shares a common homogenous identification as being uniquely a *Zemah*. J. Búda, responding to objections that *Zemah* YHWH cannot be the Sprout of David as in Jer 23:5–6, calls attention to the salient fact that this *Zemah* is a person, not vegetation.[54] In other words, the focus is upon YHWH: "the LORD" (4:4).

What justification is there for applying this term to the fourth Gospel? It is one thing to explicate the meaning of *Zemah* as it is found in Isa 4:2; it is altogether another to place this text into the substructure of the fourth Gospel. What reasonable proof can be offered for supporting the claim of this chapter linking the fourth Gospel uniquely to the prophetic reference of Isa 4:2? A defense of this proposition is hereby offered.

In general, scholarly studies incline toward the word "Branch" and consequently stick with the metaphor of a tree such as Kirsten Nielsen's *There Is Hope for a Tree: The*

---

49. For example, Otto Kaiser, *Isaiah 1–12* (1972) 54, is adamant that this cannot refer to the messianic Davidic promise.

50. J. G. Baldwin, "ṢEMAḤ" (1964) 93.

51. Ibid., 93.

52. Ibid., 94.

53. Matt 4:10: "You shall worship the LORD your God" (citing Deut 6:13).

54. J. Búda, "Ṣemaḥ Jahweh: Investigationes ad Christologiam Isaianam spectantes," *Bib* (1939) 10–26.

Tree as Metaphor in Isaiah. As in the Synoptics, the fourth Gospel does not cite the text from Isa 4:2. Yet, there are identifications, if only by piecemeal and fragmentary allusion, to the notion of a branch. Clearly, John 15:1, 5 is one such allusion: "I am the vine; you are the branches." Although the key term ἀνατολή ("branch") is not used here, the idea is present. Craig Keener even suggests: "The Targum to Ps 80.14–15 can identify the vine (as the Branch) with the Messiah . . . more important, *2 Bar* 39.7 uses the 'vine' as a symbol for the Messiah."[55] Keener does not stop there but adds that "more pervasive" references to the Branch are to be found in such texts as Isa 4:2; Jer 23:5; and Zech 3:8; 6:12.[56] Although the fourth Gospel does not make use of the term "Branch" in the same prophetic sense, the metaphorical notion of a branch does play a significant role in the Gospel of John.

Proceeding on, the Gospel of John, more than any other Gospel, identifies Jesus as God.[57] The fourth Gospel contains at least five specific references identifying Jesus as God (1:1, 14; 8:58; 10:34–36; and 20:28). I note John Ashton's comment on 8:58: "After all, the easiest and most straightforward explanation of 8:58 . . . is that Jesus is actually claiming the name of Yahweh for himself."[58] J. H. Bernard in the ICC states: "ἐγώ εἰμι is used absolutely of the solemn אֲנִי־הוּא *I (am) He*, which is the self-designation of Yahweh in the prophets . . . . Jesus Himself is reported as having said *I (am) He*, which is a definite assertion of His Godhead, and was so understood by the Jews."[59] A starting-point may be taken up with the name "Lord/LORD." C. E. B. Cranfield, commenting upon Paul's use of the name in Romans, notes: "But, if it is right to say that its use in the Septuagint (more than six thousand times) to represent the divine name YHWH . . . must surely mean that for him, the exalted Christ shared the name, the majesty, the authority, the deity of the living God himself."[60] Although a "Son of God" Christology is evident in the fourth Gospel,[61] more than any other Gospel, Jesus is identified with God himself.[62] Also, the primary motif of glory is associated with

55. Craig S. Keener, *The Gospel of John* (2003) 2.990.

56. Ibid., 990, fn. 26.

57. C. Marvin Pate, *The Writings of John* (2011) 48: "Jesus is equal to God."

58. John Ashton, *Understanding the Fourth Gospel* (1991) 146. Although Ashton credits this statement as coming from the "Johannine camp," notwithstanding his personal judgment on the origin of the statement, I believe that his observation on the meaning of the statement is correct. For a philosophical defense for the proposition that Jesus is God, see Richard Swinburne, *Was Jesus God?* (2008).

59. J. H. Bernard, *A Critical and Exegetical Commentary on the Gospel According to St. John* (1928) 322.

60. C. E. B. Cranfield, "Some Comments on Professor J. D. G. Dunn's *Christology in the Making* with Special Reference to the Evidence of the Epistle to the Romans," in *The Glory of Christ in the New Testament: Studies in Christology* (1987) 267–80, here 274.

61. See, for example, Steven B. Nash, "Psalm 2 and the Son of God in the Fourth Gospel," in *Early Christian Literature and Intertextuality* (2009) 85–102. Although Jesus is presented as both "Son," and LORD God, it is this exalted identification with God himself that makes the Gospel of John unique.

62. For additional arguments, see D. A. Fennema, "John 1.18: 'God the Only Son,'" *NTS* 31 (1985) 124–35, especially the conclusion: "By calling him θεός, the evangelist again ascribes to the Logos/

this Branch. John D. W. Watts writes: "Zechariah seems only concerned to show that Zerubbabel is a descendant of David. But here the צמח (*Zemah*) is of יהוה 'Yahweh,' not David."[63] A similar term, found in the key passage of Isa 11:1, is *neser* or *netser*. Isa 11:1 says: "A shoot will come up from the stump of Jesse; from his roots a Branch will bear fruit."

THE RELATIONSHIP BETWEEN THE FATHER AND THE SON. We turn now to consider the inner relationship between Father and Son in the Gospel of John. This relationship is highlighted in chapter 17 in which Jesus refers to this relationship as Father and Son. Six times Jesus calls God his Father: 17:1, 5, 11, 21, 24, and 25. The noun "glory" (δόξα) and the verb "to glorify" (δοξάζω) occurs a total of eight times in this single chapter: 17:1, 1, 4, 5, 5, 10, 22, and 24. Because of this emphasis upon glory, many scholars divide the Gospel of John into two parts: a "Book of Signs" (1:19–12:50) and "Book of Glory" (13–21).[64] This glory is transcendent as Jesus possessed it before the foundation of the world (17:5, 24). The idea of "oneness" (ἕν) is repeated several times: 17:11, 21, 22, 22, and 23. Jesus views himself as at "one" with the Father and prays that the disciples can come to a similar unity. Intertwined in this prayer is also the notion of a surviving remnant. All of the disciples have been kept safe from the hostility of the world. There is one exception: the son of perdition (17:12). Thus, all of the major ideas contained in the prophetic text of Isa 4:2 appear in this key chapter.

THE CONCEPT OF ONENESS. The concept of "oneness" merits further attention. The Gospel of John boldly identifies Jesus with God. More specifically, the fourth Gospel identifies Jesus with YHWH, the LORD God Almighty of the OT. This is NT Christology at its highest. In John 12:41 there is the striking assertion that Isaiah "saw his glory," thus equating Jesus with YHWH. This is a very daring claim, perhaps the most extravagant in the NT. Given the lavish nature of the claim, it is no wonder that it has generated volumes of discussion.[65] How can this claim be true? If we go outside the

---

Son the absolute deity of God himself." See also Vincent Taylor, "Does the New Testament Call Jesus 'God'?" in *New Testament Essays* (1970) 88: "The one clear ascription of Deity to Christ, 'My Lord and my God,' in the New Testament is addressed to Him in His Risen and Exalted life and breathes the atmosphere of worship." Taylor, however, cautions against seeing Jesus as fully God since this would compromise the incarnational truth that Jesus was fully Man. In our judgment, the Gospel of John shows no such reticence. See also Th. De Kruijf, "The Glory of the Only Son (John 1.14)," in *Studies in John* (1970) 111–23; and Jerome H. Neyrey, "'I Said: You are Gods': Psalm 82.6 and John 10," *JBL* 108.4 (1989) 663. Most recently, see C. Marvin Pate, *The Writings of John* (2011) 39. For an idiosyncratic interpretation arguing that Jesus is a "second" God, see Margaret Barker, *The Great Angel: A Study of Israel's Second God* (1992).

63. John D. W. Watts, *Isaiah 1–33* (1982) 49. See also Hans Wildberger, *Isaiah 1–12* (1991) 166.

64. For example, Kenneth Schenck, *Jesus Is Lord!* (2003) 286–87; Andreas J. Köstenberger, *John* (2004) 395.

65. See, for example, Peter Borgen, "The Gospel of John and Hellenism," in *Exploring the Gospel of John* (1996) 103.

Gospel of John, possibilities are not lacking for an explanation. Deut 6:4 says: "Hear, O Israel: the LORD (יהוה) our God, the LORD (אחד) is one." The so-called "shema" of ancient Israel announces that the LORD or YHWH is *one*.[66] Jesus announces that the Father and Son are *one*. A possible key for understanding this equation is the Hebrew word for *one*. The Hebrew term for "one" in Deut 6:4 is אחד (*echad*). If we track the use of this word in the OT, interesting connections open up. This same word also appears in Gen 1:5: "and there was evening and morning, one (*echad*) day." Traditional English translations of this verse do not suggest this possibility;[67] they all translate this as "first." Certainly, this is the first day; yet, the first day of creation has two parts: an evening and a morning. Together, they comprise a complete day, making a day incomplete without both elements. Stated otherwise, according to the usage here in Gen 1:5, there are two parts to an *echad*. In the particular case of the first day, these two parts have their own individual characteristics, most likely having to do with the degree of light. Together they make up an entire day. A second text exhibiting similar characteristics is Gen 2:24 which speaks of the first male and the first female. Together they are identified as "man" (Gen 1:27). Furthermore, they are to become "one" (*echad*) flesh. Although the woman comes from the man, she has her own individual characteristics as a female. Together they form the first family by becoming one flesh. The salient fact is that, though two, they form one entity. By extension, Jesus as the Son comes from the Father but has his own individual characteristics. Together, however, the Father and the Son constitute "one" YHWH or "one" God.[68]

"will be beautiful and glorious"

> MT: לצבי ולכבוד, LXX: μετὰ δόξης, NIV: "will be beautiful and glorious."

The twin words "glory/glorious" and "beautiful/splendor" are found throughout the book of Isaiah. The *Zemah*'s personal role will be that of the LORD; his defining characteristics will be beauty and glory.[69] The word for "beautiful" (צבי/*z[ts]ebi*) is used seven times in Isaiah,[70] often found with the companion term "glory" (כבוד/*kabod*)

---

66. The word *shema* comes as a transliteration of the first word in the verse: "hear" (שמע).

67. For a defense of the Hebrew in Gen 1:5 meaning "one," see Andrew E. Steinmann, "אחד as an Ordinal Number and the Meaning of Gen 1:5," *JETS* 45.4 (2002) 577–84.

68. See Daniel I. Block, "How Many Is God"? An Investigation into the Meaning of Deuteronomy 6:4–5," *JETS* 47.2 (2004) 206–7, who argues for a translation of "alone," indicating exclusive devotion to YHWH *alone*.

69. See C. F. Keil and F. Delitzsch, *Commentary on the Old Testament: Isaiah* (1975), for their case that the Branch of YHWH/Jehovah is the Messiah and not the land, 151–52: "Only compare ch. xxviii.5, where Jehovah Himself is described in the same manner, as the glory and ornament of the remnant of Israel. But if the 'sprout of Jehovah' is neither the redeemed remnant itself, nor the fruit of the field, it must be the name of the Messiah." For the argument that the Branch of YHWH *and* "the fruit of the land" both refer to the Messiah, see Edward J. Young, *The Book of Isaiah* (1974) 173–77.

70. Isa 4:2; 13:19; 23:9; 28:1, 4, 5.

which itself is used thirteen times in Isaiah.[71] Of particular interest is the text from Isa 28:5: "In *that day* (ביום ההוא) YHWH of hosts shall become a crown of *glory* (צבי) and a diadem of beauty (תפארה) for the *remnant* (לשאר) of his people." Of the four key words placed in parentheses, all four are also found in Isa 4:2. Thus 28:5 with its reference to *that day, YHWH, glory,* and *remnant* are echoes of 4:2.[72] The most significant aspect of the statement is that it describes YHWH himself. In other words, 4:2 and 28:5 potentially mirror each other by announcing YHWH is that glory. Mark Kinzer concisely states it: "Jesus is also the custodian of the divine Glory."[73] Edward J. Young adds to this profile by commenting:

> The thought of Isaiah 28 is that in place of false beauty there will be the true beauty which is the Lord Himself, and it is this comparison which shows that in the present verse [4.2] a mere reference to the land and its produce is to be excluded. A further development of the thought appears in Isaiah 60.9, where the Lord is said to have beautified Israel. In 60.19 God is said to be the nation's glory. In Zechariah 2.5 also the Lord is identified as a glory. The predicates which in 4.2 are used to describe the Sprout are those which in other passages clearly are applied to the Lord Himself.[74]

GLORY IN THE GOSPEL OF JOHN AND ISA 4:2. Jerome H. Neyrey remarks: "*Glory*. Although technically this belongs in the 'honor and shame' section, it deserves separate treatment because it is the author's favorite term to express the relationship between Jesus and God."[75] Gerhard Kittel further comments:

> It is to be noted, however, that NT usage itself takes a decisive step by using (δόξα) in relation to Christ, a word which was used in relation to God.... This emphasis is itself Johannine to the extent that John has a particularly strong sense of the causal connexion between dying and bringing forth fruit, or between the death and resurrection of Jesus, between suffering and the glorification of the Son of Man.[76]

Isaiah says that the Branch of the LORD will be "beautiful and glorious and the fruit of the land will be the pride and glory of the survivors in Israel."[77] Kittel connects the

---

71. Isa 3:8; 4:2, 5; 10:16, 18; 11:10; 14:18; 17:3; 22.18, 23, 24; 43:7; 60:13; 61:6; 66:11.

72. See Judith Lieu, "Narrative Analysis and Scripture in John," in *The Old Testament in the New* (2001) 144–63, in which Lieu argues (144) that John has only "inconsequential allusions;" yet (148), "scriptural echoes are to be found everywhere."

73. M. Kinzer, "Temple Christology in the Gospel of John," *SBLSP* 37 (1998) 453.

74. E. J. Young, *Isaiah* (1974) 175.

75. J. H. Neyrey, *The Gospel of John* (2007) 25.

76. G. Kittel, "δόξα," *TDNT* (1964) 2.248–49. See also F. F. Bruce, *The Gospel of John* (1983) 41: "'We looked on his glory'—the testimony of the Evangelist and his fellow-disciples—might serve as a sub-title for this Gospel."

77. See Gerard Van Groningen, *Messianic Revelation in the Old Testament* (1990) 520: "The Branch

concepts of glory, fruit, and beauty, thus providing a nexus of ideas compatible with the argument as presented here in this chapter.

I offer the following connections in John as potential subliminal links back to Isaiah 4:2. Although most NT scholars have noted the role that "glory" (δόξα) plays in the fourth Gospel, they do not generally link this concept back to the OT metaphor of the Branch as found in Isa 4:2.[78] However, some OT scholars have taken note of this connection and have acknowledged its vital significance.[79] While not linking the concept of glory back to Isa 4:2, yet noting the prominence giving to glory in the Gospel of John, Richard Bauckham notes this unique usage: "Above all, glory is a theme that John uses, very distinctive among the New Testament writers to highlight, by paradox, the extraordinary nature of the love of God . . ."[80] Other scholars have noted that the concept of glory is clearly attributed to the appearance of the Messiah as the long-awaited Branch.[81] In Isa 11:10, the prophet says that the Root of Jesse will provide a "glorious" place of rest. Proceeding deeper into Isaiah, at 35:1–3 the prophet says: "The desert and the parched land will be glad, the wilderness will rejoice and blossom. Like the crocus, it will burst into bloom; it will rejoice greatly and shout for joy. The glory of Lebanon will be given to it, the splendor of Carmel and Sharon; they will see the glory of the LORD, the splendor of our God." Finally, Isa 60:1–2 says: "Arise, shine, for your light has come, and the glory of the LORD rises upon you. See, darkness covers the earth and thick darkness is over the peoples, but the LORD rises upon you and his glory appears over you." This text contains a number of motifs found in the Gospel of John. Some of them are: light and darkness; shine, for your light has come; glory; and the ever present "See" or "Behold!" A similar metaphor is found in Isa 61:3 which says, "They will be called oaks of righteousness, a planting of the LORD

of Yahweh is described by Isaiah in terms of verdant growth and the rich produce of the land." Groningen does not question the genuineness of the text.

78. For example, Robert Kysar's survey of the literature in *The Fourth Evangelist and his Gospel* (1975) 185–99, turns up no connections. See also Ronald A. Piper, "Glory, Honor, and Patronage in the Fourth Gospel: Understanding the *Doxa* Given to Disciples in John 17," in *Social Scientific Models for Interpreting the Bible* (2001) 281–309. Rather than connecting *doxa* back to Isa 4:2, Piper situates the concept within the cultural milieu of the patron-client relationship. Piper does note, however, that the concept of *doxa* is of major theological significance in the fourth Gospel. See also the recent contribution by Jesper Tang Nielsen, "The Narrative Structures of Glory and Glorification in the Fourth Gospel," *NTS* 56 (2010) 343–66. Nielsen argues (354) that: "One of the salient features of the Fourth Gospel is that it applies the terminology δόξα/δοξάζω to almost all important elements of the narrative." Nielsen also argues (346) that it is beyond doubt that the Hebrew Bible forms the background for the concept of glory. There is no attempt, however, to link δόξα to Isa 4:2. Even more recent is Sanghee M. Ahn's, *The Christological Witness Function of the Old Testament Characters in the Gospel of John* (2014), who does not discuss Isa 4:2.

79. For example, Edward J. Young (1974) 172–78, and C. F. Keil and F. Delitzsch, *Isaiah* (1975) 151–53.

80. R. Bauckham, *Gospel of Glory* (2015) 43.

81. See Eduard Lohse, "Der König aus Davids Geschlecht: Bemerkungen zur messianischen Erwartung der Synagoge," in *Abraham unser Vater* (1963) 344: "Wenn der Messias erscheint, werden Herrlichkeit und Glanz anbrechen, die Gott durch sein Werkzeug seinem Volk werden lassen will."

for the display of his splendor." John Oswalt, after reviewing some 376 references to *kabod* ("glory") and its derivatives in the OT, ends with a rather surprising conclusion by linking Isa 4:2 to the "glory" mentioned in John 1:14: "But nowhere is the reality and the splendor of his presence and his character seen as in his son (Isa 4:2). Here the near blinding quality of his glory is fully portrayed: 'We beheld his glory, the glory as of the only son of the Father, full of grace and truth.'"[82] The ideas of "glory" and "beauty" are intertwined. The first mirrors the latter; the latter reflects the former, each reflecting the other. In fact, Origen uses them interchangeably.[83]

GLORY AND LIGHT. There is one further association that needs exploration. C. H. Dodd called attention to it in 1953:

> This is expressed in the Prologue in the proposition that in the incarnate Christ men saw the "glory" of the eternal Logos. To this statement we must now turn. The climax of the series of statements about the eternal light in the Prologue is that statement that the Logos . . . and the effect of this, the evangelist adds, was that (1.14). The association of δόξα with φῶς goes back to the Old Testament . . . . כבוד means the manifestation of God's being, nature and presence, in a manner accessible to human experience; and the manifestation was conceived in the form of radiance, splendor, or dazzling light . . . . It is therefore not surprising that δόξα and φῶς are found in parallelism referring to the manifestation of the power of God for the salvation of His people."[84]

This association between δόξα ("glory") and φῶς ("light") is intriguing. The Prologue to John's Gospel seems indeed to counterpoise the two. The following scheme indicates such a correspondence: 1:4, "in him was life and the life was the *light* (φῶς) of men;" 1:5, "The *light* (φῶς) shines in the darkness and the darkness has not overcome *it*;" 1:6–7, "There was a man . . . he came as a witness in order to testify regarding the *light* (φῶς);" 1:8, "That one was not the *light* (φῶς), but in order to testify in regard to the *light* (φῶς);" 1:9, "[He] was the true *light* (φῶς) who *enlightens* (φωτίζω) all men;" 1:14, "And the Word became flesh and dwelt among us, and we beheld his *glory* (δόξα), *glory* (δόξα) as the only-begotten of the Father." The evangelist thus makes a claim that the light that came into the world and enlightens men is the very light that he beheld as the glory of God. Dodd's equation that the light equals glory is a safe correlation. What is the hermeneutical value of making such a connection?

Although the metaphor of the *Zemah* betokens a kind of sapling-like growth as the likely principal idea behind the word, secondary notions can be detected, one of them being significantly the motif of light. Indeed, this is how and why the LXX translates *Zemah*. At first glance, this appears to be a strange mixing of metaphors.

---

82. John N. Oswalt, "כבד," *Theological Wordbook of the Old Testament* (1980) 1.427.
83. Origen, *Contra Celsum* 1.54.
84. C. H. Dodd, *The Interpretation of the Fourth Gospel* (1953) 206.

How can vegetative growth metaphorically suggest light? The LXX translation of Isa 4:2 may illuminate the answer to this question: Τῇ ἡμέρᾳ ἐκείνῃ ἐπιλάμψει ὁ θεὸς ἐν βουλῇ μετὰ δόξης ἐπὶ τῆς γῆς τοῦ ὑψῶσαι καὶ δοξάσαι τὸ καταλειφθὲν τοῦ Ισραηλ ("In that day God will shine in counsel with glory upon the earth"). The LXX translators (if we assume the MT as the text) take the Hebrew *Zemah* to mean "to shine." Hence, the LXX turns a noun into a verb. In the three other prophetic texts under investigation in this study, they all use the same Greek word (ἀνατολή) to translate the Hebrew *Zemah*. Why has the LXX made an exception at this point? Unless the translators have a different Hebrew text other than the MT (which I do not assume to be the case), the best explanation available to account for this variation is that *Zemah* is flexible enough so as to have it both ways. Indeed, Isa 60:1–2 says: "Arise, shine, for your light has come, and the glory of the LORD rises upon you. See, darkness covers the earth and thick darkness is over the peoples, but the LORD rises upon you and his glory appears over you." Not only do we have the association between light and glory, but the reference in the LXX to the LORD rising contains the verb ἀνατέλλω ("to arise") from which the noun ἀνατολή ("Branch") comes. Tangentially, the verb ἀνατέλλω ("to arise") is used at Matt 4:16 to describe a great light breaking over people who are sitting in darkness, and on those living in the land of the shadow of death a light has dawned (ἀνατέλλω).

"And the fruit of the land [will be] for pride and glory"

> MT: וּפְרִי הָאָרֶץ לְגָאוֹן וּלְתִפְאֶרֶת; LXX: ἐν βουλῇ δόξης ἐπὶ τῆς γῆς τοῦ ὑψῶσαι καὶ δοξάσαι τὸ καταλειφθὲν τοῦ Ισραηλ; NIV: "will be beautiful and glorious, and the fruit of the land will be the pride and glory of the survivors in Israel."

The complete text states that the Branch of YHWH will be beautiful and glorious *and* the fruit of the land will be glorious as well. A key question here is the value attached to the conjunction *and*. In other words, how parallel is the thought? It is obvious that Hebrew parallelism is at work, but we ask: what kind? Three possibilities present themselves. First, do we take the expression "fruit of the land" as being synonymous with the Branch, as if they were one and the same? If that is the case, would the Branch then become the fruit of the land? Second, is it possible to separate the subjects into two parties, but maintain a single or comparable result? Third, does the language simply suggest that one is an extension of the other? Are the two parties so closely connected that they are visualized as one? If this is the case, we are dealing with two separate subjects but just one result. On the side of synonymous parallelism is a verse such as Prov 17:17: "A friend loves at all times *and* a brother is born for adversity." Although there is a change in subject, the thought is clearly parallel. Hebrew parallelism allows for a change of subject in parallel thought, thus expressing a single idea in two lines. Sometimes the subject varies in the second clause, sometimes not.[85] Although an old work, I cite the contribution of Keil and Delitszche because of its detailed analysis:

> It is He again who is designated in the parallel clause as the "*fruit of the land*," as being the fruit which the land of Israel, and consequently the earth itself, would produce, just as in Ezek xvii.5, Zedekiah is called a "seed of the earth." The reasons already adduced to show the "the sprout of Jehovah" cannot refer to the blessings of the field, apply with equal force to the "fruit of the earth." This also relates to the Messiah Himself, regarded as the fruit in which all the growth and bloom of this earthly history would eventually reach its promised and divinely appointed conclusion. The use of this double epithet to denote "the coming One" can only be accounted for, without anticipating the New Testament standpoint, from the desire to depict his double-sided origin. He would come, on the one hand, from *Jehovah*; but, on the other hand, from *the earth*, inasmuch as He would spring from Israel.[86]

Although a lengthy citation, I have cited the above for its value in defining the double nature of the prophecy. The Branch will not only be glorious, but the "fruit of the land/earth" will likewise possess glorious qualities. What will describe or happen to the Branch is also ascribed to the fruit of the land.

The word "earth" or "land" (הארץ/*ehretz*) is used over 150 times in Isaiah alone. Since the word can easily bear one of four main definitions, context determines the meaning. *Ehretz* can refer to "country" as in the country of Assyria or Egypt (1:7; 11:16). It can refer to the earth in general as in the "whole earth" (6:3) or "the four corners of the earth" (11:12). This word can also describe the people who live in the land such as the inhabitants of the "land of Zebulun" (9:1). Less significantly perhaps in actual number of translations, the word can also simply describe the ground as, for example, the destitute who "will sit on the ground" (3:26). Admittedly, there are over-lappings. It may be a matter of splitting hairs in certain cases whether earth or land is the more appropriate definition. In some cases they can easily be interchanged. This may be the case in Isa 4:2 where fruit can come from either the earth or the land, or possibly even the ground. Since I am applying this prophetic text as the background for understanding the fourth Gospel, the reference to the land from which the Messiah will sprout is significant. The Gospel of John contains numerous references to such places as: Capernaum (5x), Galilee (17x), Jerusalem (13x), and Nazareth (5x). It is clear that this evangelist wants to situate the life and ministry of Jesus in the land of Israel.

The more critical question in regard to 4:2 is to what extent these words are to be taken figuratively. Is the prophet speaking of literal fruit, such as apples and oranges,

---

85. Isa 53:2 is a case in point: "He grew up before him like a tender shoot, and like a root out of dry ground." There is no ambiguity regarding the subject and the result. The parallelism is perfectly synonymous. The conjunction "and" indicates a single subject. The verb "grew up" is a zeugma yoking together both clauses.

86. C. F. Keil and F. Delitzsch, *Isaiah* (1975) 152.

berries and cherries? If this is the case, then the prophetic forecast is for fairer fruit and happier harvests. Or, is the meaning more figurative and metaphorical, suggesting that this fruit represents something that is produced *like* fruit? As to the second question, it is undeniable that Isaiah often describes the moral condition of Israel as a desert and dry land, suffering from drought and bereft of fruit. A prime example of this usage is the metaphor of the vine in 5:1–7. There Isaiah sings about a "loved one" who had a vineyard and went out looking for good grapes only to find "bad fruit." The parable reaches a climax when, switching from the first person voice of YHWH at v.6, the prophet then says at v.7: "The vineyard of the LORD Almighty is the house of Israel." The metaphor is precisely identified. Accordingly, the textual location of the vineyard parable in 5:1–7 should not be lost. It follows logically, not just spatially, on the heels of 4:2–6 which describe not only the Branch of YHWH but also a remnant surviving the judgment of God.[87] A similar figurative usage is found at 6:13 in which a description is given of a "holy seed" being a stump. The word "seed" (זרע) is singular, indicating an individual which may possibly be a reference to a Messiah. At 11:1 five different words come into play, none of them indicative of literal qualities. There is "shoot" (חטר), "stump" (מגזע), "branch" (נצר), "roots" (משרשיו), and a verb in the future tense, "will bear fruit" (יפרה). Then v.2 says: "The Spirit of the LORD will rest on him." Clearly, the NIV takes this passage as messianic. I see no reason to question the NIV. The NT, in fact, applies the text to Jesus (Rom 15:12).

Proceeding on, the prophet Isaiah also sees a time of bountiful fruit bearing. This fruit, like that of the YHWH Branch, would also be beautiful and glorious. Thus, what characterizes the Branch transfers to the fruit. Childs offers a caveat against taking the passage as literal: "From a strictly philological perspective, the literal rendering of the passage as a promise of renewed fertility and beauty to the land is not wrong. Yet the exalted style of the entire passage warns against a too flat and prosaic interpretation."[88] At 27:6 the prophet says: "In days to come Jacob will take root, Israel will bud and blossom and fill the world with fruit." Further along at 35:1–2, the prophet expands upon this development by means of more metaphorical language: "The desert and the parched land will be glad; the wilderness will rejoice and blossom. *Like* the crocus, it will burst into bloom; it will rejoice greatly and shout for joy. The glory of Lebanon will be given to it, the splendor of Camel and Sharon; they will see the glory of the LORD, the splendor of our God." This is patently figurative language as indicated by the word "like." *Like* the crocus, there will be a bloom. There appears to be a causal connection as people, described in terms of a desert wilderness, will take on glory as they behold glory. This is actually the claim of John 1:14: "We have beheld his glory." By beholding glory, they would then reflect glory.

---

87. E. Jenni, "Remnant," IDB (1962) 4.32 says: "The concept 'remnant' includes, accordingly, not only a destructive but also a constructive meaning. It refers to the judgment passed but at the same time to its merciful limitation by God's free grace."

88. Childs, *Isaiah* (2001) 36.

The entire book of Isaiah makes use of botanical similes, especially applying the notion of some kind of vegetative growth to the future of Israel. Isa 44:3–4 contains similar thought: "I will pour out my Spirit on your offspring, and my blessing on your descendants. They will spring up *like* grass in a meadow, *like* poplar trees by flowing streams." Isa 58:11 says: "You will be *like* a well-watered garden, *like* a spring whose waters never fail." These words are eerily similar to those in John 7:37 ("out of his inner being will flow rivers of living water").

A further text may be noted. At Isa 37:31–32 familiar motifs surface again: "Once more a remnant of the house of Judah will take root below and bear fruit above. For out of Jerusalem will come a remnant and out of Mount Zion a band of survivors. The zeal of the LORD Almighty will accomplish this." This text contains at least three relevant ideas: a remnant of Judah will take root below and bear fruit above; the people or house of Judah will bear fruit; this will happen to the survivors of Israel (this reference to survivors and a remnant anticipates the fifth and final rubric below); this survival and fecundity will occur only as a result of the LORD's intervention. This is unobstructed transparent language, unambiguously applying the metaphor of plant growth and fruit bearing to people. This language mirrors that of the Messiah from Isa 53:4: "He grew up before him *like* a tender shoot, and *like* a root out of dry ground."

J. J. M. Roberts observes how Isaiah's prophetic vision is loaded with words and notions of YHWH's indispensable role in Israel's deliverance: "Isaiah leaves no doubt that the plan and its execution are Yahweh's plan and Yahweh's work."[89] W. Robert Cook aptly observes: "Of the sixty-one times the two terms occur in John's writings only five relate to a being other than God. In all but two of the remaining fifty-six instances the glory is directed toward the Father or the Son. Two exceptions involve believers who may receive glory from God or Christ (John 5:44; 17:22)."[90] The question, of course, at this point is whether the Gospel of John is an appropriate fulfillment of the above passages. My conclusion is that the fourth Gospel provides adequate justification for such a fulfillment claim.[91] Of course, citing scholars who support your case does not thereby establish one's case. The never ending and always present question is: what is the evidence? Thus, a corollary ensues: the fruit of the branch takes on the qualities of the generative branch. Only the Gospel of John contains this kind of reflective imagery in which the disciples mirror the glory of the LORD.

---

89. J. J. M. Roberts, "The Divine King and the Human Community in Isaiah's Vision of the Future," in *The Quest for the Kingdom of God* (1983) 127–36, here 127, and also 129: "The deliverance is portrayed as pure miracle, as due to the direct intervention of Yahweh himself." I note also his conclusion (136): "In Isaiah's vision of the future the initiative belongs to Yahweh."

90. W. Robert Cook, "The 'Glory' Motif in the Johannine Corpus," *JETS* 27.3 (1984) 293.

91. G. K. Beale, "The Old Testament Background of Paul's References to 'the Fruit of the Spirit' in Galatians 5:22," *BBR* 15.1 (2005) 8, claims that the idea of "the Spirit creating fruit that is nonphysical but spiritual in character is a unique idea to Isaiah in all of the OT and to Galatians 5 in the NT." I would have to add the Gospel of John to this list, placing it next to Galatians 5.

The Survivors of Israel

MT: לפליטת ישראל, LXX: τὸ καταλειφθὲν τοῦ Ισραηλ, NIV: "the survivors of Israel."

There are four different words in Isaiah to describe a social or spiritual survivor. The most frequently used word is "remnant" (שאר/*shear*), found nine times.[92] This word can refer to survivors in the foreseeable historical time of the prophet himself. For example, in the text of Isa 10:20–22, the word is found four times in which this composite describes the eventual survival from the Assyrian invasion. Another word translated as "remnant" (שארית/*sheerith*) is found five times.[93] Our word under investigation, as translated by the NIV, is "survivor" (פליטה/*peleta*), used five times.[94] However, the NIV preference for "survivor" may be questioned. *Peleta* is better translated as "rescue" or "deliverance." The word "deliverance" or "rescue" best suits the description for several reasons. First of all, texts outside of Isaiah often describe a rescue or deliverance that is due to an act of God.[95] For example, 2 Chr 12:7 says, "In a little while I will grant them deliverance (*peleta*)." This deliverance is promised by God, yet it must be also said that the LORD is responding to the people's humility. A clearer text is that of Gen 45:7 in which Joseph is speaking to his family: "But God sent me ahead of you to preserve for you a remnant on earth and to save your lives by a great deliverance (*peleta*)." This text distinguishes the real difference between remnant and deliverance. It is God's deliverance which causes the remnant to survive. Texts inside of Isaiah also bear witness to the notion that this deliverance is conditioned upon an act of God. For example, Isa 37:31–32 juxtaposes remnant (*sheerith*) alongside deliverance (*peleta*) and then adds the words: "The zeal of YHWH will accomplish this." Thus, V. Herntrich in the *TDNT* states: "The remnant has its origin, not in the quality of those saved, but in the saving action of God."[96] Hence, the survivors compose a remnant like miners rescued from a cave-in, like a child rescued after falling into a deep well, or like trapped office workers rescued from a burning building. Without the aid of outside help there would be no escape and no surviving. The word "escape" or "survive" can imply human ingenuity, the fortitude not to give up, and fortuitous circumstances. In biblical thought, however, the notion of deliverance goes beyond mere human ability and accents the notion of divine help from an independent and gracious agent, namely YHWH.

---

92. Isa 10:20, 21, 21, 22; 11:11, 16; 14:22; 16:14; 17:3; 37:31.

93. Isa 14:30; 15:9; 37:4, 32; 46:3.

94. Isa 4:2; 15:9.

95. Victor Hamilton, "פליטה," *Theological Wordbook of the Old Testament* (1980) 2.725, states: "But those who have escaped do not owe their survival to fortuitous circumstances or luck. Their survival is only of God's mercy."

96. V. Herntrich, "λεῖμμα," *TDNT* (1967) 4.203. Herntrich never deviates from this major premise. See also (206): "If the establishment of the remnant has its basis in the gracious action of God, the conversion of men cannot be the essential presupposition for the existence of a remnant." See also (208): "If the remnant is constituted by the act of God, it is still an entity within the world."

A key question, however, involves the time that this deliverance would occur. It is clear that Isaiah foresaw in the not too distant future a national calamity befalling Israel due to her unfaithfulness to YHWH. This catastrophic event would come in the form of foreign aggression from her enemy Assyria. The biblical background for this assault can be traced through 2 Kgs 17–18 and the hostile activities of Shalmaneser and Sennacherib. But the prophet was also given assurance that a remnant of Israel would survive this national disaster. The greater question, then, is whether there is a secondary deliverance forthcoming in a yet more distant future. Although this question often yields a divided jury, I must state my own conviction: texts such as Isa 11:1–12 contain supporting references not only to a stump or branch arising from the seed of Jesse, but the text also contains the promise that "in that day" the LORD will reach out a *second* time to rescue and reclaim his remnant from all over the earth. This deliverance, in slightly different language but in similar thought, could be construed from the text of John 1:11–12: "He came to that which was his own, but his own did not receive him. Yet to all who received him, to those who believed in his name, he gave the right to become children of God." Sir Edwyn Hoskyns describes this double-edged event as a split between "where the Jews once stood and did not apprehend, and where Abraham and Isaiah once stood and did apprehend."[97] C. H. Dodd graphically depicts this polarization:

> In this gospel it is fundamental that the impact of the incarnate Logos upon the world sifts men, and selects, through their actual response, those who are given ἐξουσίαν τέκνα θεοῦ γενέσθαι ("authority to become children of God"). From one point of view, indeed, the whole story of the ministry in chs. ii–xii is a story of sifting and selection, which results in the appearance in chs. xiii–xvii of a small body of men "cleansed" by Christ's word and united to Him.[98]

B. F. Westcott, interpreting the fourth Gospel from the viewpoint of an already destroyed Jerusalem, a no longer functioning Temple system, and the Jewish race in ruins, offers this reading of the Gospel of John:

> The task of the Evangelist was to unfold the essential causes of the catastrophe, which were significant for all time, and to shew that even through apparent ruin and failure the will of God found fulfillment. Inexorable facts had revealed the rejection of the Jews. It remained to shew that this rejection was not only foreseen, but was also morally inevitable, and that it involved no fatal loss .... The true people of God survived the ruin of the Jews.[99]

---

97. E. C. Hoskyns, *The Fourth Gospel* (1947) 49.
98. C. H. Dodd, *According to the Scriptures* (1953) 353.
99. B. F. Westcott, *The Gospel according to St. John* (1881) xxxviii. For a defense of the hypothesis that the destruction of the Temple served as the occasion for the writing of the Gospel of John, see Andreas J. Köstenberger, "The Destruction of the Second Temple and the Composition of the Fourth Gospel," *TRINJ* 26 (2005) 205–42. See also J. Louis Martyn, "A Gentile Mission that Replaced an Earlier Jewish Mission?" in *Exploring the Gospel of John* (1996) 134, in which he refers to the "massive Jewish unbelief" in the Gospel of John.

Westcott's over view does not oversimplify the facts. The fourth Gospel provides assurance of the ongoing survival of the people of God as a remnant.

The Absence of a Genealogy

For a final time we turn to the issue of genealogy. Why does John omit any reference to the family tree of Jesus? All three synoptic Gospels, Matthew (10x), Mark (3x), and Luke (2x) contain incidents in which needy people call upon Jesus as the "Son of David." The Gospel of John contains no such events. Why is Jesus not addressed as the "Son of David" in John? Robert M. Grant, in his discussion of Origen's exegetical method, frames the issue:

> Everyone was aware that John does not have a genealogy of Jesus or describe his temptation. How was this difference to be explained? Origen insists upon considering the purpose the fourth evangelist had in mind when he wrote. John began his gospel with God, and as a divine being Jesus had no genealogy .... Here we seem to be on the edge of a neat explanation of this difference between the synoptics and John. The synoptics describe Jesus as a man; John describes him as God.[100]

Conclusion

George L. Parsenios has sketched a new way of approaching the fourth Gospel. Instead of seeking clues to the narrative technique of the fourth evangelist in the concerns of the Johannine community, Parsenios pursues an approach that is based upon models from Greek drama. He concludes his investigation on this note: "We can identify with greater certainty, however, a basic symmetry between the presentation of death in Greek tragedy and the presentation of the glorification and resurrection of Jesus in the fourth Gospel."[101] Parsenios acknowledges that his approach is not without some risk. He disclaims, however, a presumption to be able to identify "a debt to a particular work. The intention is not to say that John follows this or that author, but that the Fourth Gospel was influenced by broadly used tropes that were readily available."[102] In a similar fashion Christopher M. Tuckett writes of the techniques in the composition of the fourth Gospel:

---

100. R. M. Grant, *The Earliest Lives of Jesus* (1961) 62. Grant then proceeds to disclaim this explanation as "neat" by taking the reader off in a completely different direction. This evasive tactic does not allow Grant to come to terms with John's assertion about the purpose of the fourth Gospel. There is one exception: John 19:5 has Pilate saying to the crowd: ἰδοὺ ὁ ἄνθρωπος.

101. G. Parsenios, "'No Longer in the World' (John 17:11): The Transformation of the Tragic in the Fourth Gospel," *HTR* 98.1 (2005) 21. For a mediating view placing the fourth Gospel as a combination between bio and drama, see R. Alan Culpepper, "The Plot of John's Story of Jesus," *Int* 49 (1995) 356: "The Gospel of John, therefore, is an ancient biography in dramatic form."

102. Parsenios, "No Longer in the World" (2005) 3.

> But for the most part, the considerably developed presentation of John, with the greatly heightened Christology, is thought to reflect primarily a remolding of the Jesus tradition by a later Christian writer. Such remolding undoubtedly reveals the work of a Christian writer of extraordinary depth and profundity. But it is primarily the evangelist's own grasp of the truth of the Christian claims about Jesus that we see reflected in the Fourth Gospel and not so much the teaching of the pre-Easter Jesus.[103]

The above quotation is typical scholarly discourse on how the fourth evangelist writes this Gospel.[104] The emphasis in Tuckett's explanation falls not upon accurate reporting of something Jesus said or did, or even something revealed by the Spirit but, rather, something later reflected upon. It is "the evangelist's own grasp of the truth" that is highlighted. Consistent with the above approach for the other three evangelists, I would like to offer a different alternative. When we turn to consider the central theme of John, we find a set of facts that fits coherently into the possibility of divine revelation and a fourth Branch.

What is needed is an explanatory principle that will intelligently account for both the origin and the variations within the Jesus tradition.[105] What are we to conclude from the fact that we have four distinct Gospels evidencing connections with OT texts and metaphors without mentioning such texts? Also, if these four evangelists had specifically cited Jesus as the King, Servant, Man/Priest, and LORD God Branch, this might have indicated a conscious and deliberate effort on their part to participate in a conspiracy of literary collusion. Or, alternately, if they were writing completely independent of one another yet citing Branch passages, this would give rise to the criticism that they were simply retrojecting these ideas back into their texts. Having now suggested the possibility of a literary conspiracy, what is the likelihood that there was a conspiracy of silence among the four not to mention the aforementioned four prophetic texts, neither their own names, nor the names of the other evangelists? The absence of such references, however, is an invitation to inquire into the dynamics of their compositions. A frequent and longstanding claim among NT scholars is that many of the sayings of Jesus are no more than formulations created by the church, not actual statements from Jesus himself.

---

103. C. M. Tuckett, "Jesus and the Gospels" *The New Interpreter's Bible* (1995) 8.74. For a similar conclusion, see also Eric Lane Titus, "The Fourth Gospel and the Historical Jesus," in *Jesus and the Historian* (1968) 9 99: "It is not a mere reflection of the so-called Christ of faith; it is, rather, the result of profound reflection on the total event of Christ."

104. See also Ernst Käsemann, *Essays on New Testament Themes* (1971) 22.

105. Bengt Holmberg, "Questions of Method in James Dunn's *Jesus* Remembered," *JSNT* 26.4 (2004) 451: "So, we begin with data and arrive at facts, through a process of interpretation. Data have to be interpreted, that is, selected, construed, put together in a pattern that makes them meaningful, and so become historical facts. This is not a random process, however. There are scores of theoretically thinkable or possible patterns, which when screened through filters of historical verification are narrowed down to a few plausible or reasonable hypotheses about how these data are to be related to each other. The historian's task is to falsify all hypotheses, one by one, until one of them cannot be refuted, that is to say, is verified as a probable answer to the historical question."

The argument of this book proposes a different interpretative path: these four textual sublayers undergird the four Gospels with an underpinning that adequately explains the unique composition not just of John but also Matthew, Mark, and Luke.

A look back at how each Gospel begins their narrative may reinforce the conclusion of the above paragraph. Matthew *opens* his Gospel with the first two chapters being a juxtaposition of Jesus as a righteous king set against the background of the unrighteous King Herod. This contrast in righteousness hints at Jesus fulfilling the King Branch prophecy of Jer 23:5–6, especially as an antithesis to the unrighteous King Zedekiah. Mark then offers a contrast in spatial and thematic settings. Rather than starting with the conflict between Jesus and Herod, Mark *opens* his Gospel in the wilderness, away from the drama of a political intrigue. By doing so, Mark suggests a possible mnemonic reminder of ancient Israel's entrance and journey into the wilderness.[106] As Israel was to become a servant in the wilderness, so now Jesus, likewise in the wilderness, fulfills the Servant Branch prophecy of Zech 3:8. Luke *begins* by offering a further complementary contrast. By stringing together a narrative sequence of priestly associations (references to temple, priests, priestly functions, and the priesthood), Luke makes it possible to see Jesus as fulfilling the Man/Priest Branch prophecy of Zechariah 6:12–13. The Gospel of John *begins* yet in another supplementary way. Starting at the "beginning" with Jesus alongside the Father before the creation of the world, John takes the reader back before time. Jesus then enters the world in order to reveal the glory of God (1:14; 17:5). This astounding claim echoes the LORD God Branch of Isa 4:2 with its striking emphasis on glory. The fourth Gospel thus completes the fourfold prophetic image of Jesus as the foretold *Zemah* of ancient Israel. These programmatic chapter openings, rather than being discordant and clashing, present a coherent case for linking them to the four prophetic Branches of this study.

---

106. A digression here may be helpful without being a distraction to the reader. Mark 1:10 describes the heavens as being "torn" (σχίζω) as Jesus parts the waters. Mark is the only evangelist to mention this tearing or renting of the heavens. By placing this event in its rightful and specific context, an attractive connection becomes possible. This baptismal event and the accompanying divine voice punctuated, as it were, by the tearing of the heavens, occur in the wilderness. The word "wilderness" (ἔρημος) is mentioned a total of six times in chapter 1, making it the central place of action. This place of solitude, away from the intrigue of Matthew 2 and the temple activity of Luke 1, is a clear contrast to the first chapters of both Matthew and Luke. But why would Mark begin his Gospel in this manner? The following associations may provide a plausible explanation. Just as God broke into history *in the wilderness* (Exod 14:11–13) by "splitting" the sea (Exod 14:21, LXX: σχίζω), so now in the baptism of Jesus which also occurs *in the wilderness*, God breaks in with a supernatural voice that splits or tears open the heavens and inaugurates the Son's ministry of servanthood. By virtue of crossing the sea and leaving behind the land of Egypt and entering the wilderness, Israel became a servant of YHWH. As Lev 25:55 says: "For it is to me that the people of Israel are *servants*. They are my *servants* whom I brought out of the land of Egypt." Thus, we have the allusional motifs of wilderness, tearing and splitting, combined with the theme of servanthood replicated in the life of Jesus.

11

Rev 4:6–7 and the Four Living Beings around the Throne

VARIOUS ATTEMPTS HAVE BEEN made to explain the multi-faceted picture of Jesus from the four Gospels in terms of *aspect*. Three recent studies may serve as appropriate examples of aspect in that these respective book titles employ the language of "faces,"[1] "images,"[2] or "contours."[3] This gallery of scholarly portraits has one thing in common as it relates to the present investigation—none of them suggests a connection to the four living Beings in Rev 4:7.[4] In other words, current scholarship declines to see a connection between the four living Beings and the fourfold Gospel. Although Christian art has taken the step to identify the fourfold Gospel with the four living Beings of Rev 4:6–7,[5] I can find no one who has presented a scholarly and critical argument showing the unified and coherent relationship between the fourfold Gospel and the living Beings of Rev 4:6–7. Scholarly consensus eschews such a daring and provocative identification.[6]

1. Ben Witherington, *The Many Faces of the Christ* (1998).

2. See especially Craig A. Evans, "Images of Christ in the Canonical and Apocryphal Gospels," in *Images of Christ: Ancient and Modern* (1997) 34–72; and James H. Charlesworth, "Jesus Research Expands with Chaotic Creativity," in *Images of Jesus Today* (1994) 1–41.

3. For example, see the collection of essays edited by Richard N. Longenecker in *Contours of Christology in the New Testament* (2005).

4. See Paula Fredriksen, *From Jesus to Christ: The Origins of the New Testament Images of Jesus* (2000, reprint from 1988). I note also that the *Dictionary of New Testament Background* edited by Craig A. Evans and Stanley E. Porter (2000) does not list the text of Rev 4:6–7 in the Scripture Index.

5. I note the recent book by Daniel J. Harrington, *The Synoptic Gospels Set Free* (2008). The front cover is eye-catching because of the art work and its connection to the synoptic Gospels. There is a composite of a threefold portrait of a lion, an ox, and a man. Harrington, however, makes no attempt at identifying these artistic conceptions with a coherent substructure as proposed in this investigation. See also the comment by William Barclay in his *The Gospel of John* (1976) 1: "Very often on stained glass windows and the like, the gospel writers are represented in symbol by the figures of the four beasts whom the writer of the *Revelation* saw around the throne (*Revelation* 4.7)." A good example of the actual art work in the USA is the chapel at the University of the South in Sewanee, Tennessee.

6. A lone exception is the popular work by Richard Burridge in his monograph *Four Gospels, One Jesus?* (1994) 23–32. Burridge followed up this work with a collaborative effort: Richard A. Burridge and Graham Gould, *Jesus Now and Then* (2004) 53–68. This work is clearly aimed at a more popular reading market as Burridge plays with these images in order to bring out *symbolically* the various

For example, Ben Witherington, in his book entitled *The Many Faces of the Christ* (1998), does not list either Rev 4:7 or Irenaeus' *Against Heresies* in his Index of Ancient Sources. In his second work, a commentary on Revelation, Witherington makes this disclaimer even stronger, adamantly stating that the four Gospels cannot be equated with the four living Beings. He maintains that these living creatures should "be seen as heavenly archetypes of the whole of the animate creation."[7] Robert H. Mounce occupies a similar position: "All attempts to equate the living creatures with the four gospels are groundless."[8] Likewise, Mounce suggests that the four living ones could represent animate creation. Henry Barclay Swete uses comparable language when he faults the equation of the four living Beings with the four Gospels as an "unfortunate identification."[9] R. H. Charles responds to Irenaeus's identification of the four living Beings with the four Gospels by saying: "Such identifications, though popular in the early Church, and indeed in later times, are wholly fanciful."[10] A significant number of outstanding commentaries on Revelation casually dismiss a connection between the four living Beings and the four canonical Gospels.[11] This is done in spite of the testimony of the early church. Yet no concrete reason for such dismissal is given other than such a view is fanciful. The word "fanciful" is not an exegetically appropriate word. (I will return to this point later.) The purpose of this chapter is to challenge the dismissive criticism which separates the four living Beings from the fourfold Gospel.

As we momentarily shift the discussion from what the four living Beings are not to what they could possibly represent, William Hendricksen takes a less polemic position simply championing the intermediate idea of human-like qualities: "the 'living ones' are described as being in strength like *lion*, in ability to render service like the *ox*, in intelligence like *man*—noticing also their many eyes, indicating intellectual penetration, and in swiftness like the *eagle*, ever ready to obey God's commandments and to render service."[12] Swete also identifies the four living ones with "whatever is noblest, strongest, wisest, and swiftest in animate Nature."[13] David Aune, in connecting Rev 4:7 with Ezekiel 1 and 10, identifies the living ones as angelic creatures. After

---

dispositions of Jesus, as he says (p. 54): "When I was looking for a way to help people get a clearer picture of the four pictures of Jesus, I played with these images." Although Graham Gould is included in the title, Burridge writes in the first person up to p. 108. A transition occurs at p. 113 with the first reference to "we."

7. B. Witherington, *Revelation* (2003) 118. This view is also espoused by Ray Summers, *Worthy Is the Lamb* (1951) 133.

8. R. M. Mounce, *The Book of Revelation* (1977) 138.

9. H. B. Swete, *The Apocalypse of St. John* (1908) 72.

10. R. H. Charles, *A Critical and Exegetical Commentary on the Revelation of St. John* (1920) 1.124. See also the comment by Grant R. Osborne, *Revelation* (2002) 233, who also labels this view as fanciful.

11. For example, G. K. Beale, in his commentary *The Book of Revelation* (1999) 329, states: "Some early Fathers speculated without exegetical support that the beings represented the four Gospel writers."

12. W. Hendricksen, *More than Conquerors* (1963) 107. See also BADG, 431.

13. Swete, *The Apocalypse* (1908) 72.

surveying the vast literature on the subject, he offers the following linguistic conclusion: "In Ezek 1–3 the term חיות *hayyôt* is a vague, general term for living creatures ... In Ezek 10:20, the חיות *hayyôt*, 'living creatures' are explicitly identified as *kerubim*, 'cherubim'..."[14] It is not clear, however, in what precise way—if any—does a living Being differ from an angel.[15] Perhaps it does not matter. Both images partake of some heavenly essence, although the four living Beings do appear to be of a higher station in rank than the angels. Evidence of such a higher rank can be seen from the heavenly scene of Rev 7.11 which states that "all the angels" (καὶ πάντες οἱ ἄγγελοι) were standing around the throne, the Elders, and the four living Beings. This description places all the angels in a grouping by themselves, and this group is separated from the four living Beings. If we join together the exegetical views of Hendrickson and Aune, we arrive at a combination of human and divine elements—a melding that is not far removed from the composite of Jesus as presented in the fourfold Gospel.

Yet, as stated above, commentaries do not advocate a linkage between the four living Beings of Rev 4:7 and the four canonical Gospels. Leon Morris issues the following cautionary warning: "We can safely say, in view of their closeness to the throne, that these are the most important of created beings, even that they stand in some way for the whole of creation. But it is hazardous to say more."[16] Does this cautionary statement tie the hands of the interpreter? Caution, indeed, should motivate careful investigation but it should not inhibit further reflection. Is it, therefore, possible to proceed safely any farther? It is the position taken here that the text yields up more than it is given credit for. M. Eugene Boring may serve as both a summary position and a bridge or springboard to advance the discussion: "This scene is the theological fountainhead and anchor point for the whole document."[17] He elaborates:

> Around the throne are four living creatures. Their descriptions are a collage of details from Ezekiel 1 and Isaiah 6, both of which draw upon the traditional picture of the cherubim. The Israelites adopted this imagery from the winged bull or similar mythological animals that figured in Mesopotamian and Canaanite mythology as guardians of the throne of both heavenly and earthly kings. John is not interested in (or even aware of) the sources of this imagery. He is concerned with what they represent. Here we have represented before

---

14. D. Aune, *Revelation 1–5* (1982) 297. See also Rudolf Bultmann, "ζῷον," *TDNT* (1964) 2.873, who states that the word ζῷον can describe either humans or animals. He refers to Jude 10 and 2 Pet 2:12 and says, "Only where there is express emphasis on the animal level to which heretical teachers have sunk do we have ἄλογα ζῷα." In his final analysis, Bultmann prefers an identification of the living Beings as angels. Another representative of the angelic position is Margaret Barker, *The Revelation of Jesus Christ* (2000) 118–23. She makes no attempt to assign priority to either the four Living Beings or the twenty-four Elders.

15. Ned B. Stonehouse, "Elders and Living-Beings in the Apocalypse," in *Paul before the Areopagus and other New Testament Studies* (1957) 106, prefers to separate the four living Beings from angels, placing them above the angels.

16. L. Morris, *Revelation* (1969) 90.

17. M. E. Boring, *Revelation* (1989) 102.

the heavenly throne all categories of animal life, the whole animal kingdom of God's creation: wild animals, domestic animals, human beings, and birds.[18]

In view of Boring's suggestion, the following pictorial application in a collection of essays edited by Jack Dean Kingsbury is both insightful as well as puzzling. Kingsbury introduces each section or "part opening" by a symbol from the title page by Hans Holbein the Younger, from the print shop of Adam Petri, Basle, ca. 1524, plate 61 in Albert Fidelis Butsch, *Handbook of Renaissance Ornament* (1969).[19] Kingsbury does not adopt the order as given either by Irenaeus or Rev 4:7. He pictures the lion as representing Mark and the ox as representing Luke. Richard Burridge does the same thing.[20] As I will argue, this is a mistake. Given the present canonical order of the Gospels, the preferred order should be lion for Matthew, ox for Mark, man for Luke, eagle for John. But first, there are other issues to face.

An Exegetical Look at Rev 4:6–7

Is the above summary sufficient? Has anything of vital importance been left out? The following analysis may serve to fill out possible missing gaps. Although efforts have been made to consign the Ezekiel vision to an origin within Canaanite religion,[21] this assumes an iconic borrowing by an aniconic prophetic culture—a difficult premise to prove. The vision in Revelation would likely be even less explainable in terms of borrowing from the cultural world of iconography.[22] I can find no evidence outside the biblical text for iconic figures in a fourfold composite of lion, ox, man, and eagle.[23] In other words, this fourfold vision is not indebted to Canaanite imagery. Alfred Loisy, taking the discussion to the level of astrology, argues that the four do not represent the qualities of divinity but, rather, the four quadrants of the Zodiac.[24] This, I believe, is also a faulty identification, providing no hope for understanding the imagery.

---

18. Ibid., 107. For the view that Rev 4.6–7 is indebted to and dependent upon mythology, see Steven J. Friesen, *Imperial Cults and the Apocalypse of John: Reading Revelation in the Ruins* (2001), esp. his chapter "Working with Myth" (167–79).

19. J. D. Kingsbury, *Gospel Interpretation: Narrative-Critical & Social-Scientific Approaches* (1997) iv, 8, 63, 123, and 179.

20. R. A. Burridge and Graham Gould, *Jesus Now and Then* (2004) 53–68.

21. See J. Edward Wright, "Biblical Versus Israelite Images of the Heavenly Realm," *JSOT* 93 (2001) 59–75, who endeavors to tie the heavenly vision of Ezekiel to Israel's neighbors in the ancient Near East.

22. For the view that historians of religion have ignored iconography at their own peril, see T. J. Lewis, "Syro-Palestinian Iconography and Divine Image," in *Cult Image and Divine Representation in the Ancient Near East* (2005) 70.

23. Othmar Keel, *The Symbolism of the Biblical World: Ancient Near Eastern Iconography and the Book of Psalms* (1978) 85–89, focuses upon the lion, the bull, the bear, the serpent, and the dog. Although the eagle is mentioned in Psa 103:5, Keel does not treat this majestic creature.

24. A. Loisy, *L'Apocalypse de Jean* (1923) 125: "L'identification des quatre Vivants fournirait-elle la solution de l'énigme? Le premier Vivant ressemble à un lion; et ce doit être le Lion zodiacal; le second

The Order of the Living Beings. A comparison between the two texts of Ezekiel and Revelation reveals slight differences.[25] Moving in a clock-wise direction, Ezekiel's vision shows the order as: man, lion, ox, and eagle. Revelation, however, presents the order as: lion, ox, man, eagle. Only the eagle in the fourth spot remains constant; the other three are scrambled. Revelation is more precise in stating the exact sequence by adding the numerical order: *first* lion, *second* ox, *third* man, and *fourth* eagle. This systematic and itemized sequence is the order of the fourfold Gospel as handed down to us. Yet a question arises: why the change in order? An easy answer does not seem forthcoming. What is significant, though, is the obvious fact that John adds the qualifying sequential numerical order: first, second, third, and fourth. To further add to this mysterious mix is the description in Num 2:3 of the camp arrangement of ancient Israel. Judah is mentioned *first* in the configuration. Upon breaking camp, Judah sets out *first*. Also, its position faces eastward. Furthermore, of the twelve tribes, only four carry a standard. It is tempting to think that Judah's standard is the image of a lion.

The most telling characteristic against the view of an animate creation is the order: lion, ox, man, eagle. If, for example, the model was based upon the order of creation as presented in Genesis 1, a more logical sequence would be: eagle (created on day five), ox and lion (created on the early part of day six), then man (created at the end of day six). Consequently, man would be placed in the position as the climax or crown of creation. But this is not the order of Rev 4:7. Man, instead of occupying the preeminent position as in Genesis 1, takes up the third position in this vision. In terms of the biblical tradition, this makes no sense, unless something deeper is involved.

There is yet another element to this heavenly image worth exploring. Three of the four images are described as *like* a lion, *like* an ox, *like* an eagle. The word "like" invites the reader to view these images not as literal animals but only as figurative representations, perhaps pointing to inner character qualities.[26] These figures also suggest qualities for which the images are noted in the natural world: characteristics of royalty, servanthood, humanity, and majesty. The text of Rev 4:7 uses the expression "full of eyes" (γέμοντα ὀφθαλμῶν) to describe the lion, the ox, and the eagle. The third image in the sequence is described in Greek with the word "face" (πρόσωπον). This is the "face" of a *man*. Thus the three animals are not depicted with the word "face" but are

---

à un taureau, autre signe du zodiacal ..." See O. Michel's response in the *TDNT*, "μόσχος," (1967) 4:760, to the argument by A. Jeremias (*Das AT im Lichte des Alten Orients* [1930] 699ff.) that the four living creatures correspond to the signs of the zodiac. Michel concludes that such an identification is "very doubtful."

25. For a more expanded list of differences, see Christopher Roland, *The Open Heaven: A Study of Apocalyptic in Judaism and Early Christianity* (1982) 223; and Steve Moyise, *The Old Testament in the Book of Revelation* (1995) 69.

26. For an interesting comparison between animal and human, see Wolfgang Schadewaldt, "The Reliability of the Synoptic Tradition," in Martin Hengel's *Studies in the Gospel of Mark* (1985) 95: "Animals are truer to nature than human beings."

pictured as having many eyes. Only the image of the man has a face.[27] In other words, it is the image of a human face. Neither the lion nor the ox is shown as doing anything; the eagle alone is represented as flying.

We must not hurry past the picture of this flying eagle. Other than the fact the eagle is a bird, why show the eagle in the act of flying? Several reasons may explain the image. First, perhaps the imagery of flight is intended to suggest an elevated or exalted status.[28] As God is above all things, so the eagle is not only above the natural creation but also above the other three images of lion, ox, and man. Second, all four images are pictured with the ability to move. They can speak and they can bow down (7:11). This would suggest that they are not mere ornaments engraved on the throne. Of the four living Beings the eagle has the greatest movement of all as it is pictured in flight.

THE SYMBOLIC SIGNIFICANCE OF THE NUMBER FOUR. As we look deeper into the details of this text, we can count the total number of times the four living Beings are mentioned in Revelation as seventeen references.[29] Of these seventeen occasions, twelve are of a composite nature containing all four images together. Only Rev 6:1, 3, 5, 6–7; and 15:7 separates them out individually. When this breakout occurs, with the exception of 15:7, all four are mentioned specifically and all four have an active role in subsequent events of that chapter. The isolated case of 15:7 does not appear significant.

What, if any, is the symbolic significance of the number four? Richard Bauckham argues that in the book of Revelation four is the symbol of the number of the world.[30] He cites the following verses and facts: the earth has four corners (7:1; 20:8) and four winds (7:1); the created world has the four divisions of land, sea, rivers, and sky (5:13; 8:7–12; 14:7; 16:2–9). Bauckham's array of texts is rather compelling. Is his presentation of the data all-inclusive? Has he constructed an airtight compartment permitting no escape? First of all, the number four as used in Revelation describes more than earthly phenomena. The number four is also utilized to describe heavenly realities. Heavenly references in Revelation employ the number four in the following telling

---

27. For a different image, see Ben Witherington, *The Many Faces of the Christ* (1998) 3. Although the title of his book gives indications that the author will pursue the images of Rev 4:7, this is not the case. Witherington, rather, expands his treatment with a different metaphor: "like light shining through a prism, reflections on the man who fits no one formula produced a variety of colors and depths of shade that cannot and should not all be blended today into some sort of monochromatic image." Therefore, I do agree with his basic principle—Jesus cannot be confined to or captured by one single portrait. Indeed, the four Gospels do not present Jesus in a "monochromatic image."

28. W. Hendricksen, *More than Conquerors* (1963) 105, suggests that these Beings are "living ones," not beasts, brutes, or creatures. French translations likewise prefer *Vivantes*.

29. Rev 4:6, 7, 8, 9; 5:6, 8, 11, 14; 6:1, 3, 5, 6, 7; 7:11; 14:3; 15:7; and 19:4 make up a total of seventeen references, either collective or individual.

30. R. Bauckham, *The Climax of Prophecy* (1993) 31. Ian Boxall also is an advocate of this position. See his *The Revelation of St John* (2006) 90: "*Four* is often associated with the earthly created order, built into its very structure." Boxall also proposes that we understand four as "the number of the universe" (85) and "the totality of God's created order" (87).

list: a fourfold *doxology* offered to God and the Lamb (5:13), the four *angels* standing at the four corners of the earth (7:1), and the voice or sound coming from the four horns of the *altar* before God (9:13).[31] This ledger of items does not support the view which would confine the number four solely to aspects of the natural world. These angels and altars are not earthly but heavenly. The greatest omission by Bauckham, however, is that of Rev 21:16 which describes the holy city—new Jerusalem—coming down out of heaven shining with the glory of God and possessing *four* equal sides.[32] In this context, Gustav Stählin in the *TDNT* contends that the equality of the four sides is a "sign of perfection."[33] Perfection may indeed be an entirely reasonable extrapolation from this vision. An equally attractive option is that of completion. The abstract term "completion" suggests that nothing essential is missing. In the book of Revelation, the number four is often used in multiples of four (12, 24, 144, and 144,000) to indicate a complete condition of things in heaven: people, nations, the dimensions of the holy city, its foundations, and its gates. It is unreasonable to conclude that the number four is exclusively tied to the created world. It can justifiably symbolize completeness in the heavenly realm. By extension, the notion of four Gospels suggests completion not competition.

The Relationship between the Four and the Twenty-Four. These four living Beings are frequently mentioned in conjunction with twenty-four Elders.[34] What is the relationship between the four and the twenty-four? It is tempting to conclude that we are to interpret the twenty-four by the reference in Rev 21 as being a representation of the twelve tribes and the twelve apostles. Although A. Feuillet argues that the twenty-four were a picture of OT saints,[35] his arguments are not strong enough to dislodge the impression that this number is a composite of both OT and NT symbolic figures.[36] The term "Elders" could certainly symbolize the OT patriarchs but can this term also symbolize the twelve apostles? Inasmuch as Peter (1 Pet 5:1) refers to himself as an

---

31. Bruce Metzger, *A Textual Commentary on the Greek New Testament* (1971) 744, says: "The weight of the external evidence for the presence and for the absence of τεσσάρων is almost evenly balanced." The word is included in the United Bible Society Greek New Testament but enclosed in brackets. It is likely that the omission may be attributed to ellipsis owing to the OT description of the altar as having four horns. (Exod 38:2 refers to the horns upon the four corners of the altar.) The Vulgate has *ex quattor cornibus altais aurei*.

32. When used in compounds, τέσσαρες becomes τετρα-/tetra-.

33. G. Stählin, "ἰσός," *TDNT* (1965) 3.344.

34. The twenty-four Elders as a group are mentioned at 4:4, 10; 5:8; 11:16; and 19:4. With the exception of 11:16, the four living Beings are mentioned with them.

35. A. Feuillet, "Les vingt-quatre vieillards de l'Apocalypse," *RB* 65 (1958) 5: "Nous croyons que les personages en question ne sont pas des anges, mais des hommes rachetés, et plus spécialement des saints de l'Ancient Testament, les ancêtres des chrétiens dans la foi." Feuillet is concerned primarily to demonstrate that these figures are not angels. Indeed, they are never specifically identified as angels and, consequently, should not be labeled as such.

36. For a literal interpretation of the twenty-four creatures as real human beings, see Henry M. Morris, *The Revelation Record* (1983) 89.

elder, and John (2 John) also refers to himself as an elder (if he is the author), this terminology may be a suitable substitute for an apostle. Günther Bornkamm raised serious questions about this identification.[37] Bornkamm presented a threefold case arguing that these Elders are: 1) God's council of heavenly elders,[38] 2) not redeemed and transformed men,[39] and 3) a "higher class of angels."[40] I view all three points as valuable contributions to this investigation; indeed, they are perhaps unassailable. This final point is significant as it potentially elevates these Elders to a place of prominence above the angels.

Abraham Kuyper, in making an enticing case that the twenty-four Elders occupy a greater place of preeminence than do the four living Beings, says: "Evidently these four beasts are far inferior in order of rank and importance to the afore-named Presbyters, and as will appear from a closer examination of the 'beasts' themselves, this inferiority of rank goes further than superficially one would think."[41] Kuyper bases his analysis upon the fact the four living Beings are not said to wear crowns and that the Elders are placed closer to the throne than the beasts or creatures. On his first point there is no objection. It is true that the four living Beings are never pictured as wearing a crown. Since they do not wear a crown, they cannot throw down their crowns. Is there significance to this pictorial absence? I would argue that this absent imagery of not possessing a crown conveys the notion that they do not experience a temporary loss of power and authority. Kuyper's second point is without convincing proof. The text of Rev 4:6–10 indicates, in fact, just the opposite: the living Beings are not only around the throne but in the midst of it.

Larry Hurtado also champions the priority of the twenty-four Elders over the four living Beings. He places the twenty-four second only to the throne of God itself and offers the following two reasons for his interpretation: 1) the Elders are a "new and unparalleled group before the throne,"[42] and 2) the presence of the Elders "constitutes a major feature of the vision."[43] Hence, he elevates their value over the four living Beings on the basis of their cumulative weight of novelty and number of references.

---

37. G. Bornkamm, "πρεσβύτερος," *TDNT* (1968) 6.668–70.

38. Bornkamm (668) refers the reader to Isa 24:23 which mentions the presence of elders as likely part of a heavenly council.

39. Bornkamm (668) cites Rev 14:1–5 as evidence distinguishing these Elders from humans.

40. Ibid., (668): "But they are so only as a higher class of angels which is closer to the throne of God than the others and which is entrusted in a peculiar way with His secrets." Unfortunately, Bornkamm also suggests the possibility that the twenty-four are borrowed figures from astral ideas.

41. A. Kuyper, *The Revelation of St. John* (1963) 64.

42. L. Hurtado, "Revelation 4–5 in the Light of Jewish Apocalyptic Analogies," *JSNT* 25 (1985) 111: "the twenty-four elders represent a distinctive feature of the scene, not being found in any example of Jewish apocalyptic visions of heaven. But not only are the twenty-four elders a distinctive element in the author's vision, there are indications that they are a most important element."

43. Ibid., 113.

Hurtado eventually identifies the significance of these Elders as representatives of the elect. In this sense, he agrees with R. H. Charles.[44]

Looking Further into this Complex Relationship

Inasmuch as the premise of this chapter is the assertion that the four living Beings can represent the four canonical Gospels, has anything in this investigation been said so far that would justify such an interpretation? I must be candid and acknowledge that at this point conclusive evidence is still lacking. G. B. Caird even adds to this state of uncertainty by acknowledging his own personal doubts about their actual purpose.[45] This mysterious mélange of bird, human, and the two animals—one domestic, the other wild—has provoked an assortment of very diverse interpretations. It is a safe assumption that there is intention of some kind behind the symbolism. What could the symbolism mean? Can anything be advanced on a further scale that would solidify the proposed identification of the four living Beings with the four Gospels? Five additional lines of evidence within this rubric are hereby developed in support of the above thesis.

THE CONCENTRIC CONFIGURATIONS. In the section above, we looked at the sequential order of lion, ox, man, and eagle. In this present section we will explore a second kind of symmetrical order: concentricity. The clear impression this scene leaves is one of ever expanding circles. In order, these circles are: throne, four living Beings, the twenty-four Elders, and then angels. As if in ring-like fashion, each entity is encircled by a larger ring. Also, this increasing expansion moves from a single throne, to four living Beings, to the twenty-four Elders, to the even larger multitude of angels. Looking at the concentricity from this vantage point, the appearance suggests a numerical value of the smaller number over the greater. In other words, as the single throne possesses an elevated quality over the four living Beings, so the four living Beings possess a weightier quality over the twenty-four Elders. Also, this location places the four living Beings in the middle ring position, with the four living Beings situated in between the throne and the twenty-four Elders. Additionally, it is at the word of the four living Beings that the twenty-four Elders cast down their crowns (4:9–10). This action of responding to the word of the four living Beings suggests subordination on the part of the Elders to the living Beings. As we move into chapter 5, Rev 5:6–14 presents a similar scene: in the midst of the throne, there is the Lamb, surrounded first by the four living Beings, separated by a larger ring of twenty-four Elders. The only difference is

---

44. R. H. Charles, *Revelation* (1920), not dogmatic but allowing for several other viable options (129–33), finally concludes (133): "... but it is not improbable that for our author the Elders have become the heavenly representatives of the faithful, all of whom are priests, i.6."

45. C. B. Caird, *The Revelation of St. John the Divine* (1966) 64, does acknowledge slight perplexity: "What is not clear is whether the details that John takes over from the earlier prophets are used simply for their associative value or are intended by him to convey some precise symbolic idea."

the substitution of the Lamb for the throne. Also, at 5:14 when the four living Beings say "Amen," the Elders fall down and worship. Once again, the four living Beings occupy a place of preeminence, situated closer to the Lamb than the twenty-four Elders and also speaking in such a way that evokes a response from the Elders.

Rev 7:11 presents the reader with a possible exception: καὶ πάντες οἱ ἄγγελοι εἰστήκεισαν κύκλῳ τοῦ θρόνου καὶ τῶν πεσβυτέρων καὶ τῶν τεσσάρων ζῴων ("and all the angels stood in a circle around the throne as well as the Elders and the four living Beings"). At first glance, it appears that John has reversed the order of the concentricity by flipping the position of the twenty-four Elders with the four living Beings. This may not be the case. If John is viewing the rings from the outward to the inward, then he may be looking at the positions from the viewpoint of the angels. The angels, as the very outer ring, see that the next ring is the Elders, sequenced next by the four living Beings. The value of this argument hinges on the critical location of the throne in the description. If the throne had been placed last in the sequence, there would be no doubt as to the concentricity. The throne location thus prevents an airtight conclusion. Every other text in Revelation which mentions both the four living Beings and the Elders together always places the Elders outside the four living Beings. Also, the expression καὶ τῶν πεσβυτέρων καὶ τῶν τεσσάρων ζῴων indicates that not only are all the angels standing around the throne, but they are also around the twenty-four Elders and the four living Beings. The point to be made is not that the four living Beings are around the throne, but that *all* of the angels are externally around the four living Beings. This reinforces the above view that the four living Beings enjoy a status above that of the angels.

Rev 14:3 returns to the original image of throne, living Beings, and the Elders. Working with this imagery, this suggests that the four living Beings occupy a place in *between* God and the twenty-four Elders. Indeed, the Greek expression in Rev 4:6: ἐν μέσῳ τοῦ θρόνου καὶ κύκλῳ τοῦ θρόνου τέσσερα ζῷα ("and in the midst of the throne and around the throne the living Beings") can describe a middle spatial position which indicates a scene surrounded or encompassed by others.[46] Not only do the four living Beings occupy a place "in the midst of the throne," but the twenty-four Elders are situated third in the order, suggesting both a distance from and a place of lesser importance than the four living Beings.

We come now to Rev 5:6 which states: καὶ εἶδον ἐν μέσῳ τοῦ θρόνου καὶ τῶν τεσσάρων ζῴων καὶ ἐν μέσῳ τῶν πρεσβυτέρων ἀρνίον ("and I saw in the midst of the throne and of the four living Beings as well as in the midst of the twenty-four Elders a Lamb").[47] This is slightly different than Rev 4:6. Here the Elders are included, raising

---

46. BADG, 635 (1b), list one of the options as the center or middle position. Acts 4:7 shows Peter and John being placed in the middle of the Jewish leaders (ἐν τῷ μέσῳ). Peter and John are thus in the center or middle, surrounded by unfriendly faces. This environment would suggest, though, a position of hostility rather than privilege. The intent would be to threaten and intimidate, rather than honor and elevate.

47. Literally, the Greek text translates: "and I saw in the midst of the throne and of the four living

two important issues. The first is the meaning of the couplet καί . . . καί ("and . . . and" or "both . . . and").[48] The second is the double reference to ἐν μέσῳ ("in the midst"). Why repeat ἐν μέσῳ, unless it forms a line of demarcation between the four living Beings and the Elders? The double combination of καί . . . καί and ἐν μέσῳ describes not only two separate groups, but distinguishes the four living Beings as again being directly connected with the throne, yet separate from the Elders. The upshot of this vision is that the four living Beings constitute an essential part of the throne, while the Elders form only a contiguous sub-element to the four living Beings. It may be significant, too, that the Beings or Living Ones are numbered and classified as to species, but the Elders are left without numerical designation.

This is not all. The four living Beings occupy the place *closest* to the Lamb and thus would cement their position as having greater prominence over the Elders. Additionally, whenever the four living Beings give glory to God, the twenty-four Elders fall down and worship. This movement aligns the four living Beings into a more direct and mediating position to reflect the glory of the Lamb. The argument that the four living Beings represent all that is in nature dissolves in light of the greater importance attached to their close association with the Lamb. They represent the Lamb, not creation. The sharply focused scene accents the role of the Lamb, not creation. Thus, the entire vision highlights the heavenly throne, not the natural world. This interpretation, if correct, makes it possible to understand why the early church connected these four living Beings with the four canonical Gospels.

THE FUNCTION OF THE FOUR AND THE TWENTY-FOUR. While the twenty-four Elders are mentioned twelve times,[49] the four living Beings are mentioned a total of seventeen times in Revelation. A comparison of the various activities or movements of these personages reveals the following data. At 4:9–11, when the four living Beings give glory and honor to God, the twenty-four Elders are shown doing three things: 1) they fall down before the throne and worship God; 2) they lay their crowns before the throne; and 3) they say, "You are worthy our LORD and God. . ." This scene shows the Elders responding to the confessions of the four living Beings. In other words, the Four take the lead and the Twenty-four follow. At 5:8–9, the four living Beings and twenty-four Elders are again linked together. In concert, they both do the following: 1) each one has a harp; 2) each one has a golden bowl containing the prayers of the saints; and 3) they all sing together a new song to the Lamb. Here the two groups act in harmony and in unison. This scene presents no information that would tip the scales in favor of one over the other. What can be said, though, is that this text which con-

---

Beings as well as in the midst of the twenty-four Elders a Lamb"). The Lamb occupies a place of emphasis, coming as it does at the end of the sentence.

48. Surprisingly and unfortunately, BAGD do not include this specific text in their treatment of καί, although in general they do discuss this couplet.

49. 4:4, 10; 5:5, 6, 8, 11, 14; 7:11, 13; 11:16; 14:3; and 19:4.

tains five references to the Elders does not show them doing anything independent of the four living Beings.

The text at 6:1–8 shows just the opposite. The living Beings in this chapter are connected directly to the actions of the Lamb, with no mention of the Elders. Each time the Lamb opens a seal, one of the four living Beings responds to the Lamb by saying "Come!" Thus, the four living Beings function as mediating agents who execute the will of the Lamb. Once again, they serve as representatives of the Lamb. At 7:11–13 the Beings and Elders are again joined together in a posture of falling upon their faces in worship. One new element, though, emerges: one of the elders asks John a rhetorical question about the identity of the great multitude. If we place the two texts of 6:1–8 and 7:11–13 alongside each other, one possible comparative conclusion can be drawn: although the Elders (at least one of them) interface with John, the four living Beings interface with the Lamb. This interpretation, once again, enables the four living Beings to represent the Lamb.

At 11:16–17 the Elders are finally shown in a scene without the presence of the living Beings. These Elders fall down in worship and proclaim a great hymn of thanksgiving to God. At 14:1–3 the Elders and four Beings come together again, but this time they stand before the 144,000 who are singing a new song. Only the 144,000 could learn this song. 19:4 is the final scene of the living Beings and the Elders. Once again, they fall down and worship God.

What can be extracted from the above data? Each personage has movement (falling down); each has voice; each has some position of prestige. Two notable scenes portray a slight advantage accruing to the living Beings: at their voice the Elders fall down and worship God, and at the action of the Lamb in opening the seal, each one of the four Beings responds by saying "Come!"

A Puzzling Feature: The Description of the Four and the Throne. Another conclusion surfaces as we consider a puzzling feature. The creatures of Ezekiel carry the throne while the living Beings of Revelation are positioned *around* the throne and *in the midst of the throne*.[50] This description has a double significance. It not only separates the living Beings from the scene in Ezekiel but it provides a space of separation from the twenty-four Elders. Most significantly and most tellingly, the twenty-four Elders are never described as being "in the midst" of the throne. Furthermore, the twenty-four are never described as actually part of the throne of God. According to Rev 4:4, they are positioned *around* the throne of God and seated on their own individual thrones. Consequently, these Elders are never shown to occupy equally their own thrones and simultaneously the throne of the Lamb. Otherwise stated, the

---

50. Charles Homer Giblin, "From and before the Throne: Revelation 4.5–6a: Integrating the Imagery of Revelation 4–16," *CBQ* 60.3 (1998) 502: "The four living beings, who seem to constitute the throne itself." See also Christopher C. Roland, *The Book of Revelation* (1998) 592, who acknowledges that the living creatures share the throne with the elders. Giblin's conclusion is surely incorrect.

thrones of the twenty-four Elders never constitute an essential part of the throne of God. To repeat: they have their own individual thrones. This description creates yet another separation placing the Elders at a distance more remote from the four living Beings. By contrast, the four living Beings do not have a throne of their own. Neither do they have a place related to the thrones of the twenty-four Elders. Rather, they are integrally connected only to the throne of God.

The throne of the Lamb possesses very unusual characteristics. The word θρόνος occurs forty-seven times in Revelation and is one of the more frequently appearing words. The word has more than one application. It can refer to the "throne of Satan" (2:13) which is perhaps figurative language to describe a spiritual place of sinister influence. This word is also used several times to describe plural thrones occupied by the twenty-four Elders. The more relevant and principal usage that comes, though, is that the throne occupies a central place in heaven describing the seat or dwelling place of God. Furthermore, this throne possesses the unique capacity to accommodate both God and the Lamb. Not only does God himself sit upon this throne (4:9–11; 19:4), but the Lamb also sits with him (5:13; 7:17). Accordingly, the expansive character of this throne permits us to understand how it can accommodate the four living Beings as well. These data enable us to further observe that the four living Beings do not possess a throne of their own. They share in the throne of the Lamb.

There are four descriptive words that function as prepositions or adverbs of place picturing various spatial positions in their relationship to the throne. These four are: ἐνώπιον ("before"), κυκλόθεν ("around"), ἐν μέσῳ ("in the midst of"), and ἐπί ("upon"). Only God and Christ are actually described as sitting ἐπί or "upon" the throne. Only Christ and the four living Beings are actually described as ἐν μέσῳ or "in the midst of" the throne. This preposition allows another significant identification between the four living Beings and the Lamb. The prepositional phrase ἐν μέσῳ is used a total of seven times in Revelation.[51] It does not appear to imply a static description, as the Lamb is shown moving about in the midst of the seven lamps. In other words, the Lamb possesses movement; the four living Beings always seem to be connected to the throne but with limited movement or flexibility. Various beings are described as "before" (ἐνώπιον) the throne; these are: angels, the seven lamps representing the seven spirits of God, the hundred and forty-four thousand, and the twenty-four Elders. At 5:8 and 19:4 the four living Beings are also pictured before or in front of the throne. Finally, what entities are around the throne (κυκλόθεν) and encircling it? The following are said to surround or encircle the throne: the rainbow (Rev 4:3), the twenty-four Elders (Rev 4:4), all of the angels (Rev 7:11), and the four living Beings (Rev 4:6). Yet, because of the additional qualifier of also being "in the midst of the throne," this description of the four living Beings requires further comment. At this point, though, I would like to make a provisional statement: the four living Beings are never pictured in front of the throne as are other beings. The four living Beings are not envisioned

---

51. 1:13; 2:1; 4:6; 5:6, 6; 6:6; and 22:2.

solely around the throne except to show that they are also a part of it. Therefore, by inclusion they are connected to the throne as components of the throne; by exclusion they are removed from standing before the throne.

The expression "in the midst of the throne and around the throne" (ἐν μέσῳ τοῦ θρόνου καὶ κύκλῳ τοῦ θρόνου) is both perplexing and intriguing. Raymond Brewer argues that "a literal translation of the two phrases makes little sense."[52] Brewer sees that the throne was already occupied by the "Ineffable One" and, therefore, could not accommodate the four living Beings as well. The scene that John describes is one that is humanly impossible: something cannot be "around" and at the very same time also be "in the midst of."[53] Steve Moyise simply states that the vision is a "confusing picture."[54] Yet, this does not seem to confuse John. If John was merely composing ideas and scenes from an apocalyptic tradition,[55] he would be guilty of confusion. If, however, he is reporting an actual experience of seeing a heavenly vision, then the description, though straining the limits of language, may be an accurate representation. My approach will be to take the words at face value and to search out their meaning.

How can we understand this configuration? R. H. Charles noted that this description was very unusual and even concluded: "In fact, the text is unintelligible as it stands. Hence ἐν μέσῳ τοῦ θρόνου is to be taken as (1) a gloss, or as (2) a mistranslation of the Hebrew."[56] Charles could find no legitimate reason to explain the meaning of this expression and ended up throwing it out of the text as an extraneous gloss. Charles subsequently included a comment whose vital importance escaped him: "Elsewhere throughout the Apocalypse the Living Creatures are said to be 'round the throne,' never 'in the midst of it,' as here. That privilege is reserved for 'Son of Man' or 'the Lamb.'"[57]

We must pursue the trail that Charles himself pointed out but did not follow. If, as developed in this study, the four living Beings are to be taken as metaphors for the four Gospels, then an intriguing interpretation opens up. Is it possible that the vision

52. R. Brewer, "Revelation 4.6 and Translations Thereof," *JBL* 71 (1952) 231.

53. A. Loisy notes his own consternation (*L'Apocalypse de Jean* [1923] 125): "Mais d'abord il est malaiséé de comprendre comment ils peuvent être à la fois au milieu et autour du trône. L'une des indications exclut l'autre, et c'est la seconde qui est primitive." To the contrary, I note that Cameron Afzal, "Wheels of Time: *Merkavah* Exegesis in Revelation 4," *SBLSP* 37 (1998) 473, simply says: "Significantly John's living beings are depicted as a part of the throne." Afzal, however, proceeds to develop the view (echoing Austin Farrer, *Revelation of St. John the Divine* [1964] 90–91) that the four beings are related to the four elements (Rev 7) and to the four winds at the foundations of the world and "as a result stellar constellation. The latter are moreover associated specifically to the pivotal constellations of the Zodiac." That the four Living Beings are part of the throne is defensible; that they represent the signs of the Zodiac is not.

54. S. Moyise, *The Old Testament in the Book of Revelation* (1995) 69.

55. For the argument that the author of Revelation is working within an apocalyptic tradition (*1 Enoch*, *Songs of the Sabbath Sacrifice*, and the *Apocalypse of Abraham*), see Darrell D. Hannah, "Of Cherubim and the Divine Throne: Rev 5.6 in Context," *NTS* 49.4 (2003) 528–42.

56. R. H. Charles, *Revelation* (1920) 119.

57. Ibid., 120.

of the four living Beings as occupying similar space with the Lamb yet being simultaneously pictured around it may represent the incarnational view of Jesus as both Man and God? Just as it is inconceivable to understand someone being simultaneously God and Man, could this vision possibly provide an intentional heavenly image of the earthly experience of Jesus? O. Michel in the *TDNT* says:

> We are thus dealing with angelic powers who attest to God's presence in the visible world. They are in no sense representatives of creation and history before God. In the early Church the four watchers were largely understood as the four Evangelists, with some vacillation of order. In their distinction and unity these cherubim represent the perfect holiness and glory of God.[58]

Michel's suggestion that these "watchers" (to use his term) "represent the perfect holiness and glory of God" accords well with the view as developed here. This proposal leads to the next possibility.

The Four Living Beings as Components of the Throne. Robert G. Hall presents cogent arguments that the four living Beings are anchored to the Ark of the Covenant. He then says: "Hence raw materials for interpreting the living creatures as part of God's heavenly throne were well established long before the Common Era."[59] In this sense, Hall follows the exegesis of R. H. Charles, also an advocate that the heavenly vision is a mirror of the Temple containing the Ark of the Covenant.[60] If this suggestion is valid, then imagery-wise it connects the living Beings to the presence of God. Hall further suggests:

> By the first century, some Jews, represented by Josephus, conceived the living creatures not as separated from the throne by the firmament as in Ezekiel, but as ornamental constituents of the heavenly throne.... He conceives the four living creatures as an integral part of the throne.... Though part of the throne, they are not static but living creatures as John emphasizes by their name.... His intention of treating them as *living* creatures may explain why he avoids describing them as "affixed" or "sculpted" on the throne even though he considers them constituents of it.... Since the living creatures are in the midst of the throne not as occupants but as components of it, ἐν μέσῳ τοῦ θρόνου καὶ κύκλῳ τοῦ θρόνου is fully intelligible.[61]

Hall thus isolates an important aspect of these Beings: they are "living" and not sculpted; yet, they are, in fact, "occupants" as well as constituent components.

---

58. Michel, "μόσχος," *TDNT* (1967) 4.761.
59. R. G. Hall, "Living Creatures in the Midst of the Throne: Another Look at Revelation 4.6," *NTS* 36.4 (1990) 611.
60. R. H. Charles, *Revelation* (1920) 112.
61. R. G. Hall, "Living Creatures" (1990) 611.

THE ULTIMATE QUESTION: THE SYMBOLISM. A critical observation appears possible. The symbolism of the four living Beings, by virtue of their closer position to the Lamb, is a theological metaphor that commended itself to the early church suggesting that divine inspiration emanating directly from the throne may be refracted through the four living Beings as representations of the person of Christ. If Jesus is pre-existent to the NT (as the NT argues),[62] it would not be a surprise to find such pre-existence revealed in the prophetic writings of the OT. If Jesus is post-existent to the NT Gospels by virtue of his resurrection (as the NT argues), it should not be a surprise to find evidence of divine inspiration revealing the meaning of Jesus in Revelation.[63] The significance of Rev 4:7 is minor until we view the heavenly vision from the perspective of the four living Beings and their relationship with the twenty-four. We can look outward at the twenty-four Elders and see separation between Beings and Elders. We can look inward to examine the qualities that these Beings represent. From this vantage point, it is possible to see a plausible reason why the vision of Rev 4:7 is a viable heavenly mirror of the four canonical Gospels. Consequently, it is understandable why the early church was fascinated by this fourfold imagery. It gave them a visual representation of the fourfold character of Christ. This interpretation, furthermore, would lead the early church fathers to connect the fourfold Gospel to a supernatural source rather than to a human origin. This deeper source, emanating from the throne and subsequently refracted through the prism of the four living Beings, would provide a visual image of revelation.

The Testimony of the Early Church

Although there were isolated exceptions, by the year A.D. 225 the fourfold canonical Gospel was securely established in the Great Church. Irenaeus,[64] Clement of

---

62. The Dead Sea Scrolls do not offer hope of providing a human causation to explain the nature of the fourfold Gospels as advocated in this present study. Although the DSS do mention the four figures of Ezekiel 1.10, this information throws no new light upon the present thesis. For a discussion of this single DSS reference, see D. Dimant and J. Strugnell, "The Merkabah Vision in Second Ezekiel (4Q385 4)," *RevQum* 14.3 (1989–90) 339, and C. R. A. Morray-Jones, "The Temple Within: The Embodied Divine Image and its Worship in the Dead Sea Scrolls and Other Early Jewish and Christian Sources," *SBLSP* 37 (1998) 407.

63. Harry Y. Gamble, *The New Testament Canon* (1985) 24: "How, when and where the ancient church came to acknowledge four and only four Gospels is at many points obscure.... Furthermore, the Gospels did not become part of the NT canon individually. They were first shaped into a collection and then achieved canonical standing as a group." Gamble's observation about the four entering the canon together is a sound and reasonable conjecture. For further confirmation on the unlikelihood that the *titles* of the four Gospels were formulated independently, see David Trobisch, *The First Edition of the New Testament* (2000) 38. The question as to how, when, and why appears to be beyond the tools of historical criticism to recover. However, from the view point of this study an answer is provided: the early church saw the four Gospels as a reflection of the four living Beings.

64. For further discussion of the fourfold Gospel in Irenaeus, see Jeffrey D. Bingham, *Irenaeus' Use of Matthew's Gospel in Adversus Haereses* (1998) 78–79.

Alexander,[65] Origen,[66] Hippolytus,[67] and Tertullian[68] all held to a fourfold canon of the Gospel. Later on, Eusebius,[69] Ambrose,[70] and Augustine,[71] likewise, affirmed the same. Darrell D. Hannah has argued that the *Epistula Apostolorum* predates Irenaeus and provides evidence of a kind for a fourfold Gospel.[72] Justin Martyr may also serve as an earlier witness to the fourfold Gospel.[73] Irenaeus, however, is the first secure

65. For Clement, see *Stromatum* 3.93.1: πρῶτον μὲν οὖν ἐν τοῖς παραδεδομένοις ἡμῖν τέτταρσιν εὐαγγελίοις οὐκ ἔχομεν τὸ ῥητὸν ἀλλ᾽ ἐν τῷ κατ᾽ Αἰγυπτίους ("First then, we do not have this saying in our four traditional Gospels, but in the Gospel according to the Egyptians").

66. For Origen, see *Commentarii in evangelium Joannis* 1.21: Ἐγὼ δ᾽ οἶμαι ὅτι καὶ τεσσάρων ὄντων τῶν εὐαγγελίων οἰονεὶ στοιχείων τῆς πίστεως τῆς ἐκκλησίας ... τὸ κατὰ Ἰωάννην ... Ματθαῖος ... Μάρκος ... Λουκᾶς. Origen prefers the metaphor of στοιχεῖον, indicating perhaps the idea of basic element or fundamentals of faith. Lampe, "στοιχεῖον," *PGL* (1968) 1260, provides a helpful insight into how the church fathers connected this word with the four Gospels and the four living Beings. See also the more often cited text of Origen in 5.7/193D: οὕτως ἕν ἐστι τῇ δυνάμει τὸ ὑπὸ τῶν πολλῶν εὐαγγέλιον ἀναγεγραμμένον καὶ τὸ ἀληθῶς διὰ τεσσάρων ἕν ἐστιν εὐαγγέλιον. See also Origen's *Homilies on Luke* (Lk 1.1–4; *P.G.* 13.1801) in which he claims that the church has received only four Gospels: ἀλλὰ τὰ τέσσαρα μόνα ἐπελέξαντο.

67. Hippolytus, *Commentarium in Danielem* 1.17.1: "A stream of unceasing water flows and from it divides 'four streams,' watering the whole earth as may be seen in the church. For Christ, who is the stream, is proclaimed throughout the world by the fourfold Gospel..." (Sources chrétiennes 14, 1966). Hippolytus, does not refer the reader to the four living Beings of Revelation but, rather, appeals to the analogy of the four streams depicted in Gen 2:10–14.

68. For Tertullian, see *Adversus Marcionem* 4.2.2: *Denique nobus fidem ex apostolis Iohannes et Mattheus insinuant, ex apostolicis Lucas et Marcus instaurant, isdem regulis exorsi* (Sources chrétiennes 456, 2001). See also *Adversus Marcionem* 4.5.3: *eadem auctoritas ecclesiarum apostolicarum ceteris quoque patrocinabitur evangeliis, quae proinde per illas et secundum illas habemus, Iohannis dico atque Mathei, licet et Marcus, quod edidit Petri adfirmetur, cuius interpres Marcus, nam et Lucae digestum Paulo adscribere solent.*

69. Eusebius, *Historia ecclesiastica* 6.25.3. Eusebius is quoting from Origen and he makes it clear that there are only four: μόνα τέσσαρα. Eusebius next itemizes the sequential order in numerical fashion: first is Matthew; second is Mark; third is Luke, fourth is John. Eusebius, in similar numerical language, follows Rev 4:6–7 but instead of itemizing the living Beings, he inserts the Gospels. He thus reinforces the number *four* in three different ways: a specific limit of only four Gospels; a sequence of one, two, three, and four; and the four specific names of Matthew, Mark, Luke, and John.

70. For Ambrose, see *Exposito Evangelii secundum Lucam* 1.1–3. In this text, Ambrose holds to the traditional number of four evangelists, but varies the order as: *Mattheus, Marcus, Iohannes, Lucas*. See also 1.10: *Denique plurimi voluerunt scribere euangelium, sed quattuor tantummodo qui divinam meruerunt gratiam sunt recepti*. Here Ambrose returns to the identity of the "many" (*plurimi*) as those who wished to write a Gospel. Only four, however, have been accepted as divinely inspired compositions.

71. For Augustine, see *De doctrina christiana* 2.8.49: *Novi autem quattuor librorum evangelii: secundum Matthaeum, secumdum Marcum, secumdum Lucam, secumdum Iohannem*. Augustine holds to both the traditional number as well as the order. He makes no reference to the four living Beings of Rev 4:6–7.

72. See D. D. Hannah, "The Four-Gospel 'Canon' in the *Epistula Apostolorum*," *JTS* 59 (2008) 598–633, for arguments that the fourfold canon of the Gospels was probably known as early as AD. 140.

73. See Justin Martyr, *Dialogus cum Tryphone* 106.3: ἐν γὰρ τοῖς ἀπομνημονεύμασιν, ἅ φημι ὑπὸ τῶν ἀποστόλων αὐτοῦ καὶ τῶν ἐκείνοις παρακολουθησάντων συντετάχθαι ("which I say were composed in the memoirs by his apostles and by those who followed them"). The expression ὑπὸ τῶν ἀποστόλων αὐτοῦ καὶ τῶν indicates a double classification of writers. As Graham N. Stanton notes ("The Fourfold Gospel," *NTS* 45 [1997] 330): "Although Justin never refers to the number of

ancient extant witness to recognize that there are only four Gospels.[74] The third reference is that of the so-called Muratorian Canon.[75] It is Irenaeus that offers us a more promising understanding of the canon of the fourfold Gospels. In his *Against Heresies* (III.xi.8) he says: "Moreover, there are neither more Gospels in number, nor are there fewer" (*Neque autem plura numero quam haec sunt neque rursus pauciora capit esse Euangelia*).[76] That he has the number four in mind is clear from both the preceding and what follows. At 11.7 he specifically lists the four by name: Matthew, Luke, Mark, and John. He identifies these four as a *quadriforme* ("quadruple form" or "fourfold form"). It is obvious that Irenaeus has a different order than the traditional one. He has either switched the order between Mark and Luke, or this is the sequence in which he has always known them. He subsequently follows this listing by references to the *quattuor regions mundi* ("four regions of the earth") and four principal winds. These are not facts that prove his point but simply are illustrations of his argument. Irenaeus does not stop with examples from nature but moves from the natural to Scripture itself. He prefaces the scriptural point with a more serious introduction: "From which fact, it is evident that ... that Jesus has given us the Gospel under four aspects, but bound together by one Spirit." Irenaeus then combines two Scriptures, the first a citation from Psalm 80:1: "You who sit enthroned between the cherubim, shine forth." Irenaeus takes the "You" (YHWH) to be Jesus and adds that Jesus "shines forth." For his second scriptural reference, Irenaeus appeals to the words of "For the cherubim, too, were four-faced, and their faces were images of the dispensation of the Son of God." Irenaeus lists the four cherubim as a lion, a calf, a man, and an eagle, and identifies these four faces as the four aspects of the four Gospels. It is obvious that Irenaeus has before his eyes the four Gospels and/or the text of Ezek 1:10 or Rev 4:7. He further

---

the gospels he accepts, this passage implies that there were at least four." Stanton credits (fn. 46) S. Tregelles (1867): "no smaller number (than four) could be implied by the two groups." It is not clear in what precise sense the verb συντετάχθαι is to be taken. BADG list συντάσσω as meaning "to arrange." I have translated the verb as "composed." If BADG is correct, Justin implies that an orderly arrangement of some kind is to be traced back to the apostles.

74. Edgar J. Goodspeed, *A History of Early Christian Literature* (1966) 120: "Irenaeus is the first Christian writer who can be shown to have had something like what we understand by the New Testament." See also Robert M. Grant, *The Formation of the New Testament* (1965) 151: "Probably the most important statements about the New Testament in the last second century are those provided by Irenaeus." For a discussion and rebuttal of some of Irenaeus's claims, see T. C. Skeat, "Irenaeus and the Four-Gospel Canon," *NovT* 34 (1992) 194–99. Among his conclusions (197): the fourfold image was taken over by Irenaeus from an earlier source.

75. For a discussion of the Muratorian Canon, see Bruce M. Metzger, *The Canon of the New Testament* (1987) 195, and Everett Ferguson, "Canon Muratori: Date and Provenance," *SP* 17 (1982) 677–83.

76. I have used the Greek text of Adelin Rousseau and Louis Doutreleau, *Irénée de Lyon: Contre les hérésies, Livre III* (Sources chrétiennes 211, 1974). An English translation may be found in *The Ante-Nicene Fathers: The Writings of the Fathers down to A.D. 325* (1980) 1.428.

interprets these faces as the respective characteristics of royal power, sacrificial or sacerdotal order, human being, and the gift of the Spirit hovering over the Church.[77]

At this point a question comes naturally into the discussion: why did Irenaeus and others latch onto metaphors containing the number four in order to establish a fourfold Gospel? Graham Stanton asks a series of important questions relating to the four Gospels: "How did the early church come to accept as authoritative four gospels, no more, no less?"[78] Stanton brings forward three objections that the early church had to overcome in order to accept only the chosen four: 1) an abundance of rivals to challenge the elite position of the four,[79] 2) the implications of Tatian's *Diatessaron* which makes one Gospel better able to meet the "barbs of the critics" who find disagreements among the four,[80] and 3) "The early church retained four gospels in spite of the regular embarrassment over the differences in which opponents took particular delight."[81]

C. F. D. Moule writes: "Perhaps in the end it was really not so much a matter of selecting as of recognizing that only four full-length Gospels were available from within the apostolic period. And if it be asked why these maintained their independence, instead of suffering fusion (as in Tatian's *Diatessaron*) or instead of one alone coming out as sole survivor, the answer may be found in the authority of local churches or some other prestige."[82] Craig Blomberg suggests that the canonical sequence of Matthew, Mark, Luke, and John "was no doubt developed partly because of the belief that they were written in that order."[83] Historically speaking, this may indeed be the case. There is the additional reason that this reflection is simply a mirrored sequence of the divine image in heaven of the lion, ox, man, and eagle. This, however, is a theological

---

77. It is not clear why Irenaeus would allocate Luke in the servant image and Mark in the priestly. At 3.33.8/204 he says: *Id vero quod est secundum Lucam, quoniam quidem sacerdotalis characteris est, a Zacharia sacerdote sacrificante Deo inchoavit. Iam enim saginatus parabatur vitulus, qui pro inventione minoris filii inciperet mactari.* Irenaeus has the correct order in terms of Rev:4.6–7, but he identifies Luke with the calf. It is clear, therefore, that this identification in Irenaeus did not carry the day. However, his description of the calf as a *vitulus* is instructive. Tacitus in his *Annales* (15.47) describes the *vitulus* as a sacrificial animal.

78. G. N. Stanton, *The Gospels and Jesus* (2002) 135.

79. Ibid., 122. He calculates that there were at least thirty rivals.

80. Ibid., 136.

81. Ibid., 138.

82. C. F. D. Moule, *The Birth of the New Testament* (1962) 187. Moule calls attention to a belief I share along with other conservative scholars working as specialists in canon research: "It was certainly not the arbitrary decision of a single Christian body, still less of an individual. Its formal declaration, by the Church collectively, when it was made, was only the recognition, by the Church collectively, of a conviction that had long been silently growing on their consciousness." The point to be made here is not that the church created the canon but, rather, it simply and formally recognized something that was already a reality in their collective midst.

83. C. Blomberg, *Jesus and the Gospels* (1997) 97.

reflection which is not clearly stated in the book of Revelation.[84] D. Moody Smith offers the following view, a view which opens up a possible connection to the thesis of this book:

> Because of the flexibility of the process, one should not attach too great importance to the order of the Gospels. Yet the canonical order of the Gospels, like the canonical shape of the individual books makes a certain sense. It seems to bespeak an intention. To speak of "intention" in this regard is uncertain for a question is begging. Whose intention? How conscious was it? We cannot say?[85]

What D. Moody Smith acknowledges with some hesitation to be an "intention," I would like to propose to be indicative of a plan or purpose. Moody Smith's willingness, as it were, to think out loud with the word "intention" as well as dare to ask "whose" is not only charitable but a rather courageous admission.

We return now to Irenaeus. Although I will make a few modifications to Irenaeus's model, I propose to show that Irenaeus astutely may have made the correct observation. I will also amplify and build upon what Irenaeus has left us. First, we turn to his contention that there are only four Gospels. The testimony of several early church writers is in harmony over the precise number.[86] Oscar Cullman takes great exception to Irenaeus's manner and method of promoting a fourfold Gospel canon. Cullman, in very plain language, writes:

> But the way Irenaeus solved the problem was precisely the way it ought not to have been solved. He tried to show that the fourfold Gospel was in no way based simply on the historical situation of the Apostolic Church, but that the number four was a divinely ordained number essential to salvation. The fourfold Gospel tallied with the significance of the number four in all the divine institutions of creation and redemption .... Irenaeus, therefore, represents the fourfold Gospel as a miracle. He tries to show that it is not based on a purely human situation at all ....The problem under discussion cannot be

---

84. On the issue of theological reflection, see Andrew Gregory, *The Reception of Luke and Acts in the Period before Irenaeus* (2003) 49: "Justin and Papias might well believe that there only was one gospel concerning one Jesus, but is by no means apparent that either yet shared Irenaeus's articulation of one proclaimed gospel witnessed to by four written Gospels, a theological conviction that is first explicit in Irenaeus and testified to implicitly in the *subscriptions* and *inscriptions* of the earliest extant papyri. It is unclear to what extent, if at all, Irenaeus may be defending an innovation, but our evidence is such that we are unable to know if there was any earlier defense of the fourfold Gospel written by apostles and their immediate followers alongside arguments that there was one gospel of Jesus Christ."

85. D. Moody Smith, "John, the Synoptics, and the Canonical Approach to Exegesis," in *Tradition and Interpretation in the New Testament* (1987) 171.

86. See Denis Farkasfalvy, "The Presbyters' Witness on the Order of the Gospels as Reported by Clement of Alexander," *CBQ* 54 (1992) 260–70. Although Farkasfalvy shows that it is a mistake to draw firm conclusions about the *order* of the Gospels from Clement, it is clear that the fourfold canon is in view.

solved by the artificial theory of a miraculous origin of the Gospel canon exempt from human agency.[87]

Cullmann is put off by the logic of Irenaeus. However, after articulating a representative and prevailing presupposition, Cullmann does an about-face when he finally concludes (53): "Irenaeus provides a valuable hint regarding the correct theological argument for the fourfold canon . . . the fourfold Gospel is sustained by the *one Spirit* . . ." Cullmann registers his personal objections to Irenaeus's conception of the fourfold Gospel only to then backpedal into the principal logic of that second century teacher.[88] Although it is tempting not to take Irenaeus seriously and to assess him as simplistic, artificial, and arbitrary, he may very well offer the most insightful interpretation of the fourfold Gospel.[89] Everett Ferguson provides a needed correction to misunderstandings regarding Irenaeus:

> It is often stated that Irenaeus was arguing for something new and had quite weak arguments for his position. This approach misunderstands the importance of number symbolism in the ancient world and Irenaeus's use of it. He does not argue for four gospels because there are four winds or four corners of the universe. He appeals to this symbolism because he has four gospels. If he had three, five, or some other number, he would have found an appropriately fitting analogy.[90]

It is important to recognize that Irenaeus is not arbitrarily imposing a scheme of the number four over his Gospels. He has four Gospels before him which he recognizes as unique and singular. He is seeking an appropriate metaphor to highlight

---

87. O. Cullmann, "The Plurality of the Gospels as a Theological Problem in Antiquity," in *The Early Church* (1956) 51–52. See also John Webster, "The Dogmatic Location of the Canon," in *The Unity of Scripture and the Diversity of the Canon* (2003) esp. 97 and 111, who also objects to bypassing the natural and historical process of the human agency involved in establishing the canon. I refer the reader also to Graham N. Stanton, "The Fourfold Gospel," *NTS* 45 (1997) 317–46, who presents a credible case for the fourfold Gospel based upon the early church's adoption of the codex by suggesting that (345): "the four gospels are like the rivers of Paradise which flow from the Garden of Eden into the whole known earth at that time (Gen 2.10–14)." I must ask: why substitute rivers for the four heavenly images? Robert Grant, *A Historical Introduction to the New Testament* (1963) 30: "There were four gospels, neither more nor less. To be sure, the arguments of Irenaeus (*c.* 180) on this subject are not very convincing." See also Judith M. Lieu, *Christian Identity in the Jewish and Graeco-Roman World* (2004) 88, who labels the fourfold canon as a superficial construct: "Yet, in so far as recent study has emphasized the diversity that lies behind the superficially common shape of the canonical Gospels."

88. See Martin Hengel's comment in his *The Four Gospels and the One Gospel of Jesus Christ* (2000) 11: "Cullmann's criticism of Irenaeus and his grounding of the number four in an ontology of creation and in salvation history misses the point."

89. For example, Annette Yoshiko Reed, "EUAGGELION: Orality, Textuality, and the Christian Truth in Irenaeus' *ADVERSUS HAERESES*," *VC* 56 (2002) 22–23 where Reed shows that it is very uncharacteristic of Irenaeus to take the use of numbers seriously. Yet, the fact is that Irenaeus does this very thing in regard to the fourfold Gospel.

90. E. Ferguson, "Factors Leading to the Selection and Closure of the New Testament Canon: A Survey of Some Recent Studies," in *The Canon Debate* (2002) 301.

this singularity. A critical question is left begging: was the early church correct in their attempt to anchor the image of the four living Beings to the canonical four Gospels? Or, did the early church, principally Irenaeus, reach the right conclusion but for the wrong reasons? This investigation concludes that the four living Beings occupy a greater place of prominence than the twenty-four Elders; does that necessarily lead to a valid conclusion that the four Beings represent the four Gospels? On the basis of the information provided solely in the book of Revelation, such a conclusion must be considered inadequate for lack of sufficient evidence. That, however, does not provide a strong enough lever to dislodge the early church from their belief that the four living Beings accurately represent the four Gospels. There may have been other factors at work in their reasoning.

Conclusion: The Fourfold Heavenly Image

The early church from Irenaeus (A.D. 180) to Augustine (A.D. 450) was fascinated by the heavenly vision of the throne of God and the four living Beings. They constantly appealed to this image in order to find justification for the fourfold Gospel. That being said, they did not all see the symbolism alike. Theodor Zahn compiled an impressive registry of literary testimonia showing at least five different ways the early church commentators understood the four living Beings.[91] This diversity of opinion among the early Fathers does not detract from the thesis of this study; in fact, it further enhances the profile presented here. I propose this simply because these early Fathers were probably not conscious of the four prophetic texts. It will be helpful now to examine why the four images of lion, ox, man, and eagle provide an irresistible ensemble for understanding the fourfold nature of the Gospels. Each of the four living Beings is distinct in its unique characteristics. The lion is supreme on land as an animal of unparalleled courage and ferocity. The ox is unique by virtue of its supreme strength and domestic capacity as a servant to mankind. Man, of course, is the face of humanity which connects directly to humans. The eagle is considered the master of the sky and is noted for its supremacy of vision. We now examine the individual characteristics of each image.

THE LION IMAGE. Aside from the fact that Jesus is pictured as the "lion from the tribe of Judah" (Rev 5:5), the figure of a lion is often used in Scripture as a metaphor for courage and boldness. Proverbs 28:1 says, "The righteous are as bold as a lion." The twin elements of boldness and righteousness are linked together. Jesus, in the biblical tradition as the perfect embodiment of righteousness, would be the ultimate expression of boldness. YHWH is pictured in Scripture as comparing himself to the boldness and courage of a lion. Isaiah 31:4 says: "As a lion . . . so the LORD." Then Isa 32:1 opens up

---

91. T. Zahn, "*Die Thiersymbole der Evangelisten,*" in *Forschungen zur Geschichte des neutestamentlichen Canons und der altkirchlichen Literatur* (1883) 257–75.

with a statement of how a king will reign in righteousness. Both the OT and NT also make use of the lion metaphor to portray the animal as a formidable opponent.

Rev 5:5 pictures Jesus as the Lion of Heaven. This symbol when applied directly to the Gospel of Matthew is a fitting symbol. As the lion fears no enemy, backs down from no foe, and retreats from no threat, so the Lion of the tribe of Judah has entered the territory of Satan, set free the captives, and released those held prisoner to their sins. The Gospel of Matthew adequately portrays Jesus in the role of a reigning king who is august in authority and imperial in power. There is also one other possible connection. By identifying Jesus with the image of a lion, we return to our discussion of Jesus in chapter 4 in which we find numerous people bowing down in prostrate fashion before the LORD. Pliny in his *Natural History* (VIII.19.1) records the following observation about lions: "The lion alone of wild animals shows mercy to suppliants; it spares persons prostrated in front of it."[92] Pliny does not tell us upon what basis he reports this unusual behavior. Perhaps it is only anecdotal in value. Apparently, though, this is information he felt reliable enough to pass on. Lions, it may be said, are fully capable of stepping out of their wild and savage ferocity; they can rise to the level of kindness and compassion for humans.[93] The lion metaphor also reveals figuratively the concepts of Jer 23:5.

I have composed the following lines of verse as a poetic tribute to some of the intention behind the metaphors of lion, ox, man, and eagle. I begin with the lion.

> Behold the kingly Lion.
> Magnificent in majesty, regal in royalty,
> Wholly lacking in temerity, he conquers victoriously.
> He slays his enemies justly but pardons his people robustly.
> Resplendent in beauty, sovereign he is in imperial authority.
>
> Kings vow to kill him,
> People bow before him,
> Angels now come to assist him,
> Demons cow in submission to him.
>
> As the great Lion from Judah's tribe, he refuses Satan's deceitful bribe.
> Triumphant in the barren wilderness, he comes forth in the Spirit's fullness.
> Emptying himself as never before, with his life's blood our sins he bore.
> As a king leads his men in gory war, so the King of Kings defends us even more.

---

92. *Leoni tantum ex feris clementia in supplices; prostratis parcit.*

93. The fascinating account of John Randall and Ace Berg who bought a lion cub from Harrod's in 1969 and named the lion "Christian" illustrates the point.

THE IMAGE OF AN OX. The Scriptural symbol of the servant is an ox. Numbers 24:8 depends upon the metaphor of an ox to convey the idea of strength. The ox, in both art and literature, is pictured as having strong shoulders which carry the yoke, strong legs which can pull the plow, and a strong heart and lungs which can work all day in the field. The ox is the scriptural symbol for Jesus Christ as the great Servant of God. Petronius in his *Satyricon* (56) states that oxen are the most laborious workers (*laboriosissimae boves*).

As the great Servant of heaven he is the sinner's own personal Savior, the bearer of burdens, the carrier of concerns, the lifter of listless and sagging spirits. As the heavenly ox he carries the weight of the world and the guilt of our sins on his shoulders. These qualities of supernatural strength place him as the centerpiece of civilization.

I offer the following lines in order to capture the ox metaphor:

> Behold the humble Ox.
> By no means a likeness to Herod the fox,
> Stout in strength, he goes to great length
> To bear the burden of sin, in hopes our souls to win.
> His focus is fixed, his motives unmixed.
>
> As he descends from his heavenly abode,
> He comes to carry our sinful load.
> As he humbles himself to enter our lowly estate,
> He lifts us from our fallen state.
> As oxen grind out the grain,
> So the Son treads not the winepress in vain.
>
> Nailed to a prophesied cross,
> He suffers the unimaginable loss.
> The great payment to be made,
> A ransom conceived for our aid.

THE IMAGE OF A MAN. The argument developed in this study portrays Jesus as a great High Priest, and that portrait conforms to the Gospel of Luke. This portrait is further expanded into the heavenly symbol for Jesus as our high priest as illuminated by the face of a man. Jesus, as presented in the Gospels is fully Man yet fully God. As a full and complete Man he knows what it is like to be human. He, therefore, understands human weaknesses, comprehends failings, and can minister to mortal feebleness and frailty. Jesus is a divine and compassionate priest who sympathizes. He supplies strength to the weak, grace to the tempted, and comfort to the bereaving. He heals the sick, cleanses the leper, and forgives the sinner. He guides and protects the young, sustains the adult, and comforts the aged. He regards the unfortunate, lifts the needy, and helps the downtrodden. His compassion is incredible; his love is everlasting. Once again, I offer some lines that may express the symbolism of the man-metaphor:

> Behold the universal Man.
> In his heavenly function, he's endowed with keenly unction.
> Taking on our humanity, he understands our earthly frailty.
> Standing between God and man, he intercedes as no one else can.
> As the perfect Second Adam, he frees us from the dreadful damn.

> Descending from the tribe of Levi, he ministers to those who draw nigh.
> In his veins the blood of Aaron, his help is strong as iron.
> From his high priestly height, seeing his people's plight,
> He is ever at the throne, interceding as we upwardly groan.

> With his integrity unassailable, his influence remains undeniable.
> Third in a sequence of four, his place is secure forevermore.

THE IMAGE OF AN EAGLE. The Scriptural symbol for this aspect of God is an eagle. The eagle is characterized by many things, principally, though, being considered the "monarch" among birds.[94] Among Roman historians, Dionysius of Halicarnassus describes the eagle as possessing the "insignia of sovereignty" (σύμβολα τῆς ἡγεμονίας).[95] Appian in his *Civil Wars* (2.9.95) adds to this by recording that the eagle was considered "the most sovereign" (κυριώτατον) or perhaps most valued of all Roman standards and symbols. For one, the eagle flies higher than most birds, but not all. The eagle is the only bird that can look directly at the sun. The eagle flies among the highest, lives the longest, and has the greatest care for its young. In the ancient world, the eagle was especially known for its keen vision. Horace in his *Satires* (1.3.27) says: "are you as keen of sight as an eagle" (*tam cernis acutum quam aut Aquila*). The early church often associated the image of the eagle with that of Christ.[96]

But I would like to give the main reason the eagle is used as a symbol for God's eternal nature. Isaiah 40 may provide a clue: the person who waits upon the LORD rises up with the wings of an *eagle* and his youth is renewed like an *eagle*. In Scripture the eagle is a symbol for renewal in the eternal and everlasting nature of God Almighty.

---

94. There are many modern credible studies available on the eagle. Among them, Leslie Brown, *Eagles of the World* (1977), and Rebecca L. Grambo (ed.), *Masters of the Sky* (1997) 87: "No other birds, with the possible exception of the great condors, have been universally given such exalted status and treated with such reverence."

95. Dionysius, *Roman Antiquities* 3.51.1.

96. See *Acta Xanthippae* 17: ὁ ἀετός ἐστιν ὁ κύριος Ἰησοῦς Χριστός ("the eagle is the LORD Jesus Christ"). For other references, see G. W. H. Lampe, "ἀετός," *Patristic Greek Lexicon* (1968) 40.

In Psalm 103:5 it is written: "Those who wait upon the LORD will renew their youth *like* an eagle." In Prov 23:5 it is said of the eagle that it can fly toward heaven. Thus the metaphor of the eagle is used to illustrate everlasting qualities and the possibility of human renewal based upon that divine reality.

Throughout Scripture the LORD is often identified with the characteristics of an eagle. Deuteronomy 32:11–12 says, "*Like an eagle* that stirs up its nest, that flutters over its young, spreading out its wings, catching them, bearing them on its pinions, the LORD alone did lead him . . ." The image of an eagle raises a question: why the image of a bird? Josephus records that one Matthias and some of his disciples were burned alive by the Romans for having torn down an eagle from a gate in the Temple. This was clearly an act of defiance as this demolition occurred during broad daylight.[97] In the Gospel of John, Jesus reveals the very nature of God himself. The metaphor for this lofty revelation is the soaring eagle. As the eagle mirrors the majesty of grace, the loftiness of height, and is a symbol for everlasting youth, so Jesus reveals and reflects the very person of God and communicates eternal life. I conclude the eagle metaphor with the following lines:

> Behold the lofty Eagle.
> Regal is his image, honored through the age,
> As the eagle soars majestically in the sky,
> So the Son ascends on high.
> As the eagle symbolizes ebullient youth,
> So the Son reveals his eternal truth.
>
> His glory is limitless, his life is endless.
> From the shores of our temporal finity,
> He enables us to see joyful eternity.
> As the eagle sees from far away,
> So the Son opens our eyes to see,
> The glorious day of our heavenly destiny.
>
> Thus the eagle as Scripture's divine metaphor,
> Mirrors for us the glory of God in the Gospel Four.

---

97. Josephus, *Jewish Antiquities* 17.167. See also the parallel account in *Jewish Wars* 1.649–50.

12

Conclusion

THE AIM OF THIS book has been to provide a plausible explanation for the following five questions: 1) why do we have four Gospels—not three or five; 2) why is the order of the current canon: Matthew, Mark, Luke, and John; 3) why do the Gospels of Matthew and Luke have a genealogy but Mark and John do not; 4) why do the genealogies of Matthew and Luke diverge; and 5) upon what basis can we formulate the four images of Jesus in the Gospels as complementary and supplementary, rather than competitive or contradictory? In an attempt to answer the above questions, this book has proposed an argument for the underlying thematic unity of the fourfold Gospels. This unity-argument is based upon a coherent substructure tying together four prophetic texts from the Old Testament. The thesis of the book may be stated simply: it is an argument predicated upon the four prophetic texts of Jer 23:5–6; Zech 3:8; 6:12–13; and Isa 4:2 as the genetic code or DNA for understanding the four Gospels.

It may be charged that this book reduces complex literary difficulties to easy extrapolations. I have tried to show, however, that such a premise is not an artificial overlay arbitrarily imposed upon the texts. That is, the patterns developed in this investigation are not the result of haphazard cherry-picking to suit one's fancy. This study has endeavored to show how in an organizational pattern Matthew presents Jesus as the King Branch, Mark as the Servant Branch, Luke as the Priest/Man Branch, and John as the LORD God Branch. This unusual sequence of the number four (four prophetic Branches, four canonical Gospels, four heavenly Images) has been neglected in biblical studies and its very uniqueness has prompted this investigation. If one considers the plausibility of such a unique symmetry, a logical question then comes to the forefront: what is the implication of such a singular correspondence? The premise of this book is that four evangelists have not consciously and coincidentally set out to write a Gospel that would end up forming a unique quartet of Gospels. No, the argument presented here is that divine revelation is the ultimate source behind this mysterious triad of quartets (four Branches, four Gospels, and four living Beings). If one operates within a canonical interpretation of Scripture, this conclusion is not an unreasonable or unrealistic chimera. The quote by Leon Morris may again be appropriate here: "Let the Bible speak for itself without our man-made unities. But that carries with it the further consequence that where the Bible has its own unity the exegete is not at liberty to deny it on the grounds that he perceives some diversity."[1]

Robert Kysar has come up with a thought-provoking skepticism regarding hypotheses (italics his): *"simply because a hypothesis illumines the possible meaning of a passage does not necessarily prove that the hypothesis is true."*[2] This is a fair statement; there is no quarrel from this quarter. However, when a hypothesis not only explains a given text but also illuminates collectively and even synergistically a total of four books—then the accumulative weight of that hypothesis comes crashing down on competing rival theories of composition. Through chapters 4–10 I acknowledge that no Gospel *requires* us to accept that the respective evangelists were consciously in dialogue with the above four prophetic texts. Yet, the data do *allow* us to see correspondence between the Gospels and the matching prophetic texts. I now offer a conclusion predicated upon the following concessions: these permissible allowances provide a basis to see a consistent pattern building up to a literary critical mass *requiring* that the four Gospels indeed are a fulfillment of the four prophetic texts. One Gospel alone offering plausible fulfillment possibilities would not be sufficient evidence for such a thesis. Yet, the accumulation of four prophetic texts, finding a matching correspondence in the four Gospels, pins to the mat competing academic theories. Augmenting this correspondence is the additional heavenly vision of the four living Beings, each one exhibiting aspects conforming to the individual characteristics of the four Gospels.[3]

This chapter ends the investigation proper with four conclusions. Each rubric contains an analog illustrating the thesis of the book and summing up its contents. These four analogs are: *tesserae* of a mosaic, an invisible shield, a jigsaw puzzle, and the keel of a ship.

The Analog of Mosaic *Tesserae*

I introduce the first suitable analog: a *tessera* which conveys the idea of multiple expressions being treated as a single entity. A *tessera* is the smaller unit that fits coherently into a mosaic. A mosaic is a variegated pattern, a combination of diverse elements forming a coherent whole. A *tessera* is one of these elements; it contributes to the meaning of the whole but is only one part of it. To be more precise, a *tessera* of a mosaic is actually one-fourth, since this word is the Latin equivalent of the Greek word τέσσαρες, meaning "four." A theory, if it would be viewed as plausible, must accommodate itself to the facts. The salient facts of this investigation are the following:

---

1. Leon Morris, *I believe in Revelation* (1976) 30.

2. Robert Kysar, "The Whence and Whither of the Johannine Community," in *Life in Abundance* (2005) 65–81.

3. To this triad a fourth may even be added: the reference in the second chapter of the book of Numbers to four separate "standards" strikes me as yet another possible link in the sequential chain.

there are four prophetic Branches, four Gospels, and four living Beings around the heavenly throne. The most likely theory within the canon of sacred Scripture that can accommodate this unusual set of fours is that they are connected. The four prophetic texts speak of an individual person destined to appear at a time post-dating the prophets themselves; the four Gospels identify the person of Jesus as possessing the characteristics of these four prophecies; the four living Beings exhibit qualities conforming to the images as presented in the four Gospels. Therefore, my conclusion rests on the idea of canonical unity and not on a superficial or arbitrary unity. This final conclusion argues that the *only* adequate, satisfactory, and plausible explanation for the existence of the four Gospels is to be found within the biblical canon which reveals four prophetic Branches, four Gospels, and four living Beings around the throne. No other hermeneutical explanation is provided within Scripture itself. The premise of this book thus invites the reader to see the significance of the number four as an adequate lens for understanding the fourfold Gospel.

I would like to make a brief reference back to the four living Beings as treated in the previous chapter. If there is any validity—and I believe that there is—in linking the four canonical Gospels and these four heavenly images, a natural question thus surfaces: what has caused or precipitated this unusual set of relationships? The argument advanced in this study concludes that these four Gospels, the four heavenly images (Beings), and the four prophetic texts predicting the coming of a Branch all align themselves into a coherent picture which does not appear to be the result of an accidental and circumstantial phenomenon of history. Rather, this constellation of texts and images is consistent with information provided within Scripture itself. In other words, the internal design of Branches, Gospels, and Beings argues against an external and outward set of circumstantial conditions that have come together in a rather human, haphazard, or even adversarial mixture of exogenous elements. Since there is no indication within Scripture itself which supports randomness as the principle cause behind the formation of the four Gospels, belief in divine inspiration should not be dismissed as numerical chicanery or biblical buffoonery.

If a substantial connection between the Gospel of Matthew and the text of Jer 23:5–6 is admitted, this connection may be explained on other grounds than purely human and natural motivations. If so, this opens the door to the plausible idea that such a connection is due to the causation of divine revelation. The totality of Jesus' life can then be seen as an event of such supernatural proportion that only an interpretation of equal supernatural revelation could account for it. I would like to repeat C. K. Barrett's citation from chapter 5: "two swallows do not a summer make."[4] This investigation contains a mosaic of four prophetic texts articulating a smaller breakdown of twenty-eight rubrics. Twenty-eight rubrics thus surpass Barrett's standard of "two swallows." The chorus of four prophetic voices, containing within itself a total of twenty-eight rubrics, speaks of a single person, a Messiah, who was to come. Similar

---

4. C. K. Barrett, "The Background of Mark 10.45," in *New Testament Essays* (1959) 2.

to four-part harmony in which individual voices, singing soprano, alto, tenor, and bass, all sing a single hymn, so this chorus of four prophetic voices give expression to a single Savior.

Furthermore, as already presented, the thesis of this book promotes a reasonable and plausible conclusion that there was a guiding and generative force at work within the four evangelists that transcended their own natural powers of creativity. Had the prophecies of four Branches, four Gospels, and four heavenly Images been a purely human or coincidental phenomenon, this would have created a very unusual series of publishing events. It would have originated a sequence of literary synchronistic events that appear related but have no discernible causal internal relationship. Or, *au contraire*, is it possible to explain the dynamic of four Branches, four Gospels, and four Images in supernatural terms? Admittedly, there are compositional elements in the Gospels that permit explanations grounded in human and historical causes. For example, the Gospels, written not in English but Greek, present Jesus as fully God yet fully Man. As Man, he obviously had human qualities. The Gospels, therefore, may approximate this twofold identity of Jesus by likewise possessing a twofold identity of both divine and human elements. This means that each evangelist exersizes a limited autonomy. He writes as a human but he is under the power of an unusual inspiration. The issue, therefore, is not so much what can be accounted for in human terms, but what elements defy human explanation.[5] Consequently, what element (or elements) qualifies for divine explanation? "Reduced to its simplest formula, only what is humanly impossible qualifies for supernatural revelation. The evidence that has been presented so far is an argument for divine revelation based upon the several identifiable elements that do not concede to strictly human causes. Richard Bauckham, in making a direct application to the Gospel of John, states his case for the relevance of biblical numerology:

> The correspondence between Prologue and Epilogue is confirmed by an element of numerical composition (of which this is one of many in the Gospel). The prologue consists of 496 syllables, appropriately since 496 is both a triangular number and a perfect number and is also the numerical value of the Greek word *monogenes* (meaning "only son" and used in 1.14, 18). Odd though these considerations may seem to us, people in the New Testament period were fascinated by certain special sorts of numbers, including triangular and perfect numbers . . .[6]

---

5. Ernst Käsemann, *Essays on New Testament Themes* (1971) 37: "We can only count on possessing a genuine similitude of Jesus where, on the one hand, expression is given to the contrast between Jewish morality and piety and the distinctive eschatological temper which characterized the preaching of Jesus; and where on the other hand we find no specifically Christian features."

6. Richard Bauckham, *Jesus and the Eyewitnesses: The Gospels as Eyewitness Testimony* (2006) 363. His reference to the number 496 is based upon the doctoral dissertation of M. J. J. Menken, *Numerical Literary Techniques in John* (1985) 29.

I have included this citation for two reasons: 1) to indicate the relevance of biblical numbers, and 2) to demonstrate to what lengths such calculations can be pressed. Bauckham's application to the Gospel of John seems far-fetched. His main point, however, is worthy of respect: the use of biblical numbers should neither be ignored nor cavalierly disregarded as a banal proposition. Conversely, the application of the number four to this study has been much simpler: there are four prophetic texts and only four; there are four Gospels and only four; there are four living Beings and only four. This is not all. Each individual *tessera* contributes in a unique way to a composite fourfold gospel mosaic. This mosaic, in turn, portrays a single Messiah. Additionally, the precise number four, although not found in Scripture as numerically describing the fourfold Gospel or the four prophetic texts, does describe the living Beings around the heavenly throne (as first, second, third, and fourth). Thus, the number four is clearly visible, not an encoded or embedded figure, and not arbitrarily forced. Penetrating deeper within this constellation of four, there is an interior syntagmatic arrangement of theological units: there is a King Branch, a corresponding King Gospel (Matthew) which, in turn, corresponds to a lion or king Being. There is a Servant Branch, a Servant Gospel (Mark) which, in turn, corresponds to an ox Being. There is a Man/Priest Branch, a Man/Priest Gospel (Luke) which, in turn, corresponds to a man Being. Finally, there is a LORD Branch, a LORD Gospel (John), and an eagle Being.

Additionally, the four prophetic Branches find no fulfillment in the OT. That is to say, no OT text looks back and points to a human fulfillment in any of the four Branches. When the OT closes, these four branch texts are left dangling and unfulfilled. Therefore, these four prophecies regarding a Branch must be considered as either misguided failed projections or genuinely fulfilled in Christ. Indeed, as proposed in chapter 3, a NT principle for interpreting prophecy was that *all* the promises of God find their ultimate fulfillment in Christ.

An Invisible Shield

Often unnoticed is the fact that no subsequent "gospel" has succeeded in breaking into the circle of the four.[7] This fact is underscored by the fact that there was no lack of rivals to compete for gospel status.[8] Even the popularized *Gospel of Thomas* with its

---

7. Helmut H. Koester, "One Jesus and Four Primitive Gospels," *HTR* 61 (1968) 206, notes: "For this type of literature, there are no pre- nor extra-Christian parallels, and only Mark, together with the other Gospels dependent upon or related to him (Mt., Lk., and Jn.), has a genuine claim to the title 'Gospel.'" The climate is changing, however, as Lee Martin McDonald and James A. Sanders in their joint introduction to *The Canon Debate* (2002) 5, states: "In scholarly discussions these days it is not unusual to call for enlarging the traditional data base of knowledge of the historical Jesus to include, for example, the *Gospel of Thomas* and the 'Unknown Gospel' discovered in the Egerton Papyri as well as several other non-canonical writings."

8. On the numerous other "gospels" circulating about, see Christopher Tucket, "Forty other Gospels," in *The Written Gospel* (2005) 238–53.

advocates has failed to break into the sacred circle.⁹ Graham N. Stanton notes: "Today when we hear vociferous claims on behalf of the Gospels of Peter and Thomas, we need to recall that there is no manuscript evidence for the acceptance of any 'fifth' gospel alongside one or more of the writings of the fourfold Gospel."[10] As if some invisible protective shield has blocked the admission of a fifth Gospel, this elite foursome has remained intact, insulated, and inviolable for two thousand years. As Bruce Metzger once put it, "it is a clear case of the survival of the fittest."[11] Although references can be found to so-called "apocryphal" gospels (such as the Gospel of the Ebionites,[12] Gospel of Egyptians, the Gospel of Peter), none of these ever succeeded in gaining access to the status of the four.[13] These pretenders never enjoyed universal protection and they were never safeguarded under the canopy of canonicity. Rudolf Bultmann, generally recognized as one of the foremost influential international scholars of the twentieth century, raised the question of the *how*: "Though they cannot be dealt with here, the chief questions are the following: How did it happen that four Gospels were taken into the canon and that the attempts to reduce their number from four to one, either by ac-

---

9. See James M. Robinson, "The Study of the Historical Jesus after Nag Hammadi," *Semeia* 44.1 (1988) 49: "The practical exclusion of the apocryphal gospels from New Testament scholarship is indefensible on historical grounds." See also Robert W. Funk, Roy W. Hoover, and The Jesus Seminar, *The Five Gospels* (1993) and the response by Luke Timothy Johnson in his monograph, *The Real Jesus: The Misguided Quest for the Historical Jesus and the Truth of the Traditional Gospels* (1996) 29–56. The effort to insert the Gospel of Thomas into the four appears to be tied to the generational interests of aging scholars such as John Dominic Crossan, Marcus Borg, and James Robinson. It remains to be seen whether the next generation will find replacements to champion such efforts.

10. G. N. Stanton, "Jesus Traditions and Gospels in Justin Martyr and Irenaeus," in *The Biblical Canons* (2003) 370.

11. Bruce Metzger, *The Canon of the New Testament* (1987) 286. Metzger includes a fine quote from William Barclay's *The Making of the Bible* (1961)78: "It is the simple truth to say that the New Testament books became canonical because no one could stop them from doing so." This Barclean observation is intriguing, suggesting perhaps that there might have been some protective force safeguarding the canon process.

12. For the argument that the Gospel of the Ebionites is actually an attempt, prior to Tatian, to displace the fourfold Gospel, see Daniel Bertrand, "*L'Evangile des Ebionites*: une harmonie evangelique anterieure au *Diatessaron*," NTS 26.4 (1980) 561: "Le but de l'ouvrage est donc de remplacer les témoignages particuliers 'selon Matthieu,' 'selon Marc,' et 'selon Luc' par un évangile unique."

13. As Werner Georg Kümmel, *Introduction to the New Testament* (1972) 339, points out, far into the second century, apocryphal books were being consulted but not necessarily considered authoritative. See also the comment by Robert M. Grant, *The Earliest Lives of Jesus* (1961) 3: "Like most of the early Fathers, we do not consider apocryphal gospels (those not preserved in the canon of the New Testament) or 'unwritten sayings' as reliable sources of information about the life of Jesus. Too little control was exercised over the composition or transmission of these materials for us to be able to use them with any degree of confidence." See also Robert Guelich, "The Gospel Genre" (1991) 204, who refers to five of the works from Nag Hammadi which bear the label of "gospel" (Gospel of Truth, Gospel of the Egyptians, Gospel of Thomas, Gospel of Philip, and Gospel of Mary), yet he dismisses them outright as worthy of such a designation: "Furthermore, one cannot speak of these later 'gospels' generically, since they do not reflect any homogeneity in structure and/or content." For the recent debate over the Gospel of Thomas, see Simon Gathercole, *The Composition of the Gospel of Thomas* (2012).

cepting only (Luke by Marcion, Matthew by the Ebionites) or by the preparation of a Gospel harmony (Tatian), did not succeed?"[14] Although Bultmann eschews an answer to his own set of questions, he has posed an important challenge: *how* is it possible that the four canonical Gospels have been able to successfully fend off all competition and preserve their elite status?

For centuries millions and millions of readers, from beginning believer to seasoned scholar, have had their preferred favorites: some have chosen Matthew or Mark; others have opted to choose Luke or John. No one Gospel has swept away the other three. All have enjoyed a secured place in the life of the church and in the intellectual life of scholarship. James Lipovsky in his essay on the Roman historian Livy observes that Livy "swept away the competition" upon publication of his *History of Rome (Ab urbe condita)*.[15] Even more staggering is the claim expressed in the first person statement of Tacitus himself. Tacitus avows that with his own publication of the account of Roman history all previous treatments of the subject now have been rendered obsolete.[16] This cannot be said of any of the four Gospels in regard to the other three. R. Laird Harris observes: "In fact, there was not even one that gained any noticeable degree of recognition only to lose it."[17] Not one of the four need fear losing a popularity contest to any of the other three. Indeed, evidence is wholly lacking that there was a popularity contest at all. Even though approximately ninety percent of Mark is duplicated in Matthew, Mark still has his own unique identity.[18]

This is not all. While outside pretenders failed to gain entrance into the privileged set of the canonical four, it must also be acknowledged that despite efforts to eliminate one or more from the inner foursome, those attempts also have failed. Although scholarly discussion continues to be trendy regarding lost gospels,[19] no attempt to dislodge one of the four has yet prevailed. A serious attempt was made in the second century by the maverick Marcion who rejected the other three Gospels in preference to the Gospel of Luke. His industrious attempt to elevate Luke to a place of sole preeminence failed, as his views were not accepted by the wider Christian com-

---

14. R. Bultmann, *Theology of the New Testament* (1952) 2.141. Charles H. Cosgrove, "Justin Martyr and the Emerging Christian Canon: Observations on the Purpose and Destination of the Dialgoue with Trypho," *VC* 36 (1982) 226, tries to build a case that Justin Martyr opposed the fourfold Gospel on the basis that oral tradition about Jesus should take precedence over literary. If there is any merit to Cosgrove's interpretation of Justin, Justin's views did not prevail on this score.

15. James P. Lipovsky, "Livy," in *Ancient Writers: Greece and Rome* (1982) 734.

16. Tacitus, *Annals* 4.32–33: *sed nemo annals nostros cum scriptura eorum contenderit, qui veteres populi Romani res conposuere*. Tacitus claims that no history of the Roman people can contend with, rival, or parallel his own version of events and people.

17. R. Laird Harris, *Inspiration and Canonicity of the Bible* (1973) 217.

18. Morna D. Hooker, *The Gospel According to St. Mark* (1991) 398, relays the information from H. M. Humphrey's *A Bibliography for the Gospel of Mark 1954–1980* (1980) in which he lists 1,599 items for this period of time alone. Mark, indeed, casts his own definite shadow.

19. See, for example, Craig S. Keener, *The Historical Jesus of the Gospels* (2010) 47, for this acknowledgement.

munity; he was eventually branded a heretic. We must consider the reasons why the larger community of believers ("The Great Church") did not follow Marcion's logic but sustained their curatorial concern for safeguarding these four Gospels. It would have solved some problems for the church if they were spared the task of having to reconcile variations within the gospel tradition. They chose, rather, to reject Marcion's view and remain faithful to a fourfold Gospel. Why? On a superficial level, they likely preferred to face the difficulties of a fourfold Gospel rather than face the obstacle of deciding which three must be eliminated. With few exceptions, the collective voice of the early church never questioned the right of any of the four to occupy the privileged position of sacred Scripture.[20]

Tangentially, writings with a prophetic claim did not succeed in gaining entrance. F. F. Bruce observes: "Fresh revelations were not admissible: the Montanist claims to a resurgence of prophecy in the new age of the Paraclete were disallowed."[21] Even a modern attempt to create a forgery has failed.[22] So this invisible shield has worked in two directions: protecting from outside invasion and blocking from inside expulsion.[23] Or, as Francis Watson puts it, "the fixed figure four serves to exclude as well as include."

It is a peculiar phenomenon of history that what I am calling a "shield" has protected the canonical Gospels from dissolution. This shield has stood firm against the cumulative weight of early pretenders and rival claimants of such works as the Gospel of Thomas, the second-century efforts of Marcion, and the attempts of modern scholars to revise the canon. This onslaught of criticism bearing down on almost anything else likely would have caused a collapse.[24] The canonical Gospels, to this point in time,

---

20. Everett Ferguson, "Factors Leading to the Selection and Closure of the New Testament Canon," in *The Canon Debate* (2002) 303: "The continuity of these gospels with the Old Testament story contrasts with the apocryphal gospels, notably the *Gospel of Thomas*. This finding coincides with the fact that there is no time in Christian history after the writing of the four gospels when one can find evidence of their not being accepted as scripture."

21. F. F. Bruce, "New Light on the Origins of the New Testament Canon," in *New Dimensions in New Testament Study* (1974) 11. Bruce (8) acknowledges: "If we ascribe the preservation of Holy Writ to the 'singular care and providence of God,' *a fortiori* must its formation be so ascribed. And therefore the diversity within the fourfold gospel must be greeted as a divine provision." See also the suggestion by Albert C. Sundberg, "The Bible Canon and the Christian Doctrine of Inspiration," *Int* 29 (1975) 352–71, where Sundberg tries to develop a case that the early church (second century to the fourth) did not see a difference between apostolic inspiration and their own subsequent inspiration. For an earlier view, see Albert C. Sundberg, "The Protestant Old Testament Canon: Should It Be Re-Examined?" *CBQ* 28 (1966) 194–203. For a counter to Sundberg's suggestion, see F. F. Bruce, *The Canon of Scripture* (1988) 266–67.

22. As is the case of Morton Smith's *The Secret Gospel* (1974).

23. F. Watson, *The Fourfold Gospel* (2016) 90.

24. Charles William Fornara, *The Nature of History in Ancient Greece and Rome* (1983) 42, says: "No ancient writer could withstand the combined assaults of Wilamowitz, Schwartz, and Jacoby, who made Ephorus the incarnation of all that was objectionable in Greek historiography." Fornara mentions three distinguished modern historians who attack the ancient Ephorus. Has not the four Gospels withstood similar criticisms and weathered them all? Of course, there are protestations to the contrary. For example, George Aichele, "Jesus's Two Fathers: An Afterlife of the Gospel of Luke," in

have resisted any kind of makeover. From a purely human point of view, such resistance to change shows great resilience. From a spiritual point of view, such constancy shows evidence of divine protection. Of course, just as there was in the second and third centuries, there will always be marginal movements within Christianity seeking an esoteric version of the Gospels. Such is the case of the Jesus Seminar; it is both marginal and revisionist in its aims and purposes.[25]

Those who do not view the Gospels as the product of divine revelation generally advocate that the early church produced the Gospels out of motivations that are explainable in purely historical or human terms. This allegation may lead to the claim that Jesus is an embellished literary fiction which originated in the fertile imagination of the early Christian movement and has, therefore, no correlation with reality. From David Strauss to Rudolf Bultmann,[26] from Ernst Käsemann to Hans Dieter Betz, from James Robinson to Ulrich Luz and François Bovon, as though these scholars are speaking in a single united voice, they all have left clearly documented views espousing the premise that the four Gospels are solely the human creation of the early church. François Bovon may serve as a particular example. He champions the view that we need to treat the four Gospels "in the same light as we consider the apocryphal literature—for at one time the four Gospels were not canonical, but floated about in an unstable collection, not even linked together."[27] After arguing that the four evangelists dipped into earlier sources and manipulated them, he goes on to claim: "We know that they adapted and modified their sources, but because their writings are now canonical we deem their deliberate interventions as faithful, successful, and legitimate."[28] This conclusion is based upon what Bovon himself admits is "opinion." What Bovon endeavors to do is work backward from the second century into the first by supposing that canonicity gives the four Gospels an unfair façade of legitimacy. In essence, Bovon's contention is an appeal to destroy the protective shield so that the four Gospels can be placed on the same level with the apocryphal literature. Bovon's proposal is simply an old mannequin dressed up in a new skirt. The early church itself dealt with this argument. Church Fathers such as Justin Martyr, Irenaeus, Origen, Clement of Alexander, and Tertullian all recognized that there was something

---

Those Outside: Noncanonical Readings of the Canonical Gospels (2005) 23: "The disintegration of the Christian canon allows texts such as Luke to drift uncontrollably away from their canonical contexts into new and fluid juxtapositions with extra-biblical texts."

25. Robert W. Funk, Roy W. Hoover, and The Jesus Seminar, *The Five Gospels* (1993) xiii, dub their translation the Scholars Version (SV for short).

26. Rudolf Bultmann, *Theology of the New Testament* (1952) 1.26: "The scene of Peter's *Confession* (Mk. 8:27–30) is no counter-evidence—on the contrary! For it is an Easter-story projected backward into Jesus' lifetime."

27. François Bovon, *Studies in Earliest Christianity* (2003) 210. For contrary views that this period of "floating" is either minimal or non-existent, see Everett Ferguson, "Factors Leading to the Selection and Closure of the New Testament Canon," in *The Canon Debate* (2002) 304.

28. Bovon, *Studies*, 210.

intrinsically lacking in the apocryphal writings.[29] Their rejection of the apocryphal gospels as worthy of inclusion into the sacred four was linked to their understanding that these writings were not cut from the same sacred cloth as the four Gospels. Their collective decision was neither collusion nor an unfair and arbitrarily imposed one.[30] In short, they were not willing to die for the apocryphal writings. Historically, their assessment traces back to whether a particular writing could be considered apostolic in *nature*. Simply attaching the name of one of the apostles to the document did not win the day. There had to be internal grounds for acceptance as inspired.

If we probe into the possible historical causes for this protective shield, what are the available human options? Can we attribute to Irenaeus's personality or his persuasiveness the power and influence to convince the church of this pavilion of protection? Although Irenaeus is unique in the arguments he offers, no other writer within a hundred years after him adopts the same reasons. It takes approximately 200 years before we come to Ambrose and Augustine who both appeal to the heavenly images of Revelation 4 in order to understand the four Gospels. It is difficult to assign to Irenaeus the singular role of preserving the divine inspiration of the fourfold Gospel. We are still left with Justin Martyr, Tatian, Clement of Alexander, Theophylus, and Origen.

A Jigsaw Puzzle

The following analog may help to illustrate the confusion, as well as habilitate the above proposition for revelation. The dilemma may be comparable to a giant jig saw puzzle that covers the size of a large living room floor. Some of the pieces around the edge are in place and make sense. But the centerpiece is the major obstacle for correctly solving the puzzle. If a cluster of twelve smaller pieces (four prophetic Branches, four canonical Gospels, and four heavenly Images) comprising the centerpiece is allowed to represent divine revelation, a major decisive step occurs in solving the puzzle when this key cluster-piece is placed in the center. Immediately, some of the lesser pieces begin to fall into place. If, however, divine revelation is removed from the center, nothing seems to fit and the end result leads to frustration. Similarly, a hundred

---

29. I find it both encouraging and intriguing that the recent book by Elaine Pagels and Karen L. King, *Reading Judas: The Gospel of Judas and the Shaping of Christianity* (2007), is dated by these two scholars as mid second-century and is not credited with canonical status (xiii): "Because the *Gospel of Judas* was written sometimes around 150 C.E., about a century after Judas would have lived, it is impossible that he wrote it; the real author remains anonymous. Neither do we learn anything historically reliable about Judas or Jesus beyond what we already know from other early Christian literature." Thus no attempt is made to place this fictitious gospel on the same level with the canonical four.

30. Wayne G. Rollins, *The Gospels: Portraits of Christ* (1963) 14, argues that one of the stages in gospel composition "took place under the sponsorship of an earlier version of the Ford or the Rockefeller Foundation. The Gospel authors were not just free-lance writers; they were hired or appointed by communities. . . . But why were these Gospels commissioned at all?" Rollins uses a whole series of cognate words suggestive of collusion: "sponsorship," "hired," and "commissioned" by a committee.

pianos out of tune cannot be properly tuned by keying off of one another. They require the assistance of a tuning fork in order for their tuning to be restored. Efforts to understand the four Gospels can result in the same disarray when the essential piece behind their composition is left out.

In a sense, the four evangelists occupy similar ground as the OT prophets.[31] In the Jesus tradition, there is the view that the OT prophets were not always aware of whom or what they were writing.[32] Many OT scholars tend to see all prophetic texts as requiring application to the immediate situation of the prophet's own day and time. Conjoined to this view is the subordinate conviction that OT writers were fully conscious of what or who they were writing.[33] In the same manner, many NT scholars view statements that describe Jesus as the unique Son of God as creations of the early church. But the NT itself does not do this. NT texts indicate that there are OT texts that point precisely beyond the prophet's time to fulfillment in Jesus. In other words, what the OT prophets do in prospect, the NT evangelists do in retrospect. In between this double gaze is the magnetic and eye-catching person of Jesus. Similarly, the proposition presented here is that the four evangelists also give indications of being at the same disadvantage. Although the four evangelists are in a better position to understand the historical person of Jesus, they present only a part of the picture.

Is it possible that the four evangelists were not always fully conscious of all the motivations behind the selectivity of their respective writings? If so, the reason for this lack of awareness could be the presence of divine revelation working within them independent of their own volition. By not considering the possibility of a revelatory Spirit enabling biblical writers to compose their witness to the Messiah, scholars end up engaging in countless approaches trying to make the data fit their theories.[34] A

---

31. The precise number of four canonical evangelists is an integral part of this study. In the sense of a limiting number that helps to pinpoint or create a canon within a canon, the evangelists do not exactly parallel the Hebrew prophets. There are, of course, other differences between the OT prophets and the NT evangelists. In the OT, the prophet would often indicate his calling, his relationship to the king, and when and how the word of the LORD came to him (for example: Isa 1:1 and Jer 1:1). None of these details are supplied by the four evangelists.

32. For example: Matt 13:17, 16:17; John 16:12–15; 1 Pet 1:10–12, and 2 Pet 1:20–21. These texts reveal that the early Christian movement was aware of the presence of a divine Spirit revealing truth that was quite outside their own human capacity to contrive. This is how they explained their own understanding to their followers.

33. See G. Ernest Wright, "Historical Knowledge and Revelation," in *Translating & Understanding the Old Testament* (1970) 302, where the author suggests that we cannot read NT Christology back into OT texts of which those prophets "were seemingly unaware."

34. See, for example, the early assessment by Albert Schweitzer, *The Quest of the Historical Jesus* (1906) 4: "There is no historical task which so reveals a man's true self as the writing of a Life of Jesus . . . each individual created Him in accordance with his own character." Schweitzer is summing up over a century of scholarship preceding him. In a similar vein, Ernst Käsemann, *Essays on New Testament Themes* (1971) 19 says: "Did not the Jesus of the Gospels become, under the hand of the Rationalists, a figure just like ourselves, thus showing how the wealth of portraits of Jesus corresponds to the multitude of possible viewpoints and beholders?" One of the best commentaries on scholarly subjectivity can be found in Bo Reicke's "Incarnation and Exaltation: The Historic Jesus and the Kerygmatic

frequent complaint found in serious academic publishing is the confusion, endless speculation, and even pessimism over a lack of unity in scholarly activity.[35] John Dominic Crossan, in perhaps the most quoted metaphor describing the academic chaos and uncertainty in Jesus research, has labeled the discipline's lack of unity as a "bad joke."[36] As an example of this state of affairs, I cite the following observation from J. S. Kloppenborg Verbin, himself a significant scholar on the subject of Q:

> Some consensus has been achieved with respect to the authenticity of sayings such as Q 6.20b or reports such as the baptism of Jesus. But wildly divergent representations of Jesus can be constructed from the same general fund of sayings and stories. Part of the cacophony of divergent voices is simply a function of the sheer numbers of scholars at work on the problem of the historical Jesus."[37]

Christ," *Int* 16 (1962) 166: "Thus the result is merely an infinite multitude of opinions. And the picture of Jesus so produced is a work of man that must be rejected as an idol." For an interesting account of how modern Jewry has tried to assimilate itself into American culture by coming to terms with the person of Jesus, see Matthew Hoffman, *From Rebel to Rabbi* (2007). Hoffman's book presents Jesus from various Jewish angles, some sympathetic, some hostile, but never fully supernatural.

35. For hints of scholarly pessimism, see Graham Stanton, "The Origin and Purpose of Matthew's Gospel: Matthean Scholarship from 1945 to 1980," *ANRW* 25.3 (1984) 1899: "Many scholars are now prepared to concede that it is extremely difficult, if not impossible, to prove any one solution of the synoptic problem, since so many of the arguments which have been used in the past are reversible." See also the conclusion reached by Andreas Lindemann, "Die Logienquell Q Fragen an eine gut Begründete Hypothese," in *The Sayings Source Q and the Historical Jesus* (2001) 26: "Aber es bleibt die Frage, ob eine umfassende literarische Analyse und theologische Auslegung der Logienquelle, die der Analyse und Interpretation der synoptischen Evangelien vergleichbar wäre, wirklich möglich ist." For unfounded optimism, see Paul Hoffmann, "Mutmassungen uber Q: Zum Problem der literarischen Genese von Q," in *The Sayings Source Q and the Historical Jesus* (2001) 255: "James Robinson schließt seine Einführung zur *Editio Critica of* Q etwas sibyllinisch, wenn er einen Konsens der gegenwärtigen Q-Forschung darüber prognostiziert..." Richard A. Horsley, "Q and Jesus: Assumptions, Approaches, and Analyses," *Semeia* 55.1 (1991) 176: "Moreover, since meaning depends upon cultural context, the meaning discerned in sayings which we have isolated from their literary and historical contexts is highly susceptible of determination by the cultural context of the modern interpreter." John H. Leith, "The Bible and Theology," *Int* 30 (1976) 238: "Critical-historical methods of study are, as Barth protested in 1922, notoriously subjective and tentative." More recently, see Joel Willitts, "Presuppositions and Procedures in the Study of the 'Historical Jesus': Or, Why I Decided Not to Be a 'Historical Jesus' Scholar," *JSHJ* 3 (2005) 61–108. See also William John Lyons, "Hope for a Troubled Discipline? Contributions to New Testament Studies from Reception History," *JSNT* 33.2 (2010) 207–20.

36. J. D. Crossan, *The Historical Jesus* (1991) xxvii–xxviii: "*Historical Jesus research* is becoming something of a scholarly bad joke . . . . It is the number of competent and even eminent scholars producing pictures of Jesus at wide variance with one another . . . it seems we can have as many pictures as there are exegetes. . . . But that stunning diversity is an academic embarrassment." See also his comment from "Historical Jesus as Risen Lord," in *The Jesus Controversy* (1999) 2, where he takes exception to the "oft-repeated and rather cheap gibe that historical Jesus researchers are simply looking down a deep well and seeing their own reflections from below." See also Marcus J. Borg, "Reflections on a Discipline: A North American Perspective," in *Studying the Historical Jesus* (1994) 9–31, provides a running personal commentary on where he feels the discipline is divided. He includes a reference to Crossan's comment about the discipline as a "bad joke" (25).

37. J. S. Kloppenborg Verbin, "Discursive Practices in the Sayings Gospel Q and the Quest of the

He then echoes Crossan's sentiments with a reference to the current quest for the historical Jesus as a "bad joke."[38] Burton L. Mack refers to a similar lack among scholars of "any agreed-upon theoretical framework to adjudicate the differences among them. This is a serious indictment of the guild of New Testament scholarship. The guild pretends to be an academic discipline, but in fact resists the pursuit of a theoretic framework . . ."[39] Elisabeth Schussler recreates the following scene: "If Jesus, like Moses, were to return to earth, read all his biographies, and attend the Jesus Seminar or the Society of Biblical Literature annual meeting, he also would marvel and ask with amazement: 'Who is this person they are talking about?'"[40] Going back to a previous generation, George Eldon Ladd notes:

> An historical Jesus has not been found who stands the tests of scholarship . . . . This failure of the historical-critical method to discover an historical Jesus who was big enough to account for the rise of the Christian faith and the gospel portrait long ago led M. Kähler to postulate a difference between the *historische* Jesus and the *geschichtliche* Christ. The *historische* Jesus is the creation of the historical-critical methods—a *Holzweg*, a road that leads nowhere. The Jesus who lived in history is the *geschichtliche*, the biblical Christ who is portrayed in the Gospels. Kähler believed in the principle of causality; he insisted that only the Christ pictured in the Gospels, in whom dwelt the supernatural (*übergeschichtlich*), is big enough to account for the rise of the Christian faith.[41]

Historical Jesus," in *The Sayings Source Q and the Historical Jesus* (2001) 49–50. See also Terrence W. Tilley, "Remembering the Historic Jesus—A New Research Program?" *ThS* 68 (2007) 3, who argues that the "historical Jesuses" as "discovered" by scholarship are simply constructs of these individual scholars. He acknowledges indebtedness to Fiorenza. In a similar note of pessimism, see Barnhart and Kraeger, *In Search of First-Century Christianity* (2000) 117: "A careful examination of the current research among biblical scholars reveals a wide diversity of opinion regarding the details of the earthly Jesus. When the various portrayals of Jesus are explicated, no one version gains the support of most New Testament scholars. Agreement increases only as an increasing number of details are eliminated or placed in doubt."

38. Kloppenborg Verbin has borrowed this metaphor from J. D. Crossan, *The Historical Jesus* (1991) xxviii.

39. Burton Mack, *The Christian Myth* (2001) 34–35.

40. Elisabeth Fiorenza, *Jesus and the Politics of Interpretation* (2000) 1.

41. George Eldon Ladd, *A Theology of the New Testament* (1974) 179. For an insightful analogy on Ladd's point, see Morton Smith, *Jesus the Magician* (1978) 6: "Trying to find the actual Jesus is like trying, in atomic physics, to locate a submicroscopic particle and determine its charge. The particle cannot be seen directly, but on a photographic plate we see the lines left by the trajectories of larger particles it put in motion. By tracing these trajectories back to their common origin, and by calculating the force necessary to make the particles move as they did, we can locate and describe the invisible cause." The premise of this study is that the original cause, invisible though it is, was the Spirit revealing the meaning of Jesus. Smith, however, uses his analogy for an opposite application as he argues that the Gospels are legendary in nature. His analogy, however, is useful for the thesis of this investigation.

Ladd's quote from Kähler needs underscoring. The original context is: "I regard the entire Life-of-Jesus movement as a blind alley. A blind alley usually has something alluring about it, or no one would enter it in the first place."[42]

Although an appeal to revelation should not be used as an exit device to escape the difficulties encountered in historical research,[43] by the same token, an appeal to historical research should not be used as an escape mechanism to avoid facing the possibility that divine revelation is responsible for the biblical text.[44] The purpose of this study has been to consider if the omission of revelation leaves a void that cannot be filled by any other probable alternative. If, as I believe, the Gospels are ultimately the product of divine revelation, then forsaking this premise creates chaos. If divine revelation is the guiding light to understanding these writings, then an avenue opens up to better understand the basic nature of the four Gospels.[45]

I return now to a basic premise of this study: the four evangelists cannot be accused of literary collusion. For example, Matthew does not say that he is writing about a King Branch and Mark is writing about Servant Branch; neither does Luke say that he is writing about a Man/Priestly Branch and John about a LORD God Branch, as if they had entered into a conspiratorial agreement to parcel out each Branch text to one another. The four evangelists do not reveal this kind of self-conscious awareness of their own work or the work of the others. This is not the end of puzzling issues. Not one of the four evangelists mentions himself or one of the other three. Previously, so far as we know, not one of the evangelists had a reputation or even a record of past literary experience or accomplishments. Subsequent to the issuance of their Gospels, not one of the evangelists left a written record of anything outside the NT. Although some scholars question whether the four evangelists wrote their respective Gospels as a *sui generis* ("unique" or "one of its kind"),[46] the position taken here is that these

---

42. Martin Kähler, *The So-Called Historical Jesus and the Historic Biblical Christ* (1964) 46.

43. Evangelicals typically become nervous and apprehensive at the thought that something in the Gospels may not be historically accurate; rationalistic liberals become fearful that some part of the Gospels may be due to supernatural inspiration.

44. In my judgment, a skeptical approach is rather arbitrary. It could be likened to a medical student who wants to be a cardiologist yet does not want to study the heart.

45. Albert Schweitzer, *The Quest of the Historical Jesus* (1968) 7, used the expression "a fortuitous series of episodes." I borrow Schweitzer's wording but intend a different application. Schweitzer must be credited, however, with recognizing a valuable truth: if the Gospels are products of random and happy chance, then it is hopeless to understand the principles behind their composition. The argument that I have presented sets out to demonstrate that this numerical phenomenon is too unusual to be brushed aside as mere human coincidence—or "a fortuitous series of episodes." The present thesis not only involves the number four but, concurrently, it explores a significant theological symmetry employed within this number. The analysis, therefore, is based upon both a quantitative and qualitative evaluation of the sources.

46. See, for example, the defense of the genre of biography to explain the Gospels by Perry V. Kea, "Writing a *bios*: Matthew's Genre Choices and Rhetorical Situation," *SBLSP* 33 (1994) 574, in which Kea in his opening paragraph quite confidently claims that there has been a "dissolution of the old consensus that the Gospels are *sui generis*." See also Philip L. Shuler, *A Genre for the Gospels*

evangelists wrote in a genre vacuum in which they had no model, no forerunner, no exemplar or *Vorlage* to work from.⁴⁷ Certainly, it is indisputable that there is no corresponding model of four contemporary authors writing of a single influential figure.⁴⁸ I would suggest, however, that the term "unique" is appropriate because it

(1982) 27: "new genres are not created in a literary vacuum, that is, they cannot be *sui generis*." Shuler argues, ultimately, that the Gospels are encomium biography. For a mediating position, combining elements of both biography and uniqueness, see Martin Hengel, "Eye-witness Memory and Writing of the Gospels" in *The Written Gospel* (2005) 72: 'While the Gospels may not be 'biographies' in the modern sense, they are comparable, despite their unique eschatological determination, to ancient 'life descriptions' and were also understood as such in antiquity. This is shown by Justin's use of the term *apomnemoneumata ton apostolon*, the 'memoirs of the apostles,' which replaces for Gentiles the easily misunderstood term *euangelia*, and echoes Xenophon's 'memoirs of the Socrates'. This is valid, although in their intention they were and are texts *sui generis*." A further dissenting view, may be found in Ben Witherington, *The Many Faces of the Christ* (1998) 132, and his *The Gospel of Mark* (2001) 6-9, in which the author itemizes seven primary reasons along with two additional secondary reasons for viewing the Gospels as biography. See Helmut Köster, "Frühchristliche Evangelienliteratur," *ANRW* 25.2 (1984) 2.1469-75. Most recently, Craig S. Keener, *The Historical Jesus of the Gospels* (2010) 75 and 83, argues that the term *unique* is of "limited value" because it does not provide for the reader guidelines of a conventional nature. See also Keener's book *Biographies and Jesus: What Does It Mean for the Gospels to Be Biographies?* (2016).

47. Eduard Schweizer, "Mark's Contribution to the Quest of the Historical Jesus," *NTS* 10 (1964) 421: "In this situation, Mark wrote his gospel. The most astonishing fact is this decision in and of itself. For there are almost no prototypes." See also Robert H. Stein, "What Is Redaktionsgeschichte?" *JBL* 88.1 (1969) 49: "Yet we must not lose sight of the fact that the writing of the gospels was a unique event." See also E. P. Sanders and Margaret Davies, *Studying the Synoptic Gospels* (1989) 51: "Matthew, Mark and Luke are remarkably alike. There are examples from mediaeval literature of works which agree as closely, but from ancient literature no other examples of such close similarity are known." See also the very careful assessment of genre possibilities by Robert Guelich, "The Gospel Genre," in *The Gospel and the Gospels* (1991) 173-208. His treatment of encomium or "laudatory biography" is illuminating as he concludes (181): "If so, why then the anonymity of the Gospel, the absence of stated intention, and the stark contrast in the way it reads from any of the examples cited (Isocrates, Xenophon, Philo, Lucian, and Philostratus)." Guelich finally concludes (202): "To the extent that Mark first put the 'gospel' in *written* form, he created a new *literary* genre, the gospel." David Trobisch, *The First Edition of the New Testament* (2000) 38, notes that manuscripts read: εὐαγγέλιον κατά for all four Gospels, indicating a literary genre. After stating this, his argument weakens because of a lack of clarity. On the one hand, he claims that "no evidence has surfaced in pre-Christian literature, either, that the term can be used to refer to a literary genre" (thereby discounting gospel as a genre); while on the other hand, Trobisch refers to the expression εὐαγγέλιον κατά as an "unusual genre designation" (thereby implying gospel is a genre, although "unusual"). See also Paul J. Achtemeier, *Mark* (1975) 22, for similar conclusions. See also Norman Perrin, "The Interpretation of the Gospel of Mark," *Int* 30 (1976) 115-24. See also the defense of the Gospels as a unique genre peculiar to Christianity in the essay by James H. Charlesworth, "What has the Old Testament to Do with the New?" in *The Old and New Testaments: Their Relationship and the "Intertestamental" Literature* (1993) 55. See also the recent essay by M. Eugene Boring, "The Birth of Narrative Theology," in *Chalice Introduction to the New Testament* (2004) 146.

48. David Aune, *The New Testament in Its Literary Environment* (1987) 70: "The phenomenon of several biographies of the same person existing side by side and with approximately equal esteem had no parallel in antiquity." See also Eduard Norden, *Die Antike Kunstprosa: vom vi. Jahrhundert v. Chr. bis in die Zeit der Renaissance* (1998) 2.480: "Die Evangelien stehen völlig abseits von der kunstmäßigen Litteratur. Auch rein äußerlich als litterarische Denkmäler betrachtet tragen sie den Stempel des absolute Neuen zur Schau." See also Eugene E. Lemcio, "The Gospels and Canonical Criticism,"

distills the essence of these Gospels as standing apart from and above any comparable literary model.[49] Edgar Hennecke in his monumental work on the apocryphal gospels contends that any effort to connect the four Gospels with either pre-Christian or non-Christian literature would end in shipwreck.[50] Gian Biago Conte, writing from within the scholarly discipline as a classicist of Roman literature, observes what he judges to be an inviolable principle: "tradition produces a norm, which is, so to speak, the key of the genre."[51] We can see that the "tradition" of the four Gospels spawned subsequent gospels with a norm with which to work. That norm was the life of Jesus. Yet, the question remains: what precursor produced the fourfold Gospel? If we look posteriorly, we see such gospels as the Gospel of Thomas; if we look anteriorly, we see nothing that would account for the sudden origin of this genre.[52] The posterior is understandable; the anterior is a vague and empty vacuum. It is often maintained that without a proper knowledge of where a particular piece of literature falls on the genre scale, it is not possible to correctly understand the contents.[53] That premise overstates the

---

in *The New Testament as Canon* (1992) 34: "There is no other biblical sub-unit of its kind. Multiple, parallel accounts of the same person or event are not to be found elsewhere. The closest example might be the story of David in 2 Samuel and 1 Chronicles, and yet the canon separates them into different sections." Although acknowledging similarities with OT historiography, Ulrich Luz, *Matthew 1–7: A Commentary* (2007) 13–15, prefers the description of generic uniqueness, or *sui generis*: "They are proclamatory stories and are not simply to be attributed to any profane genre." Luz also discounts the genre of biography as being unknown to Matthew (15): "In this cultural circle biographies are as good as unknown; presumably even Matthew was not familiar with any ancient biography." See also Adela Yarbro Collins, *Mark: A Commentary* (2007) 1 and 18, who stakes out a mediating position for Mark as combining the OT model of sacred history and infusing it with Hellenistic historiographical traditions. See also W. D. Davies and Dale Allison, *A Critical and Exegetical Commentary on the Gospel According to Saint Matthew I–VII* (1988) 4–5, who eschew identification of Matthew with biography and find intertexuality with the OT.

49. John Ashton, "Second Thoughts on the Fourth Gospel," in *What We Have Heard from the Beginning* (2007) 12, asks an appropriate question: "When we speak of a 'carrot cake,' we mean a cake in which carrots are one of the main ingredients but they are not exactly 'fused' with the flour, the eggs, and the oil. Applied to Mark's Gospel, the term 'kerygmatic biography' seems to imply that it is a special form of biography, just as carrot cake is a special form of cake. But is this right?"

50. E. Hennecke, *New Testament Apocrypha* (1963) 1.76.

51. G. B. Conte, *Genres and Readers* (1994) 115.

52. Such is the case with the OT as well. See David Damrosch, *The Narrative Covenant: Transformations of Genre in the Growth of Biblical Literature* (1987) 41: "The thesis of this book is that the origins of Hebrew historical prose can be traced in Mesopotamian literature of the second millennium, but not through a direct comparison of historical writings alone."

53. See, for example, David A. deSilva, *An Introduction to the New Testament* (2004) 146: "If it had no connection with existing genres in the ancient world, its audience would not know how to interpret it, being without the necessary cues and clues that knowledge of genre provides." See also Richard A. Burridge, "About People, by People, for People: Gospel Genre and Audiences," in *The Gospels for All Christians: Rethinking the Gospel Audiences* (1998) 120, who bends over backwards to dispel the notion of *sui generis*. He argues that it is impossible for the Gospels to be unique because this uniqueness would thereby make it impossible to communicate to others. This argument seems strained to us. Knowing the conventions of a particular genre (comedy or tragedy, for example) does make it possible to better understand the work. However, this does not prove that a new genre cannot be understood. Admittedly, Burridge's objective is to set aside the view that the Gospels were products of

case. All genres at one time were an archetype, breaking new ground, and pioneering new literary paths. This does not necessarily imply that the original readers/listeners were confused and unable to interpret for themselves these novel contents. Although it is true, as a principle, that literary works cannot be divorced from their surrounding social conditions, this does not necessarily prove that a new genre is impossible. H. N. Roskam has recently taken a completely different tack on the issue of genre by advocating:

> The form-critical idea that Mark's Gospel is a literary product without any literary parallels presupposes that Christianity is a unique phenomenon that developed on its own, apart from its cultural surroundings. It goes without saying, however, that first-century Christianity arose from, and was part of, contemporary Hellenistic culture.[54]

Roskam uses the issue of the nature of literary productions (genre) as leverage against the uniqueness of Christianity. In his judgment, the Gospels cannot be unique because this would allow for the unthinkable conclusion that Christianity somehow "developed on its own." What Roskam considers to be unthinkable, I believe to be thinkable. In this case, the four Gospels fall in the same category as the virgin birth of Jesus and his resurrection from the dead. That is, a supernatural causative power is at work.

Illuminating this literary profile even further is evidence that the early disciples of Jesus were from Galilee—a region not noted for producing authors.[55] Although there is no internal evidence establishing actual authorship for any of the four Gospels, the testimony from the early church combined with information about the early disciples may be of some value. Consulting first the data from the four Gospels and Acts, we learn that the disciples are Galileans and not advanced in education. The surviving testimony from the early church is responsible for and attests to the received tradition that the biblical personages of Matthew, Mark, Luke, and John are the human authors of the Gospels. This tradition is not impossible, not unlikely, and not improbable. Although this early church tradition cannot be conclusively proved,

---

a community rather than individuals. To this I agree.

54. H. N. Roskam, *The Purpose of the Gospel of Mark in its Historical and Social Context* (2004) 220.

55. This is not to argue that Galileans could not read. See, for example, W. D. Davies, "Canon and Christology," in *The Glory of Christ in the New Testament* (1987) 19: "The reading of documents, written on papyrus or skin, was more widespread than is often acknowledged. Apparently, even in out-of-the-way Nazareth, Jesus could read, and assumed that his opponents in Galilee also could." See also William E. Arnal, *Jesus and the Village Scribes* (2001) 150: "Under such circumstances, even the most de facto autonomous of towns required various official and witnessed bills of sale, petitions, contracts, marriage agreements, wills, and so forth, as well as an apparatus for the administration of justice. Thus, in addition to local strong men and affluent families, a small class of literate administrators was essential to the smooth functioning of the region even prior to Roman-Herodian city building." This is the extent of Galilean literacy—essentially enough literary skills to carry on business. Arnal goes on to add that these administrators would have been few in number and certainly not available in every community of Galilee.

neither can it be disproved.[56] As Richard J. Bauckham contends, the four Gospels were never known by any other names than the four that have come down to us.[57] In fact, the lack of credible and authentic alternative documents from their own hands makes it impossible to compare their literary skills. We are left, therefore, with the testimony from the early church.[58]

The possible Galilean origin of at least three of the four evangelists is a mysterious and strange phenomenon that the backwater region of Galilee produced three (or possibly even four) very complex pieces of literature that have defied scholarly attempts to unlock its compositional secrets for the past two hundred years.[59] Further adding to the literary phenomenon of a fourfold Gospel is the general consensus that these writings arose from a non-literate culture.[60]

56. For example, Martin Hengel, "Eye-witness Memory and the Writing of the Gospels," in *The Written Gospel* (2005) 82, locates Matthew, Mark and Luke in the time period of AD 70 to 90/100. Hengel also claims (73): "We do not have any written material from Jesus himself or his immediate circle of disciples." The early church did not understand the writers in this manner. The standard scholarly response is that the early church intentionally attributed to the Gospels the biblical names of Matthew, Mark, and Luke in order to validate the authority of the writings. For a moderate view on the identity of "Mark," see D. H. Juel, "The Origin of Mark's Christology," in *The Messiah: Developments in Earliest Judaism and Christianity* (1987) 449: "We may or may not be able to establish some link between the anonymous narrator and an identifiable, flesh-and-blood person from the early Christian movement.... I am personally dubious about the historical reliability of the tradition that views the composer of this work as an intimate of Peter, but that will not be a major factor in interpreting the finished product." For an overview of possibilities for identifying when the Gospels of Matthew, Mark, and Luke came to be known by these names, see Andrew Gregory, *The Reception of Luke and Acts in the Period before Irenaeus* (2003) 45–54.

57. R. Bauckham, *Jesus and the Eyewitnesses* (2006) 303: "No evidence exists that these Gospels were ever known by other names."

58. For a defense of the tradition of early church (second century to third), see Martin Hengel, "The Gospel of Mark: Time of Origin and Situation," (1985) 1: "By contrast, I have tried below to demonstrate that the information from the early fathers of the second century is less questionable and doubtful than these relatively recent conjectures." The possibility that an eye-witness such as Nicodemus might have been an author of one of the Gospels is intriguing but not provable.

59. In order to understand the complexities and intricacies of scholarly research for solving the so-called "synoptic problem," all one has to do is to consult a workbook such as E. P. Sanders and Margaret Davies, *Studying the Synoptic Gospels* (1989) 112: "It has become clear that no one solution to the synoptic problem is without objections." These two scholars are objective enough to demonstrate that at every conclusion reached regarding the two main competing theories of composition, there are valid reasons that keep one theory from claiming a knockout blow of the other. At best, all proponents of one theory can do is claim a split decision and then hope that the next generation of scholars does not overturn their decision. Essentially, the two most attractive scholarly theories of gospel composition are deadlocked in a very interesting stalemate.

60. James D. G. Dunn, "Living Traditions," in *What Is It that the Scripture Says* (2006) 281. Dunn extrapolates from this his own understanding of the role of oral tradition in the first twenty years after Jesus. On literacy in the ancient world, see William V. Harris, *Ancient Literacy* (1989). On literacy in Roman Palestine in the first century, see M. Bar-Ilan, "Illiteracy in the Land of Israel in the First Centuries CE," in *Essays in the Social Scientific Study of Judaism and Jewish Society* (1992) 46–61; and Catherine Hezser, *Jewish Literacy in Roman Palestine* (2001). On the implications of the first century as an essentially illiterate world, see Ben Witherington, *What's In the Word: Rethinking the Socio-Rhetorical Character of the New Testament* (2009) 7–17.

It is interesting that the four evangelists do not fall victim to seeking a prominent place for themselves in their respective Gospels. Once again, we are brought face to face with another crossroads decision: since the disciples are pictured as vying for prestige and prominence in the four Gospels, and since the evangelists do not identify themselves, does this not create a wall of separation between disciples and evangelists? How can we remove the disparity between the profile of the disciples seeking honor for themselves as reported in the Gospels and the contrasting anonymity of the Gospels? Within Scripture itself, the argument for their belief in the resurrection and their experience of the power of the Spirit may provide sufficient historical reason for such a silence. Another approach may also be taken. Anonymity can lead us back to the premise of this study: the disciples were motivated by a power beyond themselves.

The consequence of this premise is the following: if one sees the Gospels as divinely inspired revelations, this would place such a reader in a position to encounter the living God. If, however, one sees the Gospels as fictitious and misguided attempts to slander Jews, hoodwink Gentiles, and fabricate an artificial Jesus, this could potentially place the interpreter in the dubious position of standing over the four Gospels in judgment rather than standing under them as a human in need of God. Such a misperception would only add more frustration to the already ever-expanding pool of academic confusion and chaos. Such nullity would not lead to God.

Has the conclusion of this study overrun the evidence and fallen victim to special pleading? Although caution is the watchword of critical study, the concept of divine revelation should not be anxiously avoided, as if such a concept implied recklessness. Unusual circumstances call for equally unusual causes. There are many items connected with the four Gospels that, at a minimum, should arouse suspicion that there is more at work than the naïve simplicity of Galilean peasants. Are we faced with only a set of fortuitous compositional circumstances? Are striking similarities simply coincidental? Or is there a deeper influence at work in the Gospels? Exciting possibilities emerge upon consideration that the four evangelists were not in a conspiracy of literary collusion, nor were their writings a result of purely historical causes; neither is there direct evidence that any of the four contradicts any of the other three. By not assigning artificiality to the four Gospels, this opens up a new way for understanding both the Gospels and revelation. It also fills a gap which struggles to be filled by any other alternative.[61]

61. I cannot bypass Marcus J. Borg's personal comment on what he refers to as "paranormal" in his article "Reflections on a Discipline" (1994) 29: "However, assigning major importance to the presence and role of the paranormal in the historical Jesus and early Christianity is not common within the discipline. Perhaps this is because of our deep-seated and in some ways healthy suspicion of accounts of the paranormal. Or perhaps we take it so much for granted that we feel it unnecessary to mention. Or perhaps we don't quite know what do with this material. Whatever the reason, it is interesting that the interdisciplinary models for illuminating the religious experience or religious 'type' of Jesus have not been used much at all." For an attempt to assign Jesus' walking on water to ASC, see John J. Pilch, "Altered States of Consciousness in the Synoptics," in *The Social Setting of Jesus and the Gospels* (2002) 103–16.

Matthew 16:18 reports that Simon Peter, upon confessing Jesus to be the "Christ, the Son of the living God" was then informed by Jesus: "Blessed are you, Simon son of Jonah, for this was not revealed to you by man, but by my Father in heaven." We have no idea how Peter experienced this confession personally and internally. Did he feel something, such as a current of harmless but illuminating energy flowing through him? The answer to this question is beyond our reach as the sources are silent. What is significant, though, is that Jesus interpreted the origin of the confession as having come from God.[62] Since Jesus informed Peter regarding the point of origination, the text as we have it in Matthew suggests that Peter may have needed this affirmation. The confession, therefore, may have surprised Peter, but we cannot be sure.[63] What we are left with is both the confession of faith, accepted by Jesus as coming from God, and the suggestion that such confession is grounded in revelation as part of the Jesus tradition. In other words, it is impossible to divorce the possibility of inspired revelation from the early history of the Jesus movement.

The Keel of a Ship

As the keel of a ship supports the entire frame of the vessel, yet is submerged underneath the water and out of sight to the crew on board, so the four prophetic pictures of the Branch are also out of sight and not specifically cited in the Gospels. Just as the keel of a ship provides structure and stability to a ship, so the four prophetic texts form the backbone of the Gospels. Just as a keel is the indispensable unifying piece which holds the hull of the ship together, so the four prophetic texts unify the presentation of Jesus in the four Gospels. The keel of a ship thus provides a suitable analog to describe an invisible yet unifying force that binds the structure of this study together. Other

---

62. I am mystified by James H. Charlesworth's statement, "From Messianology to Christology: Problems and Prospects," in *The Messiah* (1987b) 9: "Even if Mark accurately records Peter's words, we have no way of discerning what Peter meant by 'Christ.' Even if we knew exactly what he meant, we still would not be able to perceive what Jesus was thinking, since scholars throughout the world have come to agree that according to Mark Jesus did not simply accept Peter's claim that he was the Messiah (contrary to Matthew's version). If Jesus had accepted the declaration he was the Messiah, then we would be able to explain how his earliest followers came to this startling conclusion. If he did not accept this claim, as now seems obvious after years of scholars' sensitive and historical study of Mark and the Jewish literature contemporaneous with him, then we are faced with the problem of why and how his followers concluded that the title 'the Messiah' was appropriate for him. Research on such issues leads not to easy answers but to perplexing questions." It is not clear how Matthew and Mark can be pitted off against each other. Part of the purpose of this study is to provide another alternative for understanding the data. From one point of view, Charlesworth's observation is insightful; from another it resembles a scholarly shell game where the little pea under the shell is shifted about at the discretion of the mover. For a similar view, see Hans Dieter Betz, "Plutarch's *Life of Numa*: Some Observations on Graeco-Roman 'Messianism,'" in *Redemption and Resistance: The Messianic Hopes of Jews and Christians in Antiquity* (2007) 50.

63. Francis Watson, in his *Gospel Writing* (2013) 155, wonders if one evangelist would have understood another as a "proof of the common inspiration of the Holy Spirit." David E. Garland, *Luke* (2011) 54, offers the view that the verb ἔδοξε(ν) suggests a "decision that is prompted by the Holy Spirit."

than the singular and transformative person of Jesus the Christ, no other factor holds the four Gospels so tightly together as this collage of four prophetic texts.[64]

One reason that the subject of divine inspiration is no longer discussed in the forum of international scholarship is the association of revelation with infallibility. Admittedly, the proposition that Scripture is infallible and inerrant is impossible to document in historical investigation. The validity of this idea is accepted only by faith. F. F. Bruce expressed this view as follows: "The work of the Holy Spirit is not discerned by means of the common tools of the historian's trade."[65] If there is a valid point to Bruce's contention, how can the subject of inspiration be investigated? To borrow a horticultural analogy, although we cannot see the root of a tree with the unaided human eye, this does not mean the inquirer cannot study and scrutinize the fruit of the tree. Inasmuch as a tree's fruit can provide evidence of a kind regarding its root, we can likewise focus our attention on things visible as opposed to things invisible. This means that such results as the creation of belief (in the resurrection, for example), the formation of communities who engage in the worship and preaching of Jesus, the composition and preservation of sacred texts, the writing of commentaries upon such texts, the moral and spiritual transformation of lives, perseverance through Imperial persecution, and the eventual triumph of the Great Church over oppressive forces gives evidence of a kind and should not be discounted.[66] This investigation, however, considers only one of these topics: the composition of sacred texts.

There are two ultimate conclusions to this study. The first is that the four prophetic texts of Jer 23:5–6, Zech 3:8, 6:12–13, and Isa 4:2 provide the unseen structure for the four canonical Gospels. The second conclusion is that the linkage between prophetic texts, canonical Gospels, and the heavenly Images in Rev 4:7 furnish a plausible case for the divine inspiration of the four Gospels. The thesis of this study is that the totality of Jesus' life is an event of such supernatural proportion that only an interpretation of equal supernatural revelation can account for it.[67] I conclude with a thought expressed in chapter 3: the internal logic of the biblical canon (and Jesus himself) is that *everything* in the prophets concerning Jesus had to be fulfilled. Pursuing this

---

64. See Stephen Hultgren, "The Apostolic Church's Influence on the Order of Sayings in the Double Tradition," *ZNW* 99.2 (2008) 186, in a different context (arguing against the unity of Q) uses the metaphor of a submerged reef.

65. F. F. Bruce, *The Canon of Scripture* (1988) 281.

66. For example, see Richard J. Bauckham, "The Throne of God and the Worship of Jesus," in *The Jewish Roots of Christological Monotheism* (1999) 43–69; L. W. Hurtado, *Lord Jesus Christ: Devotion to Jesus in Earliest Christianity* (2003); and N. T. Wright, *The Resurrection of the Son of God: Christian Origins and the Question of God*, III (2003) 717, where Wright concludes that the bodily resurrection of Jesus is a "necessary condition" to account for subsequent events such as the creation of the church.

67. John Barton, "Unity and Diversity in the Biblical Canon," in *The Unity of Scripture and the Diversity of the Canon* (2003) 11-26, prefers to think of the diversity of Scripture as "subordinate to a higher unity" and says (19): "The texts do not all speak with a single voice, yet taken together they witness to a unified truth . . . . That is to say, the Scriptural writers really were communicating an essentially unified vision of the truth, even though they differed on points of detail."

claim for completeness farther, the Greek text of Luke 24:25–28 has a triple emphasis: *everything* (ἐπὶ πᾶσιν) that *all* the prophets spoke (ἀπὸ πάντων τῶν προφητῶν) in *all* the Scriptures regarding himself (ἐν πάσαις ταῖς γραφαῖς τὰ περὶ ἑαυτοῦ) must be fulfilled. Jesus and the early Christians held to a specific view of Scripture as containing a self-limiting structure. The very nature of Scripture requires fulfillment or else it collapses. In terms of this internal demand for fulfillment and completion, the four prophetic texts under consideration in this study offer a plausible explanation as to how fulfillment and completion could have occurred. Notable publications such as Mark L. Strauss's *Four Portraits, One Jesus* and Francis Watson's *The Fourfold Gospel* distill key images of Jesus as king, servant, priest, and God. Strauss extracts these images from a faithful literary analysis of the gospel texts; Watson bases his interpretation on a theological reading of Rev 4:6–7. Richard Burridge does a similar thing by labelling his interpretation as a "symbolic" reading of texts.[68] This present book simply takes the investigation one step further back. By taking this step back, we not only have a literary analysis, a symbolic and theological reading of texts, but also a prophetic background for understanding the four Gospels. With this fourfold foundational background of prophetic texts, this investigation ends up proposing an Old Testament precedent for understanding why we have four Gospels and four living Beings around the throne. The correlation of these four prophetic texts, the four Gospels, and the four living Beings thus argues for a relationship of causation and fulfillment.

---

68. R. A. Burridge, *Four Gospels, One Jesus?* (1994) xi.

Bibliography

Abbott, Edwin A. *The Fourfold Gospel: Introduction.* Cambridge: at the University Press, 1913.
Abegg, Martin G. "Messianic Hope and 4Q285: A Reassessment." *JBL* 113.1 (1994) 81–91.
———. "The Messiah at Qumran: Are We Still Seeing Double?" *DSD* 2.2 (1995) 125–44.
Abegg, Martin G., James E. Bowley, and Edward M.Cook, eds. *Dead Sea Scrolls Concordance: The Non-Biblical Tests from Qumran, Part One.* Leiden: Brill, 2003.
Abraham, W. "The Offense of Divine Revelation." *HTR* 95.3 (2002) 251–64.
Achtemeier, Elizabeth. *Interpretation: Nahum—Malachi.* Atlanta: John Knox, 1986.
Achtemeier, Paul, J. *Mark.* Philadelphia: Fortress, 1975.
———. "Mark as Interpreter of the Jesus Traditions." *Int* 32 (1978) 339–52.
Afzal, Cameron. "Wheels of Time: Merkavah Exegesis in Revelation 4." *SBLSP* 37 (1998) 465–82.
Ahn, Sanghee M. *The Christological Witness Function of the Old Testament Characters in the Gospel of John.* PBM. Edited by Stanley E. Porter et al. Eugene, OR: Wipf & Stock, 2014.
Aichele, George. "Literary Fantasy and the Composition of the Gospels." *Forum* 5 (1989) 42–60.
———. "Jesus's Two Fathers: An Afterlife of the Gospel of Luke." In *Those Outside: Non-canonical Readings of the Canonical Gospels.* Edited by George Aichele, 17–42. London: T &T Clark, 2005.
Aland B. "Die Rezeption des neutestamentliches Textes in den ersten Jahrhunderten." In *The New Testament in Early Christianity: La réception des écrits néotestamentaires dans le christianisme primitive.* BETL LXXXVI. Edited by Jean-Marie Sevrin, 1–38. Leuven: Leuven University Press, 1989.
Aland, Kurt. "The Problem of Anonymity and Pseudonymity in Christian Literature of the First Two Centuries." *JTS* 12.1 (1961) 39–49.
Alexander, Loveday. "Luke's Preface in the Context of Greek Preface-Writing." *NovT* 28 (1986) 48–74.
———. *The Preface to Luke's Gospel: Literary Convention and Social Context in Luke 1.1–4 and Acts 1.1.* SNTS 78. Edited by Margaret Thrall. Cambridge: Cambridge University Press, 1993.
Alkier, Stefan. "From Text to Intertext: Intertexuality as a Paradigm for Reading Matthew." *HTS/TS* 61.1 (2005) 1–18.
Allegro, John M. "Further Messianic References in Qumran Literature." *JBL* 75.3 (1956) 174–87.

———. *The Dead Sea Scrolls and the Christian Myth.* Buffalo, NY: Prometheus, 1984.
Allison, Dale C. *Scriptural Allusions in the New Testament: Light from the Dead Sea Scrolls.* DSSCOL5. North Richland Hills, TX: Bibal, 2000.
———. "Explaining the Resurrection: Conflicting Convictions." *JSHJ* 3.2 (2005) 117–33.
Amador, J. David Hester. *Academic Constraints in Rhetorical Criticism of the New Testament.* JSNTSup 174. Edited by Stanley E. Porter. Sheffield: Sheffield Academic, 1999.
Anderson, Hugh. "The Old Testament in Mark's Gospel." In *The Use of the Old Testament in the New and other Essays: Studies in Honor of William Franklin Stinespring.* Edited by James M. Efird, 280–306. Durham, NC: Duke University Press, 1972.
Anderson, Paul N. *The Fourth Gospel and the Quest for Jesus: Modern Foundations Reconsidered.* LNTS 321. Edited by Mark Goodacre. London: T & T Clark, 2006.
Arnal, William E. *Jesus and the Village Scribes:Galilean Conflicts and the Setting of Q.* Minneapolis: Fortress, 2001.
Aschim, Anders. "Melchizedek and Jesus: 11QMelchizedek and the Epistle to the Hebrews." In *The Jewish Roots of Christological Monotheism: Papers from the St. Andrews Conference on the Historical Origins of the Worship of Jesus.* Edited by J. R. Davila, C. C. Newman, and G. S. Lewis, 129–55. Leiden: Brill, 1999.
Attridge, Harold W. "Genre Bending in the Fourth Gospel." *JBL* 121.1 (2002) 3–21.
Aune, David E. *Revelation 1–5.* WBC 52. Edited by Ralph P. Martin. Dallas: Word, 1982.
———. "Christian Prophecy and the Messianic Status of Jesus." In *The Messiah: Developments in Earliest Judaism and Christianity.* FPSJCO. Edited by James H. Charlesworth, 404–22. Minneapolis: Fortress, 1987.
———. *The New Testament in Its Literary Environment.* LEC 8. Edited by Wayne A. Meeks. Philadelphia: Westminster, 1987.
———. "Greco-Roman Biography." In *Greco-Roman Literature and the New Testament: Selected Forms and Genres.* SBLSBS 21. Edited by David E. Aune, 107–26. Atlanta: Scholars, 1988.
———. "Charismatic Exegesis in Early Judaism and Early Christianity." In *The Pseudepigrapha and Early Biblical Interpretation.* JSPSup14/SSEJC 2. James H. Charlesworth and Craig A. Evans, 126–50. Sheffield: Sheffield Academic, 1993.
Auvray, Paul. *Isaïe 1–39.* Paris: J. Gabalda, 1972.
Baarda, Tjitze. "'A Staff Only, Not a Stick': Disharmony of the Gospels and the Harmony of Tatian." In *The New Testament in Early Christianity: La réption des écrits néotestamentaires dans le christianisme primitive.* Edited by Joseph Tyson, 311–33. NY: Prentice Hall, 1989.
Bachmann, M. *Jerusalem und der Tempel: Die geographisch-theologischen Elemente in der lukanischen Sicht des jüdischen Kultzentrums.* BWANT 109. Stuttgart: Kohlhammer, 1980.
Bacon, B. W. *Studies in Matthew.* New York: Henry Holt, 1930.
Bakker, Egbert J. "Time, Tense, and Thucydides." *CW* 100.2 (2007) 113–22.
Balch, David L. "Comments on the Genre and a Political Theme of Luke–Acts: A Preliminary Comparison of Two Hellenistic Historians." *SBLSP* 28 (1989) 343–61.
Baldwin, Joyce G. "ṢEMAḤ as a Technical Term in the Prophets." *VT* 14.1 (1964) 93–97.
Balla, Peter. "Evidence for an Early Christian Canon (Second and Third Century)." In *The Canon Debate.* Edited by Lee Martin McDonald and James A. Sanders, 372–85. Peabody, MA: Hendrickson, 2002.
Baltzer, K. "The Meaning of the Temple in the Lukan Writings." *HTR* 58 (1965) 263–77.

Barbour, R. S. "The Bible—Word of God?" In *Biblical Studies: Essays in Honor of William Barclay*. Edited by Johnston R. McKay and James F. Miller, 28–42. Philadelphia: Westminster, 1976.

Barclay, William. *Introduction to the First Three Gospels: A Revised Edition of the First Three Gospels*. Philadelphia: Westminster, 1975.

Bar-Ilan, M. "Illiteracy in the Land of Israel in the First Centuries CE." In *Essays in the Social Scientific Study of Judaism and Jewish Society*. Edited by Simocha Fishbane, 46–61. Montreal: Concordia University, 1992.

Barker, Margaret. "The Two Figures in Zechariah." *HeyJ* 18 (1977) 38–46.

———. The Revelation of Jesus Christ. Edinburgh: T & T Clark, 2000.

Barnhart, Joe E. and Linda A. Kraeger, *In Search of First-Century Christianity*. ANCTTBS. Edited by Paul Fiddes et al. Sydney: Ashgate, 2000.

Barr, David L. and Judith L. Wentling. "The Conventions of Classical Biography and the Genre of Luke-Acts: A Preliminary Study." In *Luke-Acts: New Perspectives from the Society of Biblical Literature Seminar*. Edited byCharles H. Talbert, 63–88. New York: Crossroad, 1984.

Barr, James. "The Theological Case against Biblical Theology." In *Canon, Theology, and Old Testament Interpretation: Essays in Honor of Brevard S. Childs*. Edited by Gene M. Tucker and David L. Petersen. Minneapolis: Fortress,1988.

———. *The Concept of Biblical Theology: An Old Testament Perspective*. Minneapolis: Augsburg Fortress, 1999.

Barrett, C. K. "Zweck des 4. Evangeliums." *ZST* 22 (1953) 257–73.

———. "The Background of Mark 10.45." In New Testament Essays: Studies in Memory of Thomas Walter Manson 1893–1958. Edited by A. J. B. Higgins, 1–18. Manchester: University Press, 1959.

———. The Gospel According to John: An Introduction with Commentary and Notes on the Greek Text. London: SPCK, 1965.

———. "The House of Prayer and the Den of Thieves." In *Jesus und Paulus: Festschrift für Werner Georg Kümmel zum 70. Geburtstag*. Edited by E. Earle Ellis and Erich GräBer, 13–20. Göttingen: Vandenhoeck & Ruprecht, 1975.

Barth, Gerhard. "Matthew's Understanding of the Law." In *Überlieferung und Auslegung im Matthäusevangelium*,1963. ET *Tradition and Interpretation in Matthew*. NTL. Translated by Percy Scott. Edited by Alan Richardson, 58–64. Philadelphia: Westminster, 1963.

Barton, John. "Marcion Revisited." In *The Canon Debate*. Edited by Lee Martin McDonald and James A. Sanders, 341–54. Peabody, MA: Hendrickson, 2002.

———. "Unity and Diversity in the Biblical Canon." In *Die Einheit der Schrift und die Vielfalt des Kanons: The Unity of Scripture and the Diversity of the Canon*. BZNW 118. Edited by John Barton and Michael Wolter, 11–26. Berlin: Walter de Gruyter, 2003.

———. "Two Types of Harmonization." In *What Is it that the Scripture Says? Essays in Biblical Interpretation, Translation, and Reception in Honour of Henry Wansbrough OSB*. Edited by Philip McCosker, 266–74. London: T & T Clark, 2006.

Batdorf, Irvin W. "Interpreting Jesus since Bultmann: Selected Paradigms and Their Hermeneutic Matrix." *SBLSP* 23 (1984) 187–215.

Bauckham, Richard J. *The Climax of Prophecy: Studies on the Book of Revelation*. Edinburgh: T & T Clark, 1993.

———. *The Theology of the Book of Revelation*. NTT. Edited by James D. G. Dunn. Cambridge: Cambridge University Press, 1993.

———, ed. *The Gospel for All Christians: Rethinking the Gospel Audiences*. Grand Rapids: Eerdmans, 1998.

———. "The Throne of God and the Worship of Jesus." In *The Jewish Roots of Christological Monotheism: Papers from the St. Andrews Conference on the Historical Origins of the Worship of Jesus*. Edited by J. R. Davila, C. C. Newman, and G. S. Lewis, 43–69. Leiden: Brill, 1999.

———. *Jesus and the Eyewitnesses: The Gospels as Eyewitness Testimony*. Grand Rapids: Eerdmans, 2006.

———. "Historiographical Characteristics of the Gospel of John." *NTS* 53 (2007) 17–36.

———. "Eyewitnesses and Critical History: A Response to Jens Schröter and Craig Evans." *JSNT* 3.2 (2008) 221–35.

———. *Gospel of Glory: Major Themes in Johannine Theology*. Grand Rapids: Baker Academic, 2015.

Bauer, David R. *The Structure of Matthew's Gospel: A Study in Literary Design*. BLS 15. David M. Gunn. Sheffield: Sheffield Academic, 1988.

———. "The Kingship of Jesus in the Matthean Infancy Narrative: A Literary Analysis." *CBQ* 57.2 (1995) 306–23.

———. "The Literary and Theological Function of the Genealogy in Matthew's Gospel." In *Treasures New and Old: Recent Contributions to Matthean Studies*. SBLSS 1. Edited by David R. Bauer and Mark Allan Powell, 129–60. Atlanta: Scholars, 1996.

Baum, Armin D. "The Anonymity of the New Testament History Books: A Stylistic Device in Context of Greco-Roman and Ancient Near Eastern Literature." *NovT* 50 (2008) 120–42.

Beasley-Murray, G. R. "The Two Messiahs in the Testaments of the Twelve Patriarchs." *JTS* 48 (1947) 1–12.

Beale, G. K. *The Book of Revelation: A Commentary on the Greek Text*. NIGTC. Edited by I. Howard Marshall and Donald A. Hagner. Grand Rapids: Eerdmans, 1999.

———. *The Temple and the Church's Mission: A Biblical Theology of the Dwelling Place of God*. Downers Grove, IL: IVP Academic, 2004.

———. "The Old Testament Background of Paul's References to 'the Fruit of the Spirit' in Galatians 5:22." *BBR* 15.1 (2005) 1–38.

Beaton, Richard C. "How Matthew Writes." In *The Written Gospel*. Edited by Markus Bockmuehl and Donald A. Hagner, 99–15. Cambridge: Cambridge University Press, 2005.

———. "Isaiah in Matthew's Gospel." In *Isaiah in the New Testament*. Edited by Steve Moyise and Maarten J. J. Menken, 63–78. London: T & T Clark, 2005.

Beckwith, Francis J. "History and Miracles." In *In Defense of Miracles: A Comprehensive Case for God's Action in History*. Edited by R. Douglas Geivett and Gary R. Habermas, 86–98. Downers Grove, IL: InterVarsity, 1997.

Begbie, Jeremy. "Who Is This God?—Biblical Inspiration Revisited." *TynB* 43.2 (1992) 259–82.

Berger, Klaus. *Qumran und Jesus: Wahrheit unter Verschluss?* Stuttgart: Quell, 1993. ET *Jesus and the Dead Sea Scrolls: The Truth under Lock and Key?* Translated by James S. Currie. Louisville: John Knox, 1995.

Bernard, J. H. *A Critical and Exegetical Commentary on the Gospel According to St. John*. ICC. Edinburgh: T & T Clark, 1928.

Bertrand, Daniel. "L'Evangile des Ebionites: une harmonie evangelique anterieure au Diatessaron." *NTS* 26.4 (1980) 548–63.

Betz, Hans Dieter. "Plutarch's Life of Numa: Some Observations on Graeco-Roman 'Messianism.'" In *Redemption and Resistance: The Messianic Hopes of Jews and Christians in Antiquity*. Edited by Markus Bockmuehl and James Carleton Paget, 44–61. London: T & T Clark, 2007.

Beuken, W. A. M. *Haggai–Sacharja 1–8: Studien zur Überlieferungsgeschichte der frühnachexilischen Prophetie*. SSN 10. Edited by M. A. Beek et al. Assen: Van Gorcum, 1967.

Beutler, Johannes. *Das Johannesevangelium: Kommentar*. Freiburg im Breisgau: Herder GmbH, 2013. ET *A Commentary on the Gospel of John*. Translated by Michael Tait. Grand Rapids: Eerdmans, 2017.

Bird, Michael F. "The Formation of the Gospels in the Setting of Early Christianity: The Jesus Tradition as Corporate Memory." *WTJ* 67 (2005) 113–34.

Black, David Alan and David R. Beck, eds. *Rethinking the Synoptic Problem*. Grand Rapids: Baker Academic, 2001.

Blaiklock, E. M. *Who Was Jesus?* Chicago: Moody, 1974.

Block, Daniel L. "My Servant David: Ancient Israel's Vision of the Messiah." In *Israel's Messiah: In the Bible and the Dead Sea Scrolls*. Edited by Richard Hess and M. Daniel Carroll, 17–56. Grand Rapids: Baker Academic, 2003.

Blomberg, Craig L. *The Historical Reliability of the Gospels*. Downers Grove, IL: IVP Academic, 1987.

———. "The Parables of Jesus: Current Trends and Needs in Research." In *Studying the Historical Jesus: Evaluations of the State of Current Research*. Edited by Bruce Chilton and Craig A. Evans, 231–54. Leiden: Brill, 1994.

———. *Jesus and the Gospels*. Nashville: Broadman & Holman, 1997.

———. "The Messiah in the New Testament." In *Israel's Messiah: In the Bible and the Dead Sea Scrolls*. Edited by Richard Hess and M. Daniel Carroll, 111–41. Grand Rapids: Baker Academic, 2003.

———. "Matthew." In *Commentary on the New Testament Use of the Old Testament*. Edited by G. K. Beale and D. A. Carson, 1–109. Grand Rapids: Baker Academic, 2007.

Bock, Darrell L. "Framing the Account: Alleviating Confusion on the Lukan Portrait of Jesus." *SBLSP* 33 (1994) 612–26.

———. "Questions about Q." In *Rethinking the Synoptic Problem*. Edited by David Alan Black and David R. Beck, 41–64. Grand Rapids: Baker Academic, 2001.

———. *Jesus according to Scripture: Restoring the Portrait from the Gospels*. Grand Rapids: Baker Academic, 2002.

———. *The Missing Gospels: Unearthing the Truth behind Alternative Christianities*. Nashville: Nelson Books, 2006.

Boda, Mark J. *Haggai & Zechariah Research: A Bibliographic Survey*. Leiden: Deo, 2003.

———. "Figuring the Future: The Prophets and Messiah." In *The Messiah in the Old and New Testaments*. MNTS 9. Edited by Stanley E. Porter, 35–74. Grand Rapids: Eerdmans, 2007.

Boecker, Hans Jochen. *Recht und Gesetz im alten Testament und im alten Orient*. NKS 10. Nuekirchen-Vluyn: Neukirchener Verlag, 1976. ET *Law and the Administration of Justice in the Old Testament and Ancient East*. Translated by Jeremy Moiser. Minneapolis: Augsburg, 1980.

Boismard, M.-E. "The Two-Source Theory at an Impasse." *NTS* 26.1 (1979–80) 1–13.

Borg, Marcus J. "Reflections on a Discipline: A North American Perspective." In *Studying the Historical Jesus: Evaluations of the State of Current Research*. NTTS 19. Edited by Bruce Chilton and Craig A. Evans, 9–31. Leiden: Brill, 1994.

Borg, Marcus and N. T. Wright. *The Meaning of Jesus: Two Visions*. San Francisco: HarperSanFrancisco, 1999.

Boring, M. Eugene. "How May We Identify Oracles of Christian Prophets in the Synoptic Tradition? Mark 3:28–29 as a Test Case." *JBL* 91 (1972) 501–21.

———. *Revelation: Interpretation, A Bible Commentary for Teaching and Preaching*. Louisville: John Knox, 1989.

———. "The Convergence of Source Analysis, Social History, and Literary Structure in the Gospel of Matthew." *SBLSP* 33 (1994) 587–611.

———. The Gospel of Matthew. NIB 8. Edited by Neil Alexander. Nashville: Abingdon, 1995.

Bornkamm, Günther. "Der Stillung der Sturm." *Wört und Dienst*. Jahrbuch der Theologischen Bethel, 1948. 49–54. Reprinted in *Überlieferung und Ausleguen im Matthäusevangelium,* 1963. ET "The Stilling of the Storm in Matthew." In *Tradition and Interpretation in Matthew*. NTL. Translated by Percy Scott. Edited by Alan Richardson, Philadelphia: Westminster, 1956.

———. *Jesus von Nazareth*. Stuttgart: Kohlhammer, 1956. ET *Jesus of Nazareth*. Translated by Irene and Fraser McLuskey. New York: Harper & Row, 1960.

Botner, Max. "The Messiah Is 'The Holy One': ὁ ἅγιος τοῦ θεοῦ as a Messianic Title in Mark 1:24." *JBL* 136.2 (2017) 417–33.

Bovon, François. "The Canonical Structure of Gospel and Apostle." In *The Canon Debate*. Edited by Lee Martin McDonald and James A. Sanders, 516–27. Peabody, MA: Hendrickson, 2002.

———. *A Commentary on the Gospel of Luke 1.1–9.50*. Hermeneia. Translated by Christine M. Thomas. Edited by Helmut Koester. Minneapolis: Fortress, 2002.

———. *Studies in Earliest Christianity*. Grand Rapids: Baker Academic, 2003.

———. *Luke the Theologian*. Waco: Baylor University Press, 2006.

Boxall, Ian. *The Revelation of St John*. BNTC. Edited by Morna D. Hooker. London: Hendrickson, 2006.

Branscome, David. "Herodotus and the Map of Aristagoras." *CA* 29.1 (2010) 1–44.

Brenneman, James E. *Canons in Conflict: Negotiating Texts in True and False Prophecy*. Oxford: Oxford University Press, 1997.

Brewer, Raymond R. "Revelation 4.6 and Translations Thereof." *JBL* 71 (1952) 227–31.

Broadhead, Edwin K. *Naming Jesus: Titular Christology in the Gospel of Mark*. JSNTSup 175. Edited by Stanley E. Porter. Sheffield: Sheffield Academic, 1999.

———. "The Extent of the Sayings Tradition (Q)." In *The Sayings Source Q and the Historical Jesus*. BETL CLVIII. Edited by A Lindemann, 719–28. Paris: Leuven University Press, 2001.

Brodie, A. "A New Temple and a New Law: The Unity and Chronicler-based Nature of Luke1:1—4:22a." *JSNT* 5 (1979) 520–39.

Brooke, George J. "Shared Intertextual Interpretations in the Dead Sea Scrolls and the New Testament." In *Biblical Perspectives: Early Use and Interpretation of the Bible in Light of the Dead Sea Scrolls*. STDJ XXVIII. Edited by Michael E. Stone and Esther G. Chazon, 35–57. Leiden: Brill, 1998.

Brown, Raymond. "The Messianism of Qumrân." *CBQ* 19 (1957) 53–82.

———. *The Birth of the Messiah: A Commentary on the Infancy Narratives in Matthew and Luke.* Garden City, NY: Doubleday & Company, 1977.
Brown, Schuyler. "The Role of the Prologues in Determining the Purpose of Luke–Acts." In *Perspectives on Luke–Acts*. PRS:SSS. Edited by Charles H. Talbert, 99–111. Edinburgh: T & T Clark, 1978.
Brown, Scott G. *A Guide to Writing Academic Essays in Religious Studies.* New York: Continuum International, 2008.
Bruce, F. F. *This Is That: The New Testament Development of Some Old Testament Themes.* Exeter: Paternoster, 1968.
———. *Tradition: Old and New.* Grand Rapids: Zondervan, 1970.
———. "New Light on the Origins of the New Testament Canon." In *New Dimensions in New Testament Study*. Edited by Richard N. Longenecker and Merrill C. Tenney, 3–18. Grand Rapids: Zondervan, 1974.
———. *The Canon of Scripture.* Downers Grove, IL: InterVarsity, 1988.
Brunner, Emil. *The Scandal of Christianity: The Gospel as a Stumbling Block to Modern Man.* Richmond: John Knox, 1965.
Búda, Josef. "ṢEMAḤ JAHWEH: Investigationes ad Christologiam Isaianam spectantes." *Bib* 20.1 (1939) 10–26.
Bultmann, Christopher. "What Do We Mean When We Talk about '(Late) Enlightenment Biblical Criticism'?" In *The Bible and the Enlightenment: A Case Study—Dr. Alexander Geddes (1737–1802)*. Edited by William Johnstone, 119–34. London: T & T Clark, 2004.
Bultmann, Rudolf. *Geschichte der synoptischen Tradition.* Göttingen: Vandenhoeck and Ruprecht, 1921. ET *The History of the Synoptic Tradition*. Translated by John Marsh. New York: Harper & Row, 1963.
———. Neues Testament und Mythologie." In *Offenbarung und Heilsgeschehen: Beiträge zur evangelischen Theologie.* VII/2. Munich, 1941. ET "New Testament and Mythology." In *Kerygma and Myth: A Theological Debate*. Translated by Reginald H. Fuller. Edited by Hans Werner Bartsch, 1–16. London: SPCK, 1953.
———. "Ist voraussetzungslose Exegese möglich?" *TZ* 13 (1957) 409–17. ET "Is Exegesis without Presuppositions Possible?" In *Existence and Faith: Shorter Writings of Rudolf Bultmann*. Translated by Schubert M. Ogden, 289–96. Cleveland: World, 1966.
———. "ζῷον." *TDNT*. Translated by Geoffrey W. Bromiley. Edited by Gerhard Kittel, 2.873. Grand Rapids: Eerdmans, 1973.
Burridge, Richard A. "About People, by People, for People: Gospel Genre and Audiences." In *The Gospel for All Christians: Rethinking the Gospel Audiences*. Edited by Richard Bauckham, 113–46. Grand Rapids: Eerdmans, 1998.
———. *What Are the Gospels? A Comparison with Graeco-Roman Biography.* BRS. Edited by John P. Meier. Grand Rapids: Eerdmans, 2004.
———. "Who Writes, Why, and for Whom?" In *The Written Gospel*. Edited by Markus Bockmuehl and Donald A. Hagner, 99–115. Cambridge: Cambridge University Press, 2005.
Burridge, Richard A. and Graham Gould. *Jesus Now and Then.* Grand Rapids: Eerdmans, 2004.
Burrows, Millar. "The Messiahs of Aaron and Israel." *ATR* 34 (1952) 202–6.
Butsch, Albert Fidelis. *Handbook of Renaissance Ornament.* New York: Dover, 1969.
Byrne, Brendan. "Jesus as Messiah in the Gospel of Luke: Discerning a Pattern of Correction." *CBQ* 65 (2003) 80–95.

Byrskog, Samuel. "A New Perspective on the Jesus Tradition: Reflections on James D. G. Dunn's Jesus Remembered." *JSNT* 26.4 (2004) 459–71.

———. "A New Quest for the Sitz im Leben: Social Memory, the Jesus Tradition and the Gospel of Matthew." *NTS* 52 (2006) 319–36.

Caird, G. B. *The Revelation of St. John the Divine*. HNTC. Edited by Henry Chadwick. New York: Harper & Row, 1966.

Calvert, D. G. A. "An Examination of the Criteria for Distinguishing the Authentic Words of Jesus." *NTS* 18 (1971–72) 209–18.

Campenhausen, Hans Freiherr Von. *Die Entstehung der christlichen Bibel*. Tübingen: J. C. B. Mohr, 1968. ET *The Formation of the Christian Bible*. Translated by J. A. Baker. Philadelphia: Fortress, 1972.

Caquot, André and Philippe de Robert. *Les Livres de Samuel*. CLT 6. Edited by A. de Pury. Genève: Labor et Fides,1994.

Carlston, Charles E. "Christology and Church in Matthew." In *The Four Gospels 1992: Festschrift Frans Neirynck*. Edited by F. Van Segroeck et al, 2.1283–95. Leuven University Press, 1992.

———. "Prologue." In *Studying the Historical Jesus: Evaluations of the State of Current Research*. NTTS 19. Edited by Bruce Metzger and Bart Ehrman, 1–9. Leiden: Brill, 1994.

Carrier, Richard. *On the Historicity of Jesus: Why We Might Have Reason for Doubt*. UK: Sheffield Phoenix, 2014.

Carroll, Robert P. "Intertextuality and the Book of Jeremiah: Animadversions on Text and Theory." In *The New Literary Criticism and the Hebrew Bible*. JSOTSup 143. Edited by J. Cheryl Exum and David J. A. Clines, 55–78. Sheffield: Sheffield Academic, 1993.

Carson, D. A. *The Gagging of God: Christianity Confronts Pluralism*. Hillsboro, OR: Goodwill, 2000.

Carter, Warren. "Evoking Isaiah: Matthean Soteriology and an Intertextual Reading of Isaiah 7–9, Matthew 1.23, and 4.15–16." *JBL* 119.3 (2000) 503–20.

———. *Matthew and Empire*. Harrisburg: Trinity International, 2001.

———. "Matthaean Christology in Roman Imperial Key: Matthew 1.1." In *The Gospel of Matthew in its Roman Imperial Context*. Edited by John Riches and David C. Sims, 143–65. London: T & T Clark, 2005.

Casey, P. Maurice. "The Deification of Jesus." *SBLSP* 33 (1994) 697–714.

———. "Culture and Historicity: The Cleansing of the Temple." *CBQ* 59 (1997) 306–32.

———. "Lord Jesus Christ: A Response to Professor Hurtado." *JSNT* 27 (2004) 83–96.

Cathcart, Kevin J. and Robert P. Gordon. *The Targum of the Minor Prophets: Translated, with a Critical Introduction, Apparatus, and Notes*. AB 14. Edited by Martin McNamara. Wilmington: Michael Glazier, 1986.

Chapman, Stephen B. *1 Samuel as Christian Scripture: A Theological Commentary*. Grand Rapids: Eerdmans, 2016.

Charette, Blaine. "'To Proclaim Liberty to the Captives': Matthew 11.28–30 in the Light of OT Prophetic Expectation." *NTS* 38.2 (1992) 290–97.

———. *The Theme of Recompense in Matthew's Gospel*. JSNTSup 79. Sheffield: Sheffield Academic, 1992.

Charles, R. H. *A Critical and Exegetical Commentary on the Revelation of St. John: With Introduction, Notes, and Indices also the Greek Text and English Translation*. New York: Charles Scribner's Son, 1920.

Charlesworth, James H. "A Prolegomenon to a New Study of the Jewish Background of the Hymns and Prayers in the New Testament." *JJS* 33.1-2 (1982) 265-85.

———. "From Messianology to Christology: Problems and Prospects." In *The Messiah: Developments in Earliest Judaism and Christianity*. FPSJCO. Edited by James H. Charlesworth, 3-35. Minneapolis: Fortress, 1987.

———. *Jesus within Judaism: New Light from Exciting Archaeological Discoveries*. ABRL. Edited by David Noel Freedman. New York: Doubleday, 1988.

———. "What has the Old Testament to Do with the New?" In *The Old and New Testaments: Their Relationship and the "Intertestamental" Literature*. FSCS. Edited by James H. Charlesworth and Walter P. Weaver, 39-87. Valley Forge: Trinity International, 1993.

———. "Hillel and Jesus: Why Comparisons Are Important." In *Hillel and Jesus: Comparative Studies of Two Major Religious Leaders*. Edited by James H. Charlesworth and Loren L. Johns, 3-30. Minneapolis: Fortress, 1997.

———. "Intertextuality: Isaiah 40.3 and the Serek ha-Yahad." In *The Quest for Context and Meaning: Studies in Biblical Intertextuality in Honor of James A. Sanders*. BIS XXVIII. Edited by Craig A. Evans and Shemaryahu Talmon, 197-224. Leiden: Brill, 1997.

———. *The Pesharim and Qumran History: Chaos or Consensus?* Grand Rapids: Eerdmans, 2002.

Chávez, Emilio. *The Theological Significance of Jesus' Temple Action in Mark's Gospel*. TST 87. Lewiston, NY: Edwin Mellen, 2002.

Chibici-Revneanu, Nicole. *Die Herrlichkeit des Verherrlichten: Das Verständnis der δόξα im Johnnesevangelium*. Tübingen, Mohr Siebeck, 2007.

Childs, Brevard S. "The *Sensus Literalis* of Scripture: An Ancient and Modern Problem." In *Beiträge zur Alttestamentlichen Theologie*. Edited by Herbert Donner, Robert Hanhart, und Rudolf Smend, 80-93. Göttingen : Vandenhoeck und Ruprecht, 1977.

———. *Biblical Theology of the Old and New Testaments: Theological Reflection on the Christian Bible*. Minneapolis: Fortress, 1993.

———. *Isaiah*. OTL. Edited by James L. Mays, Carol A. Newsom, and David L. Peterson. Louisville: Westminster/John Knox, 2001.

Chilton, Bruce A. *Galilean Rabbi and His Bible: Jesus' Use of the Interpreted Scripture of His Time*. GNS 8. Edited by Robert J. Harris. Wilmington, Michael Glazier, 1984.

———. *The Targum of Isaiah: Translated, with a Critical Introduction, Apparatus, and Notes*. AB 11. Edited by Martin McNamara. Wilmington: Michael Glazier, 1986.

———. *Targumic Approaches to the Gospels. Studies in Judaism*. New York: University Press of America, 1986.

———. "Biblical Authority, Canonical Criticism, and Generative Exegesis." In *The Quest for Context and Meaning: Studies in Biblical Intertextuality in Honor of James A. Sanders*. BIS XXVIII. Edited by Craig A. Evans and Shemaryahu Talmon, 343-55. Leiden: Brill, 1997.

Chilton, Bruce and Craig A. Evans. "Jesus and Israel's Scriptures." In *Studying the Historical Jesus: Evaluations of the State of Current Research*. NTTS XIX. Edited by Bruce Metzger and Bart Ehrman, 281-335. Leiden: Brill, 1994.

Collins, Adela Yarbro. *Mark: A Commentary*. Hermeneia. Edited by Harold W. Attridge. Minneapolis, Fortress, 2007.

Collins, John, C. *The God of Miracles: An Exegetical Examination of God's Action in the World*. Wheaton, IL: Crossway, 2000.

Collins, John, J. "Teacher and Messiah? The One Who Will Teach Righteousness at the End of Days." In *The Community of the Renewed Covenant: The Notre Dame Symposium on the Dead Sea Scrolls*. CJAS 10. Edited by Eugene Ulrich and James VanderKam, 193–210. Notre Dame: University of Notre Dame Press, 1994.

———. *The Scepter and Star: The Messiahs of the Dead Sea Scrolls and Other Ancient Literature*. New York: Doubleday, 1995.

———. "Teacher and Servant." *RHPR* 80.1 (2000) 37–50.

———. "The Eschatology of Zechariah." In *Knowing the End from the Beginning: The Prophetic, the Apocalyptic and their Relationships*. JSPSup 46. Edited by Lester L. Grabbe and James H. Charlesworth, 74–84. London: T & T Clark, 2003.

———. "A Messiah before Jesus?" In *Christian Beginnings and the Dead Sea Scrolls*. ASBT. Edited by Craig A. Evans and Lee Martin McDonald, 15–35. Grand Rapids: Baker Academic, 2006.

Combrink, H. J. Bernard. "Salvation in Mark." In *Salvation in the New Testament: Perspectives on Soteriology*. NovTSup 121. Edited by Jan G. van der Watt, 33–66. Leiden: Brill, 2005.

Connolly-Weinert, Frank. "Assessing Omissions as Redaction: Luke's Handling of the Charge Against Jesus as Detractor of the Temple." In *To Touch the Text: Biblical and Related Studies in Honor of Joseph A. Fitzmyer*. Edited by. Maurya P. Horgan and Paul J. Kobelski, 358–68. New York: Crossroad, 1989.

Conzelmann, Hans. "Jesus Christus." In *Die Religion in Geschichte und Gegenwart: Handwörterbuch für Theologie und Religionswissenschaft*. Vol. 3. Edited by Kurt Galling et al. Tübingen: J. C. B. Mohr/Paul Siebeck, 1959. ET *Jesus*. Translated by J. Raymond Lord. Edited by John Reumann. Philadelphia: Fortress, 1973.

———. *Gundriss der Theologie des Neuen Testaments*. Munich: Christian Kaiser, 1968. ET *An Outline of the Theology of the New Testament*. NTL. Translated by John Bowden. London: SCM, 1969.

Court, John M. "The Birth of Jesus Christ According to Matthew and Luke." In *New Testament Writers and the Old Testament: An Introduction*. Edited by John M. Court, 13–25. London: SPCK, 2002.

Cousland, J. R. C. *The Crowds in the Gospel of Matthew*. NovTSup CII. Edited by C. K. Barrett et al. Leiden: Brill, 2002.

Cranfield, C. E. B. "Some Comments on Professor J. D. G. Dunn's Christology in the Making with Special Reference to the Evidence of the Epistle to the Romans." In *The Glory of Christ in the New Testament: Studies in Christology*. Edited by L. D. Hurst and N. T. Wright, 267–80. Oxford: Clarendon, 1987.

Crawford, Barry S. and Merrill P. Miller, eds. *Redescribing the Gospel of Mark*. Atlanta, GA: SBL, 2017.

Crook, Zeba A. "Reflections on Culture and Social-Scientific Models." *JBL* 124.3 (2005) 515–20.

Crossan, John Dominic. "Divine Immediacy and Human Immediacy Towards a New First Principle in Historical Jesus Research." *Semeia* 44.1 (1988) 121–40.

———. *The Historical Jesus: The Life of a Mediterranean Jewish Peasant*. San Francisco: HarperSanFrancisco, 1991.

———. *The Birth of Christianity: Discovering What Happened in the Years Immediately after the Execution of Jesus*. San Francisco: HarperSanFrancisco, 1998.

———. "Historical Jesus as Risen Lord." In *The Jesus Controversy: Perspectives in Conflict*. RLS. Edited by Gerald P. McKenney, 1–47. Harrisburg, PA: Trinity International, 1999.

Cullmann, Oscar. "Die Pluralität der Evangelien als theologisches Problem im Altertum." *ThZ* i (1945) 23–42. ET "The Plurality of the Gospels as a Theological Problem in Antiquity." In *The Early Church: Five Essays*. Edited by A. J. B. Higgins, 39–54. London: SCM, 1956.

———. *Christus und die Zeit*. Zurich: Evangelischer, 1946. ET *Christ and Time: The Primitive Christian Conception of Time and History*. Translated by Floyd V. Filson. London: SCM, 1965.

Culpepper, R. Alan. *The Gospel of Luke: Introduction, Commentary, and Reflections*. NIB. Nashville: Abingdon, 1995.

Dahl, Nils Alstrup. "Contradictions in Scripture." In *Studies in Paul: Theology for the Early Christian Mission*. Edited by Nils Dahl,159–77. Minneapolis: Augsburg, 1977.

Danker, Frederick W. *Luke*. PC. Edited by Gerhard Krodel. Philadelphia: Fortress, 1976.

———. "Matthew: A Patriot's Gospel." In *The Gospels and the Scriptures of Israel*. JSNTSup 104. Edited by Craig A. Evans and W. Richard Stegner, 94–115. Sheffield: Sheffield Academic, 1994.

Davies, Philip R. "'House of David' Built on Sand: The Sins of the Biblical Maximizers." *BAR* 20.4 (1994) 54–55.

Davies, W. D. *Invitation to the New Testament*. Garden City, NY: Anchor, 1969.

———. *The Gospel and the Land: Early Christianity and Jewish Territorial Doctrine*. Berkeley: University of California Press, 1974.

———. "Canon and Christology." In *The Glory of Christ in the New Testament: Studies in Christology*. Edited by L. D. Hurst and N. T. Wright, 19–36. Oxford: Clarendon, 1987.

———. "The Jewish Sources of Matthew's Messianism." In *The Messiah: Developments in Earliest Judaism and Christianity*. FPSJCO. Edited by James H. Charlesworth, 494–511. Minneapolis: Fortress, 1987.

Davies, W. D. and Dale Allison. *A Critical and Exegetical Commentary on the Gospel According to Saint Matthew*. ICC. Edited by J. A. Emerton, C. E. B. Cranfield, and G. N. Stanton. Edinburgh: T & T Clark, 1988.

Davies, W. D. and E. P. Sanders. "Jesus: From the Jewish Point of View." In *The Cambridge History of Judaism*. Vol. 3: The Early Roman Period. Edited by William Horbury, W. D. Davies, and John Sturdy, 618–77. Cambridge: Cambridge University Press, 1984.

Day, Matthew. "Let's Be Realistic: Epistemic Probabilism, and the Cognitive Science of Religion." *HTR* 100:1 (2007) 47–64.

DeConick, April A. *Recovering the Original Gospel of Thomas: A History of the Gospel and its Growth*. London: T & T Clark, 2006.

De Jonge, Marinus. "The Use of the Word 'Anointed' in the Time of Jesus." *NovT* 8.2 (1966) 132–48.

———. ed. *The Testaments of the Twelve Patriarchs: A Critical Edition of the Greek Text*. PVTG. Edited by A. M. Denis and M. De Jonge. Leiden: Brill, 1978.

———. "Two Messiahs in the Testaments of the Twelve Patriarchs?" In *Tradition and Re-Interpretation in Jewish and Early Christian Literature*. Edited by J. W. Van, 150–62. Leiden: Brill, 1986.

———. *Jesus, the Servant-Messiah*. New Haven: Yale University Press, 1991.

De Kruijf, Th. "The Glory of the Only Son (John 1.14)." In *Studies in John Presented to J. N. Sevenster*. Editor unknown, 111–23. Leiden: Brill, 1970.

Deppe, Dean B. *The Theological Intentions of Mark's Literary Devices: Markan Intercalations, Frames, Allusionary Repetitions, Narrative Surprises, and Three Types of Mirroring*. Eugene, OR: Wipf & Stock, 2015.

deSilva, David A. *An Introduction to the New Testament: Contexts, Methods & Ministry Formation.* Downers Grove, IL: IVP, 2004.

Desrousseaux, L. "David dans la Septante: Remarques préliminaries sur la Septante." In *Messianism and the Septuagint: Collected Essays by J. Lust.* BETL CLXXVII. Edited by K Hauspie, 171–88. Leuven: Leuven University Press, 2004. Reprint from *Lectio Divina* 177 (1999) 243–63.

Deutsch, Celia. *Hidden Wisdom and the Easy Yoke: Wisdom, Torah and Discipleship in Matthew 11.25–30.* JSNTSup 18. Sheffield: Sheffield Academic, 1987.

DeVries, Simon J. *1 Kings.* WBC. Edited by John D. W. Watts. Waco, TX: Word, 1985.

Dihle, Albrecht. "The Gospels and Greek Biography." In *The Gospel and the Gospels.* Edited by Peter Stuhlmacher, 173–208. Grand Rapids: Eerdmans, 1991.

Dillion, Richard J. "Previewing Luke's Project from His Prologue (Luke 1:1–4)." CBQ 43 (1981) 205–27.

Dimant, D. and J. Strugnell. "The Merkabah Vision in Second Ezekiel (4Q385 4)." *RevQum* 14.3 (1989–90) 331–48.

Dodd, C. H. *The Interpretation of the Fourth Gospel.* Cambridge: Cambridge University Press, 1953.

———. *According to the Scriptures: The Sub-Structure of New Testament Theology.* NewYork: Charles Scribner's Son, 1953.

———. *About the Gospels.* Cambridge: Cambridge University Press, 1958.

Dommershausen, Werner. "Der 'Spross' als Messias-Vorstellung bei Jeremia und Sacharja." *TQ* 148 (1968) 321–41.

Donaldson, Terence L. "The Vindicated Son: A Narrative Approach to Matthean Christology." In *Contours of Christology in the New Testament.* Edited by Richard N. Longenecker, 100–21. Grand Rapids: Eerdmans, 2005.

Downing, F. Gerald. *Has Christianity a Revelation?* London: SCM, 1964.

———. "A Paradigm Perplex: Luke, Matthew and Mark." *NTS* 38.1 (1992) 15–36.

Drinkard, Joel, F. *Jeremiah.* WBC 26. Edited by John W. D. Watts. Dallas: Word, 1991.

Duling, Dennis C. "The Promises to David and Their Entrance into Christianity—Nailing Down a Likely Hypothesis." *NTS* 19 (1973) 55–77.

———. "Matthew and Marginality." *SBLSP* 32 (1993) 642–71.

Dunn, James D. G. "Messianic Ideas and Their Influence on the Jesus of History." In *The Messiah: Developments in Earliest Judaism and Christianity.* FPSJCO. Edited by James H. Charlesworth, 365–81. Minneapolis: Fortress, 1987.

———. *Jesus Remembered.* Grand Rapids: Eerdmans, 2003.

———. "Living Traditions." In *What Is It That the Scripture Says? Essays in Biblical Interpretation, Translation and Reception in Honour of Henry Wansbrough OSB.* Edited by Philip McCosker, 275–89. London: T & T Clark, 2006.

Du Plessis, I. I. "Once More: The Purpose of Luke's Prologue (Lk I 1–4)." *NovT* 16.4 (1974) 259–71.

Du Plessis, P. J. "Fundamentalism as Methodological Principle." In *Text and Interpretation: New Approaches in the Criticism of the New Testament.* Edited by P. J. Hartin and J. H. Petzer, 201–13. Leiden: Brill, 1991.

Dyson, A. O. *Who Is Jesus Christ?* London: SCM, 1969.

Eddy, Paul Rhodes and Gregory A. Boyd. *The Jesus Legend: A Case for the Historical Reliability of the Synoptic Jesus Tradition.* Grand Rapids: Baker Academic 2007.

Ehrman, Bart D. *The New Testament: A Historical Introduction to the Early Christian Writings*. Oxford: Oxford University Press, 1997.

———. *Misquoting Jesus: The Story Behind Who Changed the Bible and Why*. San Francisco: HarperSanFrancisco, 2005.

———. *Did Jesus Exist? The Historical Argument for Jesus of Nazareth*. New York: HarperOne, 2012.

Eisenman, Robert. *Maccabees, Zadokites, Christians and Qumran: A New Hypothesis of Qumran Origins*. Leiden: Brill, 1983.

Elliot, John H. "Social-Scientific Criticism of the New Testament: More on Methods and Models." *Semeia* 35.1 (1986) 1–34.

———. "Temple Versus Household in Luke–Acts: A Contrast in Social Institutions." In *The Social World of Luke–Acts: Models for Interpretation*. Edited by Jerome H. Neyrey, 211–40. Peabody, MA: Hendrickson, 1991.

Ellis, E. Earle. *History & Interpretation in New Testament Perspective*. BIS 54. Edited by R. Alan Culpepper and Rolf Rendtorff. Leiden: Brill, 2001.

Emerton, J. A. "Messianism and Septuagint." In *Messianism and the Septuagint: Collected Essays by J. Lust*. BETL CLXXVII. Edited by K Hauspie, 9–40. Leuven: Leuven University Press, 2004. Reprint from VTSup 36 (1985) 174–91.

Engnell, Ivan. "The 'Ebed Yahweh Songs and the Suffering Messiah in Deutero-Isaiah." *BJRL* 31 (1948) 54–93.

Enslin, Morton. "Luke and Matthew: Compilers or Authors?" *ANRW* 25.3 (1984) 2357–88.

Erickson, Richard J. "Joseph and the Birth of Isaac in Matthew 1." *BBR* 10.1 (2000) 35–51.

Esler, Philip F. "Models in New Testament Interpretation: A Reply to David Horrell." *JSNT* 78 (2000) 107–13.

Evans, Charles Stephen. *The Historical Christ and the Jesus of Faith: The Incarnational Narrative as History*. Oxford: Clarendon, 1996.

Evans, Christopher Francis. *Saint Luke*. TPIC. London: SCM, 2004.

Evans, Craig A. *Luke*. NIBC. Edited by W. Ward Gasque. Peabody, MA: Hendrickson, 1990.

———. "Luke and the Rewritten Bible: Aspects of Lukan Hagiography." In *The Pseudepigrapha and Early Biblical Interpretation*. JSPSup14/SSEJC 2. Edited by. James H. Charlesworth and Craig A. Evans, 170–201. Sheffield: Sheffield Academic, 1993.

———. "The Recently Published Dead Sea Scrolls and the Historical Jesus." In *Studying the Historical Jesus: Evaluations of the State of Current Research*. NTTS 19. Edited by. Bruce Metzger and Bart Ehrman, 535–65. Leiden: Brill, 1994.

———. *Jesus and His Contemporaries: Comparative Studies*. AGAJU XXV. Edited by Martin Hengel et al. Leiden: Brill, 1995.

———. "Images of Christ in the Canonical and Apocryphal Gospels." In *Images of Christ: Ancient and Modern*. RILP 2. Edited by Stanley E. Porter, Michael A. Hayes, and David Tombs, 34–72. London: Sheffield Academic, 1997.

———. "'The Two Sons of Oil': Early Evidence of Messianic Interpretation of Zechariah 4.14 in 4Q254 4 2." In *The Provo International Conference on the Dead Sea Scrolls: Technological Innovations, New Texts, and Reformulated Issues*. STDJ XXX. Edited by Donald W. Parry and Eugene Ulrich, 566–75. Leiden: Brill, 1999.

———. "Jesus and Zechariah's Messianic Hope." In *Authenticating the Activities of Jesus*. NTTS XXVIII.2. Edited by Bruce Chilton and Craig A. Evans, 373–88. Leiden: Brill, 1999.

———. "Diarchic Messianism in the Dead Sea Scrolls and the Messianism of Jesus of Nazareth." In *The Dead Sea Scrolls: Fifty Years after Their Discovery*. PJC. Edited by Lawrence H. Schiffman, Emanuel Tov, and James C. Vanderkam, 559–67. Jerusalem: Israel Exploration Society/Shrine of the Book Museum, 2000.

———. "The Messiah in the Dead Sea Scrolls." In *Israel's Messiah: In the Bible and the Dead Sea Scrolls*. Edited by Richard Hess and M. Daniel Carroll, 85–101. Grand Rapids: Baker Academic, 2003.

———. "The Old Testament in the New." In *The Face of New Testament Studies: A Survey of Recent Research*. Edited by Scot McKnight and Grant R. Osborne, 130–45. Grand Rapids: Baker Academic, 2004.

———. "How Mark Writes." In *The Written Gospel*. Edited by Markus Bockmuehl and Donald A. Hagner, 117–34. Cambridge: Cambridge University Press, 2005.

———. *Fabricating Jesus: How Modern Scholars Distort the Gospels*. Downers Grove, IL: IVP, 2006.

———. "The Implications of Eyewitness Tradition." *JSNT* 31.2 (2008) 211–19.

Evans, Craig A. and James A. Sanders. *Luke and Scripture: The Function of Sacred Tradition in Luke-Acts*. Minneapolis: Fortress, 1993.

Evans, Cristopher F. *Saint Luke*. TPINTC. Philadelphia: Trinity, 1990.

Evans, Mary J. *1 and 2 Samuel*. NIBC. Edited by Robert L. Hubbard. Peabody, MA: Hendrickson, 2000.

Farkasfalvy, Denis. "The Presbyters's Witness on the Order of the Gospels as Reported by Clement of Alexander." *CBQ* 54 (1992) 260–70.

Farmer, William R. *The Synoptic Problem: A Critical Analysis*. Macon, GA: Mercer University Press, 1981.

———. "State Interesse and Marcan Primacy." In *The Four Gospels 1992: Festschrift Frans Neirynck*. Edited by F. Van Segroeck et al, 3.2477–98. Leuven: Leuven University Press, 1992.

———. "Reflections on Jesus and the New Testament Canon." In *The Canon Debate*. Edited by Lee Martin McDonald and James A. Sanders, 321–40. Peabody, MA: Hendrickson, 2002.

Farrer, Austin. "Inspiration: Poetical and Divine." In *Promise and Fulfillment: Essays Presented to Professor S. H. Hooke in Celebration of his Ninetieth Birthday*. Edited by F. F. Bruce, 91–105. Edinburgh: T & T Clark, 1963.

Fennema, D. A. "John 1.18: 'God the Only Son.'" *NTS* 31 (1985) 124–35.

Ferguson, Everett. "Canon Muratori: Date and Provenance." *SP* 17 (1982) 677–83.

———. "Factors Leading to the Selection and Closure of the New Testament Canon: A Survey of Some Recent Studies." In *The Canon Debate*. Edited by Lee Martin McDonald and James A. Sanders, 295–320. Peabody, MA: Hendrickson, 2002.

Feuillet, A. "Les vingt-quatre vilillards de l'Apocalypse." *RB* 65 (1958) 5–32.

Fichtner, Johannes. *Das Erste Buch von den Königen*. BAT. Edited by Klaus DietrichFricke. Stuttgart: Calwer, 1964.

Filson, Floyd, V. The Gospel According to St. Matthew. BNTC. Edited by Henry Chadwick. London: Adam & Charles Black, 1971.

Fiorenza, Elisabeth. *Jesus and the Politics of Interpretation*. New York: Continuum, 2000.

Fitzmyer, Joseph A. "The Use of Explicit Old Testament Quotations in Qumran Literature and in the New Testament." *NTS* 7 (1960–61) 297–333. Reprint in *Essays on the Semitic*

Background of the New Testament. SBL 5. Edited by Joseph A. Fitzmyer, 3–58. London: Chapman, 1971.

———. "The Son of David Tradition and Mt 22.41–46 and Parallels." *Concilium* 10.2 (1966) 40–46.

———. "Judaic Studies and the Gospels: the Seminar." In *The Relationships among the Gospels: An Interdisciplinary Approach*. Edited by William O. Walker, 237–58. San Antonio: Trinity University Press, 1978.

———. "The Use of the Old Testament in Luke—Acts." *SBLSP* 31 (1992) 524–38.

———. *The Dead Sea Scrolls and Christian Origins*. Grand Rapids: Eerdmans, 2000.

———. *The One Who Is to Come*. Grand Rapids: Eerdmans, 2007.

Fletcher-Louis, Crispin H. T. "The Worship of Divine Humanity as God's Image and the Worship of Jesus." In *The Jewish Roots of Christological Monotheism: Papers from the St. Andrews Conference on the Historical Origins of the Worship of Jesus*. JSJSup 63. Edited by John J. Collins and Florentino Garcia Martínez, 113–28. Leiden: Brill, 1998.

———. "Jesus as the High Priestly Messiah: Part 1." *JSHJ* 4.2 (2006) 155–75.

———. "Jesus as the High Priestly Messiah: Part 2." *JSHJ* 5.1 (2007) 57–79.

Flew, Antony. "Neo-Humean Arguments About the Miraculous." In *In Defense of Miracles: A Comprehensive Case for God's Action in History*. Edited by R. Douglas Geivett and Gary R. Habermas, 45–58. Downers Grove, IL: IVP, 1997.

Flint, Peter. "Jesus and the Dead Sea Scrolls." In *The Historical Jesus in Context*. PRR. Edited by Amy-Jill Levine, Dale C. Allison, and John Dominic Crossan, 110–31. Princeton: Princeton University Press, 2006.

Floyd, Michael H. *Minor Prophets: Part 2*. FOTL 22. Edited by Rolf P. Knierim, Gene M. Tucker, and Marvin A. Sweeney. Grand Rapids: Eerdmans, 2000.

Flynn, Leslie B. *Four Faces of Jesus: The Uniqueness of the Gospel Narratives*. Grand Rapids: Kregel, 1993.

Fornara, Charles William. *The Nature of History in Ancient Greece and Rome*. SCK. Edited by Thomas G. Rosenmeyer. Berkeley: University of California Press, 1983.

Foster, Paul. "Is it Possible to Dispense with Q?" *NovT* 45.4 (2003) 313–37.

France, Richard T. "Herod and the Children of Bethlehem." *NovT* 31.2 (1979) 98–120.

———. *Matthew: Evangelist and Teacher*. Downer's Grove, IL: IVP, 1989.

Franklin, Eric. *Luke: Interpreter of Paul, Critic of Matthew*. Sheffield: Sheffield Academic, 1994.

Fredriksen, Paula. *From Jesus to Christ: The Origins of the New Testament Images of Jesus*. New Haven: Yale University Press, 2000.

Frey, Jörg. "'. . . dass sie meine Herrlichkeit schauen' (John 17.24): Zu Hintergrund, Sinn und Funktion der johanneischen Rede von der δόξα Jesu." *NTS* 54.3 (2008) 375–97.

Freyne, Seán. "The geography, Politics, and Economics of Galilee and the Quest for the Historical Jesus." In *Studying the Historical Jesus: Evaluations of the State of Current Research*. NTTS 19. Edited by. Bruce Chilton and Craig A. Evans, 75–121. Leiden: Brill, 1994.

———. *Jesus, A Jewish Galilean: A New Reading of the Jesus-Story*. London: T & T Clark International, 2004.

———. "The Herodian Period." In *Redemption and Resistance: The Messianic Hopes of Jews and Christians in Antiquity*. Edited by Markus Bockmuehl and James Carleton Paget, 29–43. London: T & T Clark, 2007.

———. "Jesus of History Vs. Jesus of Tradition." *BAR* 36. 6 (2010) 45.

Funk, Robert W., Roy W. Hoover, and The Jesus Seminar. *The Five Gospels: The Search for the Authentic Words of Jesus.* San Francisco: Harper Collins, 1993.

Gabel, John B. and Charles B. Wheeler. *The Bible as Literature: An Introduction.* Oxford: Oxford University Press, 1990.

Gamble, Harry Y. *The New Testament Canon: Its Making and Meaning.* GBS. Edited by Gene M. Tucker. Philadelphia: Fortress, 1985.

García, Martínez F. and E. J. C. Tigchelaar, eds. *Dead Sea Scrolls Study Edition.* Vol. 1: 1Q1–4Q273. Vol. 2: 4Q274–11Q31. Leiden: Brill, 1997–98.

Garland, David E. *Exegetical Commentary on the New Testament: Luke.* ZECNT. Edited by Clinton E. Arnold. Grand Rapids: Zondervan, 2011.

Gathercole, Simon J. "The Heavenly ἀνατολή (Luke 1:78–9)." *JST* 56.2 (2005) 471–88.

———. *The Preexistent Son: Recovering the Christologies of Matthew, Mark, and Luke.* Grand Rapids: Eerdmans, 2006.

———. *The Composition of the Gospel of Thomas.* Cambridge: Cambridge University Press, 2012.

Geldenhuys, Norval. *Commentary on the Gospel of Luke.* NICNT. Edited by F. F. Bruce. Grand Rapids: Eerdmans, 1960.

Gempster, Stephen G. *Dominion and Dynasty: A Biblical Theology of the Hebrew Bible.* NSBT 15. Edited by D.A. Carson. Downer's Grove, IL: InterVarsity, 2003.

Gerhardsson, Birger. *Memory and Manuscript: Oral Tradition and Written Transmission in Rabbinic Judaism and Early Christianity.* Grand Rapids: Eerdmans, 1998.

———. "The Christology of Matthew." In *Who Do You Say That I Am? Essays on Christology in Honor of Jack Dean Kingsbury.* Edited by Mark Allan Powell and David R. Bauer, 14–32. Louisville: Westminster/John Knox, 1999.

———. *The Reliability of the Gospel Tradition.* Peabody, MA: Hendrickson, 2001.

———. "The Secret of the Transmission of the Unwritten Jesus Tradition." *NTS* 51.1 (2005) 1–18.

Gesenius, William. "הנה." *A Hebrew and English Lexicon of the Old Testament.* Based on the Lexicon of William Gesenius. Translated by Edward Robinson. Edited by Francis Brown, 244. Oxford: Clarendon, 1975.

Geyer, G. W. *Fear, Anomaly, and Uncertainty in the Gospel of Mark.* Lanhan, MD: Scarecrow, 2002.

Giblin, Charles Homer. "From and before the Throne: Revelation 4.5–6a: Integrating the Imagery of Revelation 4—16." *CBQ* 60.3 (1998) 500–12.

Glasswell, M. E. "St. Mark's Attitude to the Relationship between History and the Gospel." *Studia Biblica 1978: Papers on the Gospels.* JSNTSup 2. Edited by E. A. Livingstone, 115–27. Sheffield: Sheffield Academic, 1980.

———. "The Relationship between John and Mark." *JSNT* 23 (1985) 99–115.

Globe, Alexander. "Some Doctrinal Variants in Matthew 1 and Luke 2, and the Authority of the Neutral Text." *CBQ* 42 (1980) 52–72.

Gnilka, J. "Die Erwartung des messianischen Hohenpriesters in den Schriften von Qumran und im Neuen Testament." *RevQum* 7 (1960) 395–426.

Goldenberg, Robert. *The Origins of Judaism: From Canaan to the Rise of Islam.* Cambridge: Cambridge University Press, 2007.

Goodacre, Mark. *The Synoptic Problem: A Way through the Maze.* London: Sheffield Academic, 2001.

———. *The Case Against Q: Studies in the Markan Priority and the Synoptic Problem.* Harrisburg: Trinity International, 2002.
Goodspeed, Edgar J. *A History of Early Christian Literature.* Chicago: University of Chicago Press, 1966.
Goswell, Greg. "The Fate and Future of Zerubbabel in the Prophecy of Haggai." *Bib* 91 (2010) 77–90.
Gould, J. P. "Law, Custom and Myth: Aspects of the Social Position of Women in Classical Athens." *JHS* 100 (1980) 30–49.
Grabbe, Lester L. *Priests, Prophets, Diviners, Sages: A Socio-Historical Study of Religious Specialists in Ancient Israel.* Valley Forge, PA: Trinity International, 1995.
Grambo, Rebecca, ed. *Masters of the Sky.* NY: Voyageur, 1998.
Grant, Frederick C. *The Earliest Gospel.* Nashville: Abingdon, 1943.
Grant, Robert M. *The Earliest Lives of Jesus.* New York: Harper & Brothers, 1961.
———. *A Historical Introduction to the New Testament.* London: Collins, 1963.
———. *The Formation of the New Testament.* New York: Harper & Row, 1965.
———. *Jesus after the Gospels: The Christ of the Second Century.* Hale Memorial Lectures of Seabury-Western Theological Seminary 1989. Louisville: John Knox, 1990.
Gray, George Buchanan. *A Critical and Exegetical Commentary on the Book of Isaiah I–XXXI.* ICC. Edinburgh: T & T Clark, 1928.
Green, James Leo. *Jeremiah.* BBC. Edited by Clifton J. Allen. Nashville: Broadman, 1971.
Green, Joel B. "The Death of Jesus and the Rending of the Temple Veil: A Window into Luke's Understanding of Jesus and the Temple." *SBLSP* 30 (1991) 543–57.
———. "The Death of Jesus and the Ways of God: Jesus and the Gospels on Messianic Status and Shameful Suffering." *Int* 52 (1998) 24–35.
Griffith-Jones, Robert. *The Four Witnesses: The Rebel, the Rabbi, the Chronicler, and the Mystic.* San Francisco: HarperSanFranciso, 2000.
Guelich, Robert. "The Gospel Genre." In *The Gospel and the Gospels.* Edited by Peter Stuhlmacher, 361–86. Grand Rapids: Eerdmans, 1991.
Gundry, Robert H. *The Use of the Old Testament in St. Matthew's Gospel: With Special Reference to the Messianic Hope.* NovTSup XVIII. Edited by W. C. Van Unnik. Leiden: Brill, 1967.
———. "Recent Investigations into the Literary Genre 'Genre.'" In *New Dimensions in New Testament Study.* Edited by Richard N. Longenecker and Merrill C. Tenney, 97–114. Grand Rapids: Zondervan, 1974.
———. *Matthew: A Commentary on His Literary and Theological Art.* Grand Rapids: Eerdmans, 1982.
Habel, Norman C. *The Land Is Mine: Six Biblical Land Ideologies.* OBT. Edited by Walter Brueggemann. Minneapolis: Fortress, 1995.
Hagner, Donald. "Matthew: Christian Judaism or Jewish Christianity." In *The Face of New Testament Studies: A Survey of Recent Research.* Edited by Scot McKnight and Grant R. Osborne, 263–282. Grand Rapids: Baker Academic, 2004.
Han, Kyu Sam. "Theology of Prayer in the Gospel of Luke." *JETS* 43.4 (2000) 675–93.
Hahneman, Geoffrey Mark. "The Muratorian Fragment and the Origins of the New Testament Canon." In *The Canon Debate.* Edited by Lee Martin McDonald and James A. Sanders, 405–15. Peabody, MA: Hendrickson, 2002.
Hall, Robert G. "Living Creatures in the Midst of the Throne: Another Look at Revelation 4.6." *NTS* 36.4 (1990) 609–13.

Hannah, Darrell D. "The Throne of His Glory: The Divine Throne and Heavenly Mediators in Revelation and the Similitudes of Enoch." *ZNW* 94 (2003) 68–96.

Hanson, Anthony Tyrrell. *The New Testament Interpretation of Scripture*. London: SPCK, 1980.

Hare, Douglas R. A. "How Jewish Is the Gospel of Matthew?" *CBQ* 62 (2000) 264–77.

Harrington, Daniel J. *The Synoptic Gospels Set Free: Preaching without Anti-Judaism*. SJC. Edited by Lawrence Boadt. New York: Paulist, 2008.

Harris, R. Laird. *Inspiration and Canonicity of the Bible: An Historical and Exegetical Study*. CEP. Grand Rapids: Zondervan, 1973.

Harris, Sarah. *The Davidic Shepherd King in the Lukan Narrative*. LNTS 558. Edited by Chris Keith. London: Bloomsbury, 2016.

Hartman, L. "Scriptural Exegesis in the Gospel of St. Matthew and the Problem of Communication." In *L'Évangile selon Matthieu: Rédaction et théologie*. BETL XXIX. Edited by M. Didier, 131–52. Gembloux: J. Duculot, 1971.

Harvey, A. E. *Jesus and the Constraints of History*. Philadelphia: Westminster, 1982.

Harvey, Michael G. "Science, Rationality, and Theology." *JR* 87.1 (2007) 225–47.

Harvey, Van A. *The Historian and the Believer: The Morality of Historical Knowledge and Christian Belief*. New York: MacMillan, 1966.

Hauck, Robert J. *The More Divine Proof: Prophecy and Inspiration in Celsus and Origen*. AARA Series 69. Edited by Susan Thistlewaite. Atlanta: Scholars, 1989.

Hay, David M. *Glory at the Right Hand: Psalm 110 in Early Christianity*. SBLMS 18. Edited by Robert A. Kraft. Nashville: Abingdon, 1973.

Hays, Daniel J. "If He Looks Like a Prophet and Talks Like a Prophet, Then He Must Be . . ." In *Israel's Messiah: In the Bible and the Dead Sea Scrolls*. Edited by Richard Hess and M. Daniel Carroll, 57–81. Grand Rapids: Baker Academic, 2003.

Hays, Richard B. *Echoes of Scripture in the Letters of Paul*. New Haven: Yale University Press, 1989.

———. *Reading Scripture Backwards: Figural Christology and the Fourfold Gospel Witness*. Waco: Baylor University Press, 2014.

———. *Echoes of Scripture in the Gospels*. Waco: Baylor University Press, 2016.

Hayward, Robert. *The Targum of Jeremiah: Translated, with a Critical Introduction, Apparatus, and Notes*. AB 12. Edited by Martin McNamara. Wilmington: Michael Glazier, 1986.

Heckel, Theo K. *Vom Evangelium des Markus zum viergestaltigen Evangelium*. WUNT 120. Tübingen: Mohr Siebeck, 1999.

Hendrickson, William. *New Testament Commentary: Exposition of the Gospel According to Matthew*. Grand Rapids: Baker, 1973.

Hendel, Ronald S. "Farewell to SBL: Faith and Reason in Biblical Studies." *BAR* 36.4 (July/August 2010) 28.

Hengel, Martin. "Enstehungszeit und Situation des Markusevangelium." In *Markus: Philologie, Historische, literargeschichtliche und stilistische Untersuchungen zum zweiten Evangelium*. Edited by H. Cancik. WUNT 33. J. C. B. Mohr/Paul Siebeck, 1984. ET "The Gospel of Mark: Time of Origin and Situation." In *Studies in the Gospel of Mark*. Translation by John Bowden. Edited by Martin Hengel, 1–45. Philadelphia: Fortress, 1985.

———. *Die Evangelienüberschriften. Sitzungsberichte der Heidelberger Akademie der Wissenschaften*. Carl Winter: Universitätsverlag, 1984. ET "The Titles of the Gospels and the Gospel of Mark." *Studies in the Gospel of Mark*. Translation by John Bowden. Edited by Martin Hengel, 64–84. Philadelphia: Fortress, 1985.

———. *The Four Gospels and the One Gospel of Jesus Christ: An Investigation of the Collection and Origin of the Canonical Gospels.* Translated by John Bowden. Harrisburg, PA: Trinity International, 2000.

———. "Eye-witness Memory and the Writing of the Gospels." In *The Written Gospel.* Edited by Markus Bockmuehl and Donald A. Hagner, 70–98. Cambridge: Cambridge University Press, 2005.

Henry, Carl F. H. *Frontiers in Modern Theology: A Critique of Current Theological Trends.* Chicago: Moody, 1965.

Herntrich, V. "λεῖμμα." *TDNT.* Translated by Geoffrey W. Bromiley. Edited by Gerhard Kittel, 4.196–209. Grand Rapids: Eerdmans, 1967.

Hess, Richard S. "The Image of the Messiah in the Old Testament." In *Images of Christ: Ancient and Modern.* RILP 2. Edited by Stanley E. Porter, Michael A. Hayes, and David Tombs, 22–33. London: Sheffield Academic, 1997.

Hess, Richard and M. Daniel Carroll, eds. *Israel's Messiah: In the Bible and the Dead Sea Scrolls.* Grand Rapids: Baker Academic, 2003.

Hidber, T. "Arrian." In *Narrators, Narratees, and Narratives in Ancient Greek Literature.* SNGN. Edited by Irene De Jong, René Nünlist, and Angus Bowie, 165–74. Leiden: Brill, 2004.

———. "Appian." In *Narrators, Narratees, and Narratives in Ancient Greek Literature.* SNGN. Edited by Irene De Jong, René Nünlist, and Angus Bowie, 175–85. Leiden: Brill, 2004.

Higgins, A. J. B. "The Old Testament and Some Aspects of New Testament Christology." In *Promise and Fulfillment: Essays Presented to Professor S. H. Hooke.* Edited by F. F. Bruce, 128–41. Edinburgh: T & T Clark, 1963.

———. "The Priestly Messiah." *NTS* 13 (1966–67) 211–39.

Hill, David. "The Request of Zebedee's Sons and the Johannine DOXA-Theme." *NTS* 13 (1966–67) 281–85.

Hoffman, Matthew. *From Rebel to Rabbi: Reclaiming Jesus and the Making of Modern Jewish Culture.* SSJHC. Edited by Aron Rodrique and Steven J. Zipperstein. Stanford: Stanford University Press, 2007.

Hoffman, Thomas A. "Inspiration, Normativeness, Canonicity, and the Unique Sacred Character of the Bible." *CBQ* 44.3 (1982) 447–69.

Hoffmann, Paul. "*Mutmassungen uber Q: Zum Problem der literarischen Genese von Q.*" In *The Sayings Source Q and the Historical Jesus.* BETL CLVIII. Edited by A. Lindemann, 255–88. Paris: Leuven University Press, 2001.

Holladay, William L. *Jeremiah 1: A Commentary on the Prophet Jeremiah: Chapters 1–25.* Hermeneia. Edited by Paul D. Hanson. Philadelphia: Fortress, 1986.

Holmberg, Bengt. "Questions of Method in James Dunn's Jesus Remembered." *JSNT* 26.4 (2004) 445–57.

Holmgren, Fredrick C. *The Old Testament and the Significance of Jesus.* Grand Rapids: Eerdmans, 1999.

Hooker, Morna D. *Jesus and the Servant: The Influence of the Servant Concept of Deutero-Isaiah in the New Testament.* London: SPCK, 1959.

———. "Christology and Methodology." *NTS* 17 (1970–71) 480–87.

———. "Mark." In *It is Written: Scripture Citing Scripture: Essays in Honour of Barnabas Lindars.* Edited by D. A. Carson and H. G. M. Williamson, 220–30. Cambridge: Cambridge University Press, 1988.

———. *The Gospel According to St Mark*. BNTC. Edited by Henry Chadwick. London: Adam & Charles Black, 1991.

———. "'Who Can This Be?' The Christology of Mark's Gospel." In *Contours of Christology in the New Testament*. Edited by Richard N. Longenecker, 79–99. Grand Rapids: Eerdmans, 2005.

———. "Isaiah in Mark's Gospel." In *Isaiah in the New Testament*. Edited by Steve Moyise and Maarten J. J. Menken, 35–49. London: T&T Clark, 2005.

Horbury, William. "Jewish Messianism and Early Christology." In *Contours of Christology in the New Testament*. Edited by Richard N. Longenecker, 3–24. Grand Rapids: Eerdmans, 2005.

Horrell, David G. "Models and Methods in Social-Scientific Interpretation: A Response to Philip Esler." *JSNT* 78 (2000) 83–105.

Horsley, Richard A. "'Messianic' Figures and Movements in First-Century Palestine." In *The Messiah: Developments in Earliest Judaism and Christianity*. FPSJCO. Edited by James H. Charlesworth, 276–95. Minneapolis: Fortress, 1987.

———. "Q and Jesus: Assumptions, Approaches, and Analyses." *Semeia* 55.1 (1991) 175–210.

Houlden, Leslie. "Jesus, Origins of." In *Jesus in History, Thought, and Culture: An Encyclopedia*. Edited by Leslie Houlden, 438–41. Santa Barbara: ABC-CLIO, 2003.

Houston, Walter J. "'Today, in Your Very Hearing': Some Comments on the Christological Use of the Old Testament." In *The Glory of Christ in the New Testament: Studies in Christology*. Edited by L. D. Hurst and N. T. Wright, 37–58. Oxford: Clarendon, 1987.

Hultgård, Anders. "The Ideal 'Levite,' the Davidic Messiah, and the Saviour Priest in the Testaments of the Twelve Patriarchs." In *Ideal Figures in Ancient Judaism: Profiles and Paradigms*. Edited by John J. Collins and George W. E. Nickelsburg, 93–110. Missoula, MT: Scholars, 1980.

Hultgren, Arland J. "Interpreting the Gospel of Luke." *Int* 30 (1976) 353–65.

Hultgren, Stephen. "The Apostolic Church's Influence on the Order of Sayings in the Double Tradition." *ZNW* 99.2 (2008) 185–212.

Hume, David. *Enquiries Concerning Human Understanding and Concerning the Principles of Morals: Reprinted from the 1777 Edition with Introduction and Analytical Index by L. A. Selby-Bigge*. Oxford: Clarendon, 1902.

Hunter, A. M. "Crux Criticorum—Matt 11.25–30." *NTS* 8 (1962) 241–49.

Hurtado, Larry W. "Revelation 4—5 in the Light of Jewish Apocalyptic Analogies." *JSNT* 25 (1985) 105–24.

———. *Lord Jesus Christ: Devotion to Jesus in Earliest Christianity*. Grand Rapids: Eerdmans, 2003.

———. "Devotion of Jesus and Historical Investigation: A Grateful, Clarifying and Critical Response to Professor Casey." *JSNT* 27.1 (2004) 97–104.

———. *How on Earth Did Jesus Become a God? Historical Questions about Earliest Devotion to Jesus*. Grand Rapids: Eerdmans, 2005.

Incigneri, Brian J. *The Gospel to the Romans: The Setting and Rhetoric of Mark's Gospel*. BIS 65. Edited by R. Alan Culpepper and Rolf Rendtorff. Leiden: Brill, 2003.

Ingolfsland, Dennis. "Jesus Remembered: James Dunn and the Synoptic Problem." *TrinJ* 27.2 (2006) 187–97.

Jauhianen, Marko. "Turban and Crown Lost and Regained: Ezekiel 21:29–32 and Zechariah's Zemah." *JBL* 127.3 (2008) 501–11.

Jenni, E. "Remnant." *IDB*. Edited by George Arthur Buttrick, 4.32. Nashville: Abingdon,1962.

Jensen, David H. *1 & 2 Samuel*. TCB. Edited by Amy Pantinga Pauw and William C. Placher. Louisville, KY: Westminster/John Knox, 2015.

Jeremias, J. "παῖς θεοῦ." *TDNT*. Geoffrey W. Bromiley. Edited by Gerhard Kittel, 5.678–717. Grand Rapids: Eerdmans, 1967.

Johnson, Luke Timothy. *The Real Jesus: The Misguided Quest for the Historical Jesus and the Truth of the Traditional Gospels*. San Francisco: Harper & Row, 1996.

———. "The Humanity of Jesus." In *The Jesus Controversy: Perspectives in Conflict*. RLS. Edited by Gerald P. McKenney, 48–74. Harrisburg, PA: Trinity International, 1999.

Johnson, Marshall D. "Reflections on a Wisdom Approach to Matthew's Christology." *CBQ* 36 (1974) 44–64.

Johnson, R. Frank. "Christ the Servant of the Lord." In *The Old and New Testaments: Their Relationship and the "Intertestamental" Literature*. FSCS. Edited by James H. Charlesworth and Walter P. Weaver, 107–36. Valley Forge: Trinity International, 1993.

Juel, Donald H. "The Origin of Mark's Christology." In *The Messiah: Developments in Earliest Judaism and Christianity*. FPSJCO. Edited by James H. Charlesworth, 449–60. Minneapolis: Fortress, 1987.

———. *Messianic Exegesis: Christological Interpretation of the Old Testament in Early Christianity*. Philadelphia: Fortress, 1988.

———. *A Master of Surprise: Mark Interpreted*. Minneapolis: Fortress, 1994.

Just, Arthur A. *Ancient Christian Commentary on Scripture: Luke*. Downers Grove, IL: IVP, 2003.

Kahl, Werner. *New Testament Miracle Stories in their Religious-Historical Setting: A Religionsgeschichtliche Comparison from a Structural Perspective*. FRLANT 163. Edited by Wolfgang Schrage and Rudolf Smend. Göttingen: Vandenhoeck & Ruprecht, 1994.

Kähler, Martin. *Der sogenannte historisch Jesus und der geschichtliche, biblische Christus*. München: Chr. Kaiser, 1956. Reprint from 1896. ET *The So-Called Historical Jesus and the Historic Biblical Christ*. Translated with Introduction by Carl E. Braaten. Philadelphia: Fortress, 1964.

Kaiser, Otto. *Der Prophet Jesaja/Kap. 1—12*. Göttingen: Vandenhoeck und Ruprecht, 1963. ET *Isaiah 1—12: A Commentary*. Translated by R. A. Wilson. OTL. Edited by Peter Ackroyd et al. London: SCM, 1972.

Kaiser, Walter C. "The Promise to David in Psalm 16 and its Application in Acts 2.25–33 and 13.32–37." *JETS* 23.3 (1980) 219–29.

———. "The Single Intent of Scripture." In *The Right Doctrine from the Wrong Texts? Essays on the Use of the Old Testament in the New*. Edited by G. K. Beale, 55–69. Grand Rapids: Baker Academic, 1994.

Kalin, Everett R. "The New Testament Canon of Eusebius." In *The Canon Debate*. Edited by Lee Martin McDonald and James A. Sanders, 386–404. Peabody, MA: Hendrickson, 2002.

Kant, Immanuel. "An Answer to the Question: What Is Enlightenment?" In *Perpetual Peace and Other Essays on Politics, History, and Morals*. Translated by Ted Humphreys. Indianapolis: Hackett, 1983.

Käsemann, Ernst. *Exegetische Versuche und Besinnungen*. Göttingen: Vandenhoeck und Ruprecht, 1960. ET *Essays on New Testament Themes*. SBT 41. Translated by W. T. Montague. London: SCM, 1971.

Kea, Perry V. "Writing a Bios: Matthew's Genre Choices and Rhetorical Situation." *SBLSP* 33 (1994) 574–86.

Keck, Leander E. "Toward the Renewal of New Testament Christology." *NTS* 32 (1986) 362–77.

———. "Matthew and the Spirit." In *The Social World of the First Christians*. Edited by L. Michael White and O. Larry Yarbrough, 145–55. Minneapolis: Fortress, 1995.

———. *Who Is Jesus? History in Perfect Tense*. SPNT. Edited by D. Moody Smith. Columbia: University of South Carolina Press, 2000.

———. *Why Christ Matters: Toward a New Testament Christology*. Waco. TX: Baylor University Press, 2015.

Kee, Howard Clark. "The Function of Scriptural Quotations and Allusions in Mark 11—16." In *Jesus und Paulus: Festschrift für Werner Georg Kümmel zum 70. Geburtstag*. Edited by E. Earle Ellis and Erich GräBer, 165–88. Göttingen: Vandenhoeck & Ruprecht, 1975.

Keener, Craig S. *The Gospel of John: A Commentary*. 2 vols. Grand Rapids: Baker Academic, 2003.

———. *The Historical Jesus and the Gospels*. Grand Rapids: Eerdmans, 2009.

———. *Miracles: The Credibility of the New Testament Accounts*. Grand Rapids: Baker Academic, 2012.

Keener, Craig S. and Edward T. Wright, eds. *Biographies and Jesus: What Does It Mean for the Gospels to Be Biographies?* Lexington, KY: Emeth, 2016.

Keil, C. F. and F. Delitzsch. *Commentary on the Old Testament: Isaiah*. Translated by James Martin. Grand Rapids: Eerdmans, 1975.

———. *Commentary on the Old Testament: Jeremiah and Lamentations*. Translated by David Patrick. Peabody, MA: Hendrickson, 2006. Reprint from the original English edition by T & T Clark, 1866–91.

———. *Commentary on the Old Testament: The Minor Prophets: Zechariah*. Translated by James Martin. Peabody, MA: Hendrickson, 2006. Reprint from the original English edition by T & T Clark, 1866–91.

Kelber, W. H. *The Kingdom in Mark: A New Place and a New Time*. Philadelphia: Fortress, 1974.

Keller, Ernst and Marie-Luise. *Der Streit um die Wunder*. Gütersloh: Gerd Mohn, 1968. ET *Miracles in Dispute: A Continuing Debate*. Translated by Margaret Kohl. London: SCM, 1969.

Kilpatrick, G. D. *The Origins of the Gospel according to St. Matthew*. Oxford: Clarendon, 1946.

Kim, Seyoon. "Jesus—the Son of God, the Stone, the Son of Man, and the Servant: The Role of Zechariah in the Self-Identification of Jesus." In *Tradition and Interpretation in the New Testament: Essays in Honor of E. Earle Ellis*. Edited by Gerald F. Hawthorne with Otto Betz, 134–45. Grand Rapids: Eerdmans, 1987.

Kingsbury, Jack Dean. "The Title 'Kyrios' in Matthew's Gospel." *JBL* 94 (1975) 246–55.

———. "Form and Message of Matthew." *Int* 29 (1975) 13–23.

———. "The Title 'Son of Man' in Matthew's Gospel." *CBQ* 37 (1975) 193–202.

———. *Matthew: Structure, Christology, Kingdom*. Philadelpia: Fortress, 1975.

———. "The Title 'Son of David' in Matthew's Gospel." *JBL* 95 (1976) 591–602.

———. *Matthew*. PC. Edited by Gerhard Krodel. Philadelphia: Fortress, 1977.

———. *Jesus Christ in Matthew, Mark, and Luke*. PC. Edited by Gerhard Krodel. Philadelphia: Fortress, 1981.

———. *Conflict in Luke: Jesus, Authorities, Disciples*. Minneapolis: Fortress, 1991.

———. *Gospel Interpretation: Narrative-Critical & Social-Scientific Approaches*. Harrisburg: Trinity International, 1997.

———. "The Gospel in Four Editions." *Int* 33 (1979) 363–75.

———. "The Birth Narrative of Matthew." In *The Gospel of Matthew in Current Study: Studies in Memory of William G. Thompson*. Edited by David E. Aune, 154–65. Grand Rapids: Eerdmans, 2001.

Kinzer, Mark. "Temple Christology in the Gospel of John." *SBLSP* 37 (1998) 447–64.

Kirchschläger, Walter. "Scripture and Inspiration." In *Understanding Scripture: Explorations of Jewish and Christian Traditions of Interpretation*. Edited by Clemens Thoma and Michael Wyschogrod, 36–46. New York: Paulist, 1987.

Kittel, G. "δόξα." *TDNT*. Translated by Geoffrey W. Bromiley. Edited by Gerhard Kittel, 2.248–49. Grand Rapids: Eerdmans, 1964.

Klinghardt, Matthias. "The Marcionte Gospel and the Synoptic Problem: A New Suggestion." *NovT* 50 (2008) 1–27.

Klooster, F. H. "Dogmatics." *Evangelical Dictionary of Theology*. Edited by Walter A. Elwell. 350–51. Grand Rapids: Baker Academic, 2001.

Kloppenborg Verbin, John S. "The Theological Stakes in the Synoptic Problem." In *The Four Gospels 1992: Festschrift Frans Neirynck*. Edited by F. Van Segroeck et al, 1.93–120. Leuven: Leuven University Press, 1992.

———. "Discursive Practices in the Sayings Gospel Q and the Quest of the Historical Jesus." In *The Sayings Source Q and the Historical Jesus*. BETL CLVIII. Edited by A Lindemann, 149–90. Paris: Leuven University Press, 2001.

———. "On Dispensing with Q? Goodacre on the Relation of Luke to Matthew." *NTS* 49 (2003) 210–36.

Knohl, Israel. "'By Three Days, Live': Messiahs, Resurrection, and Ascent to Heaven in Hazon Gabriel." *JR* 88.2 (2008) 147–58.

Knowles, Michael. *Jeremiah in Matthew's Gospel: The Rejected-Prophet Motif in Matthaean Redaction*. JSNTSup 68. Sheffield: Sheffield Academic, 1999.

Koester, Helmut. "One Jesus and Four Primitive Gospels." *HTR* 61 (1968) 203–47.

———. *Ancient Christian Gospels: Their History and Development*. Philadelphia:Trinity International/London: SCM, 1990.

Kohn, Risa Levitt and Rebecca Moore. *A Portable God: The Origin of Judaism and Christianity*. New York: Rowman and Littlefield, 2007.

Korteweg, Thomas. "Further Observations on the Transmission of the Text." In *Studies on the Testaments of the Twelve Patriarchs*. Edited by Marinus De Jonge, 161–82. Leiden: Brill, 1975.

Köstenberger, Andreas J. "The Destruction of the Second Temple and the Composition of the Fourth Gospel." *TRINJ* 26 (2005) 205–42.

———. "John." In *Commentary on the New Testament Use of the Old Testament*. Edited by G. K. Beale and D. A. Carson, 415–512. Grand Rapids: Baker Academic, 2007.

Kraus, Hans-Joachim. *Biblischer Kommentar, Altes Testament. Bd. 15: Psalmen 60—150*. Neukirchen-Vluyn : Neukirchener Verlag des Erziehungsvereins, 1978. ET *Psalms 60—150*. Translated by Hilton C. Oswald. Minneapolis: Augsburg, 1989.

Krentz, Edgar. *The Historical-Critical Method*. GBS. Edited by Gene M. Tucker. Philadelphia: Fortress, 1975.

Kümmel, Werner Georg. *Einleitung in das Neue Testament*. Heidelberg: Quelle & Meyer, 1965. ET *Introduction to the New Testament*. Translated by Paul Feine. Nashville: Abingdon, 1973.

Kuhn, Karl Georg. "Die Geschlechtsregister Jesus bei Lukas und Matthäus, nach ihrer Herkunft untersucht." *ZNW* 22 (1923) 206–28.

———. "Die beiden Messias Aarons und Israels." *NTS* 1 (1955) 168–79. ET "The Two Messiahs of Aaron and Israel." In *The Scrolls and the New Testament*. Edited by Krister Stendahl, 54–64. London: SCM, 1958.

Kuyper, Abraham. *Van de voleinding*. Kampen: Kok, 1931. ET *The Revelation of St. John*. Translated by John Hendrik De Vries. Grand Rapids: Eerdmans, 1963.

Kvalbein, Hans. "The Kingdom of the Father in the Gospel of Thomas." In *The New Testament and Early Christian Literature in Greco-Roman Context: Studies in Honor of David E. Aune*. NovTSup 122. Edited by John Fotopoulos, 203–30. Leiden: Brill, 2006.

Kysar, Robert. *The Fourth Evangelist and his Gospel: An Examination of Contemporary Scholarship*. Minneapolis: Augsburg, 1975.

——— "What's the Meaning of This? Reflections upon a Life and Career." In *What We Have Heard from the Beginning: Past and Present in Johannine Studies*. Edited by Tom Thatcher, 163–78. Waco, TX: Baylor University Press, 2007.

Ladd, George Eldon. *The New Testament and Criticism*. Grand Rapids: Eerdmans, 1967.

———. "The Search for Perspective." *Int* 25 (1971) 41–62.

———. *A Theology of the New Testament*. Grand Rapids: Eerdmans, 1974.

———. *I Believe in the Resurrection of Jesus*. Grand Rapids: Eerdmans, 1975.

Lampe, G. W. H. "ἀετός." *A Patristic Greek Lexicon*. Oxford: Clarendon, 1968.

Landmesser, Christof. "Interpretative Unity of the New Testament." In *One Scripture or Many? Canon from Biblical, Theological, and Philosophical Perspectives*. Edited by Christine Helmer and Christof Landmesser, 159–85. Oxford: Oxford University Press, 2004.

Lane, William L. *Commentary on the Gospel of Mark*. NICNT. Edited by F. F. Bruce. Grand Rapids: Eerdmans, 1974.

Lanier, Gregory. "'From God' or 'from Heaven'"? ἐξ ὕψους in Luke 1,78." *Bib* 97.1 (2016) 121–27.

La Sor, William Sanford. "Interpretation and Infallibility: Lessons from the Dead Sea Scrolls." In *Early Jewish and Christian Exegesis: Studies in Memory of William Hugh Brownlee*. Edited by Craig A. Evans and William F. Stinespring, 123–37. Atlanta: Scholars, 1987.

Latourelle, R. "Critères d'authenticité historique des Evangiles." *Greg* 55.4 (1974) 609–38.

Le Donne, Anthony. *The Historiographical Jesus: Memory, Typology, and the Son of David*. Waco, TX: Baylor University Press, 2009.

Leith, John H. "The Bible and Theology." *Int* 30 (1976) 227–41.

Lemcio, Eugene E. "The Gospels and Canonical Criticism." In *The New Testament as Canon: A Reader in Canonical Criticism*. JSNTSup 76. Edited by Robert W. Wall and Eugene E. Lemcio, 28–47. Sheffield: Sheffield Academic, 1992.

———. "Kerygmatic Centrality and Unity in the First Testament?" In *The Quest for Context and Meaning: Studies in Biblical Intertextuality in Honor of James A. Sanders*. Edited by Craig A. Evans and Shemaryahu Talmon, 357–73. Leiden: Brill, 1997.

Lemke, Werner E. "Revelation through History in Recent Biblical Theology." *Int* 36.1 (1982) 34–46.

Lenowitz, Harris. *The Jewish Messiahs: From the Galilee to Crown Heights*. Oxford: Oxford University Press, 1998.

Levey, Samson H. *The Messiah: An Aramaic Interpretation: The Messianic Exegesis of the Targum.* MHUC 2. Cincinnati: Hebrew Union College-Jewish Institute of Religion, 1974.

Levin, Yigal. "Jesus, 'Son of God' and 'Son of David': The 'Adoption' of Jesus into the Davidic Line." *JSNT* 28.4 (2006) 415–42.

Levine, Amy-Jill. "Introduction." In *The Historical Jesus in Context.* PRR. Edited by Amy-Jill Levine, Dale C. Allison, and John Dominic Crossan, 1–39. Princeton: Princeton University Press, 2006.

———. *The Misunderstood Jew: The Church and the Scandal of the Jewish Jesus.* San Francisco: HarperSanFrancisco, 2006.

Lewis, Jack P. *The Gospel According to Matthew Part II: 13:53—28:20.* Austin: Sweet, 1976.

Lichtenberger, H. "Jesus and the Dead Sea Scrolls." In *Hillel and Jesus: Comparative Studies of Two Major Religious Leaders.* Edited by James H. Charlesworth and Loren L. Johns, 389–96. Minneapolis: Fortress, 1997.

Licona, Michael R. *Why Are There Differences in the Gospels? What We Can Learn from Ancient Biography.* Oxford: Oxford University Press, 2017.

Lieu, Judith M. "Narrative Analysis and Scripture in John." In *The Old Testament in the New Testament.* Edited by Steve Moyise, 144–63. London: T & T Clark, 2001.

———. *Christian Identity in the Jewish and Graeco-Roman World.* Oxford: Oxford University Press, 2004.

———. "How John Writes." In *The Written Gospel.* Edited by Markus Bockmuehl and Donald A. Hagner, 171–83. Cambridge: Cambridge University Press, 2005.

Lindemann, A. "Die Logienquell Q Fragen an eine gut Begründete Hypothese." In *The Sayings Source Q and the Historical Jesus.* BETL CLVIII. Edited by A Lindemann, 3–26. Paris: Leuven University Press, 2001.

Linnemann, Eta. *Gibt es ein synoptisches Problem?* Neuhausen: Friedrich Hänssler, 1992. ET *Is There a Synoptic Problem? Rethinking the Literary Dependence of the First Three Gospels.* Translated by Robert W. Yarbrough. Grand Rapids: Baker, 1992.

Lipovsky, James P. "Livy." In Ancient Writers: Greece and Rome. Edited by T. James Luce, 2.733–64. New York: Charles Scribner's Sons, 1982.

Lohse, Eduard. "Der König aus Davids Geschlecht: Bemerkungen zur messianischen Erwartung der Synagoge." In *Abraham unser Vater. Juden und Christen im Gesprach uber die Bibel: Festschrift für Otto Michel.* Edited by Otto Betz, Martin Hengel, and Peter Schmidt, 337–45. Leiden: Brill, 1963.

Loisy, Alfred. *Le Quatrième Évangile.* Paris: Émile Nourry, 1921.

———. *L'Apocalypse de Jean.* Paris: Minerva, 1923.

Longenecker, Richard. "Literary Criteria in Life of Jesus Research: An Evaluation and Proposal." In *Current Issues in Biblical and Patristic Interpretation: Studies in Honor of Merrill C. Tenney.* Edited by Gerald F. Hawthorne, 217–29. Grand Rapids: Eerdmans, 1975.

Love, Mark Cameron. *The Evasive Text: Zechariah 1—8 and the Frustrated Reader.* JSOTSup 296. Edited by David J. A. Clines and Philip R. Davies, Sheffield: Sheffield Academic, 1999.

Loubser, J. A. "Invoking Ancestors: Some Socio-Rhetorical Aspects of the Genealogies in the Gospels of Matthew and Luke." *NeoT* 39.1 (2005) 127–40.

Lust, J. "Messianism and the Greek Version of Jeremiah." In *VII Congress of the International Organization for Septuagint and Cognate Studies: Leuven 1989.* SBLSCSS 31. Edited by Claude E. Cox, 87–122. Atlanta: Scholars, 1989.

———. "Messianism and the Greek Version of Jeremiah: Jer 23.5–6 and 33.14–26." In *Messianism and the Septuagint: Collected Essays by J. Lust.* BETL CLXXVII. Edited by K Hauspie, 41–68. Leuven: Leuven University Press, 2004.

Luz, Ulrich. "Fiktivität und Traditionstreue im Matthäusevangelium im Lichte griechischer Literatur." *ZNW* 84 (1993) 153–77.

———. *Die Jesusgeschichte des Mattäus.* Neukirchen: Neukirchen, 1993. ET *The Theology of the Gospel of Matthew.* NTT. Translated by J. Bradford Robinson. Edited by James D. G. Dunn, Cambridge: University of Cambridge Press, 1995.

———. *Evangelium nach Matthäus.* ET *Matthew 8–20: A Commentary.* Hermeneia. Translated by James E. Crouch. Edited by Helmut Koester, Minneapolis: Fortress, 2001.

———. *Evangelium nach Matthäus.* ET *Matthew 1–7: A Commentary.* Hermeneia. Translated by James E. Crouch. Edited by Helmut Koester. Minneapolis: Fortress, 2007.

Lyons, Michael A. "Marking Innerbiblical Allusion in the Book of Ezekiel." *Bib* 88.2 (2007) 245–49.

Lyons, William John. "Hope for a Troubled Discipline? Contributions to New Testament Studies from Reception History." *JSNT* 33.2 (2010) 207–20.

Ma, Wonsuk. *Until the Spirit Comes: The Spirit of God in the Book of Isaiah.* JSOT 271. Edited by David J. A. Clines and Philip R. Davies. Sheffield: Sheffield Academic, 1999.

Maccoby, Hyam. "Jesus the Pharisee." *JQ* 194 (2004) 37–42.

Mack, Burton. *The Lost Gospel: The Book of Q and Christian Origins.* San Francisco: HarperSan Francisco, 1993.

———. *The Christian Myth: Origins, Logic, and Legacy.* New York: Continuum, 2001.

MacLean, H. B. "Zimri." *IDB.* Edited by George Arthur Buttrick, 4.958. Nashville: Abingdon, 1962.

Maier, Johann. "Messias oder Gesalbter? Zu einem Übersetzungs- und Deutungsproblem in den Qumrantexten." *RevQum* 17 (1996) 587–612.

Malbon, Elizabeth Struthers. "The Jesus of Mark and the Sea of Galilee." *JBL* 103.3 (1984) 363–77.

———. "The Christology of Mark's Gospel: Narrative Christology and the Markan Jesus." In *Who Do You Say That I Am? Essays on Christology in Honor of Jack Dean Kingsbury.* Edited by. Mark Allan Powell and David R. Bauer, 33–48. Louisville: Westminster/John Knox, 1999.

Malina, Bruce J. "Social-Scientific Methods in Historical Jesus Research." In *The Social Setting of Jesus and the Gospels.* Edited by Wolfgang Stegemann, Bruce J. Malina, and Gerd Theissen, 3–26. Minneapolis: Fortress, 2002.

Manson, T. W. *The Servant-Messiah: A Study of the Public Ministry of Jesus.* Cambridge: Cambridge University Press, 1961.

Marcus, Joel. "Mark 14:61: 'Are You the 'Messiah-Son-of-God'?" *NovT* (1989) 125–41.

———. *The Way of the Lord: Christological Exegesis of the Old Testament in the Gospel of Mark.* Louisville: Westminster/John Knox, 1992.

———. "Meggitt on the Madness and Kingship of Jesus." *JSNT* 29.4 (2007) 421–24.

Marguerat, Daniel. *Le jugement dans l'évangile de Matthieu.* MB. Edited by François Bovon et Robert Martin-Achard. Geneve: Labor et Fides, 1981.

Marincola, John. *Authority and Tradition in Ancient Historiography*. Cambridge: Cambridge University Press, 1997.

———. "ἀλήθεια." *Lexicon Historio-graphicum Graecum et Latinum*. Edited by Carmine Ampolo, Ugo Fantasia, and Leone Porciani, 2.7–29. Pisa: Normale, 2007.

Marshall, I. Howard. *Luke: Historian and Theologian*. Grand Rapids: Zondervan, 1971.

———. *Commentary on Luke*. NIGTC. Edited by I. Howard Marshall and Ward Gasque, Grand Rapids, Eerdmans, 1978.

———. "Jesus as Messiah in Mark and Matthew." In *The Messiah in the Old and New Testaments*. MNTS 9. Edited by Stanley E. Porter, 117–43. Grand Rapids: Eerdmans, 2007.

Martin, Ralph P. *Mark: Evangelist and Theologian*. Grand Rapids: Zondervan, 1973.

———. *New Testament Foundations: A Guide for Christian Students*. Grand Rapids: Eerdmans, 1975.

Martínez, Florentino García. "Messianische Erwartungen in den Qumranschriften." *JBTh* 8 (1993) 171–208.

Martínez, Florentino García and Eibert J. C. Tigchelaar, eds. *The Dead Sea Scrolls Study Edition*. Leiden: Brill, 1997.

Mason, Rex. "The Messiah in the Postexilic Old Testament Literature." In *King and Messiah in Israel and the Ancient Near East: Proceedings of the Oxford Old Testament Seminar*. JSOTSup 270. Edited by David J. A. Clines and Philip R. Davies, 338–64. Sheffield: Sheffield Academic, 1998.

Massaux, Édouard. *Influence de l'Évangile de saint Matthieu sur la litérature chrétienne avant saint Irénée*. Leuven: Leuven University Press, 1986. ET *The Influence of the Gospel of Saint Matthew on Christian Literature before Saint Irenaeus*. NGS 5/2. Translated by Norman J. Belval and Suzanne Hecht. Edited by Arthur J. Bellinzoni. Macon, GA: Mercer University Press, 1992.

Massey, Preston T. "Disagreement in the Greco-Roman Literary Tradition and the Implications for Gospel Research." *BBR* 22.1 (2012) 51–80.

Matson, Mark A. "The Contribution to the Temple Cleansing by the Fourth Gospel." *SBLSP* 31 (1992) 489–506.

Matera, Frank J. *The Kingship of Jesus: Composition and Theology in Mark 15*. SBLDS 66. Edited by William Baird. Chico, CA: Scholars, 1982.

Mayordomo-Marín, Moisés. *Den Anfang hören: Leserorientierte Evangelienexegese am Beispiel von Matthäus 1–2*. FRLANT 180. Göttingen: Vandenhoeck & Ruprecht, 1998.

McCane, Byron R. *Roll Back the Stone: Death and Burial in the World of Jesus*. Harrisburg: Trinity International, 2003.

McCarter, P. Kyle. *I Samuel: A New Translation with Notes & Commentary*. Garden City, NY: Doubleday, 1980.

McCasland, S. Vernon. "Matthew Twists the Scriptures." *JBL* 80.2 (1961) 143–48.

McCown, C. C. "The Current Plight of Biblical Scholarship." *JBL* 75 (1956) 12–18.

McConville, J. Gordon. "Messianic Interpretation of the Old Testament in Modern Context." In *The Lord's Anointed: Interpretation of Old Testament Messianic Texts*. Edited by Philip E. Satterthwaite, Richard S. Hess, and Gordon J. Wenham, 1–17. Carlisle: Paternoster/Grand Rapids: Baker, 1995.

McDonald, Lee Martin. "Identifying Scripture and Canon in the Early Church: The Criteria Question." In *The Canon Debate*. Edited by Lee Martin McDonald and James A. Sanders, 416–39. Peabody, MA: Hendrickson, 2002.

McDonald, Lee Martin and James A. Sanders. "Introduction." In *The Canon Debate*. Edited by Lee Martin McDonald and James A. Sanders, 3–20. Peabody, MA: Hendrickson, 2002.

McEleney, Neil J. "Authenticating Criteria and Mark 7.1–23." *CBQ* 34 (1972) 431–60.

McKane, William. *A Critical and Exegetical Commentary on Jeremiah*. ICC. Edited by J. A. Emerton and C. E. B. Cranfield. Edinburgh: T & T Clark, 1986.

McKenzie, John L. "Royal Messianism." *CBQ* 19.1 (1957) 25–52.

———. *The Old Testament without Illusion*. Garden City, NY: Image, 1979.

McLaren, James S. "Corruption among the High Priesthood: A Matter of Perspective." In *A Wandering Galilean: Essays in Honour of Seán Freyne*. Edited by Zuleika Rogers, 141–57. Leiden: Brill, 2009.

McLay, Timothy R. *The Use of the Septuagint in New Testament Research*. Grand Rapids: Eerdmans, 2003.

McNamara, Martin S. *The New Testament and the Palestinian Targum to the Pentateuch*. AnB 27. Rome: Pontifical Biblical Institute, 1966.

Meagher, John C. *Clumsy Construction in Mark's Gospel: A Critique of Form-and Redaktionsgeschichte*. TST 3. Toronto: Edwin Mellen, 1979.

Meggitt, Justin J. "The Madness of King Jesus: Why was Jesus Put to Death, but his Followers Were Not?" *JSNT* 29.4 (2007) 379–413.

Meier, John P. *A Marginal Jew: Rethinking the Historical Jesus. Vol. 1: The Roots of the Problem and the Person*. ABRL. Edited by David Noel Freedman. New York: Doubleday, 1991.

———. "The Debate on the Resurrection of the Dead: An Incident from the ministry of the Historical Jesus?" *JSNT* 22.1 (2000) 3–23.

Menken, Maarten J. J. *Matthew's Bible: The Old Testament Text of the Evangelist*. BETL CLXXIII. Leuven: Leuven University Press, 2004.

———. "Observations on the Significance of the Old Testament in the Fourth Gospel." In *Theology and Christology in the Fourth Gospel: Essays by the Members of the SNTS Johannine Writings Seminar*. BETL CLXXXIV. Edited by Gilbert Van Belle, J. G. Van Der Watt, and P. Maritz, 155–76. Leuven: Leuven University Press, 2005.

Merenlahti, Petri. *Poetics for the Gospels? Rethinking Narrative Criticism*. SNYW. Edited by John Barclay, Joel Marcus, and John Riches. London: T & T Clark, 2002.

Merkel, Helmut. *Die Widersprüche zwischen den Evangelien: Ihre polemische und apologetisch Behandlung in der Alten Kirche bis zu Augustin*. WUNT 13. Edited by Joachim Jeremias und D. Otto Michel. Tübingen: J. C. B. Mohr/Paul Siebeck, 1971.

Metzger, Bruce M. *The Canon of the New Testament: Its Origin, Development, and Significance*. Oxford: Clarendon, 1987.

Meyers, Carol L. and Eric M. Meyers. *Haggai, Zechariah 1—8: A New Translation with Introduction and Commentary*. AB. Edited by William Foxwell Albright and David Noel Freedman. Garden City, NY: Doubleday, 1987.

Michel, O. "μόσχος." *TDNT*. Translated by Geoffrey W. Bromiley. Edited by Gerhard Kittel, 4.760–61. Grand Rapids: Eerdmans, 1967.

Miller, Merrill P. "Targum, Midrash and the Use of the Old Testament in the New Testament." *JSJ* 2 (1971) 29–82.

Miller, Patrick D. *The Book of Jeremiah*. NIB. Edited by Leader Keck. Nashville: Abingdon, 1994.

Miller, Robert J. "The (A)Historicity of Jesus' Temple Demonstration: A Test Case in Methodology." *SBLSP* 30 (1991) 235–52.

———. "The Jesus of Orthodoxy and the Jesuses of the Gospels: A Critique of Luke Timothy Johnson's The Real Jesus." *JSNT* 68 (1997) 101–20.
Mitchell, David C. "The Fourth Deliverer: A Josephite Messiah in 4QTestimonia." *Bib* 86.4 (2005) 545–53.
Mitchell, H. G. *Zechariah to Jonah*. ICC. Edited by Charles Briggs, Samuel Driver, and Alfred Plummer. New York: Charles Scribner's Sons, 1912.
Milton, Helen. "The Structure of the Prologue to St. Matthew's Gospel." *JBL* 81.2 (1962) 175–81.
M'Neile, Alan Hugh. *The Gospel According to St Matthew: The Greek Text with Introduction, Notes, and Indices*. London: MacMillan, 1915.
Miscall, Peter D. *1 Samuel: A Literary Reading*. ISBL. Edited by HerbertMarks and Robert Polzin. Bloomington, IN: Indiana University Press, 1986.
Moessner, David P. "How Luke Writes." In *The Written Gospel*. Edited by Markus Bockmuehl and Donald A. Hagner, 149–70. Cambridge: Cambridge University Press, 2005.
Montgomery, James A. *A Critical and Exegetical Commentary on the Books of Kings*. ICC. Edited by Henry Snyder Gehman. New York: Charles Scribner's Sons, 1951.
Morgan, Robert. "The Hermeneutical Significance of Four Gospels." *Int* 33.4 (1979) 376–88.
———. "The Historical Jesus and the Theology of the New Testament." In *The Glory of Christ in the New Testament: Studies in Christology*. Edited by L. D. Hurst and N. T. Wright, 187–206.Oxford: Clarendon, 1987.
———. "The New Testament Canon of Scripture and Christianity Identity." In *Die Einheit der Schrift und die Vielfalt des Kanons: The Unity of Scripture and the Diversity of the Canon*. Edited by John Barton and Michael Wolter, 151–93. Berlin: Walter de Gruyter, 2003.
Morray-Jones, C. R. A. "The Temple Within: The Embodies Divine Image and its Worship in the Dead Sea Scrolls and Other Early Jewish and Christian Sources." *SBLSP* 37 (1998) 400–31.
Morris, Leon. *Revelation: An Introduction and Commentary*. TNTC. Edited by R. V. G. Tasker. London: Tyndale, 1969.
———. *I Believe in Revelation*. Grand Rapids: Eerdmans, 1976.
Mounce, Robert H. *The Book of Revelation*. NICNT. Edited by F. F. Bruce. Grand Rapids: Eerdmans, 1977.
Moule, C. F. D. *The Birth of the New Testament*. New York: Harper & Row, 1962.
Moyise, Steve. *The Old Testament in the New: An Introduction*. New York: Continuum, 2001.
———. *Evoking Scripture: Seeing the Old Testament in the New*. London: T & T Clark, 2008.
Mussies, Gerard. "'In Those Days:' Some Remarks on the Use of 'Days' in Matthew 2.1, 3.1, and Luke 2.1." In *Early Christianity and Classical Culture: Comparative Studies in Honor of Abraham J. Malherbe*. NovTSup CX. Edited by John T. Fitzgerald, Thomas H. Olbricht, and L. Michael White, 89–101. Leiden: Brill, 2003.
Neyrey, Jerone H. "'I Said: You are Gods': Psalm 82.6 and John 10." *JBL* 108.4 (1989) 647–63.
———. "Encomium versus Vituperation: Contrasting Portraits in the Fourth Gospel." *JBL* 126.3 (2007) 529–52.
Nicholson, Ernest W. *The Book of the Prophet Jeremiah, Chapters 1–25*. Cambridge: University Press, 1973.
Nicole, Roger. "The New Testament use of the Old Testament" In *The Right Doctrine from the Wrong Texts? Essays on the Use of the Old Testament in the New*. Edited by G. K. Beale,

13–28. Grand Rapids: Baker Academic, 1994. Reprint from *Revelation and the Bible*. Edited by Carl F. Henry, 135–51. Grand Rapids: Baker, 1958.

Niebuhr, H. *The Meaning of Revelation*. New York: MacMillan, 1941.

Nielsen, Jesper Tang. "The Narrative Structures of Glory and Glorification in the Fourth Gospel." *NTS* 56 (2010) 343–66.

Nielsen, Kirsten. *There Is Hope for a Tree: The Tree as Metaphor in Isaiah*. JSOTSup 65. Translated by Christine and Frederick Crowley. Edited by David J. A. Clines and Philip R. Davies. Sheffield: Sheffield Academic, 1989.

Nolland, John. "No Son-of-God Christology in Matthew 1.18–25." *JSNT* 62 (1996) 3–12.

———. *The Gospel of Matthew: A Commentary on the Greek Text*. NIGTC. Edited by I. Howard Marshall and Donald A. Hagner. Grand Rapids: Eerdmans, 2005.

Norden, Eduard. *Die Antike Kunstprosa: vom vi. Jahrhundert v. Chr. bis in die Zeit der Renaissance*. Baltimore: Johns Hopkins University Press, 1998.

North, J. Lionel. "Reactions in Early Christianity to Some References to the Hebrew Prophets in Matthew's Gospel." *NTS* 54 (2008) 254–74.

Notley, Steven, R. "Jesus' Jewish Hermeneutical Method in the Nazareth Synagogue" In *Early Christian Literature and Intertextuality*. Edited by Craig A. Evans, 46–59. London: T & T Clark, 2009.

O'Connell, Robert H. *Concentricity and Continuity: The Literary Structure of Isaiah*. JSOT 188. Sheffield: Sheffield Academic, 1994.

O'Day, Gail. *The Gospel of John: Introduction, Commentary, and Reflections*. NIB. Edited by Neil Alexander. Nashville: Abingdon, 1995.

O'Grady, John F. *The Four Gospels and the Jesus Tradition*. New York: Paulist, 1989.

Ollenburger, Ben C. *The Book of Zechariah: Introduction, Commentary, and Reflections*. NIB 7. Edited by Leander Keck. Nashville: Abingdon, 1994.

Orchard, Bernard and Harold Riley. *The Order of the Synoptics: Why Three Gospels?* Macon: GA: Mercer University Press, 1987.

Oswalt, John N. "כבד." *Theological Wordbook of the Old Testament*. Edited by R. Laird Harris, 1.427. Chicago: Moody, 1980.

O'Toole, R. F. "How Does Luke Portray Jesus as Servant of YHWH." *Bib* 81 (2000) 328–58.

Pagels, Elaine and Karen L. King. *Reading Judas: The Gospel of Judas and the Shaping of Christianity*. New York: Viking, 2007.

Paffenroth, Kim. "Jesus as Anointed and Healing Son of David in the Gospel of Matthew." *Bib* 80.4 (1999) 547–54.

Pao, David W. and Eckhard J. Schnabel. "Luke." In *Commentary on the New Testament Use of the Old Testament*. Edited by G. K. Beale and D. A. Carson, 251–414. Grand Rapids: Baker Academic, 2007.

Paquette, Eve. "Religion as the Academic's Enemy: A Case Study of an Ineffective Discursive Strategy." *SR* 35.3 (2006) 431–46.

Parsenios, G. "'No Longer in the World' (John 17:11): The Transformation of the Tragic in the Fourth Gospel." *HTR* 98.1 (2005) 1–21.

Patterson, Stephen J. *The Gospel of Thomas and Jesus*. Salen, OR: Polebridge, 1993.

Pauck, Wilhelm. *Karl Barth: Prophet of a New Christianity*. New York: Harper & Row, 1931.

Peabody, David Barrett. *Mark as Composer*. NGS 1. Macon, GA: Mercer University Press, 1987.

Pelling, Christopher. "Is Death the End? Closure in Plutarch's Lives." In *Plutarch and History: Eighteen Studies*. London: Duckworth, 2002.

Perrin, Nicholas. "Thomas: The Fifth Gospel?" *JETS* 49.1 (2006) 67–80.

Perrin, Norman. "The Interpretation of the Gospel of Mark." *Int* 30 (1976) 115–24.

———. *What Is Redaction Criticism?* NTS. Edited by Dan O. Via. Philadelphia: Fortress, 1976.

———. "The Christology of Mark: A Study in Methodology." In *The Interpretation of Mark*. IRT 7. Edited by William Telford, 95–108. Philadelphia: Fortress, 1985.

Pervo, Richard I. "Must Luke and Acts Belong to the Same Genre?" *SBLSP* 28 (1989) 309–16.

Pesch, Rudolf. "'Er wird Nazoräer heissen': messianische Exegese in MT 1:22." In *The Four Gospels 1992: Festschrift Frans Neirynck*. Edited by F. Van Segroeck et al, 2.1385–1401. Leuven: Leuven University Press, 1992.

Petersen, D. "Zechariah's Vision: A Theological Perspective." In *Prophecy in the Hebrew Bible: Selected Studies from Vetus Testamentum*. BRBS 5. Edited by David E. Orton, 188–99. Leiden: Brill, 2000.

Peterson, Eugene H. *First and Second Samuel*. WBC. Edited by Patrick D. Miller and David L. Bartlett. Louisville: Westminster John Know, 1999.

Petrie, Stewart. "'Q' Is Only What You Make It." *NovT* 3.1 (1959) 28–33.

Petrotta, A. J. "A Closer Look at Matthew 2.6 and OT Sources." *JETS* 28 (1985) 47–52.

Pfeiffer, Charles F. *Between the Testaments*. Grand Rapids: Baker, 1959.

Philbeck, Ben F. *1—2 Samuel*. BBC. Edited by Clifton J. Allen. Nashville, TN: Broadman, 1970.

Pickup, Martin. "New Testament Interpretation of the Old Testament: The Theological Rationale of Midrashic Exegesis." *JETS* 51.2 (2008) 353–81.

Pilch, John J. "Altered States of Consciousness in the Synoptics." In *The Social Setting of Jesus and the Gospels*. Edited by Wolfgang Stegeman,103–16. Minneapolis: Fortress, 2002.

Piñero, Antonio. 'Interaction of Judaism and Hellenism in the Gospel of John: Elucidating the Ideological Frame of the Fourth Gospel." In *Hellenic and Jewish Arts: Interaction, Tradition, and Renewal*. Edited by Asher Ovadiah, 93–122. Tel Aviv: Ramot, 1998.

Piper, Ronald A. "Glory, Honor, and Patronage in the Fourth Gospel: Understanding the Doxa Given to Disciples in John 17." In *Social Scientific Models for Interpreting the Bible: Essays by the Context Group in Honor of Bruce J. Malina*. BIS 33. Edited by John J. Pilch, 281–309. Leiden: Brill, 2001.

———. "The One, the Four and the Many." In *The Written Gospel*. Edited by Markus Bockmuehl and Donald A. Hagner, 254–73. Cambridge: Cambridge University Press, 2005.

Plummer, Alfred. *A Critical and Exegetical Commentary on the Gospel According to S. Luke*. ICC. Edinburgh: T & T Clark, 1975.

Pomykala, Kenneth E. *The Davidic Dynasty Tradition in Early Judaism: Its History and Significance for Messianism*. SBLEJL 7. Edited by William Adler. Atlanta: Scholars, 1995.

Porter, Stanley E. "The Use of the Old Testament in the New Testament." In *Early Christian Interpretation of the Scriptures of Israel: Investigations and Proposals*. JSNTSup 148. Edited by C. A. Evans and J. A. Sanders, 79–96. Grand Rapids: Eerdmans, 1997.

———. "Scripture Justifies Mission: The Use of the Old Testament in Luke-Acts." In *Hearing the Old Testament in the New Testament*. Edited by Stanley E. Porter, 104–26. Grand Rapids: Eerdmans, 2006.

———. "The Messiah in Luke and Acts: Forgiveness for the Captives." In *The Messiah in the Old and New Testaments*. MNTS 9. Edited by Stanley E. Porter, 144–64. Grand Rapids: Eerdmans, 2007.

———. *John, His Gospel, and Jesus: In Pursuit of the Johannine Voice*. Grand Rapids: Eerdmans, 2015.

Powell, Eric. "The Staff of the Apostles: A Problem in Gospel Harmony." *Bib* 4 (1923) 241–66.

Powell, J. Enoch. *The Evolution of the Gospel*. New Haven: Yale University Press, 1994.

Powell, Mark Allan. "The Plot and Subplots of Matthew's Gospel." *NTS* 38.1 (1992) 187–204.

Price, C. P. "Revelation as Our Knowledge of God: An Essay in Biblical Theology." In *Faith and History: Essays in Honor of Paul W. Meyer*. Edited by John T. Carroll, Charles H. Cosgrove, and E. Elizabeth Johnson, 313–34. Atlanta: Scholars, 1990.

Price, Robert M. *The Incredible Shrinking Son of Man: How Reliable Is the Gospel Tradition?* Amherst, NY: Prometheus, 2003.

Puech, Émile. "Messianism, Resurrection, and Eschatology at Qumran and in the New Testament." In *The Community of the Renewed Covenant: The Notre Dame Symposium on the Dead Sea Scrolls*. CJAS 10. Edited by Eugene Ulrich and James VanderKam, 235–56. Notre Dame: University of Notre Dame Press, 1994.

———. "Some Remarks on 4Q246 and 4Q521 and Qumran Messianism." In *The Provo Reformulated Issues*. STDJ XXX. Edited by Donald W. Parry and Eugene Ulrich, 545–65. Leiden: Brill, 1999.

Quarles, Charles L. "The Use of the Gospel of Thomas in the Research on the Historical Jesus of John Dominic Crossan." *CBQ* 69 (2007) 517–36.

Rau, Gottfried. "Das Markusevangelium: Komposition und Intention der ersten Darstellung christlicher Mission." *ANRW* 25.3 (1985) 2037–2257.

Redditt, Paul L. "Zerubbabel, Joshua, and the Night Visions." *CBQ* 54.2 (1992) 249–59.

Reed, Annette Yoshiko. "ΕΥΑΓΓΕΛΙΟΝ: Orality, Textuality, and the Christian Truth in Irenaeus' ADVERSUS HAERESES." *VC* 56 (2002) 11–46.

Reicke, Bo. "Incarnation and Exaltation: The Historic Jesus and the Kerygmatic Christ." *Int* 16 (1962) 156–68.

———. "Christ's Birth and Childhood." In *From Faith to Faith: Essays in Honor of Donald G. Miller on his Seventieth Birthday*. PTMS 31. Edited by Dikran Y. Hadidian, 151–65. Pittsburgh: Pickwick, 1979.

Reim, Günter. "Jesus as God in the Fourth Gospel: The Old Testament Background." *NTS* 30.1 (1984) 158–60.

Rendsburg, Gary A. "The Internal Consistency and Historical Reliability of the Biblical Genealogies." *VT* 40.2 (1990) 185–206.

Reventlow, Henning Graf. *The Authority of the Bible and the Rise of the Modern World*. Philadelphia: Fortress, 1985.

Rhoads, D. "Losing Life for Others in the Face of Death: Mark's Standards of Judgment." In *Gospel Interpretation: Narrative-Critical & Social-Scientific Approaches*. Edited by Jack Dean Kingsbury, 83–94. Harrisburg: Trinity International, 1997.

Roberts, Alexander and James Donaldson, eds. *The Ante-Nicene Fathers: The Writings of the Fathers down to A.D. 325*. Vol. 1. Grand Rapids: Eerdmans, 1980.

Roberts, J. J. M. "Myth Versus History." *CBQ* 38.1 (1976) 1–13.

———. "The Old Testament's Contribution to Messianic Expectations." In *The Messiah: Developments in Earliest Judaism and Christianity*. FPSJCO. Edited by James H. Charlesworth, 39–51. Minneapolis: Fortress, 1987.

Robinson, James M. "Introduction: The Dismantling and Reassembling of the Categories of New Testament Scholarship." In *Trajectories through Early Christianity*. Edited by James Robinson, 1–19. Philadelphia: Fortress, 1971.

———. "The Impossibility and Illegitimacy of the Original Quest." In *A New Quest of the Historical Jesus and other Essays*. Edited by James M. Robinson and Helmut Koester, 26–47. Philadelphia: Fortress, 1983.

———. "The Study of the Historical Jesus after Nag Hammadi." *Semeia* 44.1 (1988) 45–55.

———. "The Critical Edition of Q and the Study of Jesus." In *The Sayings Source Q and the Historical Jesus*. BETL CLVIII. Edited by A Lindemann, 27–52. Paris: Leuven University Press, 2001.

Robinson, James M., Paul Hoffmann, and John S. Kloppenborg, eds. *The Critical Edition of Q: Synopsis including the Gospels of Matthew and Luke, Mark and Thomas with English, German, and French Translations of Q and Thomas*. Minneapolis: Fortress, 2000.

Robinson, John A. T. *Can We Trust the New Testament?* Grand Rapids: Eerdmans, 1977.

Rogers, Jack. *Biblical Authority*. Waco, TX: Word, 1977.

Roland, Christopher. *The Open Heaven: A Study of Apocalyptic in Judaism and Early Christianity*. New York: Crossroad, 1982.

Rollins, Wayne G. The Gospels: Portraits of Christ. Philadelphia: Westminster, 1963.

Rooke, Deborah. "Kingship as Priesthood: The Relationship between the High Priesthood and the Monarchy." In *King and Messiah in Israel and the Ancient Near East: Proceedings of the Oxford Old Testament Seminar*. JSOTSup 270. Edited by David J. A. Clines and Philip R. Davies, 187–208. Sheffield: Sheffield Academic, 1998.

Root, J. R. "Justin Martyr." In *Evangelical Dictionary of Theology*. Edited by Walter A. Elwell, 647. Grand Rapids: Baker Academic, 2001.

Rose, Wolter H. "Messianic Expectations in the Early Post-Exilic Period." *TynB* 49.2 (1998) 373–76.

———. *Zemah and Zerubbabel: Messianic Expectations in the Early Postexilic Period*. JSOTSup 304. Edited by David J. A. Clines and Philip R. Davies. Sheffield: Sheffield Academic, 2000.

Rosen, Klaus. "The Historian and the Gospels." *AC* 42 (1999) 139–54.

Roskam, H. N. *The Purpose of the Gospel of Mark in its Historical and Social Context*. NovTSup114. Edited by M. M. Mitchell and D. P. Moessner. Leiden: Brill, 2004.

Roth, Wolfgang. "To Invert or Not to Invert: The Pharisaic Canon of the Gospels." In *Early Christian Interpretation of the Scriptures of Israel: Investigations and Proposals*. JSNTSup 148. Edited by Craig A. Evans and James A. Sanders, 59–78. Sheffield: Sheffield Academic, 1997.

Rougier, Louis. *Celse contre les Chrétiens: la réaction païenne sous l'empire Romain*. Paris: Copernic, 1977 reprint from 1926.

Rowe, Robert D. *God's Kingdom and God's Son: The Background to Mark's Christology from Concepts of Kingship in the Psalms*. AGAJU. Edited by Martin Hengel et al. Leiden: Brill, 2002.

Rudolph, Wilhelm. *Haggai–Sacharja 1—8*. Gütersloh: Gerd Mohn, 1976.

Runnalls, Donna R. "The King as Temple Builder: A Messianic Typology." In *Spirit within Structure: Essays in Honor of George Johnston on the Occasion of His Seventieth Birthday*. PTMS 3. Edited by E. J. Furcha, 15–38. Allison Park, PA: Pickwick, 1983.

Sahlin, Harald. *Der Messias und das Gottesvolk: Studien zur protolukanischen Theologie*. Uppsala: Almqvist & Wiksells, 1945.

Saldarini, A. *Matthew's Christian-Jewish Community*. CSHJ. Edited by William Scott Green and Calvin Goldscheider. Chicago: University of Chicago Press, 1994.

Sanders, E. P. *Jesus and Judaism*. London: SCM, 1985.

Sanders, E. P. and Margaret Davies. *Studying the Synoptic Gospels*. London: SCM, 1989.
Sandmel, Samuel. "Parallelomania." *JBL* 81.1 (1962) 1–13.
Schaberg, Jane. "Daniel 7.12 and the New Testament Passion-Resurrection Predictions." *NTS* 31 (1985) 208–22.
Schaeder, H. H. "Ναζαρηνός/Ναζωραῖος." *TDNT*. Translated by Geoffrey W. Bromiley. Edited by Gerhard Kittel, 4.874–79. Grand Rapids: Eerdmans, 1965.
Schalit, Abraham. *Namenwörterbuch zu Flavius Josephus*. Leiden: Brill,1968.
Schenck, Kenneth. *Jesus Is Lord! An Introduction to the New Testament*. Marion, IN: Triangle, 2003.
Schlier, Heinrich. "Ἀνατολή." *TDNT*. Translated by Geoffrey W. Bromiley. Edited by Gerhard Kittel, 1.352–53. Grand Rapids: Eerdmans, 1974.
Shedinger, Robert F. "Kuhnian Paradigms and Biblical Scholarship: Is Biblical Studies a Science?" *JBL* 119.3 (2000) 453–71.
Schibler, Daniel. "Messianism and Messianic Prophecy in Isaiah 1–12 and 28–33." In *The Lord's Anointed: Interpretation of Old Testament Messianic Texts*. Edited by Philip E. Satterthwaite, Richard S. Hess, and Gordon J. Wenham, 87–104. Carlisle: Paternoster/ Grand Rapids: Baker, 1995.
Schiffman, Lawrence H. "Messianic Figures and Ideas in the Qumran Scrolls." In *The Messiah: Developments in Earliest Judaism and Christianity*. FPSJCO. Edited by James H. Charlesworth, 116–29. Minneapolis: Fortress, 1987.
Schiffman, Lawrence H. and James C. VanderKam. *Encyclopedia of the Dead Sea Scrolls*. 2 Vols. Oxford: Oxford University Press, 2000.
Schmidt, Karl Ludwig. "Die Stellung der Evangelien der allgemeinen Literaturegeschichte." In *Eucharistērion: Studien zur Religion und Literatur des Alten und Neuen Testaments*. Edited by Hans Schmidt, 51–134. Göttingen: Vandenhoeck & Ruprecht, 1923. ET *The Place of the Gospels in the General History of Literature*. Translated by Byron R. McCane, 51–134. Columbia: University of South Carolina Press, 2002.
Schnackenburg, Rudolf. *Matthäusevangelium*. Würzburg: Echter, 1987. ET *The Gospel of Matthew*. Translated by Robert R. Barr. Grand Rapids: Eerdmans, 2002.
Schneidau, Herbert N. "Literary Relations among the Gospels: Harmony or Conflict?" *SLI* 18 (1985) 17–32.
Schneider, Carl. "κάθημαι." *TDNT*. Translated by Geoffrey W. Bromiley. Edited by Gerhard Kittel, 3.440–44. Grand Rapids: Eerdmans, 1976.
Schniedewind, William M. "King and Priest in the Book of Chronicles and the Duality of Qumran Messianism." *JJS* 45.1 (1994) 71–78.
Schröter, Jens. "Die Frage nach dem historischen Jesus und der Charakter historischer Erkenntnis." In *The Sayings Source Q and the Historical Jesus*. Edited by A. Lindeman, 207–54. Paris: Leuven University Press, 2001.
———. "The Gospels as Eyewitness Testimony: A Critical Examination of Richard Bauckham's Jesus and the Eyewitnesses." *JSNT* 31.2 (2008) 195–209.
Schulz, Siegfried. "Markus und das Alte Testament." *ZTK* 58.2 (1961) 184–97.
Schürer, Emil. *Geschichte des jüdischen Wolkes im Zeitalter Jesus Christi*. Leipzig: J. C. Hinrich, 1901. ET *A History of the Jewish People in the Time of Jesus*. Translated by T. A. Burkill. Edited by Nahum N. Glatzer. New York: Schocken, 1961.
Schwankel, Otto. "Aspekte der johnanneischen Christologie." In *Theology and Christology in the Fourth Gospel: Essays by the Members of the SNTS Johannine Writings Seminar*.

BETL CLXXXIV. Edited by Gilbert Van Belle, J. G. Van Der Watt, and P. Maritz, 347–76. Leuven: Leuven University Press, 2005.

Schwartz, Daniel R. "Priesthood and Priestly Descent: Josephus, Antiquities 10.80." *JTS* 32 (1981) 129–35.

Schweitzer, Albert. *Von Reimarus zu Wrede: Eine Geschichte der Leben-Jesu-Forschung*. Tübingen: Mohr Siebeck, 1906. ET *The Quest of the Historical Jesus: A Critical Study of Its Progress from Reimarus to Wrede*. Translated by W. Montgomery. New York: MacMillan, 1968.

Schweizer, Eduard. "Mark's Contribution to the Quest of the Historical Jesus." *NTS* 10 (1964) 421–32.

Seeley, David. "Rulership and Service in Mark 10.41–45." *NovT* 35.3 (1993) 234–50.

Segal, Alan F. "Matthew's Jewish Voice." In *Social History of the Matthean Community: Cross-Disciplinary Approaches*. Edited by David L. Balch, 3–37. Minneapolis: Fortress, 1991.

———. *Life after Death: A History of the Afterlife in Western Religion*. New York: .Doubleday, 2004

Senior, Donald. "Between Two Worlds: Gentiles and Jewish Christians in Matthew's Gospel." *CBQ* 61 (1999) 1–23.

———. "Directions in Matthean Studies." In *The Gospel of Matthew in Current Study: Studies in Memory of William G. Thompson*. Edited by David E. Aune, 5–21. Grand Rapids: Eerdmans, 2001.

Shedinger, Robert F. "Kuhnian Paradigms and Biblical Scholarship: Is Biblical Studies a Science?" *JBL* 119.3 (2000) 466–69.

Shuler, Philip L. *A Genre for the Gospels: The Biographical Character of Matthew*. Philadelphia:Fortress, 1982.

Sieber, John, H. "The Gospel of Thomas and the New Testament." In *Gospel Origins & Christian Beginnings*. Edited by James E. Goehring et al, 64–73. CA: Polebridge, 1990.

Sim, David C. "Matthew and the Pauline Corpus: A Preliminary Intertextual Study." *JSNT* 31.4 (2009) 401–22.

Skeat, T. C. "Irenaeus and the Four-Gospel Canon." *NovT* (34 (1992) 194–99.

Smith, Dennis E. "Jesus and the Gospels." In *Chalice Introduction to the New Testament*. Edited by Dennis Smith, 117–35. Atlanta, GA: Chalice. 2004.

Smith, Moody, D. "The Use of the Old Testament in the New." In *The Use of the Old Testament in the New and Other Essays: Studies in Honor of William Franklin Stinespring*. Edited by James M. Efird, 3–65. Durham, NC: Duke University Press, 1972.

———. *John*. PC. Edited by Gerhard Krodel. Philadelphia: Fortress, 1976.

———. "John and the Synoptics." *NTS* 26.4 (1980) 425–44.

———. "John, the Synoptics, and the Canonical Approach to Exegesis." In *Tradition and Interpretation in the New Testament: Essays in Honor of E. Earle Ellis*. Edited by Gerald F. Hawthorne with Otto Betz, 166–80. Eerdmans, 1987.

———. "John and the Synoptics in Light of the Question of Faith and History." In *Faith and History: Essays in Honor of Paul W. Meyer*. Edited by John T. Carroll, Charles H. Cosgrove, and E. Elizabeth Johnson, 74–89. Atlanta: Scholars, 1990.

———. "When Did the Gospels Become Scripture?" *JBL* 119.1 (2000) 3–20.

Smith, Morton. "What Is Implied by the Variety of Messianic Figures?" *JBL* 78.1 (1959) 66–72.

———. *The Secret Gospel*. New York: Harper & Row, 1973.

———. *Jesus the Magician*. San Francisco: Harper & Row, 1978.

Snodgrass, Klyne. "The Use of the Old Testament in the New." In *The Right Doctrine from the Wrong Texts? Essays on the Use of the Old Testament in the New*. Edited by G. K. Beale, 29–51. Grand Rapids: Baker Academic, 1994. Reprint from *New Testament Criticism and Interpretation*. Edited by David Alan Black and David S. Dockery. Grand Rapids: Zondervan, 1991.

———. "The Gospel of Jesus" In *The Written Gospel*. Edited by Markus Bockmuehl and Donald A. Hagner, 31–44. Cambridge: Cambridge University Press, 2005.

Soulen, R. Kendall. "The Believer and Historical Investigation." *Int* 57.2 (2003) 174–86.

Speyer, Wolfgang. "Falschung, Pseudepigraphische freie Erfindung und 'echte religiöse Pseudepigrahphe.'" In *Pseudepigrapha I: Entretiens sur l'antiquité classique, XVIII*. Edited by Kurt von Fritz, 333–66. Genève: Fondation Hardt, 1972.

Stählin, G. "ἰσός." *TDNT*. Translated by Geoffrey W. Bromiley. Edited by Gerhard Kittel, 3.344. Grand Rapids: Eerdmans, 1965.

Stanley, Christopher D. "The Social Environment of 'Free' Biblical Quotations in the New Testament." In *Early Christian Interpretation of the Scriptures of Israel: Investigations and Proposals*. JSNTSup 148. Edited by Craig A. Evans and James A. Sanders, 18–27. Sheffield: Sheffield Academic, 1997.

Stanton, Graham N. "Introduction: Matthew's Gospel, A New Storm Center." In *The Interpretation of Matthew*. IRT 3. Edited by Graham Stanton, 1–18. Philadelphia: Fortress, 1983.

———. "The Origin and Purpose of Matthew's Gospel: Matthean Scholarship from 1945 to 1980." *ANRW* 25.3 (1985) 1889–1951.

———. "Matthew: Biblos, Euaggelion, or Bios? In *The Four Gospels 1992: Festschrift Frans Neirynck*. Edited by F. Van Segroeck et al, 2.1187–1201. Leuven: Leuven University Press, 1992.

———. "The Fourfold Gospel." *NTS* 45 (1997) 317–46.

———. "An Early Reception of Matthew's Gospel: New Evidence from Papyri?" In *The Gospel of Matthew in Current Study: Studies in Memory of William G. Thompson*. Edited by David E. Aune, 42–61. Grand Rapids: Eerdmans, 2001.

———. *The Gospels and Jesus*. OBS. Edited by P. R. Ackroyd and G. Stanton. Oxford: Oxford University Press, 2002.

———. "Jesus Traditions and Gospels in Justin Martyr and Irenaeus." In *The Biblical Canons*. BETL CLXIII. Edited by J.-M. Auwers and H. J. De Jonge, 353–70. Leuven: Leuven University Press, 2003.

———. "Messianism and Christology: Mark, Matthew, Luke and Acts." In *Redemption and Resistance: The Messianic Hopes of Jews and Christians in Antiquity*. Edited by Markus Bockmuehl and James Carleton Paget, 78–96. London: T & T Clark, 2007.

Starcky, J. "Les quatre étapes du messianisme à Qumrân." *RB* 70 (1963) 481–505.

Stavenhagen, Kurt. "Offenbarung und Erlebnistheologie." *ZTK* 36 (1927) 323–33.

Stegemann, Hartmut. "Some Remarks to IQSa, to 1QSb, and to Qumran Messianism." *RevQum* 17 (1996) 479–505.

Stein, Robert H. "What Is Redaktionsgeschichte?" *JBL* 88.1 (1969) 45–56.

———. "The Proper Methodology for Ascertaining a Markan Redaction History." *NovT* 13.3 (1971) 181–99.

———. *Difficult Passages in the New Testament: Interpreting Puzzling texts in the Gospels and Epistles*. Grand Rapids: Baker, 1990.

———. "The Matthew-Luke Agreements Against Mark: Insight from John." *CBQ* 54 (1992) 482–502.
Steinmann, Andrew E. "אחד as an Ordinal Number and the Meaning of Gen 1:5." *JETS* 45.4 (2002) 577–84.
Stendahl, Krister. "Quis et Unde?: An Analysis of Matthew 1—2." In *The Interpretation of Matthew*. IRT 3. Edited by Graham Stanton, 56–66. Philadelphia: Fortress, 1983. Reprint from *Judentum, Urchristentum: Kirche*. Edited by W Eltester, 94–105. Berlin: Topelmann, 1960.
Sterling, Gregory E. "Luke-Acts and Apologetic Historiography." *SBLSP* 28 (1989) 326–42.
———. *Historiography and Self-Definition: Josephus, Luke-Acts and Apologetic Historiography*. NovTSup LXIV. Edited by C. K. Barrett, J. K. Elliott, and M. J. J. Menken. Leiden: E.J. Brill, 1992.
———. "Mors philosophi: The Death of Jesus in Luke." *HTR* 94.2 (2001) 383–402.
Steyn, Gert J. "Soteriological Perspectives in Luke's Gospel." In *Salvation in the New Testament: Perspectives on Soteriology*. NovTSup 121. Edited by Jan G. van der Watt, 67–99. Leiden: Brill, 2005.
Stonehouse, Ned B. *The Witness of Matthew and Mark to Christ*. Grand Rapids: Eerdmans, 1944.
Strack, Hermann L and Paul Billerbeck. *Kommentar zum Neuen Testament aus Talmud und Midrash: Das Evangelium nach Markus, Lukas und Johannes*. München: Beck, 1924.
Strauss, Mark L. *The Davidic Messiah in Luke-Acts: The Promise and its Fulfillment in Lukan Christology*. JSNTSup 110. Edited by Stanley E. Porter. Sheffield: Sheffield Academic, 1995.
———. *Four Portraits, One Jesus: An Introduction to Jesus and the Gospels*. Grand Rapids: Zondervan, 2007.
Strecker, Georg. *Der Weg der Gerechtigkeit: Untersuchung zur Theologie des Matthäus*. FRLANT 82. Edited by Ernst Käsemann und Ernst Würthwein. Göttingen: Vandenhoeck & Ruprecht, 1965.
Stuckenbruck, Loren T. "Messianic Ideas in the Apocalyptic and Related Literature of Early Judaism." In *The Messiah in the Old and New Testaments*. MNTS 9. Edited by Stanley E. Porter, 90–116. Grand Rapids: Eerdmans, 2007.
Styler, G. M. "Excursus IV: The Priority of Mark." In C. F. D. Moule, *The Birth of the New Testament*. HNTC. Edited by Henry Chadwick, 223–32. New York: Harper and Row, 1962.
Stylianopoulos, Theodore. "Justin Martyr." In *Encyclopedia of Early Christianity*. Edited by Everett Ferguson, 1.647–49. New York: Garland, 1997.
Suggs, M. J. Wisdom, *Christology and Law in Matthew's Gospel*. Cambridge, MA: Harvard University Press, 1970.
Sullivan, Francis A. "Cicero and Gloria." *TAPA* 72 (1941) 382–91.
Summers, Ray. *Worthy Is the Lamb*. Nashville: Broadman, 1951.
———. *Commentary on Luke: Jesus, the Universal Savior*. Waco, TX: Word, 1975.
Sundberg, Albert C. "The Protestant Old Testament Canon: Should It Be Re-Examined?" *CBQ* 28 (1966) 194–203.
———. "The Bible Canon and the Christian Doctrine of Inspiration." *Int* 29 (1975) 352–71.
Schwartz, Daniel R. "Priesthood and Priestly Descent: Josephus, Antiquities 10.80." *JTS* 32 (1981) 129–35.

Swartley, Willard M. *Israel's Scripture Traditions and the Synoptic Gospels: Story Shaping Story*. Peabody, MA: Hendrickson, 1994.

Sweeney, Marvin A. ברית אולם *(Berit Olam): Studies in Hebrew Narrative & Poetry*. Collegeville, MN: Liturgical, 2000.

Swete, Henry Barclay. *The Apocalypse of St. John: The Greek Text with Introduction, Notes, and Indices*. Grand Rapids: Eerdmans, 1908.

Tabor, James D. "Are You the One? The Textual Dynamics of Messianic Self-Identify." In *Knowing the End from the Beginning: The Prophetic, the Apocalyptic, and their Relationships*. JSPSup 46. Edited by Lester L. Grabbe and James H. Charlesworth, 180–89. London: T & T Clark, 2003.

———. *The Jesus Dynasty: The Hidden History of Jesus, His Royal Family, and the Birth of Christianity*. New York: Simon & Shuster, 2006.

———. *Paul and Jesus: How the Apostle Transformed Christianity*. New York: Simon & Schuster, 2012.

Tabor, James D. and Simcha Jacobovici. *The Jesus Discovery: The New Archaeological Find that Reveals the Birth of Christianity*. New York: Simon Schuster, 2012.

Tabor, James D. and Michael O. Wise. "4Q521 'On Resurrection' and the Synoptic Gospel Tradition: A Preliminary Study." *JSP* 10 (1992) 149–62.

Talbert, Charles H. "Miraculous Conceptions and Births in Mediterranean Antiquity." In *The Historical Jesus in Context*. PRR. Edited by Amy-Hill Levine, Dale C. Allison Jr., and John Dominic Crossan, 79–86. Princeton: Princeton University Press, 2006.

Talmon, Shemaryahu. "The Concept of Māšîah and Messianism in Early Judaism." In *The Messiah: Developments in Earliest Judaism and Christianity*. FPSJCO. Edited by James H. Charlesworth, 79–115. Minneapolis: Fortress, 1987.

———. "The Significance of שלום and its Semantic Field in the Hebrew Bible." In *The Quest for Context and Meaning: Studies in Biblical Intertextuality in Honor of James A. Sanders*. Edited by Craig A. Evans and Shemaryahu Talmon, 75–115. Leiden: Brill, 1997.

Tannehill, Robert C. "The Disciples in Mark: The Function of a Narrative Role." In *The Interpretation of Mark*. IRT 7. Edited by William Telford, 134–57. Philadelphia: Fortress, 1985.

Tàrrech, Armand Puig i. *Jesus: A Biography*. Waco, TX: Baylor University Press, 2011.

Tasker, R. V. G. *Matthew*. Grand Rapids: Eerdmans, 1961.

Taylor, Vincent. "Does the New Testament Call Jesus 'God'?" In *New Testament Essays*. London: Epworth, 1970.

Tcherikover, Victor. *Hellenistic Civilization and the Jews*. New York: Atheneum, 1979.

Telford, William R. *The Barren Temple and the Withered Tree: A Redaction-Critical Analysis of the Cursing of the Fig-Tree Pericope in Mark's Gospel and its Relation to the Cleansing of the Temple Tradition*. JSNTSup 1. Edited by Ernst Bammel et al, Sheffield: University of Sheffield, 1980.

———. "Introduction." In *The Interpretation of Mark*. IRT 7. Edited by William Telford, 1–41. Philadelphia: Fortress, 1985.

———. *The Theology of the Gospel of Mark*. NTT. Edited by James D. G. Dunn, Cambridge: Cambridge University Press, 1999.

Tenney, Merrill C. *New Testament Survey*. Grand Rapids: Eerdmans, 1961.

ter Haar Romeny, Bas. "Hypothesis on the Development of Judaism and Christianity in Syria in the Period after 70 C.E." In *Matthew and the Didache: Two Documents from the Same Jewish-Christian Milieu?* Edited by Huub Van de Sandt, 13–33. Minneapolis/Netherlands: Fortress/Royal Van Gorcum, 2005.

Theissen G. and A. Merz. *Der historische Jesus: Ein Lehrbuch.* Göttingen: Vandenhoeck & Ruprecht, 1996.

Theissen, Gerd and Dagmar Winter. *The Quest for the Plausible Jesus: The Question of Criteria.* Louisville, KY: Westminster John Knox, 2002.

Thiemann, Ronald F. *Revelation and Theology: The Gospel as Narrated Promise.* Notre Dame: University of Notre Dame Press, 1985.

Thompson, John Arthur. *The Book of Jeremiah.* NICOT. Grand Rapids: Eerdmans, 1980.

Thompson, Marianne Meye. *John: A Commentary.* NTL. Edited by C. Clifton Black, M. Eugene Boring, and John T. Carroll. Louisville, KY: Westminster/John Knox, 2015.

Thompson, William G. "An Historical Perspective in the Gospel of Matthew." *JBL* 93.2 (1974) 243–62.

Thrall, Margaret E. *Greek Particles in the New Testament: Linguistic and Exegetical Studies.* NTTS 3. Edited by Bruce M. Metzger. Leiden: Brill, 1962.

Tilley, Terrence W. "Remembering the Historic Jesus—A New Research Program?" *JTS* 68.1 (2007) 3–35.

Tillich, D. Paul. "Die Idee der Offenbarung." *ZTK* 36 (1927) 403–12. Reprint in *Offenbarung und Glaube: Schriften zur Theologie II* (1970) 8.31–39.

Titus, Eric Lane. "The Fourth Gospel and the Historical Jesus." In *Jesus and the Historian: Written in Honor of Ernest Cadman Colwell.* Edited by Thomas Trotter, 98–113. Louisville, KY: Westminster, 1968.

Tolbert, Mary Ann. *Sowing the Gospel: Mark's World in Literary-Historical Perspective.* Minneapolis: Fortress, 1989.

Tollington, Janet E. *Tradition and Innovation in Haggai and Zechariah 1—8.* JSOTSup 150. Edited by David J. A. Clines and Philip R. Davies. Sheffield: Sheffield Academic, 1993.

Treu, Ursula. "Formen und Gattungen in der frühchristlichen Literatur." In *Spätantike und Christentum: Beiträge zur Religions- und Geistesgeschichte der griechisch-römischen Kultur und Zivilisation der Kaiserzeit.* Edited by Carsten Colpe, Ludger Honnefelder, und Matthias Lutz-Bachmann, 125–39. Berlin: Akademie, 1992.

Trobisch, David. *The First Edition of the New Testament.* Oxford: Oxford University Press, 2000.

Troeltsch, Ernst. "Ueber historische und dogmatische Methode in der Theologie." In *Gesammelte Schriften zur religiosen Lage, Religionsphilosophie und Ethik.* 2.729–53. Tübingen: J. C. B. Mohr/Paul Siebeck, 1922.

———. "Historiography." *Encyclopaedia of Religion and Ethics.* Edited by James Hastings, 6.716–23. New York: Charles Scribner's Sons, 1961.

Tucker, Gene M. *The Book of Isaiah 1—39.* NIB. Leader Keck. Nashville: Abingdon, 1994.

Tuckett, Christopher W. "Jesus and the Gospels." In *The New Interpreter's Bible.* Edited by Neil Alexander, 8.70–86. Nashville: Abingdon, 1995.

———. "Micah 5.1-3 in Qumran and in the New Testament and Messianism in the Septuagint." In *Messianism and the Septuagint: Collected Essays by J. Lust.* BETL CLXXVII. Edited by K Hauspie, 87–112. Leuven: Leuven University Press, 2004. Reprint from BETL 131 (1997) 65–88.

———. "Forty other Gospels." In *The Written Gospel.* Markus Bockmuehl and Donald A. Hagner, 238–53. Cambridge: Cambridge University Press, 2005.

Turner, H. E. W. *Historicity and the Gospels: A Sketch of Historical Method and its Application to the Gospels.* London: A. R. Mowbray, 1963.

Uffenheimer, Benjamin. *The Visions of Zechariah: From Prophecy to Apocalyptic.* Jerusalem: Kiryat Sefer, 1961.

Van Aarde, Andries G. "IJHOUS, the Davidic Messiah, as Political Saviour in Matthew's History." In *Salvation in the New Testament: Perspectives on Soteriology.* NovTSup 121. Edited by Jan G. van der Watt, 7–31. Leiden: Brill, 2005.

VanderKam, James C. "Joshua the High Priest and the Interpretation of Zechariah 3." *CBQ* 53.4 (1991) 553–68.

———. *The Dead Sea Scrolls Today.* Grand Rapids: Eerdmans, 1994.

———. "Messianism in the Scrolls." In *The Community of the Renewed Covenant: The Notre Dame Sumposium on the Dead Sea Scrolls.* CJAS 10. Edited by Eugene Ulrich and James VanderKam, 211–34. Notre Dame: University of Notre Dame Press, 1994.

———. *From Joshua to Caiaphas: High Priests after the Exile.* Minneapolis: Fortress, 2004.

Van der Woude, Adam S. "Serubbabel und die messianischen Erwartungen des Propheten Sacharja." In *Lebendige Forschung im alten Testament.* ZNWSup 100. Edited by Otto Kaiser, 138–56. Berlin: Walter de Gruyter, 1988.

Van de Sandt, Huub. "Introduction." In *Matthew and the Didache: Two Documents from the Same Jewish-Christian Milieu?* Edited by Huub van de Sandt, 1–9. Minneapolis/Netherlands: Fortress/Royal Van Gorcum, 2005.

Van Henten, Jan Willem. "The Hasmonean Period." In *Redemption and Resistance: The Messianic Hopes of Jews and Christians in Antiquity.* Edited by Markus Bockmuehl and James Carleton Paget, 15–28. London: T & T Clark, 2007.

Verheyden, J. "The Canon Muratori: A Matter of Dispute." In *The Biblical Canons.* BETL CLXIII. Edited by J.-M. Auwers and H. J. De Jonge, 487–556. Leuven: Leuven University Press, 2003.

Vermes, Geza. "Jewish Literature and New Testament Exegesis: Reflections on Methodology." *JJS* 33 (1982) 361–76.

———. *The Religion of Jesus the Jew.* London: SCM, 1993.

———. *The Authentic Gospel of Jesus.* London: Penguin, 2004.

———. *The Complete Dead Sea Scrolls in English.* London: Penguin, 2004.

Verseput, Donald. *The Rejection of the Humble Messianic King: A Study of the Composition of Matthew 11—12.* EUS XXIII. Frankfurt am Main: Peter Lang, 1986.

Veyne, Paul. *Les Grecs ont-ils cru à leurs mythes?* Paris: Editions de Seuil, 1983. ET *Did the Greeks Believe in Their Myths? An Essay on the Constitutive Imagination.* Translated by Paula Wissing. Chicago: University of Chicago Press, 1988.

Viviano, Benedict T. "The Genres of Matthew 1–2: Light from 1 Timothy 1.4." *RB* 97.1 (1990) 31–55.

Von Rad, Gerhard. *Theologie des Alten Testaments, Bd.II: Die Theolgoie der prophetischen Überlieferungen Israels.* Munich: Chr. Kaiser, 1960. ET *The Message of the Prophets.* Translated by D. M. G. Stalker. New York: Harper & Row, 1967.

———. "βασιλεύς." *TDNT.* Translated by Geoffrey W. Bromiley. Edited by Gerhard Kittel, 1.566–67. Grand Rapids: Eerdmans, 1964.

Vorster, Willem S. "The function of the Use of the Old Testament in Mark." *NeoT* 14 (1981) 62–72. Reprint in *Speaking of Jesus: Essays on Biblical Language, Gospel Narrative and the Historical Jesus.* NovTSup XCII. Edited by J. Eugene Botha, 149–60. Leiden: Brill, 1999.

Votaw, Clyde Weber. *The Gospels and Contemporary Biographies in the Graeco-Roman World*. BS 37. Philadelphia: Fortress/Facet, 1970. Reprint from *AJTh* 19 (1915) 45-73.

Waetjen, Herman C. "The Genealogy as the Key to the Gospel According to Matthew." *JBL* 95.2 (1976) 205-30.

Wagner, J. Ross. "The Septuagint and the 'Search for the Christian Bible." In *Scripture's Doctrine and Theology's Bible: How the New Testament Shapes Christian Dogmatics*. Edited by Markus Bockmuehl and Alan J. Torrance, 17-28. Grand Rapids: Baker Academic, 2007.

Watson, Francis. *Gospel Writing: A Canonical Perspective*. Grand Rapids: Eerdmans, 2013.

———. *The Fourfold Gospel: A Theological Reading of the New Testament Portrait of Jesus*. Grand Rapids: Baker Academic, 2016.

Watts, John D. W. *Isaiah 1—33*. WBC. Edited by John D. W. Watts. Waco: Word, 1982.

Watts, Rikke E. "Mark." In *Commentary on the New Testament Use of the Old Testament*. Edited by G. K. Beale and D. A. Carson, 111-249. Grand Rapids: Baker Academic, 2007.

Wcela, Emil A. "The Messiahs(s) of Qumrân." *CBQ* 26.3 (1964) 340-49.

Webster, John. "The Dogmatic Location of the Canon." In *Die Einheit der Schrift und die Vielfalt des Kanons: The Unity of Scripture and the Diversity of the Canon*. Edited by John Barton and Michael Wolter, 95-126. Berlin: Walter de Gruyter, 2003.

Weeden, Theodore J. "The Heresy that Necessitated Mark's Gospel." In *The Interpretation of Mark*. IRT 7. Edited by William Telford, 64-77. Philadelphia: Fortress, 1985.

Weinert, Francis D. "Luke, the Temple and Jesus' Saying about Jerusalem's Abandoned House." *CBQ* 44.1 (1982) 68-76.

Weinfeld, Moshe. "The King as the Servant of the People: The Source of the Idea." *JJS* 33 (1982) 189-94.

———. "'Justice and Righteousness'—משפט וצקה—The Expression and its Meaning." In *Justice and Righteousness: Biblical Themes and their Influence*. JSOTSup 137. Edited by Henning Graf Reventlow and Yair Hoffmann, 228-46. Sheffield: Sheffield Academic, 1992.

———. *The Promise of the Land: The Inheritance of the Land of Canaan by the Israelites*. TLJS. Berkeley: University of California Press, 1993.

Wells, Gary L., Amina Memon, and Steven D. Penrod. "Eyewitness Evidence: Improving Its Probative Value." *Psychological Science in the Public Interest* 7.2 (2006) 45-75.

Wendland, Paul. *Die hellenistisch-römische Kultur in ihren Beziehungen zu Judentum und Christentum: Die urchristlichen Literaturformen*. Tübingen: Mohr, 1912.

Wenham, John William. *Christ and the Bible*. Downers Grove, IL: InterVarsity. 1972.

Widengren, G. "Royal Ideology and the Testament of the Twelve Patriarchs." In *Promise and Fulfillment: Essays Presented to Professor S.H. Hooke*. Edited by F. F. Bruce, 202-12. Edinburgh: T & T Clark, 1963.

Wiebe, John M. "The Form of the 'Announcement of a Royal Savior' and the Interpretation of Jeremiah 23.5-6." *SBT* 15 (1987) 3-22.

Wildberger, Hans. *Jesaja 1—12*. BKAT. Edited by Siegfried Herrmann und Hans Walter Wolff. Wageningen, Niederlande: Neukirchen-Vluyn, 1972.

Wiles, Maurice. "Can We Still Do Christology?" In *The Future of Christology: Essays in Honor of Leander E. Keck*. Edited by Leander E. Keck, Abraham J. Malherbe, and Wayne A. Meeks, 229-38. Minneapolis: Fortress, 1993.

Willitts, Joel. "Presuppositions and Procedures in the Study of the 'Historical Jesus': Or, Why I Decided Not To Be a 'Historical Jesus' Scholar." *JSHJ* 3 (2005) 61-108.

Wilson, A. N. *Jesus A Life*. New York: W. W. Norton, 1992.

Windisch, Hans. *Johannes und die Synoptiker: Wollte der vierte Evangelist die älteren Evangelien ergänzen oder ersetzen?* Leipzig: Hinrichs, 1926.

Winter, Paul. "Some Observations on the Language in the Birth & Infancy Stories of the Third Gospel." *NTS* 1 (1954) 111–21.

Witherington, Ben. *The Christology of Jesus.* Minneaplis: Fortress, 1990.

———. *The Many Faces of the Christ: The Christologies of the New Testament and Beyond.* New York: Crossroads, 1998.

———. *The Gospel of Mark: A Socio-Rhetorical Commentary.* Grand Rapids: Eerdmans, 2001.

———. *Revelation.* NCBC. Edited by Ben Witherington. Cambridge: Cambridge University Press, 2003.

———. "The Last Man Standing." *BAR* March/April (2006) 24.

———. *What Have They Done with Jesus? Beyond Strange Theories and Bad History—Why We can Trust the Bible.* San Francisco: HarperSanFrancisco, 2006.

Wolters, Al. "The Messiah in the Qumran Documents." In *The Messiah in the Old and New Testaments.* MNTS 9. Edited by Stanley E. Porter, 75–89. Grand Rapids: Eerdmans, 2007.

Wood, Bryant G. "Let the Evidence Speak." *BAR* 33.2 (2007) 26.

Wright, G. Ernest. "Historical Knowledge and Revelation." In *Translating & Understanding the Old Testament: Essays in Honor of Herbert Gordon May.* Edited by Harry Thomas Frank and William L. Reed, 279–303. Nashville: Abingdon, 1970.

Wright, J. Edward. "Biblical Versus Israelite Images of the Heavenly Realm." *JSOT* 93 (2001) 59–75.

Wright, N. T. *The New Testament and the People of God.* Minneapolis: Fortress, 1992.

———. *Jesus and the Victory of God.* Minneapolis: Fortress, 1996.

———. "Five Gospels but no Gospel: Jesus and the Seminar." In *Authenticating the Activities of Jesus.* NTTS XXVIII.2. Edited by Bruce Chilton and Craig A. Evans, 83–120. Leiden: Brill, 1999.

———. *The Last Word: Scripture and the Authority of God—Getting Beyond the Bible Wars.* San Francisco: HarperSanFrancisco, 2006.

Xeravits, Géza. "Précisions sur le texte original et le concept messianique de CD 7:13–8.1 et 19:5–14." *RevQum* 19 (1999) 47–59.

Yarbrough, Robert W. "James Barr and the Future of Revelation in History in New Testament Theology." *BBR* 14.1 (2004) 105–26.

Young, Edward J. *The Book of Isaiah: The English Text, with Introduction, Exposition, and Notes.* NICOT. Grand Rapids: Eerdmans, 1974.

Zahn, Theodor. "Die Thiersymbole der Evangelisten." In *Forschungen zur Geschichte des neutestamentlichen Canons und der altkirchlichen Literatur.* Edited by Theodor Zahn, 2.257–75. Erlangen: Andreas Deichert, 1883.

Zahrnt, Heinz. *Es Begann mit Jesus von Nazereth.* Stuttgart: Kreuz, 1960. ET *The Historical Jesus.* Translated by J. S. Bowden. New York: Harper & Row, 1963.

Zimmerli, Walther. "παῖς θεοῦ." *TDNT.* Translated by Geoffrey W. Bromiley. Edited by Gerhard Kittel, 5.654–77. Grand Rapids: Eerdmans, 1967.

Zimmerli, Walter and Joachim Jeremias, eds. *The Servant of God.* SBT 20. London: SCM, 1965.

Zipes, Jack. "The Messianic Power of Fantasy in the Bible." *Semeia* 60.1 (1992) 7–21.

Author Index

Abbott, E., 57
Abraham, W., 2
Achtemeier, E., 182
Achtemeier, P., 128, 147, 149, 151, 155, 269
Afzal, C., 242
Ahn, S., 218
Aichele, G., 4, 11, 155, 262
Aland, K., 52
Alexander, L., 16
Alkier, S., 32, 67, 129
Allegro, J., 81–82
Allison, D., 7, 13–14, 26, 58, 65–66, 72, 91, 102, 104, 113, 125, 270
Anderson, H., 76
Anderson, P., 9, 29, 70–72
Arnal, W., 271
Attridge, H., 32, 205
Aune, D., 27, 35, 230–231, 269

Bacon, B. W., 68
Baldwin, J. G., 153, 163, 207–208
Baltzer, K., 198
Barbour, R. S., 2
Barclay, W., 95, 229, 260
Bar-Ilan, M., 272
Barker, M., 153, 163, 215, 231
Barnhart, J. E., 59
Barr, J., 2
Barrett, C. K., 83, 126, 205, 257
Barth, G., 96
Barton, J., 17, 31–33, 45, 61, 207
Batdorf, I. W., 17
Bauckham, R. J., 25–26, 52, 63, 128, 139, 174, 188, 205–206, 218, 234–235, 258–259, 272, 275
Bauer, D. R., 59, 99, 110, 126
Beasley-Murray, G. R., 189–190
Beale, G. K., 160, 168, 182–83, 223, 230
Beaton, R. C., 58, 61, 72

Beck, D. R., 23
Beckwith, F. J., 19
Begbie, J., 19
Berger, K., 198
Bernard, J. H., 205, 214
Bertrand, D., 260
Betz, H. D., 263, 274
Beuken, W. A. M., 152, 170
Billerbeck, P., 190
Bird, M. F., 25, 62, 76
Black, D., 23
Block, D. L., 216
Blomberg, C. L., 8, 31, 33, 73, 120–21, 247
Bock, D. L., 23, 26, 46, 71, 78, 146, 162, 202
Boecker, H.J., 111
Boismard, M.-E., 4
Borg, M. J., 14, 155, 260
Boring, M. E., 62, 148, 231–232, 269,
Bornkamm, G., 105, 128, 236
Botner, M., 141
Bovon, F., 51, 159, 162, 165, 184, 188, 197, 202
Boxall, I., 234
Boyd, G. A., 8
Branscome, D., 39
Brenneman, J. E., 31
Brewer, D. I., 77
Brewer, R. R., 242
Broadhead, E. K., 24, 145–148
Brodie, L. T., 198
Brooke, G. J., 78, 80, 116, 180, 188
Brown, R., 17, 121, 187, 197
Brown, S., 184
Bruce, A. B., 191
Bruce, F. F., 3, 15, 28, 78, 114, 142, 183, 206, 217, 262, 275
Brunner, E., 2
Búda, J., 213
Bultmann, C., 6
Bultmann, R., 5, 6, 8, 10, 11, 15, 17, 63, 75, 84, 86, 129, 231, 260, 263

AUTHOR INDEX

Burridge, R. A., 35, 60, 73, 84, 229, 232, 270, 276
Butsch, A. F., 232
Byrskog, S., 24, 25

Caird, G. B., 237
Calvert, D. G. A., 74
Campenhausen, H. F. V., 52
Caquot, A., 177
Carlston, C. E., 9, 105
Carrier, R., 15
Carroll, R. P., 69
Carson, D. A., 3
Carter, W., 59, 68
Casey, P. M., 44, 127, 205
Cathcart, K. J., 170
Chapman, S. B., 177
Charette, B., 96
Charles, R. H., 230, 237, 242–243
Charlesworth, J. H. xviii, 5, 8, 16, 19, 27–28, 61, 69–70, 74, 77, 84, 118, 198, 205, 229, 269, 274
Chávez, E., 174
Chibici-Revneanu, N., 74, 208
Childs, B. S., 3, 6, 82, 207–209, 222
Chilton, B. A., 44, 65, 106, 208, 211
Collins, A. Y., 34–35, 128, 150, 270
Collins, Jn. C., 6
Collins, Jn. J., 141, 148
Combrink, H. J. B., 147
Connolly-Weinert, F., 75
Conzelmann, H., 19, 62, 118, 128, 228
Cook, W. R., 223
Court, J. M., 59
Cousland, J. R. C., 118
Cranfield, C. E. B., 125, 214
Crook, Z. A., 15
Crossan, J. D., 11, 17, 25, 76, 260, 267
Cullmann, O., 10, 169, 248–249
Culpepper, R. A., 82, 199, 200, 209–210, 226

Dahl, N. A., 31
Danker, F. W., 23, 88, 185
Davies, J. A., 193
Davies, P. R., 4
Davies, W. D., 13, 35, 38, 58, 66, 91, 102, 107, 113, 118, 125, 150, 270–271
Davies, M., 55, 269, 272
Day, M., 19
DeConick, A. A., 56
De Jonge, M., 97, 195
De Kruijf, Th., 215
Delitzsch, F., 164–165, 167, 216, 218, 221
Deppe, D. B., 127, 130
de Robert, P., 117

deSilva, D. A., 27, 270
Desrousseaux, L., 113
Deutsch, C., 115
DeVries, S. J., 122, 193
Dillion, R. J., 50
Dimant, D., 244
Dodd, C. H., 16, 57, 80, 151, 219, 225
Dommershausen, W., 92, 110, 168
Donaldson, T. L., 97
Downing, F. G., 1, 2, 38
Drinkard, J. F., 111
Duling, D. C., 97, 107
Dunn, J. D. G., 8, 24–25, 47, 194, 196, 214, 227, 272
Du Plessis, I. I., 50
Du Plessis, P. J., 3
Dyson, A. O., 3

Eddy, P. R., 8
Ehrman, B. D., 2, 7, 15
Elliot, J. H., 15
Ellis, E. E., 8, 20, 107
Emerton, J. A., 113
Engnell, I., 158
Enslin, M., 35–36, 78
Erickson, R. J., 22, 194
Esler, P. F., 15
Evans, Ch. S., 9
Evans, Cr. A., ix, 15, 22, 25, 44, 59–60, 63, 65, 68, 72, 74, 78, 84–85, 88, 93, 98, 106, 107, 129, 130, 155, 164–165, 173–175, 177, 188, 193–194, 199, 210, 229
Evans, M. J., 177

Farkasfalvy, D., 2, 248
Farmer, W. R., 17
Farrer, A., 10, 242
Fennema, D. A., 215
Ferguson, E. ix, 246, 249, 262–263
Feuillet, A., 235
Fichtner, J., 193
Filson, F. V., 17, 106
Fiorenza, E., 267
Fitzmyer, J. A., 29, 33, 63, 180, 188
Fletcher-Louis, C. H. T., 100, 141–142, 150, 182
Flew, A., 6
Floyd, M. H., 130, 165
Fornara, C. W., 262
Foster, P., 24
France, R. T., 34, 133, 135, 143, 151
Franklin, E., 37, 160
Fredriksen, P., 229
Freyne, S., 22, 118, 177
Funk, R. W., 25, 43, 115, 260, 263

Gabel, J. B., 31, 129, 155–156
Gamble, H. Y., 244
García, M. F., 105
Garland, D. E., ix, 87, 185, 274
Gathercole, S. J., 20, 96, 107, 151, 260
Geldenhuys, N., 188, 193
Gempster, S. G., 172
Gerhardsson, B., 8, 24–25, 68
Gesenius, W., 90
Geyer, G. W., 147
Giblin, C. H., 240
Globe, A., 13
Gnilka, J., 194–195
Goodacre, M., 24, 32
Goodspeed, E. J., 246
Gordon, R. P., 170
Goswell, G., 152
Gould, J. P., 44
Grabbe, L. L., 170
Grambo, R., 253
Grant, F. C., 28
Grant, R. M., 24, 28, 199–200, 226, 246, 249
Gray, G. B., 212
Green, J. L., 111
Guelich, R., 144, 260, 269
Gundry, R.H., 15, 27, 65, 77, 90, 99, 125

Habel, N. C., 111
Hagner, D., 58, 96, 99
Hall, R. G., 243
Hamilton, V., 224
Han, K. S., 179
Hannah, D. D., 156, 242, 245
Hare, D. R. A., 62
Harrington, D. J., 229
Harris, R. L., 261
Harris, S., 169
Harris, W. V., 272
Hartman, L., 66, 114
Harvey, A. E., 6, 10, 11
Harvey, M. G., 20
Harvey, V. A., 6, 11
Hauck, R. J., 1, 9–10
Hay, D. M., 65, 168
Hays, D. J., 184
Hays, R. B., 19, 23–24, 57, 64–66, 72, 84, 110, 129, 212
Heckel, T. K., 52
Hendrickson, W., 175, 230–231
Hendel, R. S., 1
Hengel, M., 31, 52, 233, 249, 269, 272
Henry, C. F. H., 4
Herntrich, V., 224
Hess, R. S., 31, 183

Hidber, T., 47
Higgins, A. J. B., 98
Hoffman, M., 15, 266
Hoffmann, P., 78, 266
Hoffman, T. A., 2, 32
Holladay, W. L., 110, 112
Holmberg, B., 24, 227
Holmgren, F. C., 1, 84
Holm-Nielsen, S., 27
Hooker, M. D., 64, 70, 74, 127–128, 142, 144, 261
Hoover, R. W., 25, 43, 115, 260, 263
Horrell, D. G., 15
Horsley, R. A., 266
Hoskyns, E. C., 225
Houlden, L., 156, 198, 200
Hultgård, A., 194
Hultgren, A. J., 200–201
Hultgren, S., 78, 275
Hume, D., 6
Hurtado, L. W., 44, 61, 236–237, 275

Incigneri, B. J., 128
Ingolfsland, D., 25

Jauhianen, M., 171n50
Jenni, E., 178, 222
Jensen, D. H., 177
Jeremias, J., 22, 151
Johnson, L. T., 6, 148, 260
Johnson, M. D., 189–190
Johnson, R. F., 148–149
Juel, D. H., 60, 77, 83

Kahl, W., 17
Kähler, M., 267–268
Kaiser, O., 208, 213
Kaiser, W. C., 81, 92
Kant, I., 6
Käsemann, E., 200, 227, 258, 263, 265
Kea, P. V., 268
Keck, L. E., 9, 59–61, 79
Kee, H. C., 64, 65
Keener, C. S., ix, 7, 20, 31, 82, 136, 205–206, 214, 261, 269
Keil, C. F., 164–165, 167, 216, 218, 221
Kelber, W. H., 6, 25, 149
Keller, E., 6
Keller, M.-L., 6
Kilpatrick, G. D., 60
King, K. L., 264
Kingsbury, J. D., 7, 23, 59, 88, 98–100, 123–124, 146, 150–151, 164, 178, 197–198, 201, 232
Kinzer, M., 217

AUTHOR INDEX

Kirchschläger, W., 27
Klinghardt, M., 185
Klooster, F. H., 4
Kloppenborg Verbin, J. S., xx, 24, 78, 155, 266–267
Knowles, M., 74
Koester, H., 76, 259
Korteweg, T., 21
Köstenberger, A. J., 206, 215, 226
Kraeger, L. A., 59, 267
Kraus, H.-J., 184
Krentz, E., 5
Kümmel, W. G., 260
Kuhn, K. G., 197
Kuyper, A., 236
Kysar, R., 24, 76, 206, 218, 256

Ladd, G. E., xix, 15, 27, 267–268
Lampe, G. W. H., 245, 253
Landmesser, C., 124
Lane, N., 64
Lane, W. L., 33–34, 144–145, 174
Lanier, G., 107
LaSor, W. S., 79–81
Le Donne, A., 25, 46, 61, 63, 74, 115–116, 121
Leith, J. H., 3, 16, 266
Lemcio, E. E., 269
Lemke, W. E., 1
Levey, S. H., 211
Levin, Y., 62, 121
Levine, A-J., 33, 85
Lewis, T. J., 232
Licona, M. R., 39
Lieu, J. M., 60, 72, 118, 206, 217, 249
Lindemann, A., 24, 266
Lipovsky, J. P., 261
Lohse, E., 141, 173, 218.
Loisy, A., 190, 232, 242
Longenecker, R., 74, 77–78, 229
Love, M. C., 16, 130
Loubser, J. A., 121
Lust, J., 111
Luz, U., 39, 58, 62, 99, 116, 118, 120, 123–124, 187, 263
Lyons, M. A., 67
Lyons, W. J., 266

Ma, W., 209
Mack, B., 5, 76
MacLean, H. B., 122
Malbon, E. S., 149
Malina, B. J., 15
Manson, T. W., 128
Marcus, J., 63–64, 70, 72, 95, 104, 128, 145

Marguerat, D., 96
Marincola, J., 42, 48
Marshall, I. H., 159, 162, 187, 189, 193, 201
Martínez, F. G., 105
Mason, R., 130
Matera, F. J., 145
McCane, B. R., 32, 112
McCarter, P. K., 176
McCasland, S. V., 125
McCown, C. C., 15
McDonald, L. M., 259
McEleney, N. J., 4, 74
McKane, W., 92, 110
McKenzie, J. L., 2, 92
McLaren, J., 177
McLay, T. R., 114
McNamara, M. S., 211
Meagher, J. C., 16
Meggitt, J. J., 95
Meier, J. P., 8, 44
Menken, M. J. J., 114, 258
Merenlahti, P., 128–129
Merkel, H., 31
Merz, A., 23, 78, 200
Metzger, B. M., 61, 180, 235, 246, 260
Meyers, C. L., 137, 189
Meyers, E. M., 137, 189
Michel, O., 233, 243
Miller, R. J., 148
Mitchell, H. G., 130
Milton, H., 68
M'Neile, A. H., 58, 95, 106
Miscall, P. D., 99, 176
Moessner, D. P., 35, 70, 72
Montgomery, J. A., 122, 193
Morgan, R., 6, 31, 59
Morray-Jones, C. R. A., 244
Morris, L., 3, 69, 205–206, 231, 235, 255–256
Mounce, R. H., 230
Moule, C. F. D., 24, 77, 247
Moyise, S., 59, 63, 82, 233, 242
Mussies, G., 94

Neyrey, J. H., 215, 217
Nicholson, E. W., 110
Nicole, R., 64
Niebuhr, H., 1
Nielsen, J. T., 218
Nielsen, K., 208–209, 214
Nolland, J., 89, 93, 100, 106, 114, 120, 150, 178, 188, 192
Norden, E., 269
North, J. L., 33
Notley, S. R., 182

O'Connell, R. H., 211
O'Grady, J. F., 141
Ollenburger, B. C., 137, 165
Oswalt, J. N., 219
O'Toole, R. F., 201

Paffenroth, K., 96
Pagels, E., 264
Paquette, E., 16
Parsenios, G., 226–227
Patterson, S. J., 56
Pauck, W., 20
Peabody, D. B., 59, 74
Pelling, C., 147
Perrin, N., 60, 76, 148
Pesch, R., 106–107
Petersen, D. N., 128, 132, 136
Peterson, E. H., 176
Petrie, S., 78
Petrotta, A. J., 113
Philbeck, B. F., 177
Pickup, M., 66, 81
Pilch, J. J., 273
Piñero, A., 32
Piper, R. A., 28, 218
Plummer, A., 179–180, 187–188, 191, 201
Pomykala, K. E., 152
Porter, S. E., 4, 64, 178, 229
Powell, E., 34
Powell, J. E., 45, 46, 129
Powell, M. A., 104
Price, C. P., 3
Price, R. M., 3, 9, 47
Pesch. R., 106

Rau, G., 127, 142
Redditt, P. L., 152
Reed, A. Y., 249
Reicke, B., 5, 12, 185, 265
Rendsburg, G. A., 194
Reumann, J., xix
Reventlow, H. G., 6
Rhoads, D., 149
Roberts, J. J. M., 2, 223
Robertson, A. T., 193
Robinson, J. M., 15, 78, 260, 263, 266
Rogers, J., 3
Roland, C., 233, 240
Rollins, W. G., 146, 264
Rooke, D., 181
Rose, W. H., 106, 110, 140
Roskam, H. N., 127, 271
Roth, W., 62, 70
Rougier, L., 10

Rowe, R. D., 104, 142, 145
Rudolph, W., 152, 172
Runnalls, D. R., 168
Sahlin, H., 192
Saldarini, A., 61–62
Sanders, E. P., 15, 38, 55, 269, 272
Sanders, J. A., 259
Sandmel, S., 17, 19, 75
Schaberg, J., 138
Schaeder, H. H., 107
Schalit, A., 202
Schenck, K., 23, 71, 115, 185, 215
Schlier, H., 106
Shedinger, R. F., 16
Schnackenburg, R., 99, 116–117
Schneidau, H. N., 127
Schneider, C., 134
Schniedewind, W. M., 69
Schröter, J., 21, 25
Schwartz, D. R., 193
Schweitzer, A., xix, 29, 265, 268
Schweizer, E., 128, 148, 151, 269
Seeley, D., 127, 199
Segal, A. F., 22, 58
Senior, D., 55, 62
Shuler, P. L., 268–269
Sim, D. C., 59, 61, 67–68
Skeat, T. C., 246
Smith, D. E., 38, 71
Smith, D. M., 32, 54–55, 59, 129, 248
Smith, M., 18, 198, 262, 267
Snodgrass, K., 64, 84, 97
Speyer, W., 2
Stählin, G., 235
Stanley, C. D., 34
Stanton, G. N., 245–247, 249, 260, 266
Stein, R. H., 34, 60, 62, 95, 127, 143, 149, 269
Steinmann, A. E., 216
Stendahl, K., 117
Sterling, G. E., 159
Stonehouse, N. B., 1
Strack, H. L., 190
Strauss, M. L., 3, 71–72, 104, 145, 206, 276
Strecker, Georg., 105
Strugnell, J., 244
Suggs, M. J., 116
Summers, R., 192–193, 230
Sundberg, A. C., 262
Schwartz, D. R., 193
Swartley, W. M., 198
Sweeney, M. A., 171–172, 209
Swete, H. B., 230

Tabor, J. D., 16, 18, 39, 76, 85, 156, 159, 196–198

AUTHOR INDEX

Talbert, C. H., 20, 155
Talmon, S., 94, 181
Tannehill, R. C., 148
Tàrrech, A. P. i., 5
Tasker, R. V. G., 95
Taylor, V., 215
Tcherikover, V., 202
Telford, W. R., 61, 127-128, 142, 147
ter Haar Romeny, B., 58
Theissen G., 21, 23, 74, 78, 200
Thiemann, R. F., 1
Thompson, J. A., 92, 110
Thompson, M. M., 73
Thompson, W. G., 61
Tigchelaar, E. J. C., 105
Tilley, T. W., 26, 267
Tillich, D. P., 1
Titus, E. L., 4, 227
Tolbert, M. A., 32, 61
Tollington, J. E., 166, 189
Trobisch, D., 244, 269
Troeltsch, E., 6, 8, 9, 11
Tuckett, C. W., 56, 92, 113, 226-227
Turner, D., 58
Turner, H. E. W., 8, 21, 74

Uffenheimer, B., 152, 166

VanderKam, J.C., 56, 152-153, 165, 182
Van de Sandt, H., 60
Vermes, G., 16, 36, 60, 85
Verseput, D., 58, 95, 138
Veyne, P., 10, 14
Viviano, B. T., 90, 119
Von Rad, G., 93, 130
Vorster, W. S., 64, 129-130

Votaw, C. W., 35
Waetjen, H. C., 120, 123-124
Wagner, J. R., 111
Watson, F., 61, 123, 262, 274
Watts, John D. W., 136-137, 167, 211, 215
Webster, J., 249
Weeden, T. J., 148-149, 151
Weinert, F. D., 149, 198
Weinfeld, M., 109, 118, 158
Wells, G. L., 26
Wendland, P., 30, 128
Wenham, J. W., 3
Westcott, B. F., 2, 205, 225-226
Wheeler, C. B., 31, 129, 155-156
Wiebe, J. M., 112
Wildberger, H., 215
Willitts, J., 17, 266
Wilson, A. N., 18, 22, 84
Windisch, H., 55
Winter, D., 21, 74
Wise, M. O., 148, 159
Witherington, B., 20, 44, 127, 145-146, 229-230, 234, 269, 272
Wolters, A., 29
Wright, G. E., 265
Wright, J. E., 232
Wright, N. T., 6-7, 19, 44, 62, 155, 275

Xeravits, G., 21

Yarbrough, R. W., 2
Young, E. J., 217-218

Zahn, T., 250
Zahrnt, H., 5
Zimmerli, W. T., 22, 151

Scripture Index

Old Testament

Genesis

1:5	216, 216n67
1:27	216
1:29	162n11
2:10	245n67
18:2	101n60
23:7	101n60
24	102n66
43:26	102n63

Exodus

14:11–13	228n106
14:21	228n106
15:30	203

Leviticus

25:25	228n106

Deuteronomy

6:4	216
6:13	213n53

1 Samuel

1:9	166n32
1:11	176
2:1–10	169
2:11	176
2:18	176n66
2:21	199
2:26	199
2:30	175
2:35	176n64
2:35–36	175, 178
4:13	166n32
10:1	176
13:9–10	168n36, 184
16:1	157
16:13	176
20:41	102
21:7	156
24:9	102
30:13	157

2 Samuel

2:16	131
6:14	168, 184
7:8–11	97
7:11–16	177n69
8:18	193
9:9	156
9:10	157

2 Chronicles

33:3	101n60

Nehemiah

12:13	203

Ecclesiastes

2:6	106n87

Isaiah

4:2	xix, 73, 78, 82, 87, 126, 206, 208–215, 217–221, 224n94, 255, 275
4:3	106n91
5:1–7	222
7:11	137n53

Isaiah (continued)

7:14	23n94
8:18	136
10:20–22	224, 224n92
11:1	106
11:10	107n94
11:11, 16	224n92
14:22	224n92
14:30	224n93
15:9	224n94
16:5	109
20:3	137, 140
28:5	217
31:4	250
32:1	110, 250
35:1–3	218
37:31–32	223–224
41:9	140
42:1	144
44:3–4	223
53:2	221n87
58:11	223
60:1–2	218, 220
61:3	219
65:20	116n126

Jeremiah

23:5–6	67–68, 68n55, 73, 78–79, 82–83, 87–91, 93, 93n19, 95, 97, 103–104, 107, 109, 112, 116, 119, 125–126, 157, 161, 213, 255, 257, 275
23:5	xix, 67, 88n1, 93n19, 94–95, 106, 109–110, 162, 164, 208, 214, 251
23:6	74n85, 92, 94, 109n100, 111, 111n109, 112, 113n115, 115n130, 116–117, 119
51:10	111n110

Zechariah

3:8	xix, 72n79, 78, 90, 106, 126, 129–132, 137n56, 140, 148, 152–154, 157–158, 161–162, 164, 182, 198n47, 214, 255, 275
6:12–13	81, 81n114, 160, 164, 164n21, 182, 186, 200
6:12	90, 108n97, 153, 157, 161–165, 181, 181n84, 183, 186, 200
6:13	166, 171
9:9	90n9

New Testament

Matthew

1:2–3	117
1:6–12	124
1:16	187
1:18–24	13
1:21–23	23n94
2:1–9	107
2:1–12	109
2:6	94, 114, 117
2:13	89
2:23	107
3:1	93
4:16	22
4:16–17	107
5:1	134
5:18	xix, 87
6:33	113
7:24	113
8:2	103, 135
9:18	101–102, 135
9:27–31	46
10:10	33
11:28–30	75
12:39–42	115
13:17	63, 265
14:33	135
15:25	135
16:17	63, 265
17:24–27	99
20:20	53, 135
22:43	183
22:44	85
29:19	113
28:9	103

Mark

1:10	228n106
1:24	141–142
1:32	33
1:35	133n38
1:36	138
1:40	135
1:41	146
2:25	138
3:5	146
3:31–34	140
5:22	135
6:1–6	39n34
6:1	159
6:3	5
6:6	146

6:9	33, 33n34
7:25	135
8:22–26	46
8:31	141
9:12	114
9:35	134, 158
10:14	146
10:21	146
10:32	175
10:33	174
10:35	135
10:45	128, 133n38, 141
11:1–11	136
11:2	174
11:9	95n29
11:11	173, 175
12:18–27	43
13:2–14.31	175
14:24	141
14:36	145
14:41–42	139
15:18	135
16:1–8	60
16:5	76
16:6	141

Luke

1:1–3	37
1:1–80	186
1:2–25	168
1:1	56
1:4	38
1:5	197
1:11	161
1:17	161
1:19	161
1:27	204
1:32	99n48, 166, 173
1:36	197
1:46–55	169
1:61	202–203
1:78	81n112
1:78–79	107
1:79	107n96
2:22–38	168
2:40	199
2:48	192
2:52	199
3:23	187, 190
3:24	189
3:31	99n48
3:38	191
4:16–30	39n34

4:16	133n39
4:18–19	180
4:24	142
4:34	179
4:40	33
5:24	199
6:49	143
10:39	133
19:10	76n92
19:27	105
19:38	95n29
21:6	132n34
22:24–27	76n92
23:34	180
24:25–28	xix, 86, 276

John

1:1–18	210
1:11–12	225
1:14	219, 223
5:44	223
6:69	179
7:39	223
10:35	xix
11:49–51	83
11:51	63, 265
12:13	95n29
12:41	23n93, 215
14:20	208
14:26	63, 265
16:13	63, 265
15:1	214
19:5	226n100

Acts

1:19	185n97
2:22	185
2:30	196
3:14	179
4:7	228n46
4:27	179
7:52	228n106
17:31	185

Romans

1:3	196
15:12	81, 106, 106n89, 107n94, 222

1 Peter

1:10–12	63, 81, 207, 265

2 Peter

1:20–21	63, 265

Revelation

4:3	241
4:4	240
4:6	238
4:6–7	229, 232, 276
4:6–10	234n29, 236
4:7	29, 229, 230–234, 244–246, 275
5:5	81, 106, 106n89, 250–251
5:6	234, 238, 241n51
5:6–14	237
6:1, 3, 5, 6–7	234
7:11	238, 241
14:1–5	236n39
14:3	238
15:7	234n29
19:4	234n29
21:16	235

Ancient Document Index

Apocrypha

1 Maccabees

2:1	203n66

Pseudepigrapha

Psalms of Solomon

17.32	94n22
18:1-7	94n22

Testament of Twelve Patriarchs

TRubin

6:8	195n35

TSimeon

7.2	195

TJudah

24.1	195, 201n52

TLevi

18.1	195, 200n52
18.3	109

Dead Sea Scrolls

4Q254.4.2	129n18

Philo

On the Confusion of Tongues
(*De Confusione Linguarum*)

XIV-XV	108

On the Special Laws
(*De Specialibus Legibus*)

2.176	109n98

Josephus

Against Apion

1.36	120n3

Jewish Antiquities

4.5.3	191n18
6.195	190n14
7.43	191n18
7.196	190n14
7.250	102n64
10.80	193n29
11.333	103n72
12.266	203
17.167	254n97
20.8.6	10n38

Jewish War

1.437	203n64
1.562	203n65
1.573	203n65
2.13.45	10n38
2.361	103n73
2.575	203
4.262	103n72
4.324	103n72
5.402	103n72
6.123	103n72

Rabbinic Writings

Targum on Isaiah	211n35
Targum on Jeremiah	93n19
Targum on Zech 6:13	170n45

Greco-Roman Writings: Greek

Appian

Civil Wars 1.83	13, 49
2.9.95	253

Aristotle

Poetics 1451a	21, 35n18

Arrian

History of Alexander

1.1-2	42n41
1.1-3	52
1.12.5	53
4.11.9	102n68

Callimachus

Epigram 2	48n61

Diodorus Siculus

Library of History

1.1.5	48
1.2.3	48
4.1.4	48
4.2.1	36
4.1.7	37n25
4.3.4–5.4	37

Dio Cassius

Roman History

59.27.5	103n71

Dionysius of Halicarnassus

Roman Antiquities

1.67.1	13
2.58.1	45
2.61.1	53
3.51.1	253
4.2.2	13n47
4.6.1	45n53

Critical Essays: Thucydides

7	12

Herodotus

Histories

1.1	47

Hippocrates

Regimen in Acute Diseases

65.12	190n14

Airs, Waters, Places

22.5	11
22.53	11

Homer

Iliad

9.525	48n60

Pausanias

Description of Greece

1.30.4	12n46

Philostratus

Life of Apollonius

1.27.2	102n67
1.31.6	102n67
2.11.55	102n67
2.21.24	102n67
7.14.4	102n67
7.22.25	102n67

Plutarch

Alexander

14.5	13

Numa

4.3	12

Solon

27.1	53n80

Advice to Bride and Groom

145D	12n44

Obsolescence of Oracles

414E	12n45

On the Malice of Herodotus

854F	45n53

Polybius

Histories

1.14.1	50n67
2.56.1	41
2.56.2	42
2.58	42
2.59	42
2.61	42
2.62	42
2.63	42
4.12	44
9.1	44n48
9.2	13
10.5.8	13
10.6	44n48
12.2.1	49n66
12.4	37n27
12.7.1	44n47
12.7.6	44n48
12.13	44n49
12.15	45
15.1	50n67
35.14	4n17

Strabo

Geography

1.2.2	40
1.2.3	40
1.2.7	40
1.2.8	40
1.2.35	40
1.3.22	40
1.4.2	40
2.1.12	40
2.4.2	4n18
10.3.5	43n42

Thucydides

Histories

1.22.4	47
1.4	47
1.2.22	49n65
2.43.3	47
2.64.5	47
3.88.3	191n18

Xenophon

Anabasis

3.2.9	102n67
3.2.13	102n67
7.21	102n67

Roman Writings

Res Gestae Divi Augusti

7	201n52

Catullus

49	49n64

Cicero

Pro Archia

26	47

Ad familiares

5.12	48n62

Horace

Epodi

3.30	48
4.8	48
4.9	48

Saturae

1.3.27	253
1.10.51	35n18

Epistulae

1.2.1.56	6n27

Livy

Ab urbe condita

Prologue 9	14n51
1.4.1	14n51
1.24	38
6.12	103n69
7.40	103n69
9.45	38n32
21.17	103n69
27.16	38n32
38.43	103n69
44.45	103n69

Petronius

Satyricon

56	252

Pliny

Naturalis historia

8.19	251

Tacitus

Historia

1.36	103n70

Annales

4.32	261n16
15.47	247n77

Velleius Paterculus

Historia Romana

1.7.2	39
2.16.2	47n59
2.53.4	42n40
2.66.3	48

Early Christian Writings

Acta Xanthippae

17	253n96

Ambrose

Exposito evangelii secundum Lucam

1.1	50n70
1.1-3	245n70
1.10	245n70
3.22	108n97

Augustine

De doctrina christiana

2.8.49	245n71

Clement of Alexander

Stromatum

3.93.1	245n65

Eusebius

Historia ecclesiastica

1.2.1-17	192n26
6.25.3	245n69

Hippolytus

Commentarium in Danielem

1.12.5	195
1.17.1	245n67

Irenaeus

Adversus haereses

3.11.8	246
3.33.8	246n77

Justin Martyr

Dialogus com Tryphone

106.3	246n73
106.4	108n97

Apologia

1.32.10	108n97

Origen

Contra Celsum

1.54	219n82
2.6	82n116
2.20	13n48

Homilia in Lucam

13.18	245n66

Commentarii in evangelica Joanis

1.21	245n66

Tertullian

Adversus Marcionem

4.2.2	245n68
4.5.3	245n68

Théodoret de Cyr

Commentaire sur Isaïe

224	211n36

www.ingramcontent.com/pod-product-compliance
Lightning Source LLC
Chambersburg PA
CBHW082026300426
44117CB00015B/2370